Microsoft

WINDOWS
SERVER™ 2003
Planning Server
Deployments

PUBLISHED BY
Microsoft Press
A Division of Microsoft Corporation
One Microsoft Way
Redmond, Washington 98052-6399

Library of Congress Cataloging-in-Publication Data
Microsoft Windows Server 2003 Deployment Kit: A Microsoft Resource Kit / Microsoft Corporation.
        p. cm.
    Includes index.
    ISBN 0-7356-1486-5
    1. Microsoft Windows Server.   2. Operating systems (Computers)   I. Microsoft
Corporation.

    QA76.76.O63.M524765   2003
    005.4'4769--dc21   2003044575

Printed and bound in the United States of America.

1 2 3 4 5 6 7 8 9   QWT   8 7 6 5 4 3

Distributed in Canada by H.B. Fenn and Company Ltd.

A CIP catalogue record for this book is available from the British Library.

Microsoft Press books are available through booksellers and distributors worldwide. For further information about international editions, contact your local Microsoft Corporation office or contact Microsoft Press International directly at fax (425) 936-7329. Visit our Web site at www.microsoft.com/mspress. Send comments to *rkinput@microsoft.com*.

Acquisitions Editors: Juliana Aldous Atkinson, Martin Delre
Project Editor: Maureen Williams Zimmerman

SubAssy Part No. X08-39352
Body Part No. X08-39365

Contents at a glance

Contents

Acknowledgments

Microsoft would like to thank the following people for their contributions:

Book Lead: Jill Zoeller

Writers: Jim Bevan, Sandra Faucett, David Maguire, Douglas H Steen, Chris Wolf, Ellen Zehr, Jill Zoeller

Book Editor: Scott Turnbull

Editors: Nona Allison, Ann Becherer, Jim Becker, Bonnie Birger, Dale Callison, Carolyn Eller, Anika Nelson, Tyler Parris, Susan Sarrafan, Scott Somohano, Dee Teodoro, Scott Turnbull, Tom Winn, Paula Younkin

Documentation Manager: Pilar Ackerman

Writing Lead: Cheryl Jenkins

Editing Leads: Laura Graham, Kate O'Leary, Scott Somohano

Lab Management: Robert Thingwold, David Meyer

Project Managers: Clifton Hall, Paulette McKay, Neil Orint

Online Components Writing Team: Peter Costantini, Eve Gordon, Amy Groncznack, Lola Gunter, Sean Loosier, Irfan Mirza, Gary Moore, Chris Revelle, Kim Simmons, Greg Stemp, Dean Tsaltas, Kelly Vomacka

Online Components Editing Team: Anika Nelson, Kate Robinson, Dee Teodoro

Windows Server Resource Kit Tools Program Managers: Majdi Badarin, Clark Gilder

Resource Kit Tools Software Development and Test Team: Sameer Garde, Sunil Gummalla, Venu Somineni, Kendra Yourtee, Scott Smith, John Turner

Publishing Team: Barbara Arend, Jon Billow, Chris Blanton, Eric Camplin, Yong Ok Chung, Andrea DeGrazia, Julie Geren, Jason Hershey, Michael Howe, Richard Min, Cornel Moiceanu, Rochelle Parry, David Pearlstein, Mark Pengra, Steve Pyron, Ben Rangel, Lee Ross, Tony Ross, Gino Sega, Amy Shear, Karla van der Hoeven, Gabriel Varela, Ken Western, Matt Winberry

Indexing Team: David Pearlstein, Lee Ross, Tony Ross

Key Technical Reviewers: Arren Conner, Pasquale DeMaio, Chris Darling, David Golds, Brian Guarraci, Keith Hageman, Drew McDaniel, Tim Lytle, Venkat Ramanathan, Andrew Ritz, Tali Roth, Jim Teague, Steve West, Charlie Wickham, Chris Whitaker

Technical Reviewers: Randy Abrams, Mark Aggar, Jeff Albrecht, Sanjay Anand, Alex Angelopoulos, Zubair Ansari, Linda Apsley, Reza Baghai, Ritu Bahl, Alex Balcanquall, David Banks, Ryan Basile, Peter Bergler, Dan Boldo, Murali Brahmadesam, Shala Brandolini, John Bunn, Anil Cakir, Luis Caldeira, Laurent Cardon, Tim Cerling, Althea Champagnie, Sudarshan Chitre, Ben Christenbury, Elden Christensen, Brian Collins, Dan Conley, Judy Cowan, Shane Creamer, Mike Danseglio, Brian Dewey, David Dion, Walter Dominguez, Kumud Dwivedi, Christoph Felix, Peter Foote, Daniel Fox, Vishal Ghotge, James Gilman, Jeffrey Goldner, Amy Groncznack, William Gruber, Mukul Gupta, Costin Haigu, Clifton Hall, Uday Hegde, Adam Henderson, Atul Patel Hirpara, Matt Holle, Joe Holliday, Jari Jattu, Deborah Jay, Anjali Joshi, Mark Kieffer, Rich Knowles, Jason Leznek, Mark Licata, Alvin Loh, Paul Luber, David Martin, Steve Mathias, Michael McConnell, Thomas O. McCormick, James McIllece, Hampton Mills, Manoj Nayar, Cynthia Nottingham, Joel Oleson, Steve Olsson, Timothy Omta, David Orbits, Adam Overton, James Owusu, Rashmi Patankar, Daryl Pecelj, Rohan Phillips, Mike Plumley, Bohdan Raciborski, Letha Radebaugh, Arif Saifee, Drew Samnick, Sara Schumacher, Jamie Schwartz , Sri Seshadri, Nikhil Shrikhande, Mike Shutz, Andy Simonds, Terri Snider, Lara Sosnosky, Usha Srinivasan, David Steere, Greg Stemp, Jeff Stucky, Chittur Subbaraman, Ben Svobodny, Cristian Teodorescu, Albert Ting, Rob Trace, Catharine van Ingen, Don Velliquette, Svetlana Verthein, Michael Ward, Supriya Wickrematillake, Pascale Williams, Roland Winkler, Jon Wojan, Bruce Worthington, Ethan Zoller

Special thanks to Martin DelRe for his support and sponsorship. Without his contribution, the publication of this kit would not have been possible.

Introduction

Welcome to *Planning Server Deployments* of the *Microsoft® Windows® Server 2003 Deployment Kit*. This book provides comprehensive information about planning server storage and designing and deploying file servers, print servers, and terminal servers in medium and large organizations. You can also use the guidelines in this book to maximize the availability and scalability of your servers by planning for remote server management, designing and deploying server clusters, and designing and deploying Network Load Balancing clusters.

Deployment Kit Compact Disc

The following contents are included on the *Windows Server 2003 Deployment Kit* companion CD:

- **Windows Server 2003 Deployment Kit.** A searchable online version of the *Windows Server 2003 Deployment Kit*.

- **Resource Kit Tools for Windows Server 2003.** A collection of tools included with the Windows Deployment and Resource Kits that can help you deploy, configure, maintain, and troubleshoot Windows Server 2003.

- **Resource Kit Registry Reference for Windows Server 2003.** A searchable online reference providing detailed descriptions of the Windows Server 2003 registry, including many entries that cannot be edited by using Windows Server 2003 tools or programming interfaces.

- **Resource Kit Performance Counters Reference for Windows Server 2003.** A searchable online reference describing what each performance counter monitors. You can use performance counters to diagnose problems or detect bottlenecks in your system.

- **Deploying Internet Information Services (IIS) 6.0 & Migration Tools.** A searchable online version of *Deploying Internet Information Services (IIS) 6.0* and tools that you can use to migrate to IIS 6.0.

- **Job Aids for the Windows Server 2003 Deployment Kit.** Worksheets and resources that can help you create your deployment plan for Windows Server 2003.

- **Windows Server 2003 Help.** The searchable Help file included with the Windows Server 2003 operating system containing technical content for the IT professional, which can be installed on Microsoft® Windows® XP Professional.

- **Microsoft Office Viewers.** Viewers you can install on your computer if you do not have Microsoft® Office, which allow you to see worksheets and resources on the *Windows Server 2003 Deployment Kit* companion CD.

- **CD-ROM Release Notes.** Late breaking information about the contents of the *Windows Server 2003 Deployment Kit* companion CD.

- **Links to Microsoft Press.** Links to the Microsoft Press Support site, which you can search for Knowledge Base articles, and to the Microsoft Press product registration site, which you can use to register this book online.

Document Conventions

The following art symbols and text conventions are used throughout this book.

Flowchart Symbols

Use the following table of symbols as a resource for understanding the flowcharts included in this guide.

Symbol	Meaning	Symbol	Meaning
	Step or component process		Data stored to a database
	Predefined process or subroutine		Flowchart beginning or end
	Decision point	1	Intra-chart connector: Flow continues to next page
	Output to a document or input from a document	1	Intra-chart connector: Flow continues from previous page
	Data transfer to a file on disk	A	Inter-chart connector: Indicates an exit point to another flowchart
	Data transfer to a data store	B	Inter-chart connector: Indicates an entry point from another flowchart

Art Symbols

Use the following table of the art symbols as a resource for understanding the graphics included in this guide.

Symbol	Meaning	Symbol	Meaning
	Workstation		Macintosh client
	Portable computer		Tablet computer
	Terminal		Cellular phone
	Portable digital assistant (PDA)		Document

(continued)

(continued)

Symbol	Meaning	Symbol	Meaning
	File folder		E-mail
	Chart		Wireless network adapter
	Modem		Video camera
	Network adapter		Digital camera
	Facsimile		Printer
	Telephone		Scanner
	Hard disk		Tape drive
	Database		Tape
	Compact disc		Security key
	Digital certificate		Padlock
	Padlock		Uninterruptible power supply
	Access token		Hub
	Modem bank		Automated library

(continued)

(continued)

Symbol	Meaning	Symbol	Meaning
	Windows NT–based server		Generic server
	Mainframe computer		Host
	Server farm		Clustered servers
	Router		Switch
	Shadowed router		Windows 2000–based router
	Data jack		Input/output (I/O) filter
	Firewall		Tunnel
	Internet		An intranet
	Transceiver		Script
	Interface		Packets

(continued)

(continued)

Symbol	Meaning	Symbol	Meaning
✕	Process or communication failure	" . "	DNS root
○	Directory tree root	○	Root
⬭	Organization	○	Organizational unit
■	Common name	⬗	Generic node
△	Active Directory domain	👥	User group
△ Windows 2000 Domain	Windows 2000 domain		
△ Active Directory	Active Directory™	⬭	Site *or* Windows NT 4.0 domain

Reader Alert Conventions

Reader alerts are used throughout this guide to notify you of both supplementary and essential information. The following table explains the meaning of each alert.

Reader Alert	Meaning
💡 Tip	Alerts you to supplementary information that is not essential to the completion of the task at hand.
📝 Note	Alerts you to supplementary information.
❗ Important	Alerts you to supplementary information that is essential to the completion of a task.
🚩 Caution	Alerts you to possible data loss, breaches of security, or other more serious problems.
⚠ Warning	Alerts you that failure to take or avoid a specific action might result in physical harm to you or to the hardware.

Command-line Style Conventions

The following style conventions are used in documenting scripting and command-line tasks throughout this book.

Element	Meaning
bold font	Characters that you type exactly as shown, including commands and parameters. User interface elements are also bold.
Italic font	Variables for which you supply a specific value. For example, *Filename.ext* can refer to any valid file name.
`Monospace font`	Code samples.
`Command`	Command that is typed at the command prompt.
`Syntax`	Syntax of script elements.
`Output`	Output from running a script.

Support Policy

Microsoft does not support the software supplied in the *Windows Server 2003 Deployment Kit*. Microsoft does not guarantee the performance of the scripting examples, job aids, or tools, bug fixes for the tools, or response times for answering questions. However, we do provide a way for customers who purchase the *Windows Server 2003 Deployment Kit* to report any problems with the software and receive feedback for such issues. You can do this by sending e-mail to rkinput@microsoft.com. This e-mail address is only for issues related to the *Windows Server 2003 Deployment Kit*. For issues related to the Windows Server 2003 operating systems, please refer to the support information included with your product.

C H A P T E R   1

Planning for Storage

For many organizations today, data is their most important asset. Losing data can mean losing thousands or even millions of dollars in revenue. Organizations can help protect valuable data by ensuring adequate, available, and secure storage. To manage and secure data, you can use a number of technologies with the Microsoft® Windows® Server 2003 operating system, including direct-attached storage, storage area networks (SANs), network-attached storage, Windows server clusters, Volume Shadow Copy service, Distributed File System (DFS), and Automated System Recovery (ASR).

In This Chapter

Related Information

- For information about file servers, Distributed File System (DFS), File Replication service (FRS), Windows server clusters, NTFS file system permissions, disk quotas, shadow copies, and redundant array of independent disks (RAID) levels, see "Designing and Deploying File Servers" in this book.

- For information about high availability planning, see "Planning for High Availability and Scalability" in this book.

- For information about backup and recovery, see the *Server Management Guide* of the *Microsoft® Windows® Server 2003 Resource Kit* (or see the *Server Management Guide* on the Web at http://www.microsoft.com/reskit).

Overview of Storage Planning

Several factors have contributed to the growth of both online and offline organizational storage requirements. Among these factors are:

- Increasing amounts of data
- Increasing needs for high availability and fast recovery
- Declining costs of storage

These developments have caused many organizations to place increased priority on storage planning and design. Planning and designing a storage solution involves defining the specific requirements of your organization and carefully evaluating how those requirements can work with or benefit from operating system services and features. Windows Server 2003 includes support for critical storage technologies such as direct-attached storage, network-attached storage, and SANs, as well as features such as Automated System Recovery (ASR), shadow copies, and open file backup that should be considered as you plan to meet your organization's storage requirements. If your storage plan includes using additional storage management or backup tools, you will also need to plan for integration of the operating system's storage features with these tools.

You can use the information in this chapter to assess your organization's specific storage needs, and consider the storage technologies and operating system features that are available to meet those needs. You can then follow the processes defined here to develop a storage plan that meets your needs for scalability, security, availability, and recoverability. While this chapter does discuss how to plan for and work with various storage architectures and technologies, you should already have a working knowledge of each of these technologies.

The Storage Planning Process

A properly implemented storage infrastructure will meet your organization's needs if it is sufficiently scalable, protects valuable data, is fault tolerant, and is recoverable in the event of disaster. With this in mind, you need to address both your organizational needs and specific methods for achieving these requirements when planning for storage. Figure 1.1 shows the steps involved in planning for storage.

Figure 1.1   Planning for Storage

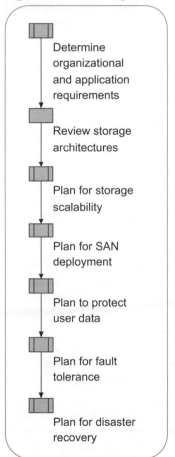

Determine organizational and application requirements

Review storage architectures

Plan for storage scalability

Plan for SAN deployment

Plan to protect user data

Plan for fault tolerance

Plan for disaster recovery

New Storage Features in Windows Server 2003

Windows Server 2003 provides many new features that aid in the planning and deployment of storage within your organization. Table 1.1 describes these features.

Table 1.1   Windows Server 2003 Storage Improvements

Feature	Description
Automated System Recovery (ASR)	ASR allows you to initiate *bare metal restores* of a system. With bare metal restores, you can boot a failed system by using the installation CD, insert an ASR floppy disk (created during an ASR backup), and recover the system state and required operating system files on the boot and system volumes from a backup. ASR can be combined with Remote Installation Services (RIS) to automate the recovery of several systems on your network.
Volume Shadow Copy service	The Volume Shadow Copy service provides an infrastructure for creating a volume that is a point-in-time image of the original volume. This image is known in the storage industry as a volume snapshot. The shadow copy can be used for the purpose of backing up the files within the volume; the copy is identical to the files at the instant the shadow copy was taken.
	Solutions built on the Volume Shadow Copy service can produce much higher quality snapshots than other technologies because of the ability to integrate with business applications and coordinate with storage hardware. As a result, high-fidelity backup recovery and data mining are possible without significantly affecting performance.
Shadow copies	You can give users access to previous versions of files by enabling shadow copies, which provide point-in-time copies of files stored on servers running Windows Server 2003. Because users can restore or roll back their files to a previous state, you can reduce the administrative burden of restoring previously backed up files for users who accidentally delete or overwrite them.
Open file backup	By integrating with the Volume Shadow Copy service, the Backup program (NTBackup.exe) available in Windows Server 2003 can now back up open files that are locked by a user or application. Previously, files had to be closed in order to be successfully backed up.
Distributed File System (DFS)	Servers running Microsoft® Windows® Server 2003, Enterprise Edition and Windows® Server 2003, Datacenter Edition support multiple DFS roots on a single server. Other new DFS features include the ability to configure DFS to choose an alternate target based on cost if no same-site targets are available.

(continued)

Table 1.1   Windows Server 2003 Storage Improvements *(continued)*

Feature	Description
File Replication service (FRS)	You can use the Distributed File System snap-in to configure the FRS replication topologies (ring, hub and spoke, and custom), and configure connection priorities. FRS suppresses excessive replication and provides better staging directory management.
SAN support	Windows Server 2003 provides many new features that make it easier to work with data and devices on a SAN. These features include improved support for booting a system from a storage device on a SAN, greater control of mounting and unmounting volumes on the SAN, including the ability to suppress the automatic mounting of volumes, and improved handling of Fibre Channel host bus adapters (HBAs) for easy SAN integration and interoperability.
Virtual Disk service (VDS)	VDS provides a standard set of application programming interfaces (APIs) to storage hardware and storage management programs that makes it easy for storage applications to work with storage hardware that includes a VDS provider. The new command-line tool DiskRaid (which is available in the *Microsoft® Windows® Server 2003 Deployment Kit*) allows you to manage hardware devices that have VDS hardware providers without the need for other management applications.
Multipathing	Multipathing provides for high availability data access by allowing a host to have up to 32 paths to access an external storage device, which facilitates failover and load balancing. Multipathing is not a feature of the operating system, but is supported through the MPIO Driver Development Kit (DDK), which provides a means for storage vendors to create interoperable multipathing solutions.
Disk Defragmenter	Disk Defragmenter performs faster and is more efficient than in the Microsoft® Windows® 2000 operating system, also now supports online defragmentation of the master file table (MFT), and can defragment NTFS volumes with any cluster size.

Determining Organizational and Application Requirements

Determining your organization's storage requirements not only involves considering your company's business needs, but also any requirements related to your line of business applications. For example, a client application might need to access data on file servers by using a single UNC path, but your storage plan calls for providing fault tolerance by storing the data on two servers. The requirements of this client application could be met by implementing DFS. The first step in planning for storage, consequently, involves determining both the needs of your organization and the needs of your applications. Collectively, they will define your storage requirements. This process is shown in Figure 1.2.

Figure 1.2   Determining Organizational and Application Requirements

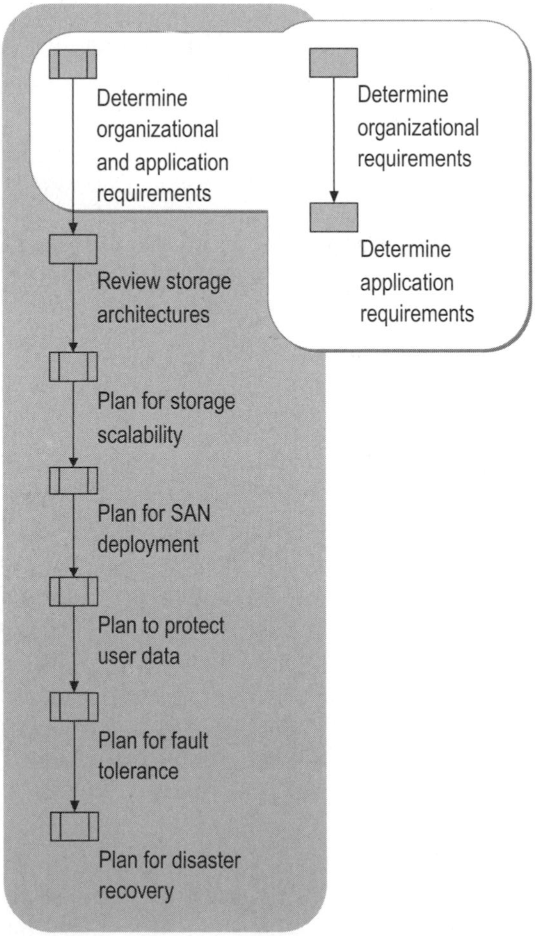

Determining Organizational Requirements

Organizational storage requirements go beyond having sufficient capacity for the data stored on each server and workstation. You must also satisfy redundancy and replication requirements. For example, to provide fault tolerance, you might decide to replicate data between two different file servers at two sites. In this case, you will need to ensure that there are sufficient storage resources at each site to store the replicated data.

To determine your organizational requirements, it will be helpful to answer the following questions:

What are your current priorities?   You should focus on prioritizing which systems to address in what order. For example, mission-critical servers are more important than individual workstations. Prioritizing systems will help to define where you should begin when defining storage requirements, and is also important when budget concerns limit the amount of storage that you can immediately upgrade. When prioritizing, focus on maximizing return on investment and distributing the benefit of improvements to the largest possible number of individuals in your organization.

What is the expected growth of data?   Do not plan only for your current volume of data. Your plan should also include estimates of the size and expected growth rate of your organization's data.

What are your budget constraints?   Budget is always a limiting factor. Understanding your budget constraints reduces wasted design efforts and helps focus on improvements that can actually be delivered. You might consider a solution that technically addresses all of your needs, but you will need to find a compromise or an alternative if the necessary funds are not available.

Can you consolidate storage?   Consolidating storage reduces the cost of managing storage on multiple servers and increases the efficiency of storage allocation and backup tasks. However, consolidation also introduces risk, because more users depend on fewer servers; so an outage affects more users than in a more distributed installation. If you plan to consolidate storage, you should also investigate ways to increase storage availability.

Will training be needed?   It might be necessary for your administrators to get additional training. For example, administrators might be comfortable with planning simple clusters, but they should not attempt state-of-the-art Fibre Channel solutions without specific training. Make plans to build necessary training into your project and budget if you plan to implement storage solutions with a high degree of complexity, or with complex management interfaces.

Will your storage needs change?   Your storage needs are probably growing. It is easier to manage a flat growth rate than an explosive one, but in either case it is best to build flexibility into your storage plan at the outset. Implementing flexible Windows storage features now lets you adapt your plan later with little or no disruption to users. For example, DFS allows you to add servers transparently to your environment, and SAN-based storage arrays and network-attached storage appliances let you achieve higher storage utilization than direct-attached storage. Look for any upcoming projects or other business changes that might require additional storage.

How many copies of data are maintained?   You need to plan adequate storage not only for primary copies of data, but also for any additional copies of the data that you need. Be sure to plan for the appropriate amount of backup media, and for sufficient online disk storage for shadow copies and replication.

What are your performance requirements?   Your choice of storage solutions is normally influenced by performance considerations. For example, your local area network (LAN) and wide area network (WAN) network components will likely need to be considered when planning for replication or data recovery between two systems in the same site, or between two or more systems in remote sites. Other considerations regarding performance include the type of server disks used, such as Enhanced Integrated Drive Electronics (EIDE) or Small Computer System Interface (SCSI), storage interfaces, and the speed of backup storage devices, such as tape drives.

What are your backup scheduling requirements?   You might have a backup window that must be met for nightly backups, or you might be able to run backups over their own network during the day. In addition to impacting the network, even backups made to direct-attached storage devices consume CPU cycles. Your backup plan should ensure that servers are available for clients and applications when they are needed most, and that backup activity does not impact network traffic during peak usage periods.

How important is ease of backup and recovery?   You might have the resources to manually back up your data nightly, and, in case of a system disaster, you might be able to bring in additional staff on an overtime basis to recover the information. Alternatively, you might require an automated approach that relies on high-end enterprise level backup software. Your plan for backup and recovery of data must balance your need for automation against the increased costs of various automated solutions.

How long can data recovery take?   Some critical systems must be continuously available. For example, an online banking enterprise might require that its system experience zero downtime. Other organizations might be able to tolerate a one-hour window of downtime. Your plan needs to take into account your organization's specific tolerance for downtime during data recovery.

Will you use legacy equipment?   Budget considerations sometimes dictate that you not replace existing equipment as you build your new storage environment. This is especially true for expensive storage libraries. The presence of older servers, disk arrays, cabling, and other equipment might save your organization money, but it might also dictate compromises in your storage plan. Also, if your plan calls for keeping existing technology, you might need to budget for any additional hardware needed to allow you to use the technology in your new storage environment.

Determining Application Requirements

When determining storage requirements, start at the application and operating system level, noting the storage and disk requirements for each system. For example, you might decide that your Microsoft® Exchange Server requires 500 gigabytes (GB) of total storage, but you also need fault-tolerance. To configure a 500 GB RAID 0+1 disk array to provide fault-tolerance, you would need 1 terabyte (TB) of physical disk storage. You would also need to allocate drives for the Exchange transaction log files.

Taking this approach server-by-server and application-by-application, you can determine the number of physical disks that you require, as well as the amount of total storage you need. When you estimate your total storage requirements, do not forget to include backup requirements. For example, you might plan to back up your Exchange server to a magnetic storage array for very fast backup and recovery performance, and then copy the backup data to tape for offsite storage. To keep a single full backup onsite would require that you double your storage estimate for the Exchange server. You will also need to estimate the growth rate of each database so that your storage meets both your immediate and future needs for a period of time as defined by your organization.

When considering storage requirements for the operating system, you should note which servers require disk mirroring to protect their boot and system volumes, and note the number of required disks along with the amount of required storage for each.

Estimating application storage requirements can be difficult without in-depth knowledge of all the applications that run in an organization. If your organization has designated specialists for your applications, consult with them to arrive at a proper estimate. The documentation for each application can also serve as an excellent source for compiling storage planning information

Reviewing Storage Architectures

When you plan a new storage configuration or reengineer your existing configuration, you will need to make decisions about the types of storage architecture to use. These architectures are direct-attached storage, network-attached storage, and storage area networks. The different storage architectures are not necessarily exclusive, but are actually complementary and often coexist on the same network. Because these architectures are well known, the discussion that follows includes only a brief overview of each architecture, and focuses on the planning considerations related to using each architecture with Windows Server 2003. The process for reviewing the storage architectures is shown in Figure 1.3.

Figure 1.3   Reviewing Storage Architectures

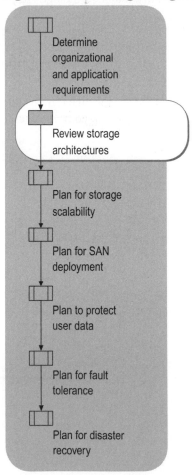

Direct-Attached Storage

Direct-attached storage refers to a storage device, such as a hard drive or tape drive, that is directly connected to a single computer. These connections are usually made by one of the following methods:

- Enhanced Integrated Drive Electronics (EIDE)

- Small Computer Systems Interface (SCSI)

- Fibre Channel

EIDE connects internal Advanced Technology Attachment (ATA) storage to a computer, SCSI provides a means to connect both internal and external storage to a computer, and Fibre Channel connects external storage to a computer. Fibre Channel is most often used with external storage in a SAN. Although Fibre Channel can be used for direct-attached storage, less expensive SCSI storage can offer similar performance, but works only over limited distances due to the physical limitations of the SCSI bus. When external direct-attached storage devices are located more than twelve meters away from a server, then Fibre Channel must be used.

Direct-attached storage retains its high popularity because of its low entry cost and ease of deployment. The simple learning curve associated with direct-attached storage technologies is also a factor many organizations consider. Direct-attached storage also makes it easy to logically and physically isolate data, because the data can only be directly accessed through a single server.

Although it is simple to deploy, there are other management considerations to take into account with direct-attached storage:

- Direct-attached storage can be more expensive to manage because you cannot redeploy unused capacity, which results in underutilization.

- Having storage distributed throughout the organization makes it difficult to get a consolidated view of storage across the organization.

- Disaster recovery scenarios are limited because a disaster will cause both server and storage outages.

- For data backup and recovery, you need to choose whether to attach local backup devices to each server, install dual network adapters in each server and back up the data over a separate LAN, or back up the server over the corporate LAN. Large organizations have found that placing stand-alone tape drives in individual servers can quickly become expensive and difficult to manage, especially when the number of servers in the organization grows into the hundreds. In this situation, it is often best to back up servers over a network to a storage library, which offers backup consolidation and eases management.

Network-Attached Storage

Network-attached storage solutions are ideal for both addressing immediate storage needs and storage consolidation projects. Their high capacity and ease of deployment allow you to implement network-attached storage with little planning. With network-attached storage, you can fulfill your storage requirements with a single purchase. This is because many network-attached storage devices are built to be *appliances*. Like home appliances, such as a refrigerator or microwave oven, you can literally purchase a network-attached storage appliance and plug it into your network. This is possible because network-attached storage appliances come prepackaged with network interfaces, storage interfaces (SCSI, Fibre Channel, or both), internal or external magnetic storage, and an operating system. Only the services required for file serving, security, and management are installed on the appliance, thus making it a high-performance file server. A network-attached storage implementation is shown in Figure 1.4.

Figure 1.4 Network-Attached Storage Implementation

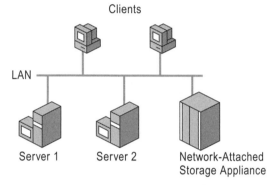

Network-attached storage has risen in popularity primarily due to the quick-and-easy nature of its implementation: Many Windows Powered Network Attached Storage appliances can be installed and running within minutes, and easily integrate into any enterprise environment.

The operating systems on Windows Powered Network Attached Storage appliances are either Windows 2000 or Windows Server 2003. Windows Powered Network Attached Storage appliances offer the file system, security, reliability, and scalability features common to all Windows operating systems, and come preconfigured with network file system (NFS), File Transfer Protocol (FTP), AppleTalk, Hypertext Transfer Protocol (HTTP), Web Distributed Authoring and Versioning (WebDAV), and NetWare protocol support. Because Windows Powered Network Attached Storage appliances support other operating system environments such as UNIX and Linux, you can seamlessly integrate them into any existing computer infrastructure, whether it uses Windows or not. They also support standard Web protocols, which allows you to manage Windows Powered Network Attached Storage appliances from a Web browser.

Windows Powered Network Attached Storage appliances are well suited for use as both departmental file servers and enterprise file servers. Network-attached storage solutions built on Windows offer data protection and high availability features like clustering and snapshots. In addition, network-attached storage appliances offer a highly scalable solution that can grow with the business. For example, storage can be added on the fly to address growing business needs.

To summarize, the key benefits of Windows Powered Network Attached Storage are:

- **Ease of deployment.** Windows Powered Network Attached Storage appliances can be installed in a heterogeneous environment within minutes.

- **Active Directory integration.** Windows Powered Network Attached Storage appliances can be integrated with the Active Directory® directory service to take advantage of features such as Kerberos authentication, Internet Protocol security (IPSec), Encrypting File System (EFS), and Group Policy objects (GPOs).

- **ISV utility support.** You can install several independent software vendor (ISV) utilities on Windows Powered Network Attached Storage appliances, including quota, backup, antivirus, and replication utilities. This is not possible with many other network-attached storage appliances.

- **Simple management.** Remote management is supported through Terminal Services sessions as well as through a Web interface. Administrators do not have to learn a new operating system to operate a network-attached storage appliance, because it uses Windows 2000 or Windows Server 2003.

- **Enhanced snapshot support.** Windows Powered Network Attached Storage appliances maximize the availability of data by supporting up to 250 snapshots, which provides an advantage compared to other network-attached storage solutions. *Snapshots* are similar to the shadow copy feature in Windows Server 2003.

- **DFS and FRS integration.** You can use DFS to build and manage a single, hierarchical view of multiple file servers and their shares. To provide redundancy and load balancing, you can store shares with identical data on multiple servers, and DFS will automatically redirect clients to alternate servers if a server becomes unavailable. To keep these shares synchronized, you can use FRS.

For more information about Windows Powered Network Attached Storage appliances, see the Windows Powered Network Attached Storage link on the Web Resources page at http://www.microsoft.com/windows/reskits/webresources.

Storage Area Networks

Unlike direct-attached or network-attached storage, SANs require careful planning before implementation. SANs differ from network-attached storage in that they store and access data at the block level, whereas network-attached storage appliances store data at the file level. File level access is preferable for users and applications needing to access a particular file, whereas block level data access is better for applications that need to quickly access data. SANs also differ from other storage architectures in that they are dedicated storage networks, and use their own network protocols and hardware components.

A simple SAN configuration is illustrated in Figure 1.5.

Figure 1.5   SAN Implementation

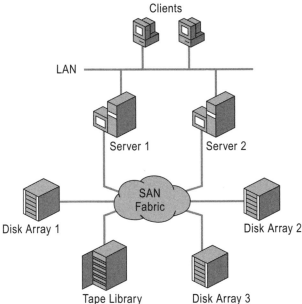

For more information about specific considerations for deploying SANs with Windows Server 2003 see "Planning for SAN Deployment" later in this chapter.

Planning for Storage Scalability

A properly planned storage infrastructure should meet both your current and future needs. It is crucial to understand the storage design and implementation limitations of your existing systems, as well as methods to overcome those limits. The general process for storage scalability planning is shown in Figure 1.6.

Figure 1.6   Planning for Storage Scalability

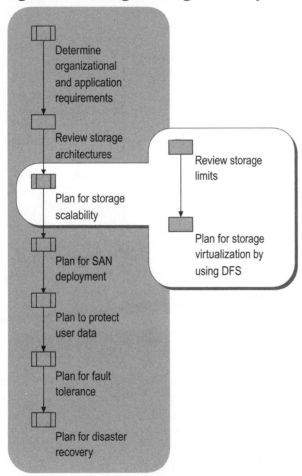

Reviewing Storage Limits

To accurately plan for storage scalability, you must take into account the physical and logical design limits of your servers. The following sections describe these limits.

Reviewing the Physical Storage Limits

From a hardware perspective, your choice of storage bus will determine the physical limits of your storage scalability. For example, local storage with two Integrated Device Electronics (IDE) controllers will allow a system to have up to four IDE storage devices; with SCSI storage, the SCSI bus type will determine the maximum amount of allowable storage devices on each bus. If you need to extend a system's local storage beyond the limitations of IDE or SCSI, you can use Fibre Channel–based storage or use SCSI protocol over TCP/IP (iSCSI), a new IP-based storage networking standard that carries SCSI commands over IP networks. However, these newer, more flexible architectures are more expensive than traditional IDE or SCSI buses.

Reviewing the Limits for Basic and Dynamic Disks

In addition to reviewing the physical storage limits, you also need to keep in mind the volume types in Windows Server 2003 and their limits. Windows Server 2003 provides enhanced volume management capabilities. You can plan for both basic disks and volumes and dynamic disks and volumes.

Basic disks use the same disk structures as those used in Microsoft® Windows NT® version 4.0 and Windows 2000. When you use basic disks, you are limited to creating four primary partitions per physical disk, or three primary partitions and one extended partition that can contain multiple logical drives. Primary partitions and logical drives on basic disks are known as *basic volumes*. As shown in Table 1.2, basic volumes are limited to 2 TB. Even if you create multiple volumes on a single logical unit, the combined size of all those volumes cannot exceed 2 TB. If you want to use volumes larger than 2 TB, you must use dynamic spanned, striped, or RAID-5 volumes.

Dynamic disks, which offer features not available in basic disks, were introduced in Windows 2000. Dynamic disks contain *dynamic volumes*, including simple volumes, spanned volumes, striped volumes, mirrored volumes, and RAID-5 volumes. Dynamic disks offer greater flexibility for volume management because they use a hidden database, instead of the disk's partition table, to track information about dynamic volumes on the disk and about other dynamic disks in the server. This flexibility allows you to create spanned, striped (RAID-0), and RAID-5 volumes that exceed the 2 TB size limit of basic volumes. Simple and mirrored volumes cannot exceed 2 TB.

Table 1.2 lists the contrasts between basic and dynamic disks.

Table 1.2   Comparison of Basic and Dynamic Disks

Storage Capabilities	Basic Disks	Dynamic Disks
Volume size (maximum)	2 TB	2 TB for simple and mirrored volumes. Up to 64 TB for spanned and striped volumes. (2 TB per disk with a maximum of 32 disks per volume.) Up to 62 TB for RAID-5 volumes. (2 TB per disk with a maximum of 32 disks per volume and 2 TB used for parity.)
Supported RAID implementation	Hardware RAID only	Hardware or software RAID
Storage of boot and system volumes	Yes	Simple or mirrored volumes only
Shared cluster storage in server clusters	Supported	Not supported*

* For more information about using dynamic disks on shared cluster storage, see article 237853, "Dynamic Disk Configuration Unavailable for Server Cluster Resources" In the Microsoft Knowledge Base. To find this article, see the Microsoft Knowledge Base link on the Web Resources page at http://www.microsoft.com/windows/reskits/webresources).

Use the following guidelines to choose between basic disks and dynamic disks.

Use basic disks if:

- You do not need to create volumes that exceed 2 TB.

- You are configuring shared cluster storage on a server cluster.

- The server runs other operating systems that cannot access dynamic disks. The only server operating systems that can access dynamic disks are Microsoft® Windows® 2000 Server and Windows Server 2003.

Use dynamic disks if:

- You want to create RAID-0 volumes or fault-tolerant volumes (RAID-1 or RAID-5) and the server does not contain hardware RAID.

- You want to combine logical units (LUNs) in a RAID array to create a volume larger than 2 TB.

- You want to extend a volume, but the underlying hardware cannot dynamically increase the size of LUNs, or the hardware has reached its maximum LUN size.

Reviewing the Limits for NTFS and the Number of Volumes Per Server

When you configure storage in Windows Server 2003–based systems, it is important to understand NTFS limits and volume limits for server storage.

Table 1.3 describes the NTFS and volume limits in Windows Server 2003.

Table 1.3   NTFS and Volume Limits for Windows Server 2003

Description	Limit
Maximum size of an NTFS volume	2^{32} clusters minus 1 cluster
	Using a 64-kilobyte (KB) cluster (the maximum NTFS cluster size), the maximum size of an NTFS volume is 256 TB minus 64 KB.
	Using a 4-KB cluster (the default NTFS cluster size), the maximum size of an NTFS volume is 16 TB minus 4 KB.
Maximum number of dynamic volumes per disk group	1,000
	A disk group is collection of dynamic disks. Windows Server 2003 supports one disk group per server.
Maximum volumes per server	Approximately 2,000 volumes
	Up to 1,000 of these volumes can be dynamic volumes; the rest are basic volumes. Boot times increase as you increase the number of volumes. In addition, the use of multipathing can reduce the number of volumes per server.

Reviewing Methods for Adding Storage Space to Volumes

If you create volumes smaller than the maximum sizes listed earlier, and you later want to add storage space to those volumes, you can do so by increasing the size of the volume or by creating a mounted drive.

Extending volumes

When a defined volume begins to reach its allocated capacity, but there is still free unallocated space on a hard disk or hardware RAID array, you can use the DiskPart command-line tool (Diskpart.exe), available in the Windows Server 2003 operating system, to extend the volume size without any loss of data. When using DiskPart, consider the following guidelines:

- You cannot use DiskPart to extend system or boot volumes; DiskPart can only be used to extend data volumes.

- The volume to be extended must be formatted with the NTFS file system.

- For basic volumes, the unallocated disk space used for the extension must be the next contiguous space on the same disk. (The disk can be a single physical disk or a group of physical disks presented by a RAID adapter to the operating system as a single disk, often referred to as a LUN.)

- For dynamic volumes, the unallocated disk space can be any empty space on any dynamic disk on the system.

- If you upgraded from Windows 2000 to Windows Server 2003, you cannot extend a simple or spanned volume that was originally created as a basic volume and converted to a dynamic volume on Windows 2000. For more information about basic and dynamic volumes, see the *Server Management Guide* of the *Windows Server 2003 Resource Kit* (or see the *Server Management Guide* on the Web at http://www.microsoft.com/reskit).

For more information about using DiskPart, see "DiskPart" in Help and Support Center for Windows Server 2003. For more information about choosing volume sizes based on Chkdsk and recovery times, see "Designing and Deploying File Servers" in this book.

Using mounted drives

Mounted drives are useful when you want to add more storage to an existing volume without having to extend the volume. A mounted drive is a local volume attached to an empty folder on an NTFS volume. Mounted drives are not subject to the 26-drive limit imposed by drive letters, so you can use mounted drives to access more than 26 drives on your computer. For more information about mounted drives, including information about creating mounted drives on server clusters, see "Using NTFS mounted drives" in Help and Support Center for Windows Server 2003.

Planning for Storage Virtualization by Using DFS

Storage virtualization is a means to organize storage virtually instead of physically. With virtualized storage, the user sees all available storage, but is insulated from the actual physical structure and processes of storage, such as the configuration, location, and capacity of the individual devices that make up the storage system. At the network level, you can achieve virtualization by using DFS. DFS allows you to move data between servers, load balance data access among servers, and change or expand your storage configuration without impacting users.

Even if your network incorporates only a single file share, you should still build your shared storage infrastructure to use DFS. This way, as your storage needs expand, the infrastructure is already in place to support that growth. With the transparency that DFS provides, you can configure and reconfigure storage at any time with no downtime or interruption to users or applications.

The benefits of using DFS include:

Unified namespace   A DFS namespace links together shared folders on different servers to create a hierarchical structure that behaves like a single high-capacity hard disk. Users can navigate the logical namespace without having to know the physical server names or shared folders that host the data.

Location transparency   DFS simplifies migrating data from one file server to another. Because users do not need to know the name of each physical server or shared folder that contains the data, you can physically move files to another server without having to reconfigure applications and shortcuts, and without having to reeducate users about where they can find their data.

Storage scalability   You can deploy additional or higher-performance file servers and present the storage on the new servers as new folders within an existing namespace.

Increased availability of file server data   When multiple servers running Windows Server 2003 host a domain-based DFS root, clients are redirected to the next available root server if any of these servers fail, which provides fault-tolerant data access. To ensure the availability of stand-alone DFS namespaces, you can create the root on a clustered file server.

Load sharing   DFS provides a degree of load sharing by mapping a single logical name to shared folders on multiple file servers. For example, suppose that \\Company\StockInfo is a heavily used shared folder. By using DFS, you can associate this location with multiple shared folders on different servers, even if the servers are located in different sites.

Simplified maintenance   Using multiple copies of shared folders also allows administrators to transparently perform preventive maintenance or upgrades on servers. A server that hosts one target can be taken offline without affecting users, because DFS automatically routes requests to a target that is online.

For more information about DFS, see "Designing and Deploying File Servers" in this book.

Planning for SAN Deployment

If your organizational and application requirements can best be satisfied by using a SAN, you need to follow the steps in this section to adequately plan for your SAN implementation. Several new or enhanced storage features are included with Windows Server 2003 to better support storage devices located on a SAN. Planning for optimal SAN deployment in a Windows Server 2003 network includes careful consideration of these SAN-related features so that you can seamlessly integrate your SAN with your Windows network. You can then plan how to configure Windows for your specific SAN implementation, and how to integrate additional storage technologies from other vendors. The process of planning for SAN deployment in a Windows network is shown in Figure 1.7.

Figure 1.7   Planning for SAN Deployment

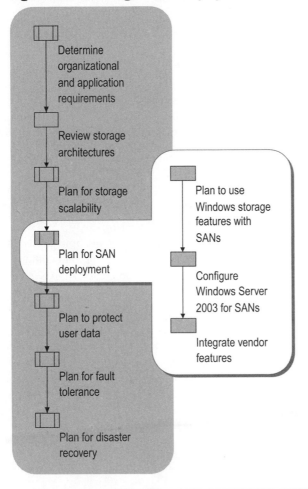

Planning to Use Windows Storage Features with SANs

As you plan your SAN implementation, consider which operating system features you can use to optimize the storage located on your SAN. Windows Server 2003 adds several services, components, and capabilities to better support storage devices located on a SAN. These include:

- Virtual Disk service (VDS)
- Volume Shadow Copy service
- Volume Automount
- Multipath Input/Output (MPIO)

Virtual Disk Service

Until recently, storage applications managed storage by directly interfacing with storage devices, based on the hardware vendor's device-specific applications. In Windows Server 2003, the Virtual Disk service (VDS) provides a standard set of APIs that storage software can use to communicate with VDS, which then sends the necessary queries or commands to the storage hardware. VDS simplifies storage management by providing a single management interface for multivendor storage devices, whether in direct-attached storage or on SANs. By using VDS, you can configure a mixed storage environment without needing to use the individual management tools supplied by each hardware vendor. To support VDS, hardware vendors must supply a VDS *provider* for the storage hardware. The provider translates the VDS APIs into instructions specific to the hardware.

VDS insulates applications from the complexities associated with storage implementations, making query and configuration operations common across all managed devices. The specific scope of VDS functionality depends on the capabilities of the underlying hardware.

Windows Server 2003 components that work with VDS as management applications include the Disk Management snap-in, the DiskPart command-line tool, and the DiskRaid command-line tool (Diskraid.exe), which is available in the *Windows Server 2003 Deployment Kit*. DiskRaid requires at least one VDS provider supplied by a storage vendor. For more information about DiskRaid, click **Tools** in Help and Support Center for Windows Server 2003, and then click Windows Resource Kit Tools.

Because of the advantages of using VDS, you should consider making VDS support a criterion when evaluating hardware or software for use in your storage infrastructure. Devices with VDS providers will be compatible with Windows Server 2003 and with other storage applications that are written for VDS. If your plan calls for storage devices that are not VDS compliant, check to ensure that the devices are compatible with Windows Server 2003 and are supported by your storage applications. For more information about device compatibility with Windows Server 2003, see the Windows Server Catalog link on the Web Resources page at http://www.microsoft.com/windows/reskits/webresources.

Volume Shadow Copy Service

The Volume Shadow Copy service adds new features for direct-attached storage and external storage arrays, including arrays that are SAN-based. It provides an infrastructure that makes possible high-fidelity backup, recovery, and data mining without significantly affecting performance.

The Volume Shadow Copy service is not a user-accessible feature, but an operating system service that works by creating a volume that can be accessed by other applications. This volume appears as a read-only point-in-time copy of the original volume. By default, the shadow copy does not appear to the server as an additional volume, but other applications can mount it and read from it. Following the creation of a shadow copy, the original volume continues to be used by the system in the same way it was used before the shadow copy was created.

The Volume Shadow Copy service can be extended with providers supplied by storage vendors, so that backup and data management applications can leverage the advanced capabilities of different storage arrays without having to deal directly with the complexities of a particular array. This allows storage management applications to more easily support a number of different hardware devices.

The Volume Shadow Copy service also enables additional capabilities in Windows Server 2003, including the following:

- **Open-file backups.** Backup applications that work with Volume Shadow Copy service, such as the Backup program in Windows Server 2003, can back up open files. For more information about backing up open files, see "Planning to Back Up Open Files" later in this chapter.

- **Shadow copies.** After an administrator has configured and enabled shadow copies, users themselves can restore earlier versions of files from point-in-time copies stored on file servers that are running Windows Server 2003. For more information about shadow copies, see "Protecting User Data by Using Shadow Copies" later in this chapter.

Volume Automount

By default, volumes automatically mount when discovered in Microsoft® Windows® Server 2003, Standard Edition and Windows® Server 2003, Web Edition operating systems. In the Windows Server 2003, Enterprise Edition and Windows Server 2003, Datacenter Edition operating systems, automount is suppressed by default to prevent these servers from aggressively mounting all volumes attached to the SAN. Automount can be enabled or disabled by using the DiskPart command-line tool. When volumes are not automounted, you can mount them and assign drive letters to them by using DiskPart.

For more information about using DiskPart, see "DiskPart" in Help and Support Center for Windows Server 2003.

Multipath Input/Output

Multipathing increases availability by providing multiple paths from the host to the external storage device. The Multipath Input/Output (MPIO) Driver Development Kit (DDK) allows storage vendors to create interoperable multipathing solutions that work with Windows Server 2003. Up to 32 paths to each logical unit are supported. For devices that can support multiple active paths, a vendor can improve performance by implementing load balancing.

To take advantage of MPIO on your SAN, you must ensure that your storage uses multipath drivers that support Microsoft MPIO technology. For more information about compatibility with Windows Server 2003, see the Windows Server Catalog link on the Web Resources page at http://www.microsoft.com/windows/reskits/webresources.

Configuring Windows Server 2003 for SANs

As you create your plan for deploying servers running Windows Server 2003 that use SAN-based storage, you need to resolve several configuration issues. In particular, consider the following:

- Is the SAN topology compatible with Windows Server 2003?
- Can the SAN storage be configured to be shared between server cluster nodes?
- Can Windows Server 2003 boot from the storage connected to the SAN?
- How will zoning and LUN masking be configured?

The sections that follow assume that you understand the basic concepts of SANs, including Fibre Channel SAN topologies and hardware components.

SAN Configurations

Your SAN configuration directly affects the speed and reliability with which your systems can access storage devices on the SAN. Two critical considerations are your choice of a Fibre Channel SAN topology and the use of redundant components in the access path to storage devices.

Supported Fibre Channel Topologies

Windows Server 2003 supports all Fibre Channel SAN topologies (point-to-point, loop, and fabric). For attaching single storage devices to Windows Server 2003 systems using a Fibre Channel host bus adapter (HBA), the point-to-point topology is ideal. There are, however, some limitations with respect to the loop (FC-AL) topology. Loop topologies are inherently limited in operation and scalability, because they often require full loop reinitialization when devices are added or removed from the SAN. This can cause data to be inaccessible for periods ranging up to minutes. Also, loops can only scale to support up to 127 devices, and, like token ring networks, only allow a single device on the SAN to transmit data at one time, which might not make full use of the available bandwidth on the SAN.

Windows Server 2003 supports FC-AL topologies when a single server is connected to storage. However, the only multiserver configuration supported on a loop is a single two-node cluster. This limitation also applies to the derivatives of FC-AL topologies: Fibre Channel Private Loop SCSI Direct Attachment (FC-PLDA), Fibre Channel Fabric Loop Attachment (FC-FLA), and Fibre Channel Private Loop Attachment (FC-PLA). This means that your SAN design should incorporate a true fabric, or switch-based fabric topology, using a fabric SAN switch (hubs or loop switches should not be used) for any SAN implementation that contains more than two components (servers or storage devices).

 Important

Placing new devices on an FC-AL–based SAN causes Loop Initialization Primitives (LIPs), which appear to the operating system as storage bus resets. LIPs can result in data unavailability and even data loss, if a LIP interrupts a write operation that is only partially committed to the storage device. LIPs can also disrupt backup operations to tape devices and can cause your devices to be assigned new addresses. Therefore, you should use persistent binding. You can limit the propagation of LIPs by using only fabric-based SAN topologies and compatible devices.

For more information about supported Fibre Channel topologies, see article 317162, "Supported Fibre Channel Configurations." To find this article, see the Microsoft Knowledge Base link on the Web Resources page at http://www.microsoft.com/windows/reskits/webresources.

Redundant Components

Although storage data on a SAN offers many benefits, it also introduces additional components whose failure can result in loss of access to data. As on a LAN, the failure of an adapter, switch, or cable can interrupt or remove access to a storage device. The best means to provide for highly available storage is to implement a SAN that uses redundant storage (such as hardware RAID), redundant data access paths (including cables and switches) and server HBAs, and MPIO storage drivers.

Server Cluster Integration

For server clusters of three or more nodes, each node must connect to shared storage over a fabric-based SAN. When planning an SAN storage solution that uses server clusters, ensure that your plan meets the following requirements:

- Each cluster on a SAN should be deployed in its own zone if possible. The mechanism the cluster uses to protect access to the disks can adversely affect other clusters or servers in the same zone. You can prevent this by using zoning to separate the SAN cluster traffic from other traffic.

- All HBAs in a single cluster must be the same type and have the same firmware, driver versions, and driver parameters. Many storage and switch vendors require that all HBAs on the same zone (and, in some cases, on the same fabric) share these features.

- All other storage drivers in the same cluster must have the same software versions.

- Only one node on a cluster should access the disks that are to be managed by the cluster when you first create the cluster, otherwise resource contention might cause the installation to fail.

  This is a requirement because, when the volume automount option is enabled, Windows Server 2003 mounts any volumes it can detect when the operating system boots (this is disabled by default on Windows Server 2003, Enterprise Edition and Windows Server 2003, Datacenter Edition).

   Caution
  If multiple nodes that are not in the same cluster access the same disk, data corruption results.

- Tape devices must not be located in the same zone as cluster disk storage devices unless Storport miniport drivers are used. A tape device will interpret a bus reset as an instruction to rewind and possibly dismount the tape, which will disrupt any backup operation. If this occurs, the backup must be restarted.

For a white paper that provides more information about using SANs with server clusters, see the Windows Clustering: Storage Area Networks link on the Web Resources page at http://www.microsoft.com/windows/reskits/webresources. For more information about Storport miniport drivers, see the MSDN Library link on the Web Resources page at http://www.microsoft.com/windows/reskits/webresources.

SAN Boot Considerations

If your plan requires servers attached to a SAN to boot from disks located on the SAN, you must verify with the disk vendor that the disks can be used to boot a Windows server. When a server's system and boot volumes are stored on a SAN, the SAN vendor must ensure that the disks are accessible during system startup. Make sure that the vendor provides specific configuration information, including needed firmware revisions and setup instructions. You will also need to ensure that each server's HBA is configured according to the disk vendor's guidelines for booting from a SAN.

Additional requirements for successfully booting servers from a SAN are:

- Proper fiber channel topology is used.

  The SAN should be configured in a fabric topology, or the host can be directly attached to the Fibre Channel storage device. For more information about Fibre Channel topologies, see "SAN Configurations" earlier in this chapter.

- Multipathing and redundant SAN links are used.

  You can avoid single points of failure in your SAN design by implementing redundant paths to the critical storage on the SAN, redundant HBAs, and MPIO-compliant drivers.

  Finally, use of the new Storport port driver and appropriate miniports from your HBA vendor will allow more flexibility in configuring your SAN. With Storport miniports, it is possible to have the boot disk and cluster disks on the same Fibre Channel connection. For more information about this configuration, see the Windows Clustering: Storage Area Networks link on the Web Resources page at http://www.microsoft.com/windows/reskits/webresources.

- The boot disk LUN is dedicated to a single host.

  A server that boots from the SAN must have exclusive access to the disk that it is booting from. Exclusively associating a storage device with a server can be accomplished either through zoning or LUN masking, which is configured at the SAN switch, HBA, or storage subsystem level. Storage-based LUN masking is the best choice when you cannot use switch zoning to isolate systems. For more information about LUN masking and zoning see "LUN Masking vs. Zoning" later in this chapter.

For more information about booting from SANs, see article 305547, "Support for Booting from a Storage Area Network (SAN)." To find this article, see the Microsoft Knowledge Base link on the Web Resources page at http://www.microsoft.com/windows/reskits/webresources.

LUN Masking vs. Zoning

The potential for any server on a SAN to mount and access any drive on the SAN can create several problems. The two most prominent ones are disk resource contention and data corruption. To deal with these problems, you can isolate and protect storage devices on a SAN by using zoning and LUN masking, which allow you to dedicate storage devices on the SAN to individual servers.

Zoning

Many devices and nodes can be attached to a SAN. When data is stored in a single *cloud*, or storage entity, it is important to control which hosts have access to specific devices. Zoning controls access from one node to another. Zoning lets you isolate a single server to a group of storage devices or a single storage device, or associate a grouping of multiple servers with one or more storage devices, as might be needed in a server cluster deployment.

Zoning is implemented at the hardware level (by using the capabilities of Fibre Channel switches) and can usually be done either on a port basis (hard zoning) or on a *World-Wide Name* (WWN) basis (soft zoning). WWNs are 64-bit identifiers for devices or ports. All devices with multiple ports have WWNs for each port, which provides more granular management. Because of their length, WWNs are expressed in hexadecimal numbers, similarly to MAC addresses on network adapters. Zoning is configured on a per-target and initiator basis. Consequently, if you need to attach multiple nonclustered nodes to the same storage port, you must also use LUN masking.

LUN masking

LUN masking, performed at the storage controller level, allows you to define relationships between LUNs and individual servers. Storage controllers usually provide the means for creating LUN-level access controls that allow access to a given LUN by one or more hosts. By providing this access control at the storage controller, the controller itself enforces access policies to the devices. LUN masking provides more granular security than zoning, because LUNs provide a means for sharing storage at the port level.

When properly implemented, LUN masking fully isolates servers and storage from events such as resets. This is critical for preventing the problems previously noted. It is important to thoroughly test your design and implementation of LUN masking, especially if you use LUN masking in server clusters.

Integrating Vendor Features

It is likely that your SAN will include applications and services from various vendors. For optimal performance and reliability, you should ensure that all devices and applications on the SAN are fully compatible with Windows Server 2003. Use the following guidelines for all applications on your SAN:

- Device drivers for SAN components should conform to Plug and Play specifications. Failure to use Plug and Play drivers can unexpectedly prevent the operating system from recognizing a device and installing the correct device drivers, which can lead to data loss.

- Drivers for all devices on the SAN, such as HBA and multipathing drivers, should have a digital signature from Microsoft or the storage vendor. Device drivers that contain a digital signature assure you that the product was tested for compatibility with Windows, comes from the specified source, and has not been altered since testing. If the driver does not contain a digital signature from Microsoft or the storage vendor, contact the vendor directly and ask for a driver that meets the Designed for Microsoft Windows Server 2003 logo requirements.

  You can use the Windows Server Catalog to check for software and hardware compatibility with Windows Server 2003. To find the Windows Server Catalog, see the Windows Server Catalog link on the Web Resources page at http://www.microsoft.com/windows/reskits/webresources. Windows Server Catalog also provides information about additional compatibility requirements for software that qualifies for the Supported & Certified for Windows Server 2003 program and hardware that qualifies for the Designed for Windows Server 2003 program. Qualifying products are specifically created to take advantage of the new features in Windows Server 2003.

- Add VDS and Volume Shadow Copy service providers for storage devices that have them. This significantly improves the compatibility of the devices with Windows Server 2003 and gives applications from various vendors the ability to use the capabilities of the devices.

- Contact your storage vendor for a Microsoft MPIO-based multipath solution.

- Make sure that all device drivers are qualified by the storage vendor for use with the specific storage products from that vendor (disk, tape or software) that you will use in your SAN.

- If you are implementing Windows Clustering, it is extremely important that you select hardware configurations that have been approved by Microsoft for Windows server clusters. Microsoft supports only complete server clusters systems chosen from the Windows Server Catalog. For more information about approved hardware configurations, see the Windows Server Catalog link on the Web Resources page at http://www.microsoft.com/windows/reskits/webresources.

For more information about using SANs with server clusters, see "Designing and Deploying Server Clusters" in this book.

Planning to Protect User Data

Windows Server 2003 provides new features that allow you to automate protecting and recovering user data. Most notably, using shadow copies provides a high level of user data protection, and also frees administrators or help desk personnel from dealing with user requests to restore single files. You will also want to consider including folder redirection in your data protection plan. The process of planning to protect user data is shown in Figure 1.8.

Figure 1.8   Planning to Protect User Data

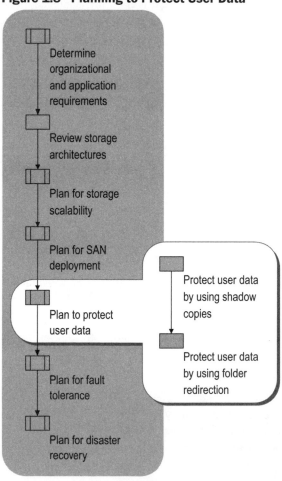

Protecting User Data by Using Shadow Copies

Shadow copies increase the availability of data and reduce the administrative burden of restoring files. After an administrator has configured and enabled shadow copies, users themselves can restore earlier versions of files from point-in-time copies stored on general-purpose file servers that are running Windows Server 2003. Shadow copies are also available on server clusters running Windows Server 2003, Enterprise Edition and Windows Server 2003, Datacenter Edition.

You can enable shadow copies by using Windows Explorer, the Disk Management snap-in, or Shared Folders extension to the Computer Management snap-in. You can also automate administrative tasks that involve making shadow copies by using the command-line tool Vssadmin.exe.

Shadow copies work by making a block-level copy of any changes that have occurred to files since the last shadow copy. Only the changes are copied, not the entire file. As a result, previous versions of files do not usually take up as much disk spacc as the current file, although the amount of disk space used for changes can vary depending on the application that changed the file. For example, some applications rewrite the entire file when a change is made, whereas other applications append changes to the existing file. If the application rewrites the entire file to disk, the shadow copy contains the entire file. Therefore, you should consider how the applications in your organization manage changes to files, as well as the frequency and number of updates to files, when you plan how much disk space to allocate for shadow copies.

Shadow copies are designed for volumes that store user data, and are best suited for protecting user data stored on servers from the following problems:

- Accidental deletion of files

- Accidental overwriting of files (for example, when a user forgets to use **Save As** to create a new version of a file)

- File corruption

Although shadow copies are made for an entire volume, users must use shared folders to access shadow copies. This is because shadow copies are designed to be accessed using the Common Internet File Sharing (CIFS) protocol. If you or your users want to access a previous version of a file that is not located in a shared folder, you must first share the folder. If you want to access shadow copies on a local server, you must use the *servername**sharename* path to access shadow copies.

The method of providing access to shadow copies from a given computer differs depending upon the operating system installed on the computer. Shadow copies can be accessed by computers running Windows Server 2003 and by computers running Microsoft® Windows® XP Professional on which you have installed the Previous Versions Client pack by running Twcli32.msi. This file is located in Windows Server 2003 in *windir*\system32\clients\twclient. You can install this file manually on clients or deploy the file by using the software distribution component of Group Policy. For more information about software distribution, see "Deploying a Managed Software Environment" in *Designing a Managed Environment* of this kit.

To access shadow copies from previous versions of Windows, including Windows 2000 and Windows XP Professional, you can download and install the Shadow Copy Client. For more information and to download the Shadow Copy Client, see the Shadow Copy Client Download link on the Web Resources page at http://www.microsoft.com/windows/reskits/webresources.

 Note

The Previous Versions Client and the Shadow Copy Client provide the same functionality, but the Shadow Copy Client can be installed on multiple operating systems, such as Windows 2000 and Windows XP Professional, whereas the Previous Versions Client can only be installed on Windows XP Professional.

If you have not yet deployed these operating systems or client packs on your clients, you can deploy one or more computers from which users can restore previous versions of files. You can also distribute the client pack on a case-by-case basis to users who request that files be restored.

For more information about shadow copies, see the following sources:

- For more information about designing a shadow copy strategy, see "Designing and Deploying File Servers" in this book.

- For more information about using shadow copies on server clusters, see "Using Shadow Copies of Shared Folders in a server cluster" in Help and Support Center for Windows Server 2003.

- For more information about using Vssadmin.exe to create shadow copies, see "Vssadmin" in Help and Support Center for Windows Server 2003.

Protecting User Data by Using Folder Redirection

If users store their data on their local workstations, you can protect it by using folder redirection. With folder redirection, user folders, such as the My Documents folder, can be redirected to a Windows Server 2003 file server. With all files located on a central server, you can configure shadow copies on the server so that users can recover earlier versions of their files, and you can back up their files in accordance with your organizational standards. You can easily implement folder redirection in your organization by using Group Policy.

Folder redirection offers the following advantages:

- Centralized user data for ease of backup

- Excellent integration and transparency with roaming user profiles

- Easily enforced disk quotas

To redirect special folders, in the Group Policy Object Editor snap-in to Microsoft Management Console (MMC), select the Group Policy object (GPO) that is linked to the site, domain, or organizational unit (OU) that contains the users whose folders you want to redirect. In the **User Configuration\Windows Settings\Folder Redirection** node of the Group Policy Object Editor, double-click **Folder Redirection**, right-click the special folder to redirect, and select **Properties**. Then you can configure redirection as either Basic or Advanced. With Basic redirection, the specified folders of all users are redirected to the same network share. With Advanced redirection, you can specify network share locations for redirection by user group.

If you have mobile users who travel with portable computers, working exclusively with folder redirection might not be feasible. To provide the benefits of folder redirection to mobile users while still making their data available to them when they travel, you can combine Offline Files with folder redirection. Offline Files allows users to download copies of their files from a server when they are connected to the network. If they modify files when they are not connected to the network, those files can be resynchronized with the server the next time the system is connected to the network. You can configure Offline Files options in a Group Policy object in the **Computer Configuration\Administrative Templates\Network\Offline Files** node of the Group Policy Object Editor.

For more information about redirecting folders, see "Implementing User State Management" in *Designing a Managed Environment* of this kit.

Planning for Fault Tolerance

Organizations are increasingly finding that any downtime that results in mission-critical data being unavailable is unacceptable. Windows Server 2003 offers several solutions to increase the availability of data. Solutions that use RAID and clustering technologies are especially suited to providing fault-tolerant storage. The process for analyzing and selecting among these solutions is illustrated in Figure 1.9.

Figure 1.9   Planning for Fault Tolerance

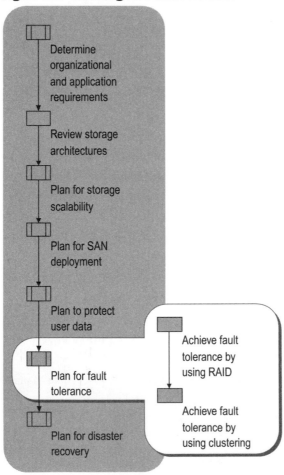

Achieving Fault Tolerance by Using RAID

RAID is commonly implemented for both performance and fault tolerance. With RAID, you can choose to assemble disks to provide fault tolerance, performance, or both, depending on the RAID level that you configure. Table 1.4 summarizes commonly available RAID levels.

Table 1.4   RAID Comparison

RAID Level	Description	Minimum Disks Required	Effective Capacity
0	Disk Striping. Two or more disks appear to the operating system as a single disk. Data is striped across each disk during read/write operations. Potentially increases disk access speeds 2X or better. Not fault tolerant.	2	S*N N = of disks in array S = Size of smallest disk in array
1	Disk mirroring. Data Is mirrored on two or more disks. Provides fault tolerance, but at a higher cost (space required is double the amount of data). Read performance is increased as well.	2	S S = Size of smallest disk in array
0+1	Combines RAID 0 and RAID 1; offers the performance of RAID 0 and the protection of RAID 1.	4	S*N/M N = of disks in array S = Size of smallest disk in array M = Number of mirror sets
5	Disk striping with parity. Provides slower performance than RAID 0, but provides fault tolerance. A single disk can be lost without any data loss. Parity bits are distributed across all disks in the array.	3	S*(N-1) N = of disks in array S = Size of smallest disk in array

From a design perspective, your choice of a RAID solution should be dictated by the type of data being stored. Although RAID 0 offers the fastest read and write performance, it does not offer any fault tolerance, so that if a single disk in a RAID 0 array is lost, all data is lost and will need to be recovered from backup. This might be a good choice for high performance workstations, but might not be suited to mission-critical servers.

RAID 1 allows you to configure two or more disks to mirror each other. This configuration produces slow writes, but relatively quick reads, and provides a means to maintain high data availability on servers, because a single disk can be lost without any loss of data. When more than two disks make up the mirror, the RAID 1 array can lose multiple disks so long as a complete mirrored pair is not lost. When planning a RAID 1 solution, remember that the amount of physical disk space required is twice the space required to store the data.

RAID 0+1 combines the performance benefit of striping with the fault tolerance of mirroring. Compared to RAID 0, writes are slower, but reads are equally fast. Compared to RAID 1, RAID 0+1 offers faster writes and reads but also requires additional storage to create the mirrored stripe sets. This configuration is often ideal for mission-critical database storage, because it offers both fast read access and fault tolerance.

RAID 5 provides fault tolerance: you can lose a single disk in an array with no loss of data. However, RAID 5 operates much more slowly than RAID 0 because a parity bit must be calculated for all write operations. RAID-5 volumes are well suited for reads and also work well in the following situations:

- In large query or database mining applications where reads occur much more often than writes. Performance degrades as the percentage of write operations increases. Database applications that read randomly work well with the built-in load balancing of a RAID 5 volume.

- Where a high degree of fault tolerance is required without the cost of the additional disk space needed for a RAID 1 volume. A RAID 5 volume is significantly more efficient than a mirrored volume when larger numbers of disks are used. The space required for storing the parity information is equivalent to 1/Number of disks, so a 10-disk array uses 1/10 of its capacity for parity information. The disk space that is used for parity decreases as the number of disks in the array increases.

Choosing Between Hardware and Software RAID

An additional consideration with RAID implementations is the choice between hardware-based and software-based RAID. With hardware RAID, a hardware RAID controller allows you to configure the RAID level of attached disks. With software RAID, the operating system manages the RAID configuration, along with data reads and writes.

Windows Server 2003 supports the following software RAID types:

- RAID 0: Up to 32 disks striped
- RAID 1: Two disks mirrored
- RAID 5: Up to 32 disks striped with parity

To configure software RAID, a disk must be configured as a dynamic disk. Although software RAID has lower performance than hardware RAID, software RAID is inexpensive and easy to configure because it has no special hardware requirements other than multiple disks. If cost is more important than performance, software RAID is appropriate. If you plan to use software RAID for write-heavy workloads, use RAID-1 instead of RAID-5. Using software-based RAID with Windows Server 2003 dynamic disks is a good choice for providing fault tolerance using SCSI or EIDE disks to non-mission-critical servers that require fault tolerance and can accommodate the added CPU load imposed by software RAID. This solution is ideal for small to medium organizations that need to add a level of fault tolerance while avoiding the cost of hardware RAID controllers.

For more information about software RAID and disk management, see the *Server Management Guide* of the *Windows Server 2003 Resource Kit* (or see the *Server Management Guide* on the Web at http://www.microsoft.com/reskit).

Using Dynamic Disks with Hardware RAID

You can also use dynamic disks with hardware-based RAID solutions. Using dynamic disks with hardware RAID can be useful in the following situations:

- You want create a large volume by using software RAID, such as RAID-0, across hardware RAID LUNs.

- You want to extend a volume, but the underlying hardware cannot dynamically increase the size of LUNs.

- You want to extend a volume, but the hardware has reached its maximum LUN size.

Before converting hardware RAID disks to dynamic disks, review the following restrictions:

- You cannot use dynamic disks on shared cluster storage. However, you can use the DiskPart command-line tool to extend basic volumes on shared cluster storage. For more information, see "Extend a basic volume" in Help and Support Center for Windows Server 2003.

- If you create a software RAID-0 volume across multiple hardware arrays, you cannot later extend the RAID-0 volume to increase its size. If you anticipate needing to extend the volume, create a spanned volume instead.

Preparing to Upgrade Servers That Contain Multidisk Fault-Tolerant Volumes

Servers running Microsoft® Windows NT® Server version 4.0 can contain volume sets, mirror sets, stripe sets, and stripe sets with parity created by using the fault-tolerant driver Ftdisk.sys. To encourage administrators to begin using dynamic volumes, Windows 2000 offers limited support for Ftdisk volumes. Completing this transition, Windows Server 2003 does not support multidisk volumes. If you plan to upgrade a server that contains multidisk volumes, review the following issues:

- If you are upgrading from Windows NT Server version 4.0 to Windows Server 2003, back up and then delete all multidisk volumes before upgrading. This is necessary because Windows Server 2003 cannot access these volumes. Be sure to verify that your backup was successful before deleting the volumes. After you finish upgrading to Windows Server 2003, create new dynamic volumes, and then restore the data from your backup.

- If you are upgrading from Windows NT Server 4.0 to Windows Server 2003, and the paging file is located on a multidisk volume, you must use **System** in Control Panel to move the paging file to a primary partition or logical drive before beginning Setup. For more information about moving the paging file, see article 123747, "Moving the Windows Default Paging and Spool File." To find this article, see the Microsoft Knowledge Base link on the Web Resources page at http://www.microsoft.com/windows/reskits/webresources.

- If you are upgrading from Windows 2000 Server to Windows Server 2003, you must use the Disk Management snap-in to convert all basic disks that contain multidisk volumes to dynamic disks before beginning Setup. If you do not do this, Setup does not continue. For information about converting basic disks to dynamic disks, see "Change a basic disk into a dynamic disk" in Help and Support Center for Windows Server 2003.

For more information about multidisk volumes, see the *Server Management Guide* of the *Windows Server 2003 Resource Kit* (or see the *Server Management Guide* on the Web at http://www.microsoft.com/reskit).

Achieving Fault Tolerance by Using Clustering

Many organizations require that critical data be continuously available. Cluster technology provides a means of configuring storage to help meet that goal. Simply put, a cluster is two or more computer systems that act and are managed as one. Clients access the cluster by using a single host name or IP address; their request is answered by one of the systems in the cluster.

The purpose of cluster technology is to eliminate single points of failure. When availability of data is your paramount consideration, clustering is ideal. Using a cluster avoids all of these single points of failure:

- Network card failure

- Processor failure

- Motherboard failure

- Power failure

- Cable failure

- Storage adapter failure

With a cluster, you can essentially eliminate nearly any hardware failure associated with using a single computer. If hardware associated with one system fails, the other system automatically takes over. Two types of clustering solutions that accomplish this are *server clusters* and *Network Load Balancing clusters*. Both types of clustering are available on Windows Server 2003, Enterprise Edition and Windows Server 2003, Datacenter Edition. In addition, Network Load Balancing clusters are available on Windows Server 2003, Web Edition and Windows Server 2003, Standard Edition.

Server Clusters

Server clusters are often implemented to offer high availability solutions to applications that need both read and write access to data, such as database, e-mail, and file servers. Server clusters can be configured with up to eight computers, or nodes, participating in the cluster. To share the same data source, server cluster nodes connect to external disk arrays by using either a SCSI or Fibre Channel connection. Fibre Channel is required for interconnecting clusters of three or more nodes to shared storage. For the 64-bit versions of Windows Server 2003, you must always use Fibre Channel hardware to connect the nodes to shared storage.

When planning to deploy server clusters in your storage solution, you must take into account the following considerations:

- The boot and system disks of each cluster node must not be located on the same storage bus as the shared storage devices, unless you use a Storport driver for your HBAs.
- Shared cluster disks cannot be configured as dynamic disks.
- Shared cluster disks must be formatted as basic disks with the NTFS file system.
- For the 64-bit versions of the Windows Server 2003 family, the shared cluster disks must be partitioned as master boot record (MBR) and not as GUID partition table (GPT) disks.
- You cannot use Remote Storage with shared cluster storage.
- You should not enable write caching on shared cluster disks unless they are logical units on an external RAID subsystem that has proper power protection (such as multiple power supplies, multiple feeds from the power grid, or adequate battery backup).
- Because cluster disks must be basic disks, you cannot use software RAID. For disk fault tolerance, you must use a hardware-based RAID solution.

For more information about server clusters, see "Designing and Deploying Server Clusters" in this book.

Network Load Balancing Clusters

Network Load Balancing clusters maintain their own local copy of data and are ideal for load balancing access to static data, such as Web pages. Up to 32 computers can participate in a Network Load Balancing cluster. Because they manage their own local data, Network Load Balancing clusters are much easier to plan and implement. By using the Network Load Balancing Manager, you can quickly configure all Network Load Balancing clusters in your enterprise from a single server.

Using Network Load Balancing clusters is the best choice for several data availability needs. For any server that has difficulty meeting the load demands of its clients, Network Load Balancing is an ideal solution, and is commonly used to provide fault tolerance and load balancing for:

- Web Servers
- FTP Servers
- Streaming Media Servers

- VPN Servers

- Terminal Servers

For each of these, Network Load Balancing is ideal, not only because it is easy to implement, but also because of how easily a Network Load Balancing cluster can scale as your company grows. Because of their simple scalability, your initial estimates of the number of servers you will require need not be perfect with Network Load Balancing clusters. As the load on a Network Load Balancing cluster grows, you can balance the increased load by simply adding additional hosts to the cluster.

Because each Network Load Balancing cluster host maintains its own local copy of storage, storage planning with Network Load Balancing clusters is not as complex as with server clusters. Many of the disk restrictions of server clusters do not apply to Network Load Balancing clusters. The general storage considerations for Network Load Balancing cluster planning are:

- Network Load Balancing cluster hosts can use any local storage space, including space on boot or system volumes.

- Local storage can consist of basic and dynamic disks.

- Hardware or software RAID can be used to add additional fault tolerance. If the Network Load Balancing cluster services a high level of traffic and you need disk fault tolerance, you must use hardware RAID.

For more information about Network Load Balancing clusters, see "Designing Network Load Balancing" and "Deploying Network Load Balancing" in this book.

Planning for Disaster Recovery

A number of technologies are available that provide fault tolerance in the event of a failure, such as fault tolerant disk configurations with hot swappable drives, server clusters, and uninterruptible power supplies, However, all of these high availability technologies cannot substitute for having a reliable backup of mission-critical data.

In a complete site disaster, for example, it is possible that both online and offline availability technologies are destroyed (for example, all cluster nodes and all disks in a RAID array). Following such a system failure or disaster at a particular site, you must be able to recover data and systems from backup. Recovering systems or sites from failure is a daunting task, unless you have thoroughly planned and prepared by implementing scheduled backups, providing for backups of open files, and configuring for Automated System Restore. You must also thoroughly test your ability to restore data. The tasks involved in planning for disaster recovery are shown in Figure 1.10.

Figure 1.10   Planning for Disaster Recovery

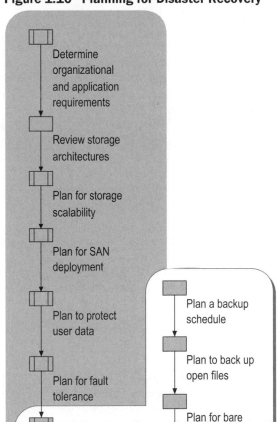

Planning a Backup Schedule

The backup schedule is perhaps the most important consideration when planning for disaster recovery. It is critical to plan your backups around your restore requirements. For example, you run only incremental backups of a file server over an extended period of time. This approach delivers very fast backups that use little network bandwidth. However, to restore the server, you would need to restore all of the incremental backups, which could take days to complete. A backup plan presumes a restore plan: Your backup plan should always be based on your requirements for restoring data. You should carefully test and document all of the processes and time required to fully recover your servers from backup data. Use the results of this testing to establish the requirements for your backup schedules.

Backup Decision Points

To plan an effective backup schedule that meets your organization's data protection and recovery requirements, consider both the available backup types and your restore plan. When considering backup types, remember that your choice must accommodate restoring a system within the time specified in your restore plan. Available backup types can be categorized as fundamental and advanced.

Fundamental Backup Types

The fundamental backup types available are:

- **Full.** Full backups are the baseline for all other backups, and contain all the data on a system (or all the data in the folders or volumes that are defined to be backed up). Because full backups secure all server data, frequent full backups can provide you with greater guarantees as to the speed and success of restore operations. Remember that when you add additional backup types to the backup set, restore jobs are prolonged.

- **Incremental.** An incremental backup stores all files that have changed since the last backup, regardless of the backup type. The advantage of incremental backups is that they take the least time to complete. However, during a restore operation, each incremental backup in the backup set is applied, which could result in a lengthy restore job.

- **Differential.** Differential backups contain all data that has changed since the last full backup. The advantage of differential backups is that they can shorten restore time compared to a backup set that includes just full and incremental backups. However, if you perform too many differential backups within a single backup set, the size of the differential backup might grow to be as large as the baseline full backup.

- **Copy.** Copy backups are identical to full backups, with the exception that they do not mark files as backed up, and thus do not impact any other backup types. A full backup marks the beginning of a new backup cycle, while a copy backup does not. Copy backups are most frequently used to create offsite copies of backup data. In this way, you can maintain a local full backup for quick restore purposes, and keep an offsite copy backup for use in the event that your local backup copy is lost.

Your backup schedule should probably include some combination of all backup types. Regular full backups take the longest to complete, but offer the quickest restore performance. Because full backups copy all files defined in the backup job, they also consume the most backup media. Incremental backups consume the least backup media and take the shortest time to complete; however, they result in lengthier restores. Consequently, it is best to balance each of the backup types so as to satisfy your organizations restore needs. For example, you might elect to perform weekly full backups of a crucial file server, and supplement that with daily differential backups, and incremental backups every two hours. This approach gives you a high degree of data protection, while keeping restore time within reasonable boundaries.

Advanced Backup Types

Advanced backup types include:

- **Backup applications that leverage the Volume Shadow Copy service.** Backup applications that support the Volume Shadow Copy service can back up open files, and all the backed-up files are from a single point-in-time. For more information about backing up open files, see "Planning to Back Up Open Files" later in this chapter.

- **Server-free backups.** In a server-free backup, a *data mover* on a SAN copies data on a SAN disk to another storage device, such as a library on the SAN. A data mover is software that can reside on a SAN device, such as a switch or router, or on a server connected to the SAN. Because the data mover performs the copy operations, the server can maintain a high level of performance for clients. Server-free backup applications must have a way of creating a point-in-time snapshot, such as by leveraging the Volume Shadow Copy service or by using some other technology.

- **Hardware-based shadow copies.** External storage arrays that support hardware-based shadow copies (also called *snapshots*) can implement Volume Shadow Copy service providers to fully utilize advanced storage array features.

Your choice of how to integrate advanced backup types into your backup schedule will be dictated by your restore requirements. Some systems might require hourly shadow copies, while other, low priority systems might only warrant weekly full backups and daily incremental backups. Your best strategy is to align your backup plan for each system with the restore plan for that system. If the system requires quick recovery of user files, frequent shadow copies are ideal. If the data on the same system is required to be retained for seven years, then you will also need to perform frequent full backups of the system to media that can be stored in an offsite location.

For more information about backup and recovery planning, see the *Server Management Guide* of the *Windows Server 2003 Resource Kit* (or see the *Server Management Guide* on the Web at http://www.microsoft.com/reskit).

Planning to Back Up Open Files

Open files are files that are normally skipped during the backup process. This is usually because the files are locked by a service or application, such as an operating system, word processing program, or application database. In Windows 2000 and Windows NT 4.0, if the operating system could not back up a file that was locked by an application, the file was skipped, and thus not backed up. In Windows Server 2003, open files are backed up by using the Volume Shadow Copy service.

When a backup is initiated by an application that can use the Volume Shadow Copy service, such as the Backup program in Windows Server 2003, the Volume Shadow Copy service makes a shadow copy of the volume to be backed up. The shadow copy constitutes a read-only copy of the volume data that is read by the backup application during the backup job. Applications can continue to access the files on the volume itself, uninterrupted by the backup. After the backup is completed, the shadow copy of the volume is deleted, because it is no longer needed. The backed-up data is stored on the backup media.

By default, Windows Server 2003 temporarily consumes free disk space on a volume for the shadow copy. The amount of disk space consumed depends on the amount of data that changes on the volume during the backup.

In the event that a shadow copy is unsuccessful, for example, when there is not enough temporary disk space available on the volume, Backup continues without using shadow copy techniques and, as in previous versions of Windows, reads files from the original volume and does not back up any open files.

To take advantage of open-file backups, purchase a backup application that works with the Volume Shadow Copy service.

Planning for Bare Metal Restores with ASR

Automated System Recovery (ASR) is a new tool for use with Backup (NTBackup.exe) and other programs created by ISVs. It has a limited but critical purpose: to help you automatically restore your system after a system failure. Previously, restoring the complete system required that you first reinstall the operating system and then restore the data. With a bare metal restore, you can boot a system from the operating system CD, and then use an ASR floppy disk to recover the system directly from a backup.

ASR works with Windows Setup to rebuild the storage configuration of the physical disks and writes the critical operating system files to the boot and system partitions in order to allow the system to boot successfully. This process is referred to as a *bare metal restore*, because the system is restored to hardware that has no installed software. The process uses an ASR floppy disk that defines the state of the storage prior to the disaster and the process to be used for restoring the server. After an ASR restore completes, you can restore any needed user or application files.

How ASR Works

ASR represents a new approach to backup and recovery. Prior to ASR, after a large-scale failure, you needed to reinstall Windows, configure all physical storage to the original settings, and then perform a complete restore of the data. The process of rebuilding the operating system could be lengthy, and you needed to perform many of these tasks at the local computer. ASR significantly automates this process. In addition to automating the restore of a single system, ASR can be used with Remote Installation Services (RIS) to automate the system state recovery of several systems across the network.

To prepare for ASR recovery, you must run the Automated System Recovery Wizard, which is part of Backup. To access this wizard when you are running Backup in Advanced Mode, click **Tools** and select **ASR Wizard**. You can start Backup in Advanced Mode by clearing the **Always start in Wizard Mode** check box when Backup starts.

The wizard backs up the operating system boot volumes and system volumes, but does not back up other volumes, such as program or data volumes. To secure data on other volumes, you must back up those volumes separately by using Backup or another backup tool. You can, however, choose to back up **All information on this computer** when running Backup. This option creates a full backup of your entire system, including ASR data. This means that you can recover the entire system through the ASR process in the event of failure.

When an ASR restore is initiated, ASR first reads the disk configurations from the ASR floppy disk and restores all disk signatures and volumes on the disks from which the system boots. In the ASR process, these are known as *critical disks*, because they are required by the operating system. Noncritical disks — disks that might store user or application data — are not backed up as a part of a normal ASR backup, and are not included in an ASR restore. If these disks are not corrupted, their data will still be accessible after the ASR restore completes. If you want to secure data on noncritical disks from disk failure, you can do so by backing it up separately.

After the critical disks are recreated, ASR performs a simple installation of Windows Server 2003 and automatically starts a restore from backup using the backup media originally created by the ASR Wizard. During an ASR restore, any Plug and Play devices on the system are detected and installed.

Before performing an ASR restore, ensure that the target system to which the restore will be made meets the following requirements:

- The target system hardware (except for hard disks, video cards, and network adapters) is identical to that of the original system.

- There are enough disks to restore all the critical system disks.

- The number and storage capacity of the critical disks are at least as great as those of the corresponding original disks.

 Caution

Do not depend on ASR to back up and recover user data files stored on the boot and system volumes. In addition, because your system volume is formatted during the ASR recovery process, any user files or directories located on those volumes are lost.

You normally access the ASR state file (Asr.sif) through a local floppy disk drive. If the computer does not have a floppy disk drive, or you want to perform an ASR restore over a network or remotely, you can use a Remote Installation Services (RIS) server to fully automate the ASR process. RIS uses Pre-boot eXecution Environment (PXE) technology to enable client computers without an operating system to boot remotely to a RIS server that performs installation of a supported operating system over a TCP/IP network connection. Consequently, the remote installation client computer must have a PXE-enabled network adapter.

For more information about using RIS to perform remote installations, see "Designing RIS Installations" in *Automating and Customizing Installations* of this kit.

 Note

ASR behaves differently from the Emergency Repair Disk feature in Windows 2000 Server, which ASR replaces. Emergency Repair Disk replaces missing or corrupt system files without formatting drives or reconfiguring storage. ASR, by contrast, always formats the boot volume and might format the system volume.

Guidelines for Using ASR

To successfully use ASR in your disaster recovery plan, you should include the following guidelines:

- Run ASR backup regularly, preferably by using automatic settings.

- Plan for making the required resources, including tape backup drives and removable and hard disks, available for ASR recovery.

- Perform any needed file system conversions before running your first ASR backup.

- Plan for conditions that might prevent a fully successful ASR restore.

  Under the following conditions, ASR might not be able to restore all disk configurations

  - If a critical volume is not accessible during an ASR restore, the restore will fail.

  - Noncritical disks that are a part of the ASR backup are not restored if they are not found during the ASR restore, but the balance of the restore will complete successfully. Disk types that might not appear to the restore process include IEEE 1394, USB, or Jaz disks.

- Plan to protect the critical files Asr.sif and Asrpnp.sif generated by Backup and copied to your ASR floppy disk.

  If the ASR floppy disk that contains these files is lost, you can recover the files from the *systemroot*\Repair folder on the host system. If these files are not accessible on the original host, you can recover them from the ASR backup media by using another system. By storing these files in three locations — the ASR floppy disk, the Repair folder, and on ASR backup media — you have three levels of protection against their loss.

For more information about ASR, see the *Server Management Guide* of the *Windows Server 2003 Resource Kit* (or see the *Server Management Guide* on the Web at http://www.microsoft.com/reskit) and see "Automated System Recovery (ASR) overview" in Help and Support Center for Windows Server 2003.

Testing Restores

The single most overlooked aspect of disaster recovery planning is testing restores. Receiving confirmation that a backup completed successfully does not guarantee that a backup can be restored. To prepare for recovery and to validate backup data, you should periodically test your backups of mission-critical servers. If a server cannot be taken offline for testing restores, you can instead restore its backup data to a test server. Practicing restore operations allows you to prepare for problems that you might encounter when recovering a complete system after a failure. These problems include the following:

- When restoring to a new server with different hardware — for example, if the original server used SCSI storage and the server where you restore the data uses IDE storage — you might need to filter files such as Boot.ini from the restore job. If the restored data replaces the Boot.ini file, the system might not be able to boot following the restore, and the parameters in the restored Boot.ini file would need to be modified.

- When restoring to a new server with different hardware, you might need different drivers, such as drivers for the network adapter or display adapter. Make sure that these drivers are available during the restore.

- The time required to restore data might exceed the time allotted in your recovery plan, which means you must change your backup schedule, your process, or your equipment to improve the speed of the restoration.

- Backup media might be corrupt. Your disaster recovery plan should specify preventive measures (such as redundant backups), and indicate the procedures to follow in the event of corrupt media (such as the location of any redundant backups, or whether out-of-date backups are to be used).

Testing restores can help you plan how to deal with such problems. For example, if your organization requires that a critical file server be returned to full operation within a four hour window, but your test restore took six hours to complete, you can plan to either adjust your backup schedule or else justify the purchase faster backup media drives or network components. Without thoroughly testing your restore procedures, you cannot conclusively document recovery procedures or recovery time, both of which are crucial to your organization's disaster recovery plan.

Additional Resources

Related Information

- "Designing and Deploying File Servers" in this book.

- "Planning for High Availability and Scalability" in this book.

- "Designing and Deploying Server Clusters" in this book.

- "Designing Network Load Balancing" in this book.

- "Deploying Network Load Balancing" in this book.

- The *Server Management Guide* of the *Windows Server 2003 Resource Kit* (or see the *Server Management Guide* on the Web at http://www.microsoft.com/reskit) for more information about disk management and file systems.

- The Windows Powered Network Attached Storage link on the Web Resources page at http://www.microsoft.com/windows/reskits/webresources.

- The Storage Services link on the Web Resources page at http://www.microsoft.com/windows/reskits/webresources.

- The Windows Clustering: Storage Area Networks link on the Web Resources page at http://www.microsoft.com/windows/reskits/webresources.

Related Help Topics

For best results in identifying Help topics by title, in Help and Support Center, under the **Search** box, click **Set search options**. Under **Help Topics**, select the **Search in title only** check box.

- "Using NTFS mounted drives" in Help and Support Center for Windows Server 2003.

- "Using Shadow Copies of Shared Folders in a server cluster" in Help and Support Center for Windows Server 2003.

- "Extend a basic volume" in Help and Support Center for Windows Server 2003.

- "Change a basic disk into a dynamic disk" in Help and Support Center for Windows Server 2003.

- "Automated System Recovery (ASR) overview" in Help and Support Center for Windows Server 2003.

Related Tools

- Diskraid.exe

  Use Diskraid.exe to manage and configure RAID subsystems that have the necessary VDS hardware providers. For more information about Diskraid.exe, in Help and Support Center for Windows Server 2003 click **Tools**, and then click Command-line reference **A-Z**.

- Diskpart.exe

  Use Diskpart.exe to manage disks and volumes from the command line. For more information about Diskpart.exe, in Help and Support Center for Windows Server 2003 click **Tools**, and then click Command-line reference **A-Z**.

C H A P T E R   2

Designing and Deploying File Servers

File servers running the Microsoft® Windows® Server 2003 operating system are ideal for providing access to files for users in medium and large organizations. Windows Server 2003 offers a number of file server solutions, such as Distributed File System (DFS), File Replication service (FRS), Windows server clusters, NTFS permissions, disk quotas, and shadow copies, for enhancing the manageability, scalability, availability, and security of file servers.

In This Chapter

Related Information

- For information about installing and managing software applications by using Group Policy, see "Deploying a Managed Software Environment" in *Designing a Managed Environment* of this kit.

- For information about managing user desktops, settings, and data by storing data and settings on network servers, see "Implementing User State Management" in *Designing a Managed Environment*.

- For information about server clusters, see "Designing and Deploying Server Clusters" in this book.

Overview of Designing and Deploying File Servers

File servers provide users a way to access shared data within their department or organization. The simplest way to create a file server is to share a folder on a server. However, this solution does not provide file server manageability, scalability, availability, or security. To achieve these goals, you can deploy the following Windows Server 2003 solutions:

Shadow copies   If users frequently require administrators to restore deleted or overwritten files from tape, shadow copies provide point-in-time copies of files in shared folders, allowing users to recover files that were accidentally deleted or overwritten.

DFS   If users need to access files on multiple file servers without having to keep track of all the server names, you can use DFS to logically group physical shared folders located on different servers by transparently connecting them to one or more hierarchical namespaces. DFS also provides fault-tolerance and load-sharing capabilities.

FRS and Windows server clusters   Windows Server 2003 provides two independent solutions, FRS and server clusters, to ensure that important business data is always available, even if a server fails or is taken offline for maintenance.

Disk quotas   By using the disk quotas feature in Windows Server 2003, you can track files on a per-volume, per-user basis to monitor disk space use and to prevent file servers from filling to capacity without warning.

NTFS permissions   To prevent unauthorized users from accessing folders, you can use NTFS file system permissions to specify the groups and users whose access you want to restrict or allow and then select the type of access.

You can use the following information to design your organization's file services. Or, if your organization already has file servers running Microsoft® Windows® NT 4.0 or Microsoft® Windows® 2000 operating systems, you can use the following information to improve the design of your existing file services to take advantage of the new and enhanced features in the Microsoft® Windows® Server 2003, Standard Edition; Windows® Server 2003, Enterprise Edition; and Windows® Server 2003, Datacenter Edition operating systems.

File Server Design and Deployment Process

Figure 2.1 outlines the general process of file server deployment. This process consists of a design phase and a deployment phase. A file services designer or design team performs the design process. The file services deployment team implements the design by deploying file servers running Windows Server 2003 and configuring the file services solutions described in this chapter. Because some features of DFS and FRS require the Active Directory® directory service, this process assumes that your organization already has an existing Active Directory infrastructure.

Figure 2.1   Designing and Deploying a File Server

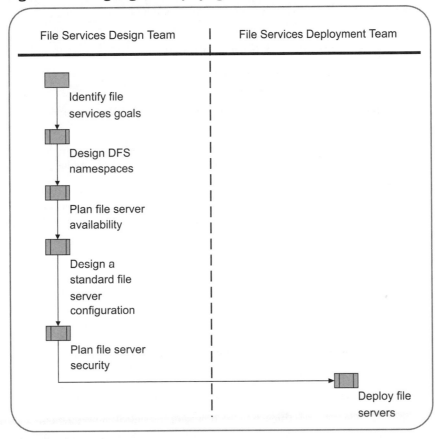

New and Enhanced File Server Features in Windows Server 2003

The following sections summarize the new and enhanced features in Windows Server 2003 that are described in this chapter.

Shadow copies

The shadow copy feature provides point-in-time copies of files on a volume, allowing users to view the contents of shared folders as they existed at points of time in the past. After you enable this feature, users can recover files that they accidentally delete or overwrite.

DFS enhancements

Windows Server 2003 includes the following DFS enhancements:

- You can create multiple DFS roots on servers running Windows Server 2003, Enterprise Edition and Windows Server 2003, Datacenter Edition.

- You can configure DFS to choose an alternate target based on the lowest connection cost if no same-site targets are available.

- You can use the Distributed File System snap-in to choose replication topologies that complement your network infrastructure.

- You can move a root target or a link target from one Active Directory site to another, and DFS will update the root or link information for the new site within 25 hours.

- To reduce network traffic to the server acting as primary domain controller (PDC) emulator master, you can configure DFS to get namespace updates from the closest domain controller, instead of from the server acting as the PDC emulator master. This mode is known as *root scalability mode*.

- By using the Offline Files feature, you can make shared folders that correspond to DFS link targets available offline to clients running Microsoft® Windows® XP Professional and Windows Server 2003. (You cannot make DFS link targets available offline to clients running Windows 2000.)

FRS enhancements

Windows Server 2003 includes the following FRS enhancements:

- FRS detects and suppresses excessive replication.

- FRS manages the staging directory to prevent it from becoming full.

- FRS supports connection priorities, which allow you to control the sequencing of the initial synchronization that occurs when you add a new member to the replica set or when you perform a *nonauthoritative restore*, which is used to bring a failed replica member back into synchronization with its partners.

Security enhancements

When you share a folder, the default permission is the Read permission for the Everyone group. This default is different from the default share permission in Windows 2000, which was the Full Control permission for the Everyone group.

Server cluster enhancements

Windows Server 2003, Enterprise Edition and Windows Server 2003, Datacenter Edition include the following server cluster enhancements:

- You can store encrypted files by using Encrypting File System (EFS) on cluster storage.

- You can create multiple stand-alone DFS roots on a clustered file server, and the roots can reside on any of the nodes in the cluster.

- You can enable client-side caching to cache files from a cluster file share onto client computers. Clients can then access these files even when the client computer is disconnected from the network.

Identifying File Services Goals

Some of the major steps for designing and deploying file servers might not apply to your organization. Therefore, the first step in the design process is to identify the goals that you want to achieve by deploying file servers running Windows Server 2003, as shown in Figure 2.2. These goals determine the design and deployment steps that are necessary for your organization.

Figure 2.2   Identifying File Services Goals

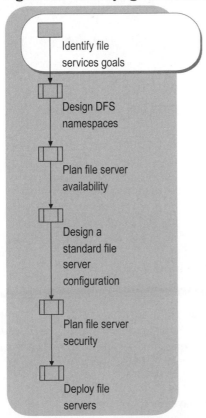

The following sections describe common goals for file services. Use the information in these sections to identify the goals for your organization and to find the relevant sections in this chapter or other sources of information to help you achieve those goals.

Improving the way users access files on file servers

If you want to improve how users access files on file servers, you might have the following goals:

- Providing an intuitive way for users to access multiple file servers throughout the organization.

- Making data on multiple file servers appear as though it were available on a single file server.

- Making data available in multiple sites so that users in each site use fast, inexpensive bandwidth to access the data.

- Reducing delays that occur when users access heavily used shared folders.

- Providing fault-tolerant access to shared folders.

- Consolidating file servers or migrating data without affecting how users locate data.

For more information about improving how users access files on file servers, see "Designing DFS Namespaces" later in this chapter.

Managing applications and user data and settings

If you are managing applications, user data, and settings, you might have the following goals:

- Enabling users to access files even when they are not connected to the network.

- Storing application files on file servers so that users can install the applications from the network to their local workstations.

- Using Group Policy–based software management to deploy, upgrade, patch, and remove users' applications without going to individual workstations.

- Allowing users to run applications from the file server.

For more information about managing applications and user data and settings, see "Implementing User State Management" and "Deploying a Managed Software Environment" in *Designing a Managed Environment* of this kit. For more information about hosting applications in a central location, see "Hosting Applications with Terminal Server" in this book.

Adding storage to file servers

If you plan to add storage to file servers, you might have the following goals:

- Transparently adding more storage to a file server.

- Making data on multiple volumes or disks in a file server appear within a single volume or drive letter.

- Creating more than 26 volumes on a server without being limited by the 26-drive letter limit.

For more information about adding storage to file servers, see "Using NTFS mounted drives" in Help and Support Center for Windows Server 2003.

Planning for file server availability and reliability

If you are planning for file server availability and reliability, you might have the following goals:

- Choosing file server hardware for reliability and availability.

- Ensuring data availability if a file server fails or is taken offline for maintenance.

- Making data available in multiple sites to provide inexpensive access to users within each site.

For more information about planning for file server availability and reliability, see "Planning File Server Availability" later in this chapter.

Choosing file server hardware and settings

If you are choosing file server hardware and settings, you might have the following goals:

- Choosing compatible file server hardware that meets your performance and storage requirements.

- Increasing file server performance.

- Consolidating file servers to reduce management costs and increase storage allocation efficiency.

- Enabling users to access previous versions of files on the file server.

- Monitoring and controlling disk space use.

For more information about choosing file server hardware and settings, see "Designing a Standard File Server Configuration" later in this chapter.

Planning for file server security

If you are planning for file server security, you might have the following goals:

- Protecting file servers from viruses.

- Preventing unauthorized users from accessing data on file servers.

- Allowing users to store encrypted files on a file server.

For more information about planning for file server security, see "Planning File Server Security" later in this chapter.

Designing DFS Namespaces

Users might have difficulty finding information in shared folders that are located on numerous file servers. Because shared folders are usually associated with physical servers, the user must first determine which physical server is hosting the shared folder. For example, a user might need to access product information on a server named \\Building 4\Marketing2\Prod_Info and on a server named \\Corporate\Floor 4\Sales\Prod_Info.

You can use DFS to address this challenge by consolidating a large set of physical shared folders into one or more virtual namespaces. You do not need to modify the shared folders to add them to the namespace, and users can navigate the namespace without having to know the physical server names or shared folders hosting the data.

Figure 2.3 outlines the general process of designing one or more DFS namespaces. For an Excel spreadsheet to assist you in documenting your DFS namespace design decisions, see "DFS Configuration Worksheet" (Sdcfsv_1.xls) on the *Microsoft® Windows® Server 2003 Deployment Kit* companion CD (or see "DFS Configuration Worksheet" on the Web at http://www.microsoft.com/reskit).

Figure 2.3   Designing DFS Namespaces

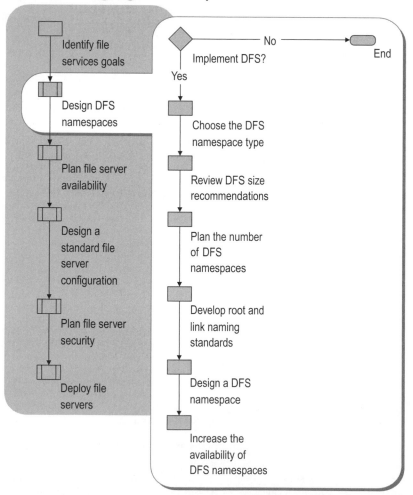

For more information about DFS security, see "Planning DFS and FRS Security" later in this chapter. For in-depth technical and troubleshooting information about DFS, see the *Distributed Services Guide* of the *Microsoft® Windows® Server 2003 Resource Kit* (or see the *Distributed Services Guide* on the Web at http://www.microsoft.com/reskit).

Deciding Whether to Implement DFS

Organizations of any size, with any number of file servers, can benefit from implementing DFS. DFS is especially beneficial for organizations in which any of the following conditions exist:

- The organization plans to deploy additional file servers or consolidate existing file servers.

- The organization has data that is stored in multiple file servers.

- The organization wants to replace physical servers or shared folders without affecting how users access the data.

- The organization has data located on servers in multiple sites and wants clients to connect to the closest servers.

- Most users require access to multiple file servers.

- Users experience delays when accessing file servers during peak usage periods.

- Users require uninterrupted access to file servers.

Even if you are busy planning your organization's migration to Windows Server 2003, you can make plans to implement DFS without immediately designing your entire namespace. You do not need to deploy DFS all at one time; you can choose to add as much or as little of your organization's physical storage as you need to the DFS namespace, at a pace that works with your overall migration schedule.

When deciding whether to implement DFS, do the following:

1. Review DFS terminology.

2. Review the benefits of using DFS.

3. Evaluate clients and servers for compatibility.

The following sections describe each of these steps.

Reviewing DFS Terminology

If you are not familiar with DFS, review the following terms and definitions to understand the important elements of a DFS configuration. For visual examples of these concepts, see Figure 2.4 through Figure 2.7 later in this section.

DFS namespace   A virtual view of shared folders on different servers as provided by DFS. A DFS namespace consists of a root and many links and targets. The namespace starts with a root that maps to one or more root targets. Below the root are links that map to their own targets.

DFS root   The starting point of the DFS namespace. The root is often used to refer to the namespace as a whole. A root maps to one or more root targets, each of which corresponds to a shared folder on a separate server. The DFS root must reside on an NTFS volume. A DFS root has one of the following formats: *servername**rootname* or *domainname**rootname*.

Root target   A physical server that hosts a DFS namespace. A domain-based DFS root can have multiple root targets, whereas a stand-alone DFS root can only have one root target.

Stand-alone DFS namespace   A DFS namespace whose configuration information is stored locally in the registry of the host server. The path to access the root or a link starts with the host server name. A stand-alone DFS root has only one root target. Stand-alone roots are not fault tolerant; when the root target is unavailable, the entire DFS namespace is inaccessible. You can make stand-alone DFS roots fault tolerant by creating them on clustered file servers.

Domain-based DFS namespace   A DFS namespace that has configuration information stored in Active Directory. The path to access the root or a link starts with the host domain name. A domain-based DFS root can have multiple root targets, which offers fault tolerance and load sharing at the root level.

DFS path   Any Universal Naming Convention (UNC) path that starts with a DFS root.

Link   A component in a DFS path that lies below the root and maps to one or more link targets.

Link target   The mapping destination of a link. A link target can be any UNC path. For example, a link target could be a shared folder or another DFS path.

Figure 2.4 illustrates the elements of a stand-alone DFS namespace in the Distributed File System snap-in. These elements include a stand-alone DFS root, a single root target, and multiple links.

Figure 2.4   Elements of a Stand-Alone DFS Namespace

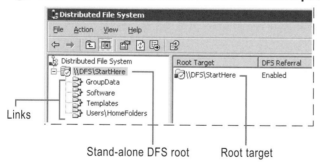

Figure 2.5 illustrates the elements of a domain-based DFS namespace in the Distributed File System snap-in. Notice that the \\Reskit.com\Public root has two root targets on different servers.

Figure 2.5   Elements of a Domain-based DFS Namespace

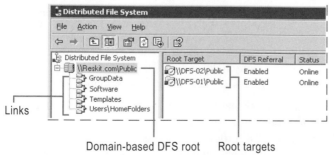

Figure 2.6 illustrates multiple link targets for the Software link. Notice that the link targets exist on three different servers and that the administrator has disabled referrals to the link target on \\dfs-03. DFS will not refer clients to the link target on \\dfs-03 until the administrator enables referrals.

Figure 2.6 Multiple Link Targets

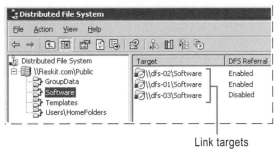

Link targets

The roots and links displayed in the Distributed File System snap-in also appear on each root server's local storage as follows:

- When you create a DFS root, you specify a shared folder to use as the root folder. If you add multiple root targets to a domain-based DFS root, you specify a shared folder on each of those root targets. (The shared folder names should always match the root name.)

- When you add links to the root, DFS creates special folders under each root folder. These folders, called *link folders*, are actually reparse points, and they display the following error message if you try to access them on the local server:

  E:\Public\GroupData is not accessible. The network location cannot be reached.

  Users who access the link folders from across the network are redirected to the appropriate link target.

Figure 2.7 illustrates volume E:\ on the local storage of one of the root targets. The volume contains root and link folders for the \\Reskit.com\Public namespace.

Figure 2.7 Root and Link Folders

Reviewing the Benefits of Using DFS

When you evaluate DFS for your organization, it is helpful to understand the benefits that your organization can gain after designing and implementing a DFS namespace. The following list describes the benefits of using DFS:

Unified namespace   A DFS namespace links together shared folders on different servers to create a hierarchical structure that behaves like a single high-capacity hard disk. Users can navigate the logical namespace without having to know the physical server names or shared folders hosting the data.

Location transparency   DFS simplifies migrating data from one file server to another. Because users do not need to know the name of each physical server or shared folder that contains the data, you can physically move data to another server without having to reconfigure applications and shortcuts, and without having to re-educate users about where they can find their data.

Storage scalability   You can deploy additional or higher-performance file servers and present the storage on the new servers as new folders within an existing namespace.

Namespace scalability   Servers running Windows Server 2003, Enterprise Edition or Windows Server 2003, Datacenter Edition can host multiple domain-based DFS roots and stand-alone DFS roots. This feature improves the scalability of DFS, enabling you to build many large namespaces without having to add file servers to host the roots.

Increased availability of file server data   When multiple servers running Windows Server 2003 host a domain-based DFS root, clients are redirected to the next available root server if any of these servers fail, providing fault-tolerant data access. To ensure the availability of stand-alone DFS namespaces, you can create the root on a clustered file server.

Alternate site selection based on cost   By default, if a target in the same site as the users fails, or if no same-site target exists, DFS refers clients to a random target. If you configure the optional site costing feature, DFS can use the site information in Active Directory to locate an alternate target that has the lowest-cost network connection as defined by the administrator in the Active Directory Sites and Services snap-in. After site costing is enabled, clients can access data on DFS targets over the optimum network connection.

Load sharing   DFS provides a degree of load sharing by mapping a given logical name to shared folders on multiple file servers. For example, suppose that \\Company\StockInfo is a heavily used shared folder. By using DFS, you can associate this location with multiple shared folders on different servers, even if the servers are located in different sites.

Intelligent client caching   When a user requests access to a target that is a part of a DFS namespace, a referral containing the target's information is cached on the client. The next time the client requires access to that portion of the namespace, the client uses the cached referral instead of obtaining a new referral, and connects directly to one of the target computers. For more information about client caching in DFS, see the *Distributed Services Guide* of the *Windows Server 2003 Resource Kit* (or see the *Distributed Services Guide* on the Web at http://www.microsoft.com/reskit).

Support for offline folders   If your clients are running Microsoft® Windows® XP or Windows Server 2003, you can make DFS link targets available offline by using the Offline Files feature. You can also use this feature to automatically cache programs so that users can run the programs locally instead of from the server. Using this feature for link targets that host applications can reduce network traffic and improve server scalability.

Simplified maintenance   If a link has multiple link targets, administrators can perform preventive maintenance, repairs, or upgrades on servers by disabling referrals to specific link targets. While the referral to the link target is disabled, DFS automatically routes new requests to the remaining link targets that are online.

Dynamic site discovery   DFS now supports dynamic site discovery. In Windows 2000, DFS maintained static site information. After the site information for a particular network resource was known, DFS used that information indefinitely, regardless of any changes in the site information of the resource. In Windows Server 2003, when you move a resource from one site to another, the information used by DFS converges to the new site information within 25 hours.

Security integration   You do not need to configure additional security for DFS namespaces, because file and folder access is enforced by existing NTFS and share permissions on each link target. For example, a user navigating a DFS namespace is permitted to access only the files or folders for which he or she has appropriate NTFS or share permissions. If you use FRS to replicate content among multiple targets, FRS also replicates access control lists (ACLs) for each file and folder. For more information about DFS and FRS security, see "Planning DFS and FRS Security" later in this chapter.

Evaluating Client and Server Compatibility

Before you implement a DFS namespace, review the types of clients and servers in your organization to make certain that the servers can host targets and that the clients can access targets in the DFS namespace. For example, if you have UNIX clients, they cannot access the DFS namespace and must instead access the files by using the UNC path to the various file servers. Table 2.1 summarizes DFS interoperability.

Table 2.1   DFS Interoperability

Platform	Act as DFS Clients?	Host DFS Roots?	Act as a Link Target?
Microsoft® Windows® Server 2003, Web Edition	Yes	Yes. Can host one stand-alone DFS root or one domain-based DFS root per server.	Yes
Windows Server 2003, Standard Edition	Yes	Yes. Can host one stand-alone DFS root or one domain-based DFS root per server.	Yes
Windows Server 2003, Enterprise Edition and Windows Server 2003, Datacenter Edition	Yes	Yes. Can host multiple stand-alone DFS roots and multiple domain-based DFS roots per server.	Yes
Windows XP	Yes	No	Yes
Windows Preinstallation Environment (WinPE)	Yes	No	No
Microsoft® Windows® 2000 Server family*	Yes	Yes, one stand-alone DFS root or domain-based DFS root per server.	Yes
Microsoft® Windows® 2000 Professional	Yes	No	Yes
Microsoft® Windows NT® Server 4.0 with Service Pack 6a	Yes	Yes, a single stand-alone DFS root per server.	Yes
Windows NT Workstation 4.0 with Service Pack 6a	Yes	No	Yes

(continued)

Table 2.1   DFS Interoperability *(continued)*

Platform	Act as DFS Clients?	Host DFS Roots?	Act as a Link Target?
Microsoft® Windows® Millenniu m Edition (Me)	Yes, client for stand-alone DFS included. Because Windows Me is designed specifically for home use, no domain-based DFS client is provided.	No	Yes
Microsoft® Windows® 98	Yes, client for stand-alone DFS included; install the Active Directory client extension for Microsoft® Windows® 95 or Microsoft Windows 98 to access domain-based DFS namespaces.	No	Yes

* Applies to general purpose servers and Windows Powered Network Attached Storage solutions running Windows Server 2003.

Note

The Active Directory client extension for Windows 95 or Windows 98 is available on the Windows 2000 operating system CD, or see the Active Directory Client Extensions link on the Web Resources page at http://www.microsoft.com/windows/reskits/webresources.

When evaluating client compatibility, review the following important considerations:

- Clients must be members of a domain before they can access a domain-based DFS namespace.

- Link targets can use other protocols, such as NetWare Core Protocol (NCP) for NetWare and Network Filesystem (NFS) for UNIX, but clients must have the appropriate redirector installed to access those link targets.

- In organizations that have a large number of domains, clients might have difficulty accessing link targets in other domains or forests. In addition, clients running Windows 98 might not be able to access any domain-based DFS namespace and might also have difficulty accessing links that point to other DFS namespaces. For more information about clients running Windows 98, see "Designing a DFS Namespace" later in this chapter.

Choosing the DFS Namespace Type

When creating a DFS namespace, you create either a stand-alone DFS root or a domain-based DFS root. Table 2.2 describes the differences between domain-based DFS namespaces and stand-alone DFS namespaces.

Table 2.2 How DFS Namespace Types Differ

Characteristic	Domain-based	Stand-Alone
Path to DFS namespace	*domainname**rootname* *Netbiosdomainname**rootname* *DNSdomainname**rootname*	*servername**rootname*
Group memberships required to create and administer namespaces	For DFS administrators who are not members of the Domain Admins group, it is recommended that you delegate permissions so that administrators can create new domain-based DFS namespaces. Administrators must also be members of the local Administrators group on each of the root targets to be able to add and delete links and add and remove the root targets.	DFS administrators must be members of the local Administrators group on the local server to create new stand-alone DFS roots and add or delete links.
Where DFS root information is stored	In Active Directory. DFS root information is replicated to all servers that host domain-based DFS roots.	In the registry of the root server.
DFS namespace size restrictions	Large domain-based DFS namespaces might cause significantly increased network traffic due to the size of the DFS Active Directory object. As a result, Microsoft recommends using fewer than 5,000 links in domain-based DFS namespaces.	The largest recommended namespace size for a stand-alone root is 50,000 links.
Supported methods to ensure DFS root availability	Create multiple DFS root targets in the same domain.	Create a stand-alone DFS root on a clustered file server.
Supported methods to ensure link target availability	Create multiple link targets and replicate files by using one of the following methods: ▪ Enabling FRS ▪ Copying files manually or by using scripts ▪ Using a third-party replication tool	Create multiple link targets and replicate files by using one of the following methods: ▪ Copying files manually or by using scripts ▪ Using a third-party replication tool

Note

For information about DFS namespace size restrictions, see "Reviewing DFS Size Recommendations" later in this chapter.

Use the following guidelines to choose a DFS namespace type.

Choose stand-alone DFS namespaces if:

- Your organization does not use Active Directory.

- You need to create a DFS namespace and are not part of the Domain Admins group, or company policy prevents you from delegating authority to manage a domain-based DFS namespace.

- You need to create a single namespace with more than 5,000 links. (If you can divide your links among two or more namespaces, domain-based DFS is an option.)

- You want to ensure the availability of the namespace by using a clustered file server.

Choose domain-based DFS namespaces if:

- You plan to use FRS to replicate data and you want to use the Distributed File System snap-in to configure and administer replication.

- You want to ensure the availability of the namespace by using multiple root targets.

As described in Table 2.2, you can increase the availability of roots and links in both types of DFS namespaces. For more information and specific guidelines about increasing the availability of roots and links, see "Increasing the Availability of DFS Namespaces" later in this chapter.

Reviewing DFS Size Recommendations

As you design your DFS namespace, use the guidelines in Table 2.3 to avoid potential performance problems that can arise when size recommendations are exceeded.

Table 2.3   DFS Size Recommendations

Description	Recommendation*	Explanation
Path limit	Less than 260 characters	Win32 application programming interfaces (APIs) have a maximum path limit of 260 characters, so applications will fail when trying to access a namespace that goes beyond that limit. If the path length of the DFS namespace exceeds the Win32 API limit of 260 characters, users must map part of the namespace to a drive letter and access the longer namespace through the mapped drive letter.
Number of DFS roots per server running Windows Server 2003, Standard Edition	One	Windows Server 2003, Standard Edition is limited to one root per server.

(continued)

Table 2.3   DFS Size Recommendations *(continued)*

Description	Recommendation*	Explanation
Number of DFS roots per server running Windows Server 2003, Enterprise Edition or Windows Server 2003, Datacenter Edition	Varies	There is no limit to the number of DFS roots you can create on a server running Windows Server 2003, Enterprise Edition or Windows Server 2003, Datacenter Edition. However, as you increase the number of roots per server, the Distributed File System service takes longer to initialize and uses more memory.
Number of root targets per domain-based DFS root	No fixed limit	If you do not enable root scalability mode, Microsoft recommends using 16 or fewer root targets to limit traffic to the server acting as the primary domain controller (PDC) emulator master.
Number of links per DFS namespace	5,000 for domain-based DFS 50,000 links for stand-alone DFS	When the number of links exceeds the recommended limit, you might experience performance degradation when making changes to the DFS configuration. For stand-alone DFS, namespace initialization after server startup might also be delayed.
Size of each DFS Active Directory object (applies to domain-based DFS namespaces only)	5 megabytes (MB)	The size of the DFS Active Directory object is determined by the number and path length of roots, links, comments, and targets in the namespace. Microsoft recommends using no more than 5,000 links in a domain-based namespace to prevent the DFS Active Directory object from exceeding 5 MB. Limiting the size of the Active Directory object is important because large domain-based DFS configurations can cause significantly increased network traffic originating from updates made to those roots, links, and targets.

* The figures in this table are based on information gathered in a test environment. The numbers in an operational DFS configuration might exceed the numbers described here and still provide acceptable performance.

 Note

You can check the size of an existing DFS namespace by using the following syntax in Dfsutil.exe:

dfsutil /root:\\domainname\rootname /view (for domain-based DFS)

dfsutil /root:\\servername\rootname /view (for stand-alone DFS)

The command output displays the number of links and, for domain-based DFS namespaces, the size of the DFS Active Directory object (described as *blob size*).

If your organization plans to create large namespaces, there are a number of strategies you can implement to work within the size recommendations shown in Table 2.3.

Keep comments to a minimum

When you add a root target or link target in the Distributed File Systems snap-in, you can enter comments that describe the target. If you plan to create a large namespace, use minimal comments, if any, because they can increase the overall size of the namespace.

> **Note**
>
> Comments are visible only within the DFS administration tools, and they are not visible to users when they navigate the namespace.

Create multiple namespaces

If you need to create more than 5,000 links in a domain-based DFS namespace, you can create multiple DFS namespaces that meet the recommended sizes and then link them together. For more information about creating multiple namespaces, see "Designing a DFS Namespace" later in this chapter.

Enable root scalability mode

You enable root scalability mode by using the /RootScalability parameter in Dfsutil.exe, which you can install from the \Support\Tools folder on the Windows Server 2003 operating system CD. When root scalability mode is enabled, DFS root servers get updates from the closest domain controller instead of the server acting as the PDC emulator master. As a result, root scalability mode reduces network traffic to the PDC emulator master at the expense of faster updates to all root servers. (When you make changes to the namespace, the changes are still made on the PDC emulator master, but the root servers no longer poll the PDC emulator master hourly for those changes; instead, they poll the closest domain controller.) With this mode enabled, you can have as many root targets as you need, as long as the size of the DFS Active Directory object (for each root) is less than 5 MB. For more information about the 5-MB limit, see the entry describing the size of the DFS Active Directory object in Table 2.3 earlier in this chapter.

Do not use root scalability mode if any of the following conditions exist in your organization:

- Your namespace changes frequently, and users cannot tolerate having inconsistent views of the namespace.

- Domain controller replication is slow. This increases the amount of time it takes for the PDC emulator master to replicate DFS changes to other domain controllers, which, in turn, replicate changes to the root servers. Until this replication completes, the namespace will be inconsistent on all root servers.

> **Note**
>
> After you enable root scalability mode in a mixed domain, root servers running Windows Server 2003 can obtain updates from the closest domain controller; however, root servers running Windows 2000 Server still obtain updates from the PDC emulator master.

For information about installing Windows Support Tools, see "Install Windows Support Tools" in Help and Support Center for Windows Server 2003.

Migrate root servers running Windows 2000 Server to Windows Server 2003

Root servers running Windows Server 2003 do not add site information to the DFS Active Directory object. As a result, if all root servers run Windows Server 2003, DFS can store more root and link information to the DFS Active Directory object before reaching the recommended 5-MB limit. For more information about using a mix of root servers running Windows 2000 Server and Windows Server 2003, see "Designing a DFS Namespace" later in this chapter.

Planning the Number of DFS Namespaces

Your next step is to plan the number of namespaces you want in your domain. For an Excel spreadsheet to assist you in documenting your namespace decisions, see "DFS Configuration Worksheet" (Sdcfsv_1.xls) on the *Windows Server 2003 Deployment Kit* companion CD (or see "DFS Configuration Worksheet" on the Web at http://www.microsoft.com/reskit).

Medium organizations might require only a single namespace, while large organizations might need multiple DFS namespaces. You can determine the number of namespaces you require by reviewing the following factors.

Scope of your domain

If your domain has a broad scope — geographically, organizationally, or functionally — you should plan for multiple DFS namespaces so that administrators in the geographical, organizational, or functional departments can define their own namespaces. On the other hand, if the domain has a narrow scope geographically, organizationally, or functionally, you might want to define a single DFS namespace.

Size of your DFS namespace

If your DFS namespace exceeds the recommended number of links per namespace, as discussed earlier in "Reviewing DFS Size Recommendations" create multiple DFS namespaces, each of which does not exceed the recommended size. In this way, you can provide a single namespace to users by creating a single DFS namespace with links that point to other DFS namespaces. For more information about linking from one namespace to another, see "Designing a DFS Namespace" later in this chapter.

Administrative boundaries

How DFS namespaces are administered can also affect the number of DFS namespaces your organization requires. For example, your organization might have the following administrative boundaries:

- **Geographic.** Geographically diverse sites can each have an administrator who creates and manages the DFS namespace located in that site.

- **Departmental or group ownership.** Individual departments or groups can create and manage a DFS namespace that is used by members of that department or group.

- **Political.** Individual departments or groups can create and manage a DFS namespace that is used by members of that department or group.

If groups in your organization will create and manage their own DFS namespaces, you can build an extensive DFS namespace out of smaller, more focused DFS namespaces. One benefit of this method is that you can present specific DFS roots to some users as the true top of the hierarchy and also present a set of those DFS roots to other users as the only DFS links in a larger hierarchy. By using a hierarchy of DFS roots, you can scale the namespace as your organization grows and tailor the namespace for distributed management.

For more information about linking from one namespace to another, see "Designing a DFS Namespace" later in this chapter.

DFS namespace depth

Limit the depth of DFS namespaces to 260 characters. The 260-character limit includes the fully qualified domain name (FQDN) of the domain hosting the DFS root as well as the DFS root name. If you exceed this limit, applications will fail when trying to access the namespace. To work around this issue, users must map part of the namespace to a drive letter and then access the longer namespace through the mapped drive letter.

Developing Root and Link Naming Standards

When you roll out DFS, you have the opportunity to implement consistent namespace designs. Developing naming standards first — and ensuring that you adhere to the naming standards during implementation — makes it easier to use and manage any DFS namespace, both from a user perspective and an administrative perspective. Even if you do not expect to implement DFS until a later phase of your Windows Server 2003 deployment, it is important to begin thinking about namespace design early in the planning process. For an Excel spreadsheet to assist you in documenting your DFS namespace design decisions, see "DFS Configuration Worksheet" (Sdcfsv_1.xls) on the *Windows Server 2003 Deployment Kit* companion CD (or see "DFS Configuration Worksheet" on the Web at http://www.microsoft.com/reskit).

Creating DFS Root Names

A DFS root name, significant primarily to users, is the point beyond the server name or domain name that is at the top of the hierarchy of the logical namespace. Standardized and meaningful names at this level are very important, especially if you have more than one DFS namespace in a domain, because the DFS root name is where users enter the namespace. The contents of a DFS namespace must be as clear as possible to the users so that they do not follow the wrong path, possibly across expensive WAN connections, and have to backtrack.

When creating the DFS root names for servers that will contain multiple roots, review the following restrictions:

- Each root requires its own shared folder.

- When you create a domain-based DFS root, the share name in the UNC path *servername\sharename* must be the same name as the DFS root name in *domainname\rootname*. For example, if you want to create a domain-based DFS root \\Reskit.com\Public on Server1, the UNC path to the shared folder must be \\Server1\Public.

- A root cannot be nested within another root. For example, if C:\Root is a shared folder that uses the share name Public, and you use this shared folder as a stand-alone DFS root (*servername*\Public) or domain-based DFS root (*domainname*\Public), you cannot create another root in the folder C:\Root\Software. Similarly, if you create a root by using the root folder C:\, you cannot create another root at C:\Root.

- On server clusters, do not create clustered DFS roots that have the same name as nonclustered DFS roots or shared folders.

- Shared folders on domain controllers must not have the same name as any domain-based DFS roots in the domain. If they do, clients who try to access the shared folder on the domain controller are redirected to the domain-based DFS root. For example, if Reskit.com has a domain controller named DC1 that contains a shared folder named Tools (\\DC1\Tools), do not create a domain-based DFS namespace using a root named Tools (\\Reskit.com\Tools). Otherwise, when users attempt to access \\DC1\Tools, they are redirected to \\Reskit.com\Tools.

Creating DFS Link Names

A DFS link is a component in a DFS namespace that lies below the root and maps to one or more link targets. Because DFS link names are exposed to users, it is important to develop standardized, meaningful names for DFS links. Another important design goal is to develop a DFS namespace that provides intuitive navigation within the hierarchy that the namespace represents. Keep in mind that comments entered in the Distributed File System snap-in are not visible to users. For this reason, the namespace must be as clear as possible at all levels.

Designing a clear naming scheme is even more important for a DFS namespace than for a physical namespace, because a user might jump to a shared folder on a different file server when he or she selects a link in the DFS namespace. As a result, a session has to be set up with that physical server (if one does not already exist), which might delay access. Therefore, you want to minimize the number of times that users traverse a wrong path. Clear and meaningful naming standards can help.

Try to keep links at the same level in the DFS namespace consistent in context. For example, you probably would not want to have links named New York, Seattle, and Milan mixed with other links named Sales, Marketing, and Consulting. To help you create a consistent namespace, DFS supports adding one or more folder names to the link name so that you can create a meaningful hierarchy of link names. In the previous example, you could create links such as the following:

- Branches\New York, Branches\Seattle, and Branches\Milan
- Departments\Sales, Departments\Marketing, and Departments\Consulting

When users browse this namespace, they will see a folder called Branches and another called Departments, which they can use to navigate to folders for branch offices (New York, Seattle, and Milan) and departments (Sales, Marketing, and Consulting).

 Note
If you want to encourage users to access the DFS namespace instead of going to individual servers, you can use a dollar sign ($) at the end of the shared folder name to hide it from casual browsers. The shared folder will still appear in the DFS namespace with the link name you specify. Doing so prevents users from accessing the shared folders by specifying individual server names. Instead, users must access the shared folders by using the namespace, which enables DFS to load share requests across multiple link targets and allows clients to be directed to another link target if the previously used target is unavailable.

Designing a DFS Namespace

As you design one or more DFS namespaces for your organization, you need to make a number of decisions about the structure and capacity of the namespaces. For an Excel spreadsheet to assist you in documenting your DFS namespace decisions, see "DFS Configuration Worksheet" (Sdcfsv_1.xls) on the *Windows Server 2003 Deployment Kit* companion CD (or see "DFS Configuration Worksheet" on the Web at http://www.microsoft.com/reskit).

Determining Who Can Manage the Namespace

You can delegate administrative authority to individual users so that they can manage a DFS namespace. Table 2.4 describes the permissions and group memberships that you must delegate before users can manage a namespace on a member server. Administering DFS namespaces on a domain controller or configuring FRS replication requires membership in the Domain Admins group.

Table 2.4   Permissions or Group Memberships Required to Administer DFS Namespaces

Task	Permissions or Group Membership Required
Creating or removing a domain-based DFS root on a member server.	One of the following: ■ Membership in the Domain Admins group. ■ Full Control permission on the DFS-Configuration container in Active Directory and membership in the local Administrators group on the root server.
Adding or removing a root target from an existing domain-based DFS root on a member server.	One of the following: ■ Membership in the Domain Admins group. ■ Full Control permission on the DFS-Configuration container in Active Directory and membership in the local Administrators group on the root server.
Creating or deleting a stand-alone DFS root on a member server.	Membership in the local Administrators group on the root server.
Adding a link to a domain-based DFS namespace or adding a target to an existing link on a member server.	Membership in the local Administrators group on each of the root target servers.
Removing a link from a domain-based DFS namespace or removing a target from an existing link on a member server.	Membership in the local Administrators group on each of the root target servers.
Changing root-related or link-related information, such as comments, referral status, and cache limits on a member server.	Membership in the local Administrators group on each of the root target servers.
Performing any of the tasks in this table on a domain controller.	Membership in the Domain Admins group.
Enabling replication on links in a domain-based DFS namespace.	Membership in the Domain Admins group.

You can also limit delegated authority to just one domain-based DFS namespace on a member server by granting a user or group Full Control permission on the DFS root object contained in the DFS-Configuration container. Doing so allows the administrator to add or remove root targets from a specific namespace. For more information about how to delegate permission to manage a DFS namespace, see "Deploying DFS" later in this chapter.

Selecting Servers to Host Roots

Table 2.5 describes the guidelines for servers hosting stand-alone DFS roots and domain-based DFS roots.

Table 2.5   Guidelines for Servers That Host DFS Roots

Server Hosting Stand-Alone DFS Roots	Server Hosting Domain-based DFS Roots
▪ Must contain an NTFS volume to host the root. ▪ Can be a member server or domain controller. ▪ Can be a general-purpose server or Windows Powered Network Attached Storage. ▪ Can be a clustered file server.	▪ Must contain an NTFS volume to host the root. ▪ Must be a member server or domain controller in the domain in which the DFS namespace is configured. (This requirement applies to every root target for a given domain-based DFS namespace.) ▪ Can be a general-purpose server or Windows Powered Network Attached Storage. ▪ Cannot be a clustered file server unless you host the domain-based DFS root on the local storage of a node in the server cluster.

The following sections provide other factors to consider when selecting root servers.

Restrictions for servers running Windows Server 2003, Standard Edition

If you are using servers running Windows Server 2003, Standard Edition, you can create only one DFS root per server, which means that you need one server for each root you plan to host.

Root servers that have the RestrictAnonymous registry value

Before you create a DFS root on a server, verify that the RestrictAnonymous registry value is not set on the server. This registry value restricts anonymous access and causes DFS referral failures. For more information about this registry value, see "Planning DFS and FRS Security" later in this chapter.

Root server performance

When evaluating the hardware specifications of the servers that host roots, note that clients access the root server to get referrals, and then the clients cache the referrals locally. Therefore, root servers do not typically experience high CPU usage. However, as the size of the namespace grows, the DFS service uses more memory, so consider using more than the minimum recommended RAM for servers that host large DFS namespaces and for servers that host multiple DFS namespaces. For more information about choosing RAM and CPU speed for file servers, see "Determining RAM and CPU Specifications" later in this chapter.

 Important

Servers running Windows Server 2003, Enterprise Edition or Windows Server 2003, Datacenter Edition can host multiple roots of any type (stand-alone or domain-based). However, as you increase the number of roots (namespaces) on a server, you also increase the number of namespaces that will be unavailable if the server fails. Therefore, devise a plan that allows you to increase the availability of the namespaces. For more information, see "Increasing the Availability of DFS Namespaces" later in this chapter.

Hosting roots on domain controllers

When deciding whether to host a DFS root on a domain controller, consider the following factors:

- Only members of the Domain Admins group can manage a DFS namespace hosted on a domain controller.

- If you plan to use a domain controller to host a DFS root, the server hardware must be sized to handle the additional load. As described earlier, root servers that host large or multiple namespaces require additional memory. For information about capacity planning for domain controllers, see "Planning Domain Controller Capacity" in *Designing and Deploying Directory and Security Services* of this kit.

Using root servers running Windows 2000 Server and Windows Server 2003

If you plan to host a domain-based DFS root on servers running a mix of Windows 2000 and Windows Server 2003, you need to understand how DFS handles site information in each of these operating systems. These differences are important because Windows Server 2003 does not store site information in the DFS Active Directory object; instead, root servers running Windows Server 2003 obtain site information directly from Active Directory. If you have root servers running Windows 2000 Server, those servers try to obtain site information from the DFS Active Directory object, and unless you use Dfsutil.exe to manually update the site info in the DFS Active Directory object, the root servers running Windows 2000 Server might provide referrals that lead to a target outside of the client's site.

Table 2.6 describes how DFS root servers handle site information.

Table 2.6   How Root Servers Handle Site Information

Site Difference	Windows 2000 Server	Windows Server 2003
Where DFS stores and retrieves site information for root and link targets	DFS stores a copy of site information for root and link targets in the DFS object in Active Directory.	DFS uses IP addresses of root and link targets to obtain site information directly from Active Directory. By default, DFS does not store site information in the Active Directory object.
Characteristic of site information	Static	Dynamic
Method for updating site information after moving a link target to a different site	Remove the link target from the namespace, and then add it back.	By default, site information automatically updates every 25 hours.
How root servers use site information for referrals	Root servers running Windows 2000 Server use the link target's site information only if the link target was created by using Windows 2000 Server. If the link target was created by using Windows Server 2003, no site information is stored, which means that the referral could lead to a target outside of the client's site.	Root servers running Windows Server 2003 ignore any site information in the Active Directory object; instead, they use site information directly from Active Directory.

Running Windows Server 2003 on every root server is recommended for a number of reasons:

- Site information is always up to date because DFS obtains site information directly from Active Directory instead of storing a copy of site information in the DFS Active Directory object.

- The DFS Active Directory object can hold additional root and link targets because it does not contain site information.

If you want referrals from root servers running Windows 2000 Server to be ordered according to site information, you can use the /UpdateWin2kStaticSiteTable parameter in Dfsutil.exe to update the static site information for all root and link targets in the DFS Active Directory object. If you plan to use this parameter, review the following issues:

- Using this parameter increases the size of the DFS Active Directory object, possibly making it exceed the 5-MB recommended size limit.

- You need to run this parameter each time you want to update site information.

- Root servers running Windows Server 2003 continue to get site information directly from Active Directory, and they ignore all site information in the DFS Active Directory object.

When all root servers are running Windows Server 2003, you can use the /PurgeWin2kStaticSiteTable parameter in Dfsutil.exe to remove site information from the DFS Active Directory object, providing you additional space for creating root and link targets.

 Important

If you are using a mix of root servers running Windows 2000 Server and Windows Server 2003, use the version of the Distributed File System snap-in available in either Windows Server 2003 or the Windows Server 2003 Administration Tools Pack to manage the namespace. Do not use the version of the Distributed File System snap-in available in Windows 2000 Server.

Determine the Root and Link Referral Time to Live Values

You can use the Distributed File System snap-in to specify the length of time that clients cache referrals to DFS root targets and link targets by adjusting the Time to Live value for each DFS root or link. When a client receives a referral to a target, the client will continue to access that target (either a particular root target or link target) until one of the following occurs: the client computer is restarted, the user clears the cache, or the Time to Live value for the root or link expires. The client will then obtain a new referral the next time it attempts to access the target. However, if the client continues to access the root or link within the Time To Live value, the Time to Live value is renewed each time and the client never requests a new referral. Clients that resume from hibernation do not request new referrals either.

Windows Server 2003 uses a default Time to Live value of 300 seconds (5 minutes) for DFS roots and 1800 seconds (30 minutes) for DFS links. The default Time to Live values work well in organizations where the namespace changes frequently and it is important that clients have up-to-date referrals. When using these values, make sure that your network has adequate bandwidth and your root servers have adequate resources to handle the traffic generated when clients contact the root servers for referrals.

Consider increasing the Time to Live value in the following situations:

- An established root or link has a single link target. In this case, you do not need to load balance requests among multiple servers, so it is appropriate to have a longer Time to Live value for that root or link.

- Your organization has clients in multiple Active Directory sites, but you do not have root servers in all sites. In this situation, you can increase the Time to Live value for the root to ensure that the client does not have to go out of its site for a root referral if more than 5 minutes have passed since the client last accessed the namespace. If your root information is static, you can set this value to be several hours.

For more information about Time to Live values, see The *Distributed Services Guide* of the *Windows Server 2003 Resource Kit* (or see the *Distributed Services Guide* on the Web at http://www.microsoft.com/reskit).

Determining the Contents of the Root Folder

The root folder of a DFS namespace is a launch point into the namespace — that is, a placeholder for the namespace. Keep the root folder as uncluttered as possible. For example, you might place a single file in the root folder (a readme file) that describes the contents and purpose of the namespace. When users access the namespace, they will see the readme file and the links that point to one or more link targets. For more information about the root folder, see "Reviewing DFS Terminology" earlier in this chapter.

Choosing Shared Folders to Add to the Namespace

Add shared folders to your namespace only if they are well established and unlikely to be retired in the near future. If you have targets whose underlying physical name is dynamic, include them in the DFS namespace only if you can tolerate the added administrative overhead or develop automated scripts to update the DFS links.

To secure files and folders, use NTFS as the underlying file system for shared folders that you add to a DFS namespace. You can add shared folders residing on file allocation table (FAT) volumes in Windows-based servers and shared folders residing on servers running other operating systems, such as UNIX or Novell NetWare servers; however, you cannot use NTFS security features to secure these folders. In addition, if you plan to use FRS to replicate the contents of shared folders, you must use NTFS as the file system.

To help users find data in DFS namespaces more easily, you can publish the UNC path for DFS links as shared folders in Active Directory. For example, if an administrator of the Reskit.com domain wants to publish the DFS link where users can install applications, the administrator can specify \\Reskit.com\Public\Apps as the path to the published folder. The administrator can also specify key words for that shared folder, such as "applications" or "Office." Domain users in a forest can locate the applications by using the Active Directory search tool in My Network Places to query for the application folder by name or key words.

For information about publishing shared folders in Active Directory, see "Publish a Shared Folder" in Help and Support Center for Windows Server 2003.

Reviewing Rules for Creating Links

When designing the namespace, review the following rules regarding link creation.

Creating new links under existing links

You cannot create a new link under an existing link. To create a hierarchy of links, specify additional folder names within the link name. For example, instead of creating a link called Groups, create links called Groups\Development, Groups\Management, Groups\Administrative, and so forth.

Creating links to shared folders in other domains or forests

If a client can access a link target in another trusted domain or trusted forest by using the target's UNC path, the client can also access the link target by using its DFS path, but only if the list of domains fits into the client's cache, which is 4 KB by default (roughly 2000 characters). If the list of domains is too large to fit into the 4-KB cache, the following actions occur:

- Clients running Windows 98 cannot access any domain-based DFS namespaces. To notify you of this issue, DFS writes an entry with the ID 14537 in the system log in Event Viewer on the domain controller that enumerates the domains.

- Computers running Windows NT 4.0, Windows 2000, Windows XP, and Windows Server 2003 automatically increase their cache size to accept the list of domains, up to a maximum of 56 KB.

If the list of domains exceeds 56 KB, DFS puts as many domains in the cache as it can until the cache reaches 56 KB. DFS then writes an entry with the ID 14536 in the system event log in Event Viewer to notify you of this issue. When populating the cache, DFS gives preference to local and explicitly trusted domains by filling the cache with their names first. Consequently, by creating explicit trust relationships with domains that host important DFS namespaces you can minimize the possibility that those domain names might be dropped from the list that is returned to the client.

Important

To make sure that clients can access link targets in other trusted domains or trusted forests, you must use DNS names for all link targets and configure DFS to use fully qualified domain names in referrals. For more information, see article Q244380, "How to Configure Dfs to Use Fully Qualified Domain Names in Referrals." To find this article, see the Microsoft Knowledge Base link on the Web Resources page at http://www.microsoft.com/windows/reskits/webresources.

Creating links to mounted drives

A mounted drive is a local volume attached to an empty folder on an NTFS volume. If C:\Root is a DFS root folder on Server1 (\\Server1\Root), and you create a folder C:\Root\Link1, where Link1 is a mounted drive (for example, Link1 points to drive D), you cannot create a link named Link1 in that DFS namespace.

Creating links to different namespaces

Windows Server 2003 supports creating links that point to other DFS namespaces. Linking to other namespaces is common in organizations that want to combine the availability benefits of domain-based DFS namespaces with the scalability of stand-alone DFS namespaces. For example, if an organization needs to create 10,000 links but does not want to divide these between two domain-based DFS namespaces, the organization can take the following steps:

1. Create a stand-alone DFS namespace with 10,000 links.

2. Create a domain-based DFS root.

3. Under the domain-based DFS root, create a link that points to the stand-alone DFS namespace.

When linking to other namespaces, you must follow these guidelines to make certain that clients can be redirected properly if a target is unavailable:

- If you plan to specify a domain-based DFS namespace as a link target (either the root or a link within that namespace), you cannot specify alternate link targets. (Windows Server 2003 enforces this restriction.)

- If you plan to specify a stand-alone DFS namespace as a link target (either the root or a link within that namespace), you can specify alternate link targets that are either stand-alone DFS roots or links within the stand-alone DFS namespace. Do not specify domain-based DFS roots or shared folders as alternate targets.

 Important

The DFS tools do not prohibit you from specifying domain-based DFS roots or shared folders as alternate targets. Therefore, follow these guidelines carefully.

When linking to other namespaces, review the following restrictions:

- A DFS path can consist of no more than eight hops through other DFS namespaces.

- Clients running Windows 98 might not correctly access links pointing to other DFS namespaces. Windows 98–based clients can only access the following types of links to other namespaces:

    - A link in a stand-alone DFS namespace that points to a stand-alone DFS root or link.

    - A link in a domain-based DFS namespace that points to a stand-alone DFS root. (This works only if the client has the latest Active Directory client installed, as described in article Q323466, "Directory Services Client Update for Windows 95 and Windows 98." To find this article, see the Microsoft Knowledge Base link on the Web Resources page at http://www.microsoft.com/windows/reskits/webresources.

For additional rules for specifying multiple link targets, see "Choosing an Availability Method for Data in Link Targets" later in this chapter.

Increasing the Availability of DFS Namespaces

After you create your initial namespace design, you need to review that design to determine whether part or all of the namespace needs to be available at all times. You can ensure DFS namespace availability at both the root and link target level. This helps prevent the situation in which the target servers are up and running but users cannot access them by using the namespace.

To increase the availability of DFS namespaces, take the following steps:

1. Choose an availability method for DFS roots.

2. Choose an availability method for data in link targets.

3. Determine where to place multiple targets.

4. Choose a replication method.

The following sections describe each of these steps.

Choosing an Availability Method for DFS Roots

If you plan to create DFS namespaces that must be highly available, such as those that provide access to business-critical data, the availability method you choose depends on the root type.

Stand-alone DFS roots

You ensure the availability of a stand-alone DFS root by creating it on the cluster storage of a clustered file server by using the Cluster Administrator snap-in. For more information about making stand-alone DFS roots highly available, see "Increasing Data Availability by Using Clustering" later in this chapter.

Domain-based DFS roots

You ensure the availability of domain-based DFS roots by creating multiple root targets on nonclustered file servers or on the local storage of the nodes of server clusters. (Domain-based DFS roots cannot be created on cluster storage.) All root targets must belong to the same domain. To create root targets, use the Distributed File System snap-in or the Dfsutil.exe command-line tool. (For information about choosing servers to host root targets, see "Designing a DFS Namespace" earlier in this chapter.)

To ensure the availability of domain-based DFS roots, you must have at least two domain controllers and two root targets within the domain that is hosting the root. If you have only one domain controller, and it becomes unavailable, the namespace is inaccessible. Similarly, if you have only a single root target, and the server hosting the root target is unavailable, the namespace is also unavailable.

Note

If you plan to use more than 16 root targets, or if you have root servers in remote sites that connect to the PDC emulator master across slow links, consider enabling root scalability mode. For more information about root scalability mode, see "Reviewing DFS Size Recommendations" earlier in this chapter.

After you determine which roots need to be highly available, document your decisions. For an Excel spreadsheet to assist you in documenting the high-availability requirements of DFS roots, see "DFS Configuration Worksheet" (Sdcfsv_1.xls) on the *Windows Server 2003 Deployment Kit* companion CD (or see "DFS Configuration Worksheet" on the Web at http://www.microsoft.com/reskit).

Choosing an Availability Method for Data in Link Targets

As you design your namespace, you need to identify link targets whose data must be highly available. There are two ways to increase the availability of data in link targets:

- Create a single link that points to a link target on a clustered file server.
- Create multiple link targets and replicate content among them.

You can create link targets that point to clustered file servers in both types of namespaces. However, if you want to replicate content among multiple link targets, the type of namespace determines your replication options.

Using replication in stand-alone DFS namespaces

In a stand-alone DFS namespace, you must replicate the files by copying them manually, using scripts, using Robocopy.exe, which is available in the *Windows Server 2003 Deployment Kit,* or by using other replication tools. The Distributed File System snap-in does not provide a user interface for configuring FRS replication in stand-alone DFS namespaces. To configure replication manually, consult the documentation supplied with your replication tools.

Using replication in domain-based DFS namespaces

The Distributed File System snap-in in Windows Server 2003 provides a user interface for creating the FRS topology and schedule on servers running Windows Server 2003. If you do not want to use FRS in a domain-based DFS namespace, you can replicate files by copying them manually or by using third-party replication tools.

For more information about replication, see "Choosing a Replication Method" later in this chapter.

 Note

The Distributed File System snap-in is also part of the Windows Server 2003 Administration Tools Pack; you can install this pack on computers running Windows XP with Service Pack 1 (SP1) or later and create FRS schedules and topologies on remote servers running Windows 2000. For more information, see article Q304718, "Administering Windows 2000-Based and Windows Server 2003-Based Computers Using Windows XP Professional-Based Clients." To find this article, see the Microsoft Knowledge Base link on the Web Resources page at http://www.microsoft.com/windows/reskits/webresources.

If you plan to use multiple link targets to ensure data availability, you need to configure link targets correctly. Each link can have targets that correspond to only one of the following options:

- One or more shared folders.

- One or more stand-alone DFS paths anywhere in the stand-alone DFS namespace, including the root.

- A single domain-based DFS path anywhere in the domain-based DFS namespace, including the root.

 Important

The DFS tools do not prohibit you from creating links that conflict with these guidelines. Therefore, follow these guidelines carefully.

After you determine which link targets need to be highly available, document your decisions. For an Excel spreadsheet to assist you in documenting which links require multiple link targets, see "DFS Configuration Worksheet" (Sdcfsv_1.xls) on the *Windows Server 2003 Deployment Kit* companion CD (or see "DFS Configuration Worksheet" on the Web at http://www.microsoft.com/reskit).

Placing Multiple Targets

When you evaluate where to place multiple targets, you should plan to place at least one target in the same Active Directory site where users access the data. Doing so enables clients to use fast, inexpensive bandwidth to access the target. Use multiple same-site targets to ensure namespace availability in each site and to avoid the need to use expensive bandwidth if one of the same-site targets fails or is taken offline. Using multiple same-site targets also provides load sharing among the targets in the site.

After you determine where to place multiple targets, you also need to consider where clients will be redirected if the primary target is unavailable. DFS supports three methods of target selection, which are described in the following sections. These methods apply to both stand-alone and domain-based DFS namespaces. After you determine the method of target selection for each link or root, document your decisions. For an Excel spreadsheet to assist you in documenting the target selection methods, see "DFS Configuration Worksheet" (Sdcfsv_1.xls) on the *Windows Server 2003 Deployment Kit* companion CD (or see "DFS Configuration Worksheet" on the Web at http://www.microsoft.com/reskit).

 Important

If you have a mix of root servers running Windows 2000 Server and Windows Server 2003, target selection is random if a root server running Windows 2000 Server provides a referral for a link target created in Windows Server 2003, regardless of which target method you configure. For more information about target selection, see "Designing a DFS Namespace" earlier in this chapter.

Default target selection

If the last (or only) target in an Active Directory site fails or is taken offline, DFS directs clients to another target in the same site, if a target is available. Clients are directed to a random target if no same-site targets are available. DFS does not consider bandwidth cost, connection speed, or the target server's processing load when choosing the random target.

Restricted same-site target selection

By using Dfsutil.exe /InSite parameter, you can limit client access to only those targets that are in the same site as the client. You enable this feature on a DFS root or on individual links in the namespace. If you enable this feature on the root, referrals for any link in the namespace return only targets that are in the same site as the client. If this functionality is disabled on the root, the individual settings on each link are used. When using this feature, plan to have at least one target (or two targets, for fault tolerance) in every site, and plan to monitor servers to make sure they are online and accessible. If no same-site targets exist, clients in that site are denied access to the data in the namespace.

 Note

The /InSite parameter takes effect after you stop and restart the Distributed File System service on each root server or when the service reads the DFS metadata, which happens every hour by default.

Least expensive target selection

If you create a stand-alone or domain-based DFS root on a server running Windows Server 2003, and the domain controller acting as the Intersite Topology Generator (ISTG) is also running Windows Server 2003, you can use the /SiteCosting parameter in Dfsutil.exe to enable DFS to choose an alternate target based on connection cost if no same-site targets are available. Windows Server 2003 uses the site and costing information in Active Directory to determine whether sites are linked by inexpensive, high-speed links or by expensive WAN links.

Site costing is not available in the following situations:

- When a stand-alone DFS namespace is hosted on a server that is not part of any domain.

- When the closest domain controller acting as the ISTG is running Windows 2000 Server.

    (This situation occurs when there are only domain controllers running Windows 2000 Server in the site of the DFS root server, or when there are no domain controllers in the site of the DFS root server and the closest site with at least one domain controller has only Windows 2000 Server domain controllers in that site. The closest site is defined in Active Directory.)

If you plan to enable site costing, review the following:

- You can enable site costing on a per-namespace basis.

- When the domain controller acting as the ISTG is running Windows 2000 Server, DFS uses the default target selection, described earlier in this section. If domain controllers running Windows 2000 Server and Windows Server 2003 exist in a site, the ISTG role is automatically given to the domain controller running Windows Server 2003.

For more information about defining sites in Active Directory, see "Designing the Site Topology" in *Designing and Deploying Directory and Security Services* of this kit.

Choosing a Replication Method

If you plan to use multiple targets and you want to synchronize data in those targets, you need to choose a replication method. You have several methods for replicating data:

- A manual replication method (such as using the command-line tool Robocopy.exe, which is available in the *Windows Server 2003 Deployment Kit*)

- FRS

- A third-party replication tool

It is not mandatory to use FRS to keep targets synchronized. In fact, by default, FRS is not enabled for DFS targets in domain-based DFS namespaces. However, in general you do want to make sure that the underlying shared folders that correspond to DFS links and targets are synchronized to present the same data to users, regardless of the folder that they want to access.

The following sections describe when to use manual replication or FRS. For an Excel spreadsheet to assist you in documenting the replication method for each target, see "DFS Configuration Worksheet" (Sdcfsv_1.xls) on the *Windows Server 2003 Deployment Kit* companion CD (or see "DFS Configuration Worksheet" on the Web at http://www.microsoft.com/reskit). For information about using third-party replication tools, consult the documentation provided by your software vendor.

When to Use Manual Replication

If the data in the shared folder is static, you can replicate the data by doing a one-time copy of the data to a target in the replica set. Even if the data in the shared folder is dynamic but changes infrequently, you might want to keep the targets synchronized by downloading the initial copies over the network and then manually updating them with changes. You must use manual replication if you plan to use a stand-alone DFS namespace or if one or more link targets for a particular link do not run Windows 2000 Server or Windows Server 2003.

When to Use FRS

FRS works by detecting changes to file and folders in a replica set and replicating those changes to other file servers in the replica set. When a change occurs, FRS replicates the entire file, not just the changed bytes. You can use FRS only if you are using a domain-based DFS namespace, and only servers running a Windows 2000 Server or Windows Server 2003 operating system can be part of a replica set. In addition, all replica sets must be created on NTFS volumes.

FRS offers a number of advantages over manually copying files, including:

Continuous replication FRS can provide continuous replication, subject to server and network loads. When a file or folder change occurs, and the file or folder is closed, FRS can begin replicating the changed file or folder to outbound partners (that is, the replica members that will receive the changed file or folder) within five seconds.

Replication scheduling   You can schedule replication to occur at specified times and durations as needed by your organization. Scheduling replication to occur during evening hours, for example, can reduce the cost of transmitting data over expensive WAN links. Replicating data during off-hours also frees up network bandwidth for other uses.

Compression   To save disk space, FRS compresses files in the staging directory by using NTFS compression. Files sent between replica members remain compressed when transmitted over the network.

Authenticated RPC with encryption   To provide secure communications, FRS uses Kerberos authentication protocol for authenticated remote procedure call (RPC) to encrypt the data sent between members of a replica set.

Fault-tolerant replication path   FRS does not rely on broadcast technology, and it can provide fault-tolerant distribution via multiple connection paths between members. If a given replica member is unavailable, the data will flow via a different route. FRS uses logic that prevents a file from being sent more than once to any given member.

Conflict resolution   FRS can resolve file and folder conflicts to make data consistent among the replica members. If two identically named files on different servers are added to the replica set, FRS uses a "last writer wins" algorithm, which means that the most recent update to a file in a replica set becomes the version of the file or folder that replicates to the other members of the replica set. If two identically named folders on different servers are added to the replica tree, FRS identifies the conflict during replication and renames the folder that was most recently created. Both folders are replicated to all servers in the replica set, and administrators can later merge the contents of two folders or take some other measure to reestablish the single folder.

Replication integrity   FRS relies on the update sequence number (USN) journal to log records of files that have changed on a replica member. Files are replicated only after they have been modified and closed. As a result, FRS does not lose track of a changed file even if a replica member shuts down abruptly. After the replica member comes back online, FRS replicates changes that originated from other replica members, as well as replicating local changes that occurred before the shutdown. This replication takes place according to the replication schedule.

When you use FRS, the link targets might not always be completely synchronized. As a result, one client's view of a link in a DFS namespace can be different from another client's view of the same link. This inconsistency can happen when clients have been referred to different link targets in the namespace. Link targets do become consistent with time, but you might experience temporary inconsistencies due to replication latency when updates are occurring. For more information about using FRS, see "Choosing an Availability Strategy for Business-Critical Data" later in this chapter.

FRS is typically used to keep link targets synchronized. It is also possible to put files and folders directly in a domain-based DFS root target and then enable replication on the root so that the files and folders are replicated to all root targets. However, avoid enabling replication on domain-based DFS roots for the following reasons:

- Morphed folders can occur under the DFS root folder. Morphed folders occur when two or more identically named folders on different servers are added to the replica tree. FRS identifies the conflict during replication, and the receiving member protects the original copy of the folder and renames (*morphs*) the later inbound copy of the folder. The morphed folder names have a suffix of "_NTFRS_xxxxxxxx," where "xxxxxxxx" represents eight random hexadecimal digits.

  Morphed folders occur in replicated roots for the following reason: When you create a link in the namespace, DFS creates a link folder under each root folder on every root server. For example, if you add 1,000 links to a namespace, DFS creates a link folder under the DFS root folder for each of those 1,000 links on every root server. When you enable FRS replication on the root, FRS attempts to replicate its local copy of the folder structure to every root server. Because each root server has a local copy of the same folder structure as the incoming changes, FRS identifies the duplicate folder names and renames the folders that were most recently created. FRS then replicates all morphed folders to all root targets in the replica set.

Note
If morphed folders do occur, you must use the /RemoveReparse:<DirectoryName> parameter in Dfsutil.exe to delete each morphed folder. For more information about morphed folders, see "Choosing an Availability Strategy for Business-Critical Data" later in this chapter.

- When adding a new root target to an FRS replicated root, you cannot replicate the contents of individual folders in the root based on business priority. Instead, the entire contents of the root are replicated to the new root target. On the other hand, if you enable replication only on individual links, you are creating multiple replica sets, which allows you to enable replication on the most important links first and then enable replication on the links in the namespace as desired.

- You cannot take individual root targets offline. For example, if you are adding a new root target, users who are referred to the new member might see incomplete data until replication is complete. On the other hand, if you enable replication on individual links, you can take a new link target offline while the initial replication takes place or whenever you want to restrict access to a particular link target.

Example: An Organization Designs a DFS Namespace

An organization with 35,000 users in one site designs a stand-alone DFS namespace to provide unified access to 1.4 terabytes (TB) of both business-critical and nonessential software. The team responsible for designing and deploying the namespace chooses a stand-alone DFS namespace for the following reasons:

- The team is not a member of the Domain Admins group, and corporate security policy prevents them from becoming members of this group.

- Corporate security policy also prohibits the team from creating a domain to host a domain-based DFS namespace.

When designing the namespace, the team needs to provide access to the following types of software:

- Business-critical software and operating systems

- Previous (archived) versions of software and operating systems

- Multimedia software that runs from the network

- Training courseware

To ensure the availability of the namespace, the team creates the stand-alone DFS root, \\software\public, on a two-node clustered file server. Each node has two Pentium III 1.26-gigahertz (GHz) CPUs and 256 MB of RAM. The root server does not provide any other services.

When evaluating users' availability requirements for the different types of software, the team determines that the business-critical software and operating systems must be available at all times. In addition, because this is the most frequently accessed software, the team wants good response times. To provide the desired availability and performance, the team uses four servers as link targets. These servers each have two Pentium III 733-MHz CPUs and 256 MB of RAM.

Although the multimedia software is not business critical, the team uses two servers as link targets for this software to improve server response times, because the client portion of the multimedia software accesses files from the server. The team does not use redundant servers for the remaining software, because it is not business critical, and users can tolerate temporary downtime of those servers.

Figure 2.8 describes the DFS namespace for this example.

Figure 2.8 A Stand-Alone DFS Namespace Used for Software Installation

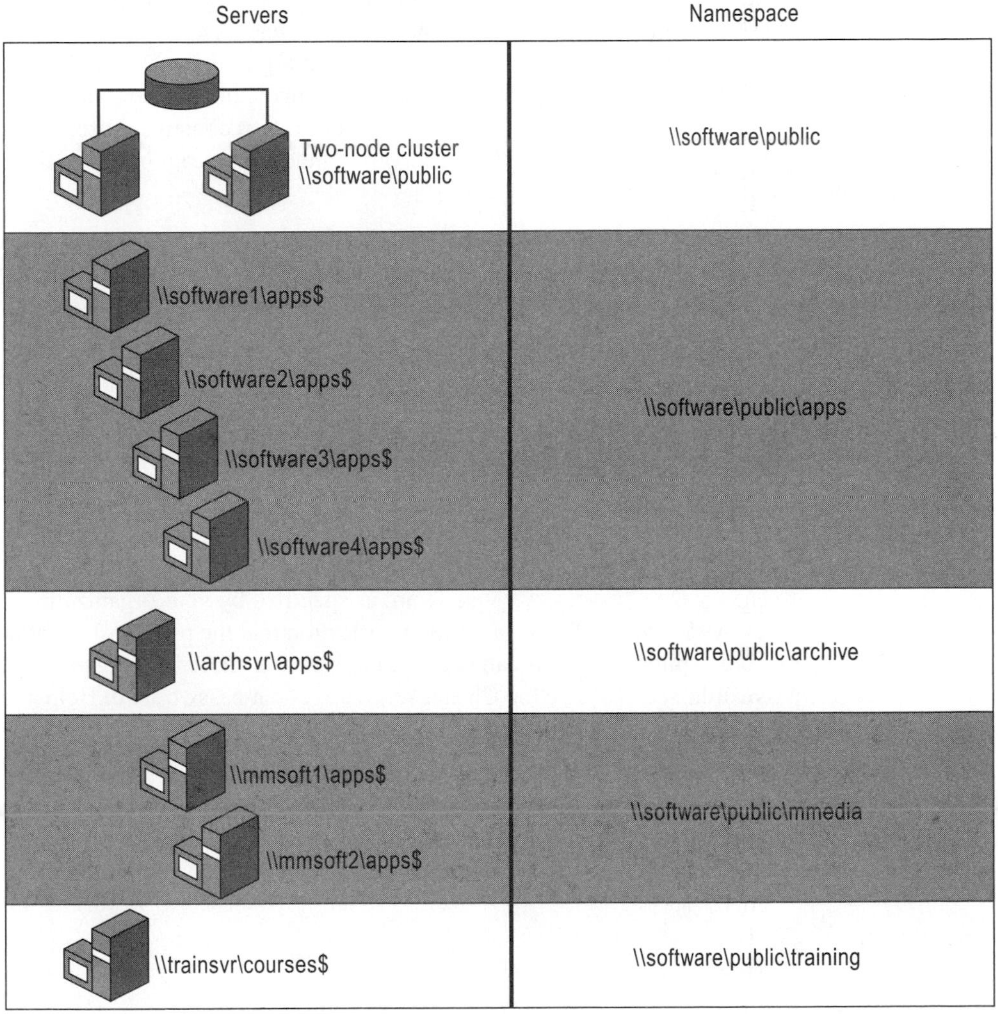

Servers	Namespace
Two-node cluster \\software\public	\\software\public
\\software1\apps$ \\software2\apps$ \\software3\apps$ \\software4\apps$	\\software\public\apps
\\archsvr\apps$	\\software\public\archive
\\mmsoft1\apps$ \\mmsoft2\apps$	\\software\public\mmedia
\\trainsvr\courses$	\\software\public\training

When updating software on the \\archsvr, \\mmsoft, and \\trainsvr servers, the team adds new files directly to the servers. To update software on the business-critical \\software servers, the team copies the new files to a staging server, \\stagesvr. The team uses Robocopy scripts on \\stagesvr to copy the data to the \\software servers. By making changes only at the staging server, the team makes sure that no accidental changes are made on the \\software servers. The team also uses the staging server as the backup source, because it contains source files for a number of servers in addition to the \\software servers. The backup team backs up the other servers individually.

To prevent the staging server from becoming overloaded, the team does not make the staging server part of the namespace, so users do not directly access the server. The team also increases the hardware specifications of this server to meet the increased disk and CPU utilization required for copying files to the \\software servers and to support backups. The hardware configuration has four Pentium III Xeon 700-MHz processors and 1 gigabyte (GB) of RAM.

While deploying the namespace in the production environment, the team learned a number of valuable lessons that can help other organizations as they test and deploy their namespaces:

- When setting permissions on the clustered root server, follow the guidelines in "Planning Cluster Security" later in this chapter. Test the clustered root server to verify that permissions work correctly after a failover occurs.

- Be sure to change the Cluster service password as specified by your organization's password policy. Windows Server 2003 does not send notification that the password is about to expire. If the password expires, problems can occur at failover. For more information about Cluster service passwords, see "Change the Cluster service account password" in Help and Support Center for Windows Server 2003.

- Stagger new software announcements so that users do not overload the servers while trying to install new software. For example, send e-mail notification to a percentage of users each day.

Planning File Server Availability

When you plan for file server availability, begin by ensuring the uptime of the physical file server. Next, determine whether the file server contains business-critical data. If it does, you need to decide whether to use an availability strategy, such as replication or clustering, to ensure the availability of the data. If data on the file server is temporary or not business critical, continue to "Planning File Server Security" later in this chapter.

Figure 2.9 describes the planning process for file server availability.

Figure 2.9   Planning File Server Availability

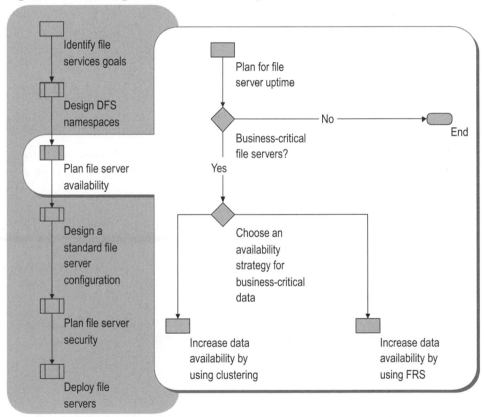

Planning for File Server Uptime

The following guidelines provide basic steps to increase the uptime of file servers. For comprehensive coverage of these topics, see "Planning for High Availability and Scalability" in this book.

Choosing Hardware for Reliability and Availability

Implement a well-planned hardware strategy to increase file server availability while reducing support costs and failure recovery times. You can choose hardware for reliability and availability by following these guidelines:

- Choose hardware from the Windows Server Catalog for products in the Windows Server 2003 family.

- Establish hardware standards.

- Keep spares or stand-by systems for redundancy.

- Use fault-tolerant network components, server cooling, and power supplies.

- Use error checking and correcting (ECC) memory. ECC memory uses a checking scheme to guarantee that the failure of any one bit out of a byte of information is corrected.

- Use fault-tolerant storage components, such as redundant disk controllers, hot-swappable disks and hot spares, and disks configured as redundant arrays of independent disks (RAID). For more information about RAID, see "Planning the Layout and RAID Level of Volumes" later in this chapter.

- Use disk resource management tools, such as disk quotas, to ensure that users always have available disk space.

- Keep a log or database of changes made to the file server. The log should contain dated entries for hardware failures and replacements, service pack and software installations, and other significant changes.

- Deploy FRS-compliant antivirus software on link target computers prior to adding files to FRS replicated links or adding new members to the replica set.

Maintaining the Physical Environment

Maintain high standards for the environment in which the file servers must run. Neglecting the environment can negate all other efforts to maintain the availability of file servers. Take the following measures to maintain the physical environment:

- Maintain proper temperature and humidity.

- Protect servers from dust or contaminates.

- For power outages, provide a steady supply of power for the servers by using uninterruptible power supply (UPS) units or standby generators.

- Maintain server cables.

- Secure the server room.

Planning for Backup and Preparing for Recovery

Backups are essential for high-availability file servers, because the ultimate recovery method is to restore from backup. To plan for backup and recovery:

- Create a plan for backup.

- Monitor backups.

- Decide between local and network backups.

- Check the condition of backup media.

- Perform trial restorations on a regular basis. A trial restoration confirms that your files are properly backed up and can uncover hardware problems that do not show up with software verifications. Be sure to note the time it takes to either restore or re-replicate the data so that you will know how long it takes to bring a server back online after a failure.

- Perform regular backups of clustered file servers and test cluster failures and failover policies. For more information about backing up server clusters and testing policies, see "Backing up and restoring server clusters" and "Test cluster failures and failover policies" in Help and Support Center for Windows Server 2003.

- If you are using DFS and FRS, put a procedure in place for recovering failed members of an FRS replica set. For more information about troubleshooting FRS, see the *Distributed Services Guide* of the *Windows Server 2003 Resource Kit* (or see the *Distributed Services Guide* on the Web at http://www.microsoft.com/reskit).

Choosing Software for Reliability

Installing incompatible or unreliable software reduces the overall availability of file servers. To choose software for reliability, follow these guidelines:

- Select software that is compatible with Windows Server 2003.

- Select signed drivers. Microsoft promotes driver signing for designated device classes as a mechanism to advance the quality of drivers, to provide a better user experience, and to reduce support costs for vendors and total cost of ownership for customers. For more information about driver signing, see the Driver Signing and File Protection link on the Web Resources page at http://www.microsoft.com/windows/reskits/webresources.

- Select software that supports the high-availability features you require, such as server clusters and online backup.

Identifying Business-Critical File Servers

After you plan for file server uptime, identify file servers that must be highly available. These file servers typically contain business-critical data that is required for an organization's central purpose, such as software distribution points, e-mail or business databases, and internal or external Web sites. File servers need to be highly available for the following reasons as well:

- **The file server contains one or more stand-alone DFS roots.** If you create a stand-alone DFS root on a file server, and the server fails or is taken offline for maintenance, the entire DFS namespace is unavailable. Users can access the shared folders only if they know the name of the file servers where the shared folders are located. To make stand-alone DFS namespaces fault tolerant, you can create the roots on clustered file servers.

- **Your organization is consolidating file servers.** Consolidation leads to a greater dependency on fewer file servers, so you must ensure the availability of the remaining file servers.

- **Your organization has existing SLAs.** Service Level Agreements (SLAs) and Organization Level Agreements (OLAs) specify the required uptime for file servers, usually defined as the percentage of time that the file server is available for use. For example, your organization might require that file servers have 99.7-percent uptime regardless of the type of data they contain. To meet these agreements, some organizations deploy clustered file servers and assign experienced administrators to manage those file servers. In addition to deploying hardware, these administrators use defined and tested processes to fulfill these agreements.

You do not need to implement additional availability strategies on file servers that store temporary or non-business-critical files. For example, if the file server fails in some way, but users can tolerate the loss of the file server for the time it takes to repair the file server or restore the data from backup, you do not need to use an availability strategy such as replication or clustering. Instead, you can work to decrease the amount of time it takes to restore the file server.

Choosing an Availability Strategy for Business-Critical Data

If a file server contains business-critical data, you need to make certain that the data is highly available. Windows Server 2003 provides two primary strategies for increasing data availability: FRS and clustering.

FRS   This strategy involves creating one or more domain-based DFS namespaces, using link targets that point to multiple file servers and using File Replication service (FRS) to synchronize the data in the link targets. This chapter describes the design and deployment process for FRS, although you can also synchronize data manually by using tools such as Robocopy or by using third-party replication tools.

Clustering   A server cluster is a group of individual computer systems working together cooperatively to provide increased computing power and to provide continuous availability of business-critical applications or resources. This group of computers appears to network clients as if it were a single system, by virtue of a common cluster name. A cluster can be configured so that the workload is distributed among the group, and if one of the cluster members fails, another cluster member automatically assumes its duties.

Both of these strategies involve using multiple file servers to ensure data availability. If for some reason you cannot use multiple file servers, follow the guidelines in "Planning for File Server Uptime" earlier in this chapter to increase the availability of the physical server.

When evaluating these two strategies, you must keep in mind your organization's tolerance for inconsistent data. FRS can cause temporary data inconsistency as data is replicated across multiple servers. Clustered file servers maintain only one copy of the data; therefore, data inconsistency does not occur.

 Note

If your organization plans to implement geographically dispersed clusters for disaster tolerance, you need to understand your data consistency needs in different failure and recovery scenarios and work with the solution vendors to match your requirements. Different geographically dispersed cluster solutions provide different replication and redundancy strategies, ranging from synchronous mirroring across sites to asynchronous replication. For more information about geographically dispersed clusters, see "Designing and Deploying Server Clusters" in this book.

Using FRS as an Availability Strategy

You can use FRS to replicate data in domain-based DFS namespaces on file servers running a Windows 2000 Server or Windows Server 2003 operating system. When evaluating FRS, you must determine whether your organization can tolerate periods of inconsistent data that can occur within a replica set. Data inconsistency can occur at the file and folder level as follows:

- FRS uses a "last writer wins" algorithm for files. This algorithm is applied in two situations: when the same file is changed on two or more servers, and when two or more different files with the same name are added to the replica tree on different servers. The most recent update to a file in a replica set becomes the version of the file that replicates to the other members of the replica set, which might result in data loss if multiple masters have updated the file. In addition, FRS cannot enforce file-sharing restrictions or file locking between two users who are working on the same file on two different replica set members.

- FRS uses a "last writer wins" algorithm when a folder on two or more servers is changed, such as by changing folder attributes. However, FRS uses a "first writer wins" algorithm when two or more identically named folders on different servers are added to the replica tree. When this occurs, FRS identifies the conflict during replication, and the receiving member protects the original copy of the folder and renames (*morphs*) the later inbound copy of the folder. The morphed folder names have a suffix of "_NTFRS_xxxxxxxx," where "xxxxxxxx" represents eight random hexadecimal digits. The folders are replicated to all servers in the replica set, and administrators can later merge the contents of the folders or take some other measure to reestablish the single folder.

Temporary data inconsistency due to replication latency is more likely to occur in geographically diverse sites with infrequent replication across slow WAN links. If you want to use replication among servers in the same site, consistency is probably not an issue, because the replication can occur quickly after the file changes — assuming that only one user makes changes to the data. If two users make changes to the data, replication conflicts occur and one user loses those changes.

Replication works well in the following scenarios.

When the data is read-only or changes infrequently

Because changes occur infrequently, the data is usually consistent. In addition, FRS has less data to replicate, so network bandwidth is not heavily affected.

When the sites are geographically dispersed and consistency is not an issue

Geographically dispersed sites might have slower bandwidth connections, but if your organization does not require the data in those sites to always be consistent with each other, you can configure replication in those sites on a schedule that make sense for your organization. For example, if your organization has sites in Los Angeles and Zimbabwe, you can place one or more replicas of the data in servers in those sites and schedule replication to occur at night or during periods of low bandwidth use. Because in this scenario replication could take hours or days to update every member, the delay must be acceptable to your organization.

When each file is changed by only one person from one location

Replication conflicts rarely occur if only a single user changes a given file from a single location. Some common scenarios for single authorship are redirected My Documents folders and other home directories. Conversely, if users roam between sites, replication latency could cause the file to be temporarily inconsistent between sites.

When replication takes place among a small number of servers in the same site

Replication latency is reduced by frequently replicating data using high-speed connections. As a result, data tends to be more consistent.

Replication should not be used in the following scenarios.

In organizations with no operations group or dedicated administrators

Organizations that do not have the staff or the time to monitor FRS event logs on each replica member should not implement FRS. Organizations must also have well-defined procedures in place to prevent the accidental or unintentional deletion of data in the replica set, because deleting a file or folder from one replica member causes the file or folder (and its contents) to be deleted from all replica members. In addition, if a folder is moved out of the replica tree, FRS deletes the folder and its contents on the remaining replica members. To avoid having to restore the files or folders from backup, you can enable shadow copies on some of the replica members so that you can easily restore a file or folder that was accidentally deleted. For more information about shadow copies, see "Designing a Shadow Copy Strategy" later in this chapter. For more information about FRS logs, see the *Distributed Services Guide* of the *Windows Server 2003 Resource Kit* (or see the *Distributed Services Guide* on the Web at http://www.microsoft.com/reskit).

In organizations that do not update virus signatures or closely manage folder permissions

A virus in FRS-replicated content can spread rapidly to replica members and to clients that access the replicated data. Viruses are especially damaging in environments where the Everyone group has share permissions or NTFS permissions to modify content. To prevent the spread of viruses, it is essential that replica members have FRS-compatible, up-to-date virus scanners installed on the servers and on clients that access replicated data. For more information about preventing the spread of viruses, see "Planning Virus Protection for File Servers" and "Planning DFS and FRS Security" later in this chapter.

When the rate of change exceeds what FRS can replicate

If you plan to schedule replication to occur during a specified replication window, verify that FRS can replicate all the changed files within the window. Replication throughput is determined by a number of factors:

- The number and size of changed files

- The speed of the disk subsystem

- The speed of the network

- Whether you have optimized the servers by placing the replica tree, the staging directory, and the FRS data on separate disks.

Each organization will have different FRS throughput rates, depending on these factors. In addition, if your data compresses extremely well, your file throughput will be higher. To determine the replication rate, perform testing in a lab environment that resembles your production environment.

If the amount of data changes exceeds what FRS can replicate in a given period of time, you need to change one of these factors, such as increasing the speed of the disk subsystem (number of disks, mechanical speed, or disk cache) or network. If no change is possible, FRS is not recommended for your organization.

In organizations that always use clustered file servers

Some organizations use clustered file servers regardless of whether the server contains business-critical data. Although storing FRS-replicated content on the cluster storage of a clustered file server might imply increased availability of the data, combining clustering and FRS is not recommended. Data might become inconsistent among the members of the replica set, thus defeating the purpose of clustering, which is to have highly available data that remains consistent because only one copy of the data exists. In addition, Windows Server 2003 does not support configuring FRS to replicate data on cluster storage.

In organizations that use Remote Storage

Remote Storage is a feature in Windows Server 2003 that automatically copies infrequently used files on local volumes to a library of magnetic tapes or magneto-optical disks. Organizations that use Remote Storage must not use FRS on the same volume. Specifically, do not perform any of the following tasks:

- Do not create a replica set on a volume that is managed by Remote Storage.

- Do not add a volume that contains folders that are part of an FRS replica set to Remote Storage.

If you use Remote Storage for volumes that contain FRS replica sets, backup tapes might be damaged or destroyed if FRS recalls a large number of files from Remote Storage. The damage occurs because FRS does not recall files in media order. As a result, files are extracted randomly, and the process can take days to complete and might damage or destroy the tape in the process. Random extraction from magneto-optical disks can also be extremely time consuming.

 Caution

Windows Server 2003 does not prevent you from using Remote Storage and FRS replica sets on the same volumes, so take extra precautions to avoid using these two features on the same volume.

When locks by users or processes prevent updates to files and folders

FRS does not replicate locked files or folders to other replica members, nor does FRS update a file on a replica member if the local file is open. If users or processes frequently leave files open for extended periods, consider using clustering instead of FRS.

When the data to be replicated is on mounted drives

If a mounted drive exists in a replica tree, FRS does not replicate the data in the mounted drive.

When the data to be replicated is encrypted by using EFS

FRS does not replicate files encrypted by using EFS, nor does FRS warn you that EFS-encrypted files are present in the replica set.

When the FRS jet database, FRS logs, and staging directory are stored on volumes where NTFS disk quotas are enabled

If you plan to store a replica set on a volume where disk quotas are enabled, you must move the staging directory, FRS jet database, and FRS logs to a volume where disk quotas are disabled. For more information, see "Planning the Staging Directory" later in this chapter.

Using Clustering as an Availability Strategy

If the data changes frequently and your organization requires consistent data that is highly available, use clustered file servers. Clustered file servers allow client access to file services during unplanned and planned outages. When one of the servers in the cluster is unavailable, cluster resources and applications move to other available cluster nodes. Server clusters do not guarantee nonstop operation, but they do provide sufficient availability for most business-critical applications, including file services. A cluster service can monitor applications and resources and automatically recognize and recover from many failure conditions. This ability provides flexibility in managing the workload within a cluster and improves overall system availability.

Server cluster benefits include the following:

High availability   Ownership of resources, such as disks and IP addresses, is automatically transferred from a failed server to a surviving server. When a system or application in the cluster fails, the cluster software restarts the failed application on a surviving server, or it disperses the work from the failed node to the remaining nodes. As a result, users experience only a momentary pause in service.

Manageability   You can use the Cluster Administrator snap-in to manage a cluster as a single system and to manage applications as if they were running on a single server. You can move applications to different servers within the cluster, and you can manually balance server workloads and free servers for planned maintenance. You can also monitor the status of the cluster, all nodes, and resources from anywhere on the network.

Scalability   Server clusters can grow to meet increased demand. When the overall client load for a clustered file server exceeds the cluster's capabilities, you can add additional nodes.

Clustered file servers work well in the following scenarios.

When multiple users access and change the files

Because only one copy of the file exists, Windows Server 2003 can enforce file locking so that only one user can make changes at a time. As a result, data is always consistent.

When large numbers of users access data in the same site

Clustered file servers are useful for providing access to users in a single physical site. In this case, you do not need a replication method to provide data consistency among sites.

When files change frequently and data consistency is a must

Even with a large number of changes, data is always consistent and there is no need to replicate the changes to multiple servers.

When you want to reduce the administrative overhead associated with creating many shared folders

On clustered file servers, you can use the Share Subdirectories feature to automatically share any folders that are created within a folder that is configured as a File Share resource. This feature is useful if you need to create a large number of shared folders.

When you want to ensure the availability of a stand-alone DFS root

Creating stand-alone DFS roots on clustered file servers allows the namespaces to remain available, even if one of the nodes of the cluster fails.

When you want to make encrypted files highly available

Windows Server 2003 supports using the EFS clustered file servers. Using EFS in FRS replica sets is not supported. For more information about using EFS on clustered file servers, see "Planning Encrypted File Storage" later in this chapter.

Some issues to consider when using clustered file servers include the following.

Dynamic disks are not available

If you want to use dynamic disks, you must use them on nonclustered file servers or on the local storage devices of the cluster. If the node hosting the local storage devices fails, the data becomes unavailable until the node is repaired and brought back online.

If you need to extend the size of basic volumes used for shared cluster storage, you can do so by using DiskPart. For more information about extending basic volumes, see "Extend a basic volume" in Help and Support Center for Windows Server 2003.

Clustered file servers must use complete cluster systems

For your server clusters to be supported by Microsoft, you must choose complete cluster systems from the Windows Server Catalog for the Windows Server 2003 family. For more information about support for server clusters, see article Q309395, "The Microsoft Support Policy for Server Clusters and the Hardware." To find this article, see the Microsoft Knowledge Base link on the Web Resources page at http://www.microsoft.com/windows/reskits/webresources.

Increasing Data Availability by Using FRS

To design an FRS replication strategy, you need to take the following steps:

1. Identify data to replicate.

2. Choose the replication topology.

3. Design the replication schedule.

4. Plan the staging directory.

5. Determine connection priorities.

The following sections describe each of these steps.

 Important

> If you configure FRS to replicate files on file servers running Windows 2000, it is highly recommended that you install the Windows 2000 Service Pack 3 (SP3) and the post-SP3 release of Ntfrs.exe, or install later service packs that include this release. For more information about updating FRS, see article 811370, "Issues That Are Fixed in the Post-Service Pack 3 Release of Ntfrs.exe." To find this article, see the Microsoft Knowledge Base link on the Web Resources page at http://www.microsoft.com/windows/reskits/webresources.

For more information about FRS security, see "Planning DFS and FRS Security" later in this chapter.

Identifying Data to Replicate

If you identify which DFS roots and links require multiple replicated targets, as described in "Increasing the Availability of DFS Namespaces" earlier in this chapter, you also need to consider the following issues.

Size of the USN journal

The default USN journal size in Windows Server 2003 is 512 MB. If your volume contains 400,000 files or fewer, no additional configuration is required. For every 100,000 additional files on a volume containing FRS-replicated content, increase the update sequence number (USN) journal by 128 MB. If files on the volume are changed or renamed frequently (regardless of whether they are part of the replica set), consider sizing the USN journal larger than these recommendations to prevent USN journal wraps, which can occur when large numbers of files change so quickly that the USN journal must discard the oldest changes (before FRS has a chance to detect the changes) to stay within the specified size limit. To recover from a journal wrap, you must perform a nonauthoritative restore on the server to synchronize its files with the files on the other replica members. For more information about USN journal wraps, see article Q292438, "Troubleshooting Journal_Wrap Errors on Sysvol and DFS Replica Sets." To find this article, see the Microsoft Knowledge Base link on the Web Resources page at http://www.microsoft.com/windows/reskits/webresources.

Where to store the replica tree

To provide the best consistency and minimize administrative intervention, carefully plan where to store the replica tree. Your choice will depend on the amount of storage on the server, the volume layout, the number of files on the volume that do not participate in a replica set, and the number of replica sets on the server.

- If you have a single replica tree, store it on its own volume if possible, or store it on a volume that also stores other user data. Adjust the USN journal size based on the total number of files on the volume.

- If you have more replica trees than volumes, store multiple replica trees on each volume and adjust the USN journal size based on the total number of files on the volume.

- If you can create a volume for each replica tree, store each replica tree on its own volume and adjust the USN journal accordingly.

The staging directory also requires careful placement. For more information, see "Planning the Staging Directory" later in this chapter.

Replicated link targets to omit from the DFS namespace

When you omit a replicated link target from the namespace, you disable referrals so that DFS does not direct clients to the link target. However, the link target still replicates with other members. Disabling DFS referrals for replica members is useful for a number of scenarios. For example, you can use such a member for any of the following purposes:

- As a backup server. For example, assume you have five servers in a replica set. You might make four of the servers part of the DFS namespace and use the fifth server as a backup source. In this scenario, DFS never refers clients to the fifth server.

- As a reference server. For example, you omit (from the namespace) the server where all changes originate, thus ensuring that you can always introduce new content without being blocked because of open files. The reference server becomes the "known good" server; all other servers should contain identical content.

- As a way to update application data. For example, you have two replica members, ServerA and ServerB, which contain application data that is frequently updated. You can disable referrals for ServerA, update the application data, and enable referrals to ServerA. You can then repeat the procedure on ServerB. In this scenario, one of the replica members is always available while the other is being updated.

To omit a replicated link target from the namespace, configure the link target within the DFS namespace and configure replication as desired by using the Distributed File System snap-in. Then use the **Enable or Disable Referral** command in the Distributed File System snap-in to disable referrals to the link targets that you want to omit from the namespace.

Files or folders to exclude from replication

You can use the Distributed File System snap-in to set filters that exclude subfolders (and their contents) or files from replication. You exclude subfolders by specifying their name, and you exclude files by using wild cards to specify file names and extensions. By default, no subfolders are excluded. The default file filters exclude the following files from replication:

- File names starting with a tilde (~) character

- Files with .bak or .tmp extensions

Filters act as exclusion filters only for new files and folders added to a replica set. They have no effect on existing files in the replica set. For example, if you change the existing file filter from "*.tmp, *.bak" to "*.old, *.bak," FRS does not go through the replica set and exclude all files that match *.old, nor does it go through the replica set and begin to replicate all files that match *.tmp. After the filter change, new files matching *.old that are added to the replica set are not replicated. New files matching *.tmp that are added to the replica set are replicated.

Any file in the replica set that was excluded from replication under the old file filter (such as Test.tmp, created when the old filter was in force) is automatically replicated under the new file filter only after the file is modified. Likewise, changes to any file that was not excluded from replication under the old filter (such as Test.old, created when the old filter was in force) continue to replicate under the new filter, until you explicitly delete the file.

These rules apply in the same manner to the directory exclusion filter. If a directory is excluded, all subdirectories and files under that directory are also excluded.

Regardless of the filters you set, FRS always excludes the following from replication:

- NTFS mounted drives

- Files encrypted by using EFS

- Any reparse points except those associated with DFS namespaces. If a file has a reparse point used for Hierarchical Storage Management (HSM) or Single Instance Store (SIS), FRS replicates the underlying file but not the reparse point.

- Files on which the temporary attribute has been set

For more information about configuring filters, see the *Distributed Services Guide* of the *Windows Server 2003 Resource Kit* (or see the *Distributed Services Guide* on the Web at http://www.microsoft.com/reskit).

Number of servers in the replica set

Will you replicate data among three servers or three hundred servers? As the number of servers increases, configuring the topology and schedule becomes more complex, and it takes longer to replicate data to all members of the replica set. If many members exist in the replica set, and if any member can originate new data, the amount of aggregate bandwidth consumed can be very high. Also note that any server with outbound connections is a server that can potentially originate content and thus requires careful monitoring.

Number of replica sets per server

Although there is no limit to the number of replica sets that can be hosted on a single server, it is recommended that you host no more than 150 replica sets on a single server to provide optimal replication performance. The optimal number of replica sets for servers in your organization depends on the CPU, memory, disk input/output (I/O) throughput, and the amount of data changed.

Network bandwidth between sites

Replicating data between sites that are connected with slow WAN links requires careful planning of the topology and schedule, because FRS does not provide bandwidth throttling. If the sites have a high-bandwidth connection, but business-critical databases and other applications use that connection as well, schedule replication so that it does not consume bandwidth that is needed for other uses.

Amount of data in the replica tree

If the replica tree includes a large amount of data, and a new member is served by a low-bandwidth link, prestage the replica tree on the new member. Prestaging a replica tree preserves security descriptors and object IDs and involves restoring the data to the new member without using the low-bandwidth link. For example, you can restore a backup of the replica tree on the new member, or you can place the new member in the same site as an existing member and prestage the replica tree by using a high-bandwidth local area network (LAN) connection. For more information about adding new replica members, see "Adding a New Member to an Existing Replica Set" later in this chapter.

How frequently the data changes

If the data that is to be replicated changes frequently, estimate the total amount of data that will be generated by each replica member over a period of time. Data that changes frequently is more difficult to keep synchronized across multiple servers, especially if those servers are located across WAN links. If replication latency is a concern, consider clustering instead of replication.

Whether you want to use single master replication

FRS is a multimaster replication engine, which means that new content and changes to existing content can originate from any member. If you want to limit the servers that can originate data, you can set up single master replication in one of the following ways:

- Set NTFS permissions on targets to control who can update data in the replica tree.

- Configure the replication topology so that a target does not have any outbound connections.

 Important

If you use this method, do not directly make changes on replica members that have no outbound connections. Changes made directly on a server that has no outbound connections will not replicate, and the server replica tree will be inconsistent and potentially unpredictable.

Speed of recovery from hardware failures

If a server contains a large amount of replicated, business-critical data, be sure to use redundant server components, such as hardware RAID, redundant disk controllers, and redundant network cards to reduce the likelihood that a hardware failure could cause the server to become unavailable. To further increase availability, use multiple servers in each site so that if a server in the site is unavailable due to hardware problems, clients in that site can access the remaining servers as you repair and restore the data on the failed server. Using multiple servers is also useful for remote sites where repair time is lengthy and in cases where the amount of replicated data is so large that it cannot be restored from a central site within the required restoration window.

Expected growth of replicated data

You need to know whether you plan to replicate larger and larger amounts of data over time so that you can make sure that your topology, schedule, and bandwidth can handle the additional data.

Expected increase in the number of replica members

If you plan to deploy a small number of servers at first and then deploy additional servers over time, you need to make sure that your topology and bandwidth can handle the new servers. For example, if you plan to add 100 more servers, and each of those servers can originate data, you must make sure that your network has the bandwidth to replicate this data. On the other hand, if you are deploying 100 new servers, but only one of those servers can originate data, bandwidth might not be a limiting factor, although you do need to make sure that your bandwidth can handle the initial synchronization of data among servers.

Choosing a Replication Topology

The replication topology describes the logical connections that FRS uses to replicate files among servers. To minimize the network bandwidth required for replication, identify where your bandwidth is highest and lowest on your network, and model your FRS replication topology after the physical topology of your network.

You use the Distributed File System snap-in to select a replication topology. After you add a second link target to a link, you are prompted to configure replication by using the Configure Replication Wizard, which allows you to perform the following tasks:

- Choose the initial master whose contents are replicated to the other targets. The initial master is only relevant during the creation of the replica set. After that, the server that acted as the initial master is treated no differently from any other server.

- Choose the location of the staging directory. By default, the staging directory is placed on a different volume than the content to be replicated.

- Choose the replication topology: ring, hub and spoke, full mesh, or custom. If you choose custom, you can add or delete connections to or from the replica set. For the other three standard topologies, you can only enable or disable connections between target servers.

The following describes the four topology types available in the Distributed File System snap-in. For an Excel spreadsheet to assist you in documenting your decision after you choose the topology, see "FRS Configuration Worksheet" (Sdcfsv_2.xls) on the *Windows Server 2003 Deployment Kit* companion CD (or see "FRS Configuration Worksheet" on the Web at http://www.microsoft.com/reskit).

Ring topology

Figure 2.10 illustrates a ring topology. In a ring topology, files replicate from one server to another in a circular configuration, with each server connected to the servers on either side of it in the ring. Choose a ring topology if your physical network topology resembles a ring topology. For example, if each server is located in a different site and has existing connectivity with neighboring servers, you can choose the ring topology so that each server connects only to neighboring servers. Because the ring topology is bidirectional, each connection is fault tolerant. If a single connection or server fails, data can still replicate to all members in the opposite direction.

Figure 2.10   Ring Topology

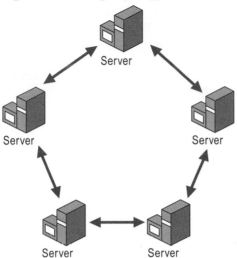

If you plan to create a ring topology with more than seven members, consider adding shortcut connections between some of the members to reduce the number of hops required for data to replicate to all members.

Hub and spoke topology

Figure 2.11 illustrates hub and spoke topology. In a hub and spoke topology, you designate one server as the *hub*. Other servers, called *spokes*, connect to the hub. This topology is typically used for WANs that consist of faster network connections between major computing hubs and slower links connecting branch offices. In this topology, files replicate from the hub server to the spoke servers and vice versa, but files do not replicate directly between two spoke servers. When you choose this topology, you must choose which server will act as the hub. If you want to set up multiple hubs, use a custom topology. Using multiple hubs is recommended, because using only one hub means that the hub is a single point of failure.

Figure 2.11   Hub and Spoke Topology

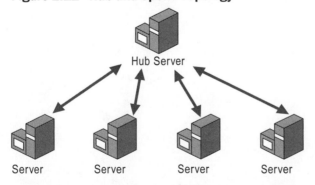

Full mesh topology

Figure 2.12 illustrates a full mesh topology. In a full mesh topology, every server connects to every other server. A file created on one server replicates directly to all other servers. Because each member connects to every other member, the propagation of change orders for replicating files can impose a heavy burden on the network. To reduce unnecessary traffic, use a different topology or delete connections you do not actually need. A full mesh topology is not recommended for replica sets with five or more members.

Figure 2.12   Full Mesh Topology

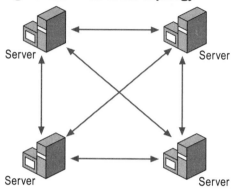

Custom topology

With a custom topology, you create the connections between the servers yourself. One example of a custom topology is a redundant hub and spoke topology. In this configuration, a hub site might contain two file servers that are connected by a high-speed link. Each of these two hub servers might connect with four branch file servers in a hub and spoke arrangement. An example of this topology is shown in "Example: An Organization Designs a Replication Strategy" later in this chapter. Figure 2.13 illustrates another type of hub and spoke topology known as a *multitier redundant hub and spoke* with an optional staging server used for introducing changes into the replica set.

Figure 2.13   Multitier Redundant Hub and Spoke Topology

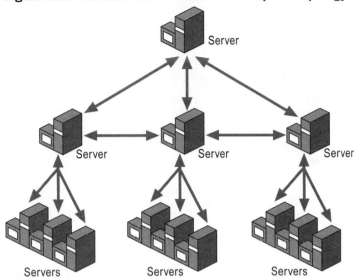

Designing a Replication Schedule

When you use the Distributed File System snap-in to configure replication, FRS schedules replication to take place 24 hours a day, seven days a week. Whenever you copy a file to a target that participates in replication, or when an existing file in the replica set is changed, FRS replicates the entire file to the other targets using the connections specified in the replication topology. Continuous replication is advised only for environments that meet the following criteria:

- The replica members are all connected by high-bandwidth connections, such as hub servers in a redundant hub and spoke topology.

- The amount of data to be replicated is not so large that it interferes with the bandwidth required for other purposes during peak or off-peak hours.

- The application whose data is being replicated needs rapid distribution of file changes, such as antivirus signature files or login scripts.

If your environment does not meet these criteria, plan to create a replication schedule so that data is replicated at night or during other times as appropriate. A replication schedule involves enabling and disabling replication so that it occurs at specified times on specified days. For example, you might schedule replication to occur beginning at 12:00 midnight and ending at 2:00 A.M. every day.

When determining the replication schedule, consider the following issues:

Amount of data to be replicated and the length of the replication window   Estimate the amount of data to be replicated so that you can choose a duration that is long enough to replicate all the data. In DFS namespaces, replication stops when the schedule window closes, and any remaining files are delayed until the next replication window opens. If you occasionally put a large amount of data into the replica set, FRS might take several replication periods to replicate all the data.

Amount of latency your organization can tolerate   If you plan to replicate data that changes frequently, consider the amount of latency that you can tolerate in keeping your targets synchronized and the amount of bandwidth that is consumed during replication.

Whether you want to stagger schedules   If you are using a redundant hub and spoke topology with several hubs, you can split the replication load among the hubs by staggering the schedule. An example of this schedule is described in "Example: An Organization Designs a Replication Strategy" later in this chapter.

For an Excel spreadsheet to assist you in documenting the replication schedule, see "FRS Configuration Worksheet" (Sdcfsv_2.xls) on the *Windows Server 2003 Deployment Kit* companion CD (or see "FRS Configuration Worksheet" on the Web at http://www.microsoft.com/reskit).

Planning the Staging Directory

The staging directory acts as a buffer by retaining copies of updated files until replication partners successfully receive them and move them into the target directory. The following sections describe the benefits and design considerations for staging directories. For an Excel spreadsheet to assist you in documenting the staging directory settings and location, see "FRS Configuration Worksheet" (Sdcfsv_2.xls) on the *Windows Server 2003 Deployment Kit* companion CD (or see "FRS Configuration Worksheet" on the Web at http://www.microsoft.com/reskit).

Why FRS Uses a Staging Directory

The staging directory acts as a queue for changes to be replicated to downstream partners. After the changes are made to a file and the file is closed, the file content is compressed, written to the staging directory, and replicated according to schedule. Any further use of that file does not prevent FRS from replicating the staging file to other members. In addition, if the file is replicated to multiple downstream partners or to members with slow data links, using a staging file ensures that the underlying file in the replica tree can still be accessed.

 Note

A new or updated file remains in the staging directory of a replica member with downstream partners even after the file has replicated to all members. The file is retained for seven days in order to optimize future synchronizations with new downstream partners. After seven days, FRS deletes the file. Do not attempt to delete any files in the staging directory yourself.

Staging Directory Size

The size of the staging directory governs the maximum amount of disk space that FRS can use to hold those staging files and the maximum file size that FRS can replicate. The default size of the staging directory is approximately 660 MB, the minimum size is 10 MB, and the maximum size is 2 TB. The largest file that FRS can replicate is determined by the staging directory size on both the upstream partner (the replica member that sends out the changed file) and downstream partners (the replica member that receives the changed file) and whether the replicated file, to the extent that it can be compressed, can be accommodated by the current staging directory size. Therefore, the largest file that FRS can replicate is 2 TB, assuming that the staging directory size is set to the maximum on upstream and downstream partners.

Managing Staging Directory Capacity

When FRS tries to allocate space for a staging file and is not successful, either because there is not enough physical disk space or because the size of the files in the staging directory has reached 90 percent of the staging directory size, FRS starts to remove files from the staging directory. Staged files are removed (in the order of the longest time since the last access) until the size of the staging directory has dropped below 60 percent of the staging directory limit. Additionally, staging files for downstream partners that have been inaccessible for more than seven days are deleted. As a result, FRS does not stop replicating if the staging directory runs out of free space. This means that if a downstream partner goes offline for an extended period of time, the offline member does not cause the upstream partner's staging directory to fill with accumulated staging files.

 Note

In Windows Server 2003, FRS detects and suppresses excessive replication that could be caused when you use Group Policy to overwrite file permissions or when you use antivirus software that overwrites security descriptors. In these examples, writes to files cause no net content changes. When FRS detects a significant increase in the number of changes made to a file, FRS logs an event with ID 13567 in the File Replication Service event log. Despite the FRS response to excessive replication caused by applications, services, or security policies, you should investigate the source of the excessive replication and eliminate it.

The fact that FRS removes files from the staging directory does not mean that the underlying file is deleted or will not be replicated. The change order in the outbound log still exists, and the file will eventually be sent to downstream partners when they process the change order. However, before replication can take place, the upstream partner must recreate the file in the staging directory, which can affect performance. Recreating the staging file can also cause a replication delay if the file on the upstream partner is in use, preventing FRS from creating the staging file.

A staging directory can reach 90 percent of its capacity in the following situations:

- **More data is being replicated than the staging directory can hold.** If you plan to replicate more than 660 MB of data, or if you expect that the largest file to replicate will be 660 MB or larger, you must increase the size of the staging directory. Use Table 2.7 for sizing guidelines.

- **A slow outbound partner.** Construct replica connections that have comparable bandwidth for all outbound partners. It is also a good idea to balance that bandwidth for inbound and outbound connections. If you cannot balance the bandwidth, increase the size of the staging directory.

- **Replication is disabled.** If a file is changed or added to the replica set while replication is disabled, the staging directory must be large enough to hold data awaiting replication during the off-time or else older staged files are removed. Replication still occurs, but less optimally.

Table 2.7 describes a range of sizing guidelines for staging directories. Use the numbers in Table 1.7 as a baseline for testing and then adjust the numbers as necessary for your environment. Also, note that the numbers in Table 1.7 apply to each replica set on a server. If a server contains multiple replica sets, you must follow these guidelines for each staging directory.

Table 2.7   Staging Directory Size Guidelines per Replica Set

Scenario	Minimum	Acceptable	Best Performance
Adding a new replica member	Whichever is larger: • 660 MB • Take the size of the 128 largest files in the replica tree, multiplied by the number of downstream partners, and then multiply that number by 1.2.	Whichever is larger: • 660 MB • Take the size of the 128 largest files in the replica tree, multiplied by the number of downstream partners, and then multiply that number by 1.2.	Whichever is larger: • 660 MB • Take the size of the 128 largest files in the replica tree, multiplied by the number of downstream partners, and then multiply that number by 1.2.
Increasing the staging directory space to account for backlog caused by replication schedules	No additional requirement	Add space equal to the maximum quantity of expected file changes in a seven-day period multiplied by 1.2.	Add space equal to the expected size of the replica tree, multiplied by 1.2.
Additional recommendations	No additional recommendations	Use dedicated disks for the staging directory.	Use dedicated, high-performance disks for the staging directory.
Suitability for large replica sets	Not recommended	Recommended	Recommended for organizations that require highest performance.

Note

The recommendations in Table 2.7 offer sufficient staging directory space for a worst-case scenario. In fact, the staging directory needs to be only as large as the largest 128 files, multiplied by the number of downstream partners that are concurrently performing a full synchronization against the replica member.

For more information about configuring the staging directory, see article Q329491, "Configuring Correct Staging Area Space for Replica Sets." To find this article, see the Microsoft Knowledge Base link on the Web Resources page at http://www.microsoft.com/windows/reskits/webresources.

For information about changing the size of the staging directory, see "Deploying FRS" later in this chapter.

Staging Directory Compression Considerations

FRS replica members running Windows 2000 Server with Service Pack 3 (SP3) or Windows Server 2003 compress the files replicated among them. Compression reduces the size of files in the staging directory on the upstream partners, over the network between compression-enabled partners, and in the staging directory of downstream partners prior to files being moved into their final location.

To maintain backward compatibility, servers running Windows 2000 Server with SP3 or Windows Server 2003 generate uncompressed staging files when they send changed files to downstream partners running Windows 2000 Server with Service Pack 2 (SP2) or earlier (or to servers running Windows 2000 Server with SP3 or Windows Server 2003 that have compression explicitly disabled in the registry).

To accommodate environments that contain a combination of compression-enabled and compression-disabled partners, the server originating or forwarding changes must generate two sets of staging files for each modified file or folder: one compressed version for servers running Windows 2000 Server with SP3 or Windows Server 2003, and one uncompressed version for partners that have compression explicitly disabled or that are running Windows 2000 Server with SP2 or earlier. To mitigate the generation of two sets of staging files, you can take one of the following steps:

- Confirm that you have sufficient disk space and an appropriately sized staging directory on all replica members.

- Explicitly disable compression in the registry until all members of the replica set are running Windows 2000 Server with SP3 or Windows Server 2003. For information about disabling replication, see article Q288160, "Error Message: Error Compressing Data," in the Microsoft Knowledge Base. To find this article, see the Microsoft Knowledge Base link on the Web Resources page at http://www.microsoft.com/windows/reskits/webresources.

- Rapidly deploy Windows 2000 Server with SP3 or Windows Server 2003 on all members of the replica set, especially if you are replicating a large amount of content.

Choosing the Staging Directory Location

You can choose the location of the staging directory when you use the Distributed File System snap-in to configure a replica set. By default, all replica sets on the server use the same staging directory, and the staging directory space limit applies to all staging directories on the local server. When the staging directory is shared among multiple replica sets, any one replica set can cause the staging directory to reach 90% capacity, at which point FRS begins to delete the oldest staging files for any of the replica sets.

To simplify staging directory management and any future recovery procedures, it is recommended that you configure replica sets in one of the following ways:

- Give each replica set its own staging directory, and place the staging directories on the same volume. This solution provides good recoverability while minimizing cost.

- Give each replica set its own staging directory, and put each staging directory on its own volume. This solution provides better recoverability, but at a higher cost.

Do not store the staging directory on a volume where NTFS disk quotas are enabled.

Improving FRS Performance

To distribute disk traffic, store the staging directory, FRS logs, the FRS jet database (Ntfrs.jdb), and replica trees on separate disks. Using separate disks for the log files is especially important when you configure FRS logging by using a high severity level. For the best replication performance, distribute disk I/O by placing the FRS logs and the staging directory on separate disks from that of the operating system and the disks containing the replica tree. In a hub and spoke topology, using separate disks is especially recommended for the hub servers.

 Important

If you store the FRS jet database on a disk that has its write cache enabled, FRS might not recover if power to the drive is interrupted and critical updates are lost. Windows Server 2003 warns you about this by adding an entry with Event 13512 in the File Replication Service event log. To leave write caching enabled for improved performance and to ensure the integrity of the FRS jet database, use an uninterrupted power supply (UPS) or a disk controller and cache with a battery backup. Otherwise, disable write caching until you can install a backup power supply.

When moving the FRS logs and FRS jet database, be sure that NTFS disk quotas are disabled on the target volume. For more information about moving the FRS logs and FRS jet database, see article Q221093, "HOW TO: Relocate the NTFRS Jet Database and Log Files," in the Microsoft Knowledge Base. To find this article, see the Microsoft Knowledge Base link on the Web Resources page at http://www.microsoft.com/windows/reskits/webresources.

Determine Connection Priorities

Connection priorities control the sequencing of the initial synchronization that occurs when you add a new member to a replica set or when you perform a nonauthoritative restore. By changing connection priorities, you can control which inbound partners go first based on resource considerations. (A server's inbound partners, also known as upstream partners, are those servers from which the new or recovered member can receive replicated content.) For example, you can specify that a new member first synchronize with a partner:

- Across a high-bandwidth network connection.

- That has low server activity.

- That has the most up-to-date files.

You configure connection priorities by using the three priority levels in the Distributed File System snap-in:

- **High.** All connections marked **High** must successfully synchronize before FRS attempts to synchronize medium-priority connections.

- **Medium.** At least one medium-priority connection must successfully complete an initial synchronization before FRS attempts to synchronize any low-priority connections. FRS attempts to synchronize all connections in the medium-priority level, but only one must be successful before FRS attempts to synchronize low-priority connections.

- **Low.** The default connection priority is low. For these connections, FRS attempts to synchronize one time, but any failure does not delay other synchronization attempts. If no medium- or high-priority connections exist, at least one low-priority connection must succeed before FRS considers the initial synchronization operation complete. If medium- or high-priority connections exist, none of the connections in the low-priority class needs to succeed for FRS to consider the initial synchronization operation complete.

 Important

Connection priorities are used for initial synchronizations only on custom topologies. If you use a ring, hub and spoke, or full mesh topology, connection priorities are used only on reinitialization during a nonauthoritative restore operation.

When evaluating your topology to determine connection priority, identify the following details for each replica member:

- All inbound connections

- The speed of those connections

Based on this data, determine which connection priority to assign to each inbound connection. The following guidelines will assist you in choosing the appropriate connection priority:

- Use medium priority or high priority only for high-bandwidth connections.

- If you plan to create a high-priority connection, note that if this connection fails, no other synchronization takes place for lower-priority partners until all high-priority connections have succeeded.

- Use low priority for low-bandwidth or unreliable connections.

 Note

Keep in mind that after the initial synchronization, connection priorities are ignored until you need to perform a nonauthoritative restore to recover a failed replica member.

For an Excel spreadsheet to assist you in documenting connection priorities, see "FRS Configuration Worksheet" (Sdcfsv_2.xls) on the *Windows Server 2003 Deployment Kit* companion CD (or see "FRS Configuration Worksheet" on the Web at http://www.microsoft.com/reskit).

Figure 2.14 illustrates an organization's planned topology. The letters A through C represent inbound connections. The hub servers are connected by a high-bandwidth network connection, and two of the hub servers connect with branch servers by using low-bandwidth network connections.

Figure 2.14   Sample FRS Topology

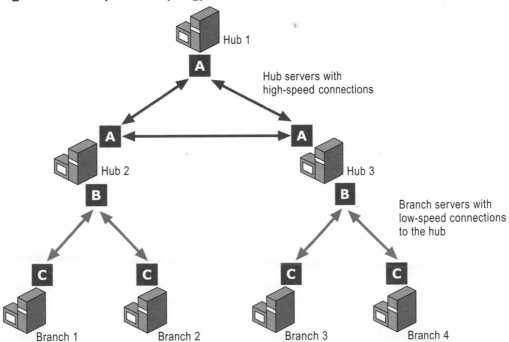

In this topology, the administrator assigns connection priorities as follows:

- "A" connections use medium priority because the hubs are connected by high-bandwidth connections and the hub servers are expected to be up to date.

- "B" and "C" connections use low priority because the branch servers connect to the hubs across a low-bandwidth network.

When the hub servers in this example are deployed, Hub1 will be the initial master. Because the "A" connections are marked as medium priority, the two other hub servers will not attempt replication with the branch servers until initial replication completes with at least one other hub server.

The administrator specifies connections "B" and "C" as low priority because the branch servers have low-bandwidth network connections. In the event of a nonauthoritative restore for any of the hubs, using low priority causes the repaired hub server to replicate first from other hubs before replicating with the branch servers.

 Note

To increase the availability of data, the administrator can place multiple servers in each branch. If the servers in the branch use high-bandwidth connections to each other, the administrator can set medium priority for those inbound connections. That way, if one of the branch servers fails and is later restored, it will first attempt to replicate with a local branch server before replicating from the hub server across a slow network connection.

Example: An Organization Designs a Replication Strategy

An organization uses Group Policy to distribute 10 GB of software to users in four sites. The software changes nightly, and it is important that clients have access to these updates the following day. To make the software files and updates highly available, the organization creates a domain-based DFS namespace for each branch and then uses the Distributed File System snap-in to configure replication. To make the updated software available even if a hub server is offline, the organization uses redundant hub servers that are connected by high-speed LAN links. The organization also uses staggered replication schedules to distribute the load between the hub servers. Figure 2.15 describes the FRS topology.

Figure 2.15   Redundant Hub and Spoke Topology for Software Distribution to Branch Offices

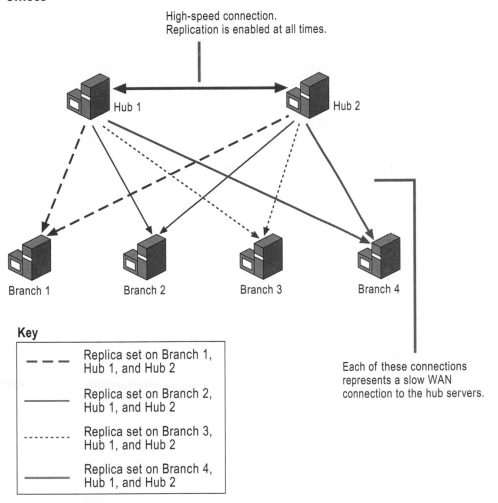

The organization uses a separate namespace for each branch so that if the local branch server is not available, the clients transparently access one of the hubs instead of another branch server. The organization enables the least-expensive target selection feature of DFS so that the clients always choose the local branch server when it is available.

In this scenario, the organization configures replication as follows:

- Each branch has its own replica set, and each replica set contains three members: the branch and the two hubs.

- Replication between the hubs is enabled at all times, so changes at one hub are immediately replicated to the other hub.

- Inbound connections between the hub servers are medium priority; all other inbound connections are low priority.

- Odd-numbered branches replicate with Hub1 from 6:00 P.M. until 7:30 P.M. and with Hub2 from 8:00 P.M. until 9:30 P.M.

- Even-numbered branches replicate with Hub2 from 6:00 P.M. until 7:30 P.M. and with Hub1 from 8:00 P.M. until 9:30 P.M.

As shown in Figure 2.15, all software updates originate at the hub servers and are replicated to the branch servers on a staggered schedule. If replication completes when the branch is connected to its primary hub, no replication takes place when the branch connects to its alternate hub, because the data will have already replicated between the hubs. Similarly, if one of the hub servers fails or is taken offline for maintenance, the branch servers replicate with the remaining hub, and when the offline hub is brought back online, the two hubs replicate immediately to synchronize their data.

Because of the large amount (10 GB) of software files, the organization prestages new branch servers by restoring the software files to the new branch servers while they are located at the staging site. The organization then transports the new branch servers to the branch sites for deployment. By prestaging the software files, the organization does not need to replicate the initial 10 GB of files across the network. For more information about prestaging replica sets, see "Adding a New Member to an Existing Replica Set" later in this chapter.

Increasing Data Availability by Using Clustering

The information presented in this section assumes an understanding of basic cluster terminology. If you are not familiar with clustering, you can refer to a number of sources for further information:

- For general information on server clusters, including terminology, procedures, checklists, and best practices, see Help and Support Center for Windows Server 2003.

- For information on designing server clusters, see "Designing and Deploying Server Clusters" in this book.

You can use clustered file servers to make sure that users can access business-critical data, such as home directories and software distribution shares. You can also use clustered servers to consolidate multiple nonclustered file servers onto a clustered file server. Each server is then re-created on the cluster as a virtual server.

 Important
Because multiple network names might belong to the same server, File Share resources might appear under these names and might also be accessible through them. To avoid client connectivity interruptions, make sure that clients use the network name that is associated with the group in which the File Share resource belongs. For more information about using the proper network name, see article Q170762, "Cluster Shares Appear in Browse List Under Other Names" in the Microsoft Knowledge Base. To find this article, see the Microsoft Knowledge Base link on the Web Resources page at http://www.microsoft.com/windows/reskits/webresources.

Choosing Virtual Server Names

If you are migrating nonclustered file servers to clustered file servers, and you do not currently use (or plan to use) DFS, you should use the IP address and network name of each migrated server to create an identical virtual server on the clustered file server. Doing so allows users to continue to access data by using the server names that they are familiar with. You also ensure that links and shortcuts continue to work as they did before the migration.

Choosing the File Share Resource Type

A clustered file server uses the File Share resource type to make data available to users. You have three options when configuring this resource type:

Normal share

Normal shares function similarly to shared folders created on nonclustered file servers, except that you use the Cluster Administrator snap-in to create them. When you create a normal share, you publish a single folder to the network under a single name. Normal shares do not have required dependencies; however, if the normal share is located on cluster storage, the normal shares should, at a minimum, have dependencies on the cluster storage device (the Physical Disk or other storage-class resource), with the preferential addition of dependencies on the network name and IP address.

You can create a maximum of 1,674 resources, including File Share resources, on a cluster. To provide good failover performance, do not approach this limit in production environments. In addition, if you need to create a large number of normal shares, it is better to use the Share Subdirectories option.

Share subdirectories (or hide subdirectories)

A share subdirectories share publishes several network names: one each for a folder and all of its immediate subfolders. For example, if you create a share subdirectories share called Users, any folder you add to the Users folder is automatically shared.

 Important

When sharing subdirectories, do not use the same name for subfolders under different folders (for example, \folder1\name1 and \folder2\name1). The first shared subdirectory to come online will remain online, but the second shared subdirectory will not be initialized and will not come online.

Share subdirectories offer a number of advantages:

- They do not require you to create a File Share resource for every folder. As a result, you reduce the potential time and CPU load needed to detect failures.

- They are an efficient way to create large numbers of related file shares on a single file server. For example, you can use this method to create a home directory for each user who has files on the server, and you can hide the subdirectory shares to prevent users from seeing the subdirectory shares when they browse the network.

- They allow administrators who are not experienced with server clusters or using the Cluster Administrator snap-in to easily create folders that are automatically shared.

When using the share subdirectories feature, determine the number of file shares you plan to host on the cluster, because the number of file shares affects server cluster capacity planning and failover policies. Specifically, you need to determine the following:

- The number of nodes you plan to have in the server cluster

- The number of node failures you want the server cluster to withstand while still providing acceptable performance

- Whether the remaining nodes can handle the load of the failed nodes

The number of nodes is important because a single node can support a limited number of file shares, which varies according to the amount of RAM in the server and which is described in "Reviewing File Server Limits" later in this chapter. If you want the cluster to be able to survive the loss of all but one node, make sure that the cluster hosts no more than the maximum number of file shares that can be hosted by a single node. This is especially important for two-node clusters, where the failure of one node leaves the single remaining node to pick up all the file shares.

In a four-node or eight-node cluster, you have other options that might be more appropriate, depending on the failure scenarios that you want to protect against. For example, if you want a four-node cluster to survive one node failing at any point, you can configure the file shares so that if one node fails, its file shares are spread across the remaining three nodes. In this scenario, each node can be loaded to 66 percent of the maximum number of file shares and still be within the maximum limit of a single node in the event of a single failure. In this case, the cluster can host three times the number of file shares that a single server can host. If you want to survive two nodes failing, a four-node cluster can hold twice as many files shares (because if two nodes fail, the remaining two nodes pick up the load from the two failed servers) and so on.

For more information about server cluster capacity planning and failover policies, see "Designing and Deploying Server Clusters" in this book.

 Note

For more information about using the Share Subdirectories option to create home directories, see article Q256926, "Implementing Home Folders on a Server Cluster," in the Microsoft Knowledge Base. To find this article, see the Microsoft Knowledge Base link on the Web Resources page at http://www.microsoft.com/windows/reskits/webresources.

DFS root

You can use the File Share resource type to create a resource that manages a stand-alone DFS root on a cluster. The DFS root File Share resource has required dependencies on a network name, which can be either the cluster name or any other network name for a virtual server. However, it is recommended that you do not use the cluster name (in the Cluster group) for any resources.

The Cluster service manages a resource group as a single unit of failover. Therefore, if you want four DFS roots to fail over independently, create them in different groups. Each group has a network name or the virtual server name with which the root is associated.

When creating a DFS root in clustered file servers, review the following issues:

- The name that you specify for one DFS root cannot overlap with the names for the other DFS roots in the same cluster. For example, if you name one DFS share C:\Dfsroots\Root1, you cannot create other roots using names that are derived from the first DFS root, such as C:\Dfsroots or C:\Dfsroots\Root1\Root2, and so forth.

- On server clusters, do not create clustered DFS roots that have the same name as nonclustered DFS roots or shared folders.

- Clustered file servers running Windows Server 2003, Enterprise Edition and Windows Server 2003, Datacenter Edition support multiple stand-alone DFS roots. These DFS roots can exist in multiple resource groups, and each group can be hosted on a different node.

- Clustered file servers running Microsoft® Windows® 2000 Advanced Server or Windows® 2000 Datacenter Server support one DFS root per server. Mixed-version clusters running Windows Server 2003, Enterprise Edition or Windows Server 2003, Datacenter Edition on some nodes and Windows 2000 on others only support one DFS root per cluster as well. For more information about mixed-version clusters and rolling upgrades, see "Deploying Clustered File Servers" later in this chapter.

 Caution

Do not make DFS configuration changes (for example, creating new roots, adding new links, new link targets, and so on) while operating a mixed-version cluster, because all DFS changes are lost upon failover.

For more information about creating DFS roots on a clustered file server, see article Q301588, "HOW TO: Use DFS on a Server Cluster to Maintain a Single Namespace," in the Microsoft Knowledge Base. To find this article, see the Microsoft Knowledge Base link on the Web Resources page at http://www.microsoft.com/windows/reskits/webresources.

Using Shadow Copies on Server Clusters

Windows Server 2003 supports creating shadow copies on cluster storage. Shadow copies are point-in-time copies of files that are stored on file servers running Windows Server 2003. By enabling shadow copies, you can reduce the administrative burden of restoring previously backed-up files for users who accidentally delete or overwrite important files.

If you plan to enable shadow copies on a server cluster, review the following issues:

- Cluster-managed shadow copies can be created only on cluster storage with a Physical Disk resource. In a cluster without cluster storage, shadow copies can be created and managed only locally.

- The recurring scheduled task that generates volume shadow copies must run on the same node that currently owns the storage volume (where the shadow copies are stored).

- The cluster resource that manages the scheduled task must be able to fail over with the Physical Disk resource that manages the storage volume.

- If you place the source volume (where the user files are stored) and the storage volume (where the shadow copies are stored) on separate disks, those disks must be in the same resource group.

- When you configure shadow copies using the procedure described in "Enable Shadow Copies of Shared Folders in a cluster" in Help and Support Center for Windows Server 2003, the resources and dependencies are set up automatically. Do not attempt to modify or delete these resources and dependencies directly.

To ensure availability, plan to enable shadow copies before you deploy the server cluster. Do not enable shadow copies in a deployed cluster. When you enable shadow copies, the shadow copy volumes (as well as all resources that directly or indirectly depend on the disk) go offline for a brief period while the resource dependencies are created. The shadow copy volumes are not accessible to applications and users while they are offline.

 Note

If you enable shadow copies before clustering your servers, you must disable, and then re-enable, shadow copies. If you cluster a disk containing a previously created shadow copy, the shadow copy might stop functioning after that disk's Physical Disk resource fails over.

For additional guidelines and information about shadow copies, see "Designing a Shadow Copy Strategy" later in this chapter. For in-depth information about using shadow copies on server clusters, see "Using Shadow Copies of Shared Folders in a server cluster" in Help and Support Center for Windows Server 2003.

Example: An Organization Designs a Clustered File Server

A large organization uses centralized file servers to store home directories for 3,000 users. The organization has an existing SLA that specifies its file servers must be 99.99 percent available, which means that the file servers can be offline no more than 53 minutes a year. To meet this level of availability, the organization implements clustered file servers in its data center, using a storage area network (SAN) for storage.

After evaluating storage and performance requirements, the organization determines that it needs one file server per 1,000 users, for a total of three file servers. The organization could implement a three-node cluster, but it decides to implement a four-node cluster instead. It will use three nodes to provide access to user directories and the fourth node to perform the following functions:

- Host a stand-alone DFS namespace to provide a unified view of the user directories on the remaining three nodes.

- Perform backups of the other three nodes in the evenings.

- Take over the resources of another node if the node fails or is taken offline for maintenance.

Figure 2.16 illustrates how the organization designs its four-node cluster.

Figure 2.16 Four-Node Cluster

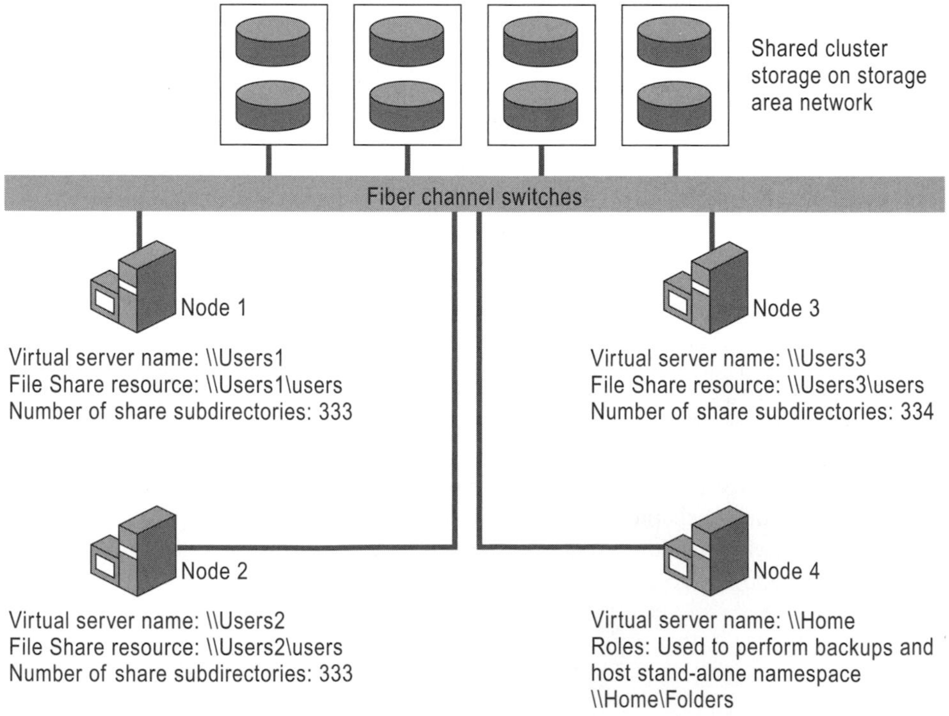

Shared cluster storage on storage area network

Fiber channel switches

Node 1
Virtual server name: \\Users1
File Share resource: \\Users1\users
Number of share subdirectories: 333

Node 3
Virtual server name: \\Users3
File Share resource: \\Users3\users
Number of share subdirectories: 334

Node 2
Virtual server name: \\Users2
File Share resource: \\Users2\users
Number of share subdirectories: 333

Node 4
Virtual server name: \\Home
Roles: Used to perform backups and host stand-alone namespace
\\Home\Folders

To create the user directories, the administrator creates a File Share resource on three nodes and specifies the Share Subdirectories option. The administrator places each File Share resource in a virtual server (a resource group containing IP address and Network Name resources) and sets up dependencies between the File Share resource and the Network Name resource. The administrator then uses a script to quickly create the user directories, which are automatically shared after creation, and to set appropriate permissions for each user directory. The administrator creates another File Share resource on the fourth node and specifies the DFS root option and then uses the Distributed File System snap-in to create a link to each user directory. Users can access their shares by using the DFS path \\Home\Folders*Username*. Logon scripts also map user shares to each user's U: drive.

 Note

If the organization needs to provide access to user data when the complete site fails, due either to a total loss of power as a result of a natural disaster or another event, the organization can implement a geographically dispersed cluster.

For more information about designing server clusters, including capacity planning, failover policies, and geographically dispersed clusters, see "Designing and Deploying Server Clusters" in this book.

Designing a Standard File Server Configuration

To maximize the reliability, availability, and performance of file servers, design one or more standard hardware and software configurations for file servers in your organization. Using a standard configuration for file servers provides a number of benefits:

- You experience less complexity managing and maintaining the hardware. Instead of learning to perform hardware tasks on multiple types of file servers, you need only to learn the task once.

- You reduce the amount of testing that must be done when updating drivers or applications on the file server. Instead of testing the fixes on multiple hardware configurations, you can test the updates on one file server and then deploy the updates to the other file servers.

- You can keep fewer spares on-site. For example, if you use the same type of hard disks in all file servers, you need fewer spare disks, reducing the cost and complexity of providing spares.

- You reduce the number of disk images or answer files you need to maintain, which is useful if you are using automated installation technologies, such as unattended installation or Remote Installation Services (RIS), to deploy your file servers.

Important

If you have read "Planning File Server Availability" earlier in this chapter and you have decided to implement clustered file servers, review the chapter "Designing and Deploying Server Clusters" in this book for important guidelines on choosing and configuring cluster hardware and storage.

Figure 2.17 outlines the process for designing a standard file server configuration.

Figure 2.17   Designing a Standard File Server Configuration

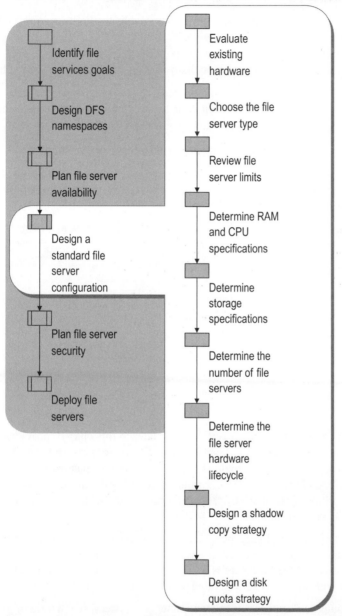

Evaluating Existing Hardware

When you evaluate your existing hardware, you must determine if the hardware meets the recommended hardware requirements for Windows Server 2003 and verify that the hardware is listed in the Windows Server Catalog for Windows Server 2003. If your hardware does not meet these requirements, you might need to acquire new hardware or upgrade your existing hardware.

Your organization might also have existing standards in place that specify the standard configuration for file servers. If so, make sure that your file servers meet those requirements as well.

Reviewing the Recommended Hardware Requirements and the Windows Server Catalog

Microsoft recommends that file servers running Windows Server 2003 should meet the hardware requirements listed in Table 2.8.

Table 2.8   Recommended Hardware Requirements for Windows Server 2003

Operating System	CPU	RAM
Windows Server 2003, Standard Edition	550 MHz	256 MB
Windows Server 2003, Enterprise Edition	550 MHz	256 MB
Windows Server 2003, Datacenter Edition	550 MHz*	512 MB minimum

*For servers on which you are upgrading from Windows 2000 Datacenter Server, the minimum processor speed is 400 MHz.

The section "Determining RAM and CPU Specifications" later in this chapter provides specific guidelines for how increasing CPU and RAM can improve file server performance. If the server provides additional services or acts as a domain controller, the server must meet higher requirements than those listed here. For more information about hardware requirements for domain controllers, see "Planning Domain Controller Capacity" in *Designing and Deploying Directory and Security Services* of this kit.

In addition to verifying that your hardware meets the recommended requirements for file servers, verify that all hardware devices on the file server are listed in the Windows Server Catalog. Only Designed for Windows Server 2003 hardware is included in the Windows Server Catalog, which means that the hardware is designed to take advantage of new features in Windows Server 2003.

For more information about hardware requirements for server clusters, see "Designing and Deploying Server Clusters" in this book.

Before you install Windows Server 2003, you can run a hardware and software compatibility check by running the Windows Upgrade Advisor from the Windows Server 2003 operating system CD. The compatibility check does not require you to actually begin an installation. To run the check, insert the Windows Server 2003 operating system CD in the CD-ROM drive and, when a display appears, follow the prompts for checking system compatibility. You will be offered the option to download the latest Setup files (by using Dynamic Update) when you run the check. If you have Internet connectivity, it is recommended that you allow the download.

Another way to run the Windows Upgrade Advisor is to insert the Windows Server 2003 operating system CD in the CD-ROM drive, open a command prompt, and type:

d:\I386\winnt32 /checkupgradeonly

In this example, **d** represents the CD-ROM drive.

For more information about hardware and software compatibility, see the following resources:

- To download the Windows Upgrade Advisor, see the Windows Upgrade Advisor link on the Web Resources page at http://www.microsoft.com/windows/reskits/webresources.

- For more information about hardware compatibility, see the Windows Server Catalog link on the Web Resources page at http://www.microsoft.com/windows/reskits/webresources.

- For more information about application compatibility, see "Planning and Testing for Application Deployment" in *Planning, Testing, and Piloting Deployment Projects* of this kit.

Verifying That Mass Storage Controllers Are Supported

If your file servers use a mass storage controller (such as a SCSI, RAID, or Fibre Channel adapter) for disks, confirm that it is compatible with products in the Windows Server 2003 family.

If your controller is compatible with products in the Windows Server 2003, but you are aware that the manufacturer has supplied a separate driver file for use with your operating system, obtain the file (on a floppy disk) before you begin Setup. During the early part of Setup, a line at the bottom of the screen prompts you to press F6. Further prompts guide you in supplying the driver file to Setup so that it can gain access to the mass storage controller.

If you are not sure whether you must obtain a separate driver file from the manufacturer of your mass storage controller, you can try running Setup. If the controller is not supported by the driver files on the Windows Server 2003 operating system CD, and it therefore requires a driver file supplied by the hardware manufacturer, Setup stops and displays a message saying that no disk devices can be found, or it displays an incomplete list of controllers. After you obtain the necessary driver file, restart Setup, and press F6 when prompted.

Verifying That Your Hardware Meets Your Requirements

If your organization has a standard configuration for file servers, verify that your existing file servers meet these requirements. If they do, proceed to "Planning File Server Security" later in this chapter. If your organization plans to update its standard file server configuration, continue to "Choosing the File Server Type."

Identifying Servers to Use as Windows Server 2003 File Servers

Identify the file servers on which you plan to run Windows Server 2003, as well as the servers that you plan to decommission as a result of consolidation or failure to meet hardware requirements.

Choosing the File Server Type

Two types of servers run Windows Server 2003: general-purpose servers and Windows Powered Network Attached Storage.

General-purpose servers   A general-purpose server can function in a number of roles, including domain controller, print server, WINS server, DHCP server, application server, or an e-mail or database server. General-purpose servers provide administrators with the flexibility to configure server software and hardware as they choose. Administrators perform the necessary configuration and optimization that the server requires to perform its role.

Windows Powered Network Attached Storage   Windows Powered Network Attached Storage solutions are dedicated file servers running Windows 2000 Server or Windows Server 2003. With built-in support for UNIX and Apple file protocols, Windows Powered Network Attached Storage solutions offer seamless integration in a heterogeneous environment.

Table 2.9 describes the features and capabilities of each file server type.

Table 2.9   Features and Capabilities of File Server Types

Description	General-Purpose Server	Windows Powered Network Attached Storage
Comes preinstalled with Windows 2000 or Windows Server 2003.	●*	●
Offers the file system, security, reliability, and scalability features of Windows 2000 or Windows Server 2003.	●	●
Can provide services for purposes other than file sharing, such as domain controller or print, WINS, or DHCP server.	●	
Can run applications, such as Microsoft® SQL Server 2000 or Exchange 2000 Server.	●	
Comes preconfigured with NFS, File Transfer Protocol (FTP), AppleTalk, HTTP, WebDAV, and NetWare protocol support.		●
Can be deployed in as little as 15 minutes.		●

* Some general-purpose servers come preinstalled with the appropriate operating system; however, other general-purpose servers require you to configure the volumes and install the operating system.

Some hardware vendors offer Windows Powered Network Attached Storage solutions in a cluster configuration. If your organization requires highly available servers, consult your hardware vendor for more information.

Reviewing File Server Limits

As you plan your file server configuration, keep in mind file system, storage, and other limits related to file servers. Table 2.10 describes these limits.

Table 2.10   File System, Storage, and File Server Limits for Windows Server 2003

Description	Limit
Maximum size of a basic volume	2 TB
Maximum size of a dynamic volume	2 TB for simple and mirrored (RAID-1) volumes. Up to 64 TB for spanned and striped (RAID-0) volumes. (2 TB per disk with a maximum of 32 disks per volume.) Up to 62 TB for RAID-5 volumes. (2 TB per disk with a maximum of 32 disks per volume and 2 TB used for parity.)
Maximum number of dynamic volumes per disk group	1,000 A disk group is collection of dynamic disks. Windows Server 2003 supports one disk group per server.
Maximum size of an NTFS volume	2^{32} clusters minus 1 cluster Using a 64-kilobyte (KB) cluster (the maximum NTFS cluster size), the maximum size of an NTFS volume is 256 TB minus 64 KB. Using a 4-KB cluster (the default NTFS cluster size), the maximum size of an NTFS volume is 16 TB minus 4 KB.
Maximum file size on an NTFS volume	16 TB (2^{44} bytes) minus 64 KB
Maximum number of files on an NTFS volume	4,294,967,295 (2^{32} minus 1 file) There is no limit to the number of files that can be stored in a folder. For recommendations on limiting the number of files stored on a volume, see "Determining Maximum Volume Size" later in this chapter.
Maximum number of clusters on an NTFS volume	4,294,967,296 (2^{32})

(continued)

Table 2.10 File System, Storage, and File Server Limits for Windows Server 2003 *(continued)*

Description	Limit
Maximum volumes per server	Approximately 2,000 volumes.
	Up to 1,000 of these volumes can be dynamic volumes; the rest are basic volumes. Boot times increase as you increase the number of volumes. In addition, you must use mounted drives to access volumes when all drive letters on a server have been used. For more information about mounted drives, see "Using NTFS mounted drives" in Help and Support Center for Windows Server 2003.
Maximum number of shared folders on a server	Varies. The number of shares on a server affects server boot time. On a server with typical hardware and thousands of shares, boot time can be delayed by minutes. Exact delays depend on server hardware.
	Shared folder information is stored in the system hive of the registry. For systems with less than 800 MB of RAM, the System hive can be as large as one-quarter of the physical memory. For systems with more than 800 MB of RAM, the maximum size of the System hive is 200 MB. If the system hive exceeds this limit, the server cannot mount the registry at startup and Windows Server 2003 cannot start.

For information about optimizing NTFS performance, see the *Server Management Guide* of the *Windows Server 2003 Resource Kit* (or see the *Server Management Guide* on the Web at http://www.microsoft.com/reskit).

Determining RAM and CPU Specifications

As hardware continues to improve, hardware vendors frequently change the RAM and CPU configurations in the servers they offer. Use the information about performance improvements and scaling factors in the sections that follow to choose the hardware that best meets your organization's needs.

When designing RAM and CPU specifications for server clusters, also consider the failover policy that you plan to use and the maximum number of File Share resources and share subdirectories that will be hosted on any one node after a failure. Each node must have the RAM and CPU resources required to host the resources of one or more failed nodes, depending on your failover policy. For more information about failover policies and server cluster capacity planning, see "Designing and Deploying Server Clusters" in this book.

 Note

Many of the figures presented in this section are derived from NetBench statistics for file server throughput. NetBench is a portable Ziff Davis Media benchmark program that measures how well a file server handles file I/O requests from 32-bit Windows clients. NetBench provides an overall I/O throughput score and average response time for servers, along with individual scores for clients. You can use these scores to measure, analyze, and predict how well your server can handle file requests from clients.

Reviewing Windows Server 2003 CPU Specifications

Table 2.11 describes the recommended CPU speed and number of processors supported by Windows Server 2003.

Table 2.11   CPU Requirements for Windows Server 2003

Specification	Windows Server 2003, Standard Edition	Windows Server 2003, Enterprise Edition	Windows Server 2003, Datacenter Edition
Minimum recommended CPU speed	550 MHz	550 MHz	550 MHz
Number of CPUs supported	1–4	1–8	8–32

Reviewing Operating System Performance Improvements

Even if you plan to use existing hardware to run Windows Server 2003, you can benefit from performance enhancements available in Windows Server 2003, as well as client and server protocol improvements available when using clients running Windows XP Professional.

Table 2.12 describes performance improvements that can be gained by migrating to new operating systems on identical hardware.

Table 2.12   Operating System Performance Improvements on the Same Hardware

Current Server and Client Operating Systems	New Server and Client Operating Systems	Improvement Factor
Windows NT Server 4.0 with Microsoft® Windows NT® Workstation 4.0 clients	Windows 2000 Server with Windows 2000 Professional clients	Up to 1.25X
Windows 2000 Server with Windows 2000 Professional clients	Windows Server 2003 with Windows XP Professional clients	Up to 2.2X
Windows NT Server 4.0 with Windows NT Workstation 4.0 clients	Windows Server 2003 with Windows XP Professional clients	Up to 2.75X

These figures are based on the following assumptions:

- The server is uniprocessor (UP), 2P, 4P, or 8P.
- For each comparison, the server hardware is the same.
- No memory, disk, or network bottlenecks prevent the processor from performing at full capacity.

Reviewing Performance Improvements Gained by Upgrading Processors

Table 2.13 describes performance improvements that can be gained by upgrading server processors. Upgrading processors improves processing power, memory bandwidth, I/O bandwidth, and the system bus. These figures are based on actual processor improvements, not operating system improvements. If you plan to use processors that are faster than those listed here, performance will be greater than the following figures show.

Table 2.13   Performance Improvements Gained by Upgrading Processors

Old Processor	New Processor (Server Class)	Improvement Factor
200 MHz Intel Pentium Pro	400 MHz Intel Pentium II Xeon	2X
400 MHz Intel Pentium II Xeon	900 MHz Intel Pentium III Xeon	2X
200 MHz Intel Pentium Pro	900 MHz Intel Pentium III Xeon	4X

Reviewing Performance Improvements Gained by Adding Processors

To increase performance, consider using more than one processor in your file servers. One advantage of using multiple processors is the ability to handle more concurrent clients, resulting in higher scaling factors at high client loads. Table 2.14 describes the NetBench throughput improvements gained by adding processors on file servers running Windows Server 2003.

Table 2.14 Performance Improvements Gained by Adding Processors

Original Number of Processors	After Upgrade	Scaling Factor*
1	2	1.4X to 1.6X
2	4	1.3X to 1.4X
1	4	1.8X to 2.3X
4	8	1.3X to 1.4X
1	8	2.4X to 3.2X

* The scaling factors are based on a range of client loads.

Determining the Client Load Based on Processor Utilization

NetBench stresses the system by applying a heavy load on the file server. Microsoft used the most intensive CPU operations — file opens and file creates (subsequently described as *opens/creates*) — to translate a NetBench client load to a more realistic client load.

To determine the client load, Microsoft observed approximately 820 opens/creates per second at peak NetBench throughput (100-percent CPU utilization) on a Xeon 900-MHz server with a single processor (UP). Table 2.15 describes active client loads for light, medium, and heavy user loads at 70-percent CPU utilization. The client loads are defined as follows:

- Light: one open/create every 10 seconds
- Medium: two opens/creates every 10 seconds
- Heavy: three opens/creates every 10 seconds

Assuming that a light user load causes one open/create every 10 seconds, a UP Xeon 900-MHz server can handle 5,700 users at 70-percent CPU utilization and 8,200 users at 100-percent CPU utilization. (These figures are derived by dividing the opens/creates per second at peak NetBench throughput by the opens/creates per second for light users.)

The figures in Table 2.15 for the UP Xeon 900-MHz server are based on the following assumptions:

- No memory, disk, or network bottlenecks prevent the processor from performing at 100-percent capacity.

- The clients are running Windows XP.

The figures for 2P, 4P, and 8P Xeon 900-MHz servers were calculated by using the scaling factors described in Table 2.14. For example, on a 4P Xeon 900-MHz server, under a heavy client load of three opens/creates every 10 seconds, the server can handle 3,400 to 4,400 active users. This figure is derived by taking the 1,900 heavy-load users supported on a UP Xeon 900-MHz server and multiplying that figure by the UP-to-4P scaling factors of 1.8X to 2.3X provided in Table 2.14.

Table 2.15   Number of Active Users Supported Based on a NetBench-Type Workload

Processor	Heavy Load	Medium Load	Light Load
UP Xeon, 900 MHz	1,900	2,800	5,700
2P Xeon, 900 MHz	2,600 to 3,000	3,900 to 4,500	8,000 to 9,100
4P Xeon, 900 MHz	3,400 to 4,400	5,000 to 6,400	10,300 to 13,100
8P Xeon, 900 MHz	4,600 to 6,100	6,700 to 9,000	13,700 to 18,200

Determining RAM Specifications

Using adequate RAM in file servers ensures that Windows Server 2003 can temporarily cache (store) files in memory, reducing the need to retrieve files from disk. Table 2.16 describes the minimum recommended RAM and maximum RAM for Windows Server 2003.

Table 2.16   Minimum and Maximum RAM for Windows Server 2003

RAM Specification	Windows Server 2003, Standard Edition	Windows Server 2003, Enterprise Edition	Windows Server 2003, Datacenter Edition
Minimum recommended RAM	256 MB	256 MB	512 MB minimum
Maximum RAM	4 GB	32 GB	64 GB

To determine the amount of RAM required to support the file server workload, review the number of remote file handles that can be efficiently supported by a file server running Windows Server 2003. Next, review how additional RAM affects the total size of files, or *file set size*, that can be held in memory at any time.

Remote concurrent file handles

A file server running Windows Server 2003 with 1 GB of RAM can efficiently support approximately 100,000 remote concurrent file handles, regardless of the size of the files. If your users are likely to have more than 100,000 files open at a time, plan to split this load across two or more servers.

File set size

On a file server with 1 GB of RAM, Windows Server 2003 can hold approximately 500 MB of file content and NTFS metadata in memory. (The amount of memory used for NTFS metadata depends on the depth of the directory hierarchy and query distribution, among other factors.) Windows Server 2003 uses the rest of the RAM for providing nonpaged pool and other operating system functions. For each additional gigabyte of RAM that you add, Windows Server 2003 can use the entire RAM capacity for storing file content in memory. For example, a file server with 3 GB of RAM can support approximately 2.5 GB of file content in memory. When the file set size exceeds the amount of memory, files are paged to disk. This paging can result in disk bottlenecks, though using a fast disk subsystem can alleviate this problem.

When determining how much RAM you plan to install in file servers, consider the following guidelines:

- When users typically access the same files, the file set is known as "hot," because the files are frequently stored in memory. For hot file sets, invest in more RAM to accommodate the entire hot file set. Typically, hot file sets are less than 1 percent of the file set, although this figure can vary.

- When users access random files, the file set is known as "cold." For cold file sets, invest in faster disks, because users typically open files that are not already in memory, and the response time is limited by disk latency. For example, if you can cut disk latency in half by using a faster disk subsystem (including number of disks, mechanical speed, and disk cache), compare the cost of doing so to the amount of RAM it would take to achieve similar performance. Using a faster disk subsystem might be less expensive.

Determining Storage Specifications

It is important to make sure that file servers have adequate, fault-tolerant storage. When determining storage specifications, perform the following tasks:

1. Estimate the amount of data to be stored.

2. Plan the amount of storage for each server configuration.

3. Determine the maximum volume size.

4. Plan the layout and RAID level of volumes.

The following sections describe each of these steps.

For more information about storage requirements for server clusters, see "Designing and Deploying Server Clusters" in this book.

Estimating the Amount of Data to Be Stored

When you estimate the amount of data to be stored on a new file server, include the following information:

- The amount of data currently stored on any file servers that will be consolidated onto the new file server.

- If the file server will be a replica member, the amount of replicated data that will be stored on the new file server.

- The amount of data that you will need to store on the file server in the future.

A general guideline is to plan for faster growth than you experienced in the past. Investigate whether your organization plans to hire a large number of people and whether any groups in your organization are planning large projects that require extra storage.

You must also take into account the amount of space used by operating system files, applications, RAID redundancy, log files, and other factors. Table 2.17 describes some factors that affect file server capacity.

Table 2.17 Factors That Affect File Server Capacity

Factor	Storage Capacity Required
Operating system files	At least 1.5 GB. To allow space for optional components, future service packs, and other items, allow an additional 3 GB to 5 GB for the operating system volume.
Paging file	1.5 times the amount of RAM by default.
Memory dump	Depending on the memory dump file option that you choose, the amount of disk space required can be as large as the amount of physical memory plus 1 MB.
Applications	Varies according to the application, which can include antivirus, backup, and disk quota software; database applications; and optional components, such as Recovery Console, Windows Services for UNIX, and Windows Services for NetWare.
Log files	Varies according to the application that creates the log file. Some applications allow you to configure a maximum log file size. You must make sure that you have adequate free space to store the log files.
RAID solution	Varies. For more information about the RAID solutions, see "Planning the Layout and RAID Level of Volumes" later in this chapter.
Shadow copies	Ten percent of the volume by default, although increasing this size is recommended. For more information about shadow copies, see "Designing a Shadow Copy Strategy" later in this chapter.
Snapshots available on Windows Powered Network Attached Storage solutions	Some Windows Powered Network Attached Storage solutions support snapshots that are similar to the shadow copies feature available in Windows Server 2003. The amount of space that these snapshots consume varies according to the frequency of the snapshots and the amount of changed data. The default setting is 20 percent of the volume.

Planning Storage for Each Server Configuration

The amount of disk space that is supported by a file server can be in the terabytes if the server is connected to high-capacity, direct-attached storage arrays or SAN-connected external storage arrays. However, your goal should not be to attach as much storage as possible to a file server. Instead, plan the amount of storage on a file server by examining your current backup solution and answering the following questions:

- How much data can your backup solution contain? Your backup solution should have the capacity to back up the entire file server.

- How much time do you have to complete your backup? You must be able to perform a full backup within a period of time that is acceptable to your organization and users. For organizations that use hardware-based snapshots and backup software that can back up open files, the backup window might not be an issue.

- How quickly do you need to restore data? In other words, do you need to be able to restore data and get the file server up and running within eight hours? Twenty-four hours? Verify that you can restore data within the required time.

If your organization provides file services to groups who have different storage requirements, you can design file server configurations with different amounts of storage. For example, a low-end file server might have 100 GB of storage, but a high-end file server might have 400 GB of storage. Because the high-end server will typically support more users, make sure that the RAM and CPU configuration is more robust than for the low-end server.

 Important

If you choose file server hardware that supports future storage expansion, answer the previous questions taking the additional storage into account. In other words, if you add more storage to an existing file server but cannot back up or restore the file server in the required time, you must deploy additional file servers or acquire a backup solution that can handle the extra storage.

Backup solutions are becoming faster and more sophisticated. If your current backup solution is not meeting your organization's needs, investigate new solutions, such as those that provide the following types of benefits:

- Many backup programs, including the Backup program that is available in Windows Server 2003, can back up files that are open, allowing administrators to back up a server without having to disconnect users or shut down processes that might have files open.

- Some backup programs offer software-based snapshots that take point-in-time images of a volume, creating virtual replicas without physically copying the data. Servers running Windows Server 2003 provide a similar feature, known as *shadow copies*. For more information about shadow copies, see "Designing a Shadow Copy Strategy" later in this chapter.

- Hardware vendors offer hardware-based snapshots (also called *split mirrors*, *snapshot mirrors*, or *clones*) that you can use to create mirror images of volumes to be used for online backup, application development, and testing purposes.

- Backup solutions designed for SAN-connected external storage arrays can perform backups without sending the data across the network. (These are known as *LAN-free backups*.) SAN backup solutions also offer serverless backups that move data directly from disk to tape.

Determining Maximum Volume Size

Volume sizes often vary, but it is important to set a maximum volume size. NTFS supports volumes up to 256 TB minus 64 KB (2^{32} clusters minus 1 cluster), but it is recommended that you take the following factors into account when you determine the size of volumes in your file servers.

Backup and restoration times

Sizing your volumes to be the same size or smaller than your backup solution's capacity is a good guideline but not an absolute rule. For example, some organizations might back up files on a per-folder basis rather than on a per-volume basis. In this case, the organization would make sure that the size of each folder is smaller than the backup solution. This method, however, requires more backups — one for every folder. In the event that you must restore the data, this method also requires more restorations to restore all the folders on the volume, increasing the overall complexity and length of the process. Because emergency restorations are often done in a hurry and under pressure, let restoration time and simplicity be your guide for sizing volumes.

Chkdsk times

Although file system errors are rare on NTFS volumes, you need to consider the time required to run Chkdsk to repair any errors that occur. Chkdsk times are determined by the number of files on the volume and by the number of files in the largest folder. Chkdsk performance has improved significantly since Windows NT 4.0 and Windows 2000. As a result, downtime due to Chkdsk should be minimal. However, it is important to avoid having volumes that contain so many files that Chkdsk requires longer to complete than the amount of downtime your users can tolerate.

To determine how long Chkdsk takes to complete, run Chkdsk on a test server with a similar number of files as those stored on a typical file server volume. Based on these results, you can limit the number of files to be stored on a volume so that Chkdsk can complete within the acceptable time limit.

Important

Windows Server 2003 provides some Chkdsk parameters that shorten the time required to run Chkdsk. However, if the volume contains file system errors, you must consider the volume at risk until you are able to run a full Chkdsk. For more information about running Chkdsk, see "Chkdsk" in Help and Support Center for Windows Server 2003.

If you need to store a large number of files on a file server and are concerned about Chkdsk times, you can distribute the files on separate volumes on the file server. If, however, you need those files to appear as though they are on a single volume, you can use mounted drives. When you create a mounted drive, you mount one local volume at any empty folder on another local NTFS volume. For example, you can create a folder called Data on volume E and then mount volume F to that folder. When you open the Data folder, the contents of volume F are displayed.

Mounted drives are also useful when you want to add more storage to an existing volume without having to extend the volume. For more information about mounted drives, including information on creating mounted drives on clustered file servers, see "Using NTFS mounted drives" in Help and Support Center for Windows Server 2003.

Planning the Layout and RAID Level of Volumes

When you design a standard hardware configuration, determine what type of data you plan to store on the file server, the RAID type and level that is appropriate for each data type, and how you plan to divide the disk space into volumes.

Evaluating Data Types

Table 2.18 describes the types of data that are typically stored on file servers and the disk I/O characteristics of the data. Knowing the I/O characteristics can help you choose the RAID level that offers the best performance for that particular type of I/O. If you have other types of data stored on the file server, be sure to estimate their I/O characteristics as well.

Table 2.18   Data Types and Their Characteristics

Data Type	Description	Disk I/O Characteristics
Operating system	The operating system, drivers, and any applications installed on the server, such as antivirus, backup, or disk quota software.	Server startup consists mostly of large reads, because the data required for startup is optimized on the disk. After startup completes, the disk I/O is mostly small reads.
Paging space	Space used by the paging file.	If the server memory is sized correctly, the disk I/O consists of small reads and writes. If the server experiences heavy reads and writes, the server needs more memory.
User and shared data	Documents, spreadsheets, graphics, and other data created by users and stored on the file server.	For user and shared data, disk I/O must be measured on a workload-by-workload basis.
Application files	Software that users install or run from the network.	For application files, disk I/O must be measured on a workload-by-workload basis.
Log files	Files used by database, communications, or transaction applications to store a history of operations (for example, the FRS log file).	Small or large writes, depending on the application.

Choosing Between Hardware and Software RAID

Many computer manufacturers provide server-class computers that support hardware-based RAID. With hardware RAID, you use the configuration utility that is provided by the hardware manufacturer to group one or more physical disks into what appears to the operating system as a single disk, sometimes called a *virtual disk* or *logical unit (LUN)*. When you create the virtual disk, you also select a RAID level. Hardware RAID typically provides a choice of RAID-0 (striped), RAID-1 (mirrored), RAID-5 (striped with parity), and in some servers, RAID-0+1 (mirrored stripe). After creating these virtual disks, you use the Disk Management snap-in or the command-line tool DiskPart.exe in Windows Server 2003 to create one or more volumes on each virtual disk.

If your server hardware does not have built-in hardware RAID support, you can use the software RAID provided in Windows Server 2003 to create RAID-0 volumes, RAID-1 volumes, and RAID-5 volumes on dynamic disks. Although software RAID has lower performance than hardware RAID, software RAID is inexpensive and easy to configure because it has no special hardware requirements other than multiple disks. If cost is more important than performance, software RAID is appropriate. If you plan to use software RAID for write-heavy workloads, use RAID-1, not RAID-5.

 Note

> Before you can use the software RAID in Windows Server 2003, you must convert basic disks to dynamic disks. In addition, dynamic disks are not supported on cluster storage. For more information about basic disks, dynamic disks, software RAID, and disk management, see the *Server Management Guide* of the *Windows Server 2003 Resource Kit* (or see the *Server Management Guide* on the Web at http://www.microsoft.com/reskit).

Choosing the RAID Level

Choosing the RAID level is a trade-off among the following factors:

- Cost
- Performance
- Availability
- Reliability

You can determine the best RAID level for your file servers by evaluating the read and write loads of the various data types and then deciding how much you are willing to spend to get the performance, reliability, and availability that your organization requires. Table 2.19 describes four common RAID levels; their relative costs, performance, and availability; and their recommended uses. The performance descriptions in Table 2.19 compare RAID performance to the performance of *just a bunch of disks (JBOD)* — a term used to describe an array of disks that is not configured using RAID.

Table 2.19 Comparing RAID Levels

Factors	RAID-0	RAID-1	RAID-5	RAID-0+1
Minimum number of disks	2	2	3	4
Usable storage capacity	100 percent	50 percent	(N-1)/N disks, where N is the number of disks	50 percent
Fault tolerance	None. Losing a single disk causes all data on the volume to be lost.	Can lose multiple disks as long as a mirrored pair is not lost.	Can tolerate the loss of one disk.	Can lose multiple disks as long as a mirrored pair is not lost.
Read performance	Generally improved by increasing concurrency.	Up to twice as good as JBOD (assuming twice the number of disks).	Generally improved by increasing concurrency.	Improved by increasing concurrency and by having multiple sources for each request.
Write performance	Generally improved by increasing concurrency.	Between 20 percent and 40 percent worse than JBOD for most workloads.	Worse unless using full-stripe writes (large requests). Can be as low as 25 percent of JBOD.	Can be worse or better depending on request size.
Best use	▪ Temporary data only	▪ Operating system ▪ Log files	▪ Operating system ▪ User and shared data[1] ▪ Application files[2]	▪ Operating system ▪ User and shared data ▪ Application files ▪ Log files

[1] Place user and shared data on RAID-5 volumes only if cost is the overriding factor.

[2] Place application files on RAID-5 volumes only if cost is the overriding factor.

When determining the number of disks to compose a virtual disk, keep in mind the following factors:

- Performance increases as you add disks.

- Mean time between failure (MTBF) decreases as you add disks to RAID-5 or RAID-0 arrays.

- RAID-0+1 almost always offers better performance than RAID-1 when you use more than two disks.

- Usable storage capacity increases as you add disks, but so does cost.

Using Dynamic Disks with Hardware RAID

Using dynamic disks with hardware RAID can be useful in the following situations:

- You want to extend a volume, but the underlying hardware cannot dynamically increase the size of LUNs.

- You want to extend a volume, but the hardware has reached its maximum LUN size.

Before converting hardware RAID disks to dynamic disks, review the following restrictions:

- You cannot use dynamic disks on cluster storage. However, you can use the command-line tool DiskPart.exe to extend basic volumes on cluster storage. For more information about extending basic volumes, see "Extend a basic volume" in Help and Support Center for Windows Server 2003.

- If you plan to use hardware snapshots of dynamic disks, you cannot import the snapshot again on the same server, although you can move the snapshot to other servers.

- If you create a software RAID-0 volume across multiple hardware arrays, you cannot extend the RAID-0 later to increase its size. If you anticipate needing to extend the volume, create a spanned volume instead.

For more information about dynamic disks, see the *Server Management Guide* of the *Windows Server 2003 Resource Kit* (or see the *Server Management Guide* on the Web at http://www.microsoft.com/reskit). For best practices on using dynamic disks, see article Q329707, "Best Practices for Using Dynamic Disks on Windows 2000-Based Computers," in the Microsoft Knowledge Base. To find this article, see the Microsoft Knowledge Base link on the Web Resources page at http://www.microsoft.com/windows/reskits/webresources.

Choosing the Cluster Size

A *cluster* (or *allocation unit*) is the smallest amount of disk space that can be allocated to hold a file. NTFS uses 4-KB clusters for volumes over 2 GB. Using a 4-KB cluster size allows you to use NTFS compression on the volume. However, in some cases you might want to use a larger cluster size to optimize NTFS performance.

To determine the cluster size, evaluate the types of files to be stored on the volume so that you can determine whether to use the default 4-KB cluster size. Some important questions to answer include the following:

- Are the files typically the same size?

- Are the files smaller than the default cluster size?

- Do the files remain the same size or grow larger?

If the files are typically smaller than the default cluster size (for example, 4 KB) and do not increase, use the default cluster size to reduce wasted disk space. However, smaller clusters can increase fragmentation, especially when files grow to fill more than one cluster. Therefore, plan to adjust the cluster size accordingly when you format the volume. If the files you store tend to be large or increase in size, and you do not want to use NTFS compression, use 16-KB or 32-KB clusters to optimize performance.

 Important

If you plan to defragment volumes on which shadow copies are enabled, it is recommended that you use a cluster size of 16 KB or larger. If you do not, the number of changes caused by defragmentation can cause shadow copies to be deleted faster than expected. Note, however, that NTFS compression is supported only if the cluster size is 4 KB or smaller. For more information about shadow copies, see "Designing a Shadow Copy Strategy" later in this chapter.

Determining the Volume Layout

When you determine the volume layout, you evaluate the type of data to be stored and the number of volumes that you want to create. For better manageability, use separate volumes for each data type where possible, though the operating system and paging file are often placed on a single volume. For example, use one volume for the operating system and paging file and one or more volumes for shared user data, applications, and log files.

If performance is important, place different data types in separate volumes on different virtual disks. Using separate virtual disks is especially important for any data types that create heavy write loads, such as log files. For example, dedicate a single set of disks (composing a virtual disk) to handling the disk I/O created by the updates to the log file. Placing the paging file on a separate virtual disk can provide some minor improvements in performance, but not typically enough to make it worth the extra cost.

To gain some performance benefits while minimizing cost, it is often useful to combine different data types in one or more volumes on the same virtual disks. A common method is to store the operating system and paging file on one virtual disk and the user data, applications, and log files in one or more volumes on the remaining virtual disk.

Note

On servers running Windows Server 2003, you can increase the size of basic volumes and dynamic volumes. If you plan to use basic volumes (primary partitions or logical drives), you can extend them on the same disk only, and the basic volume must be followed by contiguous unallocated space. If your hardware supports adding more physical disks to a virtual disk, make sure that the basic volume is the last volume on the disk. For more information about extending volumes and disk management, see the *Server Management Guide* of the *Windows Server 2003 Resource Kit* (or see the *Server Management Guide* on the Web at http://www.microsoft.com/reskit).

Determining the Number of File Servers

The following section describes reasons why you might want to deploy additional file servers and how you can determine the number of file servers that you require.

Consolidating Older File Servers

Many organizations today are consolidating older file servers throughout the organization into fewer larger, more powerful file servers. Consolidation reduces the cost of managing multiple file servers and increases the efficiency of storage allocation and backup tasks.

If you plan to consolidate file servers running Windows NT 4.0 or Windows 2000 onto new file servers running Windows Server 2003, determine the number of file servers running Windows Server 2003 that is necessary to match or exceed the performance of your existing file servers. You can derive these figures by using the scaling factors provided in "Determining RAM and CPU Specifications" earlier in this chapter.

The following scenarios describe two consolidation situations based on the scaling factors presented in "Determining RAM and CPU Specifications" earlier in this chapter.

Scenario 1: Consolidating file servers running Windows NT Server 4.0

An organization plans to migrate its file services to file servers running Windows Server 2003. It currently has 100 Windows NT 4.0 file servers with the following hardware:

- UP Pentium Pro, 200 MHz
- 256 MB RAM
- Fast Ethernet network adapters

The organization plans to use the following hardware to consolidate file servers:

- 4P 900-MHz Intel® Pentium® III Xeon™

- 3 GB RAM

- Gigabit network adapters

To determine the number of file servers the organization needs when migrating to Windows Server 2003, use the scaling factors described in Table 2.20.

Table 2.20   Consolidating File Servers Running Windows NT Server 4.0

Area of Improvement	Details	Scaling Factor
Operating system	As shown in Table 2.12, migrating from Windows NT 4.0 to Windows Server 2003 provides a 2.75X performance improvement.	2.75X
Hardware upgrade	As shown in Table 2.13, migrating from a Pentium Pro, 200 MHz, to a Xeon, 900 MHz, provides a 4X performance improvement.	4X
Processor scaling	As shown in Table 2.14, migrating from UP (one processor) servers to 4P servers provides a 1.8X performance improvement.	1.8X
Total improvements	Multiply the scaling factors (2.75 x 4 x 1.8)	19.8X

Based on these figures, the organization can migrate 100 file servers running Windows NT 4.0 to five 4P Xeon 900-MHz servers running Windows Server 2003. (To derive this number, divide 100 by 19.8.) The organization must also be sure that the five Xeon servers have adequate storage space to store the consolidated data, as well as future data, and that 3 GB of memory can handle the total workload of the 100 servers.

Scenario 2: Consolidating file servers running Windows 2000 Server

An organization plans to migrate its file services to file servers running Windows Server 2003. It currently has five Windows 2000 file servers with the following hardware:

- 4P 400-MHz Intel® Pentium® II Xeon™

- 1 GB RAM

- Gigabit network adapters

The organization plans to use the following hardware to consolidate file servers:

- 8P 900-MHz Intel® Pentium® III Xeon™

- 4 GB RAM

- Gigabit network adapters

To determine the number of file servers the organization needs when migrating to Windows Server 2003, use the scaling factors described in Table 2.21.

Table 2.21   Consolidating File Servers Running Windows 2000 Server

Area of Improvement	Details	Scaling Factor
Operating system	As shown in Table 2.12, migrating from Windows 2000 Server to Windows Server 2003 provides a 2.2X performance improvement.	2.2X
Hardware upgrade	As shown in Table 2.13, migrating from a Xeon, 400 MHz, to a Xeon, 900 MHz, provides a 2X performance improvement.	2X
Processor scaling	As shown in Table 2.14, migrating from 4P servers to 8P servers provides a 1.3X performance improvement.	1.3X
Total improvements	Multiply the scaling factors (2.2 x 2 x 1.3)	5.7X

Based on these figures, the organization can use a single 8P Xeon 900-MHz file server, assuming it has enough memory, disk, and network I/O available. To ensure the availability of the server, the organization should consider using a server cluster instead of a single stand-alone file server. For more information about increasing the availability of file servers, see "Planning File Server Availability" earlier in this chapter.

Providing Additional Storage

If your organization uses direct-attached storage for file servers, deploy as many file servers as it takes to meet your storage needs. If each of your file servers provides 500 GB of storage, and you need at least 2 TB of storage, you need a minimum of five file servers. You also need to provide the new file servers with enough processing power and memory to serve your clients. Use the factors described in "Determining RAM and CPU Specifications" earlier in this chapter.

Providing More Processing Power

If users experience delays when accessing file servers, there are a number of ways you can improve file server performance:

- Enable the Offline Files feature so that clients cache files locally instead of going to the file server whenever they need a file. You can also use this feature to enable automatic caching for programs. When you enable program caching on a shared folder, and a user runs a program from the shared folder, Windows Server 2003 copies the application .exe and .dll files as they are used and runs the files from the client's local cache, which reduces server load and network traffic. For simple programs that use a single .exe file, this feature enables the program to run correctly when the server is down or the client is not connected to the network. For programs that consist of multiple files (.exe and .dll), all files must be cached on the local computer so that the program can run while offline. The user can ensure that all files are cached by choosing the **Make Available Offline** option from the **File** menu in Windows Explorer. For more information about the Offline Files feature, see "Offline settings for shared resources" and "Make a file or folder available offline" in Help and Support Center for Windows Server 2003.

- Place copies of heavily used shared folders with primarily read-only files on multiple file servers, and use DFS to provide load sharing. If you also plan to use the Offline Files feature, note that you can use this feature in conjunction with DFS only for clients running Windows XP Professional. For more information about Offline Files, see "Offline Files overview" in Help and Support Center for Windows Server 2003.

- Upgrade the processor, RAM, or disk subsystem in your existing file servers. Use the factors described in "Determining RAM and CPU Specifications" earlier in this chapter to determine the performance improvements you can gain by upgrading existing hardware.

Providing Same-Site Data Access for Users

If you have remote sites with expensive WAN links, you can deploy one or more file servers in those sites to provide users with fast, inexpensive LAN access to the file servers. For each site, take into account the storage and processing power needed by users in the site. You also need a backup and recovery procedure in place at each site in case one of the file servers fails.

Determining the File Server Hardware Life Cycle

The hardware life cycle is the amount of time that hardware is used before it is replaced with new hardware. Typical hardware life cycles are 12, 24, or 36 months. If your organization frequently adds new file servers to increase capacity or add new functionality, consider using a relatively short replacement cycle for file servers. This recommendation is based on the high rate of change in computers, disk subsystems, and other components. Maintaining a shorter cycle prevents the problem of servers that were purchased at the beginning of the cycle becoming obsolete before the end of the cycle. However, a shorter life cycle affects the manageability of file servers, because you must replace hardware, install the operating system and applications, and migrate data more frequently.

To transparently migrate files from decommissioned servers to new servers without affecting users, implement one or more DFS namespaces. For more information about DFS, see "Designing DFS Namespaces" earlier in this chapter.

For more information about deploying new servers and migrating data, see "Deploying File Servers" later in this chapter.

Designing a Shadow Copy Strategy

You can give users access to previous versions of files by enabling shadow copies, which provide point-in-time copies of files stored on file servers running Windows Server 2003. By enabling shadow copies, you can reduce the administrative burden of restoring previously backed up files for users who accidentally delete or overwrite important files. Shadow copies work for both open and closed files; therefore, shadow copies can be taken even when files are in use.

Shadow copies work by making a block-level copy of any changes that have occurred to files since the last shadow copy. Only the changes are copied, not the entire file. As a result, previous versions of files do not usually take up as much disk space as the current file, although the amount of disk space used for changes can vary depending on the application that changed the file. For example, some applications rewrite the entire file when a change is made, whereas other applications append changes to the existing file. If the entire file is rewritten to disk, the shadow copy contains the entire file. Therefore, consider the type of applications in your organization, as well as the frequency and number of updates, when you determine how much disk space to allocate for shadow copies.

 Important

Shadow copies do not eliminate the need to perform regular backups, nor do shadow copies protect you from media failure. In addition, shadow copies are not permanent. As new shadow copies are taken, old shadow copies are purged when the size of all shadow copies reaches a configurable maximum or when the number of shadow copies reaches 64, whichever is sooner. As a result, shadow copies might not be present for as long as users expect them to be. Be sure to consider user needs and expectations when you configure shadow copies.

Shadow copies are designed for volumes that store user data, such as home directories and My Documents folders that are redirected by using Group Policy, or other shared folders where users store data. Shadow copies work with compressed or encrypted files, and they retain whatever permissions were set on the files when the shadow copies were taken. For example, if a user is denied permission to read a file, that user would not be able to restore a previous version of the file, nor would the user be able to read the file after it has been restored.

Although shadow copies are taken for an entire volume, users must use shared folders to access shadow copies. Administrators on the local server must also specify the *\\servername\sharename* path to access shadow copies. If you or your users want to access a previous version of a file that does not reside in a shared folder, you must first share the folder.

Collecting Information to Design a Shadow Copy Strategy

When you design a shadow copy strategy, review the following topics. For an Excel spreadsheet to assist you in documenting your shadow copy design decisions, see "Shadow Copy and Disk Quota Configuration Worksheet" (Sdcfsv_7.xls) on the *Windows Server 2003 Deployment Kit* companion CD (or see "DFS Configuration Worksheet" on the Web at http://www.microsoft.com/reskit).

Shadow copy support in client operating systems

Shadow copies can be accessed by computers running Windows Server 2003 and by computers running Windows XP Professional on which you have installed the Previous Versions Client pack (Twcli32.msi). This file is located in the Windows Server 2003 operating system in *windir*\system32\clients\twclient. You can install this file manually on clients or deploy the file by using the software distribution component of Group Policy. For more information about software distribution, see "Deploying a Managed Software Environment" in *Designing a Managed Environment* of this kit.

To access shadow copies from previous versions of Windows, including Windows 2000 and Windows XP Professional, you can download and install the Shadow Copy Client. For more information and to download the Shadow Copy Client, see the Shadow Copy Client Download link on the Web Resources page at http://www.microsoft.com/windows/reskits/webresources.

 Note

The Previous Versions Client and the Shadow Copy Client provide the same functionality, but the Shadow Copy Client can be installed on multiple operating systems, such as Windows 2000 and Windows XP Professional, whereas the Previous Versions Client can only be installed on Windows XP Professional.

If you have not yet deployed these operating systems or client packs on your clients, you can deploy a single computer (or as many as necessary) from which users can restore previous versions of files. You can also distribute the client pack on a case-by-case basis to users who request that files be restored.

Shadow copy support in server operating systems

Shadow copies are available only on file servers running Windows Server 2003.

Shadow copy support on server clusters

There are a number of important considerations for managing shadow copies on cluster storage. For more information about managing shadow copies on server clusters, see "Using Shadow Copies of Shared Folders in a server cluster" in Help and Support Center for Windows Server 2003.

File system requirements

Shadow copies are available only on NTFS volumes.

Recommended scenarios for using shadow copies

Shadow copies work best when the server stores user files such as documents, spreadsheets, and graphics files. Do not use shadow copies to provide access to previous versions of application or e-mail databases.

Amount of volume space to allocate to shadow copies

When you enable shadow copies on a volume, you can specify the maximum amount of volume space to be used for the shadow copies. The default limit is 10 percent of the source volume (the volume being copied). Increase the limit for volumes where users frequently change files. Also, setting the limit too small causes the oldest shadow copies to be deleted frequently, which defeats the purpose of shadow copies and which will likely frustrate users. In fact, if the amount of changes is greater than the amount of space allocated to storing shadow copies, no shadow copy is created. Therefore, carefully consider the amount of disk space that you want to set aside for shadow copies, while keeping in mind user expectations for how many versions they want to be available. Your users might expect only a single shadow copy to be available, or they might expect three days' or three weeks' worth of shadow copies. The more shadow copies the users expect, the more storage you need to allocate for storing them.

Setting the limit too small can adversely affect other programs, such as the Backup program in Windows Server 2003 and other backup programs that support the Volume Shadow Copy service. During the backup process, these programs create temporary shadow copies for consistent backups. The temporary shadow copies count towards the volume space limit you specify for shadow copies. If the available volume space remaining in the limit is too small, the Volume Shadow Copy service can delete existing shadow copies to free up space for the temporary shadow copy. If there are no existing shadow copies, and the volume space limit cannot accommodate the temporary shadow copy, the backup might fail. For more information about the Volume Shadow Copy service, see the Storage Services link on the Web Resources page at http://www.microsoft.com/windows/reskits/webresources.

Important

Regardless of the volume space that you allocate for shadow copies, you can have a maximum of 64 shadow copies for any volume. When the 65th shadow copy is taken, the oldest shadow copy is purged.

Frequency at which Windows Server 2003 creates shadow copies

By default, Windows Server 2003 creates shadow copies at 7:00 A.M. and at 12:00 noon Monday through Friday. However, you can change the schedule to better accommodate users. Keep in mind that the more shadow copies you create, the more disk space the shadow copies can consume, especially if files change frequently. When you determine the schedule, avoid scheduling shadow copies to occur more than once per hour.

Storing shadow copies on separate disks

You can dedicate a volume on separate disks for storing the shadow copies of another volume on the same file server. For example, if user files are stored on H:\, you might use another volume, such as S:\, to store the shadow copies. Using a separate volume on separate disks provides better performance, and it is recommended for heavily used file servers. If you plan to use a separate volume for the storage area (where the shadow copies are stored), be sure to change the maximum size to **No Limit** to reflect the space available on the storage area volume instead of the source volume (where the user files are stored).

Important

If you plan to store the shadow copies on the same volume as the user files, note that a burst of disk I/O can cause all shadow copies to be deleted. If you cannot tolerate the sudden deletion of shadow copies, use a volume that will not be shadow copied, preferably on separate disks, for storing shadow copies.

File servers containing mounted drives

A mounted drive is a local volume attached to an empty folder (called a *mount point*) on an NTFS volume. If you enable shadow copies on a volume that contains mounted drives, the mounted drives are not included when shadow copies are taken. In addition, if you share a mounted drive and enable shadow copies on it, users cannot access the shadow copies if they traverse from the host volume (where the mount point is stored) to the mounted drive.

For example, assume you have the folder E:\Data\Users, and the Users folder is a mount point for F:\. You enable shadow copies on both E:\ and F:\, you share E:\Data as \\Server1\Data, and you share E:\Data\Users as \\Server1\Users. In this example, users can access previous versions of \\Server1\Data and \\Server1\Users but not \\Server1\Data\Users.

Defragmenting the volume where shadow copied files are stored

If you plan to defragment volumes on which shadow copies are enabled, it is recommended that you use a cluster (or allocation unit) size of 16 KB or larger. If you do not, the number of changes caused by the defragmentation process can cause shadow copies to be deleted faster than expected. Note, however, that NTFS compression is supported only if the cluster size is 4 KB or smaller.

Note

To check the cluster size of a volume, use the **fsutil fsinfo ntfsinfo** command. If the volume contains data and you want to change the cluster size, you must back up the data on the volume, reformat it using the new cluster size, and then restore the data.

Converting basic disks to dynamic disks

If the volumes that contain the original files and the shadow copy storage area are on separate basic disks and you want to convert both of the disks to dynamic disks, you must follow these directions:

- **If the shadow copy storage area is not on the boot volume.** First dismount and take offline the volume that contains the original files. To do this, use Mountvol.exe with the /p parameter. Next, convert the disk that contains the storage area volume to a dynamic disk. After the conversion, you have 20 minutes to mount the volume that contains the original files and bring it online by using Mountvol.exe or the Disk Management snap-in; if you do not, you will lose the existing shadow copies. After you bring the volume that contains the original files back online, you can convert that disk to a dynamic disk.

- **If the shadow copy storage area is on the boot volume.** You can convert the disk that contains the storage area volume to a dynamic disk without having to dismount the volume that contains the original files. To complete the conversion, you must restart the computer twice. Next, convert the disk that contains the original files to a dynamic disk.

 Important

If the disk that contains the original files is converted to a dynamic disk first, the shadow copies are deleted when you convert the disk that contains the storage area volume to a dynamic disk.

Using DFS to provide access to volumes that contain shadow copies

You can create DFS link targets on volumes that contain shadow copies, and users can retrieve previous versions of files from the DFS link target, just as they can from a regular shared folder. However, if you use multiple link targets for a DFS link, each of those link targets can reside on a different volume with its own shadow copies. As a result, the previous versions of files can vary, depending on which link target the user last accesses to change the file.

Backing up shadow copies

Windows Server 2003 does not support backing up shadow copies. When you back up a volume, shadow copies are not backed up.

Using scripting to create shadow copies

To create shadow copies by using scripts, use Vssadmin.exe to create the shadow copies and, optionally, use Schtasks.exe to schedule the creation of shadow copies. For more information about using these command-line tools, see "Vssadmin" and "Schtasks" in Help and Support Center for Windows Server 2003.

For more information about shadow copies, see "Shadow Copies of Shared Folders" in Help and Support Center for Windows Server 2003.

Example: An Organization Designs a Shadow Copy Strategy

A large organization allows users to redirect their My Documents folders to a central file server. When a user accidentally deletes or overwrites a file and requests that the file be restored, the process requires between 1 day and 3 days and up to three escalations before the backup/restore group can restore a file. The organization determines that it costs approximately $300 for support and escalation costs plus lost productivity while the restoration takes place.

To decrease the cost associated with restoring files and to increase user satisfaction, the organization enables shadow copies on its file servers. During the pilot program, the organization determines that the default settings for the schedule and storage volume allow two weeks of previous versions. When a user contacts the support group to have a file restored, the support group provides a copy of the Previous Versions Client pack to the user. It takes the user approximately five minutes to install the software and another five minutes to restore the file. As a result, a user can restore a file in 10 minutes instead of 1 day to 3 days, and user satisfaction is greatly increased.

Designing a Disk Quota Strategy

To prevent file servers from filling to capacity without warning, use disk quotas to track and control disk space usage on file servers. Windows Server 2003 provides disk quota functionality that tracks quotas on a per-user, per-volume basis. After you enable the warning level and limit, they apply to all users who own files stored on the volume. Any user who creates a new file is automatically assigned the current warning level and limit.

Windows Server 2003 quotas are well suited for volumes that store user data, such as redirected My Documents folders or other per-user folders. For example, an organization uses Group Policy to redirect its employees' My Documents and My Pictures folders to a file server volume that stores only user data, not group data. After evaluating the storage needs of users in the organization, the administrator chooses to set storage limits by enforcing a 300-MB disk quota for each user. The administrator also sets a 270-MB warning level. If a user needs additional storage, the user must get approval from his or her manager before the administrator can increase the quota for the individual user.

Windows Server 2003 disk quotas are not designed for project-oriented scenarios in which a shared folder is given a quota that is shared among a specified set of users. A wide range of Windows Server 2003–compatible, third-party products provide group quotas, per-folder quotas, and threshold event features that this scenario requires.

To design a quota strategy for volumes that store user data, review the following topics. For an Excel spreadsheet to assist you in documenting your disk quota design decisions, see "Shadow Copy and Disk Quota Configuration Worksheet" (Sdcfsv_7.xls) on the *Windows Server 2003 Deployment Kit* companion CD (or see "DFS Configuration Worksheet" on the Web at http://www.microsoft.com/reskit).

File system requirements

Disk quotas are available only on NTFS volumes.

Tracking quotas vs. enforcing quotas

Tracking quotas is useful if you want to track use of disk space without denying users access to a volume. Enforcing quotas denies disk space to users who exceed their limit. Users can determine how much disk space they have available on the volume by viewing the properties of a mapped shared folder in Windows Explorer.

Determining how much disk space to provide to each user

You can change quotas on a per-user basis if some users require additional disk space. For example, the current limit might be 200 MB, but you can specify which users have a 500-MB limit. You cannot assign quotas on a per-group basis.

When setting quotas, make sure that you have enough disk space to accommodate existing users and that you have enough extra free space to accommodate future growth. Each file that is stored on the volume can use up to 64 KB of NTFS metadata that is not charged to a user's quota. To avoid running out of disk space, you must leave sufficient disk space to accommodate this metadata.

Using disk quotas on server clusters

Use only domain-level accounts, because local accounts cannot be resolved when the disk fails over. For more information about configuring disk quotas on shared cluster disks, see article Q278365, "HOW TO: Configure Disk Quotas for a Shared Disk in a Cluster" in the Microsoft Knowledge Base. To find this article, see the Microsoft Knowledge Base link on the Web Resources page at http://www.microsoft.com/windows/reskits/webresources.

Logging quota events

Windows Server 2003 provides quota reporting by logging events in the event log when users exceed their warning level or quota limit. You can use Windows Management Instrumentation (WMI) for customized reporting by using the WMI classes Win32_DiskQuota, Win32_QuotaSetting, and Win32_VolumeQuotaSetting. For more information about WMI, see the Microsoft Windows Management Instrumentation (WMI) SDK link on the Web Resources page at http://www.microsoft.com/windows/reskits/webresources.

Using disk quotas on DFS link targets

DFS provides a simple way to create custom quotas on different volumes that appear to users as different folders on the same volume. If you are using DFS to provide multiple link targets, note that each of these link targets can reside on a volume with different quota settings. To keep the user experience consistent, use the same quota settings for each volume.

Using disk quotas on shadow-copied volumes

You can enable shadow copies and disk quotas on the same volume, and shadow copies do not count against a user's disk quota.

 Note

For more information about file systems and Windows Server 2003 disk quotas, see the *Server Management Guide* of the *Windows Server 2003 Resource Kit* (or see the *Server Management Guide* on the Web at http://www.microsoft.com/reskit).

Planning File Server Security

Planning for file server security is vital for protecting your organization's sensitive or business-critical files. When planning for file server security, you need to protect not only the data but the physical server as well. In addition, if you plan to implement availability strategies, such as DFS or clustering, you need to take additional steps to secure the resources associated with these features.

Figure 2.18 describes the process for planning file server security.

Figure 2.18   Planning File Server Security

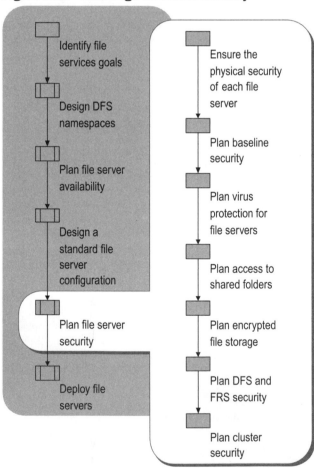

Ensuring the Physical Security of Each File Server

For file servers that must maintain high availability, restrict physical access to only designated individuals. In addition, consider to what extent you need to restrict physical access to network hardware. The details of how you implement physical security depend on your physical facilities and your organization's structure and policies. You should also implement methods to restrict access to backup media and any instruction sheets that you create, such as the instructions that go in the recovery manual for a file server. Allowing unauthorized people to study documentation or configuration manuals means that they can quickly cause harm to the system if they are able to obtain access.

Even if the physical server is in a secure room, the file server might still be accessible through remote administration tools. Therefore, implement methods for restricting access to remote administration of file servers, and ensure that remote administration tools do not weaken your organization's security model. For example, remote administration tools do not always use strong authentication protocols, such as Kerberos V5, to authenticate users across the network. You might be able to implement weaker protocols, such as NTLM, depending on the remote management tool you use and the operating system that is running on the host you are administering. In addition, certain remote administration tools might transmit unencrypted data (plaintext) across the network. This makes your data vulnerable to network sniffers.

For more information about security and remote administration, see the *Server Management Guide* of the *Windows Server 2003 Resource Kit* (or see the *Server Management Guide* on the Web at http://www.microsoft.com/reskit).

Planning Baseline Security

The Windows 2000 Server Baseline Security Checklist provides instructions for configuring a baseline level of security on servers running Windows Server 2003. The checklist contains tasks such as using NTFS, using strong passwords, disabling unnecessary services, disabling unnecessary accounts, and more. For more information about the baseline security checklist, see the Windows 2000 Server Baseline Security Checklist link on the Web Resources page at http://www.microsoft.com/windows/reskits/webresources.

Run the Microsoft Baseline Security Analyzer (Mbsa.exe for the graphical user interface version; Mbsacli.exe for the command-line version). For more information about the Microsoft Baseline Security Analyzer, see the MBSA link on the Web Resources page at http://www.microsoft.com/windows/reskits/webresources.

To further enhance security, review the Microsoft Windows Update Web site regularly for patches that fix vulnerabilities and provide security enhancements. For more information about Windows Update, see the Windows Update link on the Web Resources page at http://www.microsoft.com/windows/reskits/webresources.

Planning Virus Protection for File Servers

To protect file servers from viruses, plan to take the following precautions:

- Use Windows Server 2003–compatible antivirus software, and regularly update virus signature files.

- Back up files regularly so that damage is minimized if a virus attack does occur.

- With clustered file servers, you must use an antivirus program that is cluster aware. If it is not, failover might not occur correctly. If your organization does not have cluster-aware antivirus software, you can install antivirus software on a nonclustered server and use that server to periodically scan the drives that are mapped to the clustered file server. For more information about running antivirus software on server clusters, see article Q250355, "Antivirus Software May Cause Problems with Cluster Services," in the Microsoft Knowledge Base. To find this article, see the Microsoft Knowledge Base link on the Web Resources page at http://www.microsoft.com/windows/reskits/webresources.

- For FRS-replicated content, you must use antivirus programs that are FRS compatible and that do not change the security descriptor of files. For more information about FRS compatible antivirus programs, see article Q815263, "Antivirus, Backup and Disk Optimization Programs That Are Compatible with the File Replication Service." To find this article, see the Microsoft Knowledge Base link on the Web Resources page at http://www.microsoft.com/windows/reskits/webresources.

Planning Access to Shared Folders

When you plan access to shared folders, determine the type of permissions to use, who needs access to the folders, and the level of access that users require. You can also disable administrative shares and hide shared folders.

Determining the Type of Permissions to Use

Permissions define the type of access granted to a user or group for a file or folder. Windows Server 2003 offers two types of permissions:

- NTFS permissions restrict local and remote access to files and folders on NTFS volumes. When you create a new folder, it inherits permissions from its parent folder. When you create a file in a folder, the file inherits permissions from the parent folder.

- Share permissions restrict remote access to shared folders, but share permissions do not restrict access to users who log on to the server locally. Share permissions are available on both FAT and NTFS volumes.

To simplify administering and troubleshooting permissions, use NTFS permissions to control user and group access to file system resources.

Although NTFS is recommended as the primary method for securing folders, you must keep in mind that default share permissions are assigned when you share a folder, and the default share permissions have changed for Windows Server 2003. Windows 2000 and Windows XP grant the Everyone group the Full Control share permission, but Windows Server 2003 grants the Everyone group the Read share permission. This change increases the security of shared folders and helps prevent the spread of viruses.

Because the more restrictive permissions always apply when you use a combination of share and NTFS permissions, you might need to change the default share permissions if you want users to be able to add or change files in the folder. If you do not change the default share permissions, users will have the Read share permission even if you grant users NTFS permissions such as Write or Modify.

If you use a clustered file server, you must create share permissions by using the Cluster Administrator snap-in, not Windows Explorer. In addition, if you plan to use the Share Subdirectories option, you must use NTFS permissions to secure the subdirectories. For more information about these options, see "Planning Cluster Security" later in this chapter.

Determining Who Needs Access to the Folders

To increase security and prevent users from browsing through shared folders that are not relevant to their jobs, assign permissions only to groups that require access to the shared folders.

To reduce administrative overhead when assigning permissions, do the following:

- Assign permissions to groups rather than to users.
- Place users in global groups or universal groups, nest these groups within domain local groups, and then assign the domain local groups permissions to the folder.

You do not need to deny permissions for specific groups. When permission to perform an operation is not explicitly granted, it is implicitly denied. For example, if you allow the Marketing group, and only the Marketing group, permission to access a shared folder, users who are not members of the Marketing group are implicitly denied access. The operating system does not allow users who are not members of the Marketing group to access the folder.

Deny access to folders only in the following scenarios:

- You want to exclude a subset of a group (for example, an individual user) that has permissions.

- You want to exclude one or more special permissions when you have already granted Full Control to a user or group.

 Note

If you plan to redirect your users' My Documents folders, note that each user is granted exclusive access to his or her My Documents folder on the file server. If you need to access a user's My Documents folder, you have two choices: take ownership of the folder or follow the instructions provided in article Q288991, "Enabling the Administrator to Have Access to Redirected Folders" in the Microsoft Knowledge Base. To find this article, see the Microsoft Knowledge Base link on the Web Resources page at http://www.microsoft.com/windows/reskits/webresources.

Determining the Level of Access That Users Require

Assign the most restrictive permissions that still allow users to perform required tasks. The following descriptions explain the permissions that are associated with folders on NTFS volumes.

Write   Users can copy or paste new files and subfolders in the folder and change folder attributes. However, users cannot open or browse the folder unless you grant the Read permission. Assigning Write permission is useful for folders where users can file confidential reports, such as timesheets, that only the manager or shared folder administrator can read.

Read   Users can see the names of files and subfolders in a folder and view folder attributes, ownership, and permissions. Users can open and view files, but they cannot change files or add new files. Assign the Read permission if users need only to read information in a folder and they do not need to delete, create, or change files.

List Folder Contents   Users can see the names of files and subfolders in the folder. However, users cannot open files to view their contents.

Read & Execute   Users have the same rights as those assigned through the Read permission, as well as the ability to traverse folders. Traverse folders rights allow a user to reach files and folders located in subdirectories, even if the user does not have permission to access portions of the directory path.

Modify   Users can delete the folder and perform the actions permitted by the Write and Read & Execute permissions. Because Modify gives users the ability to delete the folder, use Modify permission only for administrators or for the group or department owner of the folder.

Full Control   Users can change permissions, take ownership, delete subfolders and files, and perform the actions granted by all other permissions. Because Full Control gives users the ability to delete the folder, use Full Control permission only for administrators or for the group or department owner of the folder.

For more information about permissions and file servers, see "Permissions on a file server" in Help and Support Center for Windows Server 2003.

Determining Whether to Disable Administrative Shares

Windows Server 2003 creates shared folders, known as *administrative shares*, by default when you start a server or when you stop and then start the Server service. These folders are shared for administrative purposes, and they allow users and applications with the appropriate administrative rights to gain access to the system remotely. For example, some backup software applications use these shares to remotely connect to systems to back up data.

Administrative shares have default share permissions that restrict access to members of only a few security groups. Each share name is appended with a dollar sign ($), which hides the share from users who browse the server. One type of administrative share is the root folder of every volume (C$, D$, and so on).

You can disable these administrative shares temporarily or permanently. For more information about disabling administrative shares and an overview of remote administration, see the *Server Management Guide* of the *Windows Server 2003 Resource Kit* (or see the *Server Management Guide* on the Web at http://www.microsoft.com/reskit).

Determining Whether to Hide Shared Folders

You can hide a shared folder by appending a dollar sign ($) to the shared folder name. Hiding shared folders is useful when you want to make a shared folder available over the network while keeping it hidden from people browsing on the network.

Hiding shared folders does not necessarily make them more secure, because anyone who knows the name of the server and the shared folder can connect to it. Therefore, you must set the necessary NTFS permissions on the shared folder so that access is granted only to the appropriate groups.

Planning Encrypted File Storage

Windows 2000, Windows XP, and Windows Server 2003 support storing files that are encrypted using EFS. However, remote decryption is a potential security risk, because files are decrypted before transmission on the local server, and they are transmitted unencrypted over the network in plaintext. Therefore, before you allow encrypted files to be stored on file servers, decide whether the risk associated with transmitting unencrypted files over the network is acceptable.

You can greatly reduce or eliminate this risk by enabling Internet Protocol security (IPSec) policies, which encrypts data that is transmitted between servers, or by using Web Distributed Authoring and Versioning (WebDAV) folders. WebDAV folders have many advantages compared to shared folders, so you should use them whenever possible for remote storage of encrypted files. WebDAV folders require less administrative effort and provide greater security than shared folders. WebDAV folders can also securely store and deliver files that are encrypted with EFS over the Internet by means of Hypertext Transfer Protocol (HTTP).

Before users can encrypt files that reside on a remote file server, you must designate the file server as trusted for delegation. Doing so allows all users with files on that server to encrypt their files. For more information about enabling encryption on a file server, see "Enable a remote server for file encryption" in Help and Support Center for Windows Server 2003. Note that when encrypting files on a WebDAV server, the server does not need to be trusted for delegation.

 Important

To enable EFS on a clustered file server, you must perform a number of steps to configure the environment correctly. For more information about enabling EFS on server clusters, see "Create a cluster-managed encrypted file share" in Help and Support Center for Windows Server 2003.

If you allow users to store encrypted files on file servers, review the following issues:

- Users can encrypt files on remote NTFS volumes only when both the user's computer and the file server are members of the same Windows Server 2003 forest. (This restriction does not apply to WebDAV folders.)

- Users must have Write or Modify permissions to encrypt or decrypt a file.

- Users cannot encrypt files that are compressed. If users encrypt a compressed file or folder, the file or folder is uncompressed.

For more information about EFS and using WebDAV folders to store encrypted files, see "Encrypting and decrypting data" and "Internet Information Services (IIS) 6.0 overview" in Help and Support Center for Windows Server 2003. For more information about configuring IPSec, see the *Networking Guide* of the *Windows Server 2003 Resource Kit* (or see the *Networking Guide* on the Web at http://www.microsoft.com/reskit).

Planning DFS and FRS Security

When planning to secure DFS namespaces and content replicated by FRS, follow these guidelines:

- Use NTFS permissions to secure DFS targets. If you are using FRS to replicate DFS link target information, any permission changes you make on one member of the replica set replicate to other members. If you are not using FRS for automatic replication, you must set the permissions on targets and manually propagate any changes that occur.

- When setting NTFS permissions, always use the path of the physical folder (*servername**sharename*) instead of navigating through the DFS namespace to set permissions. This is especially important when you have multiple link targets for a given link. Setting permissions on a folder by using its DFS path can cause the folder to inherit permissions from its parent folder in the namespace. In addition, if there are multiple link targets, only one of them gets its permissions updated when you use the DFS path.

- If you plan to use share permissions, note that FRS does not replicate share permissions; therefore, you must plan to implement identical share permissions for each shared folder in a replica set. If you do not, users might have inconsistent access to shared folders across the network.

- To prevent the spread of viruses in read-only FRS-replicated content, give the appropriate groups the NTFS Read & Execute permission, create a group for administrators who update content, and assign that group the NTFS Modify permission. Do not grant permissions to the Everyone group. For additional recommendations, see "Permissions on a file server" in Help and Support Center for Windows Server 2003.

- For FRS-replicated content, you must use antivirus programs that are FRS compatible and that do not change the security descriptor of files. For more information about FRS compatible antivirus programs, see article Q815263, "Antivirus, Backup and Disk Optimization Programs That Are Compatible with the File Replication Service." To find this article, see the Microsoft Knowledge Base link on the Web Resources page at http://www.microsoft.com/windows/reskits/webresources.

- You must have permissions on the DFS configuration object in Active Directory to add and delete roots to a domain-based DFS namespace.

- You can create DFS link targets that point to shared folders containing data that is encrypted by using EFS. However, you cannot use FRS to replicate those files among multiple link targets.

- Do not enable the RestrictAnonymous registry value on DFS root servers. Doing so restricts anonymous access and causes DFS referral failures. This registry value is also part of the HiSecWeb security template, which is designed to help secure Internet Information Services (IIS) at the operating system level. For more information about the RestrictAnonymous registry value, see article Q246261, "How to Use the RestrictAnonymous Registry Value in Windows 2000." For more information about the HiSecWeb template, see article Q316347, "IIS 5: HiSecWeb Potential Risks and the IIS Lockdown Tool," in the Microsoft Knowledge Base. To find these articles, see the Microsoft Knowledge Base link on the Web Resources page at http://www.microsoft.com/windows/reskits/webresources.

Planning Cluster Security

When planning to secure clustered file servers, follow these guidelines:

- After you create a folder by using Windows Explorer, verify that the Cluster service account has the Read permission on the folder so that you can share the folder properly by using Cluster Administrator. (Do not share the folder by using Windows Explorer.)

- Use Cluster Administrator to set share permissions. If you change file share permissions using Windows Explorer or My Computer, instead of using **Permissions** on the **Parameters** tab in Cluster Administrator, the permissions are lost when the resource is taken offline.

 Note

When you set file share permissions by using Cluster Administrator, the default permissions give the Everyone group the Read permission. When you set file share permissions by using Cluster.exe, the Everyone group has the Full Control permission.

- To secure File Share resources on the local server, use Windows Explorer to assign NTFS permissions on the physical folder, because share permissions apply only when users connect to the clustered file server across the network.

- Do not assign NTFS permissions to local groups on clustered file servers. These permissions will have no meaning when the clustered disk resource is moved to another server. Therefore, always assign permissions to a domain local group.

- By default, access to cluster file shares is disabled to anonymous users. To allow anonymous access to specific file shares, you can either enable Kerberos V5 authentication on the Network Name resource that is associated with the file share or you can change the local security policy setting. For more information about configuring these Kerberos properties, see "Enable Kerberos authentication for virtual servers" in Help and Support Center for Windows Server 2003.

- When you create File Share resources by using the Share Subdirectories option, the subdirectories inherit the permissions of the parent. If you are using the subdirectories as user folders, and you want to allow only the user and administrator to access the folder, set NTFS permissions on each subfolder.

- To enable EFS on a clustered file server, you must perform some steps to configure the environment correctly. These steps are described in "To create a cluster-managed encrypted file share" in Help and Support Center for Windows Server 2003.

For more information about server cluster security, see "Best practices for securing server clusters" in Help and Support Center for Windows Server 2003.

Deploying File Servers

Deploying file servers involves installing Windows Server 2003 on the physical servers, adding the servers to the network, and then implementing the design decisions you made throughout this chapter. Organizations that plan to deploy clustered file servers must take the additional step of configuring the clusters; all other organizations can begin by choosing the installation method. Figure 2.19 describes the file server deployment process.

Figure 2.19   File Server Deployment Process

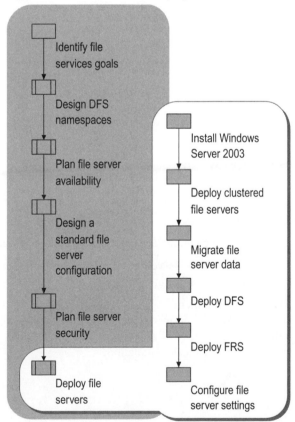

Installing Windows Server 2003

Before you install Windows Server 2003, you need to decide whether to perform clean installations or upgrades. You also need to decide if you want to perform an automated installation.

Choosing Between Clean Installations and Upgrades

If your servers are new and do not contain operating systems, you must perform clean installations. If you have existing servers, you can perform clean installations or upgrades. Consider the following points when choosing between a clean installation and an upgrade.

Choosing a new installation:

- If you reformat your hard disk and then perform a new installation, the efficiency of your disk might improve (compared to not reformatting it). Reformatting also gives you the opportunity to modify the size or number of disk partitions to make them match your requirements more closely.

- If you want to practice careful configuration management (for example, for a server where high availability is important), you might want to perform a new installation on that server instead of an upgrade. This is especially true on servers on which you have upgraded the operating system several times in the past.

Choosing an upgrade:

- With an upgrade, configuration is simpler, and you retain your existing users, settings, groups, rights, and permissions.

- With an upgrade, you do not need to reinstall files and applications. As with any major changes to the hard disk, however, it is recommended that you back up the disk before beginning an upgrade.

Preparing for a Clean Installation on Existing File Servers

Review the following issues before performing a clean installation on existing file servers:

- If you are performing a clean installation on a file server that contains a domain-based DFS root, remove the server as a DFS root before you begin the installation.

- If you are performing a clean installation on a member of an FRS replica set, use the Distributed File System snap-in (available in Windows Server 2003 or in the Windows Server 2003 Administration Tools Pack) to remove all inbound and outbound FRS connections to the server before beginning the clean installation.

Upgrading Existing File Servers

If you plan to upgrade file servers to Windows Server 2003, review the following issues:

- **Service pack requirements for servers running Windows NT 4.0.** Before you can upgrade a server that is running Windows NT 4.0 to Windows Server 2003, you must first install Windows NT 4.0 Service Pack 5 or a later version.

- **Upgrading servers that contain multidisk volumes.** If a server contains multidisk volumes, review the following issues:

  - If you are upgrading from Windows NT Server 4.0 to Windows Server 2003, verify that your backup software and hardware are compatible with both Windows NT Server 4.0 and Windows Server 2003. Next, back up and then delete all multidisk volumes (volume sets, mirror sets, stripe sets, and stripe sets with parity) before you upgrade, because Windows Server 2003 cannot access these volumes. Be sure to verify that your backup was successful before deleting the volumes. After you finish upgrading to Windows Server 2003, create new dynamic volumes, and then restore the data.

  - If you are upgrading from Windows NT Server 4.0 to Windows Server 2003, and the paging file resides on a multidisk volume, you must use System in Control Panel to move the paging file to a primary partition or logical drive before beginning Setup.

  - If you are upgrading from Windows 2000 Server to Windows Server 2003, you must use Disk Management to convert all basic disks that contain multidisk volumes to dynamic disks before beginning Setup. If you do not do this, Setup does not continue.

- **Upgrading servers that contain multiple DFS roots.** If you are running a prerelease version of Windows Server 2003, Standard Edition, and the server hosts multiple DFS roots, only one of those roots will be available after the upgrade. For more information about this and other DFS issues during upgrades, see "Deploying DFS" later in this chapter.

- **Upgrading servers that are part of FRS replica sets.** To keep the data in a replica set available during the upgrade, stagger the upgrades of replica members.

Choosing Automated Installations

Many large organizations use automated installations to install Windows Server 2003. Bulk installations are faster, easier, less expensive, more consistent, and more efficient than having users or IT professionals sit at servers and enter data manually. Windows Server 2003 provides the following tools and methods that you can use to design and deploy very simple or very sophisticated automated installations:

- Remote Installation Services (RIS)
- System Preparation Tool (Sysprep)
- Unattended Installation

These automated installation methods address a variety of specific issues, and each method has inherent advantages and disadvantages, depending on the environment in which you use these methods. To determine the best methods to use in the context of your specific environment, see "Choosing an Automated Installation Method" in *Automating and Customizing Installations* of this kit.

Deploying Clustered File Servers

The cluster installation method you choose depends on whether you have existing clustered file servers. If you do have existing clustered file servers, you have several options when upgrading server clusters:

- Perform a new installation of Windows Server 2003, Enterprise Edition or Windows Server 2003, Datacenter Edition, and configure the cluster at the same time.
- Upgrade a cluster that is running Windows NT Server 4.0, Enterprise Edition.
- Upgrade a cluster that is running Windows 2000, possibly through a rolling upgrade.

There are two major advantages to a rolling upgrade. First, there is minimal interruption of service to clients. (However, server response time might decrease during the phases in which fewer nodes handle the work of the entire cluster.) Second, you do not have to recreate your cluster configuration. The configuration remains intact during the upgrade process.

 Caution

Do not make DFS configuration changes (for example, adding new links, new link targets, and so on) while operating a mixed-version cluster, because all DFS changes are lost upon failover.

You cannot perform a rolling upgrade directly from Windows NT Server 4.0, Enterprise Edition to Windows Server 2003, Enterprise Edition or Windows Server 2003, Datacenter Edition. Instead you have two options:

- You can maintain cluster availability by performing an upgrade to Windows 2000 first (as specified in the Windows 2000 documentation), and then upgrade to Windows Server 2003, Enterprise Edition or Windows Server 2003, Datacenter Edition.

- You can perform a nonrolling upgrade directly from Windows NT 4.0 to Windows Server 2003, Enterprise Edition or Windows Server 2003, Datacenter Edition. Note that a nonrolling upgrade does not allow you to maintain cluster availability.

For comprehensive information on choosing the cluster installation method and performing the actual installation, see "Designing Server Clusters" in this book and see "Installing and upgrading on cluster nodes" in Help and Support Center for Windows Server 2003, Enterprise Edition or Windows Server 2003, Datacenter Edition.

Regardless of the installation type, evaluate your cluster hardware for compatibility with Windows Server 2003. For more information about choosing cluster hardware, see "Designing and Deploying Server Clusters" in this book.

After you have installed Windows Server 2003, Enterprise Edition or Windows Server 2003, Datacenter Edition and configured the server cluster, use the following sections for information about creating mounted drives and File Share resources on server clusters.

Creating Mounted Drives on Server Clusters

If you assign drive letters to the cluster storage devices, Windows Server 2003, Enterprise Edition, and Windows Server 2003, Datacenter Edition, limit the total number of such devices to 23. Mounted drives are not subject to this limit; you can use mounted drives to access more than 23 cluster storage devices in your server cluster.

When using NTFS mounted drives with server clusters, follow these recommendations:

- Make sure that you create unique mounted drives so that they do not conflict with existing local drives on any node in the cluster.

- Do not create mounted drives between disks on the cluster storage device (cluster disks) and local disks.

- Do not create mounted drives from the cluster disk that contains the quorum resource (the quorum disk). You can, however, create a mounted drive from the quorum disk to a clustered disk.

- Mounted drives from one cluster disk to another must be in the same cluster resource group, and they must be dependent on the root disk.

- Use Event Viewer to check the system log for any Cluster service errors or warnings indicating mount point failures. These errors are listed as ClusSvc in the **Source** column and as Physical Disk Resource in the **Category** column.

For more information about creating mounted drives, see "Create a mounted drive" in Help and Support Center for Windows Server 2003.

Creating File Share Resources

After you choose the cluster installation method and create the server cluster, migrate existing data on existing file servers, if necessary, and then create one or more File Share resources by using the Cluster Administrator snap-in or by creating scripts. For more information about creating a cluster-managed file share, see "Create a cluster-managed file share" in Help and Support Center for Windows Server 2003.

If you prefer to use scripts to create File Share resources, see article Q284838, "How to Create a Server Cluster File Share with Cluster.exe" in the Microsoft Knowledge Base. To find this article, see the Microsoft Knowledge Base link on the Web Resources page at http://www.microsoft.com/windows/reskits/webresources. For more information, see "Managing a server cluster from the command line" in Help and Support Center for Windows Server 2003.

After you create the File Share resources, you can enable shadow copies on cluster storage. For more information about enabling shadow copies on server clusters, see "Enable Shadow Copies of Shared Folders in a cluster" in Help and Support Center for Windows Server 2003.

Migrating File Server Data

If you plan to consolidate file servers or replace outdated servers with new servers, migrate existing applications and data to the new servers. To ensure the success of the migration, create a detailed and well-tested migration plan that does the following:

- Minimizes the amount of time that data is unavailable to users

- Minimizes the impact on network bandwidth

- Minimizes the cost of the migration

- Ensures that no data loss occurs during the migration

The following sections describe the tasks for creating a migration plan

Identifying Data to Migrate

Large organizations rarely have time to take all production data offline before migrating it. Instead, they typically move data gradually, migrating different classes of data in stages. A migration plan should identify which data to move, where to move it, and the order in which it should be moved. File server data can usually be classified in the following classes:

- Business-critical data

- Application data

- Personal data (such as home directories)

- Profiles or other configuration data

- Departmental or group data

- Other data types, such as special projects or temporary data

 Important

Be sure to review any legal or copyright issues that might arise when you migrate data. For example, if users are storing MP3 files on the file server, you might violate copyrights by copying those files. If you are copying applications, make sure that doing so does not violate any licensing agreements.

When creating your migration plan, determine whether you want to consolidate different classes of data at different rates, onto different hardware, onto servers with different SLAs, or to different locations. Also, consider the importance of the data when planning your migration. For example, to minimize the impact of any problems during the migration, you might choose to move nonessential data first, followed by business-critical data.

In addition to identifying which data to move, you can also identify data that you do not need to move, such as duplicate, obsolete, or non-business-related files. Eliminating these files from your migration plan decreases the number of files that you need to migrate and increases the amount of available storage on the target server after the migration.

Identifying Migration Risks

The next step is to assess the risks associated with data migration. The best way to identify these risks is to set up a test lab with clients and servers, similar to those in your production environment, and conduct trial migrations. In addition to testing your actual migration method, test any applications that are installed on client computers to determine if the applications are affected by the migration. For example, applications that depend on components stored on a particular file server might not work correctly if the file server or share is renamed after the migration is complete. If you identify problems, update your migration plan so that you prevent or mitigate those problems.

There are a number of solutions you can implement either before or during the migration to prevent problems from occurring. For example, you can ensure that shortcuts and links on client computers work correctly after the migration by doing one of the following:

- **Implementing DFS.** If you have implemented DFS before the migration, the migration is transparent to users; you just need to update the link target location.

- **Migrating to clustered file servers.** In this case, the migration is transparent if you create virtual servers that use the same name as the previously used file servers. You can also transparently migrate any stand-alone DFS namespaces to clustered file servers. Using the previous server names, create your virtual servers, and then migrate the namespaces by using Dfsutil.exe.

- **Using a third-party migration tool.** Use a tool that can identify and fix broken links, such as OLE links or application-related links in the registry.

No migration plan is complete until you develop and test "back-out" procedures to follow if the migration fails at any stage in the process. Verify that you can restore data to its previous state and location in the event that you need to roll back the migration.

The following sections describe additional risks to consider during the migration.

NTFS permissions

When evaluating migration methods, determine whether the methods support migrating NTFS permissions. If you use domain local groups to assign permissions to files and folders, members of those groups will have the same access to the files and folders after they are moved to the new server. However, if you assign permissions to computer local groups, members of those groups cannot access the files after the migration. Either reconfigure permissions to use domain local groups before the migration, or plan to create new computer local groups on the target server and give those groups the appropriate permissions to the files after the migration is complete.

NTFS compression

If you use compression on the source servers, determine if you still require compression on the target server. Hardware on the target server is typically more powerful, with greater storage capacity. Therefore, compression might not be necessary, although you do need to account for the additional space required by the uncompressed data. Also, when you copy compressed files from one server to another, the compression attribute is lost unless you enable compression on the target volume.

Files encrypted by using EFS

Migrating encrypted files has a number of risks. Only administrators who are EFS recovery agents can copy or move files that are encrypted by other users. When these administrators copy or move encrypted files to a remote shared folder, the files are decrypted locally, transmitted in plaintext, and then re-encrypted on the target server only if the remote computer is trusted for delegation and the target volume uses NTFS. When the files are encrypted again on the target server, they have new file encryption keys that are encrypted by using the administrator's public key, if it is available, or by using a new public key, which EFS generates if the profile is unavailable. As a result, the users who originally encrypt the files are no longer able to access them. Therefore, do not copy or move encrypted files from one server to another; use a backup and restore method instead.

 Important

When EFS recovery agents copy encrypted files to a target server that is not trusted for delegation, or to a target volume that uses FAT, the files become plaintext on the target server.

For more information about EFS recovery agents, see "Designing a Public Key Infrastructure" in *Designing and Deploying Directory and Security Services* of this kit.

Choosing a Migration Method

Because many migration methods require downtime to move data, migrating data can be challenging in the following situations:

- The data has high uptime requirements as specified by SLAs in your organization, and the migration method might require more downtime than the SLA allows.

- Users expect to be able to access that data throughout their workday or at all times.

When planning your migration, consider the advantages and disadvantages of each migration method that is available to you, such as those described in the following sections. Your organization might use other methods not described here.

Backup and restore data

This method involves making a backup of the source server and restoring the data on a target server. Depending on your backup method and hardware, this method might involve moving tapes from one backup device to another (for direct-attached backup hardware) or restoring data from a tape library.

Advantages:

- Large organizations routinely back up and restore data, so you can use existing backups to begin the migration.

- Backing up and restoring data does not impact network bandwidth when it is performed on the local servers.

- You can use this method to migrate encrypted files.

Disadvantages:

- Both the source server and the target server must support the backup device and its related software.

- If users are accessing files during the backup, you must make arrangements to migrate files that change while the backup occurs.

- Backup programs do not migrate shared folder information to the destination server. As a result, folders that are shared on the source server are not shared when you restore them on the destination server. You must share the destination folders manually or by using scripts, and then use Permcopy.exe, which is available on the *Windows Server 2003 Deployment Kit* companion CD, to migrate any share permissions. For more information about Permcopy.exe, click **Tools** in Help and Support Center for Windows Server 2003, and then click Windows Resource Kit Tools.

Use third-party migration tools, hardware, or services provided by hardware vendors

A number of third-party migration tools can automate the entire migration process. These migration tools typically offer features such as bandwidth throttling, scheduling, incremental file migration, and monitoring. Many hardware vendors also provide hardware solutions and services that can assist you in migrating data.

Copy the data

This method involves using Robocopy.exe to copy data from one server to another and then using Permcopy.exe to migrate share permissions. Use the **/SEC** parameter in Robocopy.exe to copy NTFS permissions from the source folder to the destination folder. After you finish moving the data, share the folders on the target server (either manually or by using scripts), and then use Permcopy.exe to copy share permissions from the source server to the target server.

Permcopy.exe and Robocopy.exe are available on the *Windows Server 2003 Deployment Kit* companion CD. For more information about Permcopy.exe and Robocopy.exe, click **Tools** in Help and Support Center for Windows Server 2003, and then click Windows Resource Kit Tools.

Advantages:

- These tools are available as part of the *Windows Server 2003 Deployment Kit.*

- This method is simple if you are migrating a small amount of data.

- Robocopy.exe gives you a number of options for migrating data, including the following:

    - Using file names, wildcard characters, paths, or file attributes to include or exclude source files as candidates for migrating.

    - Controlling the number of times that Robocopy.exe retries an operation after encountering a recoverable network error.

    - Scheduling copy jobs to run automatically.

Disadvantages:

- Files are copied across the network, which can impact network bandwidth.

- This method should not be used to migrate encrypted files.

- If users are accessing files as the files are copied, you must make arrangements to migrate files that change while the copy occurs.

- This method might take a long time to complete if you are migrating large amounts of data.

- This method does not migrate shared folder information to the destination server. As a result, folders that are shared on the source server are not shared when you copy or restore them on the destination server. You must share the destination folders manually or by using scripts, and then use Permcopy.exe to migrate any share permissions.

Completing the Migration

After you migrate data, verify that users can access the data on the new servers by completing the following tasks:

- Verify that NTFS and share permissions are migrated correctly.

- If a logon script maps drives to the old file servers, update the scripts so that they point to the new file servers.

- If the migrated folders are DFS link targets, update the link information so that it points to the new file server.

- If the migrated folders are redirected My Documents folders, use Group Policy to specify the new file server.

- If you migrate data to a clustered file server, create the necessary File Share resources.

Deploying DFS

Before you upgrade a server containing a DFS root, ensure that the namespace will be available after the upgrade. After Windows Server 2003 is installed, either through a clean installation or upgrade, you can create new DFS namespaces or migrate existing DFS namespaces to servers running Windows Server 2003. If you create a new namespace, you can use the information provided by the design team in the "DFS Configuration Worksheet" (Sdcfsv_1.xls).

Upgrading Servers That Contain DFS Namespaces

If a file server contains existing DFS roots, they are converted as follows:

- When you upgrade a server running Windows NT 4.0 to Windows Server 2003, any DFS roots are converted to Windows Server 2003 stand-alone DFS roots.

- When you upgrade a server running Windows 2000 to Windows Server 2003, stand-alone DFS roots and domain-based DFS roots are converted to Windows Server 2003 stand-alone DFS roots and domain-based DFS roots, respectively.

In the following scenarios, DFS roots are not available after upgrade:

- If you upgrade a server that hosts a root on a FAT volume, the namespace is unavailable until you convert the volume to NTFS.

- If you are running a prerelease version of Windows Server 2003, Standard Edition, and that server hosts multiple DFS roots, only one of those roots will be available after the upgrade. The other roots are unavailable because servers running Windows Server 2003, Standard Edition support only one root per server. To work around this issue, you can do either of the following:

  - Before upgrading to Windows Server 2003, Standard Edition, use Dfsutil.exe to export all but one of the namespaces to text files, and then remove the roots for the namespaces you exported. After you complete the upgrades, use Dfsutil.exe to import each namespace to a separate server running Windows Server 2003, Standard Edition.

  - Upgrade to Windows Server 2003, Enterprise Edition or Windows Server 2003, Datacenter Edition, which both support multiple roots per server.

If you do not remove the additional roots before upgrading to Windows Server 2003, Standard Server, take the following steps to remove the extra roots from the server by using Dfsutil.exe:

▷ To remove domain-based DFS roots

If the domain-based DFS root has multiple root targets, you must repeat this procedure for every root target. The DFS service will be briefly unavailable when the service is stopped and restarted, so perform this procedure during a period of low namespace usage.

1. Use the /UnmapFtRoot parameter in Dfsutil.exe to remove the extra roots from the server.

2. Use the /Clean parameter in Dfsutil.exe to remove the root-related registry entries from the server.

3. At the command prompt, type **net stop dfs & net start dfs**

▷ To remove stand-alone DFS roots

- Use the /Clean parameter in Dfsutil.exe to remove the root-related registry entries from the server.

Delegating the Administration of DFS Namespaces

Use the procedures below to allow members of the local Administrators group on each root server to create and manage domain-based DFS namespaces. For more information about delegating permission to manage a DFS namespace, see "Designing a DFS Namespace" earlier in this chapter.

The following procedure grants the selected user the ability to create new DFS namespaces as well as administer existing ones.

▷ **To delegate a user to administer DFS**

1. In the Active Directory Users and Computers snap-in, on the **View** menu, click **Advanced Features**.

2. In the console tree, double-click the **System** folder to expand it.

3. Click the **DFS-Configuration** folder.

   Any existing root objects appear in the details pane.

4. Right-click **DFS-Configuration**, and then click **Properties**.

5. On the **Security** tab, click **Add**.

6. Type the name of the user to whom you want to delegate administrative rights, and then click **OK**.

7. Select the user Full Control permission, and then click **OK**.

Use the following procedure to allow a user to have DFS administrative permissions only within a single DFS namespace.

▷ **To grant a user permission to administer only a single DFS namespace**

1. In the Active Directory Users and Computers snap-in, on the **View** menu, click **Advanced Features**.

2. In the console tree, double-click the **System** folder to expand it.

3. Click the **DFS-Configuration** folder.

   Any existing root objects appear in the details pane.

4. Right-click the root object that you want to allow the user to administer, and then click **Properties**.

5. On the **Security** tab, click **Add**.

6. Type the name of the user, and then click **OK**.

7. Verify that the user is granted the Full Control permission, and then click **OK**.

Creating New DFS Namespaces on Stand-Alone Servers

Use the Distributed File System snap-in or the command-line tools Dfscmd.exe and Dfsutil.exe to create the root and link targets on stand-alone (nonclustered) file servers. The following topics in Help and Support Center for Windows Server 2003 provide information on using these tools:

- "Checklist: Creating a distributed file system"
- "Dfscmd"

For more information about installing Dfsutil.exe, click **Tools** in Help and Support Center for Windows Server 2003, and then click Windows Support Tools.

If you plan to enable FRS on link targets in the DFS namespace, see "Deploying FRS" later in this chapter.

Creating New DFS Namespaces on Clustered Servers

Use the Cluster Administrator snap-in to create a stand-alone DFS namespace on a clustered file server. For more information about creating a DFS root on server clusters, see "Create a cluster-managed file share" in Help and Support for Windows Server 2003.

Migrating or Consolidating Existing Namespaces on New Servers

If you have namespaces on existing file servers that you want to consolidate onto a file server that is running Windows Server 2003, Enterprise Edition or Windows Server 2003, Datacenter Edition, or if you want to move a namespace from one server to another, you can use the Dfsutil.exe support tool to export the namespace from the source server to the destination server.

In the following example, an administrator wants to migrate the following namespaces on different servers to a single server running Windows Server 2003, Enterprise Edition.

- \\NT4SVR\Marketing (a stand-alone DFS root on a server running Windows NT Server 4.0)

- \\W2KSVR\Public (a stand-alone DFS root on a server running Windows 2000 Server)

First, the administrator creates the following stand-alone DFS roots on the server running Windows Server 2003, Enterprise Edition:

- \\NETSVR\Marketing

- \\NETSVR\Public

Next, the administrator installs Windows Support Tools from the Windows Server 2003 operating system CD and then uses the Dfsutil.exe tool to run the following commands:

```
Dfsutil /Root:\\NT4SVR\Marketing /export:Nt4.txt
```

```
Dfsutil /Root:\\W2KSVR\Public /export:w2k.txt
```

Finally, the administrator runs the following commands to import the namespaces onto the server running Windows Server 2003, Enterprise Edition:

```
Dfsutil /Root:\\NETSVR\Marketing /import:Nt4.txt /set
```

```
Dfsutil /Root:\\NETSVR\Public /import:w2k.txt /set
```

Using Dfsutil.exe to Customize the Namespace

Use the Dfsutil.exe parameters listed in Table 2.22 to customize the namespace. For more information about using Dfsutil.exe, in Help and Support Center for Windows Server 2003, click **Tools**, and then click Windows Support Tools.

Table 2.22   Dfsutil.exe Parameters Used to Customize the Namespace

Customization	Dfsutil.exe Parameter
Enable root scalability mode	/RootScalability
Add site information to root servers running Windows 2000 Server	/UpdateWin2kStaticSiteTable
Remove site information from root servers running Windows 2000 Server	/PurgeWin2kStaticSiteTable
Enable restricted same-site target selection	/InSite
Enable closest or least expensive target selection	/SiteCosting

Deploying FRS

After you have deployed a domain-based DFS namespace, you are ready to deploy FRS. This section describes the following FRS deployment scenarios:

- Deploying a new replica set

- Adding a new replica member to an existing replica set

This section also provides an overview of the tasks required to deploy each scenario. For detailed procedures for each scenario, see the worksheets specified in the relevant sections. The worksheets also provide information about using Sonar.exe to monitor the status of your FRS deployment. Sonar.exe is available on *Windows Server 2003 Deployment Kit* companion CD. For more information about Sonar.exe, click **Tools** in Help and Support Center for Windows Server 2003, and then click Windows Resource Kit Tools.

Deploying a New Replica Set

If you are deploying a new replica set, use the "FRS Configuration Worksheet" (Sdcfsv_2.xls) that was completed by the file services design team to begin the deployment. If the design team did not use this job aid, you will need the following information:

- The names of the link targets to be replicated. These link targets form the replica set.

- The FRS topology (ring, full mesh, hub and spoke, or custom) to use for each replica set. If the topology is custom, you also need the inbound and outbound connections for each replica member.

- The FRS replication schedule for each connection.

- The location and size of the staging directory.

- The connection priorities for each inbound connection.

Use the following information to choose the appropriate FRS deployment scenario:

- See "Deploying an Empty Replica Set" later in this section if you have two or more existing link targets on which you want to enable replication and the link targets do not contain data.

- See "Deploying a Replica Set with Existing Content" later in this section if you have two or more existing link targets that contain data and the link targets are currently in use in your organization.

- See "Adding a New Member to an Existing Replica Set" later in this chapter if you have an existing replica set and you want to add a new member.

Deploying an Empty Replica Set

This scenario requires that you have deployed your domain-based DFS namespace but you do not have any files and folders in the link targets that you plan to replicate. This scenario is the most efficient way to deploy FRS, because replica members perform their join operation on an empty tree. When you add files to the tree, FRS builds a single staging file for each file in the tree and uses those files to source all direct outbound partners.

 Important

When you deploy a new replica set using these scenarios, it is recommended that you deploy two replica members connected by high-bandwidth links and then prestage additional members, especially if they are located in remote sites with slow-bandwidth connections. For more information about adding members to a replica set, see "Adding a New Member to an Existing Replica Set" later in this chapter.

Before you begin, choose a procedure for either a standard topology (ring, hub and spoke, or full mesh) or a custom topology.

▷ **Deploying a standard FRS topology**

To deploy a ring, hub and spoke, or full mesh topology, perform the following tasks:

1. Disable referrals to the link targets to be replicated.

2. Configure the USN journal.

3. Configure replication for a standard topology, and choose the staging directory location.

4. Adjust the size of the staging directory.

5. Verify that replication is working.

6. Set the initial replication schedule.

7. Configure filters to exclude files or folders from replication (optional).

8. Copy the data into the replica tree, and verify that the data is consistent.

9. Optimize the replication schedule (optional).

10. Enable referrals to the replicated link targets.

11. Configure connection priorities (optional).

For a Word document that provides detailed instructions on completing each of these tasks, "Deploying a Standard FRS Topology for an Empty Replica Set" (Sdcfsv_3.doc) on the *Windows Server 2003 Deployment Kit* companion CD (or see "Deploying a Standard FRS Topology for an Empty Replica Set" on the Web at http://www.microsoft.com/reskit). After you complete these tasks, you can notify users that the DFS namespace is available.

▶ **Deploying a custom FRS topology**

To deploy a custom FRS topology, perform the following tasks:

1. Disable referrals to the link targets to be replicated.

2. Configure the USN journal.

3. Configure replication for a custom topology, choose the staging directory location, and configure connection priorities.

4. Adjust the size of the staging directory.

5. Verify that replication is working.

6. Set the initial replication schedule (optional).

7. Configure filters to exclude files or folders from replication (optional).

8. Copy the data into the replica tree, and verify that the data is consistent.

9. Enable referrals to the replicated link targets.

10. Optimize the replication schedule (optional).

For a Word document that provides detailed instructions on completing each of these tasks, see "Deploying a Custom FRS Topology for an Empty Replica Set" (Sdcfsv_4.doc) on the *Windows Server 2003 Deployment Kit* companion CD (or see "Deploying a Custom FRS Topology for an Empty Replica Set" on the Web at http://www.microsoft.com/reskit). After you complete these tasks, you can notify users that the DFS namespace is available.

Deploying a Replica Set with Existing Content

In this scenario, you have deployed a DFS namespace with existing content in one or more link targets, but you are not using FRS to keep those link targets synchronized. Users know about and use the namespace, and they might be accessing files from the link targets. This scenario is more complex than deploying FRS in an empty directory tree for a number of reasons:

- Users or applications might have locks on files or folders, which can prevent FRS from originating outgoing changes and receiving incoming changes.

- If files exist on the initial master, FRS builds a unique staging file for each file in the tree for each direct outbound partner. In other words, each partner gets its own set of files, which is more disk I/O and disk space intensive.

- The files in the replica tree of the initial master become authoritative, which means that after replication completes, the replica tree on each member is identical to the replica tree on the initial master. For servers that are not the initial master, FRS moves any files that existed in the replica tree to a folder named "NtFrs_PreExisting___See EventLog."

For these reasons, it is recommended that you create a new link and link targets (essentially setting up an empty replica set), configure replication as desired, and copy the existing data into the new replica tree. After replication is complete, change the name of the link that is associated with the replica set so that users can access the new replica set by using the existing link name.

 Important

This procedure requires enough disk space on each replica member to store two copies of the files — one copy is the existing data, and the second copy is the data in the newly created replica tree.

In the following procedures, "existing link" refers to the link that already contains data in its link targets, and "new link" is the link that you create with replicated link targets.

▶ **To create a new link and link targets**

1. If users can modify files in the link targets, disable referrals to the link targets for the existing link, and then close all open files.

2. Create a new link, and then follow the procedure in one of the following documents to set up an empty replica set:

   ▪ "Deploying a Standard FRS Topology for an Empty Replica Set" (Sdcfsv_3.doc) on the *Windows Server 2003 Deployment Kit* companion CD (or see "Deploying a Standard FRS Topology for an Empty Replica Set" on the Web at http://www.microsoft.com/reskit).

   ▪ "Deploying a Custom FRS Topology for an Empty Replica Set" (Sdcfsv_4.doc) on the *Windows Server 2003 Deployment Kit* companion CD (or see "Deploying a Custom FRS Topology for an Empty Replica Set" on the Web at http://www.microsoft.com/reskit).

   Be sure to disable referrals to the new link targets so that users do not access them.

3. Copy the data to be replicated into the replica tree.

   This step is complete when the files are replicated successfully to all replica members.

4. In the Distributed File System snap-in, under the existing link, add the same link targets that you added under the new link. Be sure to clear the **Add this target to the replication set** check box.

5. If you have not done so already, disable referrals, and then close all open files so that users are no longer accessing any files in the existing link targets.

6. Under the existing link, remove the link targets that are not replicated. After you complete this step, the existing link and the new link have identical link targets.

Figure 2.20 shows how two example links, Existing Link and New Link, appear in the Distributed File System snap-in at the end of this procedure.

Figure 2.20   Two Links in the Distributed File System Snap-in

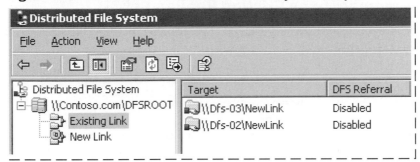

Next, use the following procedure to change the link name that is associated with the new replica set to match the existing link name.

▶ **To match the new link name with the existing link name**

1. In the Active Directory Users and Computers snap-in, click the **View** menu, and then click **Advanced Features**.

2. In the console tree, under the domain where the DFS root is located, navigate to **System**, **File Replication Service**, **DFS Volumes**.

    When you expand **DFS Volumes**, you should see existing DFS replica sets, including the one that you created in the previous procedure. The replica set is identified as **rootname|newlinkname**. Identify the correct replica set before you continue.

3. To change the name of the link that is associated with the replica set, right-click the replica set, and then click **Rename**.

4. After **rootname|**, type the name of the existing link over the name of the new link.

Figure 2.21 shows how the **rootname|newlink** name appears at Step 2 and after Step 4.

Figure 2.21   Changing the Link Name

To complete the deployment, delete the new link.

▶ **To delete the new link**

1. In the Distributed File System snap-in, locate the new link.

    The new link should no longer have replication enabled. It might be necessary to close and reopen the snap-in for the updates to appear.

2. Right-click the new link, and then click **Delete Link**.

3. Enable referrals to the link targets for the existing link.

Adding a New Member to an Existing Replica Set

Before you add a new member to an existing replica set, determine how to source the new member. You have two choices:

- **Replicate the files to the new member across the network.** When you replicate files across the network to the new member, you add the server as a link target within an existing replica set. When you add the new member to the topology, you can create a single inbound connection so that you source from a specific server, such as a server with fast connectivity, or you can add a computer with redundant inbound connections where it sources according to connection priority and schedule.

- **Prestage the files on the new member.** When you prestage files, you use a backup program to back up the replica tree and restore it on the new member. Using a backup program is required to preserve the file object IDs and security descriptors. (Command-line tools such as Copy.exe, Xcopy.exe, and Robocopy.exe do not preserve these items, and they cannot be used to prestage files.) After you restore the files, FRS replicates to the new member any files that changed since the backup was created, thus minimizing the number of files that are replicated across the network.

The method you choose typically depends on the size of the replica set and the available network bandwidth. You should replicate files over the network only if one of the following conditions exists:

- You have a high-bandwidth network, and you can afford to use part of that bandwidth for the initial replication.

- You have a low-bandwidth network, and you can afford to use that bandwidth for initial replication, and you also have the time to wait for the initial replication to complete.

If neither of these conditions exists, you should prestage the new member.

The following sections describe three possible scenarios for adding a new replica member:

- Prestaging a new replica member to avoid replicating files across the network.

- Adding a new replica member that contains no content. In this scenario, files are replicated across the network.

- Adding a new replica member that contains a copy of the content. In this scenario, the new member has an existing copy of the files, but these files are not prestaged. The files from the initial master are replicated across the network.

Prestaging a New Replica Member

In this scenario, you have an existing replica set, and you want to add a new replica member by prestaging it. After you prestage the new member and enable replication, FRS moves the prestaged files in the replica tree on the new member to the NtFrs_PreExisting____See_EventLog folder, but FRS then moves back to the replica tree any files that have the same object ID and content as the files in the master replica set. FRS replicates across the network only the files that were added or changed since you prestaged the files.

Before you can prestage a new replica member, one of the following events must occur:

- At least seven days have passed since you enabled replication between the first two members.

- You clear the outbound change log by modifying the registry on all direct upstream partners.

To prestage a new replica member, perform the following tasks:

1. Configure the USN journal.

2. Prestage the new replica member.

3. Create a new link target, add it to the replica set, and then specify the staging directory location.

4. Disable referrals to the new link target.

5. Configure connection objects, the initial schedule, and connection priorities (custom topologies only).

6. Adjust the size of the staging directory.

7. Verify that replication is working on the new member.

8. Enable referrals to the link target.

9. Optimize the replication schedule.

10. Configure connection priorities (standard topologies only).

For a Word document to assist you in completing each of these tasks, see "Prestaging a New Replica Member" (Sdcfsv_5.doc) on the *Windows Server 2003 Deployment Kit* companion CD (or see "Pre-staging a New Replica Member" on the Web at http://www.microsoft.com/reskit). After you complete these tasks, you can notify users that the DFS namespace is available.

Adding a New Replica Member That Contains No Content

In this scenario, the new replica member does not contain a copy of the replica tree. Data will replicate across the network according to the replication schedule.

To add a new replica member that contains no content, perform the following tasks:

1. Configure the USN journal.

2. Create a new link target, add it to the replica set, and then specify the staging directory location.

3. Disable referrals to the new link target.

4. Configure connection objects, the initial schedule, and connection priorities (custom topologies only).

5. Adjust the size of the staging directory.

6. Verify that replication is working on the new member.

7. Enable referrals to the link target.

8. Optimize the replication schedule (optional).

9. Configure connection priorities (standard topologies only).

For a Word document to assist you in completing each of these tasks, see "Adding a New Replica Member that Contains No Content" (Sdcfsv_6.doc) on the *Windows Server 2003 Deployment Kit* companion CD (or see "Adding a New Replica Member that Contains No Content" on the Web at http://www.microsoft.com/reskit). After you complete these tasks, you can notify users that the DFS namespace is available.

Adding a New Replica Member That Contains a Copy of the Content

In this scenario, the new replica member already contains a copy of the replica tree. You might have copied the data to the server manually (using Robocopy, for example), but you have not prestaged the new member. (Remember that prestaging preserves the file object IDs and security descriptors.) Because the data is not prestaged, the initial master replicates the entire replica tree to the new member, even if the new member already contains identical files. On the new replica member, FRS moves any files that existed in the replica tree to a folder named "NtFrs_PreExisting____See_EventLog." After replication completes, you can either delete this folder or move any unique files back into the replica tree.

To add a new replica member that contains a copy of the content, perform the following tasks:

1. Follow the procedures in "Adding a New Replica Member that Contains No Content" (Sdcfsv_6.doc) on the *Windows Server 2003 Deployment Kit* companion CD (or see "Adding a New Replica Member that Contains No Content" on the Web at http://www.microsoft.com/reskit).

2. After replication completes, locate the folder "NtFrs_PreExisting___See_EventLog" on the new replica member.

3. Do one of the following:

   ▪ If the folder contains unique files that are not part of the replica set, copy those files back into the replica tree.

   ▪ If you do not want to save any of the files, delete the folder.

Configuring File Server Settings

Many procedures for configuring file server settings are provided in Help and Support Center for Windows Server 2003. Table 2.23 lists subjects and file server topics that can be useful for configuring file server settings. For best results in identifying Help topics by title, in Help and Support Center, under the **Search** box, click **Set search options**. Under **Help Topics**, select the **Search in title only** checkbox.

Table 2.23   Help and Support Center Topics Related to File Server Settings

Subject	Topic Title
Sharing folders	"Share a drive or folder on the network"
Enabling disk quotas	"Checklist: Setting up disk quotas"
Enabling shadow copies	"Checklist: Deploying shadow copies of shared folders"
Setting NTFS permissions	"Set, view, change, or remove permissions on files and folders"
Enabling encryption on file servers	"Enable a remote server for file encryption"
Remotely managing file servers	"Using Web Interface for Remote Administration"
Managing disks and volumes	"Disk Management overview" and "DiskPart"
Enabling encryption on clustered file servers	"Create a cluster-managed encrypted file share"
Enabling client-side caching on clustered file servers	"Set client-side caching for a File Share resource"
Enabling shadow copies on cluster storage	"Enable Shadow Copies of Shared Folders in a cluster"

Additional Resources

Related Information

- "Hosting Applications with Terminal Server" in this book.

- "Planning for High Availability and Scalability" in this book.

- "Designing and Deploying Server Clusters" in this book.

- "Deploying a Managed Software Environment" in *Designing a Managed Environment* of this kit.

- "Implementing User State Management" in *Designing a Managed Environment* of this kit.

- The *Distributed Services Guide* of the *Windows Server 2003 Resource Kit* (or see the *Distributed Services Guide* on the Web at http://www.microsoft.com/reskit) for more information about the Distributed File System and the File Replication service.

- The *Server Management Guide* of the *Windows Server 2003 Resource Kit* (or see the *Server Management Guide* on the Web at http://www.microsoft.com/reskit) for more information about disk management and file systems.

- The *Internetworking Guide* in the *Windows Server 2003 Resource Kit* (or see the *Internetworking Guide* on the Web at http://www.microsoft.com/reskit) for information about interoperability with NetWare and interoperability with UNIX.

- "Deployment, Monitoring and Troubleshooting of the Windows 2000 File Replication Service Using the SONAR, TOPCHK, CONSTAT and IOLOGSUM Tools" (Troubleshooting_frs.doc), included with the version of Sonar.exe that is available from the Free Tool Downloads link on the Web Resources page at http://www.microsoft.com/windows/reskits/webresources.

- The File Services Community Center link on the Web Resources page at http://www.microsoft.com/windows/reskits/webresources for information about how Windows server technologies deliver reliable file services that are essential to enterprise computing infrastructures.

- The Windows Powered Network Attached Storage link on the Web Resources page at http://www.microsoft.com/windows/reskits/webresources.

- The Storage Services link on the Web Resources page at http://www.microsoft.com/windows/reskits/webresources.

- The File Services link on the Web Resources page at http://www.microsoft.com/windows/reskits/webresources.

- The Microsoft® SharePoint™ Products and Technologies link on the Web Resources pageat http://www.microsoft.com/windows/reskits/webresources for information about sharing information within organizations and over the Internet.

Related Job Aids

- "DFS Configuration Worksheet" (Sdcfsv_1.xls) on the *Windows Server 2003 Deployment Kit* companion CD (or see "DFS Configuration Worksheet" on the Web at http://www.microsoft.com/reskit).

- "FRS Configuration Worksheet" (Sdcfsv_2.xls) on the *Windows Server 2003 Deployment Kit* companion CD (or see "FRS Configuration Worksheet" on the Web at http://www.microsoft.com/reskit).

- "Deploying a Standard FRS Topology for an Empty Replica Set" (Sdcfsv_3.doc) on the *Windows Server 2003 Deployment Kit* companion CD (or see "Deploying a Standard FRS Topology for an Empty Replica Set" on the Web at http://www.microsoft.com/reskit).

- "Deploying a Custom FRS Topology for an Empty Replica Set" (Sdcfsv_4.doc) on the *Windows Server 2003 Deployment Kit* companion CD (or see "Deploying a Custom FRS Topology for an Empty Replica Set" on the Web at http://www.microsoft.com/reskit).

- "Prestaging a New Replica Member" (Sdcfsv_5.doc) on the *Windows Server 2003 Deployment Kit* companion CD (or see "Prestaging a New Replica Member" on the Wcb at http://www.microsoft.com/reskit).

- "Adding a New Replica Member That Contains No Content" (Sdcfsv_6.doc) on the *Windows Server 2003 Deployment Kit* companion CD (or see "Adding a New Replica Member That Contains No Content" on the Web at http://www.microsoft.com/reskit).

- "Shadow Copy and Disk Quota Configuration Worksheet" (Sdcfsv_7.xls) on the *Windows Server 2003 Deployment Kit* companion CD (or see "DFS Configuration Worksheet" on the Web at http://www.microsoft.com/reskit).

Related Help Topics

For best results in identifying Help topics by title, in Help and Support Center, under the **Search** box, click **Set search options**. Under **Help Topics**, select the **Search in title only** checkbox.

- "Disk Management overview" and "DiskPart" in Help and Support Center for Windows Server 2003 for information about managing disks and volumes.

- "Extend a basic volume" in Help and Support Center for Windows Server 2003.

- "Using NTFS mounted drives" and "Create a mounted drive" in Help and Support Center for Windows Server 2003.

- "Shadow Copies of Shared Folders" in Help and Support Center for Windows Server 2003.

- "Vssadmin" and "Schtasks" in Help and Support Center for Windows Server 2003 for information about scheduling shadow copies from the command line.

- "Checklist: Setting up disk quotas" in Help and Support Center for Windows Server 2003.

- "Share a drive or folder on the network" in Help and Support Center for Windows Server 2003.

- "Publish a Shared Folder" in Help and Support Center for Windows Server 2003 for information about publishing shared folders in Active Directory.

- "Offline Files overview," "Offline settings for shared resources," and "Make a file or folder available offline" in Help and Support Center for Windows Server 2003.

- "Permissions on a file server" in Help and Support Center for Windows Server 2003.

- "Set, view, change, or remove permissions on files and folders" in Help and Support Center for Windows Server 2003.

- "Enable a remote server for file encryption" in Help and Support Center for Windows Server 2003.

- "Encrypting and decrypting data" and "Internet Information Services (IIS) 6.0 overview" in Help and Support Center for Windows Server 2003 for information about EFS and using WebDAV folders to store encrypted files.

- "Install Windows Support Tools" in Help and Support Center for Windows Server 2003 for information about installing Windows Support Tools, including Dfsutil.exe.

- "Using Web Interface for Remote Administration" in Help and Support Center for Windows Server 2003.

- "Chkdsk" in Help and Support Center for Windows Server 2003 for information about running Chkdsk.exe.

- "Checklist: Creating a distributed file system" and "Dfscmd" in Help and Support Center for Windows Server 2003 for information about creating a DFS namespace.

- "Installing and upgrading on cluster nodes" in Help and Support Center for Windows Server 2003, Enterprise Edition or Windows Server 2003, Datacenter Edition for comprehensive information about choosing the cluster installation method and performing the actual installation.

- "Managing a server cluster from the command line" in Help and Support Center for Windows Server 2003.

- "Create a cluster-managed file share" in Help and Support for Windows Server 2003.

- "Create a cluster-managed encrypted file share" in Help and Support Center for Windows Server 2003 for information about enabling EFS on server clusters.

- "Set client-side caching for a File Share resource" in Help and Support Center for Windows Server 2003 for information about configuring client-side caching on a server cluster.

- "Using Shadow Copies of Shared Folders in a server cluster" and "Enable Shadow Copies of Shared Folders in a cluster" in Help and Support Center for Windows Server 2003 for in-depth information about using shadow copies on server clusters.

- "Change the Cluster service account password" in Help and Support Center for Windows Server 2003.

- "Enable Kerberos authentication for virtual servers" in Help and Support Center for Windows Server 2003 for information about allowing anonymous access to specific file shares on a server cluster.

- "Backing up and restoring server clusters" and "Test cluster failures and failover policies" in Help and Support Center for Windows Server 2003.

- "Best practices for securing server clusters" in Help and Support Center for Windows Server 2003.

Related Tools

- Dfscmd.exe

  Use Dfscmd.exe to create links and add link targets. For more information about Dfscmd.exe, in Help and Support Center for Windows Server 2003 click **Tools**, and then click Command-line reference **A-Z**.

- Dfsutil.exe

  Use Dfsutil.exe to configure and troubleshoot DFS namespaces. For more information about Dfsutil.exe, in Help and Support Center for Windows Server 2003 click **Tools**, and then click Windows Support Tools.

- DiskPart.exe

  Use DiskPart.exe to manage disks and volumes from the command line. For more information about DiskPart.exe, in Help and Support Center for Windows Server 2003 click **Tools**, and then click Command-line reference **A-Z**.

- Permcopy.exe

  Use Permcopy.exe to copy shared folder permissions from one shared folder to another. For more information about Permcopy.exe, click **Tools** in Help and Support Center for Windows Server 2003, and then click Windows Resource Kit Tools.

- Robocopy.exe

  Use Robocopy.exe to maintain identical copies of a folder tree in multiple locations. For more information about Robocopy.exe, click **Tools** in Help and Support Center for Windows Server 2003, and then click Windows Resource Kit Tools.

- Sonar.exe

  Use Sonar.exe to monitor key statistics about FRS members in a replica set. For more information about Sonar.exe, click **Tools** in Help and Support Center for Windows Server 2003, and then click Windows Resource Kit Tools.

- Windows Server 2003 Administration Tools Pack

Use the Windows Server 2003 Administration Tools Pack to remotely manage servers running Windows Server 2003 from computers running Windows XP. For more information about installing this tools pack, see article Q304718, "Administer Windows 2000–Based Computers Using Windows XP Professional Clients," in the Microsoft Knowledge Base. To find this article, see the Microsoft Knowledge Base link on the Web Resources page at http://www.microsoft.com/windows/reskits/webresources.

CHAPTER 3

Designing and Deploying Print Servers

Adding or upgrading print servers, consolidating servers, or creating print server clusters can increase the reliability, availability, and manageability of your printing environment. Network and print administrators in medium-to-large organizations can deploy and manage print servers more efficiently by properly planning and deploying a network printing solution.

In This Chapter

Related Information

- For conceptual information about network printing and Windows clustering, see the *Server Management Guide* of the *Microsoft® Windows® Server 2003 Resource Kit* (or see the *Server Management Guide* on the Web at http://www.microsoft.com/reskit).

- For more information about deploying Windows server clusters, see "Designing and Deploying Server Clusters" in this book.

- For information about deploying file servers, see "Designing and Deploying File Servers" in this book.

Overview of the Print Server Deployment Process

Deploying print servers running the Microsoft® Windows® Server 2003, Standard Edition or Windows® Server 2003, Enterprise Edition operating systems lets your organization share printing resources across the network, allowing client computers to send print jobs to printers attached locally to a print server and to printers accessible across the Internet. Windows Server 2003 provides a number of solutions that can benefit your organization.

Cross-platform printing support   Windows Server 2003 supports printing from Microsoft® Windows® 95, Windows® 98, Windows® Millennium Edition, Windows NT® version 4.0, Windows® 2000, Windows® XP Professional, or UNIX or Linux operating systems.

Increased availability   If your business relies on high availability of network printers, you can cluster print servers or install a standby server to increase print server availability.

Driver versioning   To improve stability, Windows Server 2003 restricts the installation of older printer drivers, which can cause the system to become unresponsive. You can override these restrictions if your network has clients that require older printer drivers.

Consolidation tools   If you have too many print servers to manage efficiently in your current printing environment, you can use the Print Migrator tool to help automate printer consolidation on Windows Server 2003. Instead of recreating all of the printer objects manually, you can back up existing printers and restore them to your new print servers.

Rich printer status reporting   If you use the standard port monitor, you can receive status reports when the printer runs out of paper, runs low on toner, or is stopped by a paper jam.

Easy location of nearby printers   If you implement the Active Directory® directory service, your users can easily find printers that are published in Active Directory based on attributes that you designate.

Improved security   New local Group Policy settings can control which individuals have access to the print queue over the network.

Centralized printer management   Windows Server 2003 lets you remotely manage and configure printers from any computer running Windows Server 2003.

If your current network environment has a mix of clients and print servers running different operating systems, you can improve the interoperability, availability, and efficiency of your print servers by properly designing your new printing environment. After the design team creates a design, and the deployment team implements that design in a test lab, you are ready to deploy your new Windows Server 2003 print servers in a production environment.

Effectively deploying print servers that run Windows Server 2003 is a three-phase process, as illustrated in Figure 3.1.

Figure 3.1   Designing and Deploying Print Servers

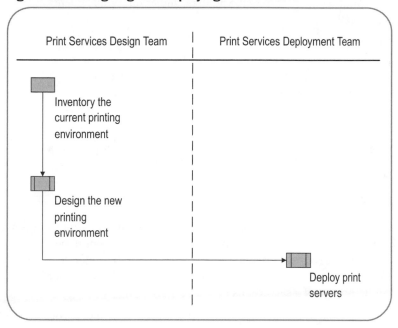

A print server design team completes the first two phases: examining your current environment and designing a new printing environment. During these phases, the design team collects information that is vital to the deployment process, determines your immediate and long-term printing needs, recommends improvements to the printing environment, and creates an appropriate printing strategy.

A print server deployment team completes the final phase of the deployment process by implementing the design team's decisions. The deployment team's responsibilities include adding printing capabilities to existing or newly created clustered servers, installing Windows Server 2003 on the print servers, creating the printers, and ensuring that clients receive the required printer connections.

 Note

For a list of the job aids that are available to assist you in deploying print servers, see "Additional Resources" later in this chapter.

Inventorying the Current Printing Environment

The first phase in moving to a Windows Server 2003–based printing environment is gathering information about your current printing environment. Document the port types, printer names, share names, IP address, driver models and driver versions of each printer that you plan to replace or migrate. This information helps you plan details of the deployment process and gives you a way to rebuild printers if a server fails.

Figure 3.2 illustrates the place of this phase in the design and deployment process.

Figure 3.2   Inventorying the Current Printing Environment

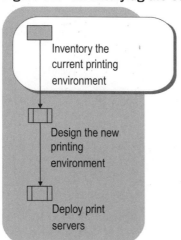

A number of tools can help you inventory your current printing environment. These tools can also be useful if you decide to migrate your existing print servers to new print servers that are running Windows Server 2003. The tools you can use depend on your current operating system:

- Windows Server 2003 includes scripts written in the Microsoft®Visual Basic® Scripting Language that you can use to inventory your current printing environment.

- If you are in a Windows NT 4.0 domain, you must use PrnAdmin to inventory your current printing environment.

 Note

For a worksheet to assist you in inventorying your printing environment, see "Print Server Inventory Worksheet" (Sdcpsv_1.doc) on the *Microsoft® Windows® Server 2003 Deployment Kit* companion CD (or see "Print Server Inventory Worksheet" on the Web at http://www.microsoft.com/reskit).

Visual Basic Scripts

Table 3.1 lists information that you might require while inventorying your printing environment and the scripts you can use to obtain that information. These scripts are located in the Windows\System32 directory.

Table 3.1   Scripts That Provide Print Server Information

Information Needed	Script
Print server name	Prnmngr.vbs
Print queue name	Prnmngr.vbs
Printer driver name	Prnmngr.vbs
Print port type	Prnport.vbs
Print port configuration	Prnport.vbs
Print device IP address	Prnport.vbs

For a list of parameters for each script listed in Table 6.1, perform the following procedure.

▶ **To list the parameters for the Visual Basic scripts listed in Table 6.1**

1. Open a **Command Prompt**, and then move to the Windows/System32 directory.

2. At the command prompt, type:

   cscript *scriptname*.**vbs**

PrnAdmin

If you are migrating from Windows NT 4.0 to Windows Server 2003, you can use Prnadmin.dll to inventory your current environment. PrnAdmin enumerates ports, drivers, printers, or forms on local or remote printers. The Visual Basic script for the PrnAdmin utility is named Prnmgr.vbs.

You can find the PrnAdmin utility on the *Windows Server 2003 Deployment Kit* companion CD. To install PrnAdmin, type the following command:

```
regsvr32 "C:\Program Files\Resource Kit\PrnAdmin.dll"
```

 Important

The preceding command syntax assumes that you installed the contents of the *Windows Server 2003 Resource Kit* companion CD in the default location, C:\Program Files\Resource Kit. If you install the contents in a different location, you must use that path in the syntax.

PrnAdmin syntax

The command-line syntax for PrnAdmin is:

```
cscript prnmgr.vbs [-adx[c]] [l] [-c server] [-b printer] [-m driver model]
[-p driver path] [-r port] [-f file]
```

PrnAdmin example

The following command lists all printers on the print server \\adminserver:

```
cscript prnmgr.vbs -l -c \\adminserver
```

Designing the New Printing Environment

After inventorying your current printing environment, your design team can start designing your new printing environment. Figure 3.3 illustrates the component tasks in this phase and its position in the design and deployment process.

Figure 3.3   Designing the New Printing Environment

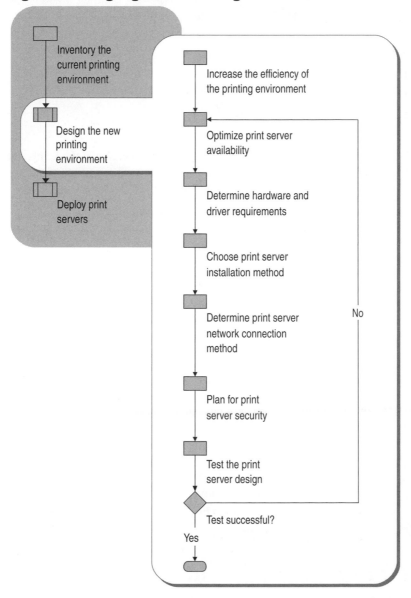

✓ **Note**

For a worksheet to assist you in designing your printing environment, see "Print Server Design Worksheet" (Sdcpsv_2.doc) on the *Windows Server 2003 Deployment Kit* companion CD (or see "Print Server Design Worksheet" on the Web at http://www.microsoft.com/reskit).

Increasing the Efficiency of the Printing Environment

When designing your new printing environment, examine your existing environment to determine if you need to make more efficient use of your resources. Examine the efficiency of both printing performance and printing management.

Printing Performance

You might need to make adjustments to servers that are not responding at the levels that you require. If users are waiting an unacceptable amount of time for jobs to print, you can improve the performance of your print servers by replacing older print devices with newer, faster devices.

Another option is to create a printer pool in which two or more of the same model printers connect to one print server and behave as a single printer. You can make the printer pool appear to users as a single printer by using multiple ports on the print server to connect the printers to one logical printer (the printer's software interface on the print server). When a user prints a document to the printer pool, the document prints to the first available printer in the pool. Users do not have to know which printer is available. The logical printer checks for an available port and then sends documents to ports in the order in which the documents are added to the print queue. A printer pool also eases administration, because you can manage multiple printers from the same logical printer on the print server.

If you have remote offices that experience bandwidth limitations while connected to a central print server, consider placing print servers in those offices. However, increasing performance in this manner has a drawback: If the print server fails, someone on-site must troubleshoot or restart the server. In addition, if your print server also hosts other services, restarting the server causes those other services to go offline as well.

Printing Management

You might also have more print servers than you need. If you have more print servers than you can manage efficiently, consider consolidating some of your print servers. For more information about consolidating print servers, see "Designing for Efficient Use of Hardware in Printing" later in this chapter.

Optimizing Print Server Availability

By evaluating your availability requirements, you can determine if you need to increase print server availability and minimize downtime if a server stops responding. Certain users or groups in your organization might need highly available network printing. An accounting group, for example, might print time-sensitive documents such as payroll checks. In such a case, you need to examine high-availability solutions for that group.

If you determine that you have users who need highly available printing, you should consider either creating a print server cluster or putting a standby system in place in the event that your print server becomes unavailable. Both of these methods have trade-offs in cost and manageability. The following sections describe these trade-offs and can help you decide which method is more appropriate for your organization.

Creating Clustered Print Servers to Increase Availability

A *cluster* is a group of individual computer systems working together to provide increased computing power and to ensure continuous availability of mission-critical applications or services. The computers in this group use a common cluster name, appear to network clients as a single system, and distribute the cluster's workload among the group.

Clustered print servers provide failover and failback capabilities, which enhance the availability of print servers by allowing individual print servers, known as *nodes*, to fill in for each other if one of them fails (although there might be a short period when the printers are unavailable while the resources fail over to the other nodes). With clustered print servers, you also can perform maintenance on one node, without interrupting printing operations, by moving the cluster resources to another node.

You can create clusters only on servers that run Windows Server 2003, Enterprise Edition or Windows Server 2003, Datacenter Edition. However, after you set up a cluster on these computers, you can administer the cluster, including installing and configuring printers, from any computer on the network that is running Windows 2000, Windows XP Professional with Service Pack 1 and the Administration Tools Pack, or Windows Server 2003. For information about installing the Administration Tools Pack, see "Windows Server 2003 Administration Tools Pack Overview" in Help and Support Center for Windows Server 2003.

Before deciding whether to use clustered print servers to increase printer availability, consider the following requirements:

- Clustered print servers have additional costs and hardware requirements. A clustered print server requires two or more physical servers running Windows Server 2003, Enterprise Edition or Windows Server 2003, Datacenter Edition. Because of the specialized hardware and the software requirements, the overall cost of implementing clustered print servers can be greater than the cost of providing a standby print server.

- Clustered print servers require administrator expertise. Implementing and maintaining clustered print servers requires experience or specialized training. Less experienced administrators might cause significant problems and delays, and mistakes can lower the availability of the print servers.

- For more information about deploying Windows server clusters, see "Designing and Deploying Server Clusters" in this book.

Creating Standby Servers to Increase Availability

Using a standby server to increase print server availability is a simple, low-cost alternative to clustering. The best method for setting up a standby server is to make sure that the hardware and software, including drivers, are exactly the same as the standard print server configuration that the design team has created. If you have a standby print server based on the standard print server configuration, you can replace any print server on your network that is based on the same configuration. In the event that a print server stops responding, rename the standby server to the same name as the server that you are replacing, and then connect the standby server to your network. For more information about standard print server configurations, see "Designing for Efficient Use of Hardware in Printing" later in this chapter.

Consider the following issues before creating standby print servers:

- Standby print servers carry additional costs. Providing a standby server requires two servers for each of the print servers that you want to be highly available. Ideally, these two servers have identical hardware and software configurations, including patches and printer drivers. The minimum requirements for a standby server are the same as the requirements for any server running Windows Server 2003.

- Standby print servers require additional maintenance. If you use standby servers, any changes that you make to the primary print server need to be made to the standby server also. If a server stops responding, you can rename the standby server and remove the primary print server from the network by using a Remote Desktop Connection.

- This method of increasing availability can result in some downtime, which is limited to the time that it takes to rename the standby print server, attach it to the network, and remove the primary print server.

- Users must resubmit any print jobs that failed to print. Print jobs that have been spooled but have not yet printed when the server stops responding must be resubmitted to the standby server after it replaces the primary print server.

Determining Hardware and Driver Requirements

Before deploying a new Windows Server 2003 print environment, examine your existing print server hardware. If any of your hardware does not meet the recommended hardware requirements for Windows Server 2003 and does not appear in Windows Server Catalog, you must acquire new hardware or upgrade your existing hardware. For more information about hardware requirements, see the Windows Server Catalog link on the Web Resources page at http://www.microsoft.com/windows/reskits/webresources

You must also consider which printer driver versions you will need. Depending on the mix of client operating systems in your environment, you might need to install different printer driver versions on different client computers in order to print to the same printer.

Designing for Efficient Use of Hardware in Printing

When determining your print server hardware requirements, consider both the sizing and placement of servers to maximize availability of printing resources, and determine whether you want to consolidate any existing print servers. After you make these design choices, consider creating a standard print server configuration to simplify the management and maintenance of your hardware.

Determining Print Server Sizing

When planning the printing strategy for your organization, consider the following factors as you estimate the number and types of printers that you need, both now and in the future:

- Determine how to divide and allocate printing resources. High-volume printers generally have more features, but a breakdown affects more users.

- Consider the printer features that you need, such as color printing, duplex printing, multibin mailboxes, envelope feeders, and stapling. Determine which users need these features and the physical locations of these users.

- Estimate any additional hardware requirements. Managing a large number of printers or many large documents requires a large amount of memory and disk space, and, potentially, a more powerful computer. If you need to store a copy of everything you print, you must provide additional disk space.

- Consider dedicating a server exclusively to printing. If you are considering using a server for both file and print sharing, remember that printing operations require a large amount of data input/output (I/O), and that the operating system gives priority to file operations over printing operations.

- Match printing volume as closely as possible to a printer's duty cycle (the number of pages the printer was designed to print per month). Maintenance problems are generally reduced if printing volume is less than or equal to the printer's duty cycle.

- Consider printing-speed requirements. In addition to the processing speed of the printer itself, network considerations also affect printing speed. Typically, printers that are attached directly to the network with network adapters offer faster throughput than printers attached with parallel buses. However, print throughput rates also depend on network traffic, the type of network adapter, and the protocol used.

- To increase the throughput of a print server, relocate the print spool folder. For best results, move the spool folder to a dedicated disk drive that does not share any files, including paging files, with the operating system.

The appropriate hardware for an organization varies widely depending on business requirements. Many businesses have relatively simple printing needs, while others have more complex printing needs. For example, when the graphics department of an advertising agency determines that it needs a high-speed color printer, the administrator locates the printer in the same area of the building as the graphics department. To avoid conflicts with other I/O operations on the server, the administrator also designates the D: drive on the print server as the print spool folder. For more information about print server sizing, see the Print Services link on the Web Resources page at http://www.microsoft.com/windows/reskits/webresources

Determining Print Server Placement

The placement of printers and print servers can affect both the efficiency of users and the congestion on your network. To minimize printing traffic in your network environment, locate printers close to the people who use them. Also, if some users print sensitive documents, consider locating their printers in an area of the building that only authorized personnel can access.

Determining Whether to Consolidate Printers

If you determine that you have more print servers than you can manage efficiently, consolidate some of them onto one of your more powerful print servers. Central print server management offers an easier way to administer print servers, and consolidation reduces the cost incurred by maintaining more print servers than you need. At the same time, consolidating servers increases the value of recovery planning and procedures.

As you consider whether or not to consolidate print servers, weigh the following advantages and disadvantages.

Advantages of consolidating printers

- You have fewer print servers to maintain.

- You can reassign the servers that no longer serve as print servers.

Disadvantages of consolidating printers

- If a server stops responding, your users have fewer servers to depend on.

- If the print server is no longer near users on the network, your users might experience delays in processing print jobs.

Using Print Migrator version 3.0 helps you automate the process of consolidating your print servers. You merely back up your existing servers and restore them to the new Windows Server 2003 print server. For more information about Print Migrator 3.0, see "Choosing a Print Server Migration Method" later in this chapter.

Creating a Standard Print Server Configuration

Creating a standard print server configuration is highly recommended. This involves defining a specific hardware and software combination that works well for your organization and operates with minimal maintenance. The specific configuration varies from business to business. The needs of your organization might necessitate more than one standard print server configuration.

Designing a standard configuration for print servers provides two important benefits:

- It reduces the complexity of managing and maintaining hardware. You need to learn hardware management and maintenance tasks for only one type of print server instead of for multiple types.

- It reduces the amount of testing that you must perform when updating drivers on the print server. Instead of testing the updates on multiple hardware and software configurations, you can test the updates on one print server and then deploy the updates to the other print servers.

If your organization has selected Cluster service to provide the highest level of availability, create a standard configuration for clustered print servers as well. For more information about clustering, see "Designing and Deploying Server Clusters" in this book.

As you design your configuration, consider creating a logical and standard naming convention for your printers, which can make it easier for users to locate printers across a network if you decide to publish your printers in Active Directory.

Designing for Printer Driver Compatibility

When designing your new printing environment, you must understand how different types of drivers work on different versions of the Windows operating system. Print servers running Windows Server 2003 use two types of drivers:

- Version 2 printer drivers operate in *kernel mode* (inside the operating system kernel memory space) and are designed for Windows NT 4.0.

- Version 3 printer drivers operate in *user mode* (outside the operating system kernel memory space) and are designed for Windows 2000, Windows XP, and Windows Server 2003.

Windows Server 2003 supports both Version 2 and Version 3 printer drivers. To ensure the stability of your print servers, use Version 3 drivers whenever possible. If some computers in your organization run Windows NT 4.0 and other computers run Windows 2000, Windows XP Professional, or Windows Server 2003, you must ensure that you have the proper mix of drivers to support all of these clients, and you might have to modify the Windows Server 2003 print server to include additional Version 2 drivers that work with Windows NT 4.0 clients.

 Note

Poorly written device drivers have been identified as a major cause of system instability. To ensure that your drivers are reliable, use drivers approved under the Windows Hardware Logo Program on your print servers.

Having the correct drivers installed on your server is important if you plan to use the Point and Print feature. By using Point and Print, a user running Windows NT 4.0, Windows 2000, Windows XP Professional, or Windows Server 2003 can create a connection to a remote printer without using disks or other installation media. All necessary files and configuration information automatically download from the print server to the client. Point and Print eases your administrative overhead by eliminating the need to visit each workstation to install the appropriate device drivers.

Windows Server 2003 also provides Point and Print support for Windows 95, Windows 98, and Windows Millennium Edition clients on your network. However, Point and Print does not support automatic driver upgrades for these clients.

Your new print servers must include printer drivers that support all the clients on your network. Maintain a list of printers that are using Version 2 drivers, so that you can replace these drivers with Version 3 drivers if you upgrade the client base to Windows 2000 or Windows XP Professional. Additionally, if you have PostScript printers, you can use PostScript drivers to increase interoperability in a mixed Windows NT 4.0, Windows 2000, and Windows XP Professional client environment.

Table 3.2 notes the compatibility of Version 2, Version 3, and PostScript drivers with different versions of the Windows operating systems.

Table 3.2   Printer Driver Compatibility with Windows Operating Systems

Driver type	Version 2	Version 3	PostScript
Windows NT 4.0	●	Supported as additional drivers*	●
Windows 2000	●	●	●
Windows XP Professional	●	●	●
Windows Server 2003	Supported as additional drivers	●	●

* Must be installed remotely from Windows 2000 and Windows XP Professional clients to allow those clients to print to a Windows NT 4.0 print server.

Version 2 and Version 3 Drivers

Version 3 drivers are recommended over Version 2 drivers because they support advanced printing features and improved performance. If a server stops responding as a result of a Version 3 driver problem, you only need to stop and restart the print spooler instead of restarting the server. Additionally, Version 3 drivers can reduce printer downtime, because Windows Server 2003 provides automatic recovery of the spooler service by default. If a Version 2 driver stops responding, you must reboot the server, taking all other services offline while the server restarts.

Often the existing Version 2 drivers on your print server function properly with Windows Server 2003. Although a default local Group Policy setting in Windows Server 2003 prohibits the installation of new Version 2 drivers, this policy setting does not affect existing Version 2 drivers when you perform an upgrade unless a driver is known to be problematic. To identify drivers that will not carry through the upgrade, use the command-line tool Fixprnsv.exe prior to upgrading.

For more information about Fixprnsv.exe, see "Identifying Interoperability Issues with Print Server Upgrades" later in this chapter. For more information about disallowing installation of printers using kernel-mode drivers, see the *Server Management Guide* of the *Windows Server 2003 Resource Kit* (or see the *Server Management Guide* on the Web at http://www.microsoft.com/reskit).

PostScript Drivers

Microsoft recommends that you consider using PostScript minidrivers (.ppd files) to increase compatibility in mixed environments with Windows NT 4.0, Windows 2000, and Windows Server 2003 systems. Computers running Windows NT 4.0, Windows 2000, Windows XP, and Windows Server 2003 can all run the same PSCRIPT5 core code, regardless of whether these computers are running Version 2 or Version 3 drivers. This offers a higher level of interoperability among clients running different versions of Windows.

Choosing Drivers for Point and Print Connectivity

If you are using Point and Print to connect clients to printers, driver compatibility is particularly important. Clients that use the same driver architecture as the print server can simply download the primary driver used on the server and therefore do not require the installation of any additional drivers on the print server for full support. For example, a Windows Server 2003 print server using a Version 3 driver for a shared printer does not require the installation of any additional drivers to provide full Point and Print support for Windows 2000 and Windows XP Professional clients, because those clients also support Version 3 drivers.

If Windows 95, Windows 98, Windows Millennium Edition, and Windows NT 4.0 clients connect to the print server, you must install the appropriate driver as an additional driver on the Windows Server 2003 print server.

For additional information about network printing, including Point and Print driver installation, see the *Server Management Guide* of the *Windows Server 2003 Resource Kit* (or see the *Server Management Guide* on the Web at http://www.microsoft.com/reskit).

Point and Print for clients running Windows NT 4.0 and earlier versions of Windows

Setting up printer drivers on a print server running Windows Server 2003 to support Point and Print is generally the same for clients running Windows NT 4.0 and earlier versions of Windows as it is for clients running Windows 2000 or Windows XP. However, you may encounter some specific differences.

You can select the printer driver versions to install on the print server on the **Drivers** tab of the **Server Properties** property sheet, or, when you install additional drivers using the Add Printer Driver Wizard, in the **Additional Drivers** dialog box shown in Figure 3.4.

Figure 3.4   Additional Drivers Dialog Box

Before you load any additional drivers on x86-based systems, one of three printer driver versions is selected by default, represented by the three following options:

- **Windows 2000, Windows XP, or Windows Server 2003.** If this option is selected before you load any additional drivers, it indicates that the server is running a Version 3 driver written specifically for the Windows 2000, Windows XP, or Windows Server 2003 platform. You cannot send that driver to a Windows NT 4.0 client for Point and Print functionality. You need to add a Version 2 driver to support Point and Print on Windows NT 4.0 client computers.

- **Windows NT 4.0.** This option indicates that a Windows NT 4.0 Version 2 driver is running on a server that is running Windows 2000 or Windows Server 2003. No additional drivers are required to support Point and Print on Windows NT 4.0–based client computers.

- **Windows 95, 98, or Windows Millennium Edition.** If this option is selected, users can connect to and download the existing driver from the server. However, those clients will not receive automatic updates when the driver on the server is updated.

Point and Print for servers running Unidrv Version 3 drivers

When a Version 3 driver written specifically for the Windows Server 2003 or Windows 2000 platforms is installed on the server, you must install a Version 2 driver with the same model name on Windows NT 4.0 clients in order to support Point and Print. Changes in the internal data structures between the Version 2 and Version 3 Unidrv.dll can cause problems in sharing or preserving settings between the clients and the server. These problems primarily manifest themselves in two ways:

- New or advanced settings on the Print Server might not be visible from the property sheet of a client printer.

- The print server might not correctly interpret the client printer properties, causing the properties to be lost. As a result, the Point and Print connection allows the client to print, but might not allow modification of certain device settings or preferences if they do not match those on the server.

Note

Incompatible data structures can cause certain printer settings — such as **Print Text as Graphics** or **Print Optimization** — to be lost between computers running Windows NT 4.0 and computers running Windows 2000. Additionally, settings such as paper tray assignments and media types might not be preserved between driver models.

Choosing the Print Server Installation Method

Print server installation includes installing or upgrading to the Windows Server 2003 operating system and creating or migrating printers. The type of installation that you choose depends on your existing printing environment. If you have new servers with no operating system installed, you must perform a clean installation of the Windows Server 2003 operating system. If you have existing servers, you can perform a clean installation or, if the server is running Windows 2000 or Windows NT 4.0, you can upgrade.

Other considerations might also play a part in your decision. For example, some organizations have software standards that prohibit upgrading the operating system on servers. These organizations choose to perform only clean installations. With a clean installation, you can install the latest printer drivers from the independent hardware vendor (IHV), thus eliminating older, potentially problematic drivers.

Consider the following points when choosing between a clean installation and an upgrade.

Choosing a clean installation

- In a clean installation, you must create all new printers or migrate existing printers.

- If you want to practice good print queue management (for example, by complying with the company's print queue naming conventions), you might want to perform a clean installation instead of upgrading a server.

Choosing to upgrade

- Configuration is simpler when you upgrade. You retain your existing print queues, drivers, and ports, minimizing the impact on users.

- You might encounter interoperability issues with your existing printer drivers.

Choosing a Print Server Migration Method

If you decide that a clean installation of Windows Server 2003 is best for your organization, you must also decide if moving some of your existing printers from other print servers makes sense. Migrating a print server is a method of moving existing printers onto your new server. If you intend to add new print servers to your existing environment, consider migrating some of your existing print servers to these new, typically more powerful servers to take full advantage of your improved hardware resources.

Three approaches are available for migrating existing print server configurations:

- Manual migration

- Automated migration

- Partially automated migration

Manual Print Server Migration

A manual print server migration requires that you document the current printing environment on your existing Windows print servers (including ports, printer names, share names, and driver models and versions). Then, using the Add Printer Wizard, recreate each printer on your new Windows Server 2003 print servers. The advantage of this method is that you can create all of the queues by using the most recent corporate standard and the newest available driver versions. The disadvantage is that this method can be very time consuming for large print environments — and it is more error-prone than the automated method.

Automated Print Server Migration with Print Migrator

Microsoft has developed a printer migration utility called Print Migrator, which can back up and restore print server configurations with minimal user intervention. Print Migrator handles the migration of print queues, drivers, and printer ports. You can also use Print Migrator to consolidate print servers.

Print Migrator does not change the driver versions when moving printers to the Windows Server 2003. For example, Print Migrator copies any Version 2 drivers used on a Windows NT 4.0 print server and recreates them on the new Windows Server 2003 print server. This process provides a much higher level of interoperability with any Windows NT 4.0 clients that might still be using print services from that server. To download Print Migrator, see the Print Services link on the Web Resources page at http://www.microsoft.com/windows/reskits/webresources.

Note

Print Migrator ships with documentation about its operation and use. Review the material carefully for more details about this tool's capabilities and limitations.

The newest version of Print Migrator, Print Migrator 3.0, provides the following functionalities:

- Version support across operating systems

- Cluster support

- Port conversion from Line Printer Remote (LPR)-to-standard port monitor (standard TCP/IP port monitor)

Version support across operating systems

Differences in the way that Version 3 and Version 2 drivers work present interoperability issues when you migrate printers across versions of the Windows operating system. Cross-version support in Print Migrator 3.0 ensures successful migration from Windows NT 4.0 to Windows 2000 or Windows Server 2003.

Cluster support

Print Migrator 3.0 also supports migrating your print cluster from a server running Windows NT 4.0 or Windows 2000 to a print server running Windows Server 2003.

LPR to standard TCP/IP port conversion

If your print servers currently have LPR ports, consider converting the ports to standard TCP/IP ports. The standard TCP/IP port is the preferred printer port in Windows Server 2003. You can use other printer ports with Windows Server 2003, but they offer limited functionality.

Partially Automated Print Server Migration

Administrators can migrate printers by using a combination of manual and automated methods. Scripts supported by Windows 2000, Windows XP, and Windows Server 2003 can perform most of the necessary tasks. For more information about using scripts to partially automate your migration, see "Managing printing from the command line" in Help and Support Center for Windows Server 2003.

Identifying Interoperability Issues with Print Server Upgrades

Upgrading print servers from previous versions of Windows can present interoperability issues because of changes in the printer driver model beginning with Windows 2000 and continuing with Windows Server 2003. For more information about driver compatibility, see "Designing for Printer Driver Compatibility" earlier in this chapter.

To handle driver-related issues more easily, use the command-line utility Fixprnsv.exe, a powerful tool for working with printer driver issues on printer servers that are running Windows NT 4.0, Windows 2000, or Windows Server 2003. The Fixprnsv.exe identifies incompatible drivers before you upgrade, finds all known bad drivers on your system, and identifies Version 2 drivers that work properly with Windows Server 2003.

The Windows Server 2003 installation CD-ROM includes Fixprnsv.exe. The executable file is located in Windows\Printers directory. To view a list of commands used with this utility, use the command **fixprnsv.exe /?** from that directory.

For more information about specific compatibility issues involved in upgrading from Windows NT or Windows 2000, see "Deploying Print Servers with Upgrade Installations" later in this chapter.

Choosing an Installation Method for Clustered Print Servers

Several options are available for upgrading a clustered print server. You can use any of the following methods:

- Upgrade a cluster that is running Windows NT Server 4.0, Enterprise Edition with Service Pack 4 or later.

- Upgrade a cluster that is running Microsoft Windows 2000 Advanced Server or Microsoft Windows 2000 Datacenter Server.

- Perform a clean installation of Windows Server 2003, Enterprise Edition and at the same time upgrade an existing stand-alone server to a server cluster.

Upgrading a Windows NT 4.0 Server Cluster

You cannot perform a rolling upgrade (upgrading the nodes sequentially) directly from Windows NT Server 4.0, Enterprise Edition to Windows Server 2003, Enterprise Edition. Instead, you have two options:

- Perform a nonrolling upgrade directly from Windows NT 4.0, Enterprise Edition with Service Pack 4 or later to Windows Server 2003, Enterprise Edition by taking the cluster resources offline and upgrading each node. With a nonrolling upgrade, you cannot maintain cluster availability during the upgrade.

- To maintain cluster availability, perform a rolling upgrade to Windows 2000 and then perform a second rolling upgrade to Windows Server 2003.

   To perform the rolling upgrade to Windows 2000, first move all of the cluster resources from the target node to other nodes. Install Windows 2000 Advanced Server or Windows 2000 Datacenter Server on the target node, and move the cluster resources back to the newly upgraded cluster node. Then install Windows 2000 Advanced Server or Windows 2000 Datacenter Server on the remaining nodes in the cluster.

   Complete the rolling upgrade by following the same process to install Windows Server 2003 on your cluster.

Upgrading a Windows 2000 Server Cluster

The easiest method for upgrading a Windows 2000 Server cluster is to perform a rolling upgrade. A rolling upgrade has two major advantages:

- Clients experience minimal interruption of service. (However, server response time might increase during the phases in which fewer nodes handle the work of the entire cluster.)

- You do not have to recreate your cluster configuration, because the configuration remains intact during the upgrade process.

Upgrading an Existing Stand-Alone Server to a Cluster

To upgrade an existing stand-alone print server to a print server cluster, use Print Migrator 3.0 to back up and restore the print server configurations to the newly created server cluster. You must create the cluster first, before adding the print spooler resource.

Additional hardware requirements exist for using the Windows Cluster service. For a list of supported cluster hardware, see the Windows Server Catalog link on the Web Resources page at http://www.microsoft.com/windows/reskits/webresources and search for "cluster."

 Note

Only Standard TCP/IP ports and LPR ports are supported on a server cluster.

For more information about clustering, see "Designing and Deploying Server Clusters" in this book.

Determining the Print Server Network Connection Method

After installing Windows Server 2003, choose one of the following three methods to connect your print servers to the network:

- Whenever possible, use the standard TCP/IP port, also know as the *standard port*. The standard port is the preferred printer port in Windows Server 2003.

- For older devices that do not function correctly with the standard port, use the Line Printer Remote (LPR) port.

- To connect to printers over the Internet or an intranet, use the Internet Printing Protocol (IPP).

When creating printer ports, Windows Server 2003 installs the associated port monitor for that port type.

Connecting Through the Standard TCP/IP Port

The standard port is designed for Windows Server 2003–based print servers that use TCP/IP to communicate with printing devices, including network-ready printers, network adapters such as Hewlett-Packard JetDirect, and external print servers such as Intel NetPort. The standard port uses the standard TCP/IP port monitor (TCPMon.dll), also known as the *standard port monitor*. The standard port monitor can support many printers on one server. It is faster and easier to configure than the LPR Port Monitor (Lprmon), and it provides rich status information and error condition reporting that eases administration of your print servers.

The standard port monitor uses Simple Network Management Protocol (SNMP) and the standard printer message information base as defined in RFC 1759, "Printer MIB." As a result, the standard port monitor provides much more detailed status information than does LPR when, for example, the printer generates an error indicating a paper jam or low toner, or a print job is not responding and must be purged.

Although Windows Server 2003 requires TCP/IP on the print server in order to communicate with the printer, clients do not need TCP/IP. Because clients communicate with the print server rather than with the printer, they can do so using any common network protocol.

For example, a Novell NetWare client might use the Internetwork Packet Exchange (IPX) protocol to send documents to a Windows Server 2003 print server. The server then passes the document to the printer using the TCP/IP protocol. Status and error information is relayed from the printer to the print server using TCP/IP, and from the print server to the client using IPX.

Connecting Through the LPR Port

The LPR port uses the LPR monitor **Lprmon**, which is provided with Print Services for UNIX. The LPR port acts as the client for printing according to guidelines defined in RFC 1179, "Line Printer Daemon Protocol." The LPR port spools to a target host enabled for Line Printer Daemon (LPD). The target is usually a computer running one of the following:

- UNIX

- Multiple Virtual Storage (MVS)

- Virtual Address Extension (VAX)/Virtual Memory System (VMS)

However, the target alternatively can be one of the following:

- A printer with a network adapter that supports LPD

- An external print server

- A computer running Windows XP Professional, Windows Server 2003, Windows 2000, or Windows NT

- A print server running Print Services for UNIX or another version of LPD.

Before you can create an LPR port, the client must have TCP/IP and Print Services for UNIX installed. The target server must be running a Berkeley Software Distribution (BSD)–compatible LPD utility that is installed according to RFC 1179. If the server is running Windows Server 2003, Windows 2000, or Windows NT 4.0, make sure that Print Services for UNIX is started.

Using the Internet Printing Protocol (IPP)

You can make Windows Server 2003 printing features accessible over the Internet. To install a printer over the Internet, use the printer's URL as the name of the printer. Within an intranet, you can alternatively use the printer's share name (for example, http://*servername*/*sharename*).

If you are connecting to a print server on the same intranet, it is recommended that users' intranet security settings for Microsoft® Internet Explorer be set to medium-low or lower. Having this setting throughout an intranet creates a true Point and Print connection, which offers many advantages over an IPP connection. You can view, connect to, and manage printers from any browser. On clients running Windows 95, Windows 98, or Windows Millennium Edition, you must install the Web Client in order to manage printers by using a browser. For clients running Windows NT 4.0, you can manage printers from a browser, but cannot connect to them for printing.

To configure a computer to print to a printer by using a URL address, perform the following procedure.

▶ **To configure a computer to print to a printer by using a URL address**

1. Install Microsoft Internet Information Services (IIS) on a computer that is running Windows XP Professional

    or

    Install Microsoft Peer Web Services (PWS) on a computer running Windows 2000 Professional.

2. Install IIS on a print server that is running Windows Server 2003.

    The low-level protocol used for job submission is Internet Printing Protocol (IPP) version 1.0, which uses the Hypertext Transfer Protocol (HTTP) protocol as a carrier.

3. Ensure that all clients use Internet Explorer version 4.0 or later to connect to a printer.

For information about Internet Printing, see "Internet Printing" in Help and Support Center for Windows Server 2003.

Planning for Print Server Security

Planning for print server security is vital in order to protect your organization's resources. As with any production server, you need to protect the physical print server and safeguard access to data stored on the server. Consequently, your security plan must address three areas:

- Physical location
- Group Policy settings
- Printer permissions

Ensuring the Physical Security of Each Print Server

Locate your print servers in a physically secure location that only designated individuals can access. Allowing unauthorized access to your print servers risks harm to the system. In addition, consider to what extent you also need to restrict physical access to network hardware. The details of implementing these security measures depend on your physical facilities as well as your organization's structure and policies.

Securing the Print Environment

Windows Server 2003 adds new Group Policy settings that affect how clients connect to print servers on the network. Two of these policy settings are particularly useful for security.

Allow print spooler to accept client connections   This Group Policy setting, which is configured on the server, determines how clients access the print server over the network. If an individual with administrative credentials creates shared printers for use by managed clients, the spooler automatically allows connections upon creation of the first shared printer. If a virtual spooler resource is created on a clustered server, the spooler likewise automatically allows connections. If no shared printers or virtual spooler resources already exist, you might need to enable this policy setting by using the Computer Management snap-in from a remote computer. To administer print services on a server running Windows Server 2003, log on to the server locally, or log on remotely through a Remote Desktop session.

Point and Print restrictions   This Group Policy setting, which is configured on client computers, determines the print servers to which the client can connect. To provide a higher level of security for managed workstations, this policy setting controls a client computer's ability to connect to and install a printer driver from specified print servers. By default, managed clients can use Point and Print only with servers that are within their forest. An administrator can use this policy to add additional servers to the list of trusted print servers. Alternatively, administrators can disable this policy to enable managed clients to connect to any accessible print server and install a printer driver from it.

Using Printer Permissions to Control Access to Shared Printers

Even if the physical server is in a secure room, the print server might still be accessible through remote administration tools. Therefore, you need to implement methods for restricting access to remote administration of print servers. You can restrict access to a print server by setting printer permissions.

You might also want to restrict access to a particular network printer. For example, the graphics department in your organization might use a high-speed color printer regularly. The cost of supplies for a color printer is substantially higher than for a black-and-white printer, so you decide to deny access to anyone outside the graphics department. The best way to restrict access is to establish a new security group. You establish a group named Graphics Department, and grant access only to members of this group.

For a procedure describing how to restrict access to printers by using printer permissions, see "Restricting Access to Printers" later in this chapter.

Testing the Print Server Design

Testing is a key part of designing your print environment. Before you deploy your print servers in a production environment, make sure that your users can print successfully in a test environment. In most cases, thorough testing of your print servers during the design phase minimizes any impact on your users' ability to print.

It is recommended that you conduct testing in two stages. During the first stage, test your Windows Server 2003 deployment in a laboratory or controlled environment. After verifying that your design is successful in the lab, conduct a pilot deployment in a controlled real-world environment in which users perform their normal business tasks using the new printing features. This two-stage approach reduces your risk of encountering problems during full-scale deployment.

Before conducting the tests, make sure that the computers used in your pilot test run the same operating systems that you have in your production environment, and that the appropriate drivers are installed.

The following are some typical scenarios that you might want to test:

- If you list your printers in Active Directory, make sure that all the printers appear as choices when users try to add a network printer.

- Make sure that all users participating in the pilot test can print after connecting to each of the printers on the new servers.

- Have several users send various print jobs to the print server to measure how well the server holds up under a typical load.

- If you implement default printer location strings by using Group Policy objects, verify that these Group Policy settings are working as expected for the various groups to which they are assigned.

  For more information about Printer Location Strings, see the *Server Management Guide* of the *Windows Server 2003 Resource Kit* (or see the *Server Management Guide* on the Web at http://www.microsoft.com/reskit).

- If you use the standard port monitor with SNMP enabled, let the printer run out of paper to ensure that you receive an "out of paper" message when you send the next print job. For more information about standard port monitor, see "Determining the Print Server Network Connection Method" earlier in this chapter.

- If you set up a print server cluster, turn off one of the servers and see if the resources fail over to the other nodes. For more information about initiating a resource failure, see "Initiate a resource failure in Help and Support Center for Windows Server 2003.

Deploying Print Servers

After your design team completes its work, the print server deployment team can implement the design for your new printing environment. Deploying print servers involves installing Windows Server 2003 on the servers, adding the servers to the network, and then adding the printers. Organizations that plan to deploy clustered print servers must take the additional step of configuring the clusters before creating the print spooler resource.

Figure 3.5 shows the tasks involved in deploying print servers.

Figure 3.5 Deploying Print Servers

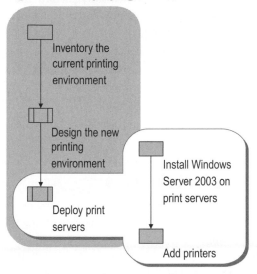

Installing Windows Server 2003 on Print Servers

The details of the print server deployment process vary depending on whether your design specifies a clean installation or an upgrade installation. If you are upgrading existing stand-alone or clustered servers, the upgrade process also differs depending on the version of the Windows operating system installed on your existing print servers.

Deploying Print Servers with Clean Installations

If you deploy print servers with clean installations of Windows Server 2003, you can decide whether to create new printers or migrate existing printers to the new servers. If you create new printers, you can enforce the standard printer naming convention that the design team developed during the design phase. If you have existing printers, it is a good idea to migrate them by using Print Migrator 3.0.

Setting Up a New Print Server

The first step in setting up a new print server is to install and configure Windows Server 2003. Identify each operating system that the printer server must support to determine any special selections that you must make while setting up your server. For example, if you support computers running Windows NT 4.0, you must install additional drivers during the upgrade process. After installing Windows Server 2003, you can begin adding printers.

Migrating Printers by Using Print Migrator 3.0

By using Print Migrator 3.0, you can back up your current print server configuration and restore the settings on a new print server, eliminating the need to manually recreate print queues and printer ports, install drivers, and assign IP addresses. Having to manually perform these tasks is a significant obstacle for most organizations. Using Print Migrator greatly reduces the manual intervention required when migrating your print servers from previous versions of Windows.

For example, an administrator obtains three new high-end servers to use as print servers. Rather than manually configure each server, the administrator uses Print Migrator 3.0 to back up three of the existing print servers and then restores the settings on the new servers. For more information about Print Migrator 3.0, see "Choosing a Print Server Migration Method" earlier in this chapter.

To ensure that your printer migration goes smoothly, read the documentation provided with Print Migrator 3.0.

Deploying Print Servers with Upgrade Installations

Deploying an upgraded installation of Windows Server 2003 can be a simple process depending on the printer drivers installed on your servers. One of the biggest challenges of upgrading is resolving any printer driver problems. Before upgrading your servers, use the command-line utility Fixprnsv.exe, provided with Windows Server 2003, to help you identify any printer driver problems. If you are upgrading from Windows NT 4.0 or Windows 2000, consider the issues presented in the following sections.

 Important

As with any major software installation, it is recommended that you back up the hard disk before beginning an upgrade.

Using Fixprnsv.exe to Resolve Driver Issues

To manage driver-related issues, use the command-line utility Fixprnsv.exe. Fixprnsv.exe automatically replaces incompatible printer drivers or those with known problems. It locates existing printer drivers that can replace unsuitable drivers. In many cases, IHVs provide new printer drivers for this purpose. If replacement drivers are available, Fixprnsv.exe replaces problem drivers with Microsoft-provided drivers. If Fixprnsv.exe does not find a suitable replacement driver, it displays a message advising you to check the printer manufacturer's Web site for a newer version of the driver. Fixprnsv.exe installs drivers only for printers that are already configured on the print server.

The Fixprnsv.exe utility is located on the Windows Server 2003 installation CD-ROM in the \Windows\Printers\ directory. For a list of commands for use with Fixprnsv.exe, use the following procedure.

▶ **To list the commands for Fixprnsv.exe**

1. Insert the Windows Server 2003 installation CD-ROM in the CD-ROM drive.
2. At the command prompt, change to the drive that contains the CD-ROM and type:

   fixprnsv.exe /?

Upgrading from Windows 2000

If you are upgrading a Windows 2000 print server that does not have Version 2 device drivers installed, your upgrade can be seamless. If your Windows 2000 print server has Version 2 drivers, you might encounter some of the issues involved in upgrading from Windows NT 4.0, which are discussed in the following section.

Upgrading from Windows NT 4.0

When upgrading from Windows NT 4.0 to Windows Server 2003, one or more of the following situations might occur:

- Windows NT 4.0 drivers that shipped with the operating system are upgraded to the new version of these drivers in Windows 2000, Windows XP, or Windows Server 2003. The Windows NT 4.0 driver remains as an additional driver.

- If the name of an IHV driver matches the name of a driver that ships with Windows 2000, Windows XP, or Windows Server 2003, the installation might upgrade the driver to the a Version 3 inbox driver (a driver that ships with Windows Server 2003). This upgrade occurs with no user intervention.

- Unstable drivers are blocked and are not carried through the upgrade. Printers that use these drivers are removed during the upgrade process. If the printer is connected directly to the computer and has a recognized Plug and Play ID, Windows searches for a suitable driver. If a suitable driver is found, the printer is installed during the upgrade as a new printer.

- Drivers that are not blocked and do not have name matches are carried through the upgrade unchanged.

Windows NT 4.0 inbox drivers

All Windows NT 4.0 Printer Control Language (PCL) drivers and Raster Device Drivers (RASDD) are upgraded to the latest Unidrv drivers as part of the upgrade process. The latest Unidrv drivers include UNIDRV5 for Windows 2000, and UNIDRV5.1 for Windows XP or Windows Server 2003. PostScript drivers that were shipped with Windows NT 4.0 are automatically upgraded to PostScript 5.0 in Windows 2000 or PostScript 5.2 in Windows XP or Windows Server 2003.

 Note

Drivers that you have installed as additional drivers for Point and Print on clients running Windows 95, Windows 98, or Windows Millennium Edition are not preserved during an upgrade from Windows NT 4.0 to Windows 2000 or Windows Server 2003. After you configure the print server, you must reinstall these additional drivers.

IHV drivers with matching names

IHV Windows NT 4.0 drivers are upgraded to Windows 2000, Windows XP, or Windows Server 2003 drivers with no user intervention if the driver name matches the existing Windows NT 4.0 driver name or if a newer version of the driver is available. In this situation, the IHV driver is treated exactly the same as the Microsoft driver.

Because of interaction problems between Windows 2000 drivers and Windows NT 4.0 drivers in Point and Print environments, many IHVs recommend that you reinstall their Windows NT 4.0 driver following the upgrade. This applies to users who plan to use Point and Print between Windows NT and Windows 2000, Windows XP, or Windows Server 2003.

Blocked IHV drivers

Microsoft designed the upgrade path from Windows NT 4.0 so that the new operating system replaces an old driver if a newer driver is available. Windows preserves a driver during an upgrade if the installation utility does not find a newer version and does not identify a driver as causing problems in Windows 2000, Windows XP, or Windows Server 2003. A driver is blocked for one of two reasons:

- Microsoft determines, through testing, that the driver causes substantial instability of the operating system.

- The IHV requests that the driver be blocked based on the IHV's own testing and available updates.

The system file Printupg.inf contains a list of known bad drivers. Drivers in this list might have an alternative inbox driver. If an alternative driver does not exist, the driver is not upgraded during the operating system installation. Instead, you need to install a newer version of the driver from the IHV. The information found in Printupg.inf can be helpful in identifying whether or not a new version from an IHV is blocked. The upgrade report also contains information about all drivers slated for removal during the upgrade.

In addition, the Fixprnsv.exe tool automatically replaces known bad drivers if inbox substitutes are available. If a compatible driver cannot be located, Fixprnsv.exe reports that fact and refers the user to the IHV's Web site. By running Fixprnsv.exe prior to upgrading, you can identify printers that are slated for deletion during the upgrade ahead of time. Otherwise, you might discover after the upgrade that some printers are unexpectedly missing.

Non-blocked IHV drivers

Certain Windows NT 4.0 drivers are not blocked and do not match the driver name of an inbox driver. These drivers proceed through the upgrade process without being altered or replaced. Use Fixprnsv.exe to identify drivers that must be replaced. For drivers that are not blocked (either because they are not in the Printupg.inf file or because they have a later date than the date of similar drivers listed in Printupg.inf), Fixprnsv.exe takes no action.

Adding Printers

After installing Windows Server 2003 on the print server, you must add the printers to the server. Depending on the decisions that the design team made, adding printers can involve the following steps:

- Adding spooler resources to server clusters
- Installing printer ports
- Adding additional printer drivers
- Publishing printers in Active Directory
- Connecting clients to printers
- Restricting access to printers
- Setting up Internet printing

Adding Spooler Resources to Server Clusters

In order to add printers to server clusters, you first need to create and configure print spooler resources. After creating the spooler resource, you can add printers, publish them in Active Directory, and add any additional drivers that your users require. You must also create and specify the spooler resource in order to use Print Migrator 3.0 to restore printers from another print server.

Creating a Spooler Resource

To create a spooler resource for a cluster, you must be the administrator of the cluster as well as of each node within the cluster. You must also have the administration software installed on your computer. Cluster Administrator is the graphical application that is supplied with the Cluster service to manage clusters. Alternatively, you can use Cluster.exe, a command-line tool, or develop custom administration tools by using the Cluster service command interfaces. Cluster Administrator is included in the Administrative Tools Pack (Adminpak.msi). The Cluster.exe tool and Adminpak.msi files are located in the Windows\System32 directory of a Windows 2003 Server.

The procedure for creating a print spooler resource is like the procedure for creating any resource in a cluster service. For more information about creating a cluster-managed printer, see "Create a cluster-managed printer in Help and Support Center for Windows Server 2003.

After you create the print spooler resource, migrate existing printers from existing print servers, if necessary, by using Print Migrator 3.0. For more information about Print Migrator, see "Choosing a Print Server Migration Method" earlier in this chapter.

Configuring the Resource

Configure the spooler resource by selecting the print spooler resource type in the Cluster Administrator window or by using Cluster.exe. Each cluster group can have only one print spooler resource, because resources are organized into interdependent groups that must fail over together.

After you create and configure the print spooler resource, you might need to install any third-party port monitors and print processors that are cluster-compatible on each node of the cluster. To do this, take each spooler resource offline, and then bring it online again so that the new resource is visible to the cluster. Then add printers to the clustered spooler. For more information about printing and the Cluster service, see "Print Spooler resource type" in Help and Support Center.

Adding a Printer to a Cluster

After creating a group and resources, you can add printers to the cluster. Each node must have connectivity to the remote print device. A printer that is locally connected to a node cannot be part of a cluster configuration, because the printer connects directly to the node and does not fail over if that node goes down.

Adding a printer to a cluster is very similar to adding the printer to any other computer, with the following exceptions:

- You never start from the local **Printers and Faxes** folder. The cluster always appears remote, even if you are working on the active cluster node. Instead type the virtual server name (for example, \\Virtual_Server_Prn) in the **Run** dialog box, and then click the remote **Printers and Faxes** folder that is displayed.

- If the Add Printer Wizard does not appear when you open the remote **Printers and Faxes** folder, you cannot continue. One of three things might be wrong:

  - The associated print spooler resource is not online or is not configured

  - You are not logged on as the administrator.

  - The spooler service is not started on the local computer. (This is unlikely.)

When a cluster group containing a print spooler resource fails over to another node, the document that is currently being sent to the printer is restarted on the other node after the failure. When you move a print spooler resource or take it offline, Cluster service waits until all documents are spooled or the configured wait time elapses. The cluster discards any documents that are submitted while the spooler resource is unavailable or the cluster is offline, and users must resubmit those print jobs.

For more information about clustering, see "Designing and Deploying Server Clusters" in this book.

Installing Printer Ports

If your users print over a network, you must create printer ports to enable connections between print servers and printers. You can install printer ports for stand-alone servers and clusters from the Printers and Faxes folder on the print server. The printer port can be one of two port types:

- Standard TCP/IP port

- LPR port

If you are using clustered print servers, you need to install the printers on each node and ensure that each node has the appropriate protocols, port monitors (not ports), and print processors installed. You can do this remotely, but you must address each node by its node name, not the cluster name. Ensure that the settings on all nodes are identical, because a specification made on one node does not carry over to the other nodes.

Standard TCP/IP Port

The standard port is the preferred printer port in Windows Server 2003. The standard port uses the standard TCP/IP port monitor (standard port monitor) and is designed for Windows Server 2003–based print servers that communicate with printers by using TCP/IP. For more information about the advantages of using the standard port and the prerequisites for installing a standard port, see "Determining the Print Server Network Connection Method" earlier in this chapter.

▷   **To install a standard port**

1. In Control Panel, open the **Printers and Faxes** folder, right-click the printer that you want to configure, and click **Properties**.

2. On the **Ports** tab, click **Add Port**.

3. In the **Printer Ports** dialog box, select **Standard TCP/IP port**, and click **New Port** to launch the **Add Standard TCP/IP Printer Port Wizard**.

4. Complete the **Add Standard TCP/IP Printer Port Wizard by** using the information provided in Table 3.3.

Table 3.3   Using the Add Standard TCP/IP Printer Port Wizard

Wizard Page	Action
Printer Name or IP Address	To identify the printer that will be connected to the port, type its name in the **Printer Name** or its IP address in the **IP Address** box.
Port Name	In the **Port Name** box, type a port name, which can be any character string, or use the default name that the wizard supplies.
Additional Port Information Required	To configure a standard port, click **Standard**, and then select one of the listed devices. If you do not know the details of the port, try using the **Generic Network Card**. To create a custom configuration, click **Custom**, and then configure the port by using the **Configure Standard TCP/IP Port Monitor** screen that appears.

If the wizard cannot determine the appropriate protocol for the port, it prompts you for the information. Follow the vendor's instructions for selecting either the RAW or LPR option.

If you are not prompted for more information, continue to step 5.Review the port information, and click **Finish**.

The new port is listed on the **Ports** tab of the **Properties** property sheet.

   Note

> With Windows Server 2003, administrators can remotely configure and manage ports from any server running Windows Server 2003. This feature applies to local ports, the standard TCP/IP port, and LPR ports. You must configure AppleTalk ports locally on the server.

You can reconfigure the standard port monitor by adjust the settings in the property sheet for the print server.

 Caution
The Configure Port dialog box does not validate the settings created in the following procedure. If they are incorrect, the port no longer works.

▷ **To reconfigure the standard TCP/IP port**

1. In Control Panel, open the **Printers and Faxes** folder, right-click the appropriate printer, and click **Properties**.

2. On the **Ports** tab, click the **Configure Port** button.

3. In the **Configure Standard TCP/IP Port Monitor** dialog box, click either the RAW or LPR protocol.

4. To configure the protocol, take one of the following actions:

   ▪ For **RAW Settings**, type the port number that the printer vendor specified (usually 9100).

   ▪ For **LPR Settings**, type the LPR queue name that the printer vendor specified.

5. If the printer supports SNMP and RFC 1759, select the **SNMP Status Enabled** check box.

6. If **SNMP Status Enabled** is selected, you can change both the SNMP community name and the host device index:

   ▪ The community name is usually "Public," but you can enter another community name if you want to limit access to the printer.

   ▪ The device index is used mainly for multiport devices that support several printers; each port on a multiport device has a different device index, specified by the device vendor.

LPR Port

If your network includes clients that are running UNIX, install LPD, which acts as the client for printing according to RFC 1179 guidelines. For more information about the LPR port, see "Determining the Print Server Network Connection Method" earlier in this chapter.

▶ **To install an LPR port**

1. In Control Panel, open the **Printers and Faxes** folder.

2. Under Printer Tasks, click **Add a printer** to open the **Add Printer Wizard**. Then click **Next**.

3. Complete the **Add Printer Wizard** by using the information provided in Table 3.4.

Table 3.4   Steps for Completing the Add Printer Wizard

Wizard Page	Action
Local or Network Printer	Click **Local printer attached to this computer**, clear the **Automatically detect and install my Plug and Play printer** check box, and then click **Next**.
Select a Printer Port	Click **Create a new port**, and then select **LPR Port**.
Add LPR compatible printer	If **LPR Port** is not available, click **Cancel** to stop the Wizard. To add the LPR Port, install the optional networking component, **Print Services for UNIX**.
Name or address of server providing LPD	Type the Domain Name System (DNS) name or Internet Protocol (IP) address of the host for the printer that you are adding. The host might be the direct-connect TCP/IP printing device or the UNIX computer to which the printing device is connected. The DNS name can be the name specified for the host in the Hosts file.
Name of printer or print queue on that server	Type the name of the printer as it is identified by the host, which is either the direct-connect printer itself or the UNIX computer.

Configuring LPR to print text files to a PostScript printer in UNIX

In some cases, sending an ASCII text file to a PostScript printer on a UNIX-based computer can cause PostScript code to be output on the printer. This can occur because the PostScript printer is processing the text as RAW data without interpreting the PostScript code.

LPR sends a processing instruction in each print job in the form of a control command indicating the data format. Table 3.5 shows the LPR commands for specific data types. Under **Lprmon**, the default is **l** (RAW data); under Lpr.exe, the default is **f** (text).

Table 3.5   Control Commands for LPR Printing

LPR Control Command	Data Format Transmitted
f, p	Text data type
L	RAW data type
0	RAW data type formatted for a PostScript printer

Using the default value of **l** can cause the PostScript code to be printed on a UNIX-based system. The **l** value sets the RAW data type, which causes the text file to be printed ignoring the PostScript instructions. To correct this, set **0** (RAW data type formatted for a PostScript printer) as the default value. This might not be necessary on some UNIX systems, which include software that scans arriving documents for PostScript code with the **l** value. If the software detects the **l** value, the document goes directly to the printer; otherwise, the software adds PostScript code. You can change the default control command that LPR sends by editing the **PrintSwitch** entry in the registry.

Caution

Do not edit the registry unless you have no alternative. The registry editor bypasses standard safeguards, allowing settings that can damage your system, or even require you to reinstall Windows. If you must edit the registry, back it up first and see the Registry Reference on the *Windows Server 2003 Deployment Kit* companion CD, or at http://www.microsoft.com/reskit.

▷ To change the default control command for a printer

1. In the registry editor, navigate to:

    HKEY_LOCAL_MACHINE\SYSTEM\CurrentControlSet\Control\Print\Monitors\LPRPort\Ports\Port-name\IP Address or Host name: Printer-name

2. Double-click **PrintSwitch**.

3. In the **Data type** box, type REG_SZ, and then in the **Value Data** box, type the control command you want to specify. (See Table 3.5 for a list of control commands and the value data types that they represent.)

Respooling

Respooling is a method of spooling a document twice to enable the print monitor to locate the appropriate LPD print server. LPR must include an accurate byte count in the control file, but it cannot get the byte count from the local print provider. After Lprmon receives a document from the local print provider, it spools the document a second time to a temporary file in the default spool directory, finds the size of that file, and then sends the size to the LPD print server.

Status reporting

LPR is a one-way protocol and does not return a detailed error status report. If a problem occurs, the message is always ERROR. For more information about LPR or LPR errors, see the Microsoft Knowledge Base link on the Web Resources page at www.Microsoft.com/windows/reskits/webresources. Search the Knowledge Base using the keywords "LPR" or "LPR Errors".

Pooling printers

Printer pooling is especially useful in high-volume printing environments. Pooled printers appear to clients as a single printer, but printing throughput is increased because the load is distributed among the printers in the pool.

Before you set up a printer pool, consider the following issues:

- Two or more printers are required; Windows Server 2003 does not limit the number of printers in a pool.

- The printers in the pool must be of the same model, and they must use the same printer driver.

- Printer ports can be of the same type or mixed (such as parallel, serial, and network).

- If you want to ensure that documents are first sent to the faster printers, add the faster printers to the pool first and the slower printers last. Print jobs are routed in the order in which you create the ports.

- Because users do not know which printer prints their documents, it is a good idea to locate all of the pooled printers in the same physical location. Otherwise, users might not be able to find their printed documents.

▷ To create a printer pool

1. In Control Panel, open the **Printers and Faxes** folder, right-click the appropriate printer, and click **Properties**.

2. On the **Ports** tab, select the **Enable printer pooling** check box.

3. In the list of ports, select the check boxes for the ports connected to the printers that you want to pool.

4. Repeat steps 2 and 3 for each additional printer to be included in the printer pool.

Adding Additional Printer Drivers

By adding additional drivers to your print server, you can support clients that are running various versions of the Windows operating systems. It is preferable to use Version 3 drivers rather than Version 2 drivers as your primary drivers, because Version 2 drivers can cause the system to become unstable or stop responding. However, you might need to use Version 2 drivers as additional drivers if you support clients running Windows NT 4.0. If your server has known bad drivers when it is upgraded, those drivers are deleted during the upgrade process. Any additional drivers that are added must have the same name as the primary driver unless they are Windows 95, Windows 98, or Windows Millennium Edition drivers.

 Note

With Windows Server 2003, you no longer need to install printer drivers on each node of a cluster. The drivers automatically propagate to the other nodes of the cluster after they are installed on the virtual server.

Publishing Printers in Active Directory

Publishing your shared printers in Active Directory can make locating printers across a network more efficient for your users. In Windows Server 2003, the print subsystem is tightly integrated with Active Directory, making it possible to search across a domain for printers at different locations. By using the standard printer object that Windows Server 2003 provides, you enable users to search for printer-based attributes such as printing capabilities (including PostScript, color, and paper size) and printer locations (allowing users to find printers located near them).

If you plan to publish printers to Active Directory, follow the naming standard that the print services design team created when you fill out the location fields on the printer properties pages across your network. This enables users to enter a standard string to search for printers by location. If you use subnets to define the sites within your organization, Active Directory can find nearby printers – a process that has formerly been difficult for both administrators and users.

For example, if you are in Los Angeles and want to find all the Los Angeles printers in your deployment, search for a network printer by using the Add Printer Wizard and type **US/LAX** in the **Location** dialog box. If **US/LAX** matches the printer location syntax in Active Directory, your search might return the following results:

- US/LAX/1/101

- US/LAX/2/103

These results indicate that two printers are available in Los Angeles, located in buildings 1 and 2, in rooms 101 and 103.

Printer publishing is controlled by the **List in the Directory** check box on the **Sharing** tab of the **Properties** sheet for each printer. Printers that are added by using the Add Printer Wizard are published by default, and the wizard does not let you change this setting. If you do not want to publish a printer in Active Directory, after adding the printer, open the printer property sheet, and clear the **List in the directory** check box on the **Sharing** tab.

The printer is placed in the **Computer** object in Active Directory on the print server. After publishing the printer in Active Directory, you can move or rename the object by using the Users and Computers snap-in in Active Directory.

▶ **To publish a printer in Active Directory**

1. In Control Panel, open the **Printers and Faxes** folder.

2. Right-click the icon for the printer that you want to publish in Active Directory, and click **Properties**.

3. On the **Sharing** tab, select the **List in the directory** check box.

Connecting Clients to Printers

Generally, clients can establish a connection to a shared network printer hosted on a Windows Server 2003 print server in one of three ways:

- **Entering the Universal Naming Convention (UNC) path.** In the **Run** dialog box, type the UNC path for the printer (for example, \\PrintServer\Printer), and then click **OK**.

- **Using the Add Printer Wizard.** From the **Printer and Faxes** folder, select **Add a Printer**. When the Add Printer Wizard opens, click **Next**, select the network printer option, and either type or browse to the path for the shared printer.

- **Using drag-and-drop.** In the **Run** dialog box, open the shared printers folder on the remote print server. Then drag the desired printer icon into the **Printers and Faxes** folder on the local workstation.

Restricting Access to Printers

If your design calls for restricting access to certain printers, you can do so by using printer permissions. To do this, it is recommended that you create a user group and then limit access to a printer to members of the group.

▶ **To create a local group**

1. Right-click **My Computer**, and click **Manage**.

2. In the console tree, double-click **Local Users and Groups**.

3. To add the group, right-click **Groups**, and click **New Group**.

4. In the **Group name** box, type the name of the new local group.

5. To add users to the group, click **Add**, and enter the user names in the **Enter the object names to select** box.

▷ **To restrict access to a specific printer**

1. In Control Panel, open the **Printers and Faxes** folder.

2. Right-click the icon for the printer to which you want to restrict access, and click **Properties**.

3. To remove extraneous group members, on the **Security** tab, remove all entries in the **Groups or user names** list box except Administrator and Creator Owner.

4. To grant access to the printer, click **Add**, and then enter the names of the groups and users that you want to grant access to this printer.

Enabling Internet Printing

By using Internet printing, you can manage print resources from your Web browser. To be able to print over the Internet, clients within the same Local Area Network (LAN) must use a remote procedure call (RPC) to connect to the print server. For more information about prerequisites for Internet printing, see the *Server Management Guide* of the *Windows Server 2003 Resource Kit* (or see the *Server Management Guide* on the Web at http://www.microsoft.com/reskit).

Installing a Printer from a Web Page

To install a printer for Internet printing, you can either view a Web page to find a printer that is identified by a URL, or — if the client is running Windows Server 2003, Windows XP Professional, Windows 2000, Windows 95, Windows 98, or Windows Millennium Edition — connect to a printer share through a Web page.

Open a web browser, and type: http://*servername*/printers. Under **Printer Actions,** click **Connect**. The installation page displays available options based on your permissions. Windows Server 2003 downloads the printer software to the client, and the printer is displayed in the **Printers and Faxes** folder on the client.

The installation route depends on whether the client and the print server are on the same intranet and are both running Windows XP Professional, Windows Server 2003, Windows 2000, or Windows NT 4.0. If they are, the client and print server communicate by means of an RPC, and the installed printer continues to use an RPC to link the client and the server even if HTTP is not specified in the address.

The installation uses HTTP instead of RPC in the following instances:

- The client and server are not on the same intranet.

- The client is not running Windows Server 2003, Windows XP Professional, Windows 2000, or Windows NT 4.0.

- The printer contains an internal network adapter, supports Internet Printing Protocol 1.0, and is not connected to a server.

With HTTP, the print server generates a .cab file containing the required .inf and installation files and sends the .cab file to the client. On the client computer, the .cab file starts the Add Printer Wizard to complete the installation. A progress report is displayed in HTML while the wizard is working.

 Important

Installation is not automatic for Web-based printers with internal network adapters. You must start the Add Printer Wizard, enter the printer's URL instead of a UNC path, and manually enter information that the wizard requires. You can use this method to install any URL-identified printer by means of HTTP.

Security for Internet Printing

Print server security is provided by IIS, which runs on the print server. IIS allows basic authentication, which all browsers support. The administrator must select basic authentication to enable the print server to support all browsers and all Internet clients. IIS and PWS allow the use of Integrated Windows authentication and Kerberos authentication, both of which are supported by Internet Explorer.

The authentication method for Internet printing in IIS or PWS is set in the print server's property sheet on the **Directory Security** tab.

By default, print jobs are sent over HTTP as RAW data. If it is important to keep this data secure, use either a Virtual Private Network (VPN) or Secure Socket Layer (SSL) connection.

▶ **To select an authentication method**

1. In the console tree of the IIS console, expand the node for the server, expand the Web Sites node, expand the Default Web Site node, and then expand the Printers node.

2. Click the icon at the Printers node.

    This node represents a virtual directory that is used to set all security for Internet printing. A list of Application Server Pages (ASP) appears in the details pane.

3. In the console tree, right-click the printer, click **Properties**, and then click the **Directory Security** tab.

4. Choose one of the following Directory Security options by clicking the respective **Edit** button:

    - **Authentication and access control**

    - **IP address and domain name restrictions**

    - **Secure communications**

Typically, administrators select **Enable anonymous access**, which allows a client to access each server resource by impersonating the Anonymous account IUSR_*computername*. No user action is required. If a user attempts to connect to another domain or proxy server that does not allow anonymous access, a dialog box prompts for the user name and password.

▶   **To choose anonymous access authentication**

1.   On the **Directory Security** tab of the **Printers Properties** page, click the **Edit** button for **Authentication and access control**.

2.   Select the **Enable Anonymous access** check box.

3.   Clear the **Windows Integrated authentication** check box.

 Note

Integrated Windows authentication is checked by default and takes precedence over other types of authentication. To ensure that users are authenticated anonymously, clear all check boxes except Enable anonymous access.

Integrated Windows authentication is more secure, because it does not send the password. During Integrated Windows authentication, IIS applies either challenge and response encryption technology, or Kerberos encryption technology, depending on the capability of the client. For more information about IIS security, see the *Internet Information Services (IIS) 6.0 Resource Guide* of the *Windows Server 2003 Resource Kit* (or see the *Internet Information Services (IIS) 6.0 Resource Guide* on the Web at http://www.microsoft.com/reskit).

Additional Resources

Related Information

- The *Server Management Guide* of the *Windows Server 2003 Resource Kit* (or see the *Server Management Guide* on the Web at http://www.microsoft.com/reskit).The Windows Deployment and Resource Kits Web site at http://www.microsoft.com/reskit, or see the MSDN Scripting Clinic link on the Web Resources page at http://www.microsoft.com/windows/reskits/webresources, for more information about scripting.

- RFC 1759: *Printer MIB* for more information about Printer Message Information Base.

- RFC 1179: *Line Printer Daemon Protocol* for more information about using an LPR port that uses the Line Printer Daemon Protocol.

Related Help topics

For best results in identifying Help topics by title, in Help and Support Center, under the **Search** box, click **Set search options**. Under **Help Topics**, select the **Search in title only** checkbox.

- "Initiate a resource failure in Help and Support Center for Windows Server 2003 for more information about initiating a resource failure.

- "Create a cluster-managed printer in Help and Support Center for Windows Server 2003 for more information about creating a cluster-managed printer.

- "Print Spooler resource type" in Help and Support Center or more information about printing and the Cluster service.

- "Windows Server 2003 Administration Tools Pack Overview in Help and Support Center for Windows Server 2003 for more information about the Administration Tools Pack.

- "Managing printing from the command line" in Help and Support Center for Windows Server 2003 for more information about managing printers from the command line.

- "Internet Printing" in Help and Support Center for Windows Server 2003 for more information about the Internet Printing.

Related Job Aids

- "Print Server Inventory Worksheet" (Sdcpsv_1.doc) on the *Windows Server 2003 Deployment Kit* companion CD (or see "Print Server Inventory Worksheet" on the Web at http://www.microsoft.com/reskit).

- "Print Server Design Worksheet" (Sdcpsv_2.doc) on the *Windows Server 2003 Deployment Kit* companion CD (or see "Print Server Design Worksheet" on the Web at http://www.microsoft.com/reskit).

Related Tools

- Print Migrator 3.0 (Printmig.exe)

  Use Printmig.exe to help automate printer consolidation on Windows Server 2003. Instead of recreating all of the printer objects manually, you can back up existing printers and restore them to your new print servers. To download Print Migrator, see the Print Services link on the Web Resources page at http://www.microsoft.com/windows/reskits/webresources.

- Fixprnsv.exe

  Use Fixprnsv.exe to help resolve printer driver compatibility issues between Windows NT 4.0, Windows 2000 and Windows Server 2003. Fixprnsv.exe is located on the Windows Server 2003 installation CD-ROM. The executable file is located in Windows\Printers directory. To view a list of commands used with this utility, use the command **fixprnsv.exe /?** from that directory.

- PrnAdmin

  Use PrnAdmin to help migrate from Windows NT 4.0 to Windows Server 2003. You can use Prnadmin.dll to inventory your current environment. PrnAdmin enumerates ports, drivers, printers, or forms on local or remote printers. The Visual Basic script for the PrnAdmin utility is named Prnmgr.vbs. PrnAdmin is located on the *Windows Server 2003 Deployment Kit* companion CD. To install PrnAdmin, type the following command:

  regsvr32 "C:\Program Files\Resource Kit\PrnAdmin.dll"

C H A P T E R   4

Hosting Applications with Terminal Server

With Terminal Server you can host applications in a central location, which saves management and deployment time and increases security because you install the applications once on a server, rather than on every desktop.

In This Chapter

Related Information

- For information about using Terminal Services and other remote management tools for remote administration, see the *Server Management Guide* of the *Microsoft® Windows® Server 2003 Resource Kit* (or see the *Server Management Guide* on the Web at http://www.microsoft.com/reskit).

- For more information about Remote Desktop, see "Configuring Remote Desktop" in *Microsoft® Windows® XP Professional Resource Kit Documentation* (or see "Configuring Remote Desktop" on the Web at http://www.microsoft.com/reskit).

Overview of the Terminal Server Deployment Process

Hosting applications from a central location with Terminal Server enables centralized management of those applications. You also gain added security because data is stored on the server, rather than on local computers. The following examples illustrate the kinds of business solutions that Terminal Server can provide.

Bandwidth-constrained locations   In areas where high bandwidth is not available or cost-effective, deploying applications on a terminal server can improve performance for remote users because large amounts of data are not being transmitted over the connection.

Applications in development or transition   You can simplify administration of crucial line-of-business applications that are in development or require frequent updating by deploying these applications on a terminal server. You can ensure that all users have access to the latest version by updating the application on the server rather than on individual client computers, reducing the total number of updates required.

Use of third-party platforms   You can reduce desktop hardware costs for users who have a primary line-of-business application that is available only on a desktop running an operating system other than a Microsoft® Windows® operating system, but who still require access to Windows-based applications. Users can connect to a terminal server to run the Windows-based applications.

Use of thin clients   Data-entry workers can access their primary application from a Windows-based terminal (or thin client) rather than a personal computer, reducing total cost of ownership. Using thin clients also minimizes work disruption for task workers. If a terminal stops running, you can replace it quickly, with minimal setup.

For more details about the solutions that Terminal Server provides, see "Identifying the Role of Terminal Server in Your Organization" later in this chapter.

Before you plan your deployment of Terminal Server, you need to design your domain infrastructure. After you complete the tasks outlined in this chapter, you can conduct a pilot test of your Terminal Server solution, adjust your design if necessary, and deploy the completed solution to the production environment. For more information about pilot testing, see Planning for Deployment in *Planning. Testing, and Piloting Deployment Projects* of this kit. For more information about implementing your Terminal Server solution, see "Terminal server role: Configuring a terminal server" in the Configure Your Server Wizard and "Checklists: Setting up Terminal Server" in Help and Support Center for the Microsoft® Windows® Server 2003 operating system.

Terminal Server is available with the Microsoft® Windows® Server 2003, Standard Edition; Windows® Server 2003, Enterprise Edition; and Windows® Server 2003, Datacenter Edition operating systems.

Process for Planning and Deploying Terminal Server

Figure 4.1 illustrates the high-level process for planning and deploying Terminal Server for hosting applications. Although the primary tasks remain the same for anyone planning to deploy Terminal Server, the steps differ depending on the solution you want to provide. Those differences are described in context throughout the chapter.

Figure 4.1   Planning and Deploying Terminal Server

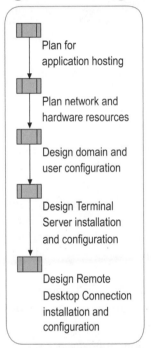

Plan for application hosting

Plan network and hardware resources

Design domain and user configuration

Design Terminal Server installation and configuration

Design Remote Desktop Connection installation and configuration

For a job aid to assist you in recording your design decisions, see "Terminal Server Planning and Design Worksheet" (SDCTS_1.xls) on the *Microsoft® Windows® Server 2003 Deployment Kit* companion CD (or see "Terminal Server Planning and Design Worksheet" on the Web at http://www.microsoft.com/reskit). For a job aid to assist you in recording your Terminal Server Group Policy configuration decisions, see "Group Policy Configuration Worksheet" (SDCTS_2.xls) on the *Windows Server 2003 Deployment Kit* companion CD (or see "Group Policy Configuration Worksheet" on the Web at http://www.microsoft.com/reskit).

Basic Terminal Server Concepts

The Terminal Server component of Windows Server 2003, which was called Terminal Services in Application Server Mode in the Microsoft® Windows® 2000 operating system, can deliver the Windows desktop, in addition to Windows-based applications, from a centralized server to virtually any desktop computing device, including those that cannot run Windows.

Terminal Server uses the Remote Desktop Protocol (RDP) to communicate between client and server. After you deploy an application on a terminal server, clients can connect over a remote access connection, local area network (LAN), wide area network (WAN), or the Internet. The client computers can run Windows (including the Microsoft® Windows® CE operating system) or run on other operating systems such as the Apple Macintosh or even UNIX (using a third-party add-on). When a user accesses an application on a terminal server that is running Windows Server 2003, all of the work of the application takes place on the server and only the keyboard, mouse, and display information are transmitted over the network to the user desktop. Each user sees only their individual session, which is managed transparently by the server operating system and is independent of any other client session.

Windows Server 2003 Terminal Server offers the following new features and improvements:

- For improved load-balancing performance, the new Session Directory feature automatically reconnects users to an existing session within a load-balanced server farm, rather than just being directed to the least loaded server when they reconnect.

- For improved logon security, you can use a smart card to log on to a terminal server running Windows Server 2003 and run applications from client computers with a smart card subsystem (including computers running the Microsoft® Windows® XP operating system, Windows 2000, and the Windows CE operating system). This provides an additional level of physical security to your network environment.

- For a better user experience, Terminal Services supports a wider variety of data redirection types (including file system, serial port, printer, audio, and time zone) and supports connections in up to 24-bit color.

- For improved management, there is an expanded set of Group Policy settings for Terminal Server and a full Windows Management Instrumentation (WMI) provider allowing for scripted configuration of Terminal Server settings.

- For improved license management, you can install Terminal Services Enterprise Licensing on either a domain controller or a member server. Terminal Services Licensing wizards have been improved to reduce the complexity of activating a terminal server and assigning it licenses. There is also a new security group that allows only specific terminal servers to request licenses from a license server in a domain.

For more information about improvements in Windows Server 2003 Terminal Server, see the "What's New in Terminal Server" white paper at the Terminal Services: Community Center link on the Web Resources page at http://www.microsoft.com/windows/reskits/webresources and "Using Terminal Server to host applications centrally" in Help and Support Center for Windows Server 2003.

Planning for Application Hosting

As shown in Figure 4.2, the first step in planning your deployment of Windows Server 2003 Terminal Server is to clearly identify the scope of your deployment. This step provides you with a high-level specification on which to base the design of your network and domain infrastructure.

Figure 4.2   Planning for Application Hosting with Terminal Server

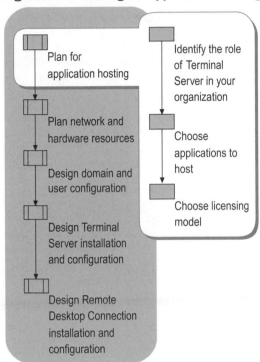

Identifying the Role of Terminal Server in Your Organization

The way in which you plan to use Terminal Server has an effect on how you deploy it. The following sections outline the various ways in which you might use Terminal Server in your organization. Use the information in these sections to clarify how you are going to use Terminal Server in your organization.

Hosting Line-of-Business Applications

If your organization or certain groups within your organization use specialized applications to do their work, it might be beneficial to host the applications with Terminal Server. For example, you might decide to use Terminal Server in the following situations:

- **Custom applications.** If your line-of-business application is developed in-house or especially for your organization, and it tends to require frequent updating or repair, deploying the application once on a terminal server can simplify administration of the application. This is especially useful if your environment is geographically dispersed or if you are deploying Terminal Server to centrally serve your organization's branch offices.

- **Large central data pool.** Applications that rely on access to a single data source often run better on a terminal server because large amounts of data do not have to travel across the network to users. Instead, the data processing takes place on the server. Only the keystrokes and display information travel across the network, so you can use lower bandwidth connections. This is especially useful if the users of the data pool are located remotely, for example in a branch office with a slow connection to the database server.

- **Task workers.** In environments where you want workers to access only the application that they need to perform their jobs, you can centralize the administration of these users by using Terminal Server.

- **IT Admin tools.** System administrators can perform tasks that require Enterprise Admin or Domain Admin permissions on a terminal server that has the necessary tools installed on it. They can also run their desktop applications on their local computer without these permissions.

- **Upgrading operating systems.** If your organization uses a line-of-business application that is not optimized for your desktop operating system, you can host the application with Terminal Server rather than change operating systems.

Hosting the Desktop

You can use Terminal Server to host users' entire desktop environments, so that when users log on, they see their usual desktop environments or desktop environments especially designed for their remote use. In this situation, users can open and close the applications they choose in the same way that they access applications from the Windows desktop on the local computer. You can host the desktop in the situations discussed in the following sections.

Remote users

Hosting the desktop with Terminal Server can provide higher levels of consistency and performance for users in remote locations because large amounts of application data are not being transmitted over the connection. For example, you might use Terminal Server in the following situations:

- **Bandwidth-constrained locations.** In areas where high bandwidth is not available or cost-effective, deploying applications on a terminal server can improve performance for users who are connecting to the network from a remote location over slow dial-up connections.

- **Mobile users.** For users who are traveling and tend to access the corporate network over connections of varying bandwidth, Terminal Server can provide a more consistent experience.

Client heterogeneity

If your organization is in the process of converting all users to the same platform or upgrading desktop hardware, you can use Terminal Server to quickly deliver the most up-to-date version of the operating system and applications to the user while enabling you to spread the desktop platform or hardware conversion over a longer period of time. You can also deliver a highly controlled standard desktop to users by using Terminal Server, as illustrated in more detail in the following list:

- **Mixed-platform environment.** If you have users who require applications based on operating systems other than Windows to perform their jobs, but your organization is transitioning to or requires a Windows-based desktop, you can host the desktop with Terminal Server. This requires the use of third-party software in conjunction with Terminal Server.

- **Upgrading hardware.** If your organization is planning to upgrade to Windows XP on the desktop, but not all of the desktop hardware is compatible, you can use Terminal Server to host the desktops of users who have older hardware while you are in the process of upgrading the hardware. All users can have the same desktop environment and run the latest versions of the applications designed for Windows XP regardless of their desktop hardware.

- **Highly controlled environments.** In situations where you want to deliver a standardized and controlled environment to users, you can host the desktop with Terminal Server to centralize management.

Hardware Considerations

You can reduce hardware costs by hosting applications with Terminal Server and using thin client devices or older hardware on your users' desktops.

- **Use of thin clients.** Windows Powered thin clients (sometimes called Windows-based terminals) offer an alternative to personal computers and traditional "green screen" terminals by enabling easy remote access to productivity and line-of-business applications that are hosted on Windows-based terminal servers.

- **Extending the life of older hardware.** Rather than replacing older hardware that is no longer capable of running new Windows-based applications, you can use that older hardware much like a thin client to access the desktop and applications on the server rather than on the local computer.

Using the Remote Desktop Web Connection

The Remote Desktop Web Connection is an ActiveX control that provides virtually the same functionality as the executable version of Remote Desktop Connection, but it delivers this functionality over the Web even if the executable version is not installed on the client computer. When hosted in a Web page, the ActiveX Client Control allows a user to log on to a terminal server through a TCP/IP Internet or intranet connection and view a Windows desktop inside Internet Explorer.

The Remote Desktop Web Connection provides an easy way to offer Terminal Server through a URL. Consider using the Remote Desktop Web Connection in the following situations:

- **Roaming users.** Users who are away from their computers can use Remote Desktop Web Connection to gain secure access to their primary workstations from any computer running Windows and Internet Explorer, provided they can reach the target computers.

- **Delivery of extranet applications.** You can use Remote Desktop Web Connection to allow business partners or customers access to internal applications over the Internet. Users who gain access in this manner do not need to reconfigure their computers, and they do not gain access to your internal network.

- **Deployment transition.** You can deploy the Remote Desktop Web Connection quickly and use it while you are deploying your full Remote Desktop Connection infrastructure.

For more information about the Remote Desktop Web Connection, see the *Server Management Guide* of the *Windows Server 2003 Resource Kit* (or see the *Server Management Guide* on the Web at http://www.microsoft.com/reskit).

Choosing Applications to Host

Before deploying applications with Terminal Server, you must determine which applications are ideal candidates for hosting in your organization, and determine if those applications will work well in a Terminal Server environment. You might also want to host the entire desktop through Terminal Server.

Identifying Ideal Candidates for Hosting

When choosing applications to host with Terminal Server, consider the compatibility of those applications with Terminal Server. Many desktop applications load and run correctly with Terminal Server. Applications that have been certified for Windows are generally compatible with Terminal Server. For more information about the Certified for Windows program, see the Certified for Windows link on the Web Resources page at http://www.microsoft.com/windows/reskits/webresources.

With any Windows-based application the definitive source of compatibility information should always be the application's vendor or developer. For more information about application compatibility with Terminal Services, see "Program compatibility" in Help and Support Center for Windows Server 2003. There are also application compatibility notes for some applications available on the VeriTest Catalog of Certified Windows Server Applications link on the Web Resources page at http://www.microsoft.com/windows/reskits/webresources.

Application Characteristics That Affect Performance with Terminal Server

Because Terminal Server is available for multisession (multiuser) use, and because the display and keystroke information travels over the network, applications that have certain characteristics might perform poorly with Terminal Server. When planning for your organization, establish a set of acceptable performance guidelines and determine through testing whether such applications run better on the user's local computer. For example:

- Multimedia applications or applications that have very large graphical output do not run well with Terminal Server. Because large amounts of display information travel over the network, the performance of these types of applications is often unacceptable, especially over low-bandwidth connections. Many computer-aided design (CAD) and streaming media applications fall into this category.

- Running 16-bit programs with Terminal Server can reduce the number of users a processor supports and increases the memory required for each user. Windows Server 2003 translates 16-bit programs in enhanced mode through a process called Windows on Windows (WOW). This causes 16-bit programs to consume additional system resources. A similar situation exists with running 32-bit applications on the 64-bit versions of Windows Server 2003.

 Note
You can prevent 16-bit applications from running on Windows Server 2003 by enabling the **Prevent access to 16-bit applications** Group Policy setting. This setting is located in Administrative Templates/Windows Components/Application Compatibility. You can set this setting for both the computer and the user.

There are third-party add-ons that you can use to help with the performance of 16-bit applications and other application compatibility issues. For more information about these add-ons, see the AppSense and Tame Software links on the Web Resources page at http://www.microsoft.com/windows/reskits/webresources.

- Applications that are based on the Microsoft® MS-DOS® operating system use keyboard polling that can consume all the available resources on a CPU.

- Applications with features that run continuously in the background (for example automatic spelling and grammar checking in Microsoft® Word) can affect performance with Terminal Server. In some cases, you can restrict user or group access to certain application types, disable unnecessary features that require the most resources, or install applications on separate servers to minimize the performance effects.

- Complex automation or macros can be CPU-intensive and are not recommended. If you use or plan to use macros with the applications you plan to host, test your plans thoroughly to ensure adequate performance.

- If you plan to use Terminal Server to host custom applications or applications developed in-house, you need to consider the specification for applications for the Certified for Windows program. For more information about the Certified for Windows program, see the Certified for Windows link on the Web Resources page at http://www.microsoft.com/windows/reskits/webresources. For information about guidelines for developing applications for use with Terminal Server, see the Optimizing Applications for Windows 2000 Terminal Services link on the Web Resources page at http://www.microsoft.com/windows/reskits/webresources.

- If you plan to host older applications with Windows Server 2003 Terminal Server, for example applications that you have hosted with the Microsoft® Windows® NT 4.0 Terminal Server Edition operating system, be aware that you might need to run Terminal Server in Relaxed Security mode, which allows access to system files and the registry on the server, in order for these applications to function properly. For more information about security modes, see "Designing the Terminal Server Configuration" later in this chapter.

After you choose the applications you want to host, analyze these applications for potential problems in a multiuser environment and thoroughly test them, including end-user testing and pilot testing, to ensure that they work in your environment. For more information about piloting and testing, see "Planning for Deployment" in *Planning, Testing, and Piloting Deployment Projects* of this kit.

Compatibility Scripts

You might have to modify or provide support for custom applications or applications that are not written to accommodate multiuser access. Such applications might not use per user data storage, the user-specific portions of the registry, or appropriate permissions. You can run compatibility scripts for these applications after you install the application. These scripts are available:

- **With the Windows Server 2003 operating system**. These scripts are located in the *systemroot*\Application Compatibility Scripts\Install folder.

- **From your application vendor**. These scripts might be available on the application CD, on the Web, or by special order from the company.

- **By developing them yourself**. Use the scripts in the *systemroot*\Application Compatibility Scripts\Install\Template folder as a template.

Information about running these scripts is available in the "Designing Application Installation" section later in the chapter. For more information about the Windows Application Compatibility Toolkit, see "Testing Application Compatibility" in *Automating and Customizing Installations* of this kit.

Hosting Full Desktops with Terminal Server

If you determine that hosting with Terminal Server is an ideal way to manage an application, consider running just the application (not the entire desktop) on the terminal server. This can save significant resources on the terminal server and can allow many more users to log on to the server simultaneously.

If, however, you want your users to access their full desktop from the terminal server as outlined in "Identifying the Role of Terminal Server in Your Organization" earlier in this chapter, be sure to fully test for performance and server capacity using the full load of applications to which your users will have access. For more information about server capacity, see "Terminal Server Capacity Planning" later in this chapter.

Choosing the Desktop Theme

If you host the full desktop with Terminal Server, the desktop environment is like the Windows desktop. The default desktop theme for Windows Server 2003, however, is Windows Classic. You can use the Windows XP default theme, however this theme affects performance for the user because it is more graphic intensive than Windows Classic. Test the responsiveness for the end user and perform real-user testing to ensure that the performance is satisfactory when using this theme. For more information about testing, see "Terminal Server Capacity Planning" later in this chapter.

You can also choose a specific theme for your end users or enforce the use of the Windows Classic theme through Group Policy. For more information, see "Configuring User Group Policy Settings" later in this chapter.

Choosing the Licensing Model

To use Terminal Server in your organization, you are required to have a Windows Server 2003 license for every terminal server that you deploy in your organization as well as Terminal Server Client Access Licenses (CALs) for devices that access the terminal servers. For terminal servers that are running Windows Server 2003, there are two types of Terminal Server CALs:

- Per Device
- Per User

Which CAL you choose depends on how you plan to use Terminal Server. By default, Terminal Server is configured in Per Device mode, but it can be switched to Per User mode using the Terminal Services Connection Configuration (TSCC) tool or by using Windows Management Instrumentation (WMI). You can serve both license types from the same license server. For more information about how to set your licensing mode, see "Designing the Terminal Server Configuration" later in this chapter.

 Note

Windows 2000 Internet Connector Licensing has been replaced by Terminal Server External Connector Licensing in Windows Server 2003. Improvements include licensing qualification extended to business partners in addition to customers, authenticated access, and unlimited concurrent users per server. For more information about External Connector Licensing, see the "Windows Server 2003 Licensing" link on the Web Resources page at http://www.microsoft.com/windows/reskits/webresources. Windows Server 2003 retains support for Windows 2000 Internet Connector Licensing.

A Terminal Server license server on your network manages the Terminal Services CALs. A license server stores all Terminal Server CAL tokens that have been installed for a terminal server and tracks the license tokens that have been issued to clients. For more information about setting up a license server, see "Planning the License Server" later in this chapter.

For more information about Terminal Server licensing, see "Terminal Server Licensing overview" in Help and Support Center for Windows Server 2003 and the "Microsoft Windows Server 2003 Terminal Server Licensing" white paper at the Terminal Services link on the Web Resources page at http://www.microsoft.com/windows/reskits/webresources. For more information about licensing, see the Licensing Programs for Enterprises link on the Web Resources page at http://www.microsoft.com/windows/reskits/webresources.

 Note

Each serviceor application that users access from the terminal server must be licensed appropriately. Typically each device requires application licenses and CALs associated with it, even if the application or service is accessed indirectly through the terminal server. For more information, check the product documentation, End User License Agreement (EULA), or any other document that specifies product usage rights.

Per Device Licensing Mode

A Per Device CAL provides each client computer the right to access a terminal server that is running Windows Server 2003. The Per Device CAL is stored locally and presented to the terminal server each time the client computer connects to the server.

Per Device licensing is a good choice for:

- Hosting a user's primary desktop for devices the customer owns or controls.

- Thin clients or computers that connect to a terminal server for a large percentage of the working day.

- Hosting line-of-business applications that are used for the bulk of your users' work.

This type of licensing is a poor choice if you do not control the device accessing the server, for example computers in an Internet café, or if you have a business partner who connects to your terminal server from outside your network.

Per User Licensing Mode

In Per User licensing mode you must have one license for every user. With Per User licensing, one user can access a terminal server from an unlimited number of devices and only needs one CAL rather than a CAL for each device.

 Note

At the release of Windows Server 2003, Per User licensing is not enforced. However the terminal server must be able to discover a license server after the 120-day grace period expires. Otherwise, clients are denied access to the terminal server. For more information about the 120-day grace period, see "Planning the License Server" later in this chapter. For more information about the enforcement of Per User licensing, see the "Microsoft Windows Server 2003 Terminal Server Licensing" white paper at the Terminal Services link on the Web Resources page at http://www.microsoft.com/windows/reskits/webresources. For more information about plans for enforcing per user licensing, see the Licensing Programs for Enterprises link on the Web Resources page at http://www.microsoft.com/windows/reskits/webresources.

Per User licensing is a good choice in the following situations:

- Providing access for roaming users.

- Providing access for users who use more than one computer, for example, a portable and a desktop computer.

- Providing ease of management for organizations that track access to the network by user, rather than by computer.

In general, if your organization has more computers than users, Per User licensing might be a cost-effective way to deploy Terminal Server because you only pay for the user to access Terminal Server, rather than paying for every device from which the user accesses Terminal Server. Check the end-user license agreement for the applications that you plan to host to determine if they support per user licensing.

Planning Network and Hardware Resources

After you select the applications to host with Terminal Server, assess your network infrastructure, hardware, and security components to be sure your network is ready to deploy and run Terminal Server. Figure 4.3 shows the steps in this process.

Figure 4.3   Planning Network and Hardware Resources

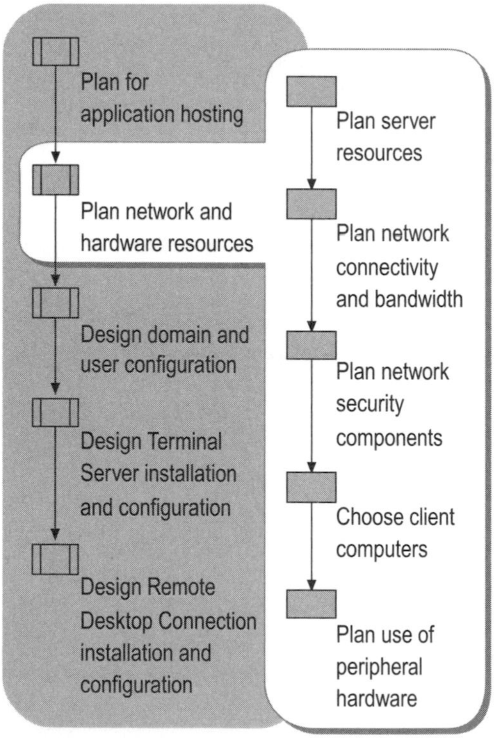

Planning Server Resources

Careful planning of the servers and server infrastructure on which you deploy Terminal Server determines the number of users who can access a terminal server at one time and the quality of their experience. You can also load balance your terminal servers for fault tolerance.

Terminal Server Capacity Planning

Size your terminal servers with sufficient CPU, memory, and disk resources to handle the client demand. For adequate performance, a terminal server requires a minimum of 128 megabytes (MB) RAM, plus additional RAM for each user running applications on the server, depending on the type of user. For more information about server capacity requirements for Terminal Server, see the Terminal Services link on the Web Resources page at http://www.microsoft.com/windows/reskits/webresources.

 Important

Guidelines outlined on this Web site are for specific server configurations, and provide a baseline for estimating server capacity. Terminal Server capacity can vary depending on factors such as type of user, server and network configuration, and the applications you are hosting. Test your design thoroughly and monitor the server load after deployment to be sure your servers have adequate capacity to provide users with an acceptable experience.

A multiprocessor configuration can maximize CPU availability. In general, processor and memory requirements scale linearly. You can support nearly double the number of users on a multiprocessor-capable Pentium system by doubling the number of processors and doubling the amount of memory. For this reason, purchasing a system that supports multiple processors, even if you initially purchase only one processor, allows you to add capacity easily as your requirements grow.

Estimating User Demand

The amount of RAM and CPU that Terminal Server users consume depends on the application features that they use, how often they use the application, and how much work they accomplish in any unit of time. If you understand the work patterns of your users, you can use the Terminal Server capacity planning tools on the *Windows Server 2003 Deployment Kit* companion CD — Roboserver (Robosrv.exe) and Roboclient (Robocli.exe) — to more accurately emulate the activity level of your users. For more information about Roboserver and Roboclient, click **Tools** in Help and Support Center, and then click Windows Resource Kit Tools. How to use the capacity planning tools to emulate the activity of your users is discussed later in this section.

Application Considerations

When determining server sizing, examine the types of applications your server runs. Check system requirements for each application carefully and consider that RAM and CPU requirements increase according to the number of sessions expected to run simultaneously. Also, a terminal server shares executable resources among individual users, just as Windows shares executable resources among individual programs. As a result, the memory requirements for additional users running the same program are typically less than the requirements for the first user who loads the application. Although you cannot make precise estimates based on these factors, they give you a basis for projecting program performance.

Testing Server Capacity

Test the servers on which you plan to host applications in order to ensure adequate server capacity. Using a server that you estimate to be of the correct capacity, construct a test environment with the appropriate number of sessions running the application for a specified period of time and at a level of activity that simulates actual use. Because adequate performance can be subjective, you need to also perform real-user testing. Ask users to identify perceived performance issues, and make sure that you establish baseline task completion times based on user feedback, and use a stopwatch to accurately measure the effect of server capacity on performance throughout testing. A good indicator of unacceptable performance is when the time to complete the tasks in the simulation takes 10 percent longer than the baseline.

Using the Capacity Planning Tools

To test the capacity of your terminal server to handle the estimated user demand, the *Windows Server 2003 Deployment Kit* provides Terminal Server capacity planning tools — Roboserver (Robosrv.exe) and Roboclient (Robocli.exe) — which include application scripting support. You can use these tools, which are available on the *Windows Server 2003 Deployment Kit* companion CD, to easily place and manage simulated loads on a server. This information can help you determine whether your environment can handle the load that users place on it. Used together, these tools make capacity planning easier and more automated. For more information about Roboserver and Roboclient, click **Tools** in Help and Support Center, and then click Windows Resource Kit Tools.

To use these tools, you will need to equip your test lab with the following hardware and software:

- A domain controller

- A server running Terminal Server

- Any additional servers needed to emulate the intended use of Terminal Server in the production environment, such as:

    - A server running Microsoft® SQL Server™ (if you are going to host an application with a SQL Server back end)

    - A server running Microsoft® Exchange (if you intend to host e-mail)

- Client computers

> **Note**
>
> The scripts included with the tools are designed for use with an Exchange server, and emulate typical usage patterns for knowledge workers and data entry workers. You can use these scripts as a template to create custom scripts for your needs. You should alter these scripts to emulate the users and infrastructure in your own environment.

The following sections summarize the hardware requirements for capacity planning tests.

For more information about using the capacity planning tools, click **Tools** in Help and Support Center for Windows Server 2003, and then click Windows Resource Kit Tools.

Note

Using these tools can also help you identify compatibility issues with the applications you plan to host with Terminal Server.

Domain controller   Roboserver runs on the domain controller. The domain controller should run Windows Server 2003, Enterprise Edition, or Microsoft® Windows® 2000 Advanced Server and be configured as the domain controller of a private domain. It should also be configured as a DNS server with both a Forward Lookup Zone and a Reverse Lookup Zone.

Terminal server   The server that runs Terminal Server should have the same hardware and be configured the same as the server planned for the production environment.

Client computers   Roboclient runs on the client computers. You need enough client computers to represent the number of users you plan to access the terminal server. You can emulate several users by using a single client computer. It is recommended that you limit the number to five, but if resources are limited, a low-end client computer can emulate as many as 20 users. In general, limit the number of users emulated on each client computer so as to keep the CPU usage of the computer below 20 percent.

Note

Emulating several users by using a single computer in the test lab alters network traffic differently than in the production environment. Network usage is higher in the production environment.

You can also use System Monitor, a Windows Server 2003 support tool, to monitor the performance on the terminal servers in your test lab. To start System Monitor, at the command line type **perfmon**. For more information about System Monitor, see "Perfmon" in Help and Support Center for Windows Server 2003.

Note

Measure disk performance from a remote computer because having the perfmon log on the disk that is being measured can affect the performance results.

Microsoft Operations Manager (MOM) is also a very useful tool for performance monitoring and scalability planning. For more information, see the Microsoft Operations Manager link on the Web Resources page at http://www.microsoft.com/windows/reskits/webresources.

Real-User Capacity Testing

Because a terminal server running at or above capacity affects performance, it is important that you also test server capacity with a sampling of real users. Also, the Terminal Server capacity planning tools simulate user activity but do not reflect actual human behavior, such as breaks and peaks and lulls in activity, and adequate performance for users is subjective. You can use your pilot test to further determine whether the capacity of your terminal servers is adequate. For more information about pilot testing, see "Planning for Deployment" in *Planning. Testing, and Piloting Deployment Projects* of this kit.

Note

It is highly recommended that you conduct a pilot test for your design before implementing it in the production environment. For Terminal Server, pilot testing is crucial for determining correct server size and satisfactory application performance levels in the production environment.

Data Storage Considerations

With Terminal Server, there are some storage access regions that you should consider distributing across several hard drives or redundant array of independent disks (RAID) array, especially for implementations serving large number of users:

- System binaries

- Application binaries

- User profiles and data

- Page files

For Terminal Server, it is best to put your page files on a dedicated hard drive. In addition, because of the multiuser nature of Terminal Server, be sure that your page file is twice the size of your RAM. For example, if your Terminal Server has 2 gigabytes (GB) of RAM, you should have a 4 GB paging file. You should also have two paging files if necessary. For information about how to change the default paging file size, see "Change the size of the virtual memory paging file" in Help and Support Center for Windows Server 2003.

For improved performance of storage devices with a backup power supply, you can use the following procedure.

▶ **To enable advanced disk performance for storage devices**

1. From the **Start** menu, click **All Programs**, click **Administrative Tools**, and then click **Computer Management**.

2. In **Computer Management**, under **Storage**, click **Disk Management**.

3. Right-click the disk for which you want to enable advanced performance and click **Properties**.

4. On the **Policies** tab, check the **Enable advanced performance** checkbox.

Load Balancing Terminal Servers

Using a load-balancing solution with Terminal Server distributes sessions across multiple servers for improved performance. Terminal Services Session Directory, which is available with Windows Server 2003, Enterprise Edition, works with your load-balancing solution. Session Directory is a database that tracks user sessions that are running on load-balanced terminal servers. It provides information when a user reconnects (after disconnecting intentionally or because of a network failure) to ensure that the user reconnects to the same session rather than starting a new session. Session Directory, which can support several thousand sessions, is also cluster-aware, so that you can support users who have concurrent sessions on different terminal server farms without confusion. For more information about Terminal Services Session Directory, see the "Session Directory and Load Balancing Using Windows Server 2003 Terminal Server" white paper at the Terminal Services link on the Web Resources page at http://www.microsoft.com/windows/reskits/webresources.

 Note

Load-balancing solutions that do not allow direct client network access to servers in the load-balanced farm need to support redirection tokens to work with Session Directory.

To implement load balancing and Session Directory with Terminal Server, you need to have the following in place:

- A load-balancing solution.

- Two or more terminal servers logically grouped into a Terminal Server farm.

- A Session Directory server.

Setting Up a Terminal Server Load-Balanced Farm

In general, set up your terminal server load-balanced farm and your load-balancing solution as you would in any other situation. Consult the documentation for your load-balancing solution.

There are a few things to consider for Terminal Server:

- Split network traffic between two network adapters — one used for Terminal Server, and the other for access to other network resources and infrastructure — placed on different subnets. By allowing RDP traffic only over the Terminal Services adapter, you can have more consistent traffic analysis and better security. More information about this is available later in this section.

- For easier administration, place load-balanced terminal servers into an organizational unit (OU) and apply Group Policy settings to that OU. If you have more than one Terminal Server load-balanced farm in your organization, place each in its own OU inside your Terminal Server OU so that you can apply Terminal Server–specific settings to the overall OU, but manage the separate farms individually.

- Configure your home directories and other user data storage in such a way that your users can easily access their data in the event of their being on a different server the next time they log on. For more information about how to do this, see "Planning Per-User Requirements" later in this chapter.

- Consider placing your terminal server farm and your clients on the same network backbone with your user profile servers and at least one domain controller. This allows for faster logon times.

Network Separation

Network separation is the separation of RDP traffic from other network traffic protocols. By dedicating one network adapter to Terminal Server traffic and the RDP, and one network adapter to application traffic, you can realize better overall performance on the Terminal Server load-balanced farms. This arrangement reduces the risk of having a network adapter bottleneck on the servers. Also, you can provide additional security by assigning different IP addresses and subnets to application traffic and to the RDP traffic. You can then constrain these separate routes as necessary by using routers, or switches and firewalls. This also tends to provide better auditing of users and traffic occurring on the network.

You can use IP packet filtering to achieve network separation. For more information about IP packet filtering, see "Designing a TCP/IP Network" in *Deploying Network Services* of this kit. You can specify the network adapter on which you want to place the RDP traffic on the **Network Adapter** tab of the TSCC. For more information about Terminal Server configuration tools, see "Designing the Terminal Server Configuration" later in this chapter.

Selecting a Host Server for Session Directory

The Session Directory server can be any server on the network that is running the Terminal Server Session Directory service. It is best if the Session Directory server is a highly available network server that is not running Terminal Server. However, you can place the Session Directory on a member of the cluster, if necessary. The Session Directory requires very little CPU, memory, and hard drive resources, so you can use a low-end member server to host the Session Directory service.

 Important

Running the Session Directory service on a domain controller is not recommended. On a member server, the Session Directory Computers group is a local group, but on a domain controller this group is a domain local group and is available on all domain controllers. The Session Directory Computers group is discussed in the following section.

One Session Directory host server can service multiple load-balanced clusters, and it is cluster-aware so it can handle users who have sessions running on different clusters seamlessly. You can also cluster the Session Directory itself for improved reliability. For more information about clustering the Session Directory, see the "Session Directory and Load Balancing Using Windows Server 2003 Terminal Server" white paper at the Terminal Services link on the Web Resources page at http://www.microsoft.com/windows/reskits/webresources.

Configuring Session Directory

After you choose a server on which to host Session Directory, you must start and configure the Session Directory service and configure the servers it will serve. You must configure the Session Directory host server to accept connections from authorized computers and you must configure the load-balanced servers to use Session Directory.

Host server configuration

When the Session Directory service starts, by default it creates the Session Directory Computers group (if one does not already exist). The group is empty and you need to add to this group the load-balanced terminal servers that will use this Session Directory server.

Session directory settings

If you are load balancing several terminal servers and using Session Directory, you can configure the servers to use Session Directory through TSCC (under Server Settings), Group Policy, or WMI. For more information about using server configuration tools, see "Designing the Terminal Server Configuration" later in this chapter.

Set the following settings to configure your load-balanced Terminal Server farm to use the session directory server:

- **Terminal Server IP Address Redirection.** When the client computer cannot connect directly to the terminal server, you can use the **Terminal Server IP Address Redirection** Group Policy setting to mask the IP address of the destination server in a load-balanced farm.

     Note
    You can only configure this setting through Group Policy or WMI.

    This policy setting is enabled by default. Disable this setting only if both of the following are true:

    - Your load-balancing solution does not allow direct connectivity from the client computer to the terminal server (for example, if your load-balancing solution is also a router).

    - Your load-balancing solution supports the use of Session Directory routing tokens.

- **Join Session Directory.** Enable this setting and apply it to your load-balanced Terminal Server OU to allow your server farm to use Session Directory. When you enable this setting, you must set the Session Directory Server and Session Directory Cluster Name settings.

- **Session Directory Server.** Enable this setting and enter the Domain Name System (DNS) name, IP address, or fully qualified domain name of the Session Directory server.

- **Session Directory Cluster Name.** Enable this setting and enter the DNS name for the load-balanced farm.

- **Network adapter and IP address session directory should redirect users to.** If your load-balanced farm is configured so that network traffic is separated between two or more network adapters, use the drop-down list in TSCC to choose the network adapter on the load-balanced server to which client computers should be directed.

 Note
You can only configure this setting through TSCC or WMI.

Implementing a Load-Balancing Solution with Session Directory

After you install and configure the terminal servers, you can set up your load-balancing solution and the Session Directory service if you are planning to use this service. To set up load balancing, consult the documentation for your solution. To use Group Policy to configure and manage your load-balanced Terminal Server farm centrally, create an OU and add each computer in the farm to the OU.

To set up Session Directory, you need to set up both the Session Directory host server and the servers that will be using Session Directory.

▶ **To set up the Session Directory host computer**

1. Right-click **My Computer** and click **Manage.**

2. Navigate to Services and Applications/Services, double-click **Terminal Services Session Directory**, and set the Startup type to Automatic.

   This service is off by default, and it is set to Manual. Starting this service and setting it to Automatic ensures that the service starts when the host server is turned on.

3. Add the computer group containing the load-balanced Terminal Server farm to the Session Directory Computers group that is created when the Session Directory service starts.

    Note
   By default, the Session Directory Computers group is empty. You can also create this group prior to starting the Session Directory service.

4. Configure the servers that will use the Session Directory service according to your plans from the previous section. For more information see the "Session Directory and Load Balancing Using Windows Server 2003 Terminal Server" white paper at the Terminal Services link on the Web Resources page at http://www.microsoft.com/windows/reskits/webresources.

Running Terminal Server with Other Applications and Services

Choosing the servers on which you deploy your applications depends on the applications you plan to host with Terminal Server and the applications and services you plan to run on the server with it. For example, you might want to conserve resources by hosting Terminal Server on a computer that also serves other purposes, or an application you plan to host might require another back-end service to run.

Sharing Terminal Servers with Other Applications and Services

To conserve resources, you can deploy Terminal Server on a server with other applications and services on the network. However, because Terminal Server is optimized for the desktop experience, this can affect the performance and scalability of both Terminal Server and the other application or service. You should, for example, avoid deploying server-based services, such as SQL Server and Exchange Server, with Terminal Server. Likewise, deploying Terminal Server on a server along with file, print, or other services can affect the performance of these services. This can cause problems especially if non-Terminal Server users access these services. Also, some services can cause conflicts with certain applications that you are hosting with Terminal Server if the client and server applications use different versions of DLLs. Test your setup if you plan to deploy Terminal Server on a server with other applications and services.

Hosting Data on a Separate Server or Drive

If you are planning to use Terminal Server to host a server-side, data-intensive application (for example a custom line-of-business application that has a SQL Server back end), you can improve performance by hosting the database and Terminal Server on separate servers. Placing the terminal server and the database on the same high-speed link or even on the same subnet increases the responsiveness of the application. You can optimize disk access performance by configuring multiple SCSI channels and distributing your operating system and application traffic across different physical drives. You can also dedicate a network adapter to operating system and application traffic, while the other network adapter handles RDP traffic.

Planning the License Server

A license server is required when Terminal Server is deployed for hosting applications and desktops. A license server stores all Terminal Server client license tokens that have been installed for a terminal server or group of terminal servers. It tracks the license tokens that have been issued by the Microsoft License Clearinghouse (the service that Microsoft maintains to activate license servers and to issue licenses to the license servers that request them). The license server manages client licenses through the terminal server. There is no direct communication between the client and the license server. For more information about Terminal Services licensing and how it works, see "Terminal Server Licensing overview" in Help and Support Center for Windows Server 2003 and the "Microsoft Windows Server 2003 Terminal Server Licensing" white paper at the Terminal Services link on the Web Resources page at http://www.microsoft.com/windows/reskits/webresources.

If you have a terminal server that is running Windows Server 2003, you must also have a license server that is running Windows Server 2003. You can use a license server that is running Windows Server 2003 to serve license tokens onto the terminal server that is running Windows Server 2003, or you can upgrade an existing license server that is running Windows 2000 to Windows Server 2003. You can set the **Prevent License Upgrade** Group Policy setting to prevent the license server from handing out Windows Server 2003 CALs to terminal servers that are running Windows 2000.

Note

For Windows Server 2003 you are no longer required to host Terminal Server licensing on a domain controller, but if you do not, you must configure the Terminal Server to discover the license server. For more information, see "Configuring the Preferred License Server" later in this section.

For information about how to transfer licenses from one license server to another, see "Repeat the installation of a client license key pack" in Help and Support Center for Windows Server 2003.

A terminal server must be able to connect to an activated license server before license tokens can be issued. To help you with your deployment planning and to give you time to install a license server and add license tokens, there is a 120-day grace period after the first client connects to a terminal server that is running Windows before you must have a license server activated. After this period, if the terminal server does not find an activated license server, clients are denied access. This grace period also ends when the first license token is issued to a client.

You can manage your license servers and Terminal Services license tokens using the Terminal Server Licensing administrative tool. For more information, see "Terminal Services administrative tools" in Help and Support Center for Windows Server 2003.

When planning your license server requirements, consider your organization's domain structure in order to choose a license server type and to select a server that is a good candidate for hosting Terminal Server Licensing. If, for example, you are deploying terminal servers for different business units or cost centers within your organization, consider deploying a license server for each Terminal Server deployment rather than a license server to service an entire domain or site. This enables each business unit to manage its own licenses and related costs. You must, however, configure your terminal servers to discover the correct license server in this situation. There is information about configuring a preferred license server later in this section.

Choosing the License Server Type

There are two types of license servers for Windows Server 2003, a domain license server and an enterprise license server. Decide which of the two types of license servers you require.

Domain license server

A domain license server is appropriate for managing Terminal Server users within a domain. Use a domain license server if you have only one domain, or if you want to manage licenses in each of your domains separately. If you have workgroups or Windows NT 4.0 domains, a domain license server is the only type that you can install, and any terminal server within the Windows NT 4.0 domain or workgroup can discover the license server. Terminal servers in a Windows 2000 or Windows Server 2003 domain can discover domain license servers only if they are in the same domain as the license server.

Enterprise license server

An enterprise license server can serve terminal servers in any domain within a site, but the domain must be a Windows Server 2003 or Windows 2000 Active Directory domain. Both the license server and Terminal Server must be within the same site.

This type of license server is appropriate if you manage users across multiple domains within a site, or if you are planning to restructure your domains. Enterprise license servers can be installed only by using Add or Remove Programs, not during Windows Server 2003 Setup. For more information about installing the license server, see "Designing Server Setting Configurations" later in this chapter.

Choosing a License Server Host Server

Servers running Windows Terminal Services can work only with license servers that are running Windows. In Windows Server 2003 domains, you can deploy the enterprise license server on either a domain controller or a member server. You are no longer required to install the license server on a domain controller, as was required in Windows 2000. For information about upgrading your license servers, see "Upgrading to Windows Server 2003 Terminal Server" later in this chapter.

 Important

If you plan to deploy a domain license server, and you choose not to deploy your license server on a domain controller, you must directly edit the registry to configure Terminal Server to locate the license server. You must do this even if the license server and the terminal server are the same computer. For more information about this process, see "Configuring the Preferred License Server" later in this section.

Take the following situations into consideration when choosing where to host Terminal Server Licensing:

- If you are deploying a license server to serve only one terminal server, consider installing the license server on the same server as Terminal Server. Terminal Server licensing causes negligible network traffic, but placement on the same server as Terminal Server eliminates the need for the server to go over the network to obtain licenses, and Terminal Server users experience no downtime if problems occur on the network.

- If you are deploying a license server for a terminal server that is hosting applications for remote clients or for users who access applications over the Internet, place the license server so that it can be accessed easily by the terminal server because there is no direct communication between the client and the license server.

Terminal Services Licensing takes about a megabyte (MB) of disk space to install, and about 10 MB of additional disk space per 1,000 licenses. If you plan to activate the license server and install subsequent license key packs automatically through the Terminal Services Licensing tool, the license server must communicate with the Microsoft License Clearinghouse using Secure Sockets Layer (SSL). SSL is a secure connection; however, as an added security precaution, avoid placing your license server on a server that hosts sensitive data that you would not otherwise want exposed to the Internet. For more information about methods to activate the license server, see "Activating a Terminal Server License Server" in Help and Support Center for Windows Server 2003. For more information about methods for installing subsequent license key packs, see "Install Client License Key Packs" in Help and Support Center for Windows Server 2003.

Setting Up Fault Tolerant License Servers

One activated license server can serve many terminal servers and Terminal Server users simultaneously. In large implementations of Terminal Services, you might want to deploy at least two licensing servers for fault tolerance. Terminal Server Licensing is not cluster-aware. However, you can improve fault tolerance for the license server by deploying two license servers per domain.

 Note
You can host Per Device and Per User licensing on the same server.

Choose two host servers for licensing and install all licenses on one license server; do not install any licenses on the backup server. The full server functions as the primary license server and can service all license requests. If the primary license server becomes unavailable, the backup license server can issue 90-day temporary license tokens to clients that need them. When the primary license server is back online, it replaces the temporary license tokens the next time the clients connect.

Configuring the Preferred License Server

If you choose not to deploy your license server on a domain controller, you must configure Terminal Services to locate the license server by directly editing the registry. For more information about the Terminal Services license server discovery process for Windows Server 2003, see article 279561, "How to Override the License Server Discovery Process in Windows Server 2003 Terminal Services." To find this article, see the Microsoft Knowledge Base link on the Web Resources page at http://www.microsoft.com/windows/reskits/webresources.

Caution

Do not edit the registry unless you have no alternative. The registry editor bypasses standard safeguards, allowing settings that can damage your system, or even require you to reinstall Windows. If you must edit the registry, back it up first and see the Registry Reference on the *Windows Server 2003 Deployment Kit* companion CD, or at http://www.microsoft.com/reskit.

▷ **To select a specific license server**

1. On each terminal server, in the **Run** dialog box, type **regedit**, and then click **OK**.

2. Locate the following path in the registry and select it:

   HKEY_LOCAL_MACHINE\SYSTEM\CurrentControlSet\Services \TermService\Parameters

3. On the **Edit** menu, point to **New**, and then click **Key** to add a subkey named LicenseServers, if one does not already exist.

4. Select the LicenseServers subkey, and on the **Edit** menu, point to **New**, and then click **Key** and type in the NetBIOS name, fully qualified domain name, or IP address of the appropriate license server to add the new subkey under LicenseServers.

5. Repeat step 4 for each license server you want the terminal server to discover.

The order of the license servers listed in the registry subkey does not guarantee the order in which the license servers are discovered. If you have more than one implementation of Terminal Server in your organization, you should also configure the license servers themselves to discover only the servers intended to service that implementation by using this procedure.

When Terminal Server discovers a license server, it continues to use that license server until it becomes unavailable. If the licence server is out of licenses, it will forward the request to a license server that has the requested type of license.

Note

If your license servers are not on domain controllers, they will only discover other license servers if their registries are configured for them to do so.

If you are deploying more than one license server to serve separate Terminal Server implementations and if you do not need to keep the licenses allocated to each implementation separate, consider adding the names of all of the license servers in your site or domain to the registry subkey LicenseServers for fault tolerance. However, if you need to keep the licenses allocated to each implementation separate, for example if they are managed by a different administrator or are in different cost centers, you should add to the registry subkey only the name of the license server or servers specific to each terminal server. In this situation, consider deploying two license servers if fault tolerance is a concern.

Planning Network Connectivity and Bandwidth

Terminal Server uses RDP to communicate between client and server. RDP works only across a TCP/IP connection, such as a local area network (LAN), wide area network (WAN), dial-up, Integrated Services Digital Network (ISDN), digital subscriber line (DSL), or virtual private network (VPN) connection. You can still use other protocols, such as Internetwork Packet Exchange (IPX) or NetBIOS Extended User Interface (NetBEUI), as the transport protocol for non–Terminal Server traffic, such as network file or printer sharing, or between the client portion of a client-server application and its server.

 Note

The Remote Desktop client requires TCP/IP to connect to the server, but after Terminal Server users connect to a terminal server, they can use IPX to gain access to Novell servers if necessary.

Bandwidth Considerations

Terminal Server works very well over low-bandwidth connections and uses whatever IP connection you provide. However, you can optimize both application and overall network performance by making sure the type of connection is appropriate to the work that is done. For example, a single user can connect over a low-bandwidth modem line and realize good performance, but it is not appropriate to share a 28.8-kilobit line among an active office of 100 people. Also, consider whether the security that an IP connection provides is appropriate to the data that you plan to transmit. For more information about bandwidth requirements, see the Terminal Services link and the Remote Desktop Protocol (RDP) Features and Performance link on the Web Resources page at http://www.microsoft.com/windows/reskits/webresources.

 Note

Printing, sound, drive redirection, and user file transfer requirements can increase the bandwidth requirement and might cause performance to drop below a level that is considered acceptable performance for users.

Access to Terminal Server over a VPN

Users can gain access to Terminal Server over a VPN by using Layer Two Tunneling Protocol (L2TP) or Point-to-Point Tunneling Protocol (PPTP). By using encryption, either one of these tunneling options provides secure access to a private network for users operating over a public medium.

Access to Terminal Server Over a Wide Area Network

Terminal Services can provide remote users with access to applications that would otherwise be unusable because of poor performance across dial-up or slow WAN connections.

Give additional consideration to applications with offline capabilities and synchronization if users will be accessing Terminal Server over a WAN. No offline synchronization of the local application is performed over the terminal server connection.

Planning Network Security Components

You can use firewalls and smart cards with Terminal Server to increase security. Use the information in the following sections to help you plan for the use of these security components in your environment. You also need to carefully choose the file system you plan to use with Terminal Server.

Using Firewalls with Terminal Server

If your organization uses a firewall for security and if you need clients to connect from the other side of the firewall, keep port 3389 open for RDP connections between the client and server and implement filter rules to ensure this traffic can reach only the terminal servers. This is not necessary if you use PPTP, L2TP, or other VPN technologies to tunnel through the firewall, because the port will be available through the tunnel, without being explicitly closed by the firewall. If you are using the Remote Desktop Web Connection, you must also check to be sure that port 80 is open.

You can change the RDP port if necessary, but you must apply the modification to both the server and clients. However changing the RDP port, for example to a well known and already open port such as 80, makes separation, identification, and audit of RDP traffic much more difficult. For more information about changing the RDP port, see article 187623, "How to Change Terminal Server's Listening Port" in the Microsoft Knowledge Base. To find this article, see the Microsoft Knowledge Base link on the Web Resources page at http://www.microsoft.com/windows/reskits/webresources.

For best results, use a firewall that uses user-based authentication. This is especially important for secure access over a WAN, because a firewall that grants access based on an IP address (rather than based on user credentials) allows users through if the IP address of the server running Terminal Services has been granted access. For more information, see "Planning Network Connectivity and Bandwidth" earlier in this chapter.

Determine if the firewall used in your organization is a packet-level or application-level firewall. Packet-level firewalls are easier to configure for new protocols. If your organization uses an application-level firewall, check to see if the vendor has defined a filter for the RDP.

Using NTFS with Terminal Server

Because of the multiuser nature of Terminal Services, it is strongly recommended that you use the Windows Server 2003 version of NTFS as the only file system on the server, rather than file allocation table (FAT). FAT does not offer any user and directory security, whereas with NTFS you can limit subdirectories to certain users or groups of users. This is important in a multiuser system such as Terminal Services. Without the security that NTFS provides, any user has access to every directory and file on the terminal server. For more information about file systems, see "Deploying File Servers" in this book.

Using Smart Cards with Terminal Server

With Windows Server 2003, you can now enable users to log on to a remote session in an Active Directory domain using a smart card. Smart cards allow you to require strong credentials from users in a manageable way, providing a more secure environment.

To use smart cards with Windows Server 2003 Terminal Server, you must have Active Directory® directory service deployed in your organization and your client computers must be running a Microsoft client operating system with built-in smart card support, such as Windows XP or Windows 2000, or most devices running Microsoft®Windows® CE .NET. You must also install smart card readers on the client computers.

Otherwise, deploying smart cards for use with Windows Server 2003 Terminal Server is the same as deploying smart cards that will not be used with Terminal Server. For more information see "Planning a Smart Card Deployment" in the *Designing and Deploying Directory and Security Services* book of this kit.

Choosing Client Computers

Client computers, or terminals, connect to a terminal server that is running Windows Server 2003 using the Remote Desktop Connection tool, which you can install on a disk or in firmware. The Remote Desktop Connection tool is installed by default when you install Windows Server 2003, Windows XP (you need to install Windows XP Service Pack 1 to benefit from features such as Auto-Reconnect), and most versions of Windows CE. On earlier versions of Windows and on the Pocket PC, you have to manually install Remote Desktop.

You can also install this tool manually from the Windows Server 2003 operating system CD or download it from the Web for use on a computer running the Microsoft® Windows® 95, Microsoft® Windows® 98, Microsoft® Windows® Millennium Edition, Windows NT 4.0, or Microsoft® Windows® 2000 Professional operating systems. Remote Desktop Connection has very low physical RAM requirements and generally works on any device that meets the minimum requirements for the operating system on which it runs. For information, see the Terminal Server link on the Web Resources page at http://www.microsoft.com/windows/reskits/webresources.

A Remote Desktop Connection Client for Mac OS X is also available from Microsoft. For more information, see the Mactopia Downloads: Remote Desktop Connection Client link on the Web Resources page at http://www.microsoft.com/windows/reskits/webresources.

For other platforms such as UNIX, you need to obtain a third-party tool to connect to a terminal server. There are a number of third-party RDP clients available. Many of these are reverse engineered and are not supported or endorsed by Microsoft. These clients might cause performance and compatibility problems, and lack of functionality. Check with the software vendor to ensure that your RDP software is a licensed client. For more information about third-party Terminal Server solutions, see the Citrix and New Moon Systems links on the Web Resources page at http://www.microsoft.com/windows/reskits/webresources.

Your choice of client platform depends on the current installed base and individual user need. Consider the following issues when choosing a client computer or platform from which to connect to your terminal server:

- You can use Windows-based terminals in the following situations:

    - Task workers can access their primary application from a Windows-based terminal (or thin client) rather than a personal computer, reducing hardware costs and work disruption. If a terminal stops responding, you can replace it quickly, with minimal setup.

    - In locations where a personal computer does not fare well — such as in exceptionally dirty, hot, or cold environments — consider deploying Windows-based thin clients, which typically have no moving parts and have a sealed-case design.

    - Windows-based thin clients can be used to replace green-screen terminals.

- You can use client computers running earlier versions of Windows to provide access to applications that require a more recent version of Windows by upgrading your terminal server and hosting the application.

- To save on hardware costs, you can use older computers that are not capable of running newer versions of Windows to access the latest application versions through Terminal Server.

- The Remote Desktop Web Connection requires a browser that supports ActiveX (available with Internet Explorer).

- Non-Windows-based computers such as Macintosh or UNIX computers need additional client software to connect to Terminal Server.

Planning Use of Peripheral Hardware

You can use desktop peripherals such as bar code readers, scanners, or card swipes with Windows Server 2003 Terminal Server if your line-of-business application requires them. You can use peripheral hardware attached to serial, universal serial bus (USB), and parallel ports of the client computer. You can also use printers attached to the client, as well as network printers, with Terminal Server. Peripherals that connect to the local computer through a specialized third-party hardware card are not recognized by the RDP-based Remote Desktop client, but they might be available using third-party software. For more information, see "Peripherals that affect performance" in Help and Support Center for Windows Server 2003.

Port Redirection

Terminal Server supports port redirection in Windows Server 2003. Using port redirection, applications running within the Terminal Server session have access to ports on the client, enabling you to use devices like bar code readers or scanners with Terminal Server. Test your devices for use with Terminal Server before deploying your solution in the production environment.

By default Windows Server 2003 Terminal Server enables LPT, USB, and COM port redirection. If you are not planning to enable these types of peripherals, you might want to disable them so that the client computer is not vulnerable to security threats that could access your computer through those ports. You can disable LPT and COM port redirection by using Terminal Server Group Policy or TSCC. For more information, see "Designing the Terminal Server Configuration" later in this chapter.

By default, Terminal Server does not allow redirection of FireWire (IEEE 1394) ports with Windows XP and Windows 2000 clients. However, you can enable FireWire port redirection on these clients by enabling all ports to be redirected by using the following procedure to modify the registry on the client computer.

Caution

Do not edit the registry unless you have no alternative. The registry editor bypasses standard safeguards, allowing settings that can damage your system, or even require you to reinstall Windows. If you must edit the registry, back it up first and see the Registry Reference on the *Windows Server 2003 Deployment Kit* companion CD or at http://www.microsoft.com/reskit.

▷ **To filter ports for redirection**

1. On the client computer, in the **Run** dialog box, type **regedit**, and then click **OK**.

2. Locate the following subkey in the registry and select it:

   HKEY_CURRENT_USER\Software\Microsoft\Terminal Server
   Client\Default\AddIns\RDPDR

3. On the **Edit** menu, point to **New**, and then click **DWORD Value**.

4. Type **FilterQueueType**, and then press **ENTER**.

5. With **FilterQueueType** selected, on the **Edit** menu, click **Modify**.

6. Type **FFFFFFFF**, and then click **OK**.

For more information about port redirection, see article 302361, "Multifunction Printers That Use DOT4 Ports Are Not Redirected By Using Remote Desktop." in the Microsoft Knowledge Base. To find this article, see the Microsoft Knowledge Base link on the Web Resources page at http://www.microsoft.com/windows/reskits/webresources.

Printer Redirection

When the user logs on to the terminal server, the server detects the client's local printer and installs the appropriate printer driver on the remote computer. If multiple printers are connected to the client computer, Terminal Services defaults to routing all print jobs to the client computer's default printer. Only printers whose drivers are available on the Windows client computer appear as available in a Remote Desktop session for local redirected printers (server-side printers are always available). If the driver for your printer is not included with the client operating system, you must manually install it on the server.

Designing Domain and User Configuration

Developing your design also involves planning the location of Terminal Server within your proposed Windows Server 2003 domain infrastructure, as shown in Figure 4.4. After you have determined how Terminal Server integrates into your domain model, you can plan the user and security settings that can be managed through Active Directory and Group Policy.

Figure 4.4   Planning Domain and Security Configuration

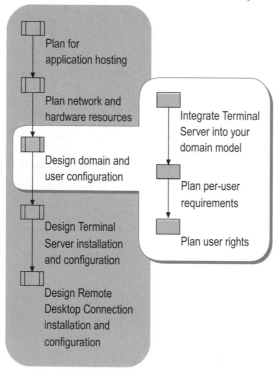

Integrating Terminal Server into Your Domain Model

Terminal Server need not be in an Active Directory domain to function, but without a domain architecture, users must have separate accounts on every computer running Terminal Server. This limits manageability and makes it more difficult to administer groups of users.

Integrating with Existing Windows NT 4.0 Domain Structure

If your organization does not currently use Active Directory, you can use an existing Windows NT 4.0 domain, which allows you to take advantage of the new features available in Windows Server 2003 Terminal Server without affecting the production environment. However, limitations apply, such as the existing Security Accounts Manager (SAM) 40,000-objects-per-domain limitation of the Windows NT 4.0 domain model. Administrators have the option of adding Terminal Server–specific attributes to users' accounts. This adds a small amount of information, typically 1 kilobyte (KB) or less, to a user's entry in the domain SAM database.

Integrating with the Windows Server 2003 and Windows 2000 Active Directory Infrastructure

This option takes full advantage of Active Directory, giving you the option of applying Group Policy settings to control the Terminal Server environment. Just as you are likely to manage your portable computers or domain controllers in a manner different from your desktop computers, you also manage your terminal servers and Terminal Server users differently. When you define your Active Directory structure, it is recommended that you place your terminal servers in a separate Terminal Services OU. Reserve this OU for Terminal Services computers. Do not include other users or non-Terminal Services computer objects. In addition, if you are deploying load-balanced server farms for Terminal Services, place each farm in a separate OU within the Terminal Services OU. It is also recommended that you place your Terminal Server users in a separate Terminal Server users OU.

In an Active Directory environment, avoid configuring Terminal Server as a domain controller for the following reasons:

- Any user rights policies you apply to such a server apply to all domain controllers in the domain. For example, to use Terminal Services, users must be authorized to log on locally to the server. If the server running Terminal Services is a domain controller, users can log on locally to all domain controllers in the Terminal Services domain, presenting a serious security risk.

- Domain controller functions place a heavy load on system resources and would thus have an effect on the user's Terminal Server experience.

- By default, enabling Terminal Services sets the server process-scheduling priority to favor interactive applications. The system does not assign top priority to critical domain-level processes such as user count replication, logon requests, logon script replication, and authentication requests.

Planning Per-User Requirements

Because of the multiuser nature of Terminal Server, it is important to plan per-user settings and data storage carefully for ease of management and an optimal user experience. How you plan to use Terminal Server in your organization affects your choice of user profile types, and your plan for using these profiles.

Using User Profiles

A profile describes the Windows Server 2003 configuration for a specific user, including the user's environment and preference settings. Profiles typically contain such user-specific information as installed applications, desktop icons, and color options. To plan for user profiles in a Terminal Server environment, choose the solution that is best for your environment, and then plan for the storage of the profiles. For more information about user profiles, see "User profiles overview" in Help and Support Center for Windows Server 2003. For information about general planning for user profiles, see "Designing Managed Desktops" in *Designing a Managed Environment* of this kit.

Unless you plan carefully for the use of user profiles, they tend to grow in size. This is a problem in a Terminal Server environment because user profiles are stored on the terminal server by default. If you have many users accessing the terminal server, the user profile files soon consume a large amount of space on the server hard drive. You should store user data and profiles on a separate drive from the system installation hard drive.

There are three different types of profiles you can use with Terminal Server:

- Terminal Server–specific profile
- Windows Server 2003 mandatory roaming profile
- Windows Server 2003 local profile

When a user logs on to a server running Terminal Server, the server first searches for the Terminal Server–specific profile. If Terminal Server cannot locate this profile, it attempts to load the user Windows Server 2003 roaming profile or Windows Server 2003 local profile.

It is recommended that you plan to use either Terminal Server–specific or roaming user profiles for your Terminal Server users, rather than local profiles, in order to better manage the size of the profiles and optimize the user experience. Terminal Server–specific profiles are recommended in most cases. Consider the following situations when choosing which type of user profile to use with Terminal Server:

- If you are planning to keep the environment for your Terminal Server users standardized and under tight control, you can use mandatory roaming user profiles to restrict access to certain applications. You can also use mandatory roaming user profiles to assign users profiles that cannot be changed.

- If you assign roaming user profiles to users who tend to access the terminal server from different computers (for example IT administrators, users who access the application from a kiosk, or users who work in certain task-worker environments), those users can retain their settings regardless of where they log on.

- If you are using Terminal Server to deliver a consistent desktop to client computers of varying platforms or configurations, you cannot use roaming user profiles unless you can group the different configurations and platforms into different OUs.

- If you are using Terminal Server in a load-balanced farm, you should plan to use roaming user profiles.

Using Terminal Server–Specific Profiles

Use Terminal Server–specific profiles to present a session to the user that is different from the user's desktop or to create user profiles optimized to the Terminal Services environment. The following are some of the situations where using Terminal Server–specific profiles might be advantageous:

- To provide users who are accessing Terminal Server with an environment that is different from the environment on their local computers.

- To provide a different look and feel for different users on the same terminal server, for example, if you have task workers and a manager on the same server.

- To better manage the size of user profiles for Terminal Services users who do not have controlled user environments that have been set through assigned or mandatory user profiles. You can use Group Policy to manage the profiles on the server that stores your Terminal Server profiles.

You can configure Terminal Services–specific profile settings for each user by using the following procedure.

▷ **To configure Terminal Services–specific profile settings**

1. Open Active Directory Users and Computers.

2. Right-click the user for which you want to set profile settings, and then click Properties.

3. Click the Terminal Services profile tab.

You can configure the following Terminal Services–specific profile settings:

- **Terminal Services User Profile path**. You can choose a place to store users' Terminal Services profiles other than the default location.

 Note

You can also set this through Group Policy under Computer Configuration\Administrative Templates\Windows Components\Terminal Services. For more information, see "Designing Terminal Server Installation and Configuration" later in this chapter.

- **Terminal Services home folder**. You can specify a path to a home folder for use with Terminal Server sessions. This directory can be either a local folder or a network share.

For information about setting Terminal Server profiles, see "Terminal Services Profile" in Help and Support Center for Windows Server 2003.

Using Roaming Mandatory User Profiles

Roaming user profiles allow users to move between different computers and maintain the same environment and preference settings. A roaming mandatory user profile is a preconfigured user profile that you assign to users. Because users cannot change a roaming mandatory profile, using this type of profile ensures that these user profiles remain at a manageable size. Additionally, you can assign one mandatory profile to all users who require identical desktop configurations. This allows you to change the desktop environments for all those users by changing only one profile.

Take the following issues into consideration when planning to use roaming mandatory user profiles with Terminal Server:

- When planning for the use of profiles for a large number of Terminal Server users, consider using Terminal Server profiles rather than roaming user profiles.

- If you are combining Folder Redirection and roaming user profiles, it is recommended you not use quotas on the profile.

- If your users roam between computers that are running Windows XP Professional, Windows XP 64-Bit Edition, Windows Server 2003, and Windows 2000, you can use the **Prevent Roaming Profile changes from being propagated to the server** Group Policy setting to be sure that each client computer receives only the profile that applies to the particular platform that the user is logged on to. For more information, see "Group Policy in multiplatform networks" in Help and Support Center for Windows Server 2003. To find this topic, click **Index** in Help and Support Center, type the keywords "Group Policy," and then select the topic "multiplatform networks."

The roaming profile information is stored on the local hard drive of the terminal server. It is recommended that this information be deleted after the user logs off. You can do this by enabling the **Delete cached copies of roaming profiles** Group Policy setting (in System/User Profiles under User Configuration in the Group Policy Object Editor) and applying the setting to your Terminal Server OU.

Important

In order to use roaming profiles on a group of Terminal Services computers, the Terminal Services computers must be identical in application and operating system configuration, such as the location of the systemroot folder and the installation location of all applications. Otherwise, group different configurations into different OUs and administer the roaming profiles separately.

For information about how to set or change a user's roaming profile path, see "Change a user's Terminal Services profile path" in Help and Support Center for Windows Server 2003.

Planning for User Profile Storage and Management

Unless you manage user profiles correctly, they can become very large and can cause problems for your Terminal Server users. In order to keep the size of your user profiles for Terminal Server under control, use the **Limit profile size** Group Policy setting or use mandatory profiles. You can find the **Limit profile size** Group Policy setting under User Configuration\Administrative Templates\System\User Profiles.

The profile path copies all user profiles to drive C of the terminal server by default. Depending on the number of users accessing your terminal server, this could greatly deplete the free space on this disk. Choose a location on a file or print server that has enough space to store the profiles and that is readily available to Terminal Server users, and then create a Windows Server 2003 share that users can access with read/write permissions. Do not store Terminal Server profiles and users' primary desktop profiles in the same location. You should store profiles in a different location from user home directories. For information, see "Change a user's Terminal Services profile path" in Help and Support Center for Windows Server 2003.

Increasing Time-out Values for Profiles with Terminal Server

Caution

Do not edit the registry unless you have no alternative. The registry editor bypasses standard safeguards, allowing settings that can damage your system, or even require you to reinstall Windows. If you must edit the registry, back it up first and see the Registry Reference on the *Windows Server 2003 Deployment Kit* companion CD, or at http://www.microsoft.com/reskit.

In a Terminal Server environment, because many users tend to access the terminal server and the profile server at the same time, the server can develop bottlenecks or the network itself can become saturated. This can cause problems with user profiles primarily because a time-out can occur during profile unloading or write back. As a result, changes to the profile are not saved. By increasing the time-out values when you set up Terminal Server, you can reduce the incidence of profile-related issues. You can increase profile time-out values by using the following procedure.

▷ **To increase profile time-out values**

1. In the Group Policy Object Editor, navigate to the **Maximum retries to unload and update user profile** policy, which is located in Computer Configuration/Administrative Templates/System/User Profiles.

2. Enable this setting and set it to 120.

3. In the **Run** dialog box, type **regedit**, and then click **OK**.

4. Locate the following subkey in the registry and select it:

    HKEY_LOCAL_MACHINE\System\CurrentControlSet\Control\Terminal Server

5. On the **Edit** menu, click **Add,** and then click **DWORD Value.**

6. Add a registry entry named LogoffTimeout with the following settings:

    ▪ Base: Decimal

    ▪ Value: 120 (4 minutes, time-out expressed in 2-second units)

 Note
Do not set this value lower than 3 minutes or higher than 15 minutes.

For more information, see article 299386, "Logoff Process May Not Be Completed Because Time-Out Is Too Slow" in the Microsoft Knowledge Base. To find this article, see the Microsoft Knowledge Base link on the Web Resources page at http://www.microsoft.com/windows/reskits/webresources.

Using Home Directories with Terminal Server

It is important that you plan for use of home directories in a Terminal Server environment because most applications must install user-specific information or copy configuration files for each user. By default, Windows Server 2003 defines a home directory for each user. For Terminal Server users, the default user's home directory is his or her user profile directory on the terminal server, for example \Wtsrv\Profiles*Username*. This directory contains user settings. Terminal Services writes user-specific application files, such as .ini files, and by default refers any application seeking the Windows system directory to the user's home directory.

Users typically save their personal files to their home directory, in the My Documents folder. This can be a problem if roaming profiles are used and the home directory is located within the user's profile directory. Windows Server 2003 copies everything in the user's profile directory to the profile cache on the local computer each time the user logs on. This can take considerable time and resources, particularly if the roaming profile is stored across the network or over a slow link. You can use Group Policy to redirect the My Documents folder to a central non–Terminal Server computer. For more information, see "Change a user's Terminal Services profile path" in Help and Support Center for Windows Server 2003.

It is recommended that you use Terminal Services–specific home directories. Choose a location on a file or print server for the home directories. Share the file and give Change permissions to Everyone, then change the home directory path for Terminal Server users. By default, users have full access to their individual home directory. Administrators can copy files into the directory, but not read or delete files there.

You can specify a location for redirecting the home directory for Terminal Services users with the **TS User Home Directory** Group Policy setting. With this setting you can specify the location of the home directory on the network or on the local computer, the root path, and the network drive letter if the root path is located on the network.

 Note

To facilitate the use of application compatibility scripts, use the same virtual drive letter for all user home directory redirection points. The first time you run an application compatibility script on a server, the server prompts you to set the drive letter that references the root of the user home directory. This drive letter is used for all subsequent application compatibility scripts. For terminal server farms, it is essential that the same drive letter be used on all the servers within the farm.

Using Folder Redirection with Terminal Server

Folder Redirection allows users and administrators to redirect the path of a folder to a new location. The new location can be a folder on the local computer or a directory on a network share. It is recommended that you redirect users' My Documents folder to a private server share by using Folder Redirection. Users can then access their My Documents folders from either a Windows XP Professional client computer or Terminal Server session as if they were accessing their local drives. This is especially useful for roaming users who access the terminal server from different computers at different times.

For general information about Folder Redirection, see "Folder Redirection" in Help and Support Center for Windows Server 2003. To find this topic, click **Index** in Help and Support Center, type the keywords "Folder Redirection," and then select the topic "overview."

When setting Folder Redirection, make sure that the user has write access to the folder in which you create the new folder for that user. If the user does not have sufficient access to the shared folder, the folder redirection fails and defaults to a dedicated folder created on the server or desktop to which the user logs on.

Configuring User Group Policy Settings

Under User Configuration in the Group Policy Object Editor, you can set several Group Policy settings that are particularly useful for Terminal Server. Use these settings to control the user experience and prevent access to areas of the terminal server. For more information about each of the settings listed here, see the Group Policy Explain text associated with each setting. For a job aid to assist you in recording your Terminal Server Group Policy configuration decisions, see "Group Policy Configuration Worksheet" (SDCTS_2.xls) on the *Windows Server 2003 Deployment Kit* companion CD (or see "Group Policy Configuration Worksheet" on the Web at http://www.microsoft.com/reskit).

See the following resources for more specific information about using Group Policy:

- For general information about Group Policy, see the Management Services link on the Web Resources page at http://www.microsoft.com/windows/reskits/webresources.

- For more information about designing a Group Policy infrastructure, see "Designing a Group Policy Infrastructure" in *Designing a Managed Environment* of this kit.

- For information about using Group Policy to lock down a Terminal Server session, see article 278295, "How to Lock Down a Windows 2000 Terminal Server Session" in the Microsoft Knowledge Base. To find this article, see the Microsoft Knowledge Base link on the Web Resources page at http://www.microsoft.com/windows/reskits/webresources.

- For more information about applying Group Policy to Terminal Server, see article 260370, "How to Apply Group Policy Objects to Terminal Services Servers." To find this article, see the Microsoft Knowledge Base link on the Web Resources page at http://www.microsoft.com/windows/reskits/webresources.

 Note

Because these settings apply to the user, and not the computer, they affect the user environment regardless of which computer the user accesses. When applying settings that you want to apply only when users have a session on the terminal server (as opposed to their own desktop computer), use computer settings that apply to the terminal server. For more information, see "Designing Terminal Server Installation and Configuration" later in this chapter.

Configuring the User Display

A graphic-intensive display can affect performance for users of Terminal Server. To ensure the best possible performance, you can control what users can put on their desktops by configuring the Group Policy settings located under User Configuration/Administrative Templates/Control Panel/Display.

Configuring desktop items

Many organizations permit users to choose their own desktop wallpaper or screen savers. However, in a Terminal Server environment, these graphics can have an effect on performance. Use the following Group Policy settings to control users' ability to change wallpaper and screen savers.

Screen savers   You can use several Group Policy settings to affect the user's screen saver. You can disable screen savers altogether by disabling the **Screen Saver** policy. You can also specify the screen saver by enabling this policy and also by enabling and specifying the screen saver executable name in the **Screen Saver executable name** policy. For more information about these Group Policy settings, see the **Explain** tab located on the property sheet for each policy.

Wallpaper   By enabling the **Prevent changing wallpaper** setting you can disable all the options in the **Desktop** tab of Display in Control Panel. This includes changing the wallpaper and changing the appearance of the desktop icons. By not allowing these changes, you can ensure that users do not choose desktop display items that might affect the performance of the server.

Configuring the desktop theme

If you are hosting the full desktop with Terminal Server, by default the desktop environment resembles a Windows Classic desktop. By default Windows Server 2003 does not have themes enabled. You can enable themes by starting the Themes service and configuring it to start automatically. For more information about starting the Themes service, see "Configure how a service is started" in Help and Support Center for Windows Server 2003.

After you have configured the Themes service to start automatically, you can enforce a specific desktop theme or the Windows XP theme for your Terminal Server users by using the following procedure. For more information about choosing to use desktop themes with Terminal Server, see "Hosting Full Desktops with Terminal Server" earlier in this chapter.

▷ **To load a specific theme for the desktop**

1. In the Group Policy Object Editor, navigate to User Configuration/Administrative Templates/Control Panel/Display/Desktop Themes.

2. Open the **Load a specific visual style file or force Windows Classic** setting.

3. Take one of the following actions, depending on what you are trying to achieve:

   - To force Windows Classic, enable this setting.

   - To load the Windows XP theme, enable the setting and type **%windir%\resources\Themes\Luna\Luna.msstyles** in the **Path to Visual Style** dialog box. For information about using the Windows XP theme with Terminal Server, see "Choosing Applications to Host" earlier in this chapter.

   - To load another theme or a custom theme, type the path to that theme in the dialog box.

Restricting Access to Drives on a Terminal Server

You can use Group Policy settings to hide and restrict access to drives on the terminal server. By enabling these settings you can ensure that users do not inadvertently access data stored on other drives, or delete or damage program or other critical system files on the C drive. The following settings are located in the Group Policy Object Editor under User Configuration/Administrative Templates/Windows Components/Windows Explorer:

- **Hide these specified drives in My Computer.** You can remove the icons for specified drives from a user's My Computer folder by enabling this setting and using the drop-down list to select the drives you would like to hide. However, this setting does not restrict access to these drives.

- **Prevent access to drives from My Computer.** Enable this setting to prevent users from accessing the chosen combination of drives. Use this setting to lock down the terminal server for users accessing it for their primary desktop.

Configuring Start Menu and Taskbar Items

You can use Group Policy settings to remove and to restrict access to items from the **Start** menu for Terminal Server users. The following settings are located in User Configuration/Administrative Templates/Start Menu and Taskbar:

- Enabling the **Remove Run menu from Start Menu** setting removes this menu from the **Start** menu. It also removes the **New Task** command from Task Manager and blocks the user from accessing Universal Naming Convention (UNC) paths, local drives, and local folders from the Internet Explorer address bar. While these are not the only methods for running applications, enabling this setting makes it difficult for users to access resources on the server or network.

- Enabling the **Remove Logoff on the Start Menu** setting prevents users from logging off the server from the Start menu. Enabling this setting does not prevent users from logging off using CTRL+ALT+DEL.

- Enabling the **Remove and Prevent access to the Shut Down command** prevents administrators from accidently shutting down the terminal server.

- Enabling the **Remove links and access to Windows Update** setting prevents users from attempting to download updates to Windows on to the server.

- Enabling the **Remove Favorites menu from Start Menu** setting reduces confusion for users who do not have access to the Internet.

Planning Terminal Server User Rights and Logon

You can use the Remote Desktop Users group to manage user rights on a terminal server. There are also special logon configurations and Internet Explorer security configurations you can set for Terminal Server.

The Remote Desktop Users Group

Before users can create a remote connection with Remote Desktop, they must have the appropriate permissions. By default, members of the Administrator group can connect remotely to the server. Members of the Remote Desktop Users built-in local group also have remote logon permissions. This built-in group gives administrators control over the resources that Terminal Server users can access. Access to Terminal Server is distributed with a default set of user rights that you can change for extra security. To provide users or groups with the appropriate rights, use the Terminal Services Configuration snap-in Permissions tab to add these groups or users and to modify permissions. For more information about managing permissions, see "Managing permissions on connections" in Help and Support Center for Windows Server 2003.

 Important

By default, the Remote Desktop Users local group for Windows Server 2003 Terminal Server is empty.

Populate the Remote Desktop Users group with your Terminal Services users group by using the Computer Management tool. For more information about populating the Remote Desktop Users group, see "Add users to the Remote Desktop Users group" in Help and Support Center for Windows Server 2003.

To control who can add members to the Remote Desktop Users group, add this group to **Restricted Groups** by using the following procedure:

▶ **To add the Remote Desktop Users group to Restricted Groups**

1. In the Security Templates Microsoft Management Console (MMC) snap-in, create a new template, or use an existing one.

2. In the navigation pane, right-click **Restricted Groups** in the template, click **Add Group**, and then type **Remote Desktop Users**.

3. In the details pane, double-click **Remote Desktop Users**, click **Add Members**, and select the users who you want to add to this group.

Planning for Automatic Logon

With Terminal Server, you can allow users to connect without entering a user name and password. You can do this on a per-user basis through the Remote Desktop Connection tool or on a per-server basis through TSCC or through Group Policy.

When you enable this, anyone with a Remote Desktop client can log on to the server. Use this connection method only in conjunction with starting users directly into a line-of-business application, especially if the application itself requires a password for access. You can enable this setting on a per-user basis through the Remote Desktop Connection tool or Group Policy or on a per-server basis through TSCC or through Group Policy. A per-server automatic logon policy is appropriate when a server is dedicated to a particular task-based application. If a server hosts more than one application, assign automatic logon on a per-user basis.

Editing User-Specific Logon Information

When users log on to the system, Terminal Services executes a batch file called UsrLogon.cmd in the system32 directory to make any modifications to the end-user environment and to ensure that users can run their applications correctly. If Terminal Server modifications are necessary to the user environment, you can make them by editing this file. Be aware that editing this file can affect the logon compatibility scripts that were written for applications. For more information about compatibility scripts, see "Identifying Ideal Candidates for Hosting" earlier in this chapter.

In your logon scripts, consider checking for the presence of the environment variables *clientname* or *sessionname*. These environment variables are Terminal Server–specific, and they only appear in a user environment when the user is logged on to a terminal server. You might choose to make changes to the user environment, for example omitting the execution of antivirus software, if the script determines that the environment is running on Terminal Server.

Internet Explorer Enhanced Security Configuration

Windows Server 2003 is installed with the Internet Explorer Enhanced Security Configuration enabled. This configuration decreases the exposure of your server to attacks that can occur through Web content and application scripts. As a result, some Web sites might not display or perform as expected. For a better user experience with Terminal Server, remove the enhanced security configuration from members of the Users group. Because these users have fewer privileges on the server, they present a lower level of risk if they are victims of an attack. This configuration allows users to browse Internet and intranet sites much as if they were using a stand-alone desktop computer.

For more information about Internet Explorer Enhanced Security Configuration settings, see "Internet Explorer Enhanced Security Configuration" in Help and Support Center for Windows Server 2003.

You can also configure Internet Explorer Enhanced Security Configuration through Unattended Setup. For more information, see "Enabling Terminal Server Using an Automated Installation Method" later in this chapter.

Designing Terminal Server Installation and Configuration

By carefully planning how you install and configure the various components of your Terminal Server solution, you can save considerable time in the installation and make management of your servers easier. Figure 4.5 describes the steps in this process. The components needed for a complete Terminal Server solution include the terminal servers themselves, the license server, and the applications that you plan to host, as well as a load-balancing solution and a Session Directory server if you plan to use them.

Figure 4.5 Designing Terminal Server Installation and Configuration

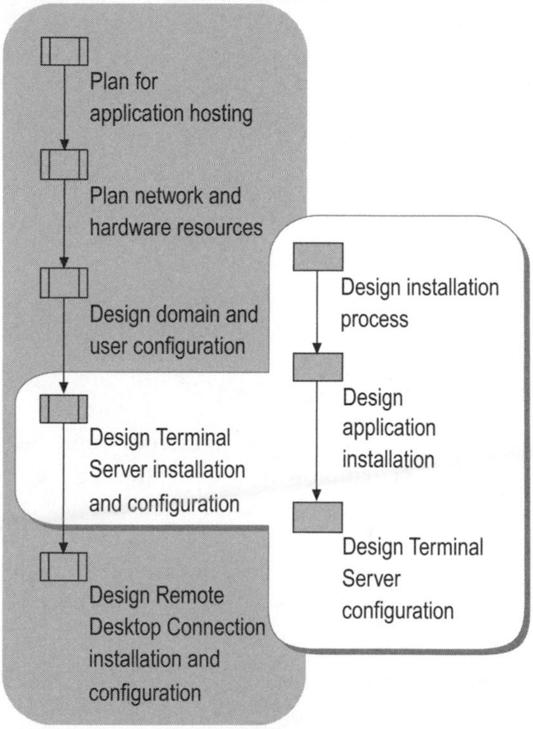

Designing the Installation Process

Selecting the best way to deploy your terminal servers depends on the scope of your use of Terminal Server. You can enable Terminal Server on a server that has Windows Server 2003 already installed by using Add or Remove Programs in Control Panel or the Configure Your Server Wizard. You can also deploy Windows Server 2003 with Terminal Server enabled by using an automated installation method. These options are discussed in further detail in the following sections.

Enabling Terminal Server Manually

If you are deploying just one terminal server, or if you are upgrading to Windows Server 2003, it might be easiest to enable Terminal Server on a server that already has the operating system installed and configure the server individually. You can accomplish this through the Configure Your Server Wizard or through Add or Remove Programs in Control Panel. For information about how to use the Configure Your Server Wizard, see "Install Terminal Server" in Help and Support Center for Windows Server 2003. To enable Terminal Server through Add or Remove Programs, open Add or Remove Programs from Control Panel, or in the **Run** dialog box, type **control appwiz.cpl**, and click Add/Remove Windows Components.

 Note
You can also install Terminal Server Licensing through Add or Remove Programs.

Internet Explorer Enhanced Security Configuration Considerations

If you choose to install Terminal Server by using Add or Remove Windows Components in Add or Remove Programs, a warning appears if the installation will proceed with Internet Explorer Enhanced Security Configuration enabled, and allows you to choose whether you want to proceed with this configuration. It is recommended that you choose No and return to Add or Remove Windows Components and disable this configuration to allow users to browse the Internet.

If you install Terminal Server through the Configure Your Server Wizard, no warning appears. When the Manage Your Server window appears after you have added the Terminal Server role, a message appears that indicates the status of the Internet Explorer Enhanced Security Configuration, and gives instructions about how to change it.

For more information about Internet Explorer Enhanced Security Configuration settings, see "Internet Explorer Enhanced Security Configuration" in Help and Support Center for Windows Server 2003.

Enabling Terminal Server Using an Automated Installation Method

One way to ensure that your servers have a consistent configuration is by using an automated installation method to install Windows Server 2003 with Terminal Server enabled. The following automated installation methods are available in Windows Server 2003:

- Unattended Setup

- Sysprep

- Remote Installation Services (RIS)

If you are deploying Terminal Server with several configurations, you can enable Terminal Server on all of the servers by using an automated installation method, and then configure the servers individually after the installation.

You cannot configure settings such as Group Policy settings within the automated installation itself. However you can set up the installation to run scripts that can configure these settings and perform a wide variety of other configurations after the setup is complete. For more information about the options for automated installations, see the design chapters for the various automated installation methods in *Automating and Customizing Installations* of this kit and the "Microsoft Windows Corporate Deployment Tools User's Guide" in the \Support\Tools folder of the Windows Server 2003 operating system CD.

 Tip

If you deploy Terminal Server for use in a load-balanced farm, an automated installation method is an easy way to ensure an identical configuration on all the servers in the farm.

Unattended Setup

Unattended Setup uses an answer file to automate the setup of Windows Server 2003. It is the only way to automate an upgrade to Windows Server 2003. Unattended Setup is a good choice for installing Terminal Server if, for example, you are planning to deploy terminal servers with a few applications for different purposes. For more information about designing an Unattended Setup, see "Designing Unattended Installations" in *Automating and Customizing Installations* of this kit.

For Terminal Server, you need to make entries in a few of sections of the answer file (Unattend.txt) in order to complete the automated installation:

[Components]

The [Components] section contains entries for installing the components of Windows XP or Windows Server 2003 operating systems. These components use the values **On** or **Off** to install or not install the component.

Note

The entries in this section can also be set in the Sysprep Factory mode, **sysprep -factory**, which is used for the preinstallation of Windows in an OEM manufacturing environment.

For Terminal Server, you can install the following components:

- **LicenseServer**. Set this to **On** if you are setting up the server as a license server for Terminal Server.

- **TerminalServer**. Set this to **On** if you are setting up the server as a terminal server.

Important

When you install Terminal Server through Unattended Setup, it is installed by default with Internet Explorer Enhanced Security Configuration enabled for administrators, and disabled for users. To change Internet Explorer Enhanced Security Configuration during Unattended Setup, you can configure IEHArdenUser and IEHArdenAdmin, also found in the [Components] section of the answer file. For more information about Internet Explorer Enhanced Security Configuration settings, see "Internet Explorer Enhanced Security Configuration" in Help and Support Center for Windows Server 2003.

- **TSWebClient**. Set this to **On** to install the ActiveX control and sample pages for hosting Remote Desktop client connections over the Web.

- **IEHardenUser.** This is set to **Off** by default, which removes the Internet Explorer Enhanced Security Configuration from members of the Restricted Users and Guests groups. For more information about Internet Explorer Enhanced Security Configuration settings, see "Internet Explorer Enhanced Security Configuration" in Help and Support Center for Windows Server 2003.

- **IEHardenAdmin**. This is set to **On** by default, which applies the Internet Explorer Enhanced Security Configuration to members of the Administrators and Power Users groups. For more information about Internet Explorer Enhanced Security Configuration settings, see "Internet Explorer Enhanced Security Configuration" in Help and Support Center for Windows Server 2003.

[TerminalServices]

If you set the TerminalServer entry to **On** in the answer file, you also need to set the following entries in the [TerminalServices] section:

 Note

You can also set these settings through the TSCC. If these settings are changed in TSCC after the installation, the new settings take precedence.

- **AllowConnections**. When set to **1** this entry enables Terminal Server by allowing connections. The default for this setting is **0**. You can also set this through Group Policy.

- **LicensingMode**. This setting configures how Terminal Services manages CALs — **PerDevice** or **PerUser**. The default for this setting is **PerDevice**. For more information about choosing a licensing mode, see "Choosing the Licensing Model" earlier in this chapter.

- **PermissionsSetting**. This setting allows you to choose the security mode for Terminal Server users during terminal server sessions. This entry maps to the Permission Compatibility setting in TSCC. The default setting for this entry is **0**, which maps to Full Security in TSCC.

 Important

Only set PermissionSetting to **1**, which maps to Relaxed Security in TSCC, if you are running older applications and your testing has determined that your applications will not run properly with the setting at **0**. For more information, see "Designing the Terminal Server Configuration" later in this chapter.

Sysprep

Sysprep is an image-based method that you can use for clean installations of Windows Server 2003 with Terminal Server enabled. Using Sysprep is the quickest way to install Terminal Server along with many applications. Sysprep is a good choice for installing Terminal Server if, for example, you are deploying a terminal server farm.

If you plan to use a single image for many server configurations, you can use Sysprep in factory mode. For Terminal Server, you can configure the entries in the [Components] section of the Winbom.ini file for use with Sysprep in factory mode. These settings are the same as for the [Components] section of the Unattend.txt file for Unattended Setup discussed earlier in this section. For more information about using Sysprep for automated installations, see "Designing Image-based Installations with Sysprep" in *Automating and Customizing Installations* of this kit.

RIS

RIS requires the deployment of a network infrastructure specifically for its use and requires that you install Active Directory in your organization. Plan to use RIS for the automated installation of Terminal Server only if you are planning to use it throughout your organization for installing Windows Server 2003. If you do plan to use RIS for installing Terminal Server, you need to be sure to image a terminal server that does not already have licenses. You need to install licenses on the servers after the installation. For more information about using RIS for automated installations, see "Designing RIS Installations" in *Automating and Customizing Installations* of this kit.

Upgrading to Windows Server 2003 Terminal Server

The best way to install Terminal Server is by performing a clean installation. However, if you already have a Windows 2000 Terminal Services in Application Mode or Windows NT 4.0 Terminal Server Edition infrastructure in place, you might want to perform an upgrade. There are a number of other reasons why you might perform an upgrade, for example, if you are transitioning gradually to Windows Server 2003 or if you want to retain the ability to use your older software and device drivers. If you are upgrading your terminal servers from Windows 2000 to Windows Server 2003, you must take into consideration a number of changes and new requirements with Windows Server 2003.

 Note

When performing an operating system upgrade on a terminal server, the security template that is applied does not reset the access control lists (ACLs). This is in contrast to a non-Terminal Server upgrade, which resets the ACLs. If you are moving from Windows NT 4.0 Terminal Server Edition or Windows 2000 in Relaxed Security mode to Windows Server 2003 Terminal Server, consider performing a clean installation.

Upgrading Terminal Server Licensing

With Windows Server 2003, you must use a license server that is running Windows Server 2003. You can still issue licenses to Windows 2000 Terminal Server with a license server that is running Windows Server 2003, if you plan to gradually upgrade your terminal servers. Also, with Windows Server 2003 you no longer need to host your license server on a domain controller. For more information about choosing a host server for Terminal Server Licensing, see "Planning the License Server" earlier in this chapter.

Table 4.1 summarizes the licensing issues to be aware of when upgrading from Windows 2000 Terminal Services to Windows Server 2003 Terminal Server.

Table 4.1   Licensing Issues for Upgrading Terminal Server

If you are...	You need to...
Gradually upgrading your terminal servers to Windows Server 2003 from Windows 2000.	Upgrade your license server to Windows Server 2003 at the same time that you upgrade the first terminal server. You can also ensure that the license server issues the appropriate CAL for Windows 2000 or Windows Server 2003 through Group Policy. For more information, see "Designing the Terminal Server Configuration" later in this chapter.
Performing an in-place upgrade of the domain controller that hosts Terminal Server Licensing.	Consider keeping your licenses on the same server whether or not you plan to host your license server on a domain controller. You can demote the domain controller either before or after you upgrade the server to Windows Server 2003 by using the Active Directory Installation Wizard (dcpromo.exe). If you upgrade your license server, you must reactivate the license server. For information about upgrading a domain controller, see "Upgrading Windows 2000 Domains to Windows Server 2003 Domains" in *Designing and Deploying Directory and Security Services* of this kit.
Performing a clean installation of the domain controller that hosts Terminal Server Licensing.	Determine where you want to host Terminal Server Licensing and whether you want an Enterprise License server or a Domain License server. You also need to migrate your licenses to the new server. For information about transferring licenses, see "Repeat the installation of a client license key pack" in Help and Support Center for Windows Server 2003.
Redeploying Terminal Server Licensing to a new server.	Determine where you want to host Terminal Server Licensing and whether you want an Enterprise License server or a Domain License server. You also need to migrate your licenses to the new server. For information about transferring licenses, see "Repeat the installation of a client license key pack" in Help and Support Center for Windows Server 2003.

Group Policy Upgrade Issues

Windows Server 2003 offers more Terminal Server–specific Group Policy settings than did earlier versions of the Windows operating system. Your initial Group Policy settings vary depending on whether you perform an upgrade or clean installation. When you upgrade your terminal servers to Windows Server 2003, the new Group Policy settings are left Not Configured rather than set to their default. When you perform a clean installation, the default settings are used. Carefully review the Group Policy settings for Terminal Server to choose the best settings for your environment. For more information, see "Designing the Terminal Server Configuration" later in this chapter.

Also new with Windows Server 2003 is the Remote Desktop Users group. Users are required to be members of this built-in local group in order to gain access to the terminal server. This group is empty by default. For more information, see "Planning Terminal Server User Rights and Logon" earlier in this chapter.

Permission Compatibility

If you are upgrading from Windows 2000 Terminal Services or Windows NT 4.0 Terminal Server Edition, and are planning to host the same applications with Windows Server 2003, be aware that, in order for them to work, some older applications require access to system resources, such as the registry, for members of the Users group on a terminal server. If your older applications require this type of access, you can control the Permission Compatibility setting in TSCC on the **Server Configuration** tab for application compatibility. This setting is set to Full Security by default, which restricts access to system resources.

 Important

Do not set this setting to Relaxed Security unless you have performed thorough testing and have determined that your applications will not work properly otherwise. Relaxed Security mode gives users access to system components on the server, such as the ability to modify the system32 directory where operating system files are stored, access to the Program Files directories, and read/write access to registry settings in HKEY_LOCAL_MACHINE.

For more information about configuring this setting, see "Designing the Terminal Server Configuration" later in this chapter.

Automated Installation

If you are planning to use an automated installation method to upgrade your terminal servers, you can do this only by using Unattended Setup. For more information about using Unattended Setup with Terminal Server, see "Designing Application Installation" later in this chapter. For more information about installing Windows Server 2003 by using an automated installation method, see *Automating and Customizing Installations* of this kit.

Internet Explorer Enhanced Security Configuration

When you upgrade from Windows 2000 Terminal Services, Internet Explorer Enhanced Security Configuration is enabled for administrators and disabled for users by default. With this configuration, users are able to browse and download files from the Internet without restriction, but administrators cannot do so. For more information about Internet Explorer Enhanced Security Configuration settings, see "Internet Explorer Enhanced Security Configuration" in Help and Support Center for Windows Server 2003.

Designing Application Installation

There are several ways in which to install the applications you plan to host on the terminal server. The size of your deployment and whether you have Active Directory installed are factors in deciding which method to use.

Installing Applications Manually

With manual installations, in order for Terminal Services to replicate the necessary registry entries or .ini files for each user, the user must install the application by using **Add or Remove Programs** in Control Panel. You can also install applications from the command line by using the **change user /install** command, but using **Add or Remove Programs** is preferable.

Installing Applications Using Group Policy and Windows Installer

A recommended way to distribute applications to a server in a Terminal Services farm is to use Group Policy. Active Directory is required for this. By separating the terminal servers into their own OU, you can create a Group Policy object that is linked to only that OU, and you can then assign Windows Installer (.msi) packages to it. Assigned applications are installed on the server when the server is turned on. For more information, see "Assigned and published programs" in Help and Support Center for Windows Server 2003. For more information about deploying software using Group Policy, see "Deploying and upgrading software" in Help and Support Center for Windows Server 2003 and "Deploying a Managed Software Environment" in *Designing a Managed Environment* of this kit.

 Note

Terminal Server cannot accept published programs because publishing occurs on a per-user basis. Additionally, you must assign programs on a per-computer basis, rather than on a per-user basis.

Some applications require a transform file (.mst) when when you install them by using Windows Installer. *Transform files* are modifications to .msi packages that you create to instruct Windows Installer to install the application and all the needed components locally on the terminal server. Test your application installation to determine if a transform file is needed. For more information about .mst files, see "Deploying a Managed Software Environment" in *Designing a Managed Environment* of this kit.

To create and install applications using an .mst file, see the Office 2000 Resource Kit at the MSDN Library link on the Web Resources page at http://www.microsoft.com/windows/reskits/webresources. Search for the topics under "Installing Office in a Windows Terminal Server Environment" in the Office 2000 Resource Kit on this Web site.

 Note

Microsoft® Office XP installs and runs on a terminal server correctly without requiring a transform file.

Running Compatibility Scripts

If it is necessary to run application compatibility scripts for any of the applications that you are hosting with Terminal Server, you must run them after you install the application, but before you restart the server. For more information about compatibility scripts, see "Identifying Ideal Candidates for Hosting" earlier in this chapter and the Optimizing Applications for Windows 2000 Terminal Services link on the Web Resources page at http://www.microsoft.com/windows/reskits/webresources.

When you run the first compatibility script, you are asked to select a drive letter to be used by this script and all future compatibility scripts. This drive letter must be the same as the users' home directory. For more information about using home directories with Terminal Server, see "Using Home Directories with Terminal Server" earlier in this chapter.

Supporting Multilingual and International Users

Windows Server 2003 with Terminal Server enabled offers multilingual support. Using this capability, Terminal Services can simultaneously serve users in any language that is installed on the server. Terminal servers that are running Windows Server 2003 can take advantage of the multilingual user interface (MUI). This interface allows you to install multiple languages on the system and configure them on a per user basis. You must load MUI to take advantage of this functionality, which simplifies the deployment of Terminal Services within a multinational organization. It is also recommended that you install the keyboard drivers for any language-specific keyboards that you use in your organization as part of the Terminal Services installation. You can support your users around the world who can understand and work in English by hosting all users on the International English version of Windows Server 2003. This ensures that the organization is not in violation of United States export laws regulating strong encryption. However, using the International English Version might be inadequate if the organization must provide support for different languages. By default, Terminal Server installs all the available keyboard layouts, including support for Asian non-Input Method Editor keyboards.

While loading the MUI, install all of the languages that you expect users to need. The installation copies the appropriate language DLLs and Help files. By using Regional and Language Options in Control Panel, users can select their default language and keyboard settings. Regional and Language Options also includes such settings as date and currency formatting. Because this setting is stored in the user profile, individual users can adjust the settings to match their locality. If a user has a roaming profile that specifies a different language than the language that is loaded in the user profile, then the system uses the default user language from the profile.

 Important

Roaming users should not use Folder Redirection with MUI. If they do, they might create multiple language versions of My Documents and other per-user folders on the computer. If the user interface (UI) language files that are needed to support the roaming user's default UI language have not been installed on the computer, the localized names of the new folders might not display correctly.

For more information about MUI, see the MultiLanguage Version link on the Web Resources page at http://www.microsoft.com/windows/reskits/webresources. For information about deploying MUI, see "Planning Multilingual Deployments" on the Web at http://www.microsoft.com/reskits.

Designing the Terminal Server Configuration

You can configure Terminal Services by using TSCC Microsoft Management Console (MMC) snap-in, Group Policy, or WMI. Some server configurations settings for Terminal Services, for example the Sessions settings, are also configurable for the user. Because the server settings can override the user settings, it is recommended that you set these settings on the server whenever possible.

Choosing a Terminal Server Configuration Tool

Choose a configuration tool based on your level of permission, the tasks you want to accomplish, and the level at which you want to apply settings. If you are a domain administrator configuring global settings on a number of terminal servers, it is recommended that you use Group Policy. WMI is a good choice for automating the configuring of global settings on a number of terminal servers if you are not a domain administrator and if you are familiar with scripting. However, you must be a local administrator on every computer you want to configure using WMI. You can also invoke WMI to configure settings automatically after you install Windows Server 2003 with an automated installation method. For more information about configuring automated installation to invoke scripts, see the design chapter in *Automating and Customizing Installations* that corresponds to the automated installation method you have chosen to use. The TSCC snap-in is an easy-to-use tool for configuring a single terminal server, and is useful for configuring unique settings for a particular server. Table 4.2 summarizes these tools, and the following sections describe each tool in further detail.

Table 4.2   Benefit and Restriction Comparison for Terminal Server Configuration Tools

Tool	Benefits	Restrictions
Group Policy	Can centrally configure terminal servers and Terminal Server users by applying policies to OUs. Always overrides configurations set by using other tools.	Administrator must be a domain administrator to apply Group Policy settings to OUs. Must have Active Directory in place.
WMI Terminal Server provider	Can configure many terminal servers or Terminal Server users using scripts.	Administrator must know how to write scripts.
Terminal Server Connection Configuration snap-in	Can configure unique per-server settings. Some configurations only available in TSCC snap-in.	Can be overwritten by Group Policy settings. Can be applied only to a single terminal server and its users. Cannot be used to configure a remote server.

Your choice of tools might also depend on your server environment or number of connections. Take the following information into consideration when making your choice:

- In an operating system environment where only Windows Server 2003 is run, you can use Terminal Server Group Policy settings to configure all settings that apply across an OU. You can also configure individual Windows Server 2003 operating systems using Group Policy on the local Group Policy object.

- In server environments where several different versions of the Windows operating system are run, you might need to use a combination of tools. For example, you might configure the Windows Server 2003 operating systems with Group Policy, while using TSCC to configure servers that are running earlier versions of Windows.

- If you have two or more connections on the same computer, and you want to configure each connection differently, you cannot use Group Policy. Instead, use the TSCC tool, which allows you to configure Terminal Services settings on a per-connection basis.

Using Group Policy

You can use Group Policy to configure Terminal Server connection settings, set user policies, configure terminal server clusters, and manage Terminal Server sessions. You can apply Group Policy settings for users of a computer through the Remote Desktop Users group, for individual computers through local Group Policy, or for groups of computers through a Terminal Server OU. To set local policies for users of a particular computer, you must be an administrator for that computer. To set policies for an OU in a domain, you must be an administrator for that domain. Settings that are specific to Terminal Server are located under Computer Configuration/Administrative Templates/Windows Components/Terminal Services. For more information, see "Configuring Terminal Services with Group Policy" in Help and Support Center for Windows Server 2003.

Note

There are many new Group Policy settings with Windows Server 2003. If you are upgrading your terminal servers from Windows 2000, the new Group Policy settings will be set to Disabled by default. For new Windows Server 2003 deployments, the defaults are stated in the "Designing Terminal Server Connection Configurations" section later in this chapter.

Using the Terminal Services WMI provider

The Terminal Services WMI provider allows administrators to create custom scripts for configuring, managing, and querying terminal servers. It contains properties and methods that can perform the same tasks as Terminal Services configuration tools and command-line tools, but remotely and through scripted applications. A *provider* is an architectural element of WMI that extends the WMI schema of classes to allow WMI to work with new types of objects. The Terminal Services provider defines classes for querying and configuring Terminal Services. The Terminal Services WMI provider is defined in *systemroot*\System32\Wbem\tscfgwmi.mof. For more information about WMI, see "Configuring Terminal Services with WMI" in Help and Support Center for Windows Server 2003.

Note

Configuration settings applied with the Terminal Services WMI provider operate in the same order of precedence as they do if applied with the corresponding configuration tool. In general, Group Policy settings always override settings applied with WMI. For more information about using WMI, see the TechNet Script Center link on the Web Resources page at http://www.microsoft.com/windows/reskits/webresources.

Using the TSCC snap-in

With the TSCC snap-in you can configure the RDP connection parameters and connection permissions for the terminal server. You can apply settings only to a single terminal server and its users, however, and you cannot use TSCC to configure a remote server. In addition, there are several settings that you can set only by using TSCC. For more information, see "Configuring Terminal Services with TSCC" in Help and Support Center for Windows Server 2003.

Designing Terminal Server Connection Configurations

Use the following guidelines to design the configuration of the connections to your terminal servers. If you are using TSCC to configure a single server, you can use the Terminal Services Connection Wizard to configure these settings when you create a new connection. For more information about configuring Terminal Server with TSCC when you create a new connection, see "Make a new connection" in Help and Support Center for Windows Server 2003. You can also use Group Policy or WMI to configure the connections to many terminal servers. For a job aid to assist you in recording your Terminal Server Group Policy configuration decisions, see "Group Policy Configuration Worksheet" (SDCTS_2.xls) on the *Windows Server 2003 Deployment Kit* companion CD (or see "Group Policy Configuration Worksheet" on the Web at http://www.microsoft.com/reskit).

Data Encryption

You can assign data transfer encryption levels between the Remote Desktop client and Terminal Server by using either Group Policy or TSCC. The default RDP encryption level is **Client Compatible**. You can choose one of the following possible choices for encryption:

- **FIPS Compliant.** Encrypts traffic between client and server to meet the Federal Information Processing Standard 140-1 (FIPS 140-1). Use this level when Terminal Services connections require the highest degree of encryption, such as those required by the U.S. federal government.

- **Client Compatible.** With Client Compatible encryption, traffic between the client and the server is encrypted using the RC4 algorithm and the strongest key the client supports (40-bit, 56-bit, or 128 bit). The server negotiates with the client to determine the key strength on connection, however the server does not accept non-encrypted client connections.

- **High.** Traffic in both directions is encrypted using the RC4 algorithm and a 128-bit key only. If a client does not support 128-bit encryption, it is not permitted to connect.

- **Low.** Traffic from the client to the server only is encrypted, at the strongest key that the client supports. This can improve performance on the client because the client does not have to decrypt the screen update data coming from the server. The client still encrypts the keystroke and mouse data that it sends to the server. This also allows you to use products to improve performance over a WAN, for example to use between a branch and a home office. Use this setting only if you are planning to use these products. A malicious user can monitor documents and data coming from the server over the link if this setting is used.

On the **General** tab of TSCC or on the Data Encryption property page of the Terminal Services Connection Wizard, the **Use standard Windows authentication** check box is cleared by default. If you select this check box, lower security authentication mechanisms are permitted.

Logon Settings

By default, users are allowed access to the terminal server using the information that they provided to log on to their remote desktop client. For a more secure system, you can require users to provide logon credentials to access the terminal server.

You can allow access to the server based on the credentials provided here by clicking the **Always use the following logon information** radio button on the **Logon Settings** tab of TSCC or by enabling the **Always prompt client for password upon connection** Group Policy setting located in the Encryption and Security folder under Terminal Services in Computer Configuration. Use one of these options only if you are hosting an application that requires a password for access. For more information, see "Planning Terminal Server User Rights and Logon" earlier in this chapter.

Remote Procedure Call (RPC) Security Policy

You can enable this Group Policy setting to allow Terminal Server to accept only authenticated and encrypted requests. It is recommended that you enable this setting for increased security.

Sessions

You can set Terminal Server time-out and reconnection settings on the server to help manage the number of sessions held by a terminal server at any one time, to help manage unreliable connections for remote users, or to reduce the impact on the CPU of many users logging on to the server at the same time. You can set most of these settings by using TSCC or Group Policy. Exceptions are noted.

 Note

You can also set these settings per user through Group Policy User Configuration and through Active Directory Users and Computers user properties. However, the Group Policy computer settings listed here take precedence over user settings.

End a disconnected session

You can set a limit on the time that a disconnected session continues to exist on the server. There can be many reasons why a session becomes disconnected, for example if a user's computer fails or if the user places the session into a disconnected state in order to access the same session from another location. The programs and processes that the user had running before the disconnection continue to run during a disconnected session. Because a user can have a disconnected session running on the server without realizing it, it is best to set a limit on how long disconnected sessions continue to run on the server. However, by setting this as high as possible you can achieve better server performance by reducing the additional CPU usage needed when a user reconnects to the server.

Active session limit

You can set a limit on how long a user can maintain an active session with the server. If you choose **Never**, the server allows an active session to continue forever.

Idle session limit

You can set a limit on how long an idle session remains open. An idle session occurs if there has been no mouse or keyboard activity for a certain period of time. This can indicate that the user has stepped away from the computer, presenting someone else with the opportunity to use his or her session. When a session has been idle for more time than you have specified, the user is notified and given two minutes to place the session back into an active state. If the two minutes elapse, the server disconnects or ends the session, depending on the settings you choose. Just as with choosing a timeframe for ending a disconnected session, it is important to understand users' work patterns and needs when choosing a limit for idle sessions.

 | **Note**
In a load-balanced farm, an idle session cannot be moved to a different server within the farm.

Session reconnection

By default, users can reconnect to a disconnected session from a computer other that the one from which they originally connected to the session. However, if a user connects from a Citrix ICA client, you can restrict the user to reconnecting only from the computer that originally connected to the session. This setting does not apply to Windows clients.

Session limit behavior

If you choose to enforce session limits for your users, you can ensure that users do not choose to have their sessions end when the connection to the server is broken for whatever reason. This way, you can be sure that all users can pick up where they left off in the event of a server failure, thereby reducing the loss of work and helpdesk incidents. If you choose to have sessions disconnect, you can use TSCC or Group Policy to specify the amount of time the session remains in a disconnected state.

Shut down options

You can use the following two Group Policy settings, found in the Terminal Services folder under Computer Configuration/Administrative Templates/Windows Components, to remove items from the **Start** menu and **Shut Down** dialog box so that users cannot use certain methods to disconnect or log off from their session:

- Enable the **Remove Windows Security item from the Start menu** policy to prevent users from unintentionally logging off of Terminal Server.

- Enable the **Remove Disconnect option from Shut Down dialog** policy to prevent users from using this method to disconnect from Terminal Server.

Automatic reconnection

You can allow a session to automatically reconnect to Terminal Server if the network connection is lost.

User Environment

Use the following settings to control the users' desktop environment.

Launch application on connection

If you are hosting a single application with Terminal Server, for example a line-of-business application or an application for task workers who use the server for only one thing, you can have that application start automatically when the user logs on. This eliminates the possibility of the user running unauthorized applications on the server or accessing other parts of the server or the network through the server. For information about how to start an application on connection, see "Specify a program to start when the user logs on" in Help and Support Center for Windows Server 2003. For more information about automatic logon, see "Planning Terminal Server User Rights and Logon" earlier in this chapter. You can configure this setting by using Group Policy (which you can apply to both computers and users), TSCC, and for users through the Remote Desktop Connection tool.

Desktop wallpaper

By default, sessions connecting to Windows Server 2003 Terminal Server do not display desktop wallpaper. For sessions connecting to servers running previous versions of Windows server operating systems and clients running Windows XP Professional or earlier, you can accomplish this by using Group Policy. For more information, see "Enforce removal of Remote Desktop wallpaper" in Help and Support Center for Windows Server 2003.

 Note

In Windows 2000 you can disable desktop wallpaper on the client from the **Environment** tab of the Terminal Services Connection Configuration tool.

Remote Control

You can use Remote Control to control or troubleshoot a user's session from a remote location. You can configure this setting by using Group Policy settings (which you can apply to both computers and users) or TSCC. If you choose to enable this in your organization, you can configure this setting in the following ways:

- Full Control with user's permission
- Full Control without user's permission
- View Session with user's permission
- View Session without user's permission

It is recommended that you configure this setting so that the user's permission is required to allow another person to access their computer through Remote Control. Keep in mind that even if you require a user to give permission, the user can choose to allow anyone who has acquired the correct permissions to access his or her computer. Also, some countries and regions have laws that do not allow the **View Session with user's permission** setting. If your organization has offices in several countries and regions, check the local laws before configuring Remote Control in this way. For more information about configuring sessions for Remote Control, see "Configure remote control settings" in Help and Support Center for Windows Server 2003.

Client Settings

You can use the settings discussed in this section to control certain aspects of the user experience and allow users to perform certain operations through their desktop computer rather than through the server.

Client/Server data redirection

You can use data redirection with Terminal Server to enable users to access and use resources from their desktop computers rather than from the terminal server. The most notable of these resources is printing, but you can also enable drive, audio, smart card, and clipboard redirection to the client computer. In general, restricting user's options to only those required to do their jobs can minimize the likelihood of introducing a vulnerability to the system. You can configure most of these settings through Group Policy (which you can apply to computers only) or TSCC. Exceptions are noted.

 Note

You can also configure redirection for disk drives, printer, and serial ports by using the Remote Desktop Connection tool on the client. For more information, see "Configuring Remote Desktop Connection" later in this chapter.

Table 4.3 summarizes the data redirection settings.

Table 4.3   Data Redirection Settings

Data redirection type	Characteristics
Time zone	Only configurable by using Group Policy.
	By default the session time zone is the same as the time zone of the terminal server. This can be an issue if you are using Terminal Server for remote or mobile users, especially when your line-of-business applications (for example, financial applications) have time dependencies.
Clipboard	By default, you can copy and paste between the terminal server and the Remote Desktop client. Disable this ability if you have sensitive data on the terminal server that should not be shared outside of the application in which it is used.
Smart card	Only configurable by using Group Policy.
	By default the ability to log on to the Remote Desktop client is allowed. For more information about using smart card with Terminal Server, see the "Planning Network Security Components" earlier in this chapter.

(continued)

Table 4.3   Data Redirection Settings *(continued)*

Data redirection type	Characteristics
Audio	By default, users cannot play audio on the Remote Desktop client. The sound plays on the server rather than the client computer. If you enable this setting, users can specify on the Remote Desktop Connection tool whether to play audio at their computer or the server, or to not have the sound play at all.
Serial port	By default, Terminal Server allows users to redirect data to peripherals attached to the serial (COM) port. Disable this capability unless there is a requirement for it. This prevents users from printing or copying sensitive data stored on the terminal server, and reduces vulnerabilities to security threats that could access your computer through these ports.
Client printer	By default, users can redirect print jobs to a printer attached to their client computer. Unless users need to print to a local printer, disable this capability so that users cannot print or copy sensitive data stored on the terminal server.
Parallel port	By default, Terminal Server allows users to redirect data to peripherals attached to the parallel (LPT) port. Disable this capability unless there is a requirement for it. This prevents users from printing or copying sensitive data stored on the terminal server, and reduces vulnerabilities to security threats that could access your computer through these ports.
Drive	By default, Terminal Server allows users to redirect data to the drives on the client computer. Unless there is a requirement for this, you should disable this capability so that users cannot copy sensitive data stored on the terminal server onto their local computer.
Default printer	By default, Terminal Server designates the client default printer as the default printer in a session. Unless users need to be able to print to a local printer, disable this capability so that users cannot print or copy sensitive data stored on the terminal server.

Color depth

You can reduce or increase the maximum color depth depending on your bandwidth and fidelity requirements (greater color depth requires more bandwidth and resources on the terminal server).

Number of connections

By default, an unlimited number of sessions are permitted on the terminal server. Restricting the number of sessions improves the performance of Terminal Server because fewer sessions are demanding system resources.

You can configure this setting in the Terminal Services folder of the Group Policy Object Editor. In TSCC, you can configure the number of settings on the **Network Adapter** tab. You can also select the network adapter you want to use for the RDP connection traffic.

Permissions

You can use TSCC to change your permissions lists by adding and removing users and groups. You can also customize the permissions for users or groups on a per-connection basis. It is recommended that you give permissions to as few users and groups as is necessary, and to give those users and groups the lowest level permissions necessary for them to do their jobs. For more information about how to set permissions, see the topics under "Managing permissions on connections" in Help and Support Center for Windows Server 2003.

Designing Server Setting Configurations

Use the following guidelines to design the configuration of your terminal servers.

Keep-Alive Connections

Configure this Group Policy setting to Enabled to ensure that the session state remains consistent with the client state. Use this setting only if you are having problems with users who cannot reconnect.

Temporary Folders

These settings can be set in the Server Settings folder of TSCC or in the Temporary Folders node of the Terminal Services administrative template in the Group Policy Object Editor. In TSCC, both of these settings are configured Yes by default, which means that temporary folders are used per session and deleted upon logging off. It is recommended that you keep the default settings unless there is a compelling business reason to change them.

Delete or retain temporary folders when exiting   It is recommended that you configure your servers so that the data stored in the temporary folder for user sessions is deleted when users log off. This provides added security by eliminating a point of access for user data. It also provides a way to manage the load on the server, because temporary folders tend to grow quickly in size in a multiuser environment. If you are using Group Policy to set this setting (set to Disable to delete temporary folders), you must also configure the server to use per-session temporary folders.

Use separate temporary folders for each session   This setting keeps each session's temporary folders in a separate folder, which enables you to configure the server to delete temporary folders when a single user logs off without affecting other users' sessions.

Active Desktop

You can restrict users from using Active Desktop by using TSCC or Group Policy under User Configuration/Administrative Templates/Desktop/Active Desktop. Active Desktop allows users to choose JPEG and HTML wallpaper, both of which can affect performance for the user because of the amount of data that needs to transfer from the server to the desktop. The default setting is Enable. It is recommended that you disable Active Desktop.

Session Directory Settings

If you are load balancing several terminal servers and using Session Directory, you can use TSCC or Group Policy to configure the servers to use Session Directory. Session Directory is a database that tracks user sessions that are running on load-balanced terminal servers. For more information about using Session Directory (including configuring Session Directory), see "Load Balancing Terminal Servers" earlier in this chapter. For more information about Session Directory, see the "Session Directory and Load Balancing Using Windows Server 2003 Terminal Server" white paper at the Terminal Services link on the Web Resources page at http://www.microsoft.com/windows/reskits/webresources.

Licensing

Use the following settings to configure the license server for Terminal Server. Most of these settings can be configured only through Group Policy. Exceptions are noted.

Licensing Mode You can set the licensing mode to Per Device or Per User through the TSCC Server Settings folder. For more information about licensing modes for Terminal Server, see "Choosing the Licensing Model" earlier in this chapter.

License Server Security Group Enabling this Group Policy setting and applying it to your license server creates a local group called Terminal Services Computers. The license server issues licenses only to the terminal servers in this group. You must add both the terminal servers for which you need to provide licenses and any license servers that might need to acquire licenses to this group for each license server. For ease of management in a large Terminal Server deployment, create an Active Directory global group named Terminal Server Licensing and add all of your terminal servers and all of your license servers to this group. Then add this group to the Terminal Services Computers group of each license server. Whenever you deploy a new terminal server or license server, if you add it to the Terminal Server Licensing group, it automatically appears in the Terminal Services Computers group for each license server.

Prevent License Upgrade In an environment with both Windows Server 2003 and Windows 2000 Terminal Server, enable this Group Policy setting to prevent the license server from handing out Windows Server 2003 CALs to terminal servers that are running Windows 2000.

Limit users to one remote session

By default, the TSCC setting that restricts users to one session is set to Yes. This ensures that a user who disconnects can reconnect to the same session. This also conserves server resources by keeping the number of sessions on your server to a known number. You can enforce this setting domain-wide by using Group Policy. Limit users to one session unless you have a valid business reason for allowing more than one.

Permission Compatibility

This TSCC setting is set to Full Security by default. It restricts access to system resources, such as the registry, to members of the Users group on a terminal server.

 Important
Although some older applications require such access, do not set this setting to Relaxed Security unless you have determined through testing that your applications do not work properly in Full Security mode.

Home Directory

Use this Group Policy setting to set the path for storing your user home directories. For more information about planning for storage of home directories, see "Using Home Directories with Terminal Server" earlier in this chapter.

Roaming Profiles

Use this Group Policy setting to set the path for storing your roaming user profiles. For more information about planning for storage of roaming user profiles, see "Using User Profiles" earlier in this chapter.

Using Software Restriction Policies

Software restriction policies, which are new with Windows XP and Windows Server 2003, enable you to identify software running on computers in your domain and to control whether a user can run them. Restricting certain types of applications can, for example, protect your organization against viruses. As a way to lock down the user environment on a terminal server, you can set up software restriction policies that allow users to run only specific applications on the server.

Software restriction policies are located in the Group Policy Object Editor under Windows Settings/Security Settings. Windows Installer operates with applications permitted by these Software Restriction Policies. For more information, see "Software restriction policies" in Help and Support Center for Windows Server 2003.

You can use software restriction policies with Terminal Server by using path rules, as shown in Table 4.4. These rules allow groups of users, when separated into different OUs, to access only the applications or application components that you want the groups of users to access on the server. For example, a company has a terminal server with a line-of-business application and a few productivity applications for the use of the accounts payable department. The company has decided that account managers need access to all of the available applications for that department, but the data-entry workers in that department need access only to the line-of-business application. The company sets the default rule to Disallowed and configures the software restriction policies as outlined in the following table.

Table 4.4   Example Software Restriction Policy Configuration

Path Rule	Security Level
Terminal Server OU	
%windir%	Unrestricted
%windir%\regedit.exe	Disallowed
%windir%\system32\cmd.exe	Disallowed
%windir%\system32\command.com	Disallowed
%windir%\system32\dllcache	Disallowed
%windir%\system32\gpresult.exe	Disallowed
%windir%\system32\gpupdate.exe	Disallowed
%ProgramFiles%\Windows NT\Accessories	Unrestricted
Data Entry OU	
%ProgramFiles%\Accounts Payable Software	Unrestricted
Account Managers OU	
%ProgramFiles%\Microsoft Office\Office	Unrestricted
%ProgramFiles%\Internet Explorer	Unrestricted

Configuring Terminal Server for Differing Time Zones

By default Terminal Server keeps track of time according to the time zone in which it has been configured, rather than on a per-user basis. This can be a problem when a user connects to a terminal server outside of the time zone in which the user is located because the local computer uses the time configured on the terminal server rather than the local time. If you are hosting time-sensitive applications on your terminal server or if you have processes in place that depend on the user's current local time, such as financial systems and calendaring, you might want to enable the Allow Time Zone Redirection Group Policy setting. This policy is located in Windows Components/Terminal Services. With this setting enabled, Terminal Services uses the server base time on the terminal server and the client time zone information to calculate the time on the session.

Designing the Remote Desktop Connection Installation and Configuration

The Remote Desktop Connection is the client-side tool that enables the connection to the terminal server. You need to install the Remote Desktop Connection on clients running Windows 2000 or earlier versions of the Windows operating system. On Windows XP clients, the Remote Desktop Connection is already installed. However you can preconfigure and distribute a connection to ensure the optimal settings for your users. For more information about the Remote Desktop Connection, see "Configuring Remote Desktop" in the *Windows XP Professional Resource Kit Documentation* (or see "Configuring Remote Desktop" on the Web at http://www.microsoft.com/reskit). Figure 4.6 shows the process for designing the Remote Desktop Connection installation and configuration.

Figure 4.6   Designing the Remote Desktop Connection Installation and Configuration

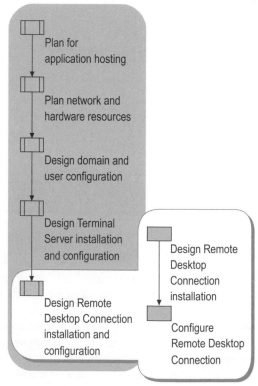

Designing the Remote Desktop Connection Installation

If you currently have Windows XP deployed to the clients, the Remote Desktop Connection is already built in. No further deployment is required unless you want to configure the connection.

The Remote Desktop Connection Windows Installer Setup package is a tool for deploying the Remote Desktop Connection and associated files for specially configured connections and on computers running Windows NT 4.0, Windows 2000 Server, Windows 2000 Professional, Windows 98, and Windows 95. You can also place the Client Windows Installer Setup package on a share for distribution through Group Policy to workstations running Windows Server 2003.

Configuring Remote Desktop Connection

By using the Remote Desktop Connection tool, you can set from the client many of the same settings that you can set on the server using TSCC, Group Policy, or WMI. Because server settings override client settings, it is recommended that you set these settings on the server for ease of management. However, there are some situations where you might need to set these settings using the Remote Desktop Connection tool. An example is if you are providing access to the same terminal server for users with slightly different user roles or purposes. These settings are summarized in Table 4.5. For detailed explanations and recommendations for these settings, see "Designing Terminal Server Installation and Configuration" earlier in this chapter.

Table 4.5   Remote Desktop Connection Tool Settings

Tab	Description
General	Enter or change logon and connection settings.
Display	Change remote Desktop size (resolution) and color depth, and choose whether to display the connection bar in full-screen mode.
Local Resources	Control sound, the behavior of keyboard combinations, and connections to local devices (drives, printers, and serial ports).
Programs	Start a program upon connection to the terminal server.
Experience	Configure the connection speed and adjust the desktop environment for optimal performance

With the Remote Desktop Connection tool you can also create and save a preconfigured Remote Desktop Connection for distribution.

Preconfiguring a Remote Desktop Connection

Remote Desktop Connection is installed by default on all versions of Windows Server 2003, most versions of Windows CE, and all versions of Windows XP operating systems. On earlier versions of Windows and on the Pocket PC you must manually install Remote Desktop Connection in order to connect to Terminal Server.

Note

Windows 2000 includes the 32-bit Terminal Services Client for connecting to Terminal Services. It is recommended that you install the latest version of the Remote Desktop Connection to get the latest performance improvements.

You can preconfigure a Remote Desktop Connection for distribution to your client computers through Group Policy as an .msi package along with associated files.

▶ **To create a preconfigured Remote Desktop Connection for distribution**

1. Open Remote Desktop Connection.

2. Expand the dialog box by clicking the **Options** button and configure the connection.

3. On the **General** tab of the Remote Desktop Connection tool, click the **Save As** button, navigate to the folder in which you want to save the configured connection, rename the file, and click **Save**.

4. Create an .msi package and distribute it to your Terminal Server users OU. For information about how to create an .msi package, see the Windows Installer documentation link on the Web Resources page at http://www.microsoft.com/windows/reskits/webresources.

Note

Users need to enter their own user name and password into the connection.

Configuring the Desktop Experience

You can configure the connection speed and fine-tune the desktop environment for optimal performance by using the settings located on the **Experience** tab of the Remote Desktop Connection tool. The settings available on this tab are summarized in

Table 4.6. Most of these settings relate to the graphical nature of the desktop. Because the processing for graphics happens on the server and must be transmitted to the desktop over the network connection, you can increase performance by allowing only the minimal settings that are necessary for your users. When you choose a connection speed, the check boxes are automatically selected to indicate the recommended settings for the richest visual experience possible at that speed.

Table 4.6   Desktop Experience Settings

Setting	Description
Desktop background	Allows user to choose a custom background or wallpaper for their desktop. Because these can be very graphic-intensive, disable this setting unless it is necessary for your users.
Show contents of window while dragging	Redraws the contents of a window rather than showing just the frame of the window when you move the window across the screen. Because this redrawing takes place on the server and needs to be transmitted over the network connection to display on the user's desktop, disable this setting unless it is necessary.
Menu and window animation	Enables cascading menus and scroll transitions for menus and tool tips. Because this rendering takes place on the server and needs to be transmitted over the network connection to display on the user's desktop, disable this setting unless it is necessary.
Themes	Allows user to choose a background plus a set of sounds, icons, and other elements for their desktop. Because many themes are graphic-intensive, disable this setting unless it is necessary for your users.
Bitmap caching	Stores frequently used images on the local computer to speed up the connection. By enabling this setting, these images do not have to be transmitted across the network connection each time they appear on the desktop. This setting is enabled by default.

Locking Down the User Session

You can configure Group Policy settings and apply them to your Terminal Server Users group to control your users sessions and user access to certain features on the server. For more information about controlling user sessions, see article 278295, "How to Lock Down a Windows 2000 Terminal Server Session." To find this article, see the Microsoft Knowledge Base link on the Web Resources page at http://www.microsoft.com/windows/reskits/webresources. You can also lock down your users' sessions by using the Security Templates MMC snap-in or the settings under Computer Configuration/Windows Settings/Security Settings in the Group Policy Object Editor.

Additional Resources

These resources contain additional information and tools related to this chapter.

Related Information

- The *Server Management Guide* of the *Windows Server 2003 Resource Kit* (or see the *Server Management Guide* on the Web at http://www.microsoft.com/reskit) for information about using Terminal Services for remote administration.

- "Configuring Remote Desktop" in the *Windows XP Professional Resource Kit Documentation* (or see "Configuring Remote Desktop" on the Web at http://www.microsoft.com/reskit).

- The Terminal Services link on the Web Resources page at http://www.microsoft.com/windows/reskits/webresources.

- The Terminal Services Community Center link on the Web Resources page at http://www.microsoft.com/windows/reskits/webresources.

- The Terminal Services Scaling link on the Web Resources page at http://www.microsoft.com/windows/reskits/webresources.

Related Tools

- Roboserver and Roboclient

  Using these tools you can easily place and manage simulated loads on a terminal server. This information can help you determine whether your environment can handle the load that users place on it. Used together, these tools make capacity planning easier and more automated. For more information about Roboserver and Roboclient, click **Tools** in Help and Support Center, and then click Windows Resource Kit Tools.

Related Help Topics

For best results in identifying Help topics by title, in Help and Support Center, under the **Search** box, click **Set search options**. Under **Help Topics**, select the **Search in title only** checkbox.

Topics under "Terminal Services Overview" in Help and Support Center for Windows Server 2003.

C H A P T E R   5

Planning for Remote Server Management

Before you deploy servers running the Microsoft® Windows® Server 2003 operating system, determine the extent to which system administrators need to manage them remotely. If you need to perform only typical administrative tasks over the network, conventional tools suffice. For *headless servers* — those having no keyboard, video display, or mouse — or for any servers having high availability requirements, you might need to use Emergency Management Services, possibly in conjunction with other hardware and software components, to remotely bring servers back into service even when they are not accessible by means of the standard network connection.

In This Chapter

Related Information

- For more information about Emergency Management Services for either headless or standard servers, see the *Server Management Guide* of the *Microsoft® Windows® Server 2003 Resource Kit* (or see the *Server Management Guide* on the Web at http://www.microsoft.com/reskit).

- For an overview of remote administration and information about associated remote management tools, see the *Server Management Guide* of the *Windows Server 2003 Resource Kit* (or see the *Server Management Guide* on the Web at http://www.microsoft.com/reskit).

Overview of Remote Management Planning

Although local administration is the most secure way to manage the computers in a networked environment, cost, staffing, and system availability requirements typically preclude this approach in medium to large organizations. Remote management can solve many of these problems by increasing productivity, decreasing time to resolution, decreasing staffing requirements, and allowing more flexibility in server placement. Remote management can also resolve physical accessibility issues for servers that are remotely located or rack mounted — whether they are headless or use keyboard-video-mouse (KVM) switches.

Windows Server 2003 provides a variety of tools and technologies to help you remotely administer the servers in your network. Conventional tools help you perform common tasks on computers that are functioning and available over the network. These tools are sometimes referred to as *in-band* tools because they function through the standard network connection. Other tools allow you to connect to a computer that is not responding to the standard network connection for some reason, such as when a Stop error occurs or the network adapter fails. These tools are sometimes referred to as *out-of-band* tools because they use a connection that does not depend on network drivers.

Emergency Management Services is a new feature in Windows Server 2003 that supports out-of-band connections. Emergency Management Services is included with Microsoft® Windows® Server 2003, Standard Edition; Windows® Server 2003, Enterprise Edition; Windows® Server 2003, Datacenter Edition; and Windows® Server 2003, Web Edition.

Before you begin managing servers remotely using in-band or out-of-band tools, you need to develop a remote management plan. A remote management plan ensures that you choose the appropriate remote management tools and management configurations for your organization and that you address all the impacts they might have on your infrastructure.

To develop your plan, you first need to know the server configuration in your organization: where the servers are located and what roles they perform. You also need to know the availability requirements for the servers you plan to manage remotely and who the administrators are.

Follow the planning process presented here to develop a plan for remotely managing the servers in your environment. This planning process addresses tools for Windows Server 2003 remote installation, in-band management tasks — such as configuring, monitoring, and troubleshooting — and out-of-band management tasks — such as restarting the computer and viewing Stop error messages. It does not address workstation management or software distribution tools for applications and updates.

Remote Management Planning Process

To produce an effective remote management plan, you need to determine which servers to manage and when to manage them remotely or locally, the tools to use, the required supporting hardware components and configurations, network and security considerations and remediation, and whether and how to deploy Windows Server 2003 remotely. These factors are included in the process presented here. Figure 5.1 illustrates the steps in the remote management planning process.

Figure 5.1   Planning Remote Management

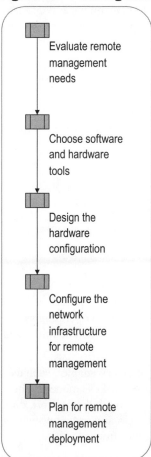

Remote Management Concepts

Conventional remote management involves establishing an in-band connection to a server to manage it across the network. As a class, in-band management tools are robust, versatile, and secure. Whenever a server is functioning and available across the network, in-band management tools are the tools of choice. In the past, this type of management was the only type of remote management available for servers running Windows operating systems.

By using Windows Server 2003, you can also manage servers by using out-of-band connections that make it possible to perform management tasks when the server is not responding to the standard network connection. When you lose the capability to manage the server with the in-band connection — such as when the firmware is initializing, a Stop error occurs, or the server stops responding — you need to use an out-of-band connection to manage it remotely.

A primary purpose of the out-of-band connection is to provide a means for you to return the server to a functioning state so that you can continue to manage it with your conventional in-band tools. Out-of-band management also makes it possible for you to configure servers for headless operation, which means the local keyboard and monitor are optional. When combined with appropriate out-of-band hardware components, Windows Server 2003–based servers need to be managed locally only for hardware installation or replacement.

 Note

For a document to assist you in setting up headless servers, see "Headless Server Quick Start" (SDCEMS_1.doc) on the *Microsoft® Windows® Server 2003 Deployment Kit* companion CD (or see "Headless Server Quick Start" on the Web at http://www.microsoft.com/reskit).

In-Band Management

Conventional remote management tools, such as Telnet, use in-band connections for communicating with the managed server. In-band connections rely on operating system network drivers for establishing connections between computers, so a server must be initialized and operational to be managed with these tools.

The most common in-band connection hardware device is a network adapter, such as an Ethernet adapter, analog modem, or Integrated Services Digital Network (ISDN) modem. The most typical method of in-band remote management is connecting through the network directly to the server, but you can also use Windows Server 2003 remote access and virtual private network (VPN) connections to manage servers through an in-band connection.

Typical tasks performed by using in-band management tools include routine configuration, monitoring, troubleshooting, and maintenance.

Out-of-Band Management

When a server is not in a functional state and cannot be accessed by using the standard network connection, you need to use an out-of-band connection to manage it remotely. Out-of-band connections do not rely on operating system network drivers for establishing connections between computers. The following are typical situations when you might need to manage a computer by using an out-of-band connection:

- The server is powered down.
- The BIOS is conducting the POST.
- A Stop error occurs.
- The server is too low on resources to respond adequately.
- The network adapter malfunctions or fails.
- The Windows loader or Recovery Console is running.
- The server is not fully initialized.

Common out-of-band connection hardware devices include serial ports, analog modems, and ISDN modems. In addition, out-of-band hardware components known as service processors can in some cases provide out-of-band connections over the network. A *service processor* is a microprocessor that functions independently of the CPU(s) in a computer and provides additional server management functionality for any operating state, whether or not the operating system is functioning.

Emergency Management Services, as well as features built into some hardware components and firmware, support out-of-band connections. Hardware components that support out-of-band connections include service processors, terminal concentrators, intelligent uninterruptible power supplies (UPSs), and intelligent power switches. A *terminal concentrator* is a hardware device that allows you to monitor multiple servers simultaneously by connecting to their out-of-band serial ports through a single network connection. An *intelligent UPS* or *intelligent power switch* is one that provides some remote functionality, such as powering up or down or resetting a computer. These components are described in detail in "Choosing Software and Hardware Tools" later in this chapter.

Console redirection is a key out-of-band feature that sends keyboard input and character-based output destined for the local display device to the out-of-band port so that you can view the information on a remote computer. Console redirection does not preclude locally attached monitors and keyboards: a computer with console redirection can still process input from a local keyboard and display output to a local monitor.

Emergency Management Services, service processors, and some system firmware provide console redirection. The extensible firmware interface (EFI) on Itanium-based computers typically provides console redirection. The BIOS on x86-based computers might or might not provide console redirection; contact your computer manufacturer to find out.

The specific component that controls console redirection changes as the operating state changes. For example, a service processor or firmware provides console redirection during power up and during the Power On Self Test (POST), and Emergency Management Services provides console redirection as soon as the Windows loader (Ntldr) starts. You can transfer control of console redirection to another component, such as a service processor, by entering specific escape sequences from the management computer.

Additional components that support out-of-band connections are described later in this chapter.

Emergency Management Services

Emergency Management Services is a new feature in Windows Server 2003 that provides out-of-band connections through a serial port or, in the case of some service processors, an alternate network connection. With Emergency Management Services, you can perform administrative tasks remotely using an out-of-band connection. When you combine Emergency Management Services with the appropriate out-of-band hardware, you can perform all administrative tasks remotely, except for installing or replacing hardware.

Emergency Management Services features are fully or partially available when the Windows Server 2003 operating system is loading, is running, or is in distress — such as when it is slow or not responding or when a Stop error occurs.

The three Emergency Management Services features that support out-of-band management are console redirection, Special Administration Console (SAC), and !Special Administration Console (!SAC). The Windows Server 2003 loader or kernel must be at least partially functioning for these features to be available.

Console redirection

Emergency Management Services can redirect keyboard input and character-based output when any of the following Windows Server 2003 components are running:

- The operating system loader on x86-based multiple-boot computers
- Recovery Console
- The Windows Server 2003 kernel
- The command prompt (cmd.exe)
- Text-mode Setup, during Windows Server 2003 installation
- Remote Installation Services (RIS) Setup

For more information about how Emergency Management Services console redirection works with these components and when it is not available, see the *Server Management Guide* of the *Windows Server 2003 Resource Kit* (or see the *Server Management Guide* on the Web at http://www.microsoft.com/reskit).

Special Administration Console

Special Administration Console (SAC) is the primary Emergency Management Services command-line environment. It provides a variety of commands for monitoring server status and troubleshooting problems during emergencies. SAC is available whenever the Windows Server 2003 kernel is running in normal mode, safe mode, and during the graphical user interface (GUI)–mode phase of Setup.

 Caution

Using SAC during an operating system upgrade or installation might cause the upgrade or installation to fail or become unstable.

Using SAC, you can establish multiple user sessions, called *channels*, and switch between them. Although SAC is separate from the Windows Server 2003 command prompt (cmd.exe), you can establish a command prompt channel from SAC and then switch between SAC and the command prompt channels by using SAC commands or escape sequences. During the GUI-mode phase of Setup, you can also establish a channel for viewing setup logs so that you can troubleshoot unresponsive or failed operating system installations. You can access only one channel at a time, which means that multiuser access to SAC is not available. To create a SAC channel, you must use a local Administrator account; therefore, all the commands that you run in a channel run as local administrator.

For more information about SAC capabilities and how to use them, see the *Server Management Guide* of the *Windows Server 2003 Resource Kit* (or see the *Server Management Guide* on the Web at http://www.microsoft.com/reskit). For more information about SAC commands, see "Special Administration Console (SAC) and SAC commands" in Help and Support Center for Windows Server 2003.

!Special Administration Console

!Special Administration Console (!SAC) is a scaled-down version of SAC that is designed to recover an unresponsive system — for example, due to a Stop error. You cannot directly invoke !SAC; it becomes available automatically when a server experiences a system failure or fault. !SAC is a last-resort tool that lets you view Stop messages, obtain computer identification information, and restart the server.

Headless Servers

Headless servers are computers that can operate without a keyboard, mouse, and local monitor. If the system firmware supports it, the video adapter and keyboard controller are also optional. Emergency Management Services, in combination with the appropriate hardware and system firmware console redirection, makes it possible for you to configure servers running Windows Server 2003 for headless operation. Redirecting firmware allows the system to pass the POST without a video adapter. When a server runs Emergency Management Services, you can manage it with both in-band and out-of-band tools, making locally attached input and output devices unnecessary.

Using headless servers does not preclude having locally attached input devices. Depending on your hardware configuration, you might be able to attach and remove local devices, such as Universal Serial Bus (USB) keyboards and mouse devices, as needed.

Computer manufactures offer preconfigured headless systems that have no keyboard controller, video adapter, and mouse. For more information about purchasing a headless computer or configuring your existing computers for headless operation, contact your computer manufacturer.

Evaluating Remote Management Needs

To implement an efficient, cost effective, secure remote management plan, you need to determine which servers to manage remotely by considering the tradeoffs — including cost, convenience, and system availability — for various ways of managing the servers in your environment. Before you decide whether or what to manage remotely, you need to evaluate remote and local management, and in-band and out-of-band management.

With Windows Server 2003, you can choose to remotely perform server management tasks that previously could be done only locally. By using Emergency Management Services with the appropriate hardware and software tools, you can remotely perform almost everything except hardware installation. When considering this type of solution, you need to weigh the level of support provided by the solution against the possible need to use legacy hardware. You might need to make a compromise between the level of support you want and the cost of additional hardware. You might also want to evaluate the savings you can obtain by configuring some of your servers for headless operation.

The first step in developing a remote management plan is to determine which servers in your environment need to be managed remotely. Figure 5.2 illustrates the place of this step in the planning process.

Figure 5.2 Evaluating Your Remote Management Needs

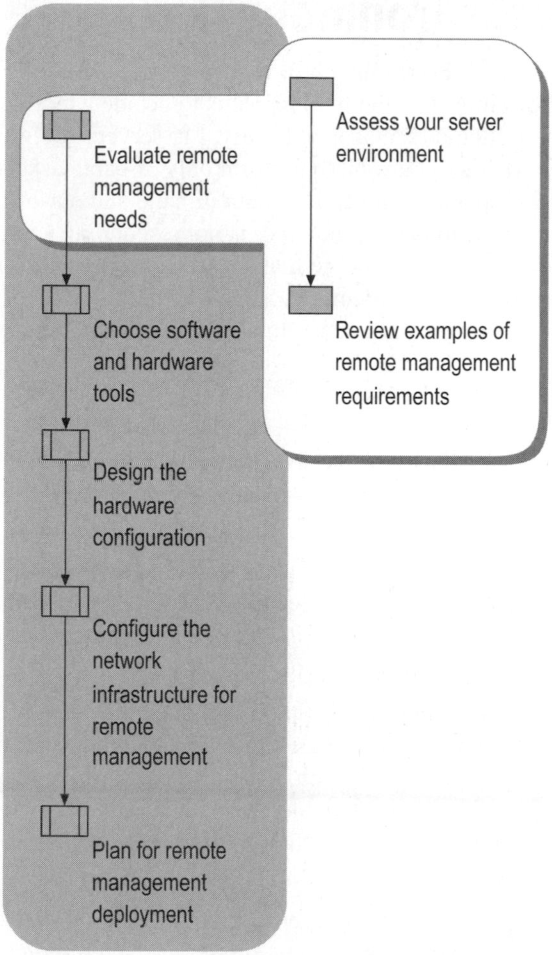

Assessing Your Server Environment

Assessing your server environment includes determining how many and what kind of servers you have, where they are located, and who administers them. The goal is to decide which servers should be managed remotely and which should be managed locally. For servers you want to manage remotely, you need to decide whether you want to perform only in-band tasks — those performed when the operating system is up and running — or both in-band and out-of-band tasks — those performed when the operating system is not running or is not responding appropriately. For example, you might want to configure some servers so that you can remotely install the operating system and perform all management tasks remotely, regardless of the state of the system, while for other servers you might only want to perform routine maintenance tasks remotely.

Identifying Computers for Remote Management

When determining which servers to manage remotely and which locally, consider the following issues:

- **Number of servers.** Does your organization have many servers or just a few? How manageable are they in relation to the number of technicians available for local support? If your organization has few servers and technicians are readily available, you might not need to manage remotely. On the other hand, if you have many servers and limited support resources, you probably want to manage at least some of them remotely.

- **Location of servers.** Are the servers in your organization consolidated in a single or a few locations where they are easily accessed by technicians, or are they widely dispersed? If the computers are distributed throughout your organization, what distances are involved? For example, are they located internationally, in different buildings in the same city, or down the hall? The more servers you have and the farther apart their locations, the greater the savings you are likely to achieve by remote management.

- **Server roles supported.** Do you have different management requirements for different types of servers, such as domain controllers, print servers, file servers, Web servers, application servers, and database servers? You might decide to manage different types of servers differently for reasons such as security or criticality to your business. For example, you might want to manage application servers remotely for mission-critical applications, but domain controllers locally for security reasons.

- **Availability requirements.** What percentage of the time must a server be up and running? For example, if you have servers with an availability rating of 99.99 percent, you can't afford a downtime of anything more than minutes. How many users typically access a server? For example, if a domain controller has a problem, many users might be affected, while if a print server in a small department fails, only a few users are affected. What is the impact to your business if a server is not available for a period of time? Remotely managing servers that have high availability requirements can significantly save downtime while waiting for someone to perform local management.

- **Reliability history.** How reliable is the server? How frequently does it typically encounter problems? The lower the reliability, the more benefit you can derive from managing it remotely.

- **Number and expertise of on-site technicians.** How many technicians do you have for local management and where are they based? For example, are there administrators on-site in branch offices? How experienced are they? If you have few technicians in certain areas, or they are inexperienced, you can probably benefit from remote management.

- **Security issues.** Do you have servers you prefer to manage locally for security reasons? For example, do you have public servers that you prefer to manage locally rather than by establishing a VPN connection? Or do have specific tasks that you prefer to perform locally and others you prefer to perform remotely?

Identifying Tasks for Remote Management

After you know which servers you want to manage remotely, the next step is to assess which kinds of management tasks to perform remotely and which to perform locally. For example, do you want to perform tasks remotely only when a server can be accessed across the network, or also when it cannot be accessed across the network?

If you have enough experienced technicians available or have highly reliable servers, in-band remote management support might be sufficient. On the other hand, if some of your servers have high availability requirements or a history of poor reliability, or if you have insufficient on-site technical support, you might need out-of-band remote management support.

If you have many servers mounted in racks and tethered to KVM switches, you might decide to configure them for headless operation and then perform all administrative tasks remotely. Because headless servers do not have monitors, keyboards, or mouse devices and might not require video adapters, they can present significant savings in space, energy consumption, and hardware costs.

Another consideration is whether your current servers are designed for out-of-band management. If you plan to use the hardware you already own and it is not designed for out-of-band support, your options might be more limited. For more information about deciding whether to use existing or new hardware, see "Planning for Remote Management Deployment" later in this chapter.

If you decide you need out-of-band remote management support, the next step is to determine how much support you need. As you determine the degree of out-of-band support you want, you need to weigh the costs of any additional hardware components — and possibly the cost of upgrading existing computers — against the savings in system uptime and reduced on-site support.

By using Emergency Management Services with nothing but a serial port, you can access nearly all Windows Server 2003 operating system states. By combining Emergency Management Services with appropriate out-of-band hardware, however, you can perform nearly every administrative task remotely — even before the operating system is fully initialized or after it stops responding — and you can effectively manage many servers from a single management computer.

To help determine the degree of out-of-band remote support you need, decide which of the following tasks you need to perform remotely:

- Start up a server

- Change BIOS settings

- View POST results

- Select which operating system to start

- View Stop error messages

- Reset a server

- Access the server when it is inaccessible through the network

- Install the Windows Server 2003 operating system

Different out-of-band tasks might require different types of hardware components. For more information about which components are needed for which tasks, see "Choosing Out-of-Band Management Tools" later in this chapter.

Identifying Responsibilities for Remote Management

As you plan for remote server management, you also need to decide whether you want different administrators to be responsible for different groups of tasks or whether you want all administrators to be authorized to perform the entire range of tasks. Depending on the size of your organization, the number and skill level of available administrators, and security requirements, you might decide to make some administrators responsible for only certain administrative tasks. To decide how to assign remote management tasks, consider the following issues:

- **Security issues.** Do you want to divide up tasks for security reasons? For example, you might decide that certain tools — based on the power of the tool or its level of built-in security — are to be used only by some administrators or that specific servers are to be accessible only to some administrators.

- **Skill level of administrators.** Do you have highly skilled administrators in all locations or only in some locations? For locations with less skilled administrators, you might decide to use remote management rather than telephone support.

Examples: Determining Remote Management Requirements

As you evaluate your needs for remote management, you develop a list of requirements. These requirements determine which tools and out-of-band configurations are most appropriate for your environment. The following descriptions illustrate three different types of remote management requirements and the level of remote management support appropriate to each. The tools and configurations appropriate to these levels of remote management are described later in this chapter.

Minimal Remote Management

You need minimal support for remote management if you have requirements such as the following:

- The site has few servers and those servers are located close together.

- The servers have low availability requirements.

- Experienced on-site technicians are typically available.

- Some routine management tasks are performed centrally.

An example business situation with minimal requirements for remote management might be a branch office that has a single, or just a few, servers running Windows Server 2003. The servers are primarily file and print servers and have low availability requirements. The branch has some on-site support available.

In this situation, on-site technicians perform most administrative tasks locally, but centrally located administrators perform some routine in-band tasks remotely over the network, such as changing a static IP address or other configuration settings,

Moderate Remote Management

You need moderate support for remote management if you have requirements such as the following:

- The site has many servers.

- The servers have availability requirements that range from low to high.

- Experienced on-site technicians are typically available to perform out-of-band tasks for servers with low to medium availability requirements.

- Many routine management tasks can be performed efficiently by using in-band remote management tools.

A situation with moderate requirements for remote management might be a data center that has many computers, some of which are legacy systems that do not support Emergency Management Services.

In this situation, the organization plans to supplement existing systems with out-of-band hardware components in order to perform some out-of-band management tasks remotely, even though the computers are not built for Emergency Management Services.

Administrators use in-band remote management tools for the systems in the data center. They use out-of-band management for some systems that have high availability requirements, but not for others that do not have such requirements. For example, the print servers are very reliable, so the organization decided it was not cost effective to support out-of-band management for these servers.

Maximum Remote Management

You need maximum support for remote management if you have requirements such as the following:

- The servers have high availability requirements.

- You need to perform a number of out-of-band tasks remotely.

- The servers are headless.

A situation with maximum requirements for remote management might exist when a group of computers has very high availability requirements. These computers support headless operation and have built-in service processors. They are mounted in racks in a highly secured room.

Administrators go into the highly secured room only when they add or replace hardware. All other administrative tasks are performed remotely, by using an in-band connection when possible and by using an out-of-band connection when a server cannot be accessed through the standard network. The Windows Server 2003 operating system is installed on these computers remotely by using RIS.

Choosing Software and Hardware Tools

After you determine how much you want to manage remotely, the next step is to select the tools and supporting components you need to accomplish your remote management tasks. Figure 5.3 illustrates the place of this step in the process.

Figure 5.3   Choosing Software Tools and Hardware Components

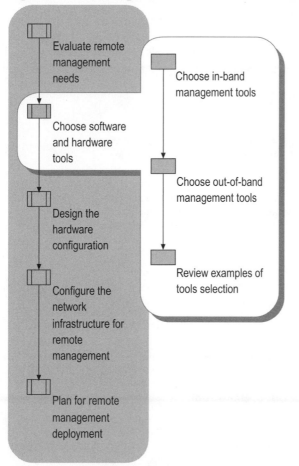

As you select your tools, think about the tasks you want to perform remotely when you have network access — by using in-band connections — and those you want to perform remotely when you do not have network access — by using out-of-band connections. As you select tools, evaluate their potential impact on your environment and build any needed environmental adjustments into your remote management plan.

Selecting In-Band or Out-of-Band Tools

In-band management is always the method of choice for managing servers when you can access them through their standard connections. If a server is functional enough to respond through the standard connection, conventional in-band management tools can provide a much broader range of functionality — and possibly greater security — than you might achieve with out-of-band management.

 Note

While the security of in-band management is highly dependent on the individual management tool, the security of out-of-band management is highly dependent on your out-of-band component configuration. For example, in a configuration that uses a remote serial connection, the security of the out-of-band management is dependent on the security built into the modem. For information about the security implications for different out-of-band configurations, see "Designing the Hardware Configuration" later in this chapter.

Keep in mind that out-of-band management is a last resort when you cannot access the server in any other way. The goal of out-of-band management is always to bring a server back into service so that you can manage it with in-band tools.

Table 5.1 shows whether to use in-band or out-of-band tools for various types of tasks during various operating states. After you know whether to use an in-band tool or an out-of-band tool, you can select the most appropriate specific tool or component, as described later in this chapter, for the tasks you want to perform remotely.

Table 5.1   Choosing In-Band or Out-of-Band Tools

During This Operating State	For This Type of Task	Use This Type of Tool
System powering on or off, or resetting	Power up, power down, reset	Out-of-band and in-band with Remote Desktop for Administration
Firmware initializing	Configure firmware, troubleshoot, restart	Out-of-band with supporting firmware
Operating system loading	Choose operating system to start, troubleshoot	Out-of-band, including Emergency Management Services
Text mode setup	Monitor, troubleshoot	Out-of-band, including Emergency Management Services
GUI mode setup	Monitor, troubleshoot	Out-of-band, including Emergency Management Services

(continued)

Table 5.1 Choosing In-Band or Out-of-Band Tools *(continued)*

During This Operating State	For This Type of Task	Use This Type of Tool
Operating system fully functional	Monitor, troubleshoot, modify configuration settings	In-band
Operating system not responding on network	Troubleshoot, restart	Out-of-band, including Emergency Management Services
Stop message occurred	Troubleshoot, restart	Out-of-band, including Emergency Management Services
System extremely slow responding on network	Troubleshoot, restart	In-band and out-of-band, including Emergency Management Services

Evaluating Tools for Environmental Impact

As you evaluate the software and hardware tools to use, consider the impact they might have on your network environment. For example, some tools present more security risks than others, and some increase network traffic more than others. Considerations such as these might influence your selection of one tool over another, or they might identify additional changes you need to make to your environment to mitigate the impact. The documentation provided with a remote management tool might contain information indicating its potential impact on your environment and any configuration changes needed for its use. For more information about configuring your environment for remote management, see "Configuring Your Infrastructure for Remote Management" later in this chapter.

As you develop your remote management plan, include the following lists:

Tasks you plan to perform remotely The more comprehensive you make this list, the easier it will be to identify all the tools you need. A task can be broad in scope (for example, manage DHCP servers), or it can be narrow in scope (for example, change the static IP address on a server). This list should include not only in-band tasks but also any required out-of-band tasks, such as remotely installing the operating system or powering up the computer.

Tools for performing the tasks Typically, you can use several different remote management tools to perform the same task. Include in your list all the tools that apply to each remote task you want to perform. In some cases, you do not need to use a specific tool to perform a remote administration task; rather, you simply need to change a configuration setting. If a task does not require a specific tool, note this in your remote administration plan. If your environment includes a mix of operating systems, you might need to look for tools that provide interoperability for some tasks. Make sure this list also includes any out-of-band tools or components you plan to obtain or install.

Network impacts to be addressed   Remote administration can have any of several impacts on your network: it can increase network traffic, decrease server performance, or create security vulnerabilities. You might need to reconfigure network, system, or security settings to mitigate or eliminate these impacts. Include in this list each potential impact and the specific steps you plan to take to address it.

Choosing In-Band Management Tools

Windows Server 2003 supports a wide variety of in-band remote management tools that you can use to manage servers. Use in-band tools when your Windows Server 2003–based server is functioning and accessible through your standard network connection.

Tools for remotely managing servers are available from many sources. Some of the tools are specific to a task, while others support a range of tasks. Some provide a command-line environment, while others provide a graphical user interface (GUI) environment. Some tools work best for managing a single computer at a time, while others support sessions with multiple computers.

In addition to the many tools built in to Windows Server 2003, management tools are available from the following sources:

- Windows Support Tools, located in the Support\Tools folder on the Windows Server 2003 operating system CD, provide command-line tools for specific management tasks in a variety of areas such as performance, security, and deployment. For more information about Windows Support Tools, in Help and Support Center for Windows Server 2003, click **Tools**, and then click Windows Support Tools.

- Resource Kit Tools provide a variety of command-line tools for specific tasks. For more information about Resource Kit Tools, click **Tools** on Help and Support Center for Windows Server 2003, and then click Windows Resource Kit Tools.

- Third-party tools available from independent software vendors (ISVs) provide a wide variety of specific or general remote management capabilities.

This section describes major characteristics of some common remote management tools for servers. Some of these tools can also be used for performing management tasks through out-of-band connections. For in-depth information about the technical considerations and potential impacts of specific remote management tools, see the *Server Management Guide* of the *Windows Server 2003 Resource Kit* (or see the *Server Management Guide* on the Web at http://www.microsoft.com/reskit) . For information about software distribution tools, see "Deploying a Managed Software Environment" in *Designing a Managed Environment* of this kit.

Table 5.2 summarizes the characteristics of common remote management tools.

Table 5.2   Common Remote Management Tools

Tool	Key Characteristics
Telnet	Command line; efficient and versatile; provides interoperability in mixed environments; in general, not secure
Windows Management Instrumentation Command-line (WMIC)	Customized applications and command-line scripts for remote management
Windows Script Host (WSH)	Customized scripts for remote management
Microsoft Management Console (MMC)	Multiple sessions; variety of snap-ins for various administrative tasks
Remote Desktop for Administration	GUI; multiple sessions; high resource usage
Group Policy	Efficient way to manage a variety of settings for groups of servers

Telnet

Telnet is a global, versatile tool that has minimal system resource and network bandwidth requirements and that provides interoperability with other operating systems. With Windows Server 2003 Telnet Server, any client that supports the Telnet protocol can connect to Windows–based systems. For example, a UNIX Telnet client can connect to a Windows–based server.

By using Telnet, you can establish a command console session on a remote computer and use it to run command-line programs and shell commands, interacting with the remote server as though you were logged on locally. Telnet can establish any number of connections and supports interactive scripts.

The Windows Server 2003 32-bit version of Telnet does not support secure logon, while the 64-bit version provides secure logon by using NTLM authentication. Some versions of Telnet provided with terminal concentrators also support secure logon. Telnet does not support encryption.

By using Telnet, you can perform out-of-band management tasks by establishing a network connection to a terminal concentrator that is connected to servers through their serial ports. For more information about terminal concentrators, see "Terminal Concentrators" later in this chapter.

Windows Management Instrumentation

Windows Management Instrumentation (WMI) is an infrastructure that enables you to access and modify standards-based information about objects — such as computers, applications, and network components — in your enterprise environment. Using WMI, you can create powerful administration applications to monitor and respond to specific events in your environment. For example, you can create applications to check CPU usage on your Windows Server 2003–based servers and notify you when it exceeds a specified level. Although WMI is a powerful tool for building customized applications, it does require a certain amount of developer time and expertise.

Windows Management Instrumentation Command-line (WMIC) provides a simplified interface to WMI. By using WMIC, you can access WMI-based information using the command line or scripts. You can use WMIC from any computer where WMIC is enabled to manage any remote computer. WMIC does not have to be available on the remote computer.

For technical information about developing applications using WMI and using WMIC, see the WMI SDK link on the Web Resources page at http://www.microsoft.com/windows/reskits/webresources.

Windows Script Host

Windows Script Host (WSH) is a language-independent scripting infrastructure that allows you to write scripts for local or remote management tasks. You can use WSH to write scripts that include WMI, Active Directory® directory service, and other application programming interface (API) calls. WSH typically is used for noninteractive scripts, such as logon and computer automation scripts.

Microsoft Management Console

Microsoft Management Console (MMC) is a framework for hosting tools, also known as snap-ins, that you can use to manage servers locally or remotely. With MMC, you can create consoles that include the tools you use most often.

Each MMC snap-in has unique advantages and disadvantages that make it suitable in some cases and unsuitable in others. For example, some are suitable for slow network connections and some transmit encrypted data. Before you use a snap-in to perform a remote management task, make sure that it is the best remote management tool for the task. For more information about using MMC snap-ins for remote management, see the *Server Management Guide* of the *Windows Server 2003 Resource Kit* (or see the *Server Management Guide* on the Web at http://www.microsoft.com/reskit).

Remote Desktop for Administration

Remote Desktop for Administration is an MMC snap-in that you can use to establish a remote console session on one or more servers and switch between sessions. By using Remote Desktop for Administration, you can log on to a remote server and use the server's desktop to perform administrative tasks, just as if you were logged on locally. Remote Desktop for Administration supports Kerberos authentication and built-in encryption.

Remote Desktop for Administration is a versatile remote management tool because it supports both GUI and command-line interfaces. Because Remote Desktop for Administration uses Remote Desktop Protocol (RDP), it efficiently transmits the user interface from the server to the client and keyboard sequences and mouse clicks from the client to the server. Nevertheless, this tool requires more memory and network bandwidth resources than many other tools.

 Important

Remote Desktop for Administration is affected by the Internet Explorer Enhanced Security Configuration, which places your server and Microsoft Internet Explorer in a configuration that decreases the exposure of your server to attacks that can occur through Web content and application scripts. As a result, some Web sites might not display or perform as expected. For more information, see "Setting up Remote Desktop Web Connection" and "Internet Explorer Enhanced Security Configuration" in Help and Support Center for Windows Server 2003.

Windows Server 2003 Administration Tools Pack

The Windows Server 2003 Administration Tools Pack includes several of the most common tools for remotely managing servers from a Microsoft® Windows® XP Professional–based computer with Service Pack 1. Many of the tools are MMC snap-ins. The tools pack is included on the 32-bit version of the Windows Server 2003 operating system CD, and the Windows Installer package — Adminpak.msi — is placed in C:\windows\system32\adminpak during the operating system installation. For 64-bit versions, use Remote Desktop for Administration instead.

For more detailed information about the tools pack, see "Windows Administration Tools Pack Overview" in Help and Support Center for Windows Server 2003. Help topics for the Administration Tools Pack are installed when you install the tools.

 Note

You cannot install the Windows Server 2003 Administration Tools Pack on a server that is running a member of the Microsoft® Windows® 2000 Server or Windows Server 2003 family operating systems. The administrative tools already exist on all servers running these systems. You can install the tools pack only on a computer that is running Windows XP Professional with Service Pack 1.

Group Policy

In an Active Directory environment, you can use Group Policy to control such things as permissions, application availability, and security for member servers, domain controllers, and any other server running Windows Server 2003 within the scope of management. You can use Group Policy to manage registry-based policy by using Administrative Templates and to assign scripts, such as for startup and shutdown. For more information about Group Policy, see the following:

- "Designing a Group Policy Infrastructure" in *Designing a Managed Environment* of this kit.

- The *Distributed Services Guide* of the *Windows Server 2003 Resource Kit* (or see the *Distributed Services Guide* on the Web at http://www.microsoft.com/reskit).

Choosing Out-of-Band Management Tools

If you cannot manage a server by using conventional in-band tools for some reason, an out-of-band connection is the only way to remotely manage it. If you configure your servers for headless operation and you cannot access them by using your in-band tools, an out-of-band connection is the only way to manage them.

To configure a server for out-of-band management, you need to consider software, firmware, and hardware. Emergency Management Services, which is included with Windows Server 2003, is the principal out-of-band component. With only Emergency Management Services and a serial port, you can manage most Windows Server 2003 operating states. When you combine Emergency Management Services with supporting firmware and hardware components, you can also perform tasks ranging from powering up computers to recovering unresponsive systems — everything, in fact, except for replacing and installing hardware.

The additional components you choose depend on which tasks you want to perform remotely, how much you are willing to spend for extra features, and how many servers you have to manage. The following tools and components work with Emergency Management Services to support out-of-band remote management:

- Firmware — BIOS for x86-based computers or EFI for Itanium-based computers — that provides console redirection

- Serial ports and modems

- Terminal concentrators

- Service processors

- Intelligent UPSs or intelligent power switches

By selecting the optional components that best meet your remote management requirements, you can capitalize on the full range of out-of-band management capabilities supported by Emergency Management Services.

For more information about selecting hardware components, see "Best practices for selecting and configuring hardware" in Help and Support Center for Windows Server 2003.

Table 5.3 shows which out-of-band tools support various operating states and remote management tasks.

Table 5.3   Components Required for Out-of-Band Situations

Operating State or Task	Type of Tool
Windows Server 2003 is starting	Emergency Management Services
Server fails to fully initialize	Emergency Management Services
Administrator needs to run Recovery Console	Emergency Management Services
Server is not functioning due to stop message	Emergency Management Services
System is low on resources, resulting in slow or no response to requests	Emergency Management Services
Network stack has malfunctioned or failed	Emergency Management Services
System is not responding on the network	Emergency Management Services
System is not responding on the network or to Emergency Management Services	Service processor
System is powered down	Wake-on-LAN network adapter*, intelligent UPS, intelligent power switch, or service processor
BIOS is conducting POST	Redirecting firmware or service processor
Change firmware configuration settings	Redirecting firmware or service processor
Operating system installation by using RIS	Emergency Management Services (see "Selecting the Installation Method" later in this chapter

* Wake-on-LAN is a combined hardware and software technology that allows you to remotely turn on Advanced Configuration and Power Interface (ACPI)–compliant computers. Several vendors provide Wake-on-LAN remote management solutions. Some vendors support this functionality across a local area network (LAN) or wide area network (WAN), while some support it over the Internet. For more information about Wake-on-LAN technology, use a Web search engine and search using the keyword "Wake-on-LAN."

Some trade-offs you might experience with out-of-band components include:

- Limited maximum throughput.
- No GUI support.
- Optionally, additional hardware requirements.

Emergency Management Services

To manage a server from a remote computer when the server is not available on the network, you must enable Emergency Management Services. Emergency Management Services is a Windows Server 2003 service that runs on the managed server. This service is not enabled by default when you install the Windows Server 2003 operating system, but you can enable it during installation or at any later time.

Emergency Management Services features are available when the Windows Server 2003 loader or kernel is at least partially running. You can access all Emergency Management Services output by using terminal emulator software that supports VT100, VT100+, or VT-UTF8 protocols on the management computer, although VT-UTF8 is the preferred protocol. For more information about terminal emulator software and the supported protocols, see "Management Software for Out-of-Band Connections" later in this chapter. For more information about enabling, configuring, and using Emergency Management Services, see the *Server Management Guide* of the *Windows Server 2003 Resource Kit* (or see the *Server Management Guide* on the Web at http://www.microsoft.com/reskit).

When Emergency Management Services is enabled:

- Console redirection automatically sends output to the out-of-band port for any supported operating state, as indicated in Table 5.4.

- You can use SAC to issue supported commands or switch to the command shell (cmd.exe) whenever the kernel is running.

- You can view logs during the GUI-mode phase of Setup.

- !SAC automatically becomes available whenever a system failure occurs.

Table 5.4 shows when you can use Emergency Management Services features for remote management, with or without special out-of-band hardware.

Table 5.4   Using Emergency Management Services Features

Task	Feature
Selecting operating system during system load	Console redirection
Running Recovery Console	Console redirection
Viewing text mode setup messages	Console redirection
Viewing GUI mode setup messages	SAC, including setup logs
Viewing RIS loading messages	Console redirection
Viewing Stop error messages	Console redirection
Monitoring and managing with out-of-band connections	SAC
Performing last-resort system recovery	!SAC

Emergency Management Services Console Redirection

Emergency Management Services console redirection redirects the output from supported Windows Server 2003 functions to the out-of-band port. When Emergency Management Services is enabled, you can perform remote management through the out-of-band port, as shown in Table 5.5.

Table 5.5 Emergency Management Services Console Redirection

Managed Operating State	Example Tasks
Windows Server 2003 Loader	▪ Select the operating system to load on x86-based multiple-boot systems. ▪ Verify the load of Windows Server 2003 components before in-band tools become available.
Kernel at least partially functioning	▪ Perform SAC commands, such as changing the priority of a process. ▪ Perform !SAC commands, such as viewing Stop messages when a system problem occurs.
Recovery Console running	▪ Troubleshoot startup problems.
Text-mode Setup	▪ View Windows Server 2003 Setup progress. ▪ Respond to text-mode Setup prompts.
GUI-mode Setup	▪ Perform SAC commands and monitor setup logs.
RIS-based Setup	▪ Respond to the **F12** prompt to initiate RIS-based Setup.

Note

You must have firmware redirection to view server information before the Windows Server 2003 operating system starts.

Special Administration Console

When Emergency Management Services is enabled, SAC is always available through the specified out-of-band port, as long as the Windows Server 2003 kernel is running. You can use SAC at any time to carry out out-of-band management commands during the following system operating states:

- Normal system operation
- Windows Server 2003 components initialization
- Safe mode
- GUI-mode during Windows Server 2003 Setup

The SAC prompt appears when you connect to a server that is running Emergency Management Services. The SAC command-line environment supports a specific set of commands. For information about SAC commands, see "Special Administration Console (SAC) and SAC commands" in Help and Support Center for Windows Server 2003.

Using SAC, you can perform management tasks such as the following:

- Gathering server information, such as computer name and IP address.

- Changing a server's TCP/IP networking information to resolve issues caused by incorrect parameters or a duplicate IP address.

- Obtaining a list of processes and threads running on the computer to determine if they are causing a system performance problem, if you cannot perform this task by using in-band tools.

- Raising or lowering the priority of a process, or ending a process that is consuming excessive server processor resources or other system resources to eliminate performance issues.

- Restarting or shutting down a server as part of unplanned maintenance task, when the in-band mechanism fails.

- Setting the system time and date, for example, for Kerberos authentication.

- Starting a command shell and running text-based tools, and switching between the command prompt and SAC.

- Viewing setup logs during GUI mode setup and switching between the setup logs and SAC.

!Special Administration Console

When Emergency Management Services is enabled and a system failure occurs, !SAC — an abbreviated form of SAC — automatically replaces SAC as the command-line environment. For information about !SAC commands, see "!Special Administration Console (!SAC) and !SAC commands" in Help and Support Center for Windows Server 2003.

 Important
!SAC is not available if the debugger is running or the system is set to restart automatically when Stop errors occur.

Using !SAC, you can perform tasks such as the following:

- View redirected Stop messages.

- Display computer identification information.

- View an abbreviated log of loaded drivers and some kernel events.

- Restart the computer.

Serial Ports

To perform out-of-band management, you need to establish a secure connection through a serial port, phone line, or an additional network connection. The serial port, also known as a COM port, is the most common out-of-band interface. It is the default out-of-band device for Emergency Management Services. You can provide remote access to an out-of-band serial port by using modems or terminal concentrators, as described later in this section.

To use the serial port as an out-of-band device with Emergency Management Services, it must meet the following requirements:

- The serial port must be a standard 16450 or 16550 Universal Asynchronous/Receive Transmit (UART) device. Windows Server 2003 tests the device for compliance before using it with Emergency Management Services.

- The serial port interface must be provided by hardware, not by a Windows driver.

- If the system firmware is compatible with Emergency Management Services, the firmware and the serial port must be configured to use the same serial port settings.

- A kernel debugger cannot share the same COM port. To avoid this problem, disable kernel debugging on servers with Emergency Management Services enabled. For more information about using kernel debuggers with Emergency Management Services, see the *Server Management Guide* of the *Windows Server 2003 Resource Kit* (or see the *Server Management Guide* on the Web at http://www.microsoft.com/reskit).

- The serial port must be the only out-of-band management port. Emergency Management Services does not support one out-of-band port for outbound communication and a second port for inbound communication.

Direct serial connections provide no logical security and therefore must be secured physically. For more information about security considerations, see "Providing Security for Remote Management" later in this chapter.

 Note

When you use Emergency Management Services with a serial port, use null modem cables that support the carrier detect signal.

For Emergency Management Services technical details and information about configuring serial port settings, see the *Server Management Guide* of the *Windows Server 2003 Resource Kit* (or see the *Server Management Guide* on the Web at http://www.microsoft.com/reskit).

Modems

A modem can provide remote access to a single server through its out-of-band serial port. Modems can be useful when you have just a few servers to manage remotely, such as a branch office with one or two servers. For an example of this type of implementation, see "Designing the Hardware Configuration" later in this chapter.

Take the following considerations into account when selecting a modem to use for out-of-band remote management:

- Security for modem connections is determined by the modem. The preferred security mechanism for modems is dial-back.

- The modem must be configurable and must not rely on initialization. Emergency Management Services does not initialize the modem, so you must configure the modem to answer or dial back automatically and pass all serial data through unchanged. For information about configuring modems for callback, see "Configure client callback options" in Help and Support Center for Windows Server 2003.

Terminal Concentrators

Terminal concentrators provide remote access to multiple servers through their out-of-band serial ports. The servers connect to the serial ports on the terminal concentrator with null modem cables. The remote management computer establishes a network connection to the terminal concentrator by using its network port. Typically, you use Telnet or a Web interface to remotely perform management tasks on the servers connected to the terminal concentrator.

Terminal concentrators facilitate remote management of servers in the following ways:

- You can manage servers using a serial connection without being within the distance of a serial cable length.

- You can monitor and manage multiple servers simultaneously from a single management computer.

- Several administrators can simultaneously view information for different servers.

Setup, configuration, and features for terminal concentrators vary by manufacturer. When choosing a terminal concentrator, assess the following features:

- Number of available serial ports.

- Built-in security features, such as use of passwords and encryption.

- Power switch capabilities.

- Number of available Ethernet ports, if important in your environment.

Some terminal concentrators support Secure Shell (SSH), which is a secure command-line alternative to Telnet. SSH is a protocol for establishing secure connections over networks. It provides logical security for the in-band connection from the management computer by supporting strong authentication and encryption and protecting against a variety of network-level attacks. Because SSH is independent of the operating system, it provides interoperability in environments with mixed operating systems. Several vendors provide Windows implementations of SSH clients and servers. Use a Web search engine and search using the keyword "SSH" to find a variety of SSH vendors, as well as frequently asked questions (FAQs) and other documentation.

You need to provide physical security for the serial connections from the servers to the terminal concentrator. Because the security features for terminal concentrators are not standardized, you might need to provide your own logical security for the in-band connection. If your terminal concentrator does not support authentication and encryption, consider using one of the following techniques to secure the connection:

- Use a secondary private management network that you can access with direct-dial remote access or with a VPN connection.

- Use a router to secure the network traffic.

- Use SSH, if the terminal concentrator supports it, instead of Telnet to provide authentication and encryption.

Firmware Console Redirection

Console redirection provided by system firmware (either BIOS for x86-based computers or EFI for Itanium-based computers) provides out-of-band access to server information before the Windows Server 2003 operating system starts. Firmware console redirection works together with Emergency Management Services console redirection to provide out-of-band support for any operating state.

If your firmware does not provide console redirection — and you do not have a service processor that provides console redirection, as described later in this chapter — you cannot remotely manage servers during the time between system restart and the initial loading of the Windows Server 2003 operating system.

If you configure your servers for headless operation, you need to have either firmware console redirection or a service processor with console redirection so that you can access the servers when the Windows Server 2003 operating system is not functioning.

 Note

Firmware console redirection typically redirects only during text mode, not during GUI mode.

By using firmware console redirection, you can perform the following out-of-band tasks from a remote computer:

- View server status before the operating system starts up. For example, you can view POST status or disk-related error messages. Firmware console redirection typically allows the POST to complete without a local keyboard, mouse, or monitor.

- View and make modifications to firmware settings, such as disabling a peripheral device or changing boot sequence, with the built-in firmware configuration program.

- View master boot record (MBR) errors.

- Start a RIS-based setup by responding to the **F12** network boot prompt. This support is required only if the **F12** prompt is presented by the firmware.

- Boot the computer from the CD drive by responding to the **Press Any Key to Boot from CD** prompt.

When assessing firmware console redirection for use in conjunction with Emergency Management Services, verify that the firmware meets the following criteria:

- Shares the serial port with Emergency Management Services and releases control to Emergency Management Services after the Windows operating system starts.

- Supports VT-UTF8, VT100+, or, at minimum, VT100 terminal emulator conventions. For more information, see "Management Software for Out-of-Band Connections" later in this chapter.

- Preferably, supports the Serial Port Console Redirection (SPCR) table.

An SPCR table is provided with some ACPI-compliant system firmware for specifying how the out-of-band management port is used. For example, if the out-of-band port is a serial port, the SPCR table contains information such as serial port number, baud rate, terminal type, and other settings used for out-of-band communication. When this table exists, Emergency Management Services uses the information in it to ensure a consistent transition between firmware console redirection and Emergency Management Services console redirection. The SPCR table is recommended for use with both 32-bit and 64-bit versions of Windows Server 2003. For more information about the SPCR table and Emergency Management Services, see the *Server Management Guide* of the *Windows Server 2003 Resource Kit* (or see the *Server Management Guide* on the Web at http://www.microsoft.com/reskit).

Service Processors

Service processors provide robust remote management support that is independent of the operating system. Because Emergency Management Services is available only when the loader or kernel is at least partially running, you might need such support when the system experiences severe problems that cause it to stop responding completely. Table 5.3, included earlier in this chapter, shows some of the operating states supported by service processors but not by Emergency Management Services. Consider a service processor if you need a high degree of reliability and availability for your servers or you decide to configure your servers for headless operation.

Typically, service processors are integrated into the system motherboard or into an add-in PCI adapter. Servers that have on-board service processors might offer higher out-of-band throughput by using higher-speed serial or Ethernet connections. Service processors operate independently from the main processor, use their own custom firmware, and sometimes include their own power supply. When you connect to a server through an out-of-band connection, you can communicate directly with the service processor.

Service processor features, client interfaces, and management tools vary by manufacturer. If you plan to use the service processor with Emergency Management Services, it is recommended that the service processor support these functions:

- Console redirection

- Remote power on and power off

- Remote reset

- Access to Emergency Management Services at all times

To be compatible with Emergency Management Services, make sure that the service processor also meets the following requirements:

- If the service process uses the serial port as its interface, it must share the serial port with Emergency Management Services and must release control to Emergency Management Services after the operating system has started.

- The UART interface must be described in the SPCR table, or in the EFI console device path for the 64-bit versions of Windows Server 2003.

- It supports VT-UTF8, VT100+, or, at minimum, VT100 terminal emulator conventions. For more information, see "Management Software for Out-of-Band Connections" later in this chapter.

Manufacturers offer a wide range of additional features. Evaluate the features and tools provided to ensure that they meet your needs. Additional features you might consider include:

- Access to Emergency Management Services through hardware interfaces other than serial, such as modem or RJ-45 Ethernet. The type of connection determines the additional components you need and the security requirements for out-of-band access to your server. For more information about configuring components for a service processor, contact the manufacturer.

- Console redirection of GUI screens.

- Any of a variety of management and troubleshooting tools.

- Client interfaces that range from simple Telnet consoles to complex Web browsers.

Intelligent UPSs and Intelligent Power Switches

An uninterruptible power supply (UPS) provides backup power to a server in the event of a power failure. Some UPS units, known as intelligent UPSs, and intelligent power switches can provide limited remote management capabilities such as powering up, powering down, and resetting a server.

If an intelligent UPS or intelligent power switch is integrated with terminal concentrator functionality, it can provide pass-through serial connection between the management computer and the server running Windows Server 2003. In this case, the port on the management computer has a serial connection to an external serial port on the UPS or power switch, which in turn has a serial connection to the server.

The situation just described can provide a more economical solution than an internal service processor: You can access the intelligent UPS, firmware console redirection, and Emergency Management Services through the same communication channel if all these components use the same terminal conventions, such as VT-UTF8. When the components share the same terminal conventions, each component can consistently interpret escape sequences passed to it. For an example of this type of configuration, see "Designing the Hardware Configuration" later in this chapter.

If the intelligent UPS or intelligent power switch shares the same management channel with Emergency Management Services, the UPS or power switch must passively monitor the serial data stream and respond only when it detects VT-UTF8, VT100+, or VT100 escape sequences that apply to it. For more information about using an intelligent UPS or intelligent power switch with Emergency Management Services, see the *Server Management Guide* of the *Windows Server 2003 Resource Kit* (or see the *Server Management Guide* on the Web at http://www.microsoft.com/reskit).

If you plan to use an intelligent UPS or intelligent power switch with Emergency Management Services, the server running Windows Server 2003 must be configured to start automatically when power is applied.

 Tip

The firmware for your server might provide a configuration option for automatically starting the computer when power is applied.

Management Software for Out-of-Band Connections

Typically, you use terminal emulation software on the management computer to connect to and communicate with a server through an out-of-band connection. The two most common methods are the following:

- Use Telnet — or a secure alternative such as SSH — to connect to a terminal concentrator through an in-band connection, which then connects to the server through an out-of-band connection.

- Use HyperTerminal to connect directly to the server.

If you use a service processor, it might require specific software to work with it and to interact with Emergency Management Services. For example, manufacturers might provide a Web browser or custom software.

Make sure that the terminal emulation software you use supports serial port and terminal definition settings that are compatible with Emergency Management Services, as well as with your service processor or system firmware. If possible, use terminal emulation software that supports the VT-UTF8 protocol because VT-UTF8 support for Unicode provides for multilingual versions of Windows. If English is the only language you need to support, the VT100+ terminal definition is sufficient. At minimum, you can use the VT100 definition, but this terminal definition requires that you manually enter escape sequences for function keys and so forth. For more information about terminal definitions and what they support, see the *Server Management Guide* of the *Windows Server 2003 Resource Kit* (or see the *Server Management Guide* on the Web at http://www.microsoft.com/reskit). For more information about the VT-UTF8 terminal definition, see the Emergency Management Services Design link on the Web Resources page at http://www.microsoft.com/windows/reskits/webresources.

If your hardware and firmware use the same terminal definition settings that Emergency Management Services uses, you can always use the same escape sequences for managing computers, regardless of what is controlling the port — hardware, firmware, or Emergency Management Services. If you use different terminal types, the escape sequences you need to use vary depending on what is controlling the serial port, making it difficult to determine the appropriate sequence to send.

Examples: Selecting Remote Management Tools

After you define your remote management requirements, you can select the tools and components you need to perform remote management tasks. The following illustrations describe the tools for the business situations and remote management levels described in "Examples: Determining Remote Management Requirements" earlier in this chapter.

Minimal Remote Management

Because the branch office in this business situation has low availability requirements and has on-site support, this situation requires no special out-of-band support. Emergency Management Services together with the basic serial port can provide out-of-band management support for the few times when administrators need to perform remote out-of-band tasks. Although this organization decided to use existing hardware, the OEM can provide a BIOS upgrade that supports console redirection. Remote Desktop for Administration provides remote in-band support in this situation.

For this branch office, administrators can perform tasks such as the following remotely:

- All in-band tasks, such as monitoring, configuring, and troubleshooting when the operating system is responding over the network.

- Monitoring operating system startup.

- Troubleshooting when the operating system is low on resources, such as when CPU usage is excessively high.

- Running Recovery Console.

- Monitoring firmware initialization and configuring firmware settings.

Administrators must perform the following types of tasks locally:

- Powering up and powering down.

- Resetting.

- Viewing POST status.

- Troubleshooting when the operating system is unresponsive.

For an illustration of out-of-band hardware configuration for this example, see "Configuring for Direct Serial Connection" later in this chapter.

Moderate Remote Management

Because the data center in this business situation has many high-availability servers, the organization does not want to incur the costs of upgrading to new computers to obtain out-of-band management support. The BIOS for some of the existing servers can be upgraded to provide console redirection; for other servers, such an upgrade is not available. Emergency Management Services together with a serial port provides out-of-band support when the Windows Server 2003 operating system is functioning.

This data center is configured with terminal concentrators to consolidate access to many servers by using a single in-band network connection. These terminal concentrators have SSH built in to provide authenticated and encrypted remote console sessions. They also have a built-in intelligent UPS for power backup and remote power functionality.

In this data center, administrators can perform tasks such as the following remotely:

- All in-band tasks, such as monitoring, configuring, and troubleshooting when the operating system is responding over the network.

- Monitoring operating system startup.

- Troubleshooting when the operating system is not responding over the network, such as when CPU usage is excessively high.

- Running Recovery Console.

Administrators must perform the following tasks locally:

- For servers without firmware console redirection, viewing POST results.

- For servers without firmware console redirection, monitoring firmware initialization and configuring firmware settings.

- Troubleshooting when the operating system is not responding to Emergency Management Services or the network.

For an example configuration for this example, see "Configuring for Terminal Concentrator Connections" later in this chapter.

Maximum Remote Management

In this business situation, the headless servers support Emergency Management Services and include firmware console redirection and built-in service processors. The servers are configured with a terminal concentrator that has built-in intelligent UPS functionality and built-in SSH for secure communications.

Administrators perform all tasks — except hardware replacement — remotely. The Windows Server 2003 operating system is also installed remotely by using RIS.

For possible out-of-band hardware configurations that are appropriate for this business situation, see "Configuring for Intelligent UPS and Terminal Concentrator" and "Configuring for Network Service Processor" later in this chapter.

Designing the Hardware Configuration

Because in-band management occurs through the standard network connection to a responding operating system, in-band management tools are typically software applications and tools. Out-of-band management, on the other hand, might require hardware components to access a non-responding server or to consolidate access to multiple servers. After you have determined which tasks you want to perform remotely and which tools and components to use, the next step is to determine how to configure the components, as Figure 5.4 illustrates.

Figure 5.4   Designing the Hardware Configuration

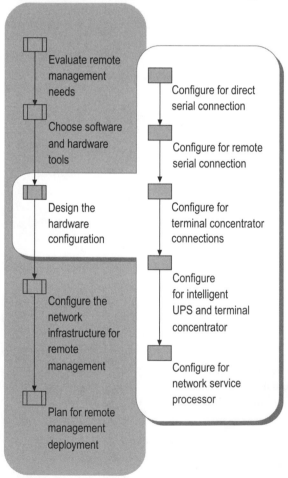

This section describes and illustrates ways to configure various out-of-band components. These configurations are only sample solutions. Depending on your hardware, you might require a different solution. For more detailed information about setting up out-of-band connections in an Emergency Management Services installation, see the *Server Management Guide* of the *Windows Server 2003 Resource Kit* (or see the *Server Management Guide* on the Web at http://www.microsoft.com/reskit).

Although you can use Emergency Management Services with only a serial port or modem to manage most Windows Server 2003 operating states, this minimal configuration is useful only if you are managing just one or two servers. If you are managing many servers, this minimal configuration might be of limited practical application.

When you combine Emergency Management Services with additional components, such as a terminal concentrator, an intelligent UPS or intelligent power switch integrated with terminal concentrator functionality, or a network-enabled service processor, you can use a single network connection from your management computer to manage multiple servers through their out-of-band ports. This configuration can be effective when you need to manage many servers in a single location.

The following configurations are described in order from least to most robust.

Configuring for Direct Serial Connection

Figure 5.5 illustrates a direct serial connection. Using a null modem cable, you can connect the management computer to the server that has Emergency Management Services enabled. This configuration is the simplest out-of-band configuration.

Figure 5.5   Direct Serial Connection

Serial

Server

Management Computer

The management computer runs terminal emulation software that preferably supports VT-UTF8 terminal conventions.

Because null modem connections have no built-in security, this configuration depends on physical security. For more information about planning for security, see "Providing Security for Remote Management" later in this chapter.

This type of configuration has the following advantages:

- No need to buy additional hardware

- Easiest to set up and configure

- Good for situations with very few servers to manage

Disadvantages of this type of configuration include:

- Management computer must be in close proximity for physical security

- Least robust configuration

- Logical security is not supported

- Ineffective in situations with many servers to manage

A variant of this configuration might be a server with a service processor that provides the serial connection. If a service processor and firmware console redirection are included in the configuration, you can manage all operating states through the out-of-band connection. If Emergency Management Services is the sole provider of console redirection, you can perform out-of-band management only when the Windows Server 2003 loader or kernel is at least partially running.

With this configuration, you can be ready to quickly connect a laptop to a headless server to perform management tasks.

Configuring for Remote Serial Connection

Figure 5.6 illustrates a remote serial connection using a modem. The modem is connected to the server that is running Emergency Management Services, and the remote management computer connects over the phone line.

Figure 5.6   Serial Connection with Modem

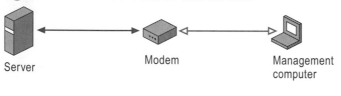

Server   Modem   Management
                                         computer

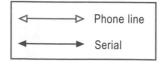

The management computer runs terminal emulation software that preferably supports VT-UTF8 terminal conventions. The modem functionality might be provided by an external modem or by a service processor with built-in modem functionality.

This configuration depends on physical security between the server and the modem and modem-based security for the phone connection. For security, modems that support dial-back are preferred. If you use a service processor, it might provide additional security options.

This type of configuration has the following advantages:

- No need to buy additional hardware

- Easy to set up and configure

- Good for situations with very few servers to manage

- Management computer can be in a remote location

Disadvantages of this type of configuration include:

- Security is not robust

- Ineffective in situations with many servers to manage

This configuration can be used for the minimal remote management example described in "Examples: Selecting Remote Management Tools" earlier in this chapter.

Configuring for Terminal Concentrator Connections

Figure 5.7 illustrates a terminal concentrator with direct serial connections to multiple servers running Emergency Management Services. The optional modem connects to the terminal concentrator. The remote management computer can connect to the terminal concentrator over the network for an in-band connection or over the phone line for an out-of-band connection when the network is not available.

Figure 5.7   Remote Connections with Terminal Concentrator

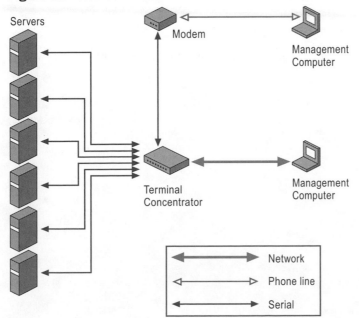

The servers running Emergency Management Services connect to the terminal concentrator with serial connections using the VT-UTF8 terminal definition. The serial connections might be provided by null modem cables or by service processors. The number of serial ports provided by the terminal concentrator determines the number of servers that can be supported in this configuration. If the terminal concentrator is integrated with intelligent power switch functionality, you can use this configuration to power servers off and on.

The remote management computer connects to the terminal concentrator over the standard network by using an in-band tool, such as Telnet or SSH, that supports the VT-UTF8 terminal definition.

This configuration requires physical security between the servers and the terminal concentrator. In addition, it is important to provide logical security for the terminal concentrator. Because access to a terminal concentrator provides access to multiple servers, it is important to ensure that only authorized persons can gain access, as described in "Providing Security for Remote Management" later in this chapter, thus protecting the connected servers from denial-of-service attacks. The terminal emulation software supported by the terminal concentrator helps determine the logical security between the management computer and terminal concentrator. For example, some terminal concentrators have SSH built in to provide authentication and encryption. If the terminal emulation software does not support authentication and encryption and the network is accessible to outsiders, an unauthorized person can sniff the network to obtain credentials for your servers. Another solution is to use a private, secondary network for remote management.

The advantages of this type of configuration are:

- Supports remote management for multiple servers
- Combined with firmware console redirection, provides broad functionality
- Supports logical security
- Can support the use of legacy computers

The primary disadvantage of this configuration is that it requires additional hardware.

This configuration is an excellent alternative to service processors. When combined with firmware redirection, this configuration provides functionality comparable to service processors without the additional costs. It provides a way to obtain state-of-the-art technology with legacy computers. For a document to assist you in setting up headless servers in this type of configuration, see "Headless Server Quick Start" (SDCEMS_1.doc) on the *Windows Server 2003 Deployment Kit* companion CD (or see "Headless Server Quick Start" on the Web at http://www.microsoft.com/reskit).

This configuration can be used for the moderate remote management example described in "Examples: Selecting Remote Management Tools" earlier in this chapter.

Configuring for Intelligent UPS and Terminal Concentrator

Figure 5.8 illustrates a remote management computer with a network connection to an intelligent UPS that also functions as a terminal concentrator.

Figure 5.8   Intelligent UPS and Terminal Concentrator

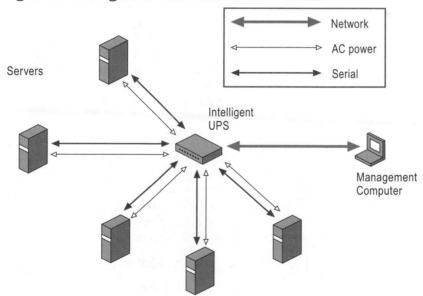

The servers running Emergency Management Services have two connections to the intelligent UPS/terminal concentrator: an AC power connection and a serial connection that supports the VT-UTF8 convention. The serial connection can be provided by a null modem cable or by a service processor. The number of ports provided by the UPS determines the number of servers that can be supported in this configuration. The remote management computer connects to the UPS over the standard network by using an in-band tool, such as Telnet.

In this configuration, terminal concentrator and intelligent UPS functionality are combined, allowing you to manage multiple servers, as well as remotely control power to them.

This configuration requires physical security between the servers and the intelligent UPS. The network connection requires logical security, as described for the terminal concentrator configuration.

This configuration can provide an economical alternative to internal service processors for legacy computers that do not support service processors.

Advantages of this configuration include:

- Provides much of the functionality of a service processor

- Does not require a new component for each server (as service processors do)

- Supports remote management of multiple servers

- Supports logical security

The primary disadvantage of this configuration is that it requires additional hardware.

This configuration can be used for the moderate remote management example described in "Examples: Selecting Remote Management Tools" earlier in this chapter.

Configuring for Network Service Processor

Figure 5.9 illustrates a remote management computer connected to servers with network-enabled service processors.

Figure 5.9   Network Service Processor

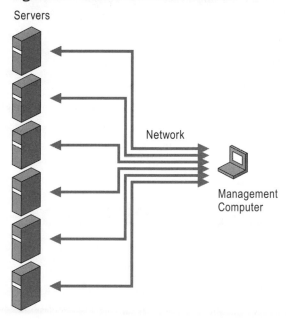

The servers in this configuration each have an internal network-enabled service processor. The service processors might be integrated into the motherboard or on an add-in PCI card.

The remote management computer connects to the servers through the network using an in-band tool such as Telnet or a proprietary tool provided by the service processor manufacturer.

The security in this configuration depends on the service processors. Using the Secure Sockets Layer (SSL) protocol is the preferred method. Using a secondary management network is another option for providing security.

Advantages of this configuration include:

- Does not require physical security for connections to servers
- Supports remote management for multiple servers

The primary disadvantage of this configuration is the cost of service processors, which are needed for each managed server.

This configuration can be used for the maximum remote management example described in "Examples: Selecting Remote Management Tools" earlier in this chapter.

Configuring Your Infrastructure for Remote Management

Remote administration, whether in-band or out-of-band, might require changes to your environment in areas such as network connectivity, memory and processor resources, and security. After you select the tools you plan to use for remote management, assess the impact they have on your environment, and decide how to configure hardware components, the next step is to determine the changes you need to make to your infrastructure to mitigate any potential negative impacts. The place of this step in the process is illustrated in Figure 5.10.

Figure 5.10   Configuring Your Infrastructure for Remote Management

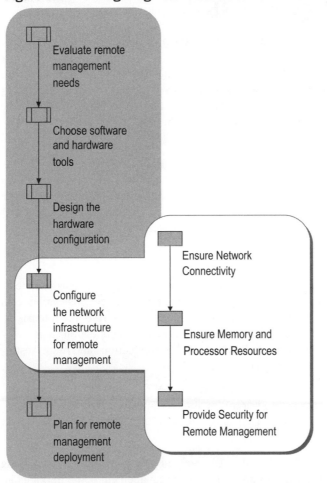

For more information about ways that remote administration might affect your environment, see the *Server Management Guide* of the *Windows Server 2003 Resource Kit* (or see the *Server Management Guide* on the Web at http://www.microsoft.com/reskit).

Ensuring Network Connectivity

Remote administration requires a stable, unrestricted connection between the management computer and the server being managed. In some cases, you also might need a high-speed connection. The tools you select and the location of the management computer in relation to the server being managed determine the network connectivity issues you need to address. Issues you need to address include available network bandwidth, the type of connection you plan to use, firewalls that might prevent access, and routers that might prevent access due to IP packet filtering.

Network bandwidth

Because remote administration tools can increase network traffic, you need to assess your current traffic levels and the capacity of your network to handle additional traffic that might result from the tools you decide to use. Typically, remote administration tools increase traffic only by a small amount, but some tools can increase traffic significantly. Remote Desktop for Administration, for example, is resource intensive and can create a significant amount of traffic.

Type of connection

If you select resource intensive remote management tools, you also need to assess the type of connection you plan to use with the tool. Typically, high-speed connections available on a LAN or WAN can, depending on your current traffic level, accommodate resource intensive tools. Dial-up, digital subscriber line (DSL), or broadband digital cable connections across a VPN, however, are relatively slow compared to LAN and WAN connections and might result in poor performance for some remote management tools.

If you plan to perform remote management tasks across a VPN, you need to configure the networking settings for the connection. For information about specifying these settings, see "VPN remote access for employees" in Help and Support Center for Windows Server 2003.

Firewalls

Because firewalls restrict network traffic, they can prevent you from remotely managing computers from outside the firewall. If you plan to use a management computer outside the firewall to manage servers inside the firewall, ensure that you can connect to them remotely through the firewall and that the firewall supports the network protocols and ports used by your tools. You might need to reconfigure firewall settings to permit remote management through the firewall.

For more information about the impact of firewall settings on remote management, see the *Server Management Guide* of the *Windows Server 2003 Resource Kit* (or see the *Server Management Guide* on the Web at http://www.microsoft.com/reskit).

IP packet filtering

If you use routers that filter IP packets based on source and destination IP addresses and TCP ports, ensure that you can remotely access the servers you need to manage remotely. You might need to reconfigure IP packet filtering settings on your routers to permit remote management from your management computer.

For more details about configuring your network for remote management, see the *Server Management Guide* of the *Windows Server 2003 Resource Kit* (or see the *Server Management Guide* on the Web at http://www.microsoft.com/reskit).

Ensuring Memory and Processor Resources

Remote management software tools that run on a management computer use memory, disk, and processor resources. Remote management services that run on a managed server use memory and processor resources. Although you typically do not need to add memory or processor resources for remote management, you might want to ensure that the tools you choose do not degrade server performance, especially on critical servers such as domain controllers.

Remote management tools that support graphical user interfaces use more processor resources than command-line tools do. If you are concerned about the effect of a specific remote management tool on server performance, test the tasks you plan to perform with the tool to ensure that the current memory and processor resources can accommodate remote management. The task you perform with a tool affects processor activity more than the tool itself.

Remote management tools use memory on both the management computer and the server. If the computers meet minimum hardware requirements, remote management tools typically do not cause memory usage performance problems. If you optimize memory by terminating all nonessential services and processes, such as on a Web server, you might want to verify that your remote management tools do not have an impact on performance. For more information about assessing memory usage on remote management computers and servers, see the *Server Management Guide* of the *Windows Server 2003 Resource Kit* (or see the *Server Management Guide* on the Web at http://www.microsoft.com/reskit).

Providing Security for Remote Management

Remote administration introduces new security considerations into your environment. When you manage servers remotely, sensitive information that normally is not transmitted across a network is sent over your network. For example, server identifying information, configuration information, and other sensitive management information such as user names and passwords can be transmitted. You need to ensure that your remote management tools and tasks do not expose this sensitive data to someone sniffing or eavesdropping on your network. In addition, when you use serial ports for out-of-band management, the null modem connections between the servers and the management computer or other out-of-band hardware component provide no logical security against unauthorized access.

When planning security solutions for remote management, you need to protect against intentional acts as well as accidents. For in-band remote management, you need to consider solutions such as authentication and encryption. If you plan to use dial-up, DSL, or broadband digital cable connections across a VPN, you also need to plan your firewall configuration. For out-of-band remote management, you need to plan physical security solutions to protect the inherently insecure serial connections. Finally, you need to determine a strategy for user rights and shared folder permissions so that only authorized administrators can perform authorized management tasks.

As you plan your remote management security strategy, you need to make sure that:

- The server allows administrative commands only from an authenticated computer.

- The server accepts administrative commands only from an authenticated administrator.

- Confidential information — including administrative commands and configuration settings — cannot be intercepted, read, or changed by intruders.

- Log files are viewed by using a secure method.

A secondary network built specifically for remote management can increase security, performance, and availability. You can control access to such a management network by using a secure router.

For more detailed information about assessing security risks inherent in remote management and an overview about how to mitigate or eliminate these security vulnerabilities, see the *Server Management Guide* of the *Windows Server 2003 Resource Kit* (or see the *Server Management Guide* on the Web at http://www.microsoft.com/reskit).

Authentication

When you perform remote administration, you need to log on to the remote computer you want to manage. Remote management tools use several different authentication protocols — some stronger than others — to ensure that only authorized users can access computers remotely. For example, some tools use the Kerberos version 5 authentication protocol and others use the NTLM authentication protocol. Kerberos authentication is more secure than NTLM authentication.

You can mitigate the vulnerabilities of less secure authentication protocols by configuring one or more Group Policy settings. Configure these policy settings for maximum protection if either of the following is true:

- You are administering remote computers in an environment that forces NTLM authentication.

- You are administering remote computers with remote management tools that use NTLM authentication.

For information about environments that force NTLM authentication and the description and location of Group Policy settings you can use with NTLM, see the *Server Management Guide* of the *Windows Server 2003 Resource Kit* (or see the *Server Management Guide* on the Web at http://www.microsoft.com/reskit).

Encryption

Some remote management tools encrypt data — including passwords — before transmitting it across the network, while others do not. Unencrypted data makes your network vulnerable to eavesdropping and sniffing.

If you decide to use a remote management tool that does not encrypt or otherwise secure data, you can mitigate the security vulnerability by using Internet Protocol security (IPSec) to encrypt the communication between the management computer and the server. When you use IPSec, IP packets can pass securely through routers or other computers that do not support IPSec. You administer IPSec by using policies, which you can configure for the specific security requirements of individual computers, domains, organizational units, sites, or your entire enterprise. If you plan to support dial-up remote management, consider using IPSec across a VPN connection. For more information about VPN and about using IPSec with VPN, see the *Internetworking Guide* of the *Windows Server 2003 Resource Kit* (or see the *Internetworking Guide* on the Web at http://www.microsoft.com/reskit).

For information about IPSec policies, see "Internet Protocol security (IPSec)" in Help and Support Center for Windows Server 2003. For more information about IPSec in general, see the *Networking Guide* of the *Windows Server 2003 Resource Kit* (or see the *Networking Guide* on the Web at http://www.microsoft.com/reskit).

For detailed information about using encryption for remote management, see the *Server Management Guide* of the *Windows Server 2003 Resource Kit* (or see the *Server Management Guide* on the Web at http://www.microsoft.com/reskit).

Physical Security

Although corporate servers must always be situated in secure locations, out-of-band management introduces another physical security issue: the serial connections between servers and out-of-band management components, such as a remote management computer or a terminal concentrator, need to be protected physically because null modem connections provide no logical security. Some ways to provide physical security include:

- Keeping server rooms locked with secured access, such as keys, smart cards, or passwords.

- Using terminal concentrators or intelligent UPSs to consolidate access to servers and keeping these out-of-band hardware components in the same secured room with the servers.

- Keeping cable lengths short to prevent the possibility of extending them outside the secured room.

Rights and Permissions

After you know which servers you plan to manage remotely and which administrators are responsible for specific administrative tasks, you need to set up security groups and assign administrators membership in order to grant them access to remote resources. As you define your security groups, set up administrative tasks with the minimum necessary administrative credentials. By using this technique, you can avoid assigning users a higher security level than they need to perform the tasks for which they are responsible. For recommendations about assigning permissions and user rights, see "Best practices for permissions and user rights" in Help and Support Center for Windows Server 2003.

Two types of security considerations are important in remote administration: user rights and shared folder permissions.

User rights   User rights control the tasks you can perform on a computer, such as setting up user accounts or installing hardware. Depending on the security model and the group structure you use, you might have to configure user rights on each server and management computer, or you might be able to configure them on the domain controller.

Shared folder permissions   Shared folder permissions control which users or groups can gain access to the contents of a shared folder remotely over the network, as well as which actions users or groups can perform on the contents of those folders. You can configure shared folder permissions on the server and enable users to gain access to the folders remotely over the network. For example, you can assign Read or Full Control.

You need to configure user rights and shared folder permissions if administrators need to do the following:

- Access the administrative shares on a remote computer.

- Log on to computers remotely by using terminal emulation or command console programs.

- Access files or folders on a remote computer.

You can centrally control remote management by using Group Policy settings related to remote management. Group Policy settings for computer configuration include security settings that restrict how a user can access files, folders, and computers, as well as administrative template settings that change the behavior and appearance of remote management tools and technologies, such as Terminal Services.

 Important

Terminal Services is affected by the Internet Explorer Enhanced Security Configuration, which places your server and Microsoft Internet Explorer in a configuration that decreases the exposure of your server to attacks that can occur through Web content and application scripts. As a result, some Web sites might not display or perform as expected. For more information, see "Before installing Terminal Server" and "Internet Explorer Enhanced Security Configuration" in Help and Support Center for Windows Server 2003.

For information about groups, user rights, permissions, and authorization and access control, see the *Distributed Services Guide* of the *Windows Server 2003 Resource Kit* (or see the *Distributed Services Guide* on the Web at http://www.microsoft.com/reskit). For information about configuring user rights and permissions for remote management, see the *Server Management Guide* of the *Windows Server 2003 Resource Kit* (or see the *Server Management Guide* on the Web at http://www.microsoft.com/reskit).

Secondary Management Network

In addition to authentication, encryption, and user rights, you can add an extra layer of network security by placing your remote management system on a separate network segment and control access by using a secure router, as shown in Figure 5.11. You can use this configuration to control exactly which users and computers are allowed access to the management system.

Figure 5.11   Secondary Management Network

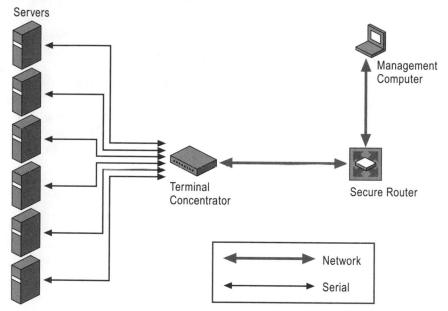

In this configuration, the servers are connected to the terminal concentrator with null modem cables, and all these components are located in a secure room. The management computer can access the servers by connecting to the terminal concentrator through the secure router. The management computer can use an in-band connection or a remote access connection through a remote access server.

Planning for Remote Management Deployment

After you create your remote management strategy and determine your tools and configurations, the remaining step is to plan for deployment, as illustrated in Figure 5.12.

Figure 5.12   Planning for Remote Management Deployment

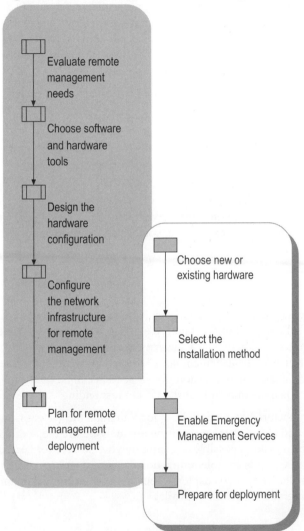

If you decide to use Emergency Management Services for out-of-band management, evaluate your existing server hardware to determine whether it supports the out-of-band functionality you need. After you decide whether to use your existing hardware or to purchase new servers or components, you can decide how you want to install the Windows Server 2003 operating system on your remote servers. Then you need to test your plan in a lab environment and identify the tasks that you need to perform to implement your plan.

Choosing New or Existing Hardware

If you have older server hardware, it might not support some of the enhanced remote management capabilities provided by newer hardware. For many computers, however, you can purchase hardware components that provide enhanced out-of-band features. If you plan to purchase new servers, you can purchase ones that have been designed for compatibility with Emergency Management Services.

As you compare your existing server hardware with your remote management needs, choose one of the following approaches:

- Use existing servers only

- Use existing servers and purchase new peripherals

- Purchase new servers

These three choices are not mutually exclusive; you can decide the most cost-effective solution for each situation on a case-by-case basis. If you want to eventually replace existing servers with new ones but do not want to incur the entire cost at once, you can also plan to prestage new servers, and gradually deploy them over time.

Using Existing Servers

You might be able to use your existing servers, even if they include legacy hardware, but they might provide more limited out-of-band options. If you use existing servers, out-of-band management functionality is limited to Emergency Management Services functionality, which means that you can perform out-of-band management tasks remotely only when the operating system is functioning. You might decide on this option if your servers can be easily and quickly accessed for local management when the operating system is not responding.

If your server was recently manufactured, you might be able to upgrade the system firmware. Firmware that supports console redirection lets you manage remotely before the operating system starts. Upgraded firmware can also make it possible to configure your servers for headless operation. Without firmware that supports console redirection, it is not possible to start your server without a keyboard controller and video adapter. Check with your original equipment manufacturer (OEM) to see if upgraded firmware is available.

If you decide to use existing servers, advantages include the following:

- You save on the cost of purchasing new servers.

- You can gain experience with the technology before investing in new hardware.

- You might be able to upgrade the operating system instead of performing a new installation, and you might not need to reinstall all the applications.

For more information about considerations for upgrading computers, see "Choosing an Automated Installation Method" in *Automating and Customizing Installations* in this kit.

Disadvantages of this approach include the following:

- You have only limited out-of-band functionality: with only Emergency Management Services, you can manage remotely only when the loader or kernel is at least partially running.

- You might experience compatibility issues with older hardware. Check the Windows Server Catalog to verify that all installed devices are listed. To find the Windows Server Catalog, see the Windows Server Catalog link on the Web Resources page at http://www.microsoft.com/windows/reskits/webresources.

Using Existing Servers with New Peripherals

You might decide to use your existing servers but purchase out-of-band peripherals to provide enhanced out-of-band functionality. For example, you can purchase an intelligent UPS to provide remote power options or a terminal concentrator to provide access to multiple servers from a network connection. Devices such as a PCI adapter with a service processor are also available.

Advantages of this approach include the following:

- You save on the cost of new hardware because new peripherals cost less than new servers.

- You might be able to upgrade to Windows Server 2003 instead of performing a new installation.

- You can gain experience with the new technology as you phase in new servers and components.

- You can obtain increased out-of-band functionality.

Disadvantages of this approach include the following:

- You incur the cost of new hardware components.

- If your OEM does not provide out-of-band support, your out-of-band functionality is limited.

If your OEM does not provide out-of-band-related hardware upgrades, or does not support use of such devices, then your options are limited to using existing servers or purchasing new ones. If you need out-of-band management support when the operating system is not functioning, you need to purchase new hardware. Newer systems that are compliant with Emergency Management Services typically have some or all of the out-of-band management features described in this chapter.

Using New Servers

If you plan to purchase new servers as part of an organization-wide Windows Server 2003 deployment and you plan to implement remote out-of-band management, look for features that enhance Emergency Management Services when you purchase the new computers. Newer computers that are compliant with Emergency Management Services typically include firmware that provides console redirection and might include service processors.

Advantages of purchasing new servers include the following:

- You can simplify the hardware configuration if the servers have components such as service processors or intelligent power switches built in.

- You are much less likely to encounter component incompatibilities because the Emergency Management Systems–compliant computers packaged by OEMs are sold as a single entity and tested together for compatibility.

- Servers that are compliant with Emergency Management Services might have features such as console redirection, a service processor, and an intelligent power switch built in, providing immediate access to enhanced out-of-band features.

- Servers that are compliant with Emergency Management Services typically are compatible with in-band Windows Server 2003 remote management technologies, including RIS.

- Headless server configurations are an option.

The primary disadvantage of purchasing new servers is the cost of the new hardware.

Prestaging Servers

When you prestage servers you gradually replace existing servers in your organization with new ones preconfigured and tested in your lab. With this approach, you can use existing servers for your initial Windows Server 2003 deployment. Then, as servers reach approximately 90 percent usage, a technician can go onsite to replace the existing servers with new ones that are built to support out-of-band management.

Advantages of this approach include the following:

- You can spread out the cost of new hardware over time.

- You can gain experience with the technology before investing in new hardware and refine your buying criteria as you phase out old equipment and replace it with new servers.

- You gradually get increased out-of-band functionality as servers are replaced.

- You might be able to upgrade to Windows Server 2003 during the initial deployment, instead of performing new installations and reinstalling applications.

The primary disadvantage of prestaging is that you have the possibility of interim compatibility issues.

Selecting the Installation Method

Your decision to use existing servers or to purchase new ones might influence the method you choose to install Windows Server 2003. If you decide to use existing servers, you might be able to upgrade the operating system.

There are many issues in addition to upgrade or new installation to consider when you choose an installation method. For a complete discussion of the considerations when deciding on a method, see "Choosing an Automated Installation Method" in *Automating and Customizing Installations* of this kit. This section covers only the installation issues involved with Emergency Management Services and headless servers.

Selecting RIS for Installation

On 32-bit and 64-bit systems, you can use Remote Installation Services (RIS) to start a network-based Windows Server 2003 installation on a computer without an operating system. To install the Windows Server 2003 operating system by using RIS, you must have a network adapter that is Pre-Boot eXecution Environment (PXE) capable. A PXE-capable network adapter lets you boot the server from the network.

Special versions of Startrom.com support Emergency Management Services console redirection and let you perform an unattended installation on a server from a remote management computer. These versions of Startrom.com let you perform a remote unattended installation even if the firmware on the server does not provide console redirection. Without the Emergency Management Services version of Startrom.com, you cannot respond to the **Press F12 for network boot** prompt unless the server has firmware that provides console redirection. If you have firmware console redirection, however, it is preferable to rely on it instead of Emergency Management Services console redirection and to use the standard Startrom.com file, because the standard version supports a wider variety of baud rates. The special versions of Startrom.com support only a baud rate of 9600.

Note

If you use one of the special versions of Startrom.com, you must also configure the management computer to use a baud rate of 9600 baud in order to read the redirected output.

For more information about using RIS with Emergency Management Services, see the *Server Management Guide* of the *Windows Server 2003 Resource Kit* (or see the *Server Management Guide* on the Web at http://www.microsoft.com/reskit). For more information about RIS in general, see "Designing RIS Installations" in *Automating and Customizing Installations* of this kit.

Selecting Network-Based Unattended Installations

If you want to fully automate Setup and enable Emergency Management Services, you can use a network-based unattended installation. If your firmware supports the Serial Port Console Redirection (SPCR) table, Setup automatically detects the out-of-band port parameters and enables Emergency Management Services. If your firmware does not support the SPCR table or you want to fully automate Setup, you can configure Setup by using the Unattend.txt file. You can also use the Unattend.txt file to disable Emergency Management Services if your firmware supports the SPCR table, but you do not want to enable Emergency Management Services.

When Emergency Management Services is enabled, you can use Emergency Management Services console redirection to remotely monitor text-mode setup. Although you cannot use either firmware or Emergency Management Services console redirection to redirect GUI-mode setup graphics such as windows and cursors, you can avoid pauses for user input by specifying parameters in your Unattend.txt file. For headless computers, you need to use an Unattend.txt file or run Setup by using a Remote Desktop for Administration connection.

If your Unattend.txt file does not contain the information necessary for GUI-mode setup to proceed — such as your accepting the the End User License Agreement (EULA), entering a 25-digit product key, and providing an administrator password — you will be prompted through the serial port to provide that input. If the server has a local monitor, a dialog will show that the system is waiting for input through the serial port. You can optionally use the local keyboard to cancel this. If more information is missing from your answer file, a default answer is created so that you are not prompted again. For example, if the computername parameter is missing, the random computer name, "computername=*" is automatically generated. You can then change this information after GUI-mode setup is complete.

A sample Unattend.txt file is on the Windows Server 2003 operating system CD. You can use default settings or create customized installations by modifying or adding parameters. For more details about Emergency Management Server parameters for the Unattend.txt file, see the *Server Management Guide* of the *Windows Server 2003 Resource Kit* (or see the *Server Management Guide* on the Web at http://www.microsoft.com/reskit). For more information about network-based unattended installations, see "Designing Unattended Installations" in the *Automating and Customizing Installations* book of this kit.

Selecting Unattended CD-Based Installations

If your system supports firmware console redirection, you can enable Emergency Management Services as part of a CD-based installation. If your firmware supports the SPCR table, Setup automatically detects the out-of-band port parameters and enables Emergency Management Services. You can then use Windows Emergency Management Services console redirection to remotely monitor text-mode setup, but you cannot use console redirection to monitor GUI-mode setup. To fully automate a CD-based installation that includes customized parameters, you need to configure an unattended setup by using the Winnt.sif file.

If your firmware supports the SPCR table, console redirection is enabled, and you do not plan to use unattended files during setup, you can use Express Setup. When you boot a headless server from CD and do not use the Winnt.sif file, Setup automatically provides default parameters for the computer configuration so that the GUI-mode phase can complete without displaying any prompts. After Setup is complete, you can use SAC to set parameters such as IP address or view the computer name, if the IP address was assigned using DHCP. Then you can use a Remote Desktop for Administration connection to complete your custom configuration.

To begin a CD-based Windows Server 2003 setup, you must enable firmware console redirection to remotely view and respond to the **Press any key to boot from CD-ROM** prompt that appears when starting the computer by using the Windows Server 2003 operating system CD.

 Tip
CD-based setups are most useful for local installations during testing.

For more details about using CD-based setups and configuring the Winnt.sif file for Emergency Management Services, see the *Server Management Guide* of the *Windows Server 2003 Resource Kit* (or see the *Server Management Guide* on the Web at http://www.microsoft.com/reskit).

Selecting Unattended Image-Based Installations

You can also use an Unattend.txt file to fully automate Setup and enable Emergency Management Services as part of an image-based installation on headless servers. You can distribute the CD image you create to a remote server, power on that server, and proceed through an unattended GUI-mode setup just as you would proceed through an unattended, network-based installation. You can also use Express Setup if your firmware supports the SPCR table, console redirection is enabled, and you do not plan to use unattended files during setup

Enabling Emergency Management Services

Emergency Management Services functionality is built into Windows Server 2003 and is installed, but not enabled, when the operating system is installed. You can enable Emergency Management Services at any of the following times:

- During a new Windows Server 2003 installation, including RIS-based setups.
- During a Windows Server 2003 upgrade (x86-based systems only).
- After you complete a Windows Server 2003 installation.

For information about how to enable Emergency Management Services during or after installation, see the *Server Management Guide* of the *Windows Server 2003 Resource Kit* (or see the *Server Management Guide* on the Web at http://www.microsoft.com/reskit).

Preparing for Deployment

After you have followed the planning steps in this chapter to identify your organization's remote management requirements and to design a solution that meets those requirements, you need to test your solution in a lab environment that emulates your production environment as closely as possible. Because out-of-band management and support for headless servers is new to the Windows environment, it is particularly important to test your headless server and out-of-band configurations. Then develop a list of tasks you need to perform before you can implement your plan. Include tasks for preparing your network, hardware and software configurations, and security.

Network connectivity

Identify the steps you need to take to prepare your network infrastructure to ensure connectivity and stable access. Include tasks to accomplish the following:

- Configure your network for increased bandwidth, or establish a secondary network for remote management, if necessary.

- Configure Dial-up Networking settings, if you plan to support dial-up remote management.

- Configure firewall settings, if you plan to remotely manage across a firewall.

- Configure IP packet filter settings, if you plan to remotely manage across a router that filters packets.

Server resources

Identify the steps for assessing computer resources and for upgrading them, if necessary, such as:

- Upgrade server and management computer memory and processor, if necessary, to support remote management tools.

- Upgrade or purchase new computers that provide enhanced out-of-band support, if necessary.

Security

Identify the steps for ensuring both physical and logical security, for both in-band and out-of-band management, such as:

- Provide secured access to servers.

- Provide physical security for out-of-band serial connections.

- Provide for authentication and encryption protocols.

- Configure Group Policy settings to mitigate vulnerabilities of less secure authentication protocols.

- Configure IPSec policies to provide security if you plan to use tools without encryption or dial-up connections through a VPN.

- Establish a secondary management network or configure secured routers, if necessary.

- Set up security groups and assign membership for administrators.

- Set up shared folders as necessary, and assign permissions.

- Configure Group Policy settings to restrict the types of administrative tasks remote users can perform.

Configure out-of-band settings

Identify the steps for configuring computers for out-of-band management:

- Enable firmware console redirection.

- Verify and, if necessary, configure hardware resource settings for serial ports.

- Configure SPCR table settings.

- Configure the service processor, if necessary.

- Select consistent terminal definition settings for firmware, Emergency Management Services, and client terminal software.

For more information about specific settings for Emergency Management Services, see the *Server Management Guide* of the *Windows Server 2003 Resource Kit* (or see the *Server Management Guide* on the Web at http://www.microsoft.com/reskit).

Connect out-of-band hardware components

Identify the steps for configuring the out-of-band infrastructure:

- Set up serial port null modem connections.

- Connect terminal concentrators, modems, service processors, and intelligent UPSs.

For more information about setting up null modem connections in an Emergency Management Services installation, see the *Server Management Guide* of the *Windows Server 2003 Resource Kit* (or see the *Server Management Guide* on the Web at http://www.microsoft.com/reskit).

Install and enable Emergency Management Services

Identify the steps for installing Windows Server 2003 and enabling Emergency Management Services:

- Build and test files and directories for unattended network, unattended CD, or RIS installations of Windows Server 2003.

- Enable Emergency Management Services during or after Windows Server 2003 installation.

For more information about enabling Emergency Management Services, see the *Server Management Guide* of the *Windows Server 2003 Resource Kit* (or see the *Server Management Guide* on the Web at http://www.microsoft.com/reskit).

Additional Resources

These resources contain additional information and tools related to this chapter.

Related Information

- The *Server Management Guide* of the *Windows Server 2003 Resource Kit* (or see the *Server Management Guide* on the Web at http://www.microsoft.com/reskit) for more information about remote management, remote management tools, and configuring and using Emergency Management Services.

- "Deploying a Managed Software Environment" in *Designing a Managed Environment* of this kit for information about software distribution tools.

- "Designing a Group Policy Infrastructure" in *Designing a Managed Environment* of this kit for more information about Group Policy.

- The *Distributed Services Guide* of the *Windows Server 2003 Resource Kit* (or see the *Distributed Services Guide*" on the Web at http://www.microsoft.com/reskit) for more information about Group Policy, and also for more information about groups, user rights, permissions, and authorization and access control.

- The *Internetworking Guide* of the *Windows Server 2003 Resource Kit* (or see the *Internetworking Guide* on the Web at http://www.microsoft.com/reskit) for more information about VPN and about using IPSec with VPN.

- "Choosing an Automated Installation Method" in *Automating and Customizing Installations* in this kit for more information about choosing an installation method for the Windows Server 2003 operating system.

- "Designing RIS Installations" in *Automating and Customizing Installations* of this kit for more information about Remote Installation Services (RIS).

- "Designing Unattended Installations" in *Automating and Customizing Installations* of this kit for more information about network-based unattended installations.

- The WMI Software Development Kit (SDK) link on the Web Resources page at http://www.microsoft.com/windows/reskits/webresources for more information about developing applications using WMI.

Related Tools

- Windows Server 2003 Administration Tools Pack

  This set of tools includes several of the most common tools for remotely managing servers from a Windows XP Professional–based computer. Install the tools pack by running C:\windows\system32\adminpak\adminpak.msi.

Related Help Topics

For best results in identifying Help topics by title, in Help and Support Center, under the **Search** box, click **Set search options**. Under **Help Topics**, select the **Search in title only** check box.

- "Special Administration Console (SAC) and SAC commands" in Help and Support Center for Windows Server 2003 for information about SAC commands.

- "!Special Administration Console (!SAC) and !SAC commands" in Help and Support Center for Windows Server 2003 for information about !SAC commands.

- "Windows Administration Tools Pack Overview" in Help and Support Center for Windows Server 2003 for more information about the Administration Tools Pack. This topic is installed when you install the tools.

- "Configure client callback options" in Help and Support Center for Windows Server 2003 for information about configuring modems for callback.

- "VPN remote access for employees" in Help and Support Center for Windows Server 2003 for information about network settings for VPN connections.

- "Best practices for selecting and configuring hardware" in Help and Support Center for Windows Server 2003 for information about selecting hardware components to use with Emergency Management Services.

- "Internet Protocol security (IPSec)" in Help and Support Center for Windows Server 2003 for information about IPSec policies.

- "Best practices for permissions and user rights" in Help and Support Center for Windows Server 2003 for information about assigning permissions and user rights for remote management.

Related Job Aids

For a document to assist you in setting up headless servers with a terminal concentrator, see "Headless Server Quick Start" (SDCEMS_1.doc) on the *Windows Server 2003 Deployment Kit* companion CD (or see "Headless Server Quick Start" on the Web at http://www.microsoft.com/reskit).

CHAPTER 6

Planning for High Availability and Scalability

Business-critical applications such as corporate databases and e-mail often need to reside on systems and network structures that are designed for high availability. The same is true for retail Web sites and other Web-based businesses. Knowing about high availability concepts and practices can help you to maximize the availability (extremely low downtime) and scalability (the ability to grow as demand increases) of your server systems. Using sound IT practices and fault-tolerant hardware solutions in your deployment can increase availability and scalability. Additionally, the Microsoft® Windows® Server 2003 operating system offers two clustering technologies — server clusters and Network Load Balancing — that provide both the reliability and scalability that most enterprises need.

In This Chapter

Related Information

- For more information about planning for server clusters, see "Designing and Deploying Server Clusters" in this book.

- For more information about Network Load Balancing, see "Designing Network Load Balancing" in this book.

- For more information about fault-tolerant storage solutions, see "Planning for Storage" in this book.

- For information on deploying Emergency Management Services for managing remote servers, see "Planning for Remote Server Management" in this book.

Overview of Planning for High Availability and Scalability

A highly available system reliably provides an acceptable level of service with minimal downtime. Downtime penalizes businesses, which can experience reduced productivity, lost sales, and lost faith from clients, partners, and customers.

By implementing recommended IT practices, you can increase the availability of key services, applications, and servers. These practices also help you minimize both planned downtime, such as for maintenance or service pack installations, and unplanned downtime, such as downtime caused by a server failure.

Additionally, the clustering technologies available in Windows Server 2003 can provide added levels of availability and scalability. A cluster is a group of independent computers that work together to provide a common set of services. If a cluster node (a computer in a cluster) fails, other nodes in the cluster assume the functions of the failed node. Clusters enhance the availabilityof critical applications and services. Clusters also increase the scalabilityof your deployment by allowing you to scale your solution over time to support additional clients or increased client demands. In most deployments, server clustersprovide availability, and Network Load Balancing clustersincrease scalability.

If you need the highest levels of availability (and if your budget can accommodate the expense), use both recommended IT practices and clustering for a truly comprehensive high availability deployment that is also scalable. If you determine that your organization needs to increase availability and scalability, this chapter can help you create an effective plan for implementing a high availability and scalability solution that meets your organization's current and future needs.

 Note

Server clusters are supported by the Microsoft® Windows® Server 2003, Enterprise Edition, and Windows® Server 2003, Datacenter Edition, operatings systems. Network Load Balancing is supported by all Windows Server 2003 operating systems, including Windows® Server 2003, Standard Edition, and Windows® Server 2003, Web Edition.

High Availability and Scalability Planning Process

Figure 6.1 illustrates the high availability design process and defines the steps you can take to ensure a deployment that meets your requirements for high availability.

Figure 6.1   Planning for High Availability and Scalability

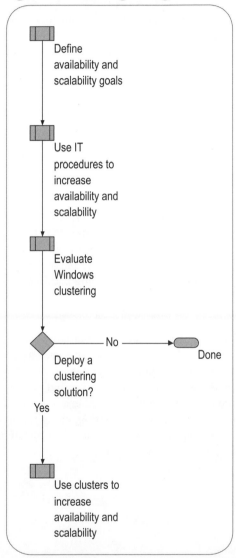

Basic High Availability and Scalability Concepts

To begin designing a Windows Server 2003 deployment for maximum availability and scalability, familiarize yourself with these fundamental high availability and scalability concepts.

Basic High Availability Concepts

An integral part of building large-scale, mission-critical systems that your business and your users can rely on is to ensure that no single point of failure can render a server or network unavailable. There are several types of failures you must plan against to keep your system highly available.

Storage failures

There are many ways to protect against failures of individual storage devices using techniques such as Redundant Array of Independent Disks (RAID). Storage vendors provide hardware solutions that support many different types of hardware redundancy for storage devices, allowing devices as well as individual components in the storage controller itself to be exchanged without losing access to the data. Software solutions also provide similar capabilities.

Network failures

There are many components to a computer network, and there are many typical network topologies that provide highly available connectivity. All types of networks need to be considered, including client access networks and management networks. In storage area networks (SANs), failures might include the storage fabrics that link the computers to the storage units. For more information about SANs, see "Planning for Storage" and "Designing and Deploying Server Clusters" in this book.

Computer failures

Many enterprise-level server platforms provide redundancy inside the computer itself, such as through redundant power supplies and fans. Vendors also allow components such as peripheral component interconnect (PCI) cards and memory to be swapped in and out without removing the computer from service. In cases where a computer fails or needs to be taken out of service for routine maintenance or upgrades, clustering provides redundancy to enable applications or services to continue. This redundancy happens automatically in clustering, either through failover of the application (transferring client requests from one computer to another) or by having multiple instances of the same application available for client requests.

Site failures

In extreme cases, a complete site can fail due to a total power loss, a natural disaster, or other unusual occurrences. More and more businesses are recognizing the value of deploying mission-critical solutions across multiple geographically dispersed sites. For disaster tolerance, a data center's hardware, applications, and data can be duplicated at one or more geographically remote sites. If one site fails, the other sites continue offering service until the failed site is repaired. Sites can be *active-active*, where all sites carry some of the load, or *active-passive*, where one or more sites are on standby.

You can prevent most of these failures by using the following methods:

- **Proven IT practices.** IT strategies can help your organization avoid some or all of the above failures. IT practices take on added importance when a clustering solution is not applicable to, or even possible in, your particular deployment. Whether or not you choose to deploy a clustering solution, all Windows deployments should at a minimum follow the guidelines and reference the resources listed in this chapter for fault-tolerant hardware solutions.

- **Clustering.** This chapter introduces Windows Server 2003 clustering technologies and provides an overview of how they work. Different kinds of clusters can be used together to provide a true end-to-end high availability and scalability solution. For more information about end-to-end solutions, see "Using Clusters to Increase Availability and Scalability" later in this chapter. For complete information about designing clusters, see "Designing and Deploying Server Clusters" and "Designing Network Load Balancing" in this book.

Basic Scalability Concepts

In general deployments, scalability is the measure of how well a service or application can grow to meet increasing performance demands. When applied to clustering, scalability is the ability to incrementally add systems to an existing cluster when the overall load of the cluster exceeds the cluster's capabilities.

Scaling up

Scaling up involves increasing system resources (such as processors, memory, disks, and network adapters) to your existing hardware or replacing existing hardware with greater system resources. Scaling up is appropriate when you want to improve client response time, such as on a Network Load Balancing cluster. If the required number of users are not properly supported, adding random access memory (RAM) or central processing units (CPUs) to the server is one way to meet the demand.

Windows Server 2003 supports single or multiple CPUs that conform to the symmetric multiprocessing (SMP) standard. Using SMP, the operating system can run threads on any available processor, which makes it possible for applications to use multiple processors when additional processing power is required to increase the capability of a system. For more information about scaling up, see "Using Clusters to Increase Availability and Scalability" later in this chapter.

Scaling out

Scaling out involves adding servers to meet demand. In a server cluster, this means adding nodes to the cluster. Scaling out is also appropriate when you want to improve client response time with your servers, and when you have the hardware budget to purchase additional servers as needed. For more information about scaling out, see "Using Clusters to Increase Availability and Scalability" later in this chapter.

Testing and Pilot Deployments

Before you deploy any new solution, whether it is a fault-tolerant hardware or networking component, a software monitoring tool, or a Windows clustering solution, you should thoroughly test the solution before deploying it. After testing in an isolated lab, test the solution in a pilot deployment in which only a few users are affected, and make any necessary adjustments to the design. After you are satisfied with the pilot deployment, perform a full-scale deployment in your production environment. Depending on the number of users you have, you might want to perform your full-scale deployment in stages. After each stage, verify that your system can accommodate the increased processing load from the additional users before deploying the next group of users.

Clusters in particular need to be tested and then deployed in a pilot environment before you deploy them in a production environment. For more information about testing clusters, see "Designing and Deploying Server Clusters" and "Deploying Network Load Balancing" in this book.

For complete information about setting up a test environment for your Windows Server 2003 deployment and implementing a pilot deployment see "Designing a Test Environment" and "Designing a Pilot Project" in *Planning, Testing, and Piloting Deployment Projects* in this kit.

Defining Availability and Scalability Goals

Defining availability and scalability goals is the first step toward ensuring that your efforts are focused on the elements of the system that matter the most to your organization. Figure 6.2 shows how to quantify and determine your availability goals.

Figure 6.2   Defining Availability and Scalability Goals

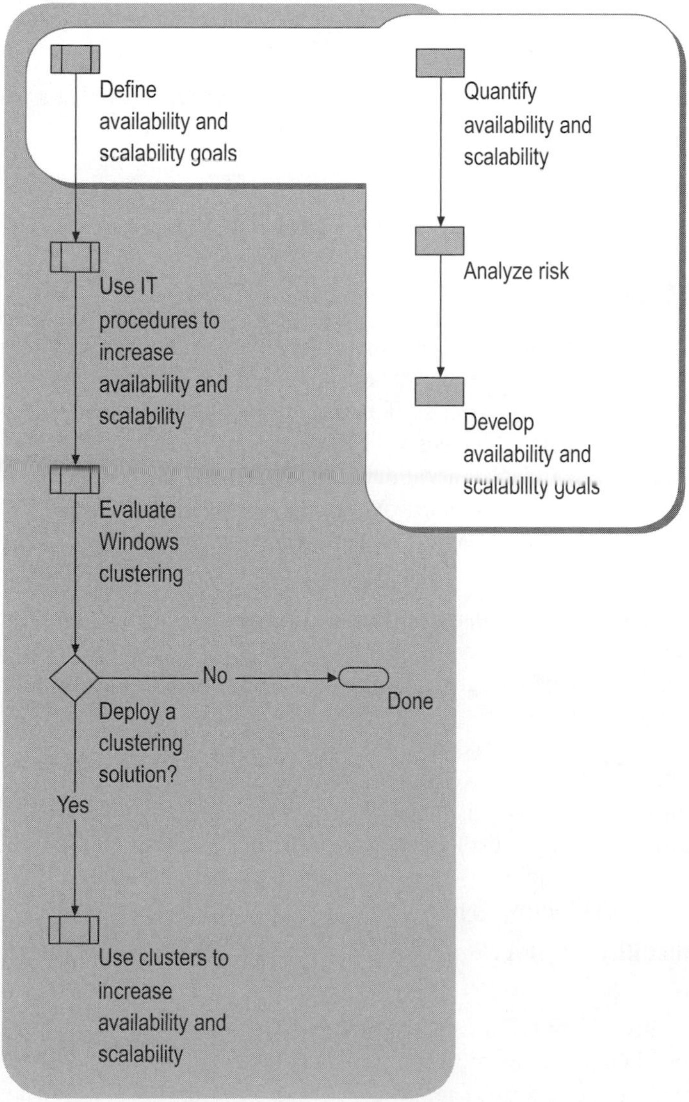

Availability goals allow you to accomplish the following tasks:

- Design, operate, and evaluate your systems in relationship to a consistent set of priorities, and place new requests or problems in context.

- Keep efforts focused where they are needed. Without clear goals, efforts can become uncoordinated, or resources can be spread so thin that none of the organization's most important needs are met.

- Limit costs. You can direct expenditures toward the areas where they make the most difference.

- Recognize when tradeoffs must be made, and make them in appropriate ways.

- Clarify areas where one set of goals might conflict with another, and avoid making plans that require a system to handle two conflicting goals simultaneously.

- Provide a way for operators and support staff to prioritize unexpected problems when they arise by referring to the availability goals for that component or service.

Quantifying Availability and Scalability for Your Organization

Your goal in quantifying availability is to compare the costs of your current IT environment — including the actual costs of outages — and the cost of implementing high availability solutions. These solutions include training costs for your staff as well as facilities costs, such as costs for new hardware. After you have calculated the costs, IT managers can use these numbers to make business decisions, not just technical decisions, about your high availability solution. For information about monitoring tools that can help you measure the availability of your services and systems, see "Implementing Software Monitoring and Error-Detection Tools" later in this chapter.

Scalability is more difficult to quantify because it is based on future needs and therefore requires a certain amount of estimation and prediction. Remember, though, that scalability is tied to availability because if your system cannot grow to meet increased demand, certain services will become less available to your users.

Determining Availability Requirements

Availability can be expressed numerically as the percentage of the time that a service is available for use. The exact level of availability must be determined in the context of the service and the organization that uses the service. Table 6.1 displays common availability levels that many organizations try to achieve. The following formula is used to calculate these levels:

Percentage of availability = (total elapsed time – sum of downtime)/total elapsed time

Table 6.1   Availability Measurements and Yearly Downtime

Availability	Yearly Downtime
99.999%	5 minutes
99.99%	53 minutes
99.9%	8 hours, 45 minutes

Availability requirements can vary depending on the server role. Your users can probably continue to work if a print server is down, for example, but if a server hosting a mission-critical database fails, your business might feel the effects immediately.

Determining Reliability Requirements

Reliability is related to availability, and it is generally measured by computing the time between failures. Mean time between failures (MTBF) is calculated by using the following equation:

MTBF = (total elapsed time – sum of downtime)/number of failures

A related measurement is mean time to repair (MTTR), which is the average amount of time that it takes to bring an IT service or component back to full functionality after a failure.

A system is more reliable if it is *fault tolerant*. Fault tolerance is the ability of a system to continue functioning when part of the system fails. This is achieved by designing the system with a high degree of hardware redundancy. If any single component fails, the redundant component takes its place with no appreciable downtime. For more information about fault-tolerant components, see "Planning and Designing Fault-Tolerant Hardware Solutions" later in this chapter.

Determining Scalability Requirements

You need to consider scalability now to provide your organization a certain amount of flexibility in the future. If you believe your hardware budget will be sufficient, you can plan to purchase hardware at regular intervals to add to your existing deployment. The amount of hardware you purchase depends on the exact increase in demand. If you have budget limitations, purchase servers that you can scale up later by adding RAM or CPUs to meet a rise in users or client requests.

Looking at past growth can help you determine how demand on your IT system might grow. However, because business technology is becoming increasingly complex, and reliance on that technology is growing every year, you must consider other factors as well. If you anticipate growth, realize that some aspects of your deployment may grow at different rates. You might need many more Web servers than print servers, for example, over a certain period of time. For some types of servers, it might be sufficient to add CPU power when network traffic increases, while in other cases, such as with a Network Load Balancing cluster, the most practical scaling solution might be to add more servers.

Recreate your Windows deployment as accurately as possible in a test environment and, either manually or through a simulation program, put as much workload as possible on different areas of your deployment. Observing your system under such circumstances can help you formulate scaling priorities and anticipate where you might need to scale first.

After your system is deployed, software-monitoring tools can alert you when certain components of your system are near or at capacity. Use these tools to monitor performance levels and system capacity so that you know when a scaling solution is needed. For more information about monitoring performance levels, see "Implementing Software Monitoring and Error-Detection Tools" later in this chapter.

Analyzing Risk

When planning a highly available Windows Server 2003 environment, consider all available alternatives and measure the risk of failure for each alternative. Begin with your current organization and then implement design changes that increase reliability to varying degrees. Evaluate the costs of each alternative against its risk factors and the impact of downtime to your organization.

Often, achieving a certain level of availability can be relatively inexpensive, but to go from 98 percent availability to 99 percent, for example, or from 99.9 percent availability to 99.99 percent, can be very costly. This is because bringing your organization to the next level of availabity might entail a combination of new or costly hardware solutions, additional staff, and support staff for non-peak hours. As you determine how important it is to maintain productivity in your IT environment, consider whether those added days, hours, and minutes of availability are worth the price.

Every operations center needs a risk management plan. When assessing risks in your proposed Windows Server 2003 deployment, remember that network and server failures can cause considerable loss to businesses. After you evaluate risks versus costs, and after you design and deploy your system, your IT staff needs sound guidelines and plans of action in case a failure in the system does occur.

For more information about designing a risk management plan for your Windows Server 2003 deployment, see the Microsoft Operations Framework (MOF) link on the Web Resources page at http://www.microsoft.com/windows/reskits/webresources. The MOF Web page provides complete information about creating and maintaining a flexible risk management plan, with emphasis on change management and physical environment management, in addition to staffing and team role recommendations.

Developing Availability and Scalability Goals

Begin establishing goals by reviewing information that is readily available within your organization. Existing Service Level Agreements, for example, define the availability goals for specific IT services or systems. Gather information from those individuals and groups who are most directly affected, such as the users or departments that depend on the services and the people who make decisions about IT staffing.

The following questions provide a starting point for developing a list of availability goals. These goals, and the factors that influence them, vary from organization to organization. By identifying the goals appropriate to your situation, you can clarify your priorities as you work to increase system availability and reliability.

Organization's Central Purposes

These fundamental questions will help you prioritize the applications and services that are most important to your organization and the extent to which you rely on your IT infrastructure for certain key tasks.

- What are the organization's central purposes?
- What must the organization accomplish to survive and flourish?

Details on Record That Help Define Availability Requirements

The questions in this section can help you quantify your availability needs, which is the first step in addressing those needs.

- If your organization has attempted to evaluate the need for high availability in the past, do you have existing documents that already outline availability goals?
- Do you have current or previous Service Level Agreements, Operating Level Agreements, or similar agreements that define service levels?
- Have you defined acceptable and unacceptable service levels?
- Do you have data about the cost of outages or the effect of service delays or outages (for example, information about the cost of an outage at 9 A.M. versus the cost of an outage at 9 P.M.)?
- Do you have any data from groups that practice incident management, problem management, availability management, or similar disciplines?

Users of IT Services

It is important to define the needs of your users to provide them with the availability they need to do their work. There is often a tradeoff between providing high availability and paying the cost of hardware, training, and support. Categorizing your users can make these kinds of business decisions easier.

- Who are the end users? What groups or categories do they fall into? What expertise levels do they have?

- How important is each user group or category to the organization's central goals?

Requirements and Requests of End Users

These questions help pinpoint the needs of your users. You can more easily customize your high availability solutions and anticipate scalability issues if you know exactly what your users need.

- Among the tasks that users commonly perform, which are the most important to the organization's central purposes?

- When end users try to accomplish the most important tasks, what do they expect to see on their screens (or access through some other device)? Described another way, what data (or other resources) do users need to access, and what applications or services do they need when working with that data?

- For the users and tasks most important to the organization, what defines a satisfactory level of service?

Requirements for User Accounts, Networks, or Similar Types of Infrastructure

It is important to know about supporting services — even services that you do not control — when evaluating availability needs and defining availability goals. Your system will be only as fault tolerant as the systems that support it.

- What types of network infrastructure and directory services are required so that users can accomplish the tasks that you have identified as requirements for end users? In other words, what types of behind-the-scenes services do users require?

- For these behind-the-scenes services, what defines the difference between satisfactory and unsatisfactory results for the organization?

Time Requirements and Variations

Keeping support staff on-site to maintain a system can be expensive. Costs can be minimized if support personnel are on-site only during critical periods. Similarly, knowing when workload is highest can help you anticipate when availability is most important, and possibly when a failure is likely to occur.

- Are services needed on a 24-hours-a-day, 7-days-a-week basis, or on some other schedule (such as 9 A.M. to 5 P.M. on weekdays)?

- What are the normal variations in load over time?

- What increments of downtime are significant (for example, five seconds, five minutes, an hour) during peak and nonpeak hours?

Using IT Procedures to Increase Availability and Scalability

The following sections introduce best practices for optimizing your Windows Server 2003 deployment for high availability and scalability. A well-planned deployment strategy can increase system availability and scalability while reducing the support costs and failure recovery times of a system. Figure 6.3 displays the process for deploying your servers and network infrastructure in a fault-tolerant manner that also provides manageability.

Figure 6.3   Using IT Procedures to Increase Availability and Scalability

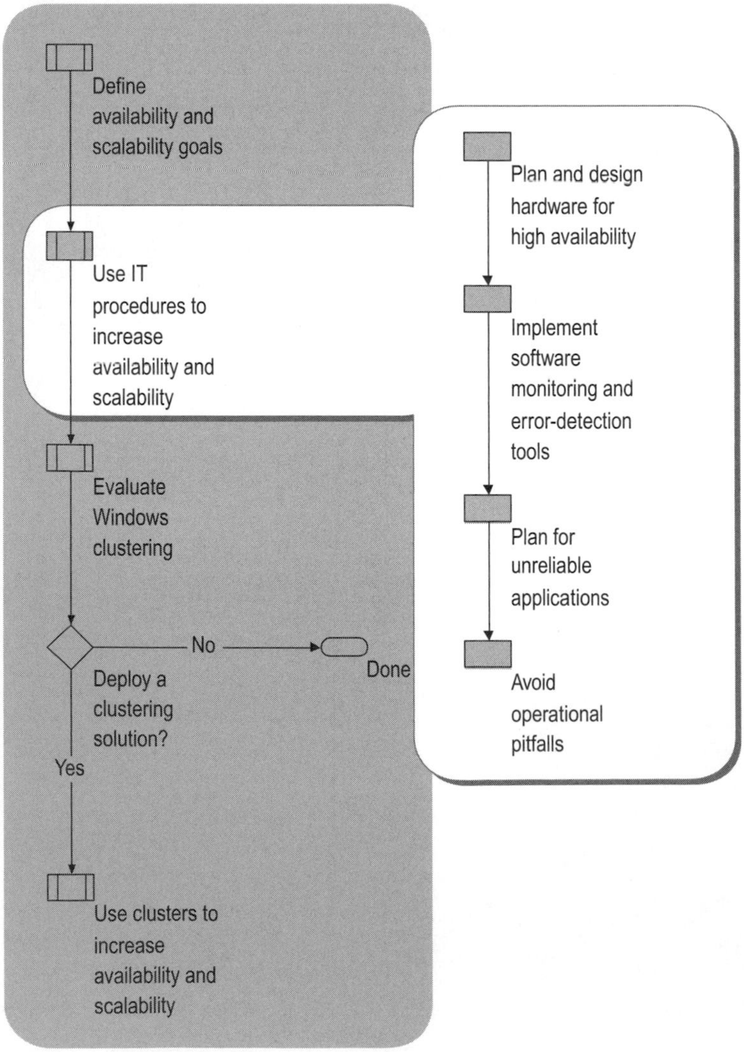

To aid in this planning, Microsoft recommends the Microsoft Operations Framework (MOF). MOF is a flexible, open-ended set of guidelines and concepts that you can adapt to your specific operations needs. Adopting MOF practices provides greater organization and contributes to regular communication between your IT department, your end users, and other departments in your company that might be affected. For complete information about MOF and how to implement it in your organization, see the Microsoft Operations Framework (MOF) link on the Web Resources page at http://www.microsoft.com/windows/reskits/webresources.

Planning and Designing Hardware for High Availability

Fault tolerance means there can be no single point of failure that can cause system failures. The following sections contain highlights of IT practices for ensuring reliable hardware performance and a fault-tolerant IT infrastructure. Included is a summary of ways to safeguard your servers for optimal performance. For detailed information on IT fault-tolerant hardware strategies and highly available system designs, see the Microsoft Solutions Framework link on the Web Resources page at http://www.microsoft.com/windows/reskits/webresources.

Planning and Designing Fault-Tolerant Hardware Solutions

An effective hardware strategy can improve the availability of a system. These strategies can range from adopting commonsense practices to using expensive fault-tolerant equipment.

Using Standardized Hardware

To ensure full compatibility with Windows operating systems, choose hardware from the Windows Server Catalog only. For more information, see the Windows Server Catalog link on the Web Resources page at http://www.microsoft.com/windows/reskits/webresources.

When selecting your hardware from the Windows Server Catalog, adopt one standard for hardware and standardize it as much as possible. To do this, pick one type of computer and use the same kinds of components, such as network cards, disk controllers, and graphics cards, on all your computers. Use this computer type for all applications, even if it is more than you need for some applications. The only parameters that you should modify are the amount of memory, number of CPUs, and the hard disk configurations.

Standardizing hardware has the following advantages:

- Having only one platform reduces the amount of testing needed.

- When testing driver updates or application-software updates, only one test is needed before deploying to all your computers.

- With only one system type, fewer spare parts are required.

- Because only one type of system must be supported, support personnel require less training.

For help choosing standardized hardware for your file and print servers, see "Designing and Deploying File Servers" and "Designing and Deploying Print Servers" in this book.

Using Spares and Standby Servers

This chapter discusses clustering as a means of providing high availability for your applications and services to your end users. However, there are two clustering alternatives that provide flexibility or redundancy in your hardware design: spares and standby systems.

Spares

Keep spare parts on-site, and include spares in any hardware budget. One of the advantages of using a standard configuration is the reduced number of spares that must be kept on-site. If all of the hard drives are of the same type and manufacturer, for example, you can keep fewer drives in stock as spares. This reduces the cost and complexity associated with providing spares.

The number of spares that you need to keep on hand varies according to the configuration and failure conditions that users and operations personnel can tolerate. Another concern is availability of replacement parts. Some parts, such as memory and CPU, are easy to find years later. Other parts, like hard drives, are often difficult to locate after only a few years. For parts that may be hard to find, and where exact matches must be used, plan to buy spares when you buy the equipment. Consider using service companies or contracts with a vendor to delegate the responsibility, or consider keeping one or two of each of the critical components in a central location.

Standby Systems

Consider the possibility of maintaining an entire standby system, possibly even a hot standby to which data is replicated automatically. For file servers, for example, the Windows Server 2003 Distributed File System (DFS) allows you to logically group folders located on different servers by transparently connecting them to one or more hierarchical namespaces. When DFS is combined with File Replication service (FRS), clients can access data even if one of the file servers goes down, because the other servers have identical content. DFS and FRS are discussed in detail in "Designing and Deploying File Servers" in this book.

If the costs of downtime are very high and clustering is not a viable option, you can use standby systems to decrease recovery times. Using standby systems can also be important if failure of the computer can result in high costs, such as lost profits from server downtime or penalties from a Service Level Agreement violation.

A standby system can quickly replace a failed system or, in some cases, act as a source of spare parts. Also, if a system has a catastrophic failure that does not involve the hard drives, it might be possible to move the drives from the failed system to a working system (possibly in combination with using backup media) to restore operations relatively quickly. This scenario does not happen often, but it does happen, in particular with CPU or motherboard component failures. (Note that this transfer of data after a failure is performed automatically in a server cluster.)

One advantage to using standby equipment to recover from an outage is that the failed unit is available for careful after-the-fact diagnosis to determine the cause of the failure. Getting to the root cause of the failure is extremely important in preventing repeated failures.

Standby equipment should be certified and running on a 24-hours-a-day, 7-days-a-week basis, just like the production equipment. If you do not keep the standby equipment operational, you cannot be sure it will be available when you need it.

Using Fault-Tolerant Components

Using fault-tolerant technology improves both availability and performance. The following sections describe some basic fault-tolerant considerations in two key areas of your deployment: storage and network components. In both cases you should also consult hardware vendors for details specific to each product, especially if you are considering deploying server clusters. For more information about storage options and strategies for server clusters, see "Designing and Deploying Server Clusters" in this book.

Storage Strategies

When planning how to store your data, consider the following points:

- The type and quantity of information that must be stored. For example, will a particular computer be used to store a large database needing frequent reads and writes?

- The cost of the equipment. It does not make sense to spend more money on the storage system than you expect to recover in saved time and data if a failure occurs.

- Specific needs for protecting data or making data constantly available. Do you need to prevent data loss, or do you need to make data constantly available? Or are both necessary? For preventing data loss, a RAID arrangement is recommended. For high availability of an application or service, consider multiple disk controllers, a RAID array, or a Windows clustering solution. (Clustering is discussed later in this chapter.)

- A good backup and recovery plan is essential. Downtime is inevitable, but a sound and proven backup and recovery plan can minimize the time it takes to restore services to your users. For more information, see "Backing up and recovering data" in Help and Support Center for Windows Server 2003.

- Physical memory copying, or memory *mirroring*, provides fault tolerance through memory replication. Memory-mirroring techniques include having two sets of RAM in one computer, each a mirror of the other, or mirroring the entire system state, which includes RAM, CPU, adapter, and bus states. Memory mirroring must be developed and implemented in conjunction with the original equipment manufacturer (OEM).

For more information about storage strategies, see "Planning for Storage" in this book.

Network Components

The network adapter is a potential single point of failure. Fortunately, the network adapter is, on average, very reliable. However, other components outside the computer can fail, causing the same effect that you would experience with the loss of the network adapter. These include the network cable to the computer; the switch or hub; the router; and the Dynamic Host Configuration Protocol (DHCP), Domain Name System (DNS), and Windows Internet Name Service (WINS) systems. Any one of these components can fail and cause the failure of one or more servers and, potentially, all the servers.

You can contend with such failures through redundancy in your network design. Many components lend themselves to backup or load-sharing strategies. The following list describes redundancy strategies for the network hardware (hub or switch, network adapter, and wiring), the routers, and DNS or WINS.

 Note

The following is a list of general planning considerations for all networks. For more information about network considerations for specific cluster types, see "Designing Network Load Balancing" and "Designing and Deploying Server Clusters" in this book.

Network hardware   Although hubs, switches, network adapters, and wiring are very reliable, if a service must be guaranteed, it is still important to use redundancy for these components. Consult with the vendors who provide your network hardware and support for recommendations on how to build redundancy into your network. For more information about building redundancy into your network, see "Designing a TCP/IP Network" in *Deploying Network Services* of this kit.

Routers   Routers do not frequently fail, but when they do, entire computer centers can go down. Having redundant routing capability in the computer center is critical. Your router vendor is a recommended source of information about how to protect against router failures.

DHCP   For the servers on which you must maintain the highest degree of availability, use fixed IP addresses on servers and do not use DHCP. This prevents an outage due to the failure of the DHCP server. This can improve address resolution by DNS servers that do not handle the dynamic address assignment provided by DHCP. For more information about DHCP, see "Deploying DHCP" in *Deploying Network Services* of this kit.

DNS and WINS   DNS and WINS infrastructure components are easy to replicate. Both were designed to support replication of their name tables and other information. Make sure that when you use multiple DNS and WINS servers, you place them on different network segments. For information about WINS and DNS servers and replication, see "Deploying DNS" and "Deploying WINS" in *Deploying Network Services* of this kit.

For information about replication options for WINS servers, see "Configuring WINS replication" in Help and Support Center for Windows Server 2003. For information about replicating DNS zones, see "DNS zone replication in Active Directory" in Help and Support Center for Windows Server 2003.

For more information about network infrastructure, see the Microsoft Systems Architecture link on the Web Resources page at http://www.microsoft.com/windows/reskits/webresources.

Safeguarding the Physical Environment of the Servers

An important practice for high availability of servers is to maintain high standards for the environment in which the servers must run. The following list contains information to consider if you want to increase the longevity and reliability of your hardware:

- **Temperature and humidity.** Install mission-critical servers in a room set aside for that purpose, where you can carefully control temperature and humidity. Computers perform best at approximately 70 degrees Fahrenheit. In an office, temperature is not normally an issue, but be aware of the effect of a long holiday weekend in the summer with the air conditioning turned off.

- **Dust or contaminants.** Protect servers and other equipment from dust and contaminants where possible, and check for dust periodically. Dust and other contaminants can cause components to short-circuit or overheat, which can cause intermittent failures. Whenever the case of a server is opened for any reason, perform a quick check to determine whether the unit needs cleaning. If so, check all the other units in the area.

- **Power supplies.** Planning for power outages, like any disaster-recovery planning, is best done long before you anticipate outages, and it involves identifying the resources that are most critical to the operation of the company. When possible, provide power from at least two different circuits to the computer room and divide redundant power supplies between the power sources. Ideally, the circuits should originate from two different sources external to the building. Be aware of the maximum amount of power a location can provide. It is possible that a location could have so many servers that there is not sufficient power for any additional servers you might want to install. Consider a backup power supply for use in the event of a power failure in your computer center. It may be necessary to continue providing computer service to other buildings in the area or to areas geographically remote from the computer center. Short outages can be dealt with through uninterruptible power supply (UPS) units. Longer duration outages can be handled using standby generators. Include network equipment, such as routers, when reviewing equipment that requires backup power during an outage.

- **Maintenance of cables.** Prevent physical damage to cables in the computer room by making sure cables are neat and orderly, either with a cable management system or tie wraps. Cables should never be loose in a cabinet, where they can be disconnected by mistake. Make sure all cables are securely attached at both ends where possible, and make sure pull-out, rack-mounted equipment has enough slack in the cables, and that the cables do not bind and are not pinched or scraped. Set up good pathways for redundant sets of cables. If you use multiple sources of power or network communications, try to route the cables into the cabinets from different points. If one cable is severed, the other can continue to function. Do not plug dual power supplies into the same power strip. If possible, use separate power outlets or UPS units (ideally, connected to separate circuits) to avoid a single point of failure.

- **Security of the computer room.** For servers that must maintain high availability, restrict physical access for all but designated individuals. In addition, consider the extent to which you need to restrict physical access to network hardware. The details of how you implement this depend on your physical facilities and your organization's structure and policies. When reviewing the security in place for the computer room, also review your methods for restricting access to remote administration of servers. Make sure that only designated individuals have remote access to your configuration information and your administration tools.

Implementing Software Monitoring and Error-Detection Tools

Constant vigilance of your network and applications is essential for high availability. Software-monitoring tools and techniques allow you to determine the health of your system and identify potential trouble spots before an error occurs.

This section assumes that you have selected software that supports the high availability features you require. Not all software supports features such as redundancy or clustering. For an application that requires 99 percent uptime, this might not matter. An application that requires 99.9 percent or greater availability must support such features. Monitoring tools can reveal performance trends and other indications that a potential loss of service is eminent before an error actually occurs. If an error does occur, monitoring tools can provide analytic data that administrators can use to prevent the problem from happening again.

Before deploying software, check the application's hardware requirements and consult the documentation or software vendor to be sure the application supports online backup. When your monitoring tools detect a problem or error in an application, online backup allows you to fix the problem with no disruption of service.

Planning Long-Term Monitoring for Trend Analysis

Whenever possible, establish monitoring over the long term so you can carry out trend analysis and capacity planning. The advantages of long-term monitoring include:

- Increasing your ability to predict when expansion of the system is necessary.
- Helping with troubleshooting for problems such as memory leaks or abnormal disk consumption.
- Assisting in identifying strategies for load balancing.

Capacity planning plays an important part in the long-term success of a high availability system. A good capacity plan can limit avoidable failures by anticipating system usage, scalability, and growth requirements. Do not limit capacity planning to items such as disks. Ensure that your plans encompass all parts of a system that could become bottlenecks.

Potential bottlenecks for a server include the CPU, memory, disks, and networking components such as cables, routers, switches, and telecommunications carriers.

CPU As a general guideline, provide enough processing power to keep CPU utilization below 75 percent.

Memory It is important to understand physical memory and its relation to caching, virtual memory, and disk paging. The goal is to provide enough memory to avoid excessive paging, because paging can never be as efficient as directly transferring information to or from physical memory.

Disks A general observation for disks is that utilization above 85 percent tends to cause longer seek times, adding to overall response time. As a general guideline, size your disks, and distribute the load between them, to keep utilization below 85 percent.

Networking, including cabling, routers, switches, and telecommunications carriers
Create a logical map that includes each type of network component and its location along with servers and user access points. This type of diagram provides an understanding of how information travels back and forth between a given user and a given server. Along with using the diagram, gather and organize as much information as possible about the capacities of your network components and about the network loads generated in your enterprise.

Domain controller traffic When monitoring network performance, be sure to consider domain controllertraffic and other services inherent in your networking infrastructure. The number of domain controllers that you deploy and their location in your topology can affect performance. For more information about domain controllers, see "Planning Domain Controller Capacity" in *Designing and Deploying Directory and Security Services* of this kit.

Choosing Monitoring Tools

After you deploy your software, establish routine and automated monitoring and error detectionfor your operating system and applications. If you can detect application and system errors immediately after they occur, you have a better chance of responding before a system shutdown. Monitoring can also alert you if scaling is necessary somewhere in your organization. For example, if one or more servers are operating at capacity some or all of the time, you can decide if you need to add more servers or increase the CPUs of existing servers.

You can use the following tools and methods to monitor your programs. For more information about monitoring, consult "Monitoring and status tools" in Help and Support Center for Windows Server 2003.

When choosing software to run in a server cluster or Network Load Balancing cluster, see "Designing Network Load Balancing" and "Designing and Deploying Server Clusters" in this book. For additional information, see "Choosing applications to run on a server cluster" and "Determining which applications to use with Network Load Balancing" in Help and Support Center for Windows Server 2003.

Windows Management Instrumentation

Windows Management Instrumentation (WMI) helps you manage your network and applications as they become larger and more complex. With WMI, you can monitor, track, and control system events that are related to software applications, hardware components, and networks. WMI includes a uniform scripting application programming interface (API), which defines all managed objects under a common object framework that is based on the Common Information Model (CIM). Scripts use the WMI API to access information from different sources. WMI can submit queries that filter requests for very specific information, and it can subscribe to WMI events based on your particular interests, rather than being limited to events predefined by the original developers. For more information, see " Windows Management Instrumentation overview" in Help and Support Center for Windows Server 2003.

Microsoft Operations Manager 2000

The Microsoft® Operations Manager 2000 management packs have a full set of features to help administrators monitor and manage both the events and performance of their IT systems based on the Microsoft® Windows® 2000 or Windows Server 2003 operating systems. Microsoft Operations Manager 2000 Application Management Pack improves the availability of Windows-based networks and server applications. Microsoft Operations Manager 2000 and Windows Server 2003 are sold separately. For information about Microsoft Operations Manager 2000 and the Application Management Pack, see the Microsoft Operations Manager (MOM) link on the Web Resources page at http://www.microsoft.com/windows/reskits/webresources.

Simple Network Management Protocol

Simple Network Management Protocol (SNMP) allows you to capture configuration and status information on systems in your network and have the information sent to a designated computer for event monitoring. For more information, see "SNMP" in Help and Support Center for Windows Server 2003.

Event logs

When you diagnose a system problem, event logs are often the best place to start. By using the event logs in Event Viewer, you can gather important information about hardware, software, and system problems. Windows Server 2003 records this information in the system log, the application log, and the security log. In addition, some system components such as the Cluster serviceand FRS also record events in a log. For more information about event logs, see "Checking event logs" in Help and Support Center for Windows Server 2003.

Service Control Manager

Service Control Manager (SCM), a tool introduced with the release of the Microsoft® Windows NT® version 4.0 operating system, maintains a database of installed services in the registry. SCM can provide high availability because you can configure it to autorestart services after they have failed. For more information about SCM, see the topic "Service Control Manager" in the Windows Platform SDK documentation.

Performance Logs and Alerts

Performance Logs and Alerts collects performance data automatically from local or remote computers. You can collect a variety of information on key resources such as CPU, memory, disk space, and the resources needed by the application. When planning your performance logging, determine the information you need and collect it at regular intervals. Be aware, however, that performance sampling consumes CPU and memory resources, and that excessively large performance logs are hard to store and hard to extract useful information from. For more information about automatically collecting performance data, see "Performance Logs and Alerts overview" in Help and Support Center for Windows Server 2003.

Shutdown Event Tracker

You can document the reasons for shutdowns and save the information in a standard format by using Shutdown Event Tracker. You can use codes to categorize the major and minor reasons for each shutdown and record a comment for the shutdown. For more information, see "Shutdown Event Tracker overview" in Help and Support Center for Windows Server 2003.

Planning for Unreliable Applications

An unreliable application is an application, usually proprietary to an organization, that your business cannot do without, but that does not meet high standards for reliability. There are two basic approaches you can take if you must work with such an application:

- Remove the unreliable applications from the servers that are most critical to your enterprise. If an application is known to be unreliable, take steps to isolate it, and do not run the application on a mission-critical server.

- Provide sufficient monitoring, and use automatic restarting options where appropriate. Sufficient monitoring requires taking snapshots of important system performance measurements at regular intervals. You can set up automatic restarting of an application or service by using the Services snap-in. For more information about services, see " Services overview" in Help and Support Center for Windows Server 2003.

Avoiding Operational Pitfalls

The following sections describe operational practices that can limit the availability of applications and computers, in both clustered and nonclustered environments.

Supporting multiple versions of the operating system, service packs, and out-of-date applications

Support of a highly available system becomes much more difficult when multiple combinations of different versions of software (and hardware) are used together in one system or in systems that interact on the network. Older software, protocols, and drivers (and the associated hardware) become impractical when they do not support new technologies.

Set aside resources and time for planning, testing, and installing new operating systems, applications, and (where appropriate) hardware. When planning software upgrades, work with users to identify the features they require. Provide training to ease users through software transitions. In your budget for software and support, provide funds for upgrading applications and operating systems in the future.

Installing incompatible hardware

Maintain and follow a hardware standard for new systems, spare parts, and replacement parts.

Failing to plan for future capacity requirements

Capacity planning is critical to the success of highly available systems. Study and monitor your system during peak loads to understand how much extra capacity currently exists in the system.

Performing outdated procedures

Make sure you remove any outdated procedures from operation and support schedules when a root system problem is fixed. For example, when software is replaced or upgraded, certain procedures might become unnecessary or no longer be valid. Pay special attention to procedures that may have become routine. Be sure that all procedures are necessary and not simply temporary fixes for issues for which the root cause has not been found.

Failing to monitor the system

If you do not use adequate monitoring, you might not have the ability to catch problems before they become critical and cause system failures. Without monitoring, an application or server failure may be the only notification you receive of a problem.

Failing to determine the nature of the problem before reacting

If the operations staff is not trained and directed to analyze problems carefully before reacting, your personnel can spend large amounts of time responding inappropriately to a problem. They also might not use monitoring tools effectively in the crucial time between the first signs of a problem and an actual failure.

Treating symptoms instead of root cause

Symptom treatment is an effective strategy for restoring service when an unexpected failure occurs or when performing short-term preventative maintenance. However, symptom treatments that are added to standard operating procedures can become unmanageable. Support personnel can be overwhelmed with symptom treatment and might not be able to react properly to new failures.

Stopping and restarting to end error conditions

Stopping and restarting a computer may be necessary at times. However, if this process temporarily fixes a problem but leaves the root cause untouched, it can create more problems than it solves.

Evaluating Windows Clustering

Windows Server 2003 provides two clustering technologies: server clusters and Network Load Balancing. The clustering technologies in Windows Server 2003 provide different availability and scalability solutions, and they can be implemented throughout your organization.

You can also utilize an additional type of clustering, Component Load Balancing (CLB) clusters, in your Windows Server 2003 deployment. CLB clusters, however, are a feature of Microsoft® Application Center 2000, and they are not discussed in detail here.

 Note

You can use CLB clusters on Windows Server 2003, provided that you use Application Center 2000 Service Pack 2 or later.

For complete information on CLB clusters, see your Microsoft Application Center 2000 documentation. Figure 6.4 illustrates the high-level process for evaluating clustering technologies.

Figure 6.4   Evaluating Clustering

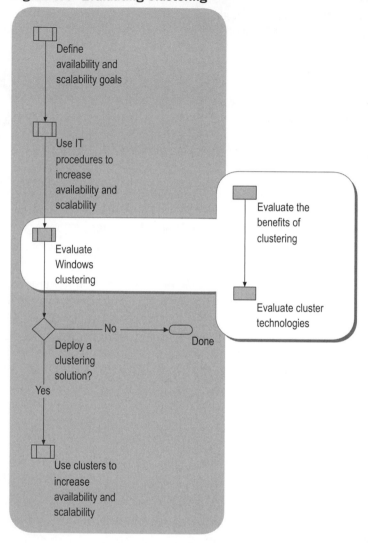

Evaluating the Benefits of Clustering

A cluster is two or more computers working together to provide higher availability, reliability, and scalability than can be obtained by using a single system. When failure occurs in a cluster, resources are redirected and the workload is redistributed. Microsoft cluster technologies guard against three specific types of failure:

- Application and service failures, which affect application software and essential services.

- System and hardware failures, which affect hardware components such as CPUs, drives, memory, network adapters, and power supplies.

- Site failures in multisite organizations, which can be caused by natural disasters, power outages, or connectivity outages.

Benefits of Clustering

If one server in a cluster stops working, a process called *failover* automatically shifts the workload of the failed server to another server in the cluster. Failover ensures continuous availability of applications and data.

This ability to handle failure allows clusters to meet two requirements that are typical in most data center environments:

- **High availability.** The ability to provide end users with access to a service for a high percentage of time while reducing unscheduled outages.

- **High reliability.** The ability to reduce the frequency of system failure.

Additionally, Network Load Balancing clusters address the need for high scalability, which is the ability to add resources and computers to improve performance.

Limitations of Clustering

Server clusters are designed to keep applications available, rather than keeping data available. To protect against viruses, corruption, and other threats to data, organizations need solid data protection and recovery plans. Cluster technology cannot protect against failures caused by viruses, software corruption, or human error.

The Cluster service, the service behind server clusters, depends on compatible applications and services to operate properly. The software must respond appropriately when a failure occurs. Administrators must be able to configure where an application stores its data on the server cluster. Also, clients that are accessing a clustered application or service must be able to reconnect to the cluster virtual server after a failure has occurred and a new cluster node has taken over the application.

Only services and applications that use TCP/IP for client-server communication are supported on Network Load Balancing clusters and server clusters.

You cannot use Windows Server 2003 File Replication service (FRS) on shared cluster storage. You also cannot create domain-based Distributed File System (DFS) roots on shared cluster storage. Finally, without the proper management tools, you also cannot use dynamic disks on shared cluster storage. For more information about using dynamic disks on shared cluster storage, see article 237853, "Dynamic Disk Configuration Unavailable for Server Cluster Resources" In the Microsoft Knowledge Base. To find this article, see the Microsoft Knowledge Base link on the Web Resources page at http://www.microsoft.com/windows/reskits/webresources). DFS and FRS are discussed in detail in "Designing and Deploying File Servers" in this book.

Clustering vs. Fault-Tolerant Hardware Components

Both clustering and fault-tolerant hardware protect your system from failures of components such as the CPU, memory, fan, or PCI bus. Fault-tolerant hardware is discussed in the section "Planning and Designing Fault-Tolerant Hardware Solutions" earlier in this chapter. Clustering and fault tolerance can be used together in a complete end-to-end solution, but be aware that the two technologies provide high availability in different ways.

Clustering can protect your system against an application or operating system failure, but a fault-tolerant standby server (or a server that uses *hot-swappable* hardware, which allows a device to be added while the server is running) cannot. It is also possible to upgrade an application or operating system or to install a service pack, Quick Fix Engineering (QFE) update, or hotfix without taking a cluster offline. Upgrades on standby servers, however, are only possible by taking that hardware offline.

Evaluating Cluster Technologies

If you decide to deploy clustering with Windows Server 2003, choosing a cluster technology depends greatly on the application or service that you want to host on the cluster. Server clusters and Network Load Balancing both provide failover support for IP-based applications and services that require high scalability and availability. Each type of cluster, however, is intended for different kinds of services. Your choice of cluster technologies depends primarily on whether you run *stateful* or *stateless* applications:

- **Server clusters are designed for stateful applications.** Stateful applications have long-running in-memory state, or they have large, frequently updated data states. A database such as Microsoft® SQL Server™ 2000 is an example of a stateful application.

- **Network Load Balancing is intended for stateless applications.** Stateless applications do not have long-running in-memory state. A stateless application treats each client request as an independent operation, and therefore it can load-balance each request independently. Stateless applications often have read-only data or data that changes infrequently. Web front-end servers, virtual private networks (VPNs), and File Transfer Protocol (FTP) servers typically use Network Load Balancing.

Server Clusters

Server clusters provide high availability for more complex, stateful applications and services by allowing the failover of resources. Server clusters also maintain client connections to applications and services. If your application is stateful, with frequent changes to data, a server cluster is a more appropriate solution. Server clusters run on Windows Server 2003, Enterprise Edition, and Windows Server 2003, Datacenter Edition.

Server clusters, which use the Cluster service, maintain data integrity and provide failover support and high availability for mission-critical applications and services on your back-end servers, including databases, messaging systems, and file and print services. Organizations can use server clusters to make applications and data available on multiple servers that are linked together in a server cluster configuration. Back-end applications and services, such as messaging applications like Microsoft Exchange or database applications like Microsoft SQL Server, are ideal candidates for server clusters.

In server clusters, nodes share access to data. Nodes can be either active or passive, and the configuration of each node depends on the operating mode (active or passive) and how you configure failover in the cluster. A server that is designated to handle failover must be sized to handle the workload of the failed node in addition to its own workload.

In Windows Server 2003, Enterprise Edition, and Windows Server 2003, Datacenter Edition, server clusters can contain up to eight nodes. Each node is attached to one or more cluster storage devices, which allow different servers to share the same data. Because nodes in a server cluster share access to data, the type and method of storage in the server cluster is very important.

For information about server clusters, including resource groups, failover and failover policies, storage configurations, cluster-aware applications, and optimizing your network for server clusters, see "Planning your server cluster" in Help and Support Center for Windows Server 2003 and "Designing and Deploying Server Clusters" in this book.

Network Load Balancing

If your application is stateless or can otherwise be cloned with no decline in performance, consider deploying Network Load Balancing. Network Load Balancing provides failover support for IP-based applications and services that require high scalability and availability. Network Load Balancing can run on all editions of Windows Server 2003.

Network Load Balancing addresses bottlenecks caused by front-end services, providing continuous availability for IP-based applications and services that require high scalability. Network Load Balancing clusters are used to provide scalability for Web services and other front-end servers, such as VPN servers and firewalls. Organizations can build groups of clustered computers to support load balancing of TCP and User Datagram Protocol (UDP) traffic requests.

Network Load Balancing clusters are groups of identical, typically cloned computers that, through their numbers, enhance the availability of Web servers, Microsoft® Internet Security and Acceleration (ISA) servers (for proxy and firewall servers), and other applications that receive TCP and UDP traffic. Because Network Load Balancing cluster nodes are usually identical clones of each other and can therefore operate independently, all nodes in a Network Load Balancing cluster are active.

You can scale out Network Load Balancing clusters by adding additional servers. As demand on the cluster increases, you can scale out Network Load Balancing clusters to as many as 32 servers if necessary. Each node runs a copy of the IP-based application or service that is being load balanced and stores all the data necessary for the application or service to run on local drives.

In clusters, stateless applications are typically cloned, so that multiple instances of the same code are executed on the same dataset. Figure 6.5 shows a cloned application (called "App") deployed in a cluster. Each instance of the cloned application is self-contained, so that a client can make a request to any instance and will always receive the same result.

Figure 6.5   Cloned Application

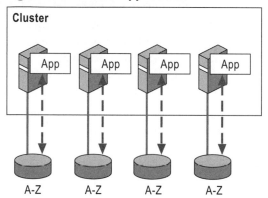

Changes made to one instance of a cloned stateless application can be replicated to the other instances, because the dataset of stateless applications is relatively static. Because stateful applications such as Microsoft Exchange or Microsoft SQL Server are updated with new data frequently, they cannot be easily cloned and they are not good candidates for hosting on Network Load Balancing clusters.

For more information about Network Load Balancing, see "Designing Network Load Balancing" and "Deploying Network Load Balancing" in this book.

Component Load Balancing

CLB clusters address the unique scalability and availability needs of middle-tier (business) applications that use the COM+programming model. Organizations can load balance COM+ components over more than one node to dramatically enhance the availability and scalability of software applications. CLB clusters, however, are a feature of Microsoft Application Center 2000. For information about CLB clusters, see your Microsoft Application Center 2000 documentation.

Using Clusters to Increase Availability and Scalability

Different types of clusters provide different benefits. Network Load Balancing clusters are designed to provide scalability because you can add nodes as your workload increases. Server clusters increase availability of stateful applications, and they can also allow you to consolidate servers and save on hardware costs. Figure 6.6 shows the steps for planning cluster deployment.

Figure 6.6   Planning Cluster Deployment

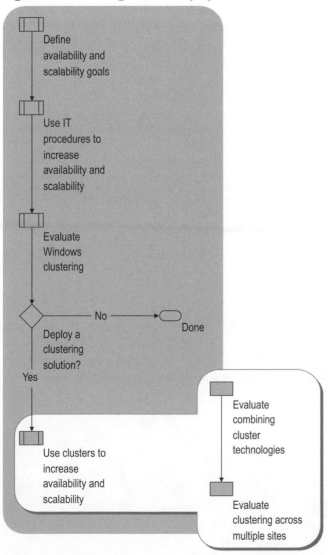

Scaling by Adding Servers

Scaling by adding servers to a Network Load Balancing cluster is also known as *scaling out*. In Windows Server 2003, Network Load Balancing clusters can contain up to 32 nodes. Windows Server 2003, Enterprise Edition, and Windows Server 2003, Datacenter Edition, support server clusters containing up to eight nodes. For this reason, it is recommended that you use Network Load Balancing rather than server clusters to increase scalability. Additional servers allow you to meet increased demand on your Network Load Balancing clusters; however, not every organization has the budget to readily add hardware.

Table 6.2 summarizes the number of servers a cluster can contain, by cluster type and operating system.

Table 6.2   Maximum Number of Nodes in a Cluster

Operating System	Network Load Balancing	Component Load Balancing*	Server Cluster
Microsoft® Windows® 2000 Advanced Server	32	12	2
Microsoft® Windows® 2000 Datacenter Server	32	12	4
Windows Server 2003, Standard Edition	32	12	N/A
Windows Server 2003, Enterprise Edition	32	12	8
Windows Server 2003, Datacenter Edition	32	12	8

* Component Load Balancing is not included with the Windows Server 2003 operating system and runs only on Windows Application Center 2000. You can use CLB clusters with Windows Server 2003, provided that you use Windows Application Center 2000 Service Pack 2 or later. For complete information about Component Load Balancing, see your Windows Application Center 2000 documentation.

Network Load Balancing Clusters also run on Windows Server 2003, Web Edition; the maximum number of nodes is 32.

Scaling by Adding CPUs and RAM

Your options for adding CPUs and RAM, also known as *scaling up*, depend on the server operating system. This is a less expensive scaling option than adding nodes, but you are limited by the capacity of the operating system.

Table 6.3 illustrates the CPU and RAM capacity in Windows 2000 and Windows Server 2003.

Table 6.3   Maximum Number of Processors and RAM

Operating System	Number of Processors	Maximum RAM
Windows 2000 Advanced Server	8	8 GB
Windows 2000 Datacenter Server	32	64 GB
Windows Server 2003, Enterprise Edition	8	32 GB
Windows Server 2003, Datacenter Edition	32	64 GB

Availability and Server Consolidation with Server Clusters

While Network Load Balancing can meet your scaling needs, server clusters provide high availability for hosted applications by reducing the interruption of service due to unplanned outages and hardware failure.

Increasing the number of nodes in a server cluster proportionally increases the availability of the services and applications running on that server cluster. This is because spreading the workload over a greater number of nodes allows each node to run at a lower capacity. When failover occurs in a server cluster with many nodes, there are more servers available to accept the workload of the failed node. Similarly, when a server running at low capacity takes on additional processing after a failover, the failover is less likely to result in a decline in performance.

The hardware required for server cluster nodes is expensive, however. In some cases, it might be possible for you to save money on hardware by consolidating the number of servers or nodes you have deployed in your server clusters. You can still provide high availability of your mission-critical applications after server consolidation, but be aware that combining clusters to reduce the total number of nodes also reduces availability. This is a tradeoff that your organization should evaluate.

Figure 6.7 shows two clusters before consolidation, where two separate two-node clusters, each with one active and one passive node, provide service for a group of clients.

Figure 6.7   Two Server Clusters Before Consolidation

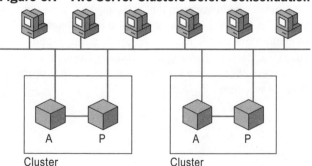

Two clusters, each dedicated to a separate application, generally have higher availability than one cluster hosting both applications. This is depends on, among other factors, the available capacity of each server, other programs that may be running on the servers, and the hosted applications themselves. However, if a potential loss in availability is acceptable to your organization, you can consolidate servers.

Figure 6.8 shows what the clusters in Figure 6.7 would look like if they were consolidated into a single three-node cluster. There is a potential loss in availability because in the event of a failure, both active clusters will fail over to the same passive node, whereas before consolidation, each active node had a dedicated passive node. In this example, if both active nodes were to fail at the same time, the single passive node might not have the capacity to take on the workloads of both nodes simultaneously. Your organization must consider such factors as the likelihood of multiple failures in the server cluster, the importance of keeping the applications in this server cluster available, and if potential loss in services is worth the money saved by server consolidation.

Figure 6.8   Consolidated Server Cluster

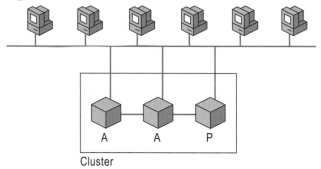

Evaluating Combining Cluster Technologies

You can use several Windows clustering solutions together, depending on the services and applications that you need to make highly available. Each cluster type performs a different role in a multicluster deployment. The most common scenario that combines all three clusters is an e-commerce Web site, where the front-end Web servers are configured in Network Load Balancing clusters that receive client requests, the middle-tier applications (such as the Microsoft® BizTalk® Server) use CLB clusters running on Windows Application Center 2000, and the back-end SQL database servers operate in a server cluster. Figure 6.9 illustrates a typical deployment, utilizing all three Windows clustering technologies.

Figure 6.9   E-Commerce Clustering Scenario

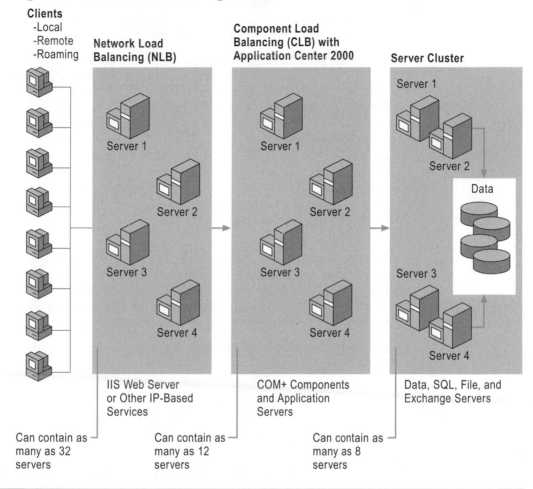

Evaluating Clustering Across Multiple Sites

Many organizations build disaster recovery and increased availability into their infrastructure by using multiple physical sites. Most designs involve a primary siteand one or more remote sites, where a remote site mirrors the primary site. The level at which components are mirrored between sites depends on the Service Level Agreement and the business requirements.

Geographically Dispersed Clusters

Geographically dispersed server clusters are possible in Windows Server 2003 by using virtual local area networks (VLANs)to connect SANs over long distances. Majority node set, a new type of quorum resource in Windows Server 2003, makes it easier for cluster servers to be geographically separated while maintaining consistency in the event of a node failure.

A geographically dispersed cluster is a combination of pieces supplied by hardware OEMs and software vendors. The configurations required can be complex, and the clusters must use only components supported by Microsoft. Geographically dispersed clusters should be deployed only in conjunction with vendors who provide qualified configurations.

For more information about geographically dispersed clusters and SANs, see "Designing and Deploying Server Clusters" in this book. For complete information on geographically dispersed clusters, see the Geographically Dispersed Clusters link on the Web Resources page at http://www.microsoft.com/windows/reskits/webresources.

MultiSite Network Load Balancing Clusters

Like geographically dispersed server clusters, Network Load Balancing clusters that span more than one physical site (sometimes known as *stretch clusters*) are intended to protect data in the event of a disaster. Additionally, multisite configurations can be used to provide local access to clients that are spread nationally or globally. For example, a Network Load Balancing cluster split between a data center on the East Coast and a data center on the West Coast can provide services to users in either location.

Unlike geographically dispersed server clusters, in most cases a single Network Load Balancing cluster is not deployed across multiple sites. Instead, multiple, independent Network Load Balancing clusters are deployed, typically with one cluster at each location. The sites are then combined into a single service using features such as DNS round robinto load balance client requests across the sites. Figure 6.10 illustrates a simple version of this scenario.

Figure 6.10   Multisite Network Load Balancing Configuration

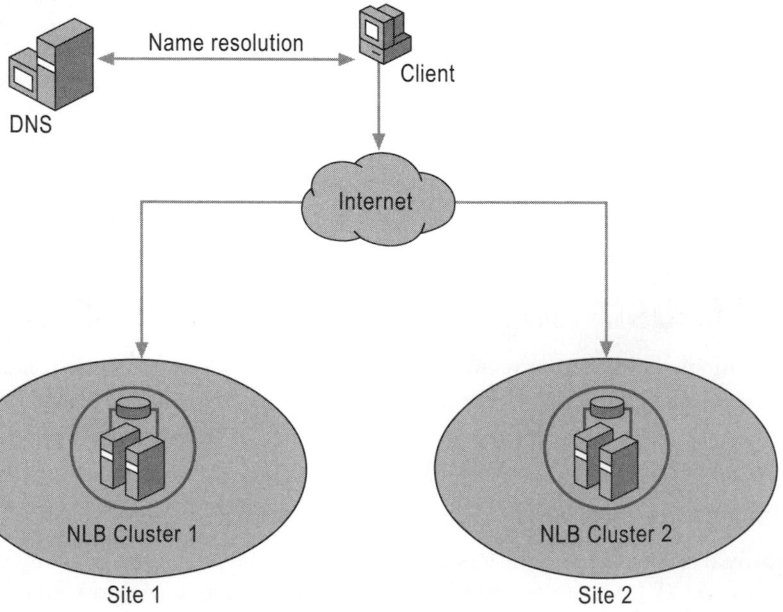

In Figure 6.10, the client uses DNS to resolve the service name to an IP address. Depending on the IP address that the client receives, the request is sent to Site 1 or Site 2. In this type of configuration, the sites are essentially clones of each other, and the sites provide the same set of services. A Web site, for example, would be identical at either site, and clients receive the same response to a given query regardless of the site they are directed to. Not only are client requests load-balanced between the sites, but in the event that one site fails, the other site can continue responding to client requests. It is worth noting that when one site goes down, there is potential for a longer response time to individual requests, depending on geographical factors and network demand.

Additional Resources

Related Information

- "Designing and Deploying Server Clusters" in this book for more information about planning and deploying server clusters.

- "Designing Network Load Balancing" in this book for more information about designing Network Load Balancing clusters.

- "Deploying Network Load Balancing" in this book for information about deploying Network Load Balancing clusters.

- "Designing and Deploying File Servers" in this book for information about clustered file servers.

- "Designing and Deploying Print Servers" in this book for information about clustered print servers.

- "Deploying DHCP" in *Deploying Network Services* of this kit for information about deploying clustered DHCP servers.

- "Deploying WINS" in *Deploying Network Services* of this kit for information about deploying clustered WINS servers.

Related Help Topics

For best results in identifying Help topics by title, in Help and Support Center, under the **Search** box, click **Set search options**. Under **Help Topics**, select the **Search in title only** checkbox.

- "Configuring WINS replication" in Help and Support Center for Windows Server 2003.

- "DNS zone replication in Active Directory" in Help and Support Center for Windows Server 2003.

- "Planning your server cluster" in Help and Support Center for Windows Server 2003.

- "Choosing applications to run on a server cluster" in Help and Support Center for Windows Server 2003.

- "Determining which applications to use with Network Load Balancing" in Help and Support Center for Windows Server 2003.

- "WMI overview" in Help and Support Center for Windows Server 2003 for information about Windows Management Instrumentation, which is used to manage networks and networked applications.

- "Services" in Help and Support Center for Windows Server 2003 for information about the Services snap-in.

- "Backing up and recovering data" in Help and Support Center for Windows Server 2003.

- "Monitoring and status tools" in Help and Support Center for Windows Server 2003.

- "Performance Logs and Alerts overview" in Help and Support Center for Windows Server 2003.

- "SNMP" in Help and Support Center for Windows Server 2003.

- "Checking event logs" in Help and Support Center for Windows Server 2003.

- "Shutdown Event Tracker overview" in Help and Support Center for Windows Server 2003.

Designing and Deploying Server Clusters

Server clusters ensure that applications continue to run in the event of planned service downtime due to maintenance or during unplanned downtime due to hardware or network failure. In order to design server clusters, organizations need to understand the applications that they intend to host on a server cluster, namely the best way to deploy and configure the application in a clustering environment, and they also need to know the server cluster's storage and capacity requirements.

In This Chapter

Related Information

- For more information about planning for high availability see "Planning for High Availability and Scalability" in this book.

- For more information about Network Load Balancing clusters, see "Designing Network Load Balancing" in this book.

- For more information about clustered print servers, see "Designing and Deploying Print Servers" in this book.

- For more information about clustered file servers, see "Designing and Deploying File Servers" in this book.

- For more information about designing storage systems, see "Planning for Storage" in this book.

Overview of the Server Clusters Design Process

Mission-critical applications, such as corporate databases and e-mail, must reside on systems that are designed for high availability and scalability. Deploying server clusters with the Microsoft® Windows® Server 2003, Enterprise Edition or the Windows® Server 2003, Datacenter Edition operating system minimizes the amount of planned and unplanned server downtime. Server clusters can benefit your organization if:

- Your users depend on regular access to mission-critical data and applications to do their jobs.

- Your organization has established a limit on the amount of planned or unplanned service downtime that you can sustain.

- The cost of the additional hardware that server clusters require is less than the cost of having mission-critical data and applications offline during a failure.

Windows Server 2003 provides two different clustering technologies: server clusters (discussed in this chapter) and Network Load Balancing. An overview of these cluster solutions is provided in "Planning for High Availability and Scalability" in this book. For more information about Network Load Balancing, see "Designing Network Load Balancing" and "Deploying Network Load Balancing" in this book. Note that this chapter focuses on using server clusters to make applications highly available. For information about using server clusters with resources such as file and print services, see "Designing and Deploying Print Servers" and "Designing and Deploying File Servers" in this book.

A third clustering technology, Component Load Balancing (CLB), is available in Microsoft® Application Center 2000 but not in Windows Server 2003. CLB clusters enable COM+ applications to be distributed across multiple servers. For more information about CLB, see the documentation for Microsoft Application Center 2000.

If your business is considering server clusters to provide increased availability for one or more applications, and you plan to use Windows Server 2003 — either Enterprise Edition or Datacenter Edition — this chapter will help you evaluate, design, and implement a server cluster compatible with those applications. If you are already running server clusters on Windows NT 4.0 or Windows 2000, this chapter helps you prepare to upgrade those clusters to Windows Server 2003.

Server Cluster Design and Deployment Process

You begin the server cluster design and deployment process by defining your high-availability needs. After you determine the applications or services you want to host on a server cluster, you need to understand the clustering requirements of those applications or services. Next, design your server cluster support network, making sure that you protect your data from failure, disaster, or security risks. After you evaluate and account for all relevant hardware, software, network, and security factors, you are ready to deploy a server cluster. Figure 7.1 illustrates the server cluster design process.

Figure 7.1   Designing and Deploying Server Clusters

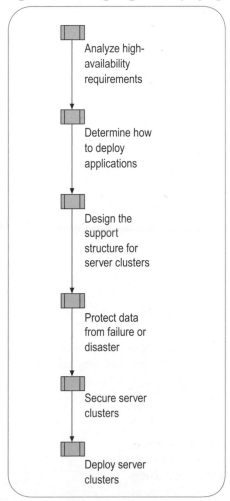

Analyze high-availability requirements

Determine how to deploy applications

Design the support structure for server clusters

Protect data from failure or disaster

Secure server clusters

Deploy server clusters

Server Cluster Fundamentals

The following sections provide an overview of key clustering concepts and summarize new clustering features that have been added to Windows Server 2003.

A *cluster* is a group of individual computer systems working together cooperatively to provide increased computing power and to ensure continuous availability of mission-critical applications or services. From the client viewpoint, an application that runs on a server cluster is no different than an application that runs on any other server, except that availability is higher.

Clustering Terms

The following terms are fundamental clustering concepts that are common to almost every clustering decision. For more information about the following terms and for an overview of server clusters, see "Server cluster components" and "Cluster objects" in Help and Support Center for Windows Server 2003.

Node   A computer system that is a member of a server cluster. Windows Server 2003 supports up to eight nodes in a server cluster.

Resource   A physical or logical entity that is capable of being managed by a cluster, brought online, taken offline, and moved between nodes. A resource can be owned only by a single node at any point in time.

Resource groups   A collection of one or more resources that are managed and monitored as a single unit. Resource groups can be started and stopped independently of other groups (when a resource group is stopped, all resources within the group are stopped). In a server cluster, resource groups are indivisible units that are hosted on one node at any point in time. During failover, resource groups are transferred from one node to another.

Virtual server   A collection of services that appear to clients as a physical Windows-based server but are not associated with a specific server. A virtual server is typically a resource group that contains all of the resources needed to run a particular application and can be failed over like any other resource group. All virtual servers must include a Network Name resource and an IP Address resource.

Failover   The process of taking resource groups offline on one node and bringing them back online on another node. When a resource group goes offline, all resources belonging to that group go offline. The offline and online transitions occur in a predefined order. Resources that are dependent on other resources are taken offline before and brought online after the resources upon which they depend.

Failback   The process of moving resources, either individually or in a group, back to their original node after a failed node rejoins a cluster and comes back online.

Quorum resource   The quorum-capable resource selected to maintain the configuration data necessary for recovery of the cluster. This data contains details of all of the changes that have been applied to the cluster database. The quorum resource is generally accessible to other cluster resources so that any cluster node has access to the most recent database changes. By default there is only one quorum resource per cluster.

Cluster Hardware Requirements

The following are general hardware requirements for building Windows Server 2003 clusters. More detailed information is provided throughout this chapter where applicable. In order for server clusters to be supported by Microsoft, all hardware must be selected from a list of qualified clustering solutions. See the Windows Server Catalog link on the Web Resources page at http://www.microsoft.com/windows/reskits/webresources. For more information about support for server clusters, see article Q309395, "The Microsoft Support Policy for Server Clusters and the Hardware." To find this article, see the Microsoft Knowledge Base link on the Web Resources page at http://www.microsoft.com/windows/reskits/webresources.

- Use a minimum of two computers running Windows Server 2003, Enterprise Edition or Windows Server 2003, Datacenter Edition (computer hardware must also be listed in the Windows Server Catalog). You cannot mix x86-based and Itanium architecture–based computers in the same server cluster.

- Meet minimum storage requirements. Minimum storage requirements depend on a number of factors, such as whether or not your server cluster uses storage area network (SAN) technology, or the type of quorum resource used in the server cluster. For more information about storage solutions, see "Designing the Support Structure for Server Clusters" later in this chapter. Note that all storage solutions must also be listed in the Windows Server Catalog.

- Use a minimum of two network adapters for each node. In recommended configurations, one network adapter connects the node to the other nodes in the cluster for communication and configuration purposes (private network). The second adapter connects the cluster to both an external network (public network) and the private network.

 Important

Server clusters do not protect against hardware failures. Microsoft recommends a redundant array of independent disks (RAID) solution for all cluster disks to eliminate disk drives as a potential single point of failure.

New in Windows Server 2003

Windows Server 2003 introduces a number of new clustering features that are highlighted below.

More nodes in a cluster   Windows Server 2003 supports up to eight nodes per cluster.

Support for 64-bit versions of Windows Server 2003 operating system   The 64-bit versions of Windows Server 2003, Enterprise Edition and Windows Server 2003, Datacenter Edition support the Cluster service. Note that you cannot use GUID partition table (GPT) disks for shared cluster storage. A GPT disk is an Itanium–based disk partition style in the 64-bit versions of Windows Server 2003. For 64-bit versions of Windows Server 2003, you must partition cluster disks on a shared bus as master boot record (MBR) disks and not as GPT disks.

Simplified cluster configuration and setup   Server cluster system files are installed by default with Windows Server 2003. New features include the ability to create new server clusters — or add nodes to an existing cluster — remotely. Another new feature, the New Server Cluster Wizard, analyzes hardware and software configurations to identify potential problems before installation.

Security enhancements   You can reset the Cluster service account password without stopping the Cluster service, allowing you to maintain corporate password policies without compromising availability. In addition, server clusters now support the Kerberos version 5 authentication protocol. For more information, see "Securing Server Clusters" later in this chapter.

Scripting   An application can be made server cluster-aware through scripting (both VBScript and Jscript are supported), rather than through resource dynamic-link library (DLL) files. Unlike DLLs, scripting does not require knowledge of the C or C++ programming languages, which means scripts are easier for developers and administrators to create and implement. Scripts are also easier to customize for your applications.

Majority node set clusters   In every cluster, the quorum resource maintains all configuration data necessary for the recovery of the cluster. In majority node set clusters, the quorum data is stored on each node, allowing for, among other things, geographically dispersed clusters. For more information about quorums, see "Designing the Support Structure for Server Clusters" later in this chapter. For more information about majority node set clusters, see "Protecting Data from Failure or Disaster" later in this chapter.

Analyzing High-Availability Requirements

After determining that you have mission-critical applications or services that need to be highly available, analyze your business needs to determine if clustering is the best solution. You must then evaluate your applications for compatibility with clustering. Figure 7.2 illustrates the process for determining if server clusters are appropriate for your needs.

Figure 7.2   Analyzing High-Availability Requirements

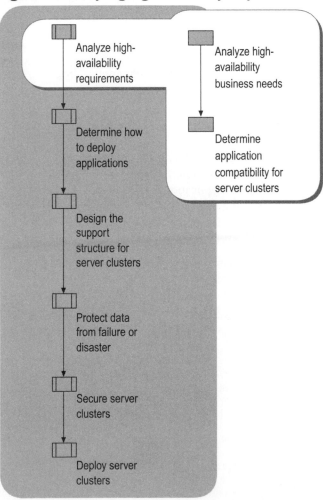

Analyzing High-Availability Business Needs

This chapter assumes that you have already decided to make one or more applications or services highly available, based on your organization's business needs. You need high availability if users require regular access to data or if your organization cannot tolerate downtime from an application or service for more than a minimal amount of time. Other common business motivations for high availability include contractual obligations, concern about losing sales during the time it takes to rebuild a server, and the potential for lost employee productivity when data is inaccessible.

If your business or organization requires high availability, answer the following questions before you begin designing a server cluster:

- How many users depend on a particular application?

- Are your users located at more than one physical site?

- What is the minimum acceptable downtime for a particular application?

- How many failures does your cluster need to tolerate? One node failure? Two nodes or more?

- How much hardware (particularly cluster nodes) can be dedicated to the server cluster?

Additionally, if you have more than one application that needs to be made highly available, do some applications take priority over other applications that will be running on the server cluster? If the answer is yes, consider prioritizing the applications. For example, if more than one node fails in your server cluster, and the remaining hardware is not sufficient to take on every failed node's workload, which applications and services must continue working?

Understanding the business requirements that must be handled by your server cluster is important, particularly later in the server cluster design process when you design failover policies. For more information about these requirements, see "Determining How to Deploy Applications" later in this chapter.

If a server cluster is the most appropriate high-availability solution for your business or organization, the next step is to make sure your application can run on a server cluster.

Determining Application Compatibility for Server Clusters

Not all applications can be adapted to run on a server cluster. If your application meets all the following conditions, it will likely work in a server cluster:

- Your application uses a protocol based on Internet Protocol (IP).

- Your application can specify where application data is stored.

- Your application attempts to reconnect or recover from network failures.

IP-based protocols include Transmission Control Protocol (TCP), User Datagram Protocol (UDP), Distributed Component Object Model (DCOM), named pipes, and remote procedure call (RPC) over TCP/IP. NetBEUI and Internetwork Packet Exchange (IPX) protocols do not work on a server cluster.

 Tip

For information about pretesting to determine if your application is cluster ready, or for information about whether your application supports failover, whether clients can survive failure and subsequent restart of your application, and if clients can survive a failure without a restart of your application, see "Choosing applications to run on a server cluster" in Help and Support Center for Windows Server 2003.

Additionally, some applications do not react to cluster events. An application must be *cluster-aware* (must communicate with the Cluster application programming interface) to receive status and notification information from the server cluster. The Cluster application programming interface (API) is a collection of functions that are implemented by the cluster software and used to manage the cluster, cluster objects, and the cluster database.

Most older applications are not cluster-aware, but they can still run in a server cluster and fail over. These applications respond to only the most basic methods of failure detection and shutdown, and they are not capable of the more advanced initialization and cleanup tasks performed by applications that can react to cluster events. For this reason, these applications might not be as highly available in a server cluster as are applications that can interact with the cluster.

For more information about applications that can run on a cluster, see the Software Development Kit (SDK) link on the Web Resources page at http://www.microsoft.com/windows/reskits/webresources and search for the help topic "Server Cluster Application Types."

Before designing your server cluster, contact the software vendor or consult the documentation to see if your application can run on a cluster. This information can affect how you install your application in a server cluster, and might also determine the best way to upgrade an application once it is installed in a server cluster.

Determining How to Deploy Applications

Some of your deployment decisions are dictated by the application you plan to deploy in the server cluster. Figure 7.3 displays the process for analyzing your application and determining the best way to deploy the application in a server cluster.

Figure 7.3   Determining How to Deploy Applications

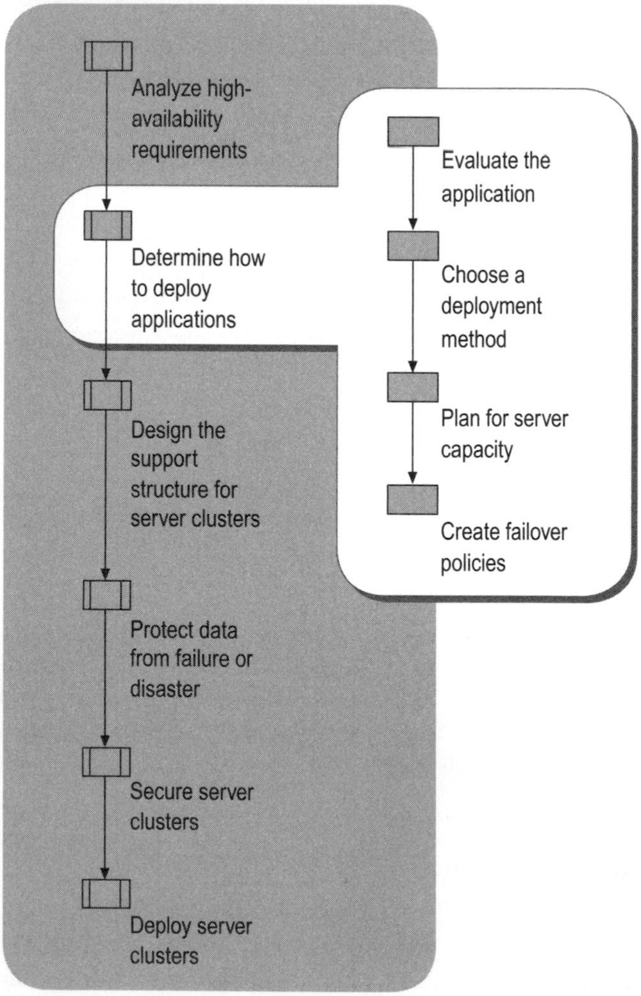

Evaluating the Application

You need a thorough understanding of your application's installation needs before deploying the application in a server cluster. For every application that you intend to install in a server cluster, check the documentation or contact the software vendor about installation issues in general and clustering considerations in particular.

The information you need before deploying an application in a server cluster includes:

- **Setup information.** How the application setup works, such as where the application is installed and where supporting data for the application is installed. When installing Microsoft® Exchange 2000 Server on a server cluster, for example, the log files and database in each storage group must be on the cluster's shared disk. This allows the log files and the storage group databases to fail over to another node if the Exchange virtual server goes offline.

- **Upgrade information.** When it is time to upgrade the application, can the application be upgraded online, or will the server cluster need to be taken offline?

- **Application behavior during failover.** Anticipating application behavior during failover will also help to optimize your deployment. In Microsoft® SQL Server™, Microsoft recommends making all transactions as small as possible because the startup process for SQL virtual servers includes going through the transaction log for each database and rolling transactions back or forward. Therefore, larger transactions, especially with a large volume of transactions, could result in slower failover time.

Choosing a Method for Deploying an Application on a Server Cluster

The best method for deploying an application on a server cluster depends greatly on what type of application it is. Applications running on a cluster can be characterized in two ways: single-instance and multiple-instance. The way your application behaves in a server cluster depends on which type (single-instance or multiple-instance) it is. This means that your deployment method can also vary by application type.

Deploying Single-Instance Applications

With single-instance applications, only one application instance is running on the cluster at any time, and the application typically has data sets that cannot be partitioned across multiple nodes. The Dynamic Host Configuration Protocol (DHCP) service is an example of a single-instance application. The set of leased IP addresses that the application provides is small, but would be complicated to replicate across a cluster. Therefore the DHCP instance exists as a single instance, and high availability is provided by failing over the instance to another node in the cluster.

Figure 7.4 illustrates a single-instance application, named "App," in a four-node cluster. Only one node is currently hosting the application. If that node fails, the application can fail over to one of the other three nodes (the failover options are represented by dotted lines). All four nodes are connected to the application data source, but only the node currently hosting the application can access the data source.

Figure 7.4   Single-Instance Application

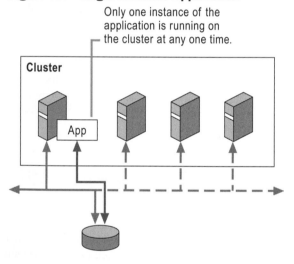

Deploying Multiple-Instance Applications

With a multiple-instance application, either multiple instances of the same code, or different pieces of code that cooperate to provide a single service, can run on a cluster. In both cases, the client or end user sees only one partition of an application. Applications can be either *cloned* or *partitioned* to create multiple instances in a cluster.

Cloned Applications

In a cloned deployment, multiple instances of the same code are executed on the same data set. Cloned applications are more commonly deployed in Network Load Balancing clusters than in server clusters, because cloning is ideal for *stateless* applications, which are applications with data that is rarely updated or that is read-only. Server clusters are designed for applications such as databases and messaging systems that have frequently updated data. For more information about Network Load Balancing clusters, see "Designing Network Load Balancing" in this book.

Partitioned Applications

Server clusters are designed for *stateful* applications, which are applications with frequently updated data sets and long-running in-memory states. Most stateful applications can be partitioned. A large database, for example, can be partitioned so that names beginning with A through L are in one database partition, and those beginning with M through Z are in another database partition. In other applications, functionality — rather than data — is partitioned. After they are partitioned, the different functions are deployed across a set of nodes in a cluster.

In order to represent a single application instance to clients or end users, a partitioned application requires an application-dependent decomposition, routing, and aggregation mechanism that allows a single client request to be distributed across the set of partitions. Then the results from the partitions need to be combined into a single response back to the client. This mechanism depends on the type of application and type of data returned, and is therefore application-specific. The query engine in SQL Server performs this splitting and aggregating. In Exchange 2000 Server clusters, the Exchange front-end server uses the Active Directory® directory service to perform this task.

Figure 7.5 shows an example of a partitioned application in which a database of customer names has been partitioned on a four-node cluster. The solid lines represent each node's connection to its partition of the database; the dotted lines represent the application's access to a given partition as needed.

Figure 7.5   Data Partitioning for an Application on a Cluster

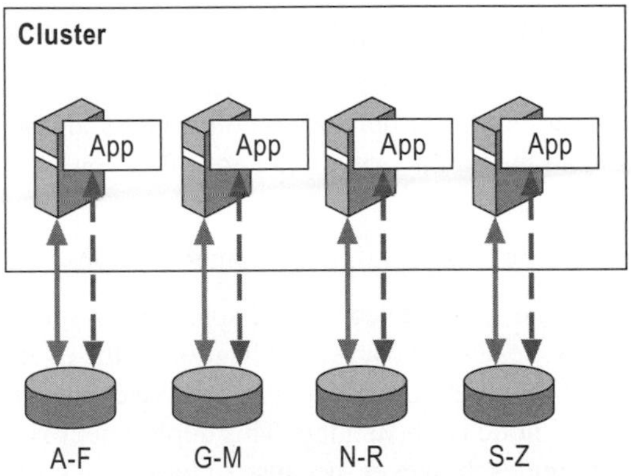

When a client issues a query such as "return all records" across multiple instances, the request is split across the instances and — after results are collected — aggregated back into a single result, which is passed back to the client.

A deployment such as the one in Figure 7.5 allows for scalability, because more servers can be added to house additional partitions, but it does not provide high availability. If one of the nodes fails, that part of the data set is no longer accessible.

As mentioned above, an application can also be partitioned by functionality. Figure 7.6 shows a multiple-instance application deployment, where functionality, not data, is shared among the nodes.

Figure 7.6 Functional Partitions

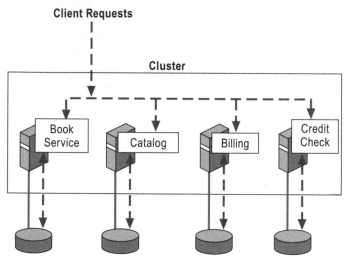

When a client request is introduced to the server cluster in Figure 7.6, the request is directed to the appropriate node, depending on the nature of the request. A billing inquiry, for example, is handled by the node designated for that function. The billing node is the only node with access to the billing database.

The deployment of an application across a server cluster depends on the style of application (single-instance versus multiple-instance) and the number of applications that you plan to deploy in the same cluster.

The following sections describe the most common application deployment options.

One single-instance application One node in the cluster executes the application, servicing user requests. The remaining nodes are on standby, ready to host the application in the event of failover. This type of deployment is well suited for a two-node active-passive cluster in which one node runs the applications and the second node is on standby. This deployment is not typically used in clusters with three or more nodes, however, because of hardware costs. In a cluster of N nodes, only $1/N$ of total processing power is used. Although availability of the single application is high, even in a two-node cluster hardware costs are higher than with other deployment options because of the cost of purchasing standby servers. Some multiple-instance applications, such as SQL Server, can be deployed as a single instance. In the case of SQL Server, when a node in the cluster running SQL Server fails, the entire SQL Server workload is transferred to another, identically configured node.

Several single-instance applications Each application is independent from the others, and different applications can fail over to different nodes in the cluster. For more information about defining failover targets, see "Creating Failover Policies" later in this chapter. This type of deployment provides high availability for applications, but careful capacity planning is required to ensure that each node has sufficient processing capacity, memory, and bandwidth to accommodate additional loads in the event of failover.

One multiple-instance application The cluster supports only one application, with pieces of the application hosted on different nodes. When there is a failover with a partitioned application, a node can host multiple partitions until failback. In SQL Server and other multiple-instance applications, it is important to make sure that each node has the capacity to take on additional partitions in the event of failover.

Several multiple-instance applications Each node hosts one instance of each application. In such a deployment, both capacity planning and defining failover targets become increasingly important and complex.

Planning for Server Capacity

Before deploying your application on a high-availability server cluster, you need to answer some key business questions:

- How many servers are available for your cluster and what is the capacity of each server?

- In the case of a failover, what kind of performance is acceptable until failback returns the cluster to full processing capacity?

- Given that it is possible for more than one node in a cluster to fail, how many failures do you want your cluster to be able to withstand before the application becomes unavailable?

The workload of a server both before and after failover is closely tied to your server resource planning. The way your application adapts to the server cluster depends on how much of the server resources it consumes. The consumption of server resources affects the number of servers you need to ensure high availability for the application, in addition to how many servers are required to pick up the workload for a given node in the event of a failover.

Consider a simple example: a two-node cluster, with Node A and Node B. If Node A fails over, Node B has to continue processing its own jobs in addition to processing the jobs that fail over from Node A. This means that prior to failover, both nodes can operate at a maximum of 50 percent capacity. After failover, Node B operates at 100 percent capacity. When any server operates at maximum capacity, performance is compromised. However, even reduced performance is preferable to completely losing Node A's workload, which is what would happen in a nonclustered environment. In this example, an organization would have to determine if this level of availability is sufficient for its needs, or if an expenditure on more hardware is warranted.

If you add a third node to the above example and all three nodes operate at 50 percent, the two remaining nodes can divide the workload of a failed node. If Node A fails over, Node B and Node C assume Node A's work and operate at 75 percent capacity, which provides better application performance than a single server operating at 100 percent capacity. However, if two nodes in this cluster were to fail over, the remaining node would not have sufficient capacity to assume the processing for the entire cluster.

Windows Server 2003 supports up to eight nodes in a cluster. With additional nodes, you have more options for distributing the workload in a cluster.

Cluster Server Capacity Examples

The following illustrations of a simple four-node cluster demonstrate how server load can be balanced across nodes. These examples also demonstrate the relationship between hardware resources, fault tolerance, and availability.

 Important

The examples in this section are theoretical and intended for discussion purposes only. Be aware that in an actual server cluster deployment, applications cannot always be distributed as evenly as they are in the following examples.

In Figure 7.7, all four nodes are operational, each running at 25 percent capacity.

Figure 7.7   Cluster Under Normal Operating Conditions

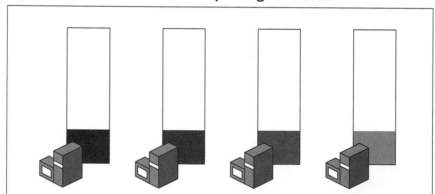

Server Cluster

Figure 7.8 shows the cluster after one of the nodes fails. The remaining three nodes each receive a share of the failed node's work.

Figure 7.8   Cluster After a Single Node Failure

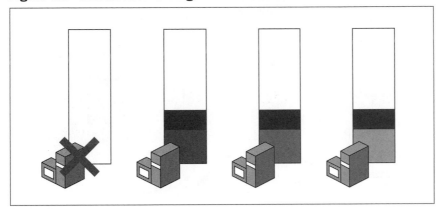

Server Cluster

After two nodes fail, shown in Figure 7.9, the remaining two nodes are each operating at approximately 50 percent capacity.

Figure 7.9   Cluster After Two Failures

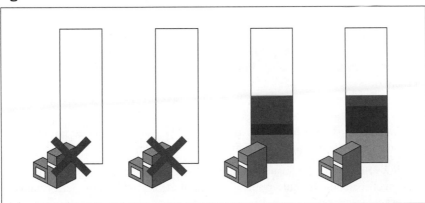

Server Cluster

Finally, when three nodes fail, as shown in Figure 7.10, the remaining node has enough capacity to take over the clusters' entire workload (though application performance might be degraded somewhat with the server operating at 100 percent capacity).

Figure 7.10   Cluster After Three Failures

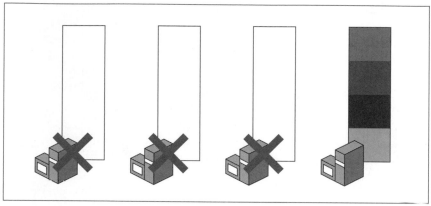

Server Cluster

Deployment Considerations

When determining the appropriate size of your server cluster (the number of nodes and their capacity) and the failover policies for one or more applications, consider the following points:

- The cluster configuration in Figure 7.7 through Figure 7.10 is able to tolerate three failures with no loss of availability for clients and users. The cost of this availability is the price of four servers of sufficient capacity. For example, if the above nodes were running at 50 percent or 75 percent capacity, the same amount of work could be done with fewer nodes (or the same number of nodes could do more work). However, the cluster would then be unable to accommodate three failures; the remaining nodes would already be at full capacity by the time the third node failed. If you don't need to anticipate three failures, you could use fewer nodes running at a higher capacity than 25 percent.

- In Windows Server 2003, Cluster Administrator allows you to designate applications to fail over to specific nodes. If your application cannot afford to lose any performance when it fails over to another node, configure failover distribution so that the application fails over to a node with plenty of room (running at low capacity). Again, this requires a hardware investment in order to have a server standing by for the purpose of failover.

- If some decline in performance is acceptable for your application, specifically during the time it takes to get the failed node restarted, you can fail over the application to a node that is operating at a higher capacity. This means you can use fewer nodes, but the chances are higher that performance on the new node will decrease after failover.

- If some applications are a higher priority than others to your organization, you can use Cluster Administrator to fail over the high-priority applications before the others. This is useful in deployments where multiple failures cannot be tolerated due to capacity limitations. In this case, if both a high-priority application and a lower-priority application fail over and need to find room elsewhere in the cluster, the high-priority application always takes precedence.

- In planning server capacity (and in all other aspects of cluster deployment planning), it is important that you consider scalability and future demands on your cluster. It is very likely that over time your applications will grow, or you will need to deploy more applications on a cluster, or both. When calculating how many servers you will need and how much capacity each server needs to have, a general IT principal is to increase your estimates by 30 percent, and then add capacity for anticipated future growth. The extra 30 percent provides a safety buffer against calculation error or unforeseen load additions.

Creating Failover Policies

To provide high availability, single-instance applications — and the individual partitions of multiple-instance applications — fail over from one cluster node to another. In a two-node cluster, failover involves transferring the resources of one node to the remaining node. As the number of nodes in a cluster increases, different failover policies are possible.

When you create failover policies, you must perform each of the following tasks:

1. Make key failover policy decisions.
2. Evaluate N+I failover policies.
3. Evaluate random versus customized failover control.

Making Key Decisions in Failover Policies

You need to make the following decisions when planning and configuring your failover policies:

- How many nodes, such as standby servers, do you deploy for failover?

- What resources do you fail over to which nodes?

- Do you partition applications and services across cluster nodes, or do you distribute the load differently?

- How do you consolidate resources into resource groups? A group is the indivisible unit (a collection of resources) that fails over from one node to another.

Note

A failover policy often involves targeting a specific node for a given application. Such targeting can be configured through Cluster Administrator. For more information about targeting failover nodes, see "Determining failover and move policies for groups" in Help and Support Center for Windows Server 2003.

Many of the key decisions in failover policies involve weighing the benefits of implementing the best possible solution against the cost of purchasing and maintaining hardware. For example, do your applications and services need the highest level of availability, or is your organization willing to settle for a slightly lower level of availability at a greatly reduced cost? If you decide to purchase standby servers that are dedicated to receiving specific applications in the event of failover, be sure your budget can accommodate the additional cost.

Evaluating N+I Failover Policies

The most common modeling used for failover policies is *N+I,* where *N* nodes are hosting applications and *I* (idle) nodes are standing by as spares. The simplest method for providing failover is to match each node with its own idle failover node: in a three-node cluster that would be 3+3. This design achieves the highest level of availability, but requires an investment in hardware that remains idle much of the time.

A failure on a cluster might result in an impact on users that can range from slow performance to application unavailability. When deploying an N+I solution, extensive testing must be done to ensure that, in the case of a massive failure, one node can run all applications and services with little or no user impact.

N+I configurations are scalable and good for handling multiple failures. An example of an N+I configuration is shown in Figure 7.11.

Figure 7.11   N+I Configuration

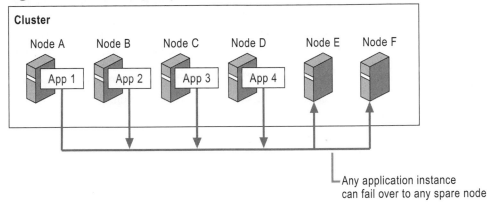

Any application instance
can fail over to any spare node

The configuration shown in Figure 7.11 is a good configuration if your application must continue running without any decrease in performance after failover. This configuration guarantees that the application will fail over to a node with 100 percent available resources and not to a node already in use by another application or another partition (assuming there has not already been another failover in the same server cluster).

Exchange 2000 Server is a good example of an application suited for an N+I server cluster deployment. In a four-node cluster, Microsoft recommends three active nodes and one node on standby (3+1). Because Exchange can have large memory and processing requirements, it is better to have a resource group in an Exchange cluster fail over to a node with 100 percent available resources. The potential drawback is that only one node failure is supported in this scenario.

Standby Server

A variation of N+I, a standby server configuration has idle nodes prepared to take on the work of one or more active nodes. Standby servers are effective for maintaining a consistent performance level for your users even after failover. A three-node version of a standby server configuration is illustrated in Figure 7.12.

Figure 7.12   Standby Server Configuration

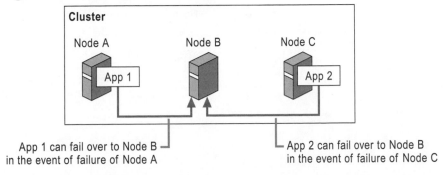

App 1 can fail over to Node B
in the event of failure of Node A

App 2 can fail over to Node B
in the event of failure of Node C

Standby servers are good for larger applications that require a lot of resources such as processing power, memory, and input/output (I/O) bandwidth. In the event of a failure on one node, all applications are still hosted on separate servers. In Figure 7.12, for example, App1 and App2 are large applications. Combining them on the same node might require more processing or capacity than a single node could provide. With a standby server configuration, if Node A were to fail, App1 would move to Node B and the applications would remain on separate nodes. It is easy to plan server capacity for this failover policy; the size of each node is based on the application that it will be running, and the capacity of the spare server is sized to the maximum of the other nodes.

The drawback of this failover policy is that there is a single point of failure. In Figure 7.12, for example, if Node A failed, and App1 moved to Node B, no failover could take place if Node B were to also fail. This type of configuration also does not support multiple failures well. For example, if both Node A and Node C were to fail, Node B would not have sufficient resources to run both applications. This example shows a three-node cluster, however. In larger clusters (up to eight nodes) you can configure a variety of standby combinations to eliminate a single point of failure.

Failover Pairs

Failover pairs are another common N+I variation. Failover pairs are often used in clusters with four or more nodes, and they are ideal for ensuring performance consistency after failover. Failover policies can be defined so that each application can fail over between two nodes, such as in the four-node cluster illustrated in Figure 7.13. Here, Node A is paired with Node B, and Node C is paired with Node D.

Figure 7.13   Failover Pair Server Configuration

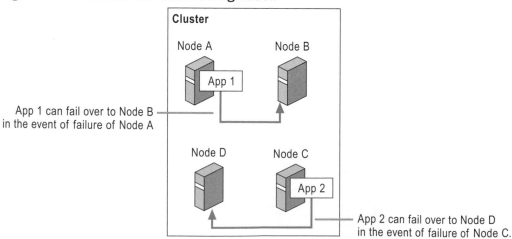

Failover pairs are also good for larger, resource-intensive applications such as databases. For capacity planning, you must ensure that each node in the pair can accommodate the application in question. Compared to a standby server policy, failover pairs have the added benefit of being part of a larger cluster. If the failover node needs to be brought down for maintenance, for example, a different failover node for the application can be assigned dynamically.

The disadvantage of failover pairs is that in simpler configurations, such as the one illustrated in Figure 7.13, only 50 percent of the cluster resources are ever in use. Also, depending on the number of nodes and the specific failover policies configured on the nodes, multiple failures in this kind of cluster might require administrators to manually failback resources when nodes are restored.

Evaluating Random vs. Customized Failover Control

Depending on the size and complexity of your server cluster, and the resources at your disposal, you might want to enact precise control over failover policies. Alternatively, you can let Windows Server 2003 determine the failover location for an application randomly.

Random Failover Policies

In clusters that run several small application instances, where the capacity of any node is large enough to support several instances at a time, random failover policies work well. Random failover policies are not recommended for large clusters (four or more nodes) because, given the great number of combinations of nodes, resources, and failures, there is no way to prevent some nodes from becoming overloaded while other nodes are underused.

When a resource group has an empty preferred owners list, and the node hosting that group fails, Windows clustering randomizes the failover target for the group. Assuming there are sufficient resources and application instances in a cluster, random failover in a small cluster can actually load balance applications across cluster nodes. Random failover is also well able to handle multiple failures.

The disadvantage of random failover policies is that you might find it difficult to plan capacity because statistically there is no guarantee that applications will be equally divided across nodes. Similarly, the effect on the performance of an application after failover is also difficult to predict. Random failover policies are not recommended in clusters with large, resource-intensive applications.

Customized Failover Policies

Targeting specific applications to specific nodes gives the administrator full control over what happens when a failure occurs. It also makes capacity planning easy, because you know which application is going to run on which server.

Group affinity is an attribute of a dependency between groups that determines the groups' relative location in the server cluster. For resources and resource groups that have no requirements for specific hardware or configurations, it might not matter where the resource groups are hosted on the cluster. There are circumstances, however, where the location of one group can affect the location of other groups. Groups can be set up to have strong or weak *affinity*. With strong affinity, they will be placed together on the same node, if possible. They can also be set up to have strong or weak *anti-affinity*. With strong anti-affinity, groups will be kept apart if at all possible. Exchange virtual servers are an example of groups that use anti-affinity, because running more than one instance of Exchange on the same node is not recommended.

If you have multiple applications, defining good policies for each can be difficult. In the event of multiple failures, it is difficult to account for all the possible combinations of application and server failures. For more information about configuring group affinity, see article Q296799, "How to Configure Windows Clustering Groups for Hot Spare Support." To find this article, see the Microsoft Knowledge Base link on the Web Resources page at http://www.microsoft.com/windows/reskits/webresources.

Designing the Support Structure for Server Clusters

A server cluster depends on network connectivity for communication with clients and end users, and for intra-cluster configuration information between nodes. The other fundamental requirement for a server cluster is storage — the storage of application information that is shared and failed over between nodes, and the storage of cluster configuration data. Note that your storage design, in addition to providing sufficient storage capacity, must be able to deliver information to the cluster in a timely and efficient manner.

Before you design the support structure for your server clusters, assemble the information that you collected during the steps outlined earlier in this chapter, including:

- Usage statistics, such as the number of users and clients who will be using applications running on your clusters.

- The number of clusters you plan to run on your network, and the number of nodes in each cluster.

- The amount of storage your applications need.

- The scalability needs in your organization, particularly projections for anticipated growth in storage needs and network traffic in the near future.

Figure 7.14 shows the high-level process for analyzing your network and infrastructure needs.

Figure 7.14   Designing the Support Structure for Server Clusters

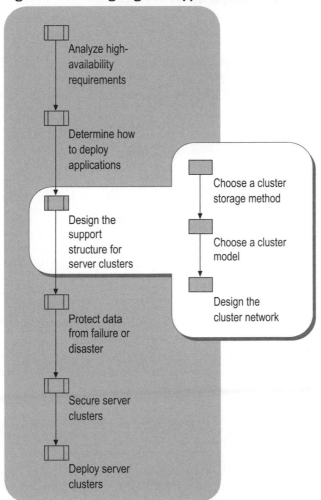

> ⚠ **Important**
>
> All storage and networking solutions for a server cluster must be supported by Microsoft. For more information about qualified storage and networking solutions, see the Windows Catalog link on the Web Resources page at http://www.microsoft.com/windows/reskits/webresources.

Choosing a Cluster Storage Method

Currently, the most common storage I/O technologies used with Windows Server 2003 clusters are Parallel SCSI and Fibre Channel.

Beginning with the Windows Server 2003 release, SCSI interconnects are supported only on two-node clusters running the 32-bit version of Windows Server 2003, Enterprise Edition. SCSI is not supported on Windows Server 2003, Datacenter Edition, or any 64-bit version of the Windows Server 2003 family.

SCSI storage and two types of Fibre Channel — arbitrated loops and switched network — are currently qualified storage configurations in the Windows Catalog. Both SCSI and Fibre Channel are discussed later in this section.

Note

This section provides an overview of storage technology and implementation recommendations. The information here is intended to provide deployment guidelines and help administrators make informed deployment decisions. For procedural information about installing or configuring storage in your server cluster, see "Storage configuration options" in Help and Support Center for Windows Server 2003.

In addition to configuring adequate storage for applications, you also need a dedicated disk to use as the quorum device. This disk must have a minimum capacity of 50 megabytes (MB). For optimal NTFS file system performance, it is recommended that the quorum disk have at least 500 MB. For more information about the quorum device, see "Choosing a Cluster Model" later in this chapter. It is recommended that you do not use the quorum disk for storing applications or anything other than quorum data.

Using RAID in Server Clusters

It is strongly recommended that you use a RAID solution for all disks running the Windows Server 2003 operating system. A RAID configuration prevents disk failure from being a single point of failure in your server cluster.

It is possible to use hardware-based RAID with Windows Server 2003. By using a controller provided by the hardware vendor or RAID solution provider, you can configure physical disks into fault-tolerant sets or volumes. The sets can be made visible to clusters either as whole disks or as smaller partitions.

Cluster nodes are unaware of the physical implementation of disks and treat each volume as a physical disk. For an ideal configuration, it is recommended that you associate the logical volume size as closely as possible with the actual physical disk size. This practice avoids taxing the physical disk with too many I/O operations from multiple logical volumes.

If your RAID controller supports dynamic logical unit (LUN) expansion, cluster disks can be extended without rebooting, providing excellent scalability for your organization's needs. The command-line tool DiskPart.exe lets administrators apply the physical extension of the disks to the logical partitions with no disruption of service. For more information about DiskPart.exe, in Help and Support Center for Windows Server 2003, click **Tools**, and then click **Command-line reference A-Z**.

Using Storage Interconnects with Server Clusters

Make sure that all interconnects used on a server cluster are supported by Microsoft by checking the Windows Catalog. This also applies to any software that is used to provide fault tolerance or load balancing for adapters or interconnects. For more information about qualified interconnects and software, see the Windows Catalog link on the Web Resources page at http://www.microsoft.com/windows/reskits/webresources.

Consider establishing redundant access routes to stored data. Providing multiple paths to your storage is another way to provide high availability. With versions of Windows operating systems earlier than Windows Server 2003, vendors and storage providers implemented two or more storage fabrics that were configured for load balancing and fault tolerance. The specific solution was designed by the vendor and required specially designed configurations and drivers. With the release of Windows Server 2003, Microsoft developed and supplied vendors with a multipath driver, which they can use in place of customized drivers.

Using SCSI Storage with Server Clusters

SCSI is supported only on two-node clusters running the 32-bit version of Windows Server 2003, Enterprise Edition. Server clusters using SCSI are not supported on the 64-bit version of Windows Server 2003. General guidelines for deploying SCSI in your server cluster are listed below:

- All devices on the SCSI bus, including disks, must have unique SCSI IDs (for example, by default, most SCSI adapters have an ID of 7).
- SCSI hubs are not supported in server clusters.
- The SCSI bus must be terminated. Use physical terminating devices, and do not use controller-based or device-based termination.

Using Fibre Channel Storage with Server Clusters

There are two supported methods of Fibre Channel-based storage in a Windows Server 2003 server cluster: arbitrated loops and switched fabric.

 Important

When evaluating both types of Fibre Channel implementation, read the vendor's documentation and be sure you understand the specific features and restrictions of each.

Although the term *Fibre Channel* implies the use of fiber-optic technology, copper coaxial cable is also allowed for interconnects.

Arbitrated Loops (FC-AL)

A Fibre Channel arbitrated loop (FC-AL) is a set of nodes and devices connected into a single loop. FC-AL provides a cost-effective way to connect up to 126 devices into a single network. As with SCSI, a maximum of two nodes is supported in an FC-AL server cluster configured with a hub. An FC-AL is illustrated in Figure 7.15.

Figure 7.15   FC-AL Connection

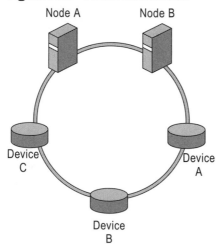

FC-ALs provide a solution for two nodes and a small number of devices in relatively static configurations. All devices on the loop share the media, and any packet traveling from one device to another must pass through all intermediate devices.

If your high-availability needs can be met with a two-node server cluster, an FC-AL deployment has several advantages:

- The cost is relatively low.

- Loops can be expanded to add storage (although nodes cannot be added).

- Loops are easy for Fibre Channel vendors to develop.

The disadvantage is that loops can be difficult to deploy in an organization. Because every device on the loop shares the media, overall bandwidth in the cluster is lowered. Some organizations might also be unduly restricted by the 126-device limit.

Switched Fabric (FC-SW)

For any cluster larger than two nodes, a switched Fibre Channel fabric (FC-SW) is the only supported storage technology. In an FC-SW, devices are connected in a many-to-many topology using Fibre Channel switches (illustrated in Figure 7.16).

Figure 7.16   FC-SW Connection

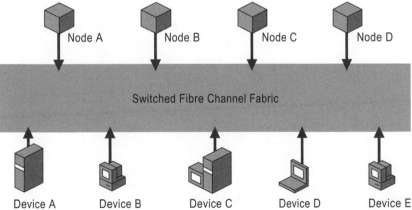

When a node or device communicates with another node or device in an FC-SW, the source and target set up a point-to-point connection (similar to a virtual circuit) and communicate directly with each other. The fabric itself routes data from the source to the target. In an FC-SW, the media are not shared, any device can communicate with any other device, and communication occurs at full bus speed. This is a fully scalable enterprise solution and, as such, is highly recommended for deployment with server clusters.

FC-SW is the primary technology employed in SANs. Other advantages of FC-SW include ease of deployment, the ability to support millions of devices, and switches that provide fault isolation and rerouting. Also, there are no shared media as there are in FC-AL, allowing for faster communication. However, be aware that FC-SWs can be difficult for vendors to develop, and the switches can be expensive. Vendors also have to account for interoperability issues between components from different vendors or manufacturers.

Using SANs with Server Clusters

For any large-scale cluster deployment, it is recommended that you use a SAN for data storage. Smaller SCSI and stand-alone Fibre Channel storage devices work with server clusters, but SANs provide superior fault tolerance.

A SAN is a set of interconnected devices (such as disks and tapes) and servers that are connected to a common communication and data transfer infrastructure (FC-SW, in the case of Windows Server 2003 clusters). A SAN allows multiple server access to a pool of storage in which any server can potentially access any storage unit.

The information in this section provides an overview of using SAN technology with your Windows Server 2003 clusters. For more information about deploying server clusters on SANs, see the Windows Clustering: Storage Area Networks link on the Web Resources page at http://www.microsoft.com/windows/reskits/webresources.

 Note
Vendors that provide SAN fabric components and software management tools have a wide range of tools for setting up, configuring, monitoring, and managing the SAN fabric. Contact your SAN vendor for details about your particular SAN solution.

The following sections provide an overview of SAN concepts that directly affect a server cluster deployment.

HBAs

Host bus adapters (HBAs) are the interface cards that connect a cluster node to a SAN, similar to the way that a network adapter connects a server to a typical Ethernet network. HBAs, however, are more difficult to configure than network adapters (unless the HBAs are preconfigured by the SAN vendor).

Zoning and LUN Masking

Zoning and LUN masking are fundamental to SAN deployments, particularly as they relate to a Windows Server 2003 cluster deployment. Both methods provide isolation and protection of server cluster data within a SAN, and in most deployments one or the other is sufficient. Work with your hardware vendor to determine whether zoning or LUN masking is more appropriate for your organization.

Zoning

Many devices and nodes can be attached to a SAN. With data stored in a single *cloud*, or storage entity, it is important to control which hosts have access to specific devices. Zoning allows administrators to partition devices in logical volumes and thereby reserve the devices in a volume for a server cluster. That means that all interactions between cluster nodes and devices in the logical storage volumes are isolated within the boundaries of the zone; other noncluster members of the SAN are not affected by cluster activity.

Figure 7.17 is a logical depiction of two SAN zones (Zone A and Zone B), each containing a storage controller (S1and S2, respectively).

Figure 7.17   Zoning

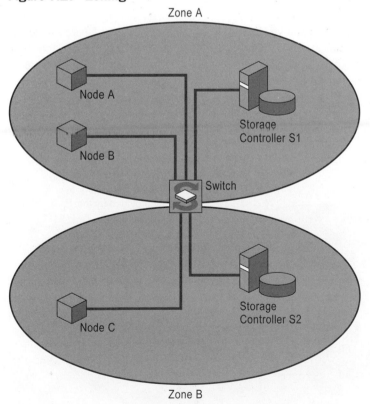

In this implementation, Node A and Node B can access data from the storage controller S1, but Node C cannot. Node C can access data from storage controller S2.

Zoning needs to be implemented at the hardware level (with the controller or switch) and not through software. The primary reason is that zoning is also a security mechanism for a SAN-based cluster, because unauthorized servers cannot access devices inside the zone (access control is implemented by the switches in the fabric, so a host adapter cannot gain access to a device for which it has not been configured). With software zoning, the cluster would be left unsecured if the software component failed.

In addition to providing cluster security, zoning also limits the traffic flow within a given SAN environment. Traffic between ports is routed only to segments of the fabric that are in the same zone.

LUN masking

A LUN is a logical disk defined within a SAN. Server clusters see LUNs and think they are physical disks. LUN masking, performed at the controller level, allows you to define relationships between LUNs and cluster nodes. Storage controllers usually provide the means for creating LUN-level access controls that allow access to a given LUN to one or more hosts. By providing this access control at the storage controller, the controller itself can enforce access policies to the devices.

LUN masking provides more granular security than zoning, because LUNs provide a means for zoning at the port level. For example, many SAN switches allow overlapping zones, which enables a storage controller to reside in multiple zones. Multiple clusters in multiple zones can share the data on those controllers. Figure 7.18 illustrates such a scenario.

Figure 7.18   Storage Controller in Multiple Zones

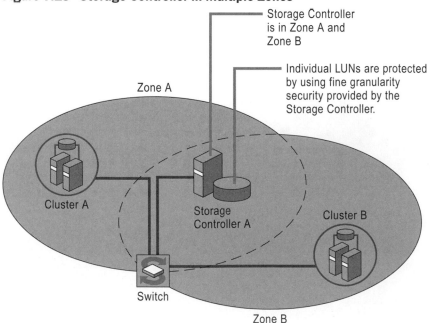

LUNs used by Cluster A can be masked, or hidden, from Cluster B so that only authorized users can access data on a shared storage controller.

Requirements for Deploying SANs with Windows Server 2003 Clusters

The following list highlights the deployment requirements to meet when using a SAN storage solution with your server cluster. For a white paper to provide more complete information about using SANs with server clusters, see the Windows Clustering: Storage Area Networks link on the Web Resources page at http://www.microsoft.com/windows/reskits/webresources.

Note

A utility that might be helpful in deploying SANs with server clusters is Mountvol.exe. Mountvol.exe is included with the Windows Server 2003 operating system, and provides a means of creating volume mount points and linking volumes without requiring a drive letter. For more information about Mountvol.exe, see "Mountvol" in Help and Support Center for Windows Server 2003.

- Each cluster on a SAN must be deployed in its own zone. The mechanism the cluster uses to protect access to the disks can have an adverse effect on other clusters that are in the same zone. By using zoning to separate the cluster traffic from other cluster or noncluster traffic, there is no chance of interference.

- All HBAs in a single cluster must be the same type and have the same firmware version. Many storage and switch vendors require that all HBAs in the same zone — and, in some cases, the same fabric — share these characteristics.

- All storage device drivers and HBA device drivers in a cluster must have the same software version.

- Never allow multiple nodes access to the same storage devices unless they are in the same cluster.

Caution

If multiple nodes in different clusters can access a given disk, data corruption will result.

- Never put tape devices into the same zone as cluster disk storage devices. A tape device could misinterpret a bus rest and rewind at inappropriate times, such as during a large backup.

Guidelines for Deploying SANs with Windows Server 2003 Clusters

In addition to the SAN requirements discussed in the previous section, the following practices are highly recommended for server cluster deployment:

- In a highly available storage fabric, you need to deploy clustered servers with multiple HBAs. In these cases, always load the multipath driver software. If the I/O subsystem sees two HBAs, it assumes they are different buses and enumerates all the devices as though they were different devices on each bus. The host, meanwhile, is seeing multiple paths to the same disks. Failure to load the multipath driver will disable the second device, because the operating system sees what it thinks are two independent disks with the same signature.

- Hardware snapshots can go either to a server outside the server cluster or to a backup *clone* disk. When the original disk fails, you can replace it in the server cluster with its clone. When using cloned disks, it is very important that only one disk with a given disk signature be exposed to the server cluster at one time. Many controllers provide snapshots at the controller level that can be exposed to the cluster as a completely separate LUN. Cluster performance is degraded when multiple devices have the same signature. If a hardware snapshot is exposed back to the node with the original disk online, the I/O subsystem attempts to rewrite the signature. However, if the snapshot is exposed to another node in the cluster, the Cluster service does not recognize it as a different disk and the result could be data corruption. Although this is not specifically a SAN issue, the controllers that provide this functionality are typically deployed in a SAN environment.

 Caution
Exposing a hardware snapshot to a node on the cluster might result in data corruption.

Choosing a Cluster Model

The term *cluster model* refers to the manner in which the quorum resource is used in the server cluster. Server clusters require a quorum resource, which contains all of the configuration data necessary for recovery of the cluster. The cluster database, which resides in the Windows Server 2003 registry on each cluster node, contains information about all physical and logical elements in a cluster, including cluster objects, their properties, and configuration data. When a cluster node fails and then comes back online, the other nodes update the failed node's copy of the cluster database. It is the quorum resource that allows the Cluster service to keep every active node's database up to date.

The quorum resource, like any other resource, can be owned by only one node at a time. A node can form a cluster only if it can gain control of the quorum resource. Similarly, a node can join a cluster (or remain in an existing cluster) only if it can communicate with the node that controls the quorum resource.

Servers negotiate for ownership of the quorum resource in order to avoid split-brain scenarios, which occur when nodes lose communication with one another and multiple partitions of the cluster converge with a well-defined set of members, each partition believing that it is the one and only instance of the cluster. In such a case, each partition would continue operating in the belief that it had control of any cluster-wide shared resources or state, ultimately leading to data corruption.

The concept of a quorum ensures that only one partition of a cluster survives a split-brain scenario. When the cluster is partitioned, the quorum resource is used as an arbiter. The partition that owns the quorum resource is allowed to continue. The other partitions of the cluster are said to have *lost quorum*, and Cluster service — along with any resources hosted on the nodes that are not part of the partition that has quorum — is terminated.

The Cluster service stores cluster configuration data in a quorum log file. This file is usually located on a shared disk that all nodes in the cluster can access, and it acts as the definitive version of the cluster configuration. It holds cluster configuration information such as which servers are part of the cluster, what resources are installed in the cluster, and the state of those resources (for example, online or offline). Because the purpose of a cluster is to have multiple physical servers acting as a single virtual server, it is critical that each of the physical servers has a consistent view of how the cluster is configured.

A quorum resource can be any resource that:

- Provides a means for arbitration leading to membership and cluster state decisions.
- Provides physical storage to store configuration information.
- Uses NTFS.

The quorum resource you choose is dictated by the server cluster model you deploy (number of servers, number of sites, and so on). Do not build your server cluster around a particular type of quorum resource; instead, design the cluster that best supports your applications, and then choose one of the cluster models described in the following sections.

Three types of cluster models are available for deployment with server clusters:

- Local quorum
- Single quorum device
- Majority node set

For more information about the cluster database and the quorum resource, see "Quorum resource" in Help and Support Center for Windows Server 2003.

Local Quorum Cluster

This cluster model is for clusters that consist of only one node. This model is also referred to as a local quorum. It is typically used for:

- Deploying dynamic file shares on a single cluster node, to ease home directory deployment and administration.

- Testing.

- Development.

Single Quorum Device Cluster

The most widely used cluster model is the single quorum device cluster (also referred to as the standard quorum model), which is illustrated in Figure 7.19. The definitive copy of the cluster configuration data is on a single cluster storage device connected to all nodes.

Figure 7.19   Single Quorum Device Cluster

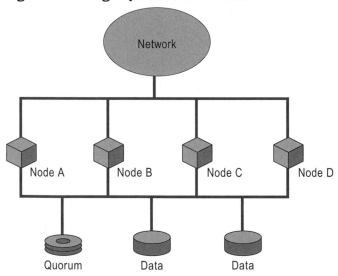

Majority Node Set Cluster

With Windows Server 2003, Microsoft introduces the majority node set cluster. The majority node set quorum model is intended for sophisticated, end-to-end clustering solutions. Each node maintains its own copy of the cluster configuration data. The quorum resource ensures that the cluster configuration data is kept consistent across the nodes. For this reason, majority node set quorums are typically found in geographically dispersed clusters. Another advantage of majority node set quorums is that a quorum disk can be taken offline for maintenance and the cluster will continue to operate.

The major difference between majority node set clusters and single quorum device clusters is that single quorum device clusters can survive with just one node, but majority node set clusters need to have a majority of the cluster nodes survive a failure for the server cluster to continue operating. A majority node set cluster is illustrated in Figure 7.20.

Figure 7.20   Majority Node Set Cluster

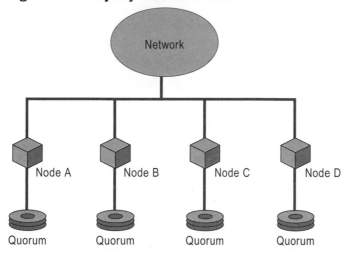

A majority node set cluster is a good solution for controlled, targeted scenarios as part of a cluster solution offered by an independent software vendor (ISV) or independent hardware vendor (IHV). By abstracting storage from the Cluster service, majority node set clusters provide ISVs with much greater flexibility for designing sophisticated cluster scenarios.

There are strict requirements to adhere to when you deploy majority node set clusters. The deployment of majority node set clusters is appropriate in some specialized configurations that need tightly consistent cluster features and do not have shared disks, for example:

- Clusters that host applications that can fail over, but that use other, application-specific methods to keep data consistent between nodes. Database log shipping and file replication for relatively static data are examples of this kind of application.

- Clusters that host applications that have no persistent data, but that need to cooperate in a tightly coupled manner to provide consistent volatile state.

- Multisite clusters, which span more than one physical site.

For more information about majority node sets and geographically dispersed clusters, see "Protecting Data From Failure or Disaster" later in this chapter.

Designing the Cluster Network

A network performs one of the following roles in a cluster:

- A private network carries internal cluster communication.

- A public network provides client systems with access to cluster application services.

- A mixed network (public and private) carries internal cluster communication and connects client systems to cluster application services.

Figure 7.21 shows a typical four-node server cluster deployment with a public (intranet) and private network.

Figure 7.21   Four-Node Cluster Service Cluster with Private and Public Networks

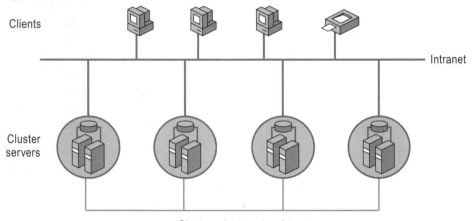

A network might have no role in a cluster; this is also known as disabling a network for cluster use. In the case of single quorum device clusters, the Cluster service will not use the network for internal traffic, nor will it bring IP Address resources online. Other cluster-related traffic, such as traffic to and from a domain controller for authentication, might or might not use this network.

Use these guidelines for designing the network segments of the server clusters:

- You can provide fault tolerance in your network by grouping network adapters on multiple ports to a single physical segment. This practice is known as *teaming network adapters* and is described in "Eliminating Single Points of Failure in Your Network Design" later in this chapter.

- You can use any network adapter that is certified for Network Driver Interface Specification (NDIS).

- Use only network adapters that comply with specifications for the Peripheral Component Interconnect (PCI) local bus. Do not use network adapters compatible with an Industrial Standard Architecture (ISA) or Extended Industrial Standard Architecture (EISA) bus.

- For each server cluster network, use only identical network adapters on all nodes (that is, the same make, model, and firmware version). This is not a requirement, but it is strongly recommended. Consider the loads on each type of adapter and plan accordingly; for example, the private network adapters can require 10 MB to 100 MB of throughput, although the public network adapters can require 1 gigabyte (GB) of throughput.

Eliminating Single Points of Failure in Your Network Design

You must incorporate failsafe measures within the cluster network design. To achieve this end, adhere to the following rules:

- Configure at least two of the cluster networks for internal cluster communication to eliminate a single point of failure. A server cluster whose nodes are connected by only one network is not supported.

- Design each cluster network so that it fails independently of other cluster networks. This requirement implies that the components that make up any two networks must be physically independent. For example, the use of a multiport network adapter to attach a node to two cluster networks does not meet this requirement if the ports share circuitry.

- If using multihoming nodes, make sure the adapters reside on separate subnets.

- Do not connect multiple adapters on one node to the same network; doing so does not provide fault tolerance or load balancing.

Note

If a cluster node has multiple adapters attached to one network, the Cluster service will recognize only one network adapter per node per subnet.

The best way to guard against network failure in your server cluster is by teaming network adapters. By grouping network adapters on multiple ports to a single physical segment, you can provide fault tolerance to your cluster network. If a port fails — whether the failure occurs on the adapter, cable, switch port, or switch — another port takes over automatically. To the operating system and other devices on the network, this failover is transparent.

An important consideration, however, is that networks dedicated to internal server cluster communication cannot be teamed. Teaming network adapters is supported only on networks that are not dedicated to internal cluster traffic. Teaming network adapters on all cluster networks concurrently is not supported. There are alternative methods for achieving redundancy on networks that are dedicated to internal cluster traffic. These alternatives include adding a second private network, which avoids the cost of adding network adapters (however, this second network must be for intra-cluster network traffic only).

Teaming network adapters on other cluster networks is acceptable; however, if communication problems occur on a teamed network, it is recommended that you disable teaming.

Determining Domain Controller Access for Server Clusters

For Windows Server 2003 clusters to function properly, any node that forms part of the cluster must validate the Cluster service account in the local domain. To do this, each node must be able to establish a secure channel with a domain controller. If a domain controller cannot validate the account, the Cluster service does not start. This is also true for other clustered applications that need account validation, such as SQL Server and Microsoft® Exchange 2000. There are three ways to provide the necessary access, presented here in order of preference:

- Configure cluster nodes as member servers within a Windows domain and give them fast, reliable connectivity to a local domain controller.

- If the connectivity between cluster nodes and domain controllers is slow or unreliable, locate a domain controller within the cluster.

- Configure the cluster nodes as domain controllers, so that the Cluster service account can always be validated.

The security rights applicable to a domain controller administrator are often inappropriate or nonfunctional for a cluster administrator. A domain controller administrator can apply global policy settings to a domain controller that might conflict with the cluster role. Domain controller administrative roles span the network; this model generally does not suit the security model for clusters.

It is strongly recommended that you do not configure the cluster nodes as domain controllers, if at all possible. But if you must configure the cluster nodes as domain controllers, follow these guidelines:

- If one node in a two-node cluster is a domain controller, both nodes must be domain controllers. If you have more than two nodes, you must configure at least two nodes as domain controllers. This gives you failover assurance for the domain controller services.

- A domain controller that is idle can use between 130 MB and 140 MB of Random Access Memory (RAM), which includes running the Cluster service. If these domain controllers have to replicate with other domain controllers within the domain and across domains, replication traffic can saturate bandwidth and degrade overall performance.

- If the cluster nodes are the only domain controllers, they must be Domain Name System (DNS) servers as well. You must address the problem of not registering the private interface in DNS, especially if the interface is connected by a crossover cable (two-node cluster only). The DNS servers must support dynamic updates. You must configure each domain controller and cluster node with a primary — and at least one secondary — DNS server. Each DNS server needs to point to itself for primary DNS resolution and to the other DNS servers for secondary resolution.

- If the cluster nodes are the only domain controllers, they must also be global catalog servers.

- The first domain controller in the forest takes on all single-master operation roles. You can redistribute these roles to each node; however, if a node fails over, the single-master operation roles that the node has taken on are no longer available.

- If a domain controller is so busy that the Cluster service is unable to gain access to the quorum as needed, the Cluster service might interpret this as a resource failure and cause the resource group to fail over to the other node.

- Clustering other applications, such as SQL Server or Exchange 2000, in a scenario where the nodes are also domain controllers can result in poor performance and low availability due to resource constraints. Be sure to test this configuration thoroughly in a lab environment before you deploy it.

- You must promote a cluster node to a domain controller by using the Active Directory Installation Wizard before you create a cluster on that node or add it to an existing cluster.

- Practice extreme caution when demoting a domain controller that is also a cluster node. When a node is demoted from a domain controller, security settings are changed. For example, certain domain accounts and groups revert back to the default built-in accounts and groups originally on the sever. This means the security ID (SID) of the Domain Admins group changes to that of the local Administrators group. As a result, the Administrators entry in the security descriptor for the Cluster service is no longer valid because its SID still matches the Domain Admins group, and not the SID for the local Administrators group.

Protecting Data from Failure or Disaster

You must take steps to protect and ensure the integrity of your data. If your organization spans more than one physical site, for example, you might want to cluster resources across sites in what is known as a geographically dispersed cluster. Geographically dispersed clusters maintain high availability even when communication with another site is disrupted or lost. And all server clusters, whether in a single site or spread across two sites, need a plan for backing up application data regularly, and for recovering data in the event of a failure or disaster.

Figure 7.22 displays the process for ensuring the data integrity for your server cluster.

Figure 7.22   Protecting Data from Failure or Disaster

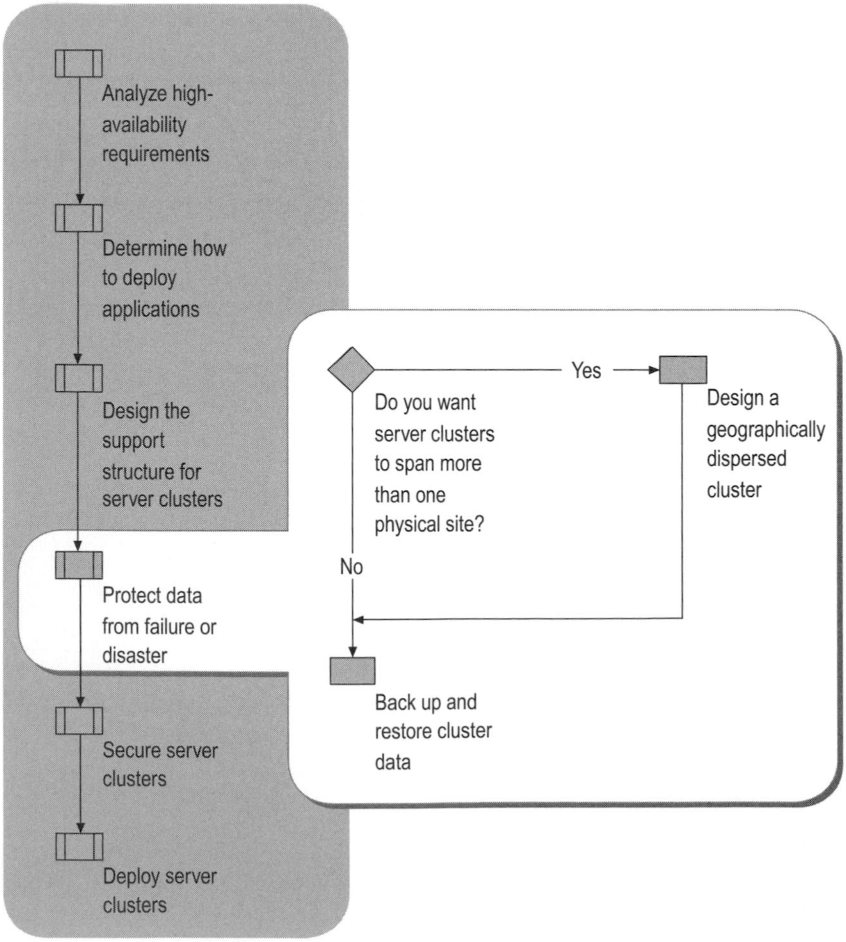

Designing a Geographically Dispersed Cluster

Geographically dispersed server clusters ensure that a complete outage at one site does not cause a loss of access to the application being hosted. All nodes hosting an application must exist within the same cluster. Therefore, to provide fault tolerance, a single cluster spans multiple sites.

Important

Windows Server 2003 supports two-site geographically dispersed clusters. However, Microsoft does not provide a software mechanism for replicating application data from one site to another. Instead, Microsoft works with hardware and software vendors to provide a complete solution. For more information about qualified clustering solutions, see the Windows Server Catalog link or the Geographically Dispersed Clusters link on the Web Resources page at http://www.microsoft.com/windows/reskits/webresources.

A geographically dispersed cluster requires multiple storage arrays, at least one in each site, to ensure that in the event of failure at one site, the remaining site will have local copies of the data. In addition, the nodes of a geographic cluster are connected to storage in such a way that when there is a failure at one site or a failure in communication between sites, the functioning nodes can still connect to storage at their own site. For example, in the simple two-site cluster configuration shown in Figure 7.23, the nodes in Site A are directly connected to the storage in Site A, so they can access data with no dependencies on Site B.

Figure 7.23 Geographically Dispersed Cluster

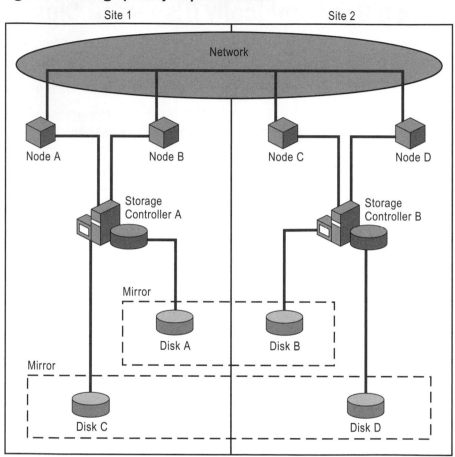

In Figure 7.23, Nodes A and B are connected to one array in Storage Controller A, while Node C and Node D are connected to another array in Storage Controller B. These storage arrays present a single view of the disks spanning both arrays. In other words, Disks A and B are combined into a single logical device (by using mirroring, either at the controller level or the host level). Logically, the arrays appear to be a single device that can fail over between Nodes A, B, C, and D.

Note

For a job aid to assist you in gathering your requirements for a multisite server cluster and organizing the necessary, preparatory information, see "Planning Checklist for Geographically Dispersed Clusters" (Sdcclu_1.doc) on the Microsoft® Windows® Server 2003 Deployment Kit companion CD (or see "Planning Checklist for Geographically Dispersed Clusters" on the Web at http://www.microsoft.com/reskit).

Design Requirements for Geographically Dispersed Clusters

Although there are many requirements in setting up a geographically dispersed cluster, at the most fundamental level your design has to meet two requirements:

- Both sites must have independent copies of the same data. The goal of a geographically dispersed cluster is that if one site is lost, such as from a natural disaster, the applications can continue running at the other site. For read-only data, the challenge is relatively simple: the data can be cloned, and one instance can run at each site. However, in a typical stateful application, in which data is updated frequently, you must consider how changes made to the data at one site are replicated to the other site.

- When there is a failure at one site, the application must restart at the other site. Even if the application data is replicated to all sites, you need to know how the application is restarted at an alternate site when the site that was running the application fails.

 Important

The hardware and software configuration of a geographically dispersed cluster must be certified and listed in the Windows Server Catalog. Also, be sure to involve your hardware manufacturer in your design decisions. Frequently, third-party software and drivers are required for geographically dispersed clusters to function correctly. Microsoft Product Support Services might not be aware of how these components interact with Windows Clustering. For more information about hardware and software configurations, see the Windows Server Catalog link on the Web Resources page at http://www.microsoft.com/windows/reskits/webresources.

Network Requirements for Geographically Dispersed Clusters

The following network requirements pertain to all server clusters, but are particularly important with regard to geographically dispersed clusters:

- All nodes must be on the same subnet. The nodes in the cluster can be on different physical networks, but the private and public network connections between cluster nodes must appear as a single, nonrouted Local Area Network (LAN). You can do this by creating virtual LANs (VLANs).

- Each VLAN must fail independently of all other cluster networks. The reason for this rule is the same as for regular LANs — to avoid a single point of failure.

- The roundtrip communication latency between any pair of nodes cannot exceed 500 milliseconds. If communication latency exceeds this limit, the Cluster service assumes the node has failed and will potentially fail over resources.

Data Replication in Geographically Dispersed Clusters

Data can be replicated between sites with different techniques, and at different levels in the clustering infrastructure. At the block level (known as *disk-device-level replication* or *disk-device-level mirroring*), replication is performed by the storage controllers or by mirroring the software. At the file-system level (replication of file system changes), the host software performs the replication. Finally, at the application level, the applications themselves can replicate data. An example of application-level replication is Microsoft SQL Server log shipping.

The method of data replication that is used depends on the requirements of the application and the business needs of the organization that owns the cluster.

Synchronous vs. Asynchronous Replication

When planning geographically dispersed clusters, you need to understand your data consistency needs in different failure and recovery scenarios and work with the solution vendors to meet your requirements. Different geographically dispersed cluster solutions provide different replication and redundancy strategies. Determine the support requirements of your applications with regard to replication -- in geographically dispersed server clusters, the type of data replication is just as important as the level at which it occurs. There are two types of data replication: synchronous and asynchronous.

Synchronous replication is when an application performs an operation on one node at one site, and then that operation is not completed until the change has been made on the other sites. Using synchronous, block-level replication as an example, if an application at Site A writes a block of data to a disk mirrored to Site B, the I/O operation will not be completed until the change has been made to both the disk on Site A and the disk on Site B. Because of this potential latency, synchronous replication can slow or otherwise detract from application performance for your users.

Asynchronous replication is when a change is made to the data on Site A and that change eventually makes it to Site B. In asynchronous replication, if an application at Site A writes a block of data to a disk mirrored to Site B, then the I/O operation is complete as soon as the change is made to the disk at Site A. The replication software transfers the change to Site B (in the background) and eventually makes that change to Site B. With asynchronous replication, the data at Site B can be out of date with respect to Site A at any point in time.

Different vendors implement asynchronous replication in different ways. Some preserve the order of operations and others do not. This is very important, because if a solution preserves ordering, then the disk at Site B might be out of date, but it will always represent a state that existed at Site A at some point in the past. This means Site B is *crash consistent*: the data at Site B represents the data that would exist at Site A if Site A had crashed at that point in time. Conversely, if a solution does not preserve ordering, the I/O operations might be applied at Site B in an arbitrary order. In this case, the data set at Site B might never have existed at Site A. Many applications can recover from crash-consistent states; very few can recover from out-of-order I/O operation sequences.

 Caution

Geographically dispersed server clusters must never use asynchronous replication unless the order of I/O operations is preserved. If this order is not preserved, the data that is replicated to the second site can appear corrupt to the application and be totally unusable.

Mirroring and replication solutions are implemented differently, depending on the vendor, the business needs of the organization, and the logistics of the cluster. In general terms, however, for every disk there is a master copy and one or more secondary copies. The master is modified, and then the changes are propagated to the secondary copies.

In the case of disk-device-level replication, the secondary disk might not be visible to the applications. If it is visible, it will be a read-only copy of the device. When there is a failover, a cluster resource typically designates one of the secondary disks to be the new primary, and the old primary becomes a secondary. In other words, most of the mirroring solutions are master-secondary, one-way mirror sets. This is usually on a per-disk basis, so some disks might have the master at one site and others might have the master at another site.

Majority Node Set Quorum in Geographically Dispersed Clusters

Although geographically dispersed clusters can use a standard quorum, presenting the quorum as a single logical shared drive between sites can create design issues. Majority node set clusters solve these issues by allowing the quorum to be stored on the local hard disk of each node.

Applications in a geographically dispersed cluster are typically set up to fail over in the same manner as those in a single-site cluster; however, the total failover solution is inherently more complex. The Cluster service provides health monitoring and failure detection of the applications, the nodes, and the communications links, but there are cases where it cannot differentiate between various failure modes.

Consider two identical sites, each having the same number of nodes and running the same software. If a complete failure of all communication (both network and storage fabric) occurs between the sites, neither site can continue without human intervention because neither site has sufficient information about the other site's continuity.

As discussed in "Choosing a Cluster Model" earlier in this chapter, the server cluster architecture requires that a single-quorum resource in the cluster be used as the tiebreaker to avoid split-brain scenarios. Although split-brain scenarios can happen in single-site clusters, they are much more likely to occur in geographically dispersed clusters.

If communication between two sites in a geographically dispersed server cluster were to fail, none of the cluster nodes in either site could determine which of the following is true:

- Communication between sites failed and the other site is still alive.

- The other site is dead and no longer available to run applications.

This problem is solved when one of the partitions takes control of the quorum resource. However, with majority node set clusters, the process is different than in a traditional (single-site, single-quorum) server cluster. Traditional clusters can continue as long as one of the nodes owns the quorum disk, and traditional server clusters can therefore continue even if only one node out of the configured set of nodes is running (if that node owns the quorum disk). By contrast, a server cluster running with a majority node set quorum resource will start up (or continue running) only if a majority of the nodes configured for the cluster are running, and if all nodes in that majority can communicate with each other.

When designing your server cluster with a majority node set quorum, consider this difference, because it can affect how majority node set clusters behave when the server cluster is partitioned and during split-brain scenarios. This "more than half" quorum requirement makes the number of nodes in your server cluster very important. For more information about majority node set quorum cluster models, see "Model 3: Majority node set server cluster configuration" in Help and Support Center for Windows Server 2003.

Single Quorum in Geographically Dispersed Clusters

It is possible to use a single quorum disk resource in a geographically dispersed cluster, provided the quorum is replicated across sites, such as through disk mirroring. When a single quorum is used across multiple sites, the quorum data must always use synchronous replication, although application data can be replicated either synchronously or asynchronously (assuming there are no application-specific restrictions). This is because the quorum could become corrupt during asynchronous replication, rendering different quorum data on each site, and your server cluster would then fail.

Backing Up and Restoring Cluster Data

In order to maintain high availability on your server clusters, it is important to back up server cluster data on a regular basis. The Backup or Restore Wizard in Windows Server 2003 (Ntbackup.exe) has been enhanced to enable backups and restores of the local cluster database, in addition to the capacity to restore configurations locally and to all nodes in a cluster.

 Note

In addition to the Backup or Restore Wizard, Ntbackup.exe is also available as a command-line tool. For more information about Ntbackup.exe, in Help and Support Center for Windows Server 2003, click **Tools**, and then click **Command-line reference A-Z.**

Although there are some scenarios in which you can restore data without having a backup data set available, your options are limited. Providing true high availability to your users is possible only by backing up your data on a regular basis. For information about what you can do to restore your server cluster without a backup, see the Server Cluster (MSCS) Backup and Recovery Best Practices link on the Web Resources page at http://www.microsoft.com/windows/reskits/webresources.

A new backup and restore feature in Windows Server 2003 is Automated System Recovery (ASR), which helps you recover a system that will not start. ASR is a two-part recovery option consisting of ASR backup and ASR restore, both of which are accessed through the Advanced mode of the Backup or Restore Wizard. Note that ASR backs up only the partition used by the operating system. You must back up other partitions by using the standard Backup or Restore Wizard.

You can use ASR to recover a cluster node, the quorum disk, and the signatures on any lost shared disks. You can use ASR to restore a Windows Server 2003 installation when:

- A node cannot start as the result of damaged or missing Windows Server 2003 system files. ASR verifies and replaces damaged critical system files.

- There is a hardware failure, such as disk failure. ASR restores the installation to the state of your most recent ASR backup.

- The Cluster service will not start on the local node because the Cluster database is corrupt or missing.

- The disk signature has changed on one of the shared disks as a result of a disk replacement or other disk-related issue, causing a shared disk to fail to come online.

For more information about ASR, see "Automated System Recovery (ASR) overview" in Help and Support Center for Windows Server 2003.

For specific information about backing up cluster disk signatures and partition layouts, the cluster quorum, and data on cluster nodes, see "Backing up and restoring server clusters" in Help and Support Center for Windows Server 2003. Details include how to restore the cluster database on a local node, how to restore the contents of a cluster quorum disk for all nodes in a cluster, and how to repair a damaged cluster node by using ASR.

Help and Support Center for Windows Server 2003 also includes:

- The specific permissions that a cluster administrator needs in order to perform each backup and restore procedure. For example, to back up the data on cluster nodes or to restore a damaged cluster node using Automated System Recovery, you must be a member of the Administrators group on the local computer, or you must have been delegated the appropriate authority. For the specific access control permissions you need to perform each backup and restore operation, see "Backing up and restoring server clusters" in Help and Support Center for Windows Server 2003.

- Ten failover and restore scenarios that describe failure from cluster disk data loss, cluster quorum corruption, cluster disk corruption or failure, and complete cluster failure. Scenarios include symptoms that are common indications of a server cluster failure, and methods for recovering from such failures. For more information see "Backing up and restoring server clusters" in Help and Support Center for Windows Server 2003.

 Important

For information about backing up applications that run on your server cluster, consult the documentation for the application.

Securing Server Clusters

Security considerations must be present in all aspects of your cluster design. After your clustering infrastructure is in place, you need to consider a number of recommended policies and configurations to ensure that your server clusters are secure. Figure 7.24 shows an overview of security deployment considerations.

Figure 7.24   Securing Your Server Clusters

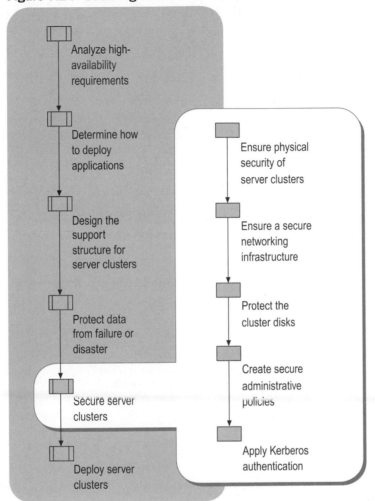

Before beginning your security design, see "Best practices for securing server clusters" in Help and Support Center for Windows Server 2003.

> **Note**
>
> Do not weaken the default security settings for clustering objects in the operating system. This includes registry keys, files, and devices.

Ensuring the Physical Security of Server Clusters

For servers that must maintain high availability, it is recommended that you restrict physical access to a small number of essential, designated individuals. Locate server clusters and their storage in physically secure locations.

When you review your policies for keeping your computer room secure, be sure to include the following:

- Restrict access to the instruction sheets that you create, such as the directions for server recovery.

- Review your administration practices to ensure that only trusted, authorized personnel have access to restricted data, such as logs and backup and restore media.

Ensuring a Secure Networking Infrastructure

Standard security devices — such as firewalls, network probes, and management tools to detect irregular traffic — must be in place before you put sensitive data on server clusters (or any other servers).

 Note

Although you can use IP security (IPSec) with server clusters, IPSec was not designed for use in failover situations. You can, however, use IPSec if your business need for secure connectivity outweighs your need for continuous client access during failover. For more information about IPSec and clusters, see article Q306677, "IPSec Is Not Designed for Failover," in the Microsoft Knowledge Base. To find this article, click the Microsoft Knowledge Base link on the Web Resources page at http://www.mmicrosoft.com/windows/reskits/webresources.

In order to create a secure environment for your server clusters, begin with the following basic network precautions:

- Secure your network with firewalls and management tools that can detect irregular network traffic.

- Restrict physical access to network hardware (routers, hubs, and switches) to protect them from unauthorized individuals.

- Make sure administrative permissions are adhered to, and that logs and other resources are protected by access control lists (ACLs).

- Ensure that network services such as the Active Directory, DNS, and DHCP, and Windows Internet Name Service (WINS) are protected from compromise. Any compromise of these infrastructure services can lead to a compromise of the Cluster service itself.

Protecting Server Clusters from Network Flooding

The Cluster service uses User Data Protocol (UDP) port 3343 for intracluster communication. This communication includes heartbeat traffic, which detects node failure, and cluster control operations. Some of this communication (such as heartbeats) is time sensitive. If there is a significant load on the ports due to network flood attacks, the result can be false node-failure detection, which can cause unnecessary failover operations, leading to application downtime. To ensure that node-failure detection cannot be compromised in this way, secure the private network or networks between cluster nodes so that only trusted nodes can send data.

Protecting Server Clusters from Unauthorized Access

The Cluster service provides remote management capabilities through the Cluster API so that you can manage the cluster from a management workstation. If you are administrating clusters remotely, be sure to use only trusted computers. The Cluster API uses the NTLM authentication protocol to authenticate the administrator on the cluster. This allows the cluster to verify that the administrator has sufficient administrative credentials to manage the cluster; however, it does not provide mutual authentication. In other words, the client has no guarantee that the node or cluster it is connected to is the real cluster.

If an unauthorized computer appears on the network with the same IP address or network name assigned to the cluster (assuming DNS information was compromised), the unauthorized computer can masquerade as the cluster. If that unauthorized computer also appears to implement the Cluster API, the unauthorized computer can intercept any management commands sent to the cluster. In many cases, this might not represent a threat because the administrator simply receives a false positive or negative that an action was performed. However, there are some sensitive operations (such as changing the cluster configuration) during which an unauthorized recipient could potentially collect cluster configuration data that might help to extend the attack surface.

This type of masquerade attack cannot occur until a number of conditions are met:

- The unauthorized computer must be visible on the same subnet as the target cluster and respond to traffic to the cluster IP address (this can be the IP address of the physical computers or the IP address of virtual servers hosted by the computer).

- In a typical environment, the unauthorized computer can take over the IP address only if the cluster node or virtual server is not running.

- The unauthorized computer must appear to implement the Cluster API.

- The administrator or an operational procedure must change the configuration that includes the sensitive data (for example, the administrator must change the Cluster service account password).

To protect against such attacks, the subnets on which the server clusters reside must be protected in the following ways:

- The subnet used by the cluster nodes must not extend beyond the set of nodes that can be physically secured or trusted. You must ensure that unauthorized or potentially compromised computers cannot attach to the subnet that contains the clusters. Because this network typically contains domain controllers, DNS servers, WINS servers, DHCP servers, and other network infrastructure, you must take steps to ensure that these infrastructure servers are also secure.

- Make sure that only nodes in the cluster are visible on a private network (multiple clusters can use the same private network). Make sure that no other network infrastructure servers or other application servers exist on the private subnet. This can be achieved by physically constraining the network itself (for example, ensuring that the private network is a LAN that is only connected to the cluster nodes), or by isolating the private networks by using VLAN-capable switches.

Protecting the Cluster Disks

Windows Clustering supports only NTFS on cluster disks. This ensures that file protection can be used to safeguard data on the cluster disks. Because the cluster disks can fail over between nodes, you must use only domain user accounts (or Local System, Network Service, or Local Service) to protect files. Local user accounts on one computer have no meaning on other computers in the cluster.

Cluster disks are periodically checked for health. The Cluster service account must have Write access to the top-level directory of all cluster disks. If the Cluster service account does not have Write access, the disk might be mistakenly declared as failed.

Evaluating Upgrade Risks

On the Microsoft® Windows® 2000 Server and Microsoft® Windows NT® version 4.0 operating systems, the default security attributes of the cluster log files in the *windir*\Cluster directory and the default security attributes of the quorum directory allow any authenticated user to read the contents. The security of these directories has been tightened in Windows Server 2003 to stop nonadministrator access altogether, ensuring that unauthorized users cannot gain information about the cluster configuration. However, these security attributes are not modified when you upgrade to Windows Server 2003, so on an upgraded Windows Server 2003 cluster node, all authenticated users might have Read access to these directories. Be sure to manually set the permissions to conform to the minimum access requirements.

 Note

Be aware that if you install any service packs in the future, the service packs might reset permissions that have been configured manually.

Protecting the Quorum Disk

Never store other application data on the quorum disk. The quorum disk should contain only quorum data.

The quorum disk health determines the health of the entire cluster. If the quorum disk fails, the Cluster service becomes unavailable on all cluster nodes. The Cluster service checks the health of the quorum disk and negotiates for exclusive access to the physical drive by using standard I/O operations. These operations are queued to the device along with any other I/O operations to that device. If extremely heavy traffic delays the Cluster service I/O operations, the Cluster service declares the quorum disk as failed and forces a regroup event to bring the quorum back online somewhere else in the cluster.

To protect against malicious applications that could fill up the quorum disk, or flood the quorum disk with I/O operations, restrict access to the quorum disk to the local Administrators group on the local computer and the Cluster service account. If the quorum disk fills up, the Cluster service might be unable to log required data. In this case, the Cluster service fails, potentially on all cluster nodes.

Protecting the Server Cluster Data Disks

As it does with the quorum disk, the Cluster service periodically checks the health of the cluster data disks. If malicious applications flood the cluster data disks with I/O operations, the Cluster service health check can fail, thereby causing the disk (and any applications that depend on the disk) to fail over to another cluster node, which can result in a denial-of-service attack. To avoid this possibility, restrict access to the cluster data disks to only those applications that store data on the specific disks.

Creating Secure Administrative Policies for Server Clusters

To provide adequate and manageable security for sever clusters, you need to implement appropriate administrative practices and policies. The most important secure administrative policy is to permit only trusted, specially designated workstations to access the Cluster service. Any compromise on computers used to administer the cluster can compromise the cluster. For example, if a workstation from which administrative tools are run can be accessed by unauthorized users, these users can run unreliable or malicious code on the cluster without the knowledge of the cluster administrator. For this reason, it is important to audit both administrative access to the server cluster and changes to the Cluster service account.

The following sections describe best practices for securely administrating a server cluster.

 Note

To change the password of the Cluster service account without taking any nodes offline, it is essential that each node in the cluster have the same Cluster service account.

Verifying Permissions for the Cluster Service Account

The nodes in a server cluster use authenticated communication mechanisms to ensure that only valid members of the cluster can participate in intra-cluster protocols. Authentication of the communication is based on the Cluster service account. The Cluster service creates and maintains files, devices, registry keys, and other objects in the operating system. The default security setting of these objects ensures that unauthorized users cannot impact the cluster configuration or the applications running on the cluster. Making these security settings less restrictive can lead to the cluster being compromised and application data being corrupted.

For the server cluster to function properly, the Cluster service account must have certain permissions associated with it. During cluster installation, some of these rights are granted directly to the Cluster service account while others are inherited when the Cluster service account is made a member of the local Administrators group. The Cluster service account must have rights that allow it to perform the following actions:

- Act as part of the operating system.

- Back up files and directories.

- Adjust memory quotas for a process.

- Increase scheduling priority.

- Log on as a service.

- Restore files and directories.

- Debug programs.

- Manage auditing and security logs.

- Impersonate a client after authentication.

In Windows Server 2003, the Cluster service can publish virtual servers as computer objects in Active Directory. To ensure correct operation, the Cluster service account needs appropriate permissions to manipulate these objects in the Active Directory Computers container.

 Note

Although the Network Name resource publishes a computer object in Active Directory, that computer object must not be used for administrative tasks such as applying Group Policy settings. The only roles for the virtual server computer object are to support Kerberos authentication, and for cluster-aware services that can use Active Directory (such as Message Queuing) to publish service provider information.

Administering Clusters

Cluster administrators can grant permissions to groups or individuals to manage the cluster. There is no fine granularity of control: Either a user has credentials to administer the cluster, or the user does not. Because of the high degree of impact administrators can have on your system's security, granting administrative credentials to a user must be done with careful consideration.

The security descriptor for the Cluster service contains the accounts that are authorized to administrate the cluster. By default, a cluster node's local Administrators group is added to the Cluster service security descriptor. The service accounts LocalSystem and NetworkService are also added to the security descriptor. The local Administrators group and the two accounts cannot be removed from the security descriptor. Be aware that adding a domain user or global group to the local Administrators group gives cluster administrator permissions to that group or account. If a node is evicted from a cluster, or if the last node is removed, the Cluster service account is not removed from the local Administrators group. When you remove a node from the cluster, you must manually remove the Cluster service account from the local Administrators group.

Cluster administrators can manage all aspects of the cluster configuration, including:

- Taking resources offline and bringing resources online.
- Adding and removing nodes from the cluster.
- Adding and removing resources from the cluster.

In addition, cluster administrators are able to shut down the Cluster service on nodes, provided they are also member of the local Administrators group. Apart from the local Administrators group on a node, all other members of the cluster security descriptor must be either domain user accounts, built-in local accounts such as System or NetworkService, or global groups. This ensures that the account is an identical, well-defined, and authorized account on all nodes in the cluster.

The Cluster service account does not need to be a member of the Domain Admins group, because the Cluster service account does not need domain administrator permissions. As a general security guideline, give all accounts the minimal possible permissions.

If you are deploying multiple clusters in a single domain, you can make administration easier by using the same Cluster service account on all nodes. However, you must balance ease of management against the potential security risks associated with using a single account for many clusters. If the account is compromised, the scope of the impact might exceed the benefits you gain by increasing the ease of management. With Windows Server 2003, the Cluster service account password on multiple clusters can be changed at the same time, as long as every node in the cluster is using the same Cluster service account.

Cluster administrators and the Cluster service need to use different accounts to administer the cluster. This allows finer granularity of auditing and allows policy settings (such as password expiration) to be applied to the Cluster service account and the accounts used to administer the cluster.

If you plan to deploy multiple clusters that have different Cluster service accounts, create a global group or universal group that implements all the policy settings described earlier in this section. Then place each Cluster service account into the group. This eases management of the Cluster service accounts by providing a single container for all Cluster service accounts, and a single point of management for changing account policy settings. For example, you could put all cluster nodes and the Cluster service accounts into a single organizational unit (OU) in Active Directory.

Your OU model depends on your Active Directory implementation. If your Windows Server 2003 clusters reside in a Windows NT 4.0 domain, OUs and universal groups are not available.

Follow these guidelines for ease of use and best security:

- If there are multiple clusters in a single domain, use the same Cluster service account on all nodes to make administration easier.

- If you have password expiration policy settings on your Cluster service account, do not use this account for other services.

- Do not use the Cluster service account for SQL Server or Exchange 2000 if you have password expiration policy settings. When multiple services use the same account, coordinating the password change across the Cluster service and other services is complex and can cause the entire cluster or service to become unavailable during a password rotation. It is recommended that you use a dedicated account, which can be maintained independently, for each service.

- With Windows Server 2003, the Cluster service account password can be changed online without taking down the cluster, but only if the Cluster service account is not used by other services.

 Caution
Be sure to change the Cluster service account password before it expires. The cluster will stop functioning when the password expires, because intra-cluster communication can no longer be successfully authenticated.

Applying Kerberos Authentication in a Clustered Environment

Carefully plan your use of Kerberos authentication in a server cluster. By default, Kerberos authentication support for the network name resource is turned off. When Kerberos authentication support is enabled, the Cluster service account must be able to create a virtual computer object in Active Directory.

By default, all users have **Add workstations to the domain** permissions, which allows the creation of computer objects in Active Directory.

> **Note**
>
> By default, authenticated users can join up to ten machine accounts to the domain. This limit does not apply to members of the Administrators or Domain Admins groups, and to those users who have delegated permissions on containers in Active Directory to create and delete computer accounts.

If the **Add workstations to the domain** permission has been removed from the Cluster service account, before enabling Kerberos authentication, a member of the Domain Administrators group must perform one of the following actions:

- Grant the Cluster service account the **Create Computer Objects** permission on the Computers organizational unit in Active Directory.

- Create the computer object manually in Active Directory before enabling Kerberos authentication. If the object is manually created, the Cluster service account must have **Write all properties** access permission to allow it to manipulate the computer object.

> **Caution**
>
> Although the Network Name resource supports the changing of its **Name** property, many services, such as Message Queuing and Microsoft® SQL Server™ 2000, do not support changing the Network Name resource **Name** property. Do not change this property unless you fully understand the implications of doing so. In some cases, changing the Network Name resource **Name** property can lead to loss of data or service failure.

Before you allow clients to access a server cluster, or before failing over the resources to another node, ensure that the domain controllers have replicated newly created computer objects associated with Network Name resources. Until replication is complete, clients might fail to authenticate, or they could authenticate with the default NTLM authentication protocol and not with Kerberos authentication. One way to avoid replication issues with your clients is to not notify clients that the service is available until you are sure replication is complete. The amount of time it takes your directory to replicate information depends on many factors, such as the topology and the amount of network traffic. If you are not sure of the time necessary to allow for replication, replication can be forced with tools such as Ntdsutil.exe. For more information about Ntdsutil.exe, see "Using Ntdsutil" in Help and Support Center for Windows Server 2003.

After you enable Kerberos authentication on a server cluster, do not disable Kerberos authentication on a virtual server without knowing the effects the disabling will have on other services that use that virtual server. Microsoft® Message Queuing (MSMQ), for example, relies on the presence of a virtual computer object and ceases to function if its dependent Network Name resource has Kerberos authentication support disabled.

Use extreme care when you remove Kerberos authentication from a Network Name resource. When you disable Kerberos authentication from a Network Name resource, the computer object is disabled, leaving the system administrator with an explicit decision to delete the computer object. If the object remains in Active Directory, the Network Name resource does not go online. If the computer object is deleted, properties attached by applications that can use Active Directory are also deleted, and the applications might no longer function correctly.

For more information about enabling Kerberos authentication on a virtual server, see "Enable Kerberos authentication for virtual servers" in Help and Support Center for Windows Server 2003, or see articles Q302389, "Description of the Properties of the Cluster Network Name Resource in Windows Server 2003," and Q307532, "How to Troubleshoot the Cluster Service Account When It Modifies Computer Objects," in the Microsoft Knowledge Base. To find these articles, see the Microsoft Knowledge Base link on the Web Resources page at http://www.microsoft.com/windows/reskits/webresources.

Deploying Server Clusters

After your application has been evaluated for server cluster deployment, and your hardware and network are in place, you can deploy your server cluster on Windows Server 2003, Enterprise Edition or Windows Server 2003, Datacenter Edition. Figure 7.25 illustrates the process for installing or upgrading a server cluster.

Figure 7.25 Deploying a Server Cluster

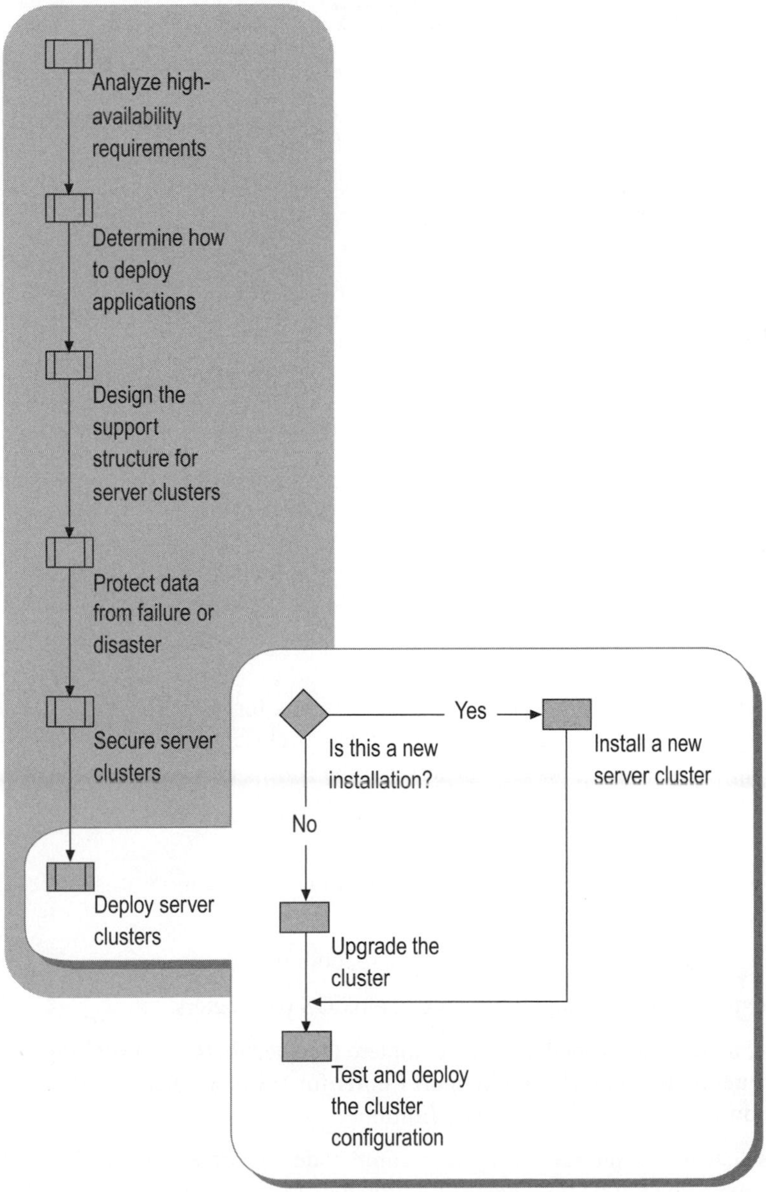

Important

Server clusters have very specific hardware requirements. It is extremely important that you select hardware configurations approved by Microsoft for Windows server clusters. For more information about approved hardware configurations, see the Windows Server Catalog link on the Web Resources page at http://www.microsoft.com/windows/reskits/webresources.

Installing a New Server Cluster

This section is designed as an overview of the new server cluster installation process and is not intended as an installation guide. For detailed information about creating server clusters, see "Checklists: Creating server clusters" in Help and Support Center for Windows Server 2003.

Before installing Windows Server 2003, Enterprise Edition or Windows Server 2003, Datacenter Edition on your cluster nodes, consult "Planning for Deployments" in *Planning, Testing, and Piloting Deployment Projects* in this kit. Information in that chapter includes methods for taking inventory of your current IT environment and how to create a functional specification that you can use to create a clear and thorough cluster deployment plan. In addition, gather the following materials and have them available for reference during installation:

- A list of all services and applications to be deployed on server clusters.

- A plan that defines which applications are to be installed on which nodes.

- Failover policies for each service or application, including resource group planning.

- A selected quorum model.

- A physical and logical security plan for the cluster.

- Specifications for capacity requirements.

- Documentation for your storage system.

- The Windows Server Catalog — approved device drivers for network hardware and storage systems. For more information about support for server clusters, see article Q309395, "The Microsoft Support Policy for Server Clusters and the Hardware Compatibility List." To find this article, see the Microsoft Knowledge Base link on the Web Resources page at http://www.microsoft.com/windows/reskits/webresources.

- Documentation supplied with all cluster hardware and all applications or services that will be deployed on the server cluster.

- An IP addressing scheme for the cluster networks, both private and public.

- A selected cluster name, its length limited by NetBIOS parameters.

Before installing, it is recommended that you complete the checklists in " Installing and upgrading on cluster nodes" in Help and Support Center for Windows Server 2003, Datacenter Edition and Windows Server 2003, Enterprise Edition.

Completing these checklists and reviewing the recommended information in Help and Support Center for Windows Server 2003, Datacenter Edition and Windows Server 2003, Enterprise Edition ensures that your hardware and network components are compatible and supported by Microsoft.

Additionally, be sure to read " Best practices" and the conceptual topics under "Installing Windows Server 2003, Enterprise Edition on cluster nodes" in Help and Support Center for Windows Server 2003, Enterprise Edition

Upgrading a Cluster

If you are upgrading an existing server cluster from the Microsoft® Windows NT Server 4.0, Enterprise Edition or Windows® 2000 Advanced Server operating system, you have a choice of the following:

- Take the servers offline, upgrade the operating system, and rebuild the server cluster.

- Perform a rolling upgrade.

A *rolling upgrade* is the process of upgrading cluster nodes by turns while the other nodes continue to provide service. The server cluster downtime is reduced to a few minutes, which is the time needed to move resources from one node to another. Note that you cannot perform a rolling upgrade directly from Windows NT 4.0 to Windows Server 2003, but you can upgrade to Windows 2000 Advanced Server and then upgrade to Windows Server 2003, Enterprise Edition. Rolling upgrades are described in "Rolling Upgrades" later in this chapter.

 Important

Consult with the software vendors, or your software documentation, to be certain that all applications and services currently running on your server clusters will be able to function on Windows Server 2003.

Upgrading by Rebuilding a Server Cluster

The process of upgrading a server cluster by taking the nodes offline, upgrading the operating system, and then rebuilding the cluster requires the same preparation as described in "Installing a New Server Cluster" earlier in this chapter.

Checklists for Upgrading a Server Cluster

Before upgrading a Windows NT Server 4.0, Enterprise Edition server cluster or a Windows 2000 Advanced Server cluster, it is recommended that you complete the checklist Preparation for upgrading a cluster" in Help and Support Center for Windows Server 2003, Datacenter Edition and Windows Server 2003, Enterprise Edition.

Additionally, be sure to read the relevant conceptual topics under "Upgrading to Windows Server 2003, Enterprise Edition on cluster nodes" in Help and Support Center for Windows Server 2003, Enterprise Edition and "Upgrading to Windows Server 2003, Datacenter Edition on cluster nodes" in Help and Support Center for Windows Server 2003, Enterprise Edition. Also available is information specific to Windows NT 4.0 server clusters running the Microsoft Distributed Transaction Coordinator (DTC) and MSMQ applications, and Windows NT 4.0 server clusters running Internet Information Services (IIS).

For information about upgrading clusters from Windows 2000 Server, see "Upgrade a cluster from Windows 2000" in Help and Support Center for Windows Server 2003, Enterprise Edition. In Help and Support Center forWindows Server 2003, Datacenter Edition, search for this title to view individual topics about how to upgrade clusters containing IIS and clusters containing Message Queueing.

Upgrading from Windows NT Server 4.0, Enterprise Edition

There are extra considerations when upgrading directly to Windows Server 2003, Enterprise Edition from Windows NT Server 4.0, Enterprise Edition. You must be running Windows NT Server 4.0, Enterprise Server, Service Pack 5 or later, and you have to make sure that your server cluster hardware is compatible with Windows Server 2003 (and has enough processing power and memory). Check the Windows Server Catalog to be certain Microsoft will support your Windows NT 4.0 Server cluster after you upgrade to the new operating system.

It is also important to check with your software and service vendors, or the supporting documentation, to be certain that your services and applications still function after you upgrade.

For information about upgrading and reinstating your cluster nodes, see "Upgrade a cluster from Windows NT 4.0" in Help and Support Center for Windows Server 2003, Enterprise Edition. Note that by upgrading directly to Windows Server 2003, there is no way for you to provide service to your users until the upgrade of the entire cluster is complete. For more information about supported hardware for server clusters, see the Windows Server Catalog link on the Web Resources page at http://www.microsoft.com/windows/reskits/webresources.

Rolling Upgrades

Rolling upgrades allow you to upgrade your server clusters while continuing to provide service to your users. Rolling upgrades can be performed for the following scenarios only:

- From Windows 2000 Advanced Server to Windows Server 2003, Enterprise Edition.

- From the Microsoft® Windows® 2000 Datacenter Server operating system to Windows Server 2003, Datacenter Edition.

You cannot perform a rolling upgrade directly from Windows NT 4.0 to Windows Server 2003. To upgrade from Windows NT 4.0, you can perform a rolling upgrade to Windows 2000 and then perform another rolling upgrade to Windows Server 2003. Consult your Windows 2000 documentation for the best way to upgrade your server cluster to Windows 2000 Advanced Server.

As with a standard (offline) upgrade, before performing a rolling upgrade you have to check the Windows Server Catalog to make sure your cluster hardware is supported, and then you have to confirm that your clustered applications and services will be able to run in a Windows Server 2003 cluster. For more information about cluster hardware support, see the Windows Server Catalog link on the Web Resources page at http://www.microsoft.com/windows/reskits/webresources.

For detailed procedures for performing a rolling upgrade, see "Perform a rolling upgrade from Windows 2000" in Help and Support Center for Windows Server 2003. Also available is specific information for upgrading Windows 2000 clusters running IIS and MSMQ, and for upgrading a print spooler resource.

During the process of a rolling upgrade, some of your nodes will be upgraded to Windows Server 2003 while others will still be running Windows 2000, temporarily resulting in a mixed-version cluster. Although mixed version clusters are supported by Windows Server 2003, Datacenter Edition, this is not a desirable configuration. You should upgrade all nodes to the same operating system as soon as possible.

The operation of a mixed-version cluster is complicated if a resource type that you add to the cluster is supported in one version of the operating system but not in the other. For example, the Cluster service in Windows Server 2003, Datacenter Edition supports the Generic Script resource type. However, older versions of the Cluster service do not support it. A mixed-version cluster can run a Generic Script resource on a node running Windows Server 2003, Datacenter Edition, but not on a node running Windows 2000. The Cluster service transparently sets the possible owners of new resource types to prevent these resources from failing over to a Windows 2000 node of a mixed-version cluster. Consequently, when you view the possible owners of a new resource type, a Windows 2000 node will not be in the list, and you will not be able to add this node to the list. If you create such a resource during the mixed-version phase of a rolling upgrade, the resource groups containing those resources will not fail over to a Windows 2000 node.

For information about which services support rolling upgrades, see "Resource behavior during rolling upgrades" in Help and Support Center for Windows Server 2003. Also, before you perform a rolling upgrade, read Relnotes.htm in the \Docs folder of the Windows Server 2003, Enterprise Edition operating system CD, in addition to the product documentation that comes with each application or resource.

If you have a service that is not fully supported during rolling upgrade, you can still perform a last node rolling upgrade. For more information, see "Perform a last node rolling upgrade from Windows 2000" in Help and Support Center for Windows Server 2003. This process entails moving all the applications and resources on your server cluster that do not support rolling upgrades to a single Windows 2000 node. You then upgrade the remaining nodes in the cluster, transfer the applications and resources to the newly upgraded nodes, and upgrade the final node to Windows Server 2003.

Testing and Deploying the Cluster Configuration

You must always test a server cluster configuration prior to live deployment. Ensure that your failover policies work and that the receiving nodes have the required capacity for all failover resources. Perform a benchmark on each server upon initial installation, and monitor the servers to ensure they are staying within operational guidelines. Collect performance data at peak and off-peak periods.

For information about ensuring that your server cluster is ready for a test environment, see "Test cluster failures and failover policies" in Help and Support Center for Windows Server 2003.

After verifying that your servers are running within acceptable tolerances and that failover is properly achieved, pilot test your server clusters in a production environment. A small pilot deployment in a production environment lets you test the effectiveness of your clusters in an environment that simulates the conditions of a full deployment. This allows you to make any necessary adjustments to your cluster design before performing the full deployment.

Complete information about testing and piloting Windows Server 2003 deployments is available in "Designing a Test Environment" and "Designing a Pilot Project" in *Planning, Testing, and Piloting Deployment Projects* of this kit.

Additional Resources

Related Information

- "Designing Network Load Balancing" and "Deploying Network Load Balancing" in this book for more information about designing and deploying Network Load Balancing clusters.

- "Deploying DHCP" in *Deploying Network Services* of this kit for information about deploying clustered DHCP servers.

- "Deploying WINS" in *Deploying Network Services* of this kit for information about deploying clustered WINS servers.

- The SQL Server 2000 Failover Clustering link on the Web Resources page at http://www.microsoft.com/windows/reskits/webresources for more information about deploying clustering solutions with SQL Server 2000.

- The Deploying Microsoft Exchange 2000 Server Service Pack 2 Clusters link on the Web Resources page at http://www.microsoft.com/windows/reskits/webresources for more information about using Exchange 2000 Server clusters running on Windows 2000 Server.

- Article 814607, "Microsoft Support for Server Clusters with 3rd Party System Components." To find this article, see the Microsoft Knowledge Base link on the Web Resources page at http://www.microsoft.com/windows/reskits/webresources.

- Article 309395, "The Microsoft Support Policy for Server Clusters and the Hardware Compatibility List." To find this article, see the Microsoft Knowledge Base link on the Web Resources page at http://www.microsoft.com/windows/reskits/webresources.

Related Tools

- DiskPart.exe

  You can use DiskPart.exe to manage objects (disks, partitions, or volumes) by using scripts or direct input from a command prompt. For more information about DiskPart.exe, in Help and Support Center for Windows Server 2003, click **Tools**, and then click **Command-line reference A-Z**.

- Mountvol.exe

  You can use this command-line utility to create, delete, or list a volume mount point. Mountvol.exe is a way to link volumes without requiring a drive letter. For more information, see "Mountvol" in Help and Support Center for Windows Server 2003.

- Ntbackup.exe

  You can use this backup tool to perform backup operations at a command prompt or from a batch file using the ntbackup command followed by various parameters. For more information about Ntbackup.exe, in Help and Support Center for Windows Server 2003, click **Tools**, and then click **Command-line reference A-Z**.

- Clusdiag.exe

  You can use the Cluster Diagnostics and Verification Tool (ClusDiag.exe) to run diagnostic tests. These tests will help you verify the functionality of a cluster and troubleshoot cluster failures using the generated log files. For more information about Clusdiag.exe, in Help and Support Center for Windows Server 2003, click **Tools**, and then click **Command-line reference A-Z**.

Related Job Aids

- "Planning Checklist for Geographically Dispersed Clusters" (Sdcclu_1.doc) on the *Windows Server 2003 Deployment Kit* companion CD (or see "Planning Checklist for Geographically Dispersed Clusters" on the Web at http://www.microsoft.com/reskit).

Related Help Topics

For best results in identifying Help topics by title, in Help and Support Center, under the **Search** box, click **Set search options**. Under **Help Topics**, select the **Search in title only** checkbox.

- "Server cluster components" and "Cluster objects" in Help and Support Center for Windows Server 2003 for an overview of server clusters.

- "Choosing applications to run on a server cluster" in Help and Support Center for Windows Server 2003.

- "Determining failover and move policies for groups" in Help and Support Center for Windows Server 2003.

- "Storage configuration options" in Help and Support Center for Windows Server 2003.

- "Mountvol" in Help and Support Center for Windows Server 2003.

- "Quorum resource" in Help and Support Center for Windows Server 2003.

- "Model 3: Majority node set server cluster configuration" in Help and Support Center for Windows Server 2003.

- "Automated System Recovery (ASR) overview" in Help and Support Center for Windows Server 2003.

- "Backing up and restoring server clusters" in Help and Support Center for Windows Server 2003.

- "Best practices for securing server clusters" in Help and Support Center for Windows Server 2003.

- "Enable Kerberos authentication for virtual servers" in Help and Support Center for Windows Server 2003.

- "Using Ntdsutil" in Help and Support Center for Windows Server 2003.

- " Best practices" and the conceptual topics under "Installing Windows Server 2003, Enterprise Edition on cluster nodes" in Help and Support Center for Windows Server 2003, Enterprise Edition

- "Installing Windows Server 2003, Enterprise Edition on cluster nodes in Help and Support Center for Windows Server 2003, Enterprise Edition

- "Upgrading to Windows Server 2003, Enterprise Edition on cluster nodes" in Help and Support Center for Windows Server 2003, Enterprise Edition.

- "Checklists: Creating server clusters" in Help and Support Center for Windows Server 2003.

- "Upgrade a cluster from Windows 2000" in Help and Support Center for Windows Server 2003, Enterprise Edition. In Help and Support Center forWindows Server 2003, Datacenter Edition, search for this title to view individual topics telling how to upgrade clusters containing IIS and clusters containing Message Queueing.

- "Upgrade a cluster from Windows NT 4.0" in Help and Support Center for Windows Server 2003, Enterprise Edition and Windows Server 2003, Datacenter Edition.

- "Perform a rolling upgrade from Windows 2000" in Help and Support Center for Windows Server 2003, Enterprise Edition and Windows Server 2003, Datacenter Edition.

- "Resource behavior during rolling upgrades" in Help and Support Center for Windows Server 2003, Enterprise Edition and Windows Server 2003, Datacenter Edition.

- "Perform a last node rolling upgrade from Windows 2000" in Help and Support Center for Windows Server 2003, Enterprise Edition and Windows Server 2003, Datacenter Edition.

- "Test cluster failures and failover policies" in Help and Support Center for Windows Server 2003.

CHAPTER 8

Designing Network Load Balancing

Many of your deployments will include mission-critical applications and services. The servers that host your applications and services must be able to support projected increases in the number of users, and they must ensure that users can access mission-critical applications. To fulfill these requirements, your solution must be highly available and scalable. Network Load Balancing (NLB) improves availability and scalability in your solutions by distributing application load across multiple servers.

In This Chapter

Related Information

- For information about deploying Network Load Balancing, see "Deploying Network Load Balancing" in this book.

- For information about server clusters, see "Designing and Deploying Server Clusters" in this book.

Overview of the NLB Design Process

Improving availability and scalability in your solution depends on the applications and services in your organization. A computer running the Microsoft® Windows® Server 2003 operating system can provide a high level of reliability and scalable performance. However, a Network Load Balancing cluster can achieve the higher levels of availability and performance required by mission-critical servers.

A Network Load Balancing cluster comprises multiple servers running any version of the Windows Server 2003 family, including the Microsoft® Windows® Server 2003, Standard Edition; Windows® Server 2003, Enterprise Edition; Windows® Server 2003, Datacenter Edition; and Windows® Server 2003, Web Edition operating systems. The servers are combined to provide greater scalability and availability than is possible with an individual server. Network Load Balancing distributes client requests across the servers to improve scalability. If a server fails, client requests are redistributed to the remaining servers to improve availability. Network Load Balancing can improve scalability and availability for applications and services that communicate with clients that use Transmission Control Protocol (TCP) or User Datagram Protocol (UDP).

The Network Load Balancing design process assumes that you are creating new clusters or that you are redesigning existing Windows Load Balancing Service (WLBS) or Network Load Balancing clusters. Upon completion of the Network Load Balancing design process, you will have a solution that meets or exceeds your scalability and availability requirements.

Note

For a list of additional information to assist you in designing Network Load Balancing clusters, see "Additional Resources" later in this chapter.

NLB Design Process

Creating a Network Load Balancing design involves more than documenting Windows Server 2003 and Network Load Balancing settings on the individual application servers. You must identify the applications and services that can benefit from Network Load Balancing, determine the core set of specifications in your design, ensure that your solution is secure, and provide for scalability and availability. The process for creating your Network Load Balancing design is shown in Figure 8.1.

Figure 8.1   Designing a Network Load Balancing Solution

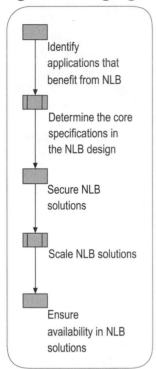

As you create your Network Load Balancing design, document your decisions and use that information to deploy your Network Load Balancing solution.

Note

For a Word document to assist you in documenting your Network Load Balancing design decisions, see "NLB Cluster Host Worksheet" (Sdcnlb_1.doc) on the *Microsoft® Windows® Server 2003 Deployment Kit* companion CD (or see "NLB Cluster Host Worksheet" on the Web at http://www.microsoft.com/reskit).

NLB Fundamentals

To create a successful Network Load Balancing design and to ensure that Network Load Balancing is correct for your solution, you need to know the fundamentals of how Network Load Balancing provides improved scalability and availability, and how Network Load Balancing compares with other strategies for providing scalability and availability.

How NLB Provides Improved Scalability and Availability

Network Load Balancing improves scalability and availability by distributing client traffic across the servers that you include in the Network Load Balancing cluster. Each *cluster host* (a server running on a cluster) runs an instance of the applications supported by your cluster. Network Load Balancing transparently distributes client requests among the cluster hosts. Clients access your cluster by using one or more virtual IP addresses. From the perspective of the client, the cluster appears to be a single server that answers the client request.

As the scalability and availability requirements of your solution change, you can add or remove servers from the cluster as necessary. Network Load Balancing automatically distributes client traffic to take advantage of any servers that you add to the cluster. In addition, when you remove a server from the cluster, Network Load Balancing redistributes the client traffic among the remaining servers in the cluster.

As an example, assume that your organization has a Web application farm running Microsoft® Internet Information Services (IIS) version 6.0 that hosts your organization's Internet presence. As seen in Figure 8.2, Network Load Balancing allows your individual Web application servers to service client requests from the Internet by distributing them across the cluster. On each of the servers, you install IIS 6.0 and Network Load Balancing. By combining the individual Web application servers into a Network Load Balancing cluster, you can load balance the requests to improve client response times and to provide improved fault tolerance in the event that one of the Web application servers fails.

Figure 8.2   Network Load Balancing Cluster in a Web Farm

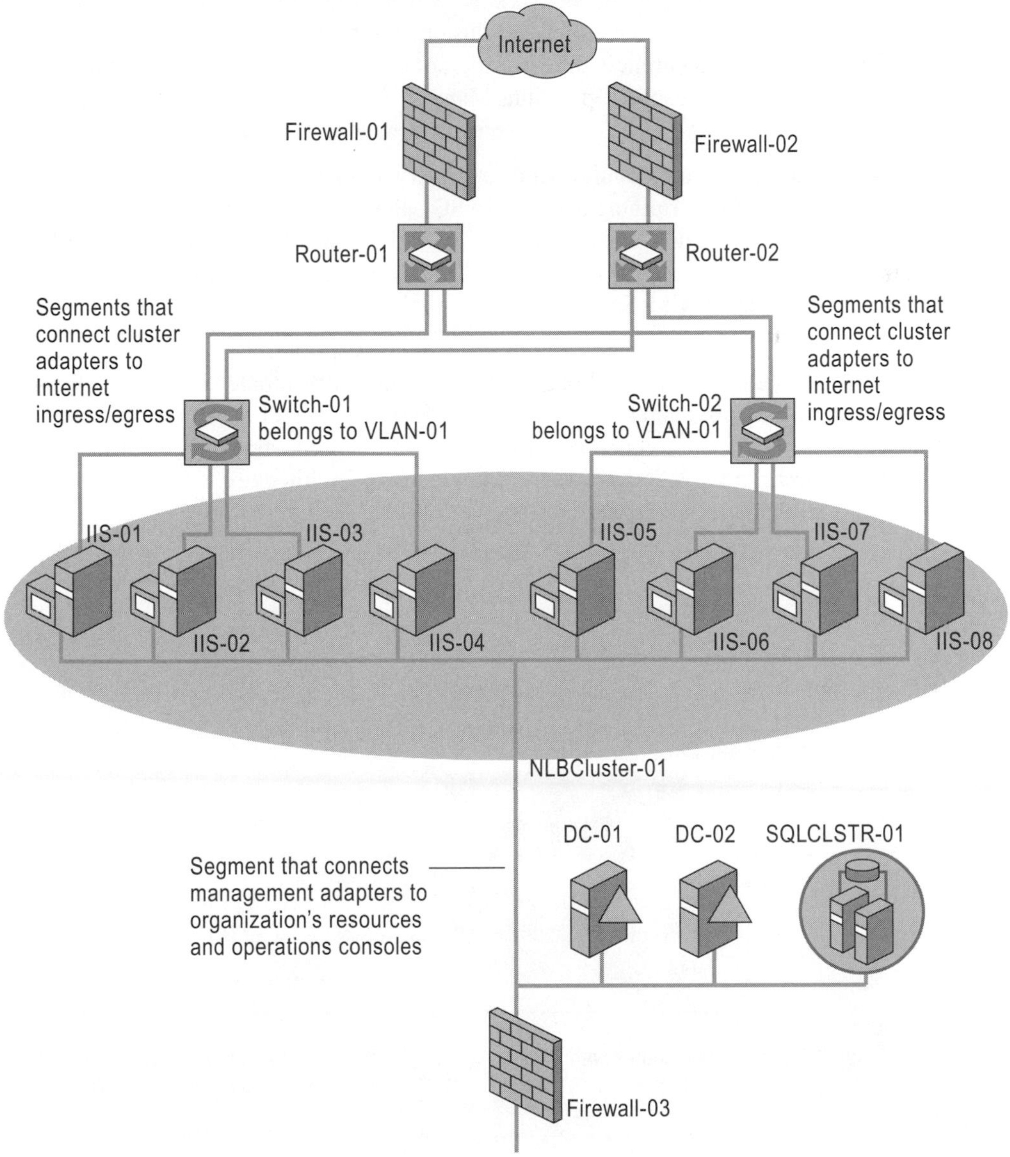

Network Load Balancing automatically detects and recovers when the entire server fails or is manually disconnected from the network. However, Network Load Balancing is unaware of the applications and services running on the cluster, and it does not detect failed applications or services. To provide awareness of application or service failures, you need to add management software, such as Microsoft® Operations Manager (MOM) 2000, Microsoft® Application Center 2000, a third-part party application, or software developed by your organization.

When your design requires fault tolerance for servers that support your Network Load Balancing cluster, such as servers running Microsoft® SQL Server™ 2000, include Microsoft server clusters. For example, you can improve the availability of the network database (SQLCLSTR-01 in Figure 8.2) by creating a two-node server cluster. For more information on server clusters, see "Designing and Deploying Server Clusters" in this book.

Network Load Balancing runs as an intermediate network driver in the Windows Server 2003 network architecture. Network Load Balancing is logically situated beneath higher-level application protocols, such as Hypertext Transfer Protocol (HTTP) and File Transfer Protocol (FTP), and above the network adapter drivers. Figure 8.3 illustrates the relationship of Network Load Balancing in the Windows Server 2003 network architecture.

Figure 8.3   Network Load Balancing in the Windows Server 2003 Network Architecture

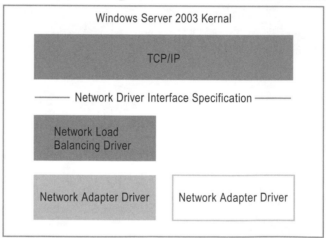

To maximize throughput and to provide high availability in your solution, Network Load Balancing uses a distributed software architecture. A copy of the Network Load Balancing driver runs on each host in the cluster. The Network Load Balancing drivers allow all hosts in the cluster to concurrently receive incoming network traffic for the cluster.

On each host in the cluster, the driver acts as an intermediary between the network adapter driver and the TCP/IP stack. This allows a subset of the incoming network traffic to be received by the host. Network Load Balancing uses this filtering mechanism to distribute incoming client requests among the servers in the cluster.

Network Load Balancing architecture maximizes throughput by using a common media access control (MAC) address to deliver incoming network traffic to all hosts in the cluster. As a result, there is no need to route incoming packets to the individual hosts in the cluster. Because filtering unwanted network traffic is faster than routing packets (which involves receiving, examining, rewriting, and resending), Network Load Balancing delivers higher network throughput than dispatcher-based software load balancing solutions. Also, as you add hosts to your Network Load Balancing cluster, the scalability grows proportionally, and any dependence on a particular host diminishes.

Because Network Load Balancing load balances client traffic across multiple servers, it provides higher availability in your solution. One or more cluster hosts can fail, but the cluster continues to service client requests as long as any cluster hosts are running.

NLB and Round Robin DNS

Round robin Domain Name System (DNS) is a software method for distributing workload among multiple servers, but does not prevent clients from detecting server outages. If one of the servers fails, round robin DNS continues sending client requests to the server until a network administrator detects the failure and removes the server from the DNS address list. This results in service disruption for clients.

In contrast, Network Load Balancing automatically detects servers that have been disconnected from the cluster and redistributes client requests to the remaining servers. Unlike round robin DNS, this prevents clients from sending requests to the failed servers.

For more information about methods for improving availability and scalability, see "Planning for High Availability and Scalability" in this book.

Identifying Applications That Benefit from NLB

The first step in creating your Network Load Balancing design, as illustrated in Figure 8.4, is to determine if any of your applications can benefit from the improved scalability and availability provided by Network Load Balancing. Your applications include not only applications in the traditional sense, such as Web applications, but also Windows Server 2003 network services, such as virtual private network (VPN) remote access.

Figure 8.4   Identifying Applications That Benefit from Network Load Balancing

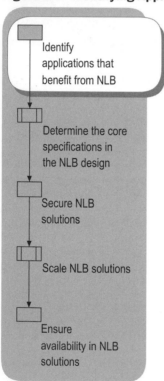

Beyond using TCP/IP, an application that works well with Network Load Balancing has one or more of the following characteristics:

- Avoids instructing the client to open a subsequent connection that must be serviced by the same cluster host.

  For example, a Web application sends a response instructing a client to open an additional Secure Sockets Layer (SSL) session, and the application expects the SSL session to be established with the same cluster host that originated the response.

- Avoids retaining application state on a specific server in the cluster, such as session state saved by Active Server Pages (ASP).

  For example, some Web applications use a common database, or service, to maintain session state. A cookie is sent to the client on the initial request. On subsequent requests, the client sends the cookie to the cluster. Any cluster host in the cluster is capable of restoring the application session state by using the cookie sent by the client to retrieve the session state from the session database, or service. Applications that use a common database, or service, in conjunction with client-side cookies to maintain session state are more likely to work with Network Load Balancing than those that retain application state on a specific host in the cluster.

Applications and services that are stateless are the most likely to run without modifications on Network Load Balancing. Applications and services are said to be *stateless* when each client request is considered to be a new request that is unrelated to any previous request. Anytime a client request is considered to be a continuation of a previous request, the applications and services maintain *session state*.

Applications that maintain session state are said to be *stateful*. Stateful applications require *affinity* with the cluster host, when the session state is maintained locally.

You can set affinity between the client computer and a specific server within your cluster by using the port rules in Network Load Balancing. For more information about port rules, see "Identifying Applications or Services That Require Custom Port Rules" later in this chapter.

Regardless of which category your application belongs to, always test the application with Network Load Balancing in your lab environment during the proof-of-concept stage in your design. Ensure that your application is compatible with Network Load Balancing before continuing with the design process.

Some of the common applications and services that run on Network Load Balancing include:

- Web applications running on IIS 6.0

  One of the most common of the solutions that use Network Load Balancing is an IIS 6.0 Web farm. A typical challenge in supporting Web applications occurs when an application must maintain a persistent connection to a specific cluster host. For example, if a Web application uses Hypertext Transfer Protocol Secure (HTTPS), the application should contact the same cluster hosts within the cluster, for efficiency. Connecting to a different cluster host requires establishing a new SSL session, which creates excess network traffic and overhead on the client and server. Network Load Balancing maintains affinity and reduces the possibility that a new SSL session needs to be established.

- VPN remote access running on Routing and Remote Access

  Another solution that uses Network Load Balancing involves using the Routing and Remote Access service in Windows Server 2003 to provide VPN remote connectivity. In the VPN solution, you combine multiple remote access servers running Windows Server 2003 and Routing and Remote Access to create a VPN remote access server farm.

- Web content caching and firewall running on Microsoft® Internet Security and Acceleration (ISA) Server 2000

  You can also use Network Load Balancing in solutions that include ISA Server to provide network security, network isolation, network address translation, or Web content caching. In ISA Server solutions, the design and deployment are integral parts of the ISA Server design and deployment process.

  For more information on creating ISA Server designs and deploying ISA Server in your organization, see "Deploying ISA Server" in *Deploying Network Services* of this kit and see the documentation that accompanies ISA Server.

- Application hosted on Terminal Services

  When you run applications on Terminal Services, the Terminal Services clients can be load balanced across a number of computers running Terminal Services. Network Load Balancing is combined with the Session Directory service in Terminal Server to provide improved scalability and availability for Terminal Services.

  For more information about creating Terminal Services designs to host applications, see "Hosting Applications with Terminal Server" in this book, or see the Session Directory and Load Balancing Using Terminal Server link on the Web Resources page at http://www.microsoft.com/windows/reskits/webresources.

 Note

Network Load Balancing is an inappropriate solution if you are using Terminal Services to provide remote administration for specific servers, because Network Load Balancing can distribute your administration traffic to any one of the cluster hosts within the cluster. When you want to use Terminal Services to remotely administer cluster hosts, connect to the specific cluster host through the dedicated IP address on the cluster adapter or through a separate management adapter. For more information about the adapters in a cluster host, see "Selecting the Number of Network Adapters in Each Cluster Host" later in this chapter.

- Custom applications

  Network Load Balancing might be an appropriate method of improving scalability and availability for applications that your organization or third-party organizations have developed. Custom applications must adhere to the same criteria listed earlier in this section.

  The considerations for custom applications are similar to those for Web applications running on IIS 6.0. For example, any application behavior that maintains local session state across multiple TCP connections is less likely to benefit from Network Load Balancing. For more information about determining if an application requires cluster host affinity, see "Identifying Applications or Services That Require Custom Port Rules" later in this chapter.

  In addition to being compatible with Network Load Balancing, custom applications must be compatible with Windows Server 2003. For help in determining if your application is compatible with Windows Server 2003, use the Windows Application Compatibility Toolkit on the *Windows Server 2003 Deployment Kit* companion CD. For more information about the Windows Application Compatibility Toolkit, in Help and Support Center for Windows Server 2003, click **Tools**, and then click Windows Resource Kit Tools.

Determining the Core Specifications in the NLB Design

After you identify applications that can benefit from Network Load Balancing, you are ready to design the core specifications for your Network Load Balancing design. These core specifications form the foundation on which you create your cluster. They include the design process steps that are required for all Network Load Balancing solutions. Figure 8.5 illustrates the current step in the process for creating your Network Load Balancing design. The steps that occur later in the design process depend on the design decisions that you make about these essential aspects of your design.

Figure 8.5   Determining the Core Specifications in the NLB Design

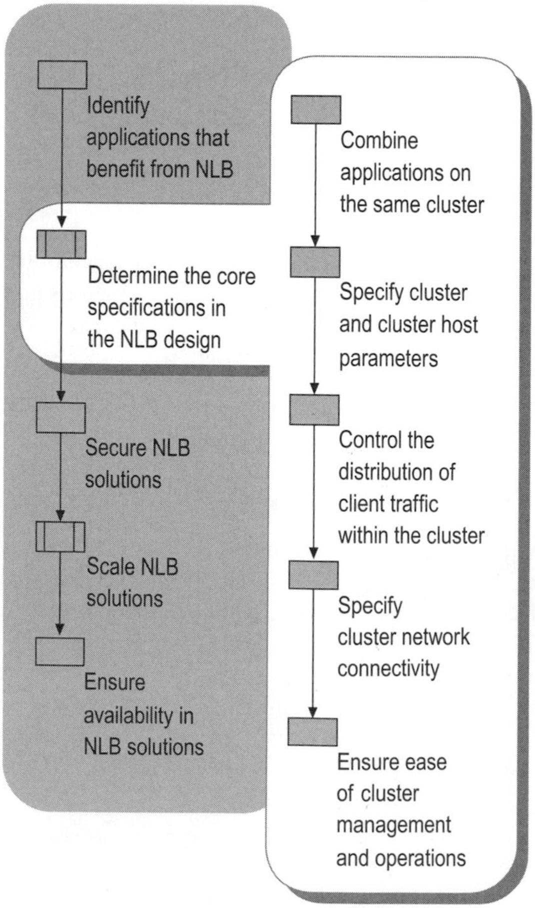

Combining Applications on the Same Cluster

When you create your Network Load Balancing design, one of the first steps is to determine if you can combine the applications and services in your solution on the same cluster. One of the primary concerns when combining applications on the same cluster is determining if the applications are compatible with each other. Table 8.1 lists the categories of common applications and services that run on Network Load Balancing, and it describes how you can combine them on the same cluster.

Table 8.1   Compatibility of Applications and Services on a Cluster

Application or Service	Combined on the Same Cluster
IIS 6.0 Web applications	▪ Can be combined on the same cluster; however, might require customized port rules.[1]
Terminal Services	▪ Can run any combination of applications as long as the applications are compatible with Terminal Services. ▪ Avoid combining Terminal Services (when Terminal Services is hosting applications) with other application platforms or services, such as IIS 6.0 or VPN remote access.[2]
VPN remote access	▪ Can be combined with ISA Server to combine remote access server and firewall features in the same server. ▪ Otherwise, avoid combining with other application platforms and services, such as IIS 6.0.
ISA Server	▪ Can be combined with Routing and Remote Access to combine remote access server and firewall features. ▪ Can be combined with IIS 6.0 to provide default Web site redirection to a Web site that is local to the server running ISA Server and IIS 6.0.
Custom applications	▪ Can be combined on the same cluster; however, might require customized port rules.[1]

[1] For more information, see "Identifying Applications or Services That Require Custom Port Rules" later in this chapter.

[2] If you are not hosting applications with Terminal Services, you can combine Terminal Services with IIS 6.0 Web applications, VPN remote access servers, ISA Server, and your custom applications to provide remote administration of those servers.

As mentioned in Table 8.1, avoid running some applications and services, such as Terminal Services and VPN remote access, on the same cluster. The reasons for not running these applications and services on the same cluster include system resource constraints, security constraints, and ease of management.

In some instances, the cluster hosts might not have sufficient system resources to run the combined applications. For example, if you use Terminal Services to host applications, Terminal Services consumes a significant amount of processor and memory resources. Hosting applications with Terminal Services on the same cluster as IIS 6.0 might cause significant delays in running Web applications. For more information on scaling applications and services on Network Load Balancing clusters, see "Scaling NLB Solutions" later in this chapter.

Also, security considerations might require running the applications and services on separate clusters. For example, you might want to avoid running an FTP site that allows anonymous access on a cluster that also runs a secured e-commerce Web application.

Finally, combining applications on the same cluster can make the applications unmanageable and difficult to administer. The complexity of combining applications can correspondingly increase the complexity of managing and operating the cluster. For more information about creating clusters that are easy to manage and operate, see "Ensuring Ease of Cluster Management and Operations" later in this chapter.

Example: Combining Applications on the Same Cluster

A fictitious organization, Contoso, is in the process of restructuring its existing network infrastructure and application platforms. Contoso wants to reduce the number of Network Load Balancing clusters required to support its new network infrastructure and application platforms. The company plans to run the following applications and services on Network Load Balancing clusters:

- A VPN remote access server farm, based on Routing and Remote Access

- Three e-commerce Web applications, based on IIS 6.0

  One of the applications is based on static Hypertext Markup Language (HTML) content with Common Gateway Interface (CGI) scripts, another application is an ASP application, and the third application is an ASP.NET application.

- A customer support FTP site, based on IIS 6.0

  The customer support FTP site supports the downloading of information and documents to customers and the uploading of customer documents, files, and other information to the FTP site. The customer support FTP site allows anonymous access for users who want to download and upload files.

For each of these applications and services, Contoso must determine if the application can be combined with other applications and services or if the application requires its own cluster. Table 8.2 lists the clusters required to support the applications and services and the reasons for including those clusters in the design.

Table 8.2   Clusters Required by Contoso

Cluster Required	Applications Running on the Cluster	Reason for Inclusion
NLBClusterA	VPN remote access server farm	VPN remote access servers should not be combined with other applications platforms or services.
NLBClusterB	E-commerce Web applications	The three e-commerce Web applications are compatible with one another.
NLBClusterC	Customer support FTP site	The customer support FTP site supports anonymous user access and cannot be combined with the e-commerce Web applications.

Specifying Cluster and Cluster Host Parameters

For each Network Load Balancing cluster, there are settings that are common to all cluster hosts and there are other settings that are unique to each cluster host. The cluster parameters define the cluster and establish cluster-wide configurations, such as the virtual IP address assigned to the cluster. The cluster host parameters define the cluster host role and identity within the cluster, such as the cluster host's priority within the cluster or the dedicated IP address that is unique to the cluster host.

Specify the cluster and cluster host parameters by completing the following steps:

1. Specify the settings that are common to all cluster hosts within the same cluster.

2. Specify the settings that are unique to each cluster host.

 Note

For a Word document to assist you in documenting cluster and cluster host parameters, see "NLB Cluster Host Worksheet" (Sdcnlb_1.doc) on the *Windows Server 2003 Deployment Kit* companion CD (or see "NLB Cluster Host Worksheet" on the Web at http://www.microsoft.com/reskit).

Specifying the Cluster Parameters

Cluster parameters are the configuration settings that define the cluster and the configuration settings common to all cluster hosts within the cluster. The cluster parameters must be unique within your organization's network.

Specify the cluster parameters by completing the following steps:

1. Specify the cluster IP address.

2. Specify the cluster fully qualified domain name (FQDN).

3. Specify the cluster operation mode.

4. Specify the remote control settings.

 Tip

When you configure cluster parameters by using Network Load Balancing Manager, enter the cluster parameters once during the creation of the cluster. As cluster hosts are added to the cluster, Network Load Balancing Manager automatically configures the cluster parameters for the new cluster hosts. When you configure them by using other methods, configure the cluster parameters identically for all cluster hosts within the same cluster. For more information about configuring the cluster parameters, see "Network Load Balancing parameters" in Help and Support Center for Windows Server 2003.

Specifying the Cluster IP Address

The cluster IP address is the virtual IP address that is assigned to the cluster. Client requests are sent to the cluster IP address. The cluster IP address has a corresponding subnet mask that is part of the cluster IP address specifications. The criteria for specifying the cluster IP address and subnet mask are the same as for all other IP addresses. When you configure the cluster manually, you must configure the cluster IP address and subnet mask identically on all cluster hosts within the cluster.

 Tip

The cluster IP address must appear in the list of IP addresses in the TCP/IP properties. Network Load Balancing Manager automatically configures the TCP/IP properties so that the cluster IP address is in the list. When you configure the TCP/IP properties by other methods, you must ensure that the cluster IP address is in the list of IP addresses in the TCP/IP properties.

Specifying the Cluster FQDN

For each cluster, you must designate the FQDN to be assigned to the cluster. The FQDN is registered in DNS later in the deployment process, when the cluster is deployed and ready to service client requests. The cluster FQDN refers to the cluster as a whole.

 Tip

You can enter the cluster FQDN in the full Internet name setting. The full Internet name is not automatically registered in DNS or used by other Windows components. As a result, treat the full Internet name setting as a comment that allows administrators to easily identify the cluster's FQDN. If you elect to leave the full Internet name setting blank, the operation of any Windows component, including Network Load Balancing, is not affected.

In addition to the cluster FQDN, designate a FQDN for each application and service running on the cluster. Ultimately these FQDNs become DNS entries as you deploy the corresponding application or service.

Specify the Cluster Operation Mode

The cluster operation mode determines the method, *unicast* or *multicast*, that is used to propagate incoming client requests to all the cluster hosts. For more information about determining which method to select for the cluster, see "Selecting the Unicast or Multicast Method of Distributing Incoming Requests" later in this chapter.

Specify the Remote Control Settings

The remote control settings provide the ability to perform certain remote administration tasks, such as starting and stopping a cluster host, from the command line utility Nlb.exe. Because of security-related concerns, avoid enabling the remote control settings. Nlb.exe can only perform limited administrative tasks. Network Load Balancing Manager can perform all administrative tasks, and is the preferred method for administering clusters. Remotely administering a cluster by using Network Load Balancing Manager is not affected by the remote control settings. For more information about specifying the remote control settings, see "Securing NLB Solutions" later in this chapter.

Specifying the Cluster Host Parameters

The cluster host parameters are the configuration settings that define each cluster host, including the configuration settings that are unique to each cluster host within the cluster. The cluster host parameters must be unique within a cluster and within your organization's network.

Specify the cluster host parameters by completing the following steps:

1. Specify the cluster host priority.

2. Specify the dedicated IP address configuration.

3. Specify the initial host state.

For more information about configuring the cluster host parameters, see "Network Load Balancing parameters" in Help and Support Center for Windows Server 2003.

Tip

Network Load Balancing Manager prevents common cluster host configuration errors, such as duplicate cluster host priorities or duplicate dedicated IP addresses. When you use other methods to configure the cluster host parameters, you must ensure that the cluster host parameters are configured appropriately for all cluster hosts within the cluster.

Specifying the Cluster Host Priority

For each cluster host, you must specify a cluster host priority that is unique within the cluster. During cluster convergence, the cluster host with the lowest numeric value for the cluster host priority triggers the end of convergence. For example, if three cluster hosts have the priorities of 3, 16, and 22, 3 is the cluster host with the highest priority and it will trigger the end of convergence.

Specify the cluster host priority for your cluster by using any unique identifier between 1 and 32. Any sequence can be used as long as the cluster host priorities are unique.

Note

If you specify the same cluster host priority for two cluster hosts, the last cluster host that starts fails to join the cluster. An error message describing the problem is written to the Windows system event log. The existing cluster hosts continue to operate as before.

Specifying the Dedicated IP Address Configuration

The dedicated IP address is an IP address that is assigned to each cluster host for network traffic that is not associated with the cluster, such as Telnet access to a specific host within a cluster. This IP address is used to individually address each host in the cluster; therefore, it should be unique for each host. Enter this parameter in standard Internet dotted notation (for example, w.x.y.z).

Traffic that is sent to the dedicated IP address is not load balanced by Network Load Balancing. Network Load Balancing ensures that all traffic to the dedicated IP address is unaffected by the Network Load Balancing current configuration, including:

- When a host is running as part of the cluster.

- When Network Load Balancing is disabled as a result of parameter errors in the registry.

 Tip

The dedicated IP address must be the first IP address in the list of IP addresses in the TCP/IP properties. Network Load Balancing Manager automatically configures the TCP/IP properties so that the dedicated IP address is first. When you use other methods to configure the TCP/IP properties, you must ensure that the dedicated IP address is the first IP address listed in the TCP/IP properties.

Specifying the Initial Host State

The *initial host state* specifies whether Network Load Balancing starts and whether the cluster host joins the cluster when the operating system starts. You need to determine the correct initial host state for the applications and services running on the cluster.

Network Load Balancing starts very early in the system start sequence. As a result, a cluster host can join the cluster before the applications and services running on the cluster host are ready to handle traffic. In this situation, clients might be directed to the cluster host and experience outages.

In some instances, management software, such as MOM or Applications Center 2000, is responsible for starting Network Load Balancing. The management software monitors the applications and services running on the cluster host and starts Network Load Balancing when the applications are fully operational.

In other instances, you might decide to start Network Load Balancing manually to ensure that applications and services are running before Network Load Balancing starts.

Table 8.3 lists the possible settings for the initial host state and the reasons for selecting the specific initial host state.

Table 8.3 Selecting the Appropriate Initial Host State

Initial Host State	Reasons for Selecting the Initial Host State
Started	▪ The applications and services running on the cluster start before Network Load Balancing. ▪ The length of time between the start of Network Load Balancing and the start of applications and services running on the cluster is negligible.
Stopped	▪ Management software, such as MOM or Application Center 2000, is responsible for starting Network Load Balancing automatically. ▪ The applications and services running on the cluster start after Network Load Balancing, and you want to start the cluster host manually.
Suspended	▪ You have performed maintenance on the cluster host, and you want to prevent the cluster from responding to clients after a restart of the cluster host.

Example: Specifying Cluster and Cluster Host Parameters

A fictitious organization, Contoso, is designing a VPN remote access solution, based on Routing and Remote Access and Network Load Balancing. The VPN remote access solution provides remote access to Contoso's private network by establishing Point-to-Point Tunneling Protocol (PPTP) and Layer Two Tunneling Protocol (L2TP) VPN tunnels through the Internet. The VPN remote access server farm contains five servers that have identical system resources.

Table 8.4 lists the cluster parameter design decisions for the VPN remote access server farm and the reasons for making those decisions.

Table 8.4   Cluster Parameter Settings for the VPN Remote Access Server Farm

Decision	Reason for the Decision
The cluster IP address and subnet mask is assigned an IP address and subnet mask that is accessible from the Internet.	Remote access users need to access the VPN server farm running on the cluster from the Internet.
The cluster is assigned the FQDN of vpn.contoso.com.	The FQDN assigned to the cluster is the name used by remote access users when accessing the VPN server farm running on the cluster.
The cluster operation mode is set to unicast.	The network infrastructure supports the unicast cluster operation mode. For more information about the decisions regarding setting this mode, see "Selecting the Unicast or Multicast Method of Distributing Incoming Requests" later in this chapter.
The remote control settings are not enabled.	The remote control settings are not required, because Network Load Balancing Manager will be used to administer the cluster.

Table 8.5 lists the cluster host parameter design decisions for the VPN remote access server farm.

Table 8.5   Cluster Host Parameter Settings for the VPN Remote Access Server Farm

Cluster Host Name	Host Priority	Dedicated IP Address	Initial Host State
NLBClusterA-01	1	Not specified	Started
NLBClusterA-02	2	Not specified	Started
NLBClusterA-03	3	Not specified	Started
NLBClusterA-04	4	Not specified	Started
NLBClusterA-05	5	Not specified	Started

A unique cluster host priority is assigned to each cluster host. The cluster host initial host state is set to Started to ensure that Network Load Balancing starts automatically and that the cluster host automatically joins the cluster.

Controlling the Distribution of Client Traffic Within the Cluster

One of the intended purposes of Network Load Balancing is to distribute incoming client traffic within the cluster. You can control the distribution of client traffic within the cluster by using Network Load Balancing port rules. Port rules are criteria-based policies that allow you to direct client requests to specific cluster hosts, based on TCP and UDP port numbers.

A default port rule is created during the installation of Network Load Balancing. In many instances, the default port rule is sufficient for some of the applications and services that use Network Load Balancing. When the default port rule is insufficient, you can create custom port rules. For more information about the default port rule, see "Identifying the Behavior of the Default Port Rule" later in this chapter.

The default port rule is sufficient for the following applications and services:

- VPN remote access farms with Routing and Remote Access

- Load-balancing application hosting with Terminal Services

 Tip
The ISA Server setup process defines the port rules that are necessary for ISA Server. No custom port rules are necessary for ISA Server.

If the default port rule is sufficient for your solution, and creating custom port rules is unnecessary, see "Specifying Cluster Network Connectivity" later in this chapter.

For IIS 6.0 Web farms or for custom applications, custom port rules might be required.

In some instances, the applications and services might require that the same client traffic be handled differently for the same or different applications and services. The virtual IP address assigned to the cluster can handle client traffic only in one way. However, you can specify a *virtual cluster* for each of the applications, allowing each application to have its own load-balancing behavior. Virtual clusters are a logical construct within the cluster, and they require no additional hardware.

For example, two Web applications might require different load-balancing behavior for HTTP (TCP port 80). You can create a virtual cluster for each Web application that allows different load-balancing behavior for the HTTP client traffic.

You can create a virtual cluster by specifying a virtual IP address in a Network Load Balancing port rule. The virtual IP address that is assigned in the port rule is associated with the application that requires the different load-balancing behavior.

Figure 8.6 illustrates the relationship between a Network Load Balancing cluster and the virtual clusters specified for the cluster. Each of the applications — Web applications A, B, and C — requires different load-balancing behavior. A virtual IP address is assigned to each virtual cluster and associated with each application. A DNS entry associates the virtual IP address with a URL for the corresponding application.

Figure 8.6   Relationship Between an NLB Cluster and Virtual Clusters

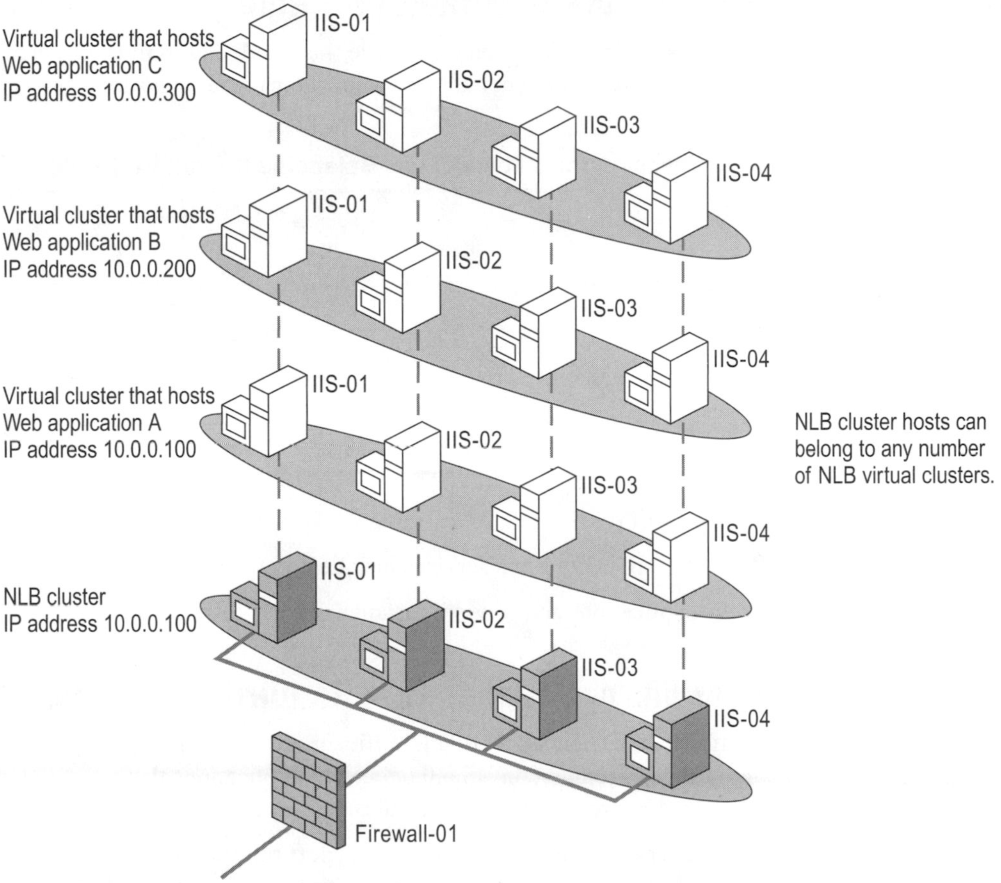

Virtual cluster that hosts
Web application C
IP address 10.0.0.300

IIS-01

IIS-02

IIS-03

IIS-04

Virtual cluster that hosts
Web application B
IP address 10.0.0.200

IIS-01

IIS-02

IIS-03

IIS-04

Virtual cluster that hosts
Web application A
IP address 10.0.0.100

IIS-01

IIS-02

IIS-03

IIS-04

NLB cluster hosts can
belong to any number
of NLB virtual clusters.

NLB cluster
IP address 10.0.0.100

IIS-01

IIS-02

IIS-03

IIS-04

Firewall-01

For more information about including Network Load Balancing port rules in your design, see "Identifying Applications or Services That Require Custom Port Rules" later in this chapter.

Control the distribution of client traffic within a cluster by completing the following steps:

1. Identify the behavior of the default port rule.

2. Identify applications or services that require custom port rules.

3. Specify the client traffic to be affected by the custom port rule.

4. Specify the affinity and load-balancing behavior of the custom port rule.

◆ Important

The port rules applied to each cluster host must be identical, with the exception of the load weight (in the multiple hosts filter mode) and the handling priority (in the single hosts filter mode). If there is a discrepancy between port rules on existing cluster hosts, the cluster will not converge.

Identifying the Behavior of the Default Port Rule

When Network Load Balancing is installed on a cluster host, a default port rule is created. Table 8.6 lists the configuration of the default port rule that is created during Network Load Balancing installation.

Table 8.6   Specifications for the Network Load Balancing Default Port Rule

Default Port Rule Setting	Set to This Value
Cluster IP address	All
Port range: From	0
Port range: To	65535
Protocols	Both
Filtering Mode	Multiple Hosts with Single affinity and Equal load weight

Specify that the default port rule be deleted unless the default port rule is:

- Appropriate for the applications and services installed on the cluster.

- Modified for the applications and services installed on the cluster.

Identifying Applications or Services That Require Custom Port Rules

As previously mentioned, the default port rule is sufficient for some applications and services. However, many applications running on IIS 6.0 or custom applications that are developed by your organization might require customized port rules.

These applications and services can require customized port rules to influence how load is directed to hosts in the cluster. In addition, the applications and services might require a virtual cluster when the same client traffic must be handled differently for the same or different applications and services. With virtual clusters, you can use different port rules for different Web sites or applications hosted on the cluster, provided each Web site or application has a different virtual IP address.

Identifying Applications and Services That Need Persistent Sessions

The applications and services that run on Network Load Balancing include stateful applications (those that maintain session state) and stateless applications. Maintaining session state means that the application or service establishes information on the initial connection to a cluster host and then retains the information for subsequent requests. During a user session, the same server must handle all the requests from the user in order to access that information. Applications and services that are stateless maintain no user or communication information for subsequent connections.

With a single server, maintaining session state presents no difficulty, because the user always connects to the same server. However, when client requests are load balanced within a cluster, without some type of persistence, the client might not be directed to the same cluster host for a series of client requests.

In Network Load Balancing, you maintain session state with a *port rule affinity* between the client and a specific cluster host. Port rule affinity directs all client requests from the same IP address to the same cluster host. You can use port rules to specify the port rule affinity between clients and cluster hosts. For more information about specifying port rule affinity between clients and cluster hosts, see "Specifying the Affinity and Load-Balancing Behavior of the Custom Port Rule" later in this chapter.

Port rule affinity might be required by the following:

- An application or service running on the cluster
- Session-oriented protocols that are used by the application or service running on the cluster if the session lifetime extends across multiple TCP connections

Identifying applications that require affinity

Applications and services require persistent sessions when the application or service retains information established in a client request that is used in subsequent client requests. In some instances, the application or service is aware that load balancing is occurring, and it uses an application-specific method, such as client-side cookies, for maintaining session state. In other instances, the application or service is unaware that load balancing is occurring, and it requires Network Load Balancing to maintain affinity between the client and specific cluster hosts.

An example of an application that maintains session state is a Web application that requires a user to log on to buy products through a shopping cart application. After the application authenticates the user, the user's information, including shipping information, billing information, and items in the shopping cart, is retained for subsequent requests. The session state is maintained until the user completes or cancels the purchase.

Table 8.7 lists common Web application types and their requirements for affinity provided by cluster port rules.

Table 8.7 Web Applications and Their Requirements for Port Rule Affinity

Web Application	Description	Requires Port Rule Affinity
Static, HTML-based applications	Application maintains no user information.	
Static, HTML-based applications with CGI	CGI portion of the application might retain user information.	●
Web application that uses client-side cookies	Application sends a cookie to the client when the application session is initiated. On subsequent requests, the client sends the cookie along as part of the request. The instance of the application running on individual cluster hosts is capable of retrieving application session state by using the cookie in the request.	
ASP.NET applications with session state persistence	ASP.NET applications support a method for maintaining session state on a centralized session state server or on a server running SQL Server 2000. Because the session state is managed centrally, any cluster host can recover session state information, and affinity is not required. For more information about ASP.NET application session state, see "Deploying ASP.NET Applications in IIS 6.0" in *Deploying Internet Information Services (IIS) 6.0* of this kit (or see "Deploying ASP .NET Applications in IIS 6.0" on the Web at http://www.microsoft.com/reskit).	
ASP applications and ASP.NET applications without session state	These applications create session information when the user first starts the application. The session information is managed by the instance of the ASP or ASP.NET dynamic-link libraries (DLLs) running on the cluster host. On subsequent requests, the session state is maintained for the application on that specific cluster host. No session state information is shared among cluster hosts.	●

For applications that are written by your organization, consult with the application developers to determine if, or how, any session information is retained. When your applications run on Terminal Services, port rule affinity is required.

Identifying session-oriented protocols that require affinity

Even when the application or service is stateless, the protocol required by the application or service might be session-oriented. For example, an application might be based on static HTML, but it might use SSL to provide security.

However, other session-oriented protocols, such as SSL, can operate correctly without affinity, but they incur a significant decrease in performance. When an SSL session is established with a cluster host, an SSL session ID is exchanged between the cluster host and the client. If the client makes a subsequent request to the same cluster host, the same session ID can be used.

If the client makes a subsequent request to a different cluster host, a new session ID must be obtained. The overhead for obtaining a new SSL session ID is five times more than for reusing a session ID. By using port rule affinity, SSL session IDs are reused whenever possible.

Compensating for Differences in System Resources

During the IT life cycle of your cluster, new cluster hosts might be added to the cluster. These new cluster hosts are typically new computers with improved system resources, such as processor speed, number of processors, or memory. Because of the improved system resources, the new cluster hosts are capable of servicing more clients.

The default port rule, created during the installation of Network Load Balancing, evenly distributes network requests among cluster hosts, regardless of the available system resources on individual cluster hosts. Cluster hosts with inadequate system resources can provide slower response times to clients than other cluster hosts with adequate system resources. You can compensate for differences in available system resources on individual cluster hosts by directing a higher percentage of client requests to the cluster hosts with adequate system resources.

The method of compensating for the differences in system resources is based on the filter mode in the port rule. Only the Multiple Hosts port filter mode supports compensating for differences in cluster host resources. For more information about port rule filter modes and, specifically, the Multiple Hosts port filter mode, see "Specifying the Affinity and Load-Balancing Behavior of the Custom Port Rule" later in this chapter.

Deciding to Include Virtual Clusters

In some instances, you might want a cluster to appear logically as multiple Network Load Balancing clusters. In Network Load Balancing, you can define virtual clusters that allow you to apply a unique set of port rules to each virtual cluster.

Include virtual clusters in the following situations:

- An application or service running on a cluster must exhibit different affinity behavior.

  For example, you might have an FTP site hosted on multiple servers running IIS 6.0. You want FTP downloads to be load balanced across all cluster hosts. However, you want FTP uploads to be sent only to one cluster host. You can create a virtual cluster that supports FTP downloads with no affinity and another virtual cluster that directs FTP uploads to a specific cluster host.

- Multiple applications or services running on the same cluster require different affinity behaviors for the same client traffic type (same TCP/UDP port number).

  For example, you might have two Web applications hosted on the same cluster running IIS 6.0. Both applications use HTTP (TCP port 80), but one application maintains session state while the other application does not. You can create a virtual cluster that supports the application that maintains session state with affinity and another virtual cluster that supports the stateless application without affinity.

- The maintenance and operations of an application or service must be independent of other applications and services running on the cluster.

  For example, you might have two applications hosted on the same cluster. For ease of maintenance, upgrade, or other operations tasks, you can create a virtual cluster for the application. You can stop client communication with the virtual cluster and then perform application maintenance without affecting other applications running on the cluster.

Tip

You can stop client communications with a virtual cluster by using the **drain** parameter from Nlb.exe or Network Load Balancing Manager, both of which are a part of Windows Server 2003.

Virtual clusters are specialized port rules that require a virtual IP address, which is assigned to the virtual cluster. You define a virtual cluster by specifying one or more port rules that share the same virtual IP address. As with regular port rules, the port rules that define the virtual cluster must be the same for all cluster hosts in the cluster. For more information about port rule specifications, see "Specifying Client Traffic To Be Affected by the Custom Port Rule" later in this chapter.

Specifying Client Traffic To Be Affected by the Custom Port Rule

Port rules can be divided into two parts. The first part of a port rule identifies the client traffic to be affected by the port rule. You identify the client traffic affected by the port rule by specifying the cluster IP address and the TCP (or UDP) port range. Network Load Balancing examines all client requests and determines if a port rule applies to the client request.

The second part of a port rule determines the affinity and load-balancing characteristics of the cluster. For more information about the affinity and load-balancing characteristics of the cluster, see "Specifying the Affinity and Load-Balancing Behavior of the Custom Port Rule" later in this chapter.

Specify the client traffic to be affected by the port rule by completing the following steps:

1. Designate the value for the cluster IP address.

2. Specify the port range for the port rule as a starting port number (From) and an ending port number (To).

3. Specify the protocol for the port range that you specified.

> **Note**
>
> For a Word document to assist you in documenting your port rule settings, see "NLB Cluster Host Worksheet" (Sdcnlb_1.doc) on the *Windows Server 2003 Deployment Kit* companion CD (or see "NLB Cluster Host Worksheet" on the Web at http://www.microsoft.com/reskit).

Designating the Value for the Cluster IP Address

If you are specifying a:

- Global port rule for a cluster, specify All.

- Port rule for a virtual cluster, specify the virtual IP address for the virtual cluster.

For more information about deciding when to include virtual clusters in your design, see "Identifying Applications or Services That Require Custom Port Rules" earlier in this chapter.

Specifying the Port Range

Specify the port range for the port rule:

- Based on the TCP and UDP ports used by the applications and services running on the Network Load Balancing cluster.

- As a starting port number (From) and an ending port number (To).

For example, if your Network Load Balancing cluster supports Web applications that use only TCP port 80, you specify a starting port number of 80 and an ending port number of 80.

Specifying the Protocol for the Port Range

If the applications and services are using:

- TCP, specify TCP.
- UDP, specify UDP.
- Both TCP and UDP, specify Both.

Specifying the Affinity and Load-Balancing Behavior of the Custom Port Rule

The second part of a port rule affects the affinity and load-balancing behavior of the port rule. The affinity and load-balancing behavior of a port rule are specified by the filter mode of the port rule. Only one filter mode can be selected for each port rule. Table 8.8 describes the filter modes that are available.

Table 8.8   Selecting the Filter Mode for the Port Rule

Filter Mode	Description
Multiple Hosts	Permits all cluster hosts to actively respond to client requests. This is the most common filter mode, because it allows the affinity and load-balancing characteristics to be customized.
Single Host	Allows only one cluster host in the cluster to actively respond to client requests. Could be useful when providing backup servers. For example, in an FTP site where users upload files, single host mode allows one host to receive FTP uploads. If the host fails, the host with the next highest priority takes over for the failed host.
Disable	Prevents the cluster from responding to a specific type of client traffic.

Note

For a Word document to assist you in documenting your port rule settings, see "NLB Cluster Host Worksheet" (Sdcnlb_1.doc) on the *Windows Server 2003 Deployment Kit* companion CD (or see "NLB Cluster Host Worksheet" on the Web at http://www.microsoft.com/reskit).

Specifying Multiple Hosts Filter Mode Settings

The Multiple Hosts filter mode provides load balancing across multiple cluster hosts. One of the complexities introduced by load balancing is persistent relationships (affinity) between clients and cluster hosts. For more information about affinity, see "Identifying Applications or Services That Require Custom Port Rules" earlier in this chapter.

Another complexity introduced by load balancing is compensation for differences in cluster host system resources on the cluster over time. Based on differences in available system resources or applications, specific cluster hosts might not be capable of managing the same number of client requests. For more information about compensating for differences in cluster host system resources, see "Identifying Applications or Services That Require Custom Port Rules" earlier in this chapter.

Specify the settings for the Multiple Hosts filter mode by completing the following steps:

1. Preserve persistent application sessions by specifying the affinity between a client and a specific cluster host.

2. Compensate for differences in system resources by specifying the load weight settings.

Selecting the affinity between a client and a specific cluster host

You can override the default behavior by selecting other port rule affinity options. Table 8.9 lists the port rule affinity options and the reasons for selecting them.

Table 8.9   Including Port Rule Affinity Options in Your Design

Option	Reasons for Selecting This Option
None	▪ You want to ensure even load balancing among cluster hosts. ▪ Client traffic is stateless (for example, HTTP traffic).
Single	▪ You want to ensure that requests from a specific client (IP address) are sent to the same cluster host. ▪ Client state is maintained across TCP connections (for example, HTTPS traffic).
Class C	▪ Client requests from a Class C IP address range (instead of a single IP address) are sent to the same cluster host. ▪ Clients use multiple proxy servers to access the cluster, and they appear to have multiple IP addresses within the same Class C IP address range. ▪ Client state is maintained across TCP connections (for example, HTTPS traffic).

Single affinity is the most common selection when applications require that information about the user state be maintained across TCP connections. Examples of these types of applications include applications that use SSL or applications that retain user information, such as e-commerce shopping cart applications.

Applications that use SSL with Single affinity are efficient because the SSL session IDs are reused. Negotiating a new SSL session ID requires five times the amount of overhead as reusing a SSL session ID. Although negotiating the SSL session ID is transparent to the client, the cumulative increase in overhead could degrade the performance of the cluster.

Applications that retain user information can resolve the affinity requirement by using Network Load Balancing affinity or by using a common session state database or server. Applications that have a common session state database or server are combined with cookie-based affinity to allow any cluster host to restore the appropriate session state. If an application has a common session state database or server, you can select a port rule affinity of **None** if SSL is not part of the solution.

If an application retains user information by requiring that client transactions are completed on the same cluster host, select a port rule affinity of Single. For a discussion of when an application requires persistent connections to specific cluster hosts, along with an explicit discussion regarding SSL, see "Identifying Applications or Services That Require Custom Port Rules" earlier in this chapter.

Class C is used when Internet clients connect through proxy servers with different IP addresses within the same Class C IP address range. Some Internet service providers, such as America Online (AOL) in the United States, have proxy servers with different Class C IP addresses. Using different Class C IP addresses on the proxy servers can break the affinity between the client and the cluster host. In situations like this, other methods might be required to preserve cluster host affinity. For example, Application Center 2000 supports cookie-based affinity, which solves the problem of proxy servers with different Class C IP addresses. Alternatively, the application can be redesigned to maintain application session state in a common database or session state server, such as that provided by IIS 6.0 and ASP.NET. When possible, allow the application to maintain session state in this manner because the application will be more robust and scalable.

Specifying the load weight settings for each cluster host

The default port rule that is created during the installation of Network Load Balancing uses equal load weights. To override the default behavior, you can specify a custom load weight to be handled by each cluster host, as shown in Table 8.10.

Table 8.10   Selecting the Method for Distributing Client Requests

Method	Description
Equal	Evenly distributes client requests across all cluster hosts when the available system resources are the same.
Load weight	Distributes client requests based on the available system capacity because of differences in the: ■ Hardware configuration of each cluster host. ■ Applications and services running on each cluster host.

Specify the amount of client requests to be handled by each cluster host by completing one of the following steps:

■ Specify Equal to ensure that client requests are evenly distributed across all cluster hosts, unless the cluster hosts do not have the same available system capacity.

■ Otherwise, specify the load weight value for the cluster host.

The load weight value can range from 0 (zero) to 100. You can prevent a cluster host from handling any client requests by specifying a load weight of 0.

The percentage of client requests that are handled by each cluster host is computed by dividing the local load weight by the sum of all load weights across the cluster. Table 8.11 shows an example of the relationship between load weight and the percentage of client requests that are handled by each cluster host.

Table 8.11   Using Load Weights and Client Request Percentages

Cluster Host	Load Weight	Percentage of Client Requests
ClusterHost-A	50	40%
ClusterHost-B	50	40%
ClusterHost-C	25	20%

Specifying Single Host Filter Mode Settings

As with the cluster host priority setting for Network Load Balancing, which is discussed in "Specifying the Cluster Host Parameters" earlier in this chapter, you must specify the handling priority value for each cluster host that has the port rule.

Specify the handling priority for Single Host filter mode by completing the following steps:

1. Specify a value of 1 as the priority for the cluster host that will always handle the client traffic designated in the port rule criteria.

2. Increase the value assigned to the previous cluster host by 1, assign that value to the next cluster host, and repeat the process until you have specified the handling priority for all cluster hosts.

 Important

If you specify the same handling priority for two cluster hosts, the last cluster host that starts will fail to join the cluster. An error message describing the problem will be written to the Windows system event log. The existing cluster hosts will continue to operate as before if cluster convergence completed previously. Otherwise, convergence must complete before traffic is handled by the cluster.

Specifying Disable Filter Mode Settings

As previously mentioned, the Disabled filter mode means that the client traffic corresponding to the port rule is blocked. Unlike the other filter modes, after you select this mode, no additional settings or values are required.

Example: Controlling the Distribution of Client Traffic Within the Cluster

An organization implements the following solutions, which include Network Load Balancing, to reduce outages and improve performance:

- VPN remote access, based on Routing and Remote Access

- E-commerce Web applications, based on IIS 6.0

- A customer support FTP site, based on IIS 6.0

VPN remote access solution with Routing and Remote Access

The VPN remote access solution, based on Routing and Remote Access, provides remote access to the organization's private network by establishing PPTP and L2TP VPN tunnels through the Internet.

The VPN remote access server farm contains five servers that have identical system resources. Network Load Balancing is enabled on the network adapters connected to the Internet. A cluster IP address has been configured for the cluster, and the appropriate DNS entries have been determined but not yet created.

Because the default port rule provides the appropriate affinity and load balancing, no custom port rules are required for the cluster.

E-commerce Web application solution with IIS 6.0

The e-commerce Web application solution, based on IIS 6.0, includes the following applications:

- Web-based, e-commerce application built with static HTML

- Web-based, e-commerce application built with ASP

Both applications use:

- HTTPS (TCP port 443)

- HTTP (TCP Port 80)

The application that uses ASP maintains user session information after the user is authenticated.

The two e-commerce Web application solutions are combined on the same IIS 6.0 Web farm and, subsequently, the same Network Load Balancing cluster. The IIS 6.0 Web farm contains four computers that have identical system resources. Network Load Balancing is enabled on the network adapters connected to the Internet. A cluster IP address is configured for the cluster, and the appropriate DNS entries have been determined but not yet created.

To facilitate the combination of the two e-commerce Web applications into a single Web farm and cluster, each e-commerce application is assigned to a virtual cluster. By assigning each e-commerce application to a virtual cluster, client access can be stopped individually to allow operations tasks, such as upgrades, to be performed without disrupting client access to the other e-commerce application.

Table 8.12 lists the cluster, virtual cluster, and cluster hosts in the organization's e-commerce solution.

Table 8.12   Network Load Balancing Clusters and Cluster Hosts in the E-Commerce Solution

Cluster Name	Solution	Type	Cluster Host
NLBCluster-B	Web-based, e-commerce applications	Cluster	▪ NLBClusterB-01 ▪ NLBClusterB-02 ▪ NLBClusterB-03 ▪ NLBClusterB-04
VirCluster-A	IIS 6.0 and HTML	Virtual cluster	Same as NLBCluster-B
VirCluster-B	IIS 6.0 and ASP	Virtual cluster	Same as NLBCluster-B

Table 8.13 lists the port rules that meet the requirements of the e-commerce Web application solution that includes IIS 6.0 and Network Load Balancing.

Table 8.13 Port Rules for IIS 6.0 E-Commerce Solution on NLBCluster-B

Cluster IP Address	Start	End	Protocol	Filtering Mode	Load Weight	Affinity
VirtualIP-A	80	80	TCP	Multiple	Equal	None
VirtualIP-A	443	443	TCP	Multiple	Equal	Single
VirtualIP-B	80	80	TCP	Multiple	Equal	Single
VirtualIP-B	443	443	TCP	Multiple	Equal	Single

Because the port rules, listed in Table 8.13, have a specified load weight of Equal, the same port rules are used for all the cluster hosts. The virtual clusters, VirtualIP-A and VirtualIP-B, are dedicated to the respective e-commerce applications. Because both applications use HTTP (TCP port 80) and HTTPS (TCP port 443), port rules must be specified for each protocol in each virtual cluster.

Customer support FTP site solution with IIS 6.0

The customer support FTP site solution:

- Is based on IIS 6.0.

- Provides secured and unsecured access to files.

- Allows users to upload files to specified areas on the FTP site.

- Requires file uploads that are centralized on one FTP server to avoid users uploading duplicate files.

- Uses TCP port 20 for FTP.

- Uses TCP port 21 for FTP.

The customer support FTP site runs on an IIS 6.0 farm and, subsequently, a Network Load Balancing cluster. The IIS 6.0 farm contains three computers that have identical system resources. Network Load Balancing is enabled on the network adapters connected to the Internet. A cluster IP address has been configured for the cluster, and the appropriate DNS entries have been determined but not yet created.

To support the number of simultaneous users who are performing FTP downloads, all FTP download requests must be load balanced across the entire IIS 6.0 farm. However, to ensure that users upload files to only one location, FTP uploads must be directed to only one server in the IIS 6.0 farm.

To facilitate the differences in cluster host affinity between FTP uploads and downloads, each direction of FTP transfer is assigned to a different virtual cluster. By assigning FTP uploads to a virtual cluster and FTP downloads to another virtual cluster, the organization ensures that FTP downloads can be load balanced across all cluster hosts, while FTP uploads are sent to only one cluster host in the cluster.

Table 8.14 lists the cluster, virtual cluster, and cluster hosts selected in the organization's customer support FTP site solution.

Table 8.14   Clusters and Cluster Hosts in the Customer Support FTP Site Solution

Cluster Name	Solution	Type	Cluster Host
NLBCluster-C	FTP site	Cluster	▪ NLBClusterC-01 ▪ NLBClusterC-02 ▪ NLBClusterC-03
VirCluster-C	FTP download	Virtual cluster	All cluster hosts can be used for download.
VirCluster-D	FTP upload	Virtual cluster	NLBClusterC-03 is to be used for upload.

Table 8.15 lists the port rules that meet the requirements of the organization's customer support FTP site solution, which includes IIS 6.0 and Network Load Balancing.

Table 8.15   Port Rules for an IIS 6.0 FTP Site Solution on NLBCluster-C

Cluster IP Address	Start	End	Protocol	Filtering Mode	Load Weight	Affinity	Handling Priority
VirtualIP-C	20	21	TCP	Multiple Hosts	Equal	Single	NA
VirtualIP-D	20	21	TCP	Single Host			▪ NLBClusterC-03 = 1 ▪ NLBClusterC-01 = 2 ▪ NLBClusterC-02 = 3

The port rules that define VirCluster-C are identical for all the cluster hosts in NLBCluster-C. The port rules that define VirCluster-D are unique for each cluster host in NLBCluster-C, because the handling priority for each cluster host is unique. NLBClusterC-03 is the cluster host that is designated for FTP uploads, and it is assigned a handling priority of 1 to ensure that all file uploads are sent to NLBClusterC-03. The handling priority for NLBClusterC-01 and for NLBClusterC-02 must be unique and of a lower priority than for NLBClusterC-03.

Specifying Cluster Network Connectivity

The scalability and availability improvements provided by your cluster depend on the network connectivity that is provided to the cluster. An improperly designed network infrastructure can cause client response-time problems and application outages. Specify the connections between the cluster and the client computers, the other servers within your organization's network, and the operation consoles to achieve the connectivity goals of your network.

The goals of network connectivity to the cluster are to provide:

- High-capacity network connectivity to ensure adequate client response time.

- Redundant routing and switching infrastructure.

- Restricted management of the cluster and cluster resources.

- Valid IP configuration for each network interface in each cluster host.

Specify the cluster network connectivity by completing the following steps:

1. Select the number of network adapters in each cluster host.

2. Select the unicast method or the multicast method of distributing incoming client requests to cluster hosts.

3. Include support for teaming network adapters.

4. Determine the network infrastructure requirements.

After you have specified the cluster network connectivity, document your decisions on your organization's network diagram (for example, on a Microsoft® Visio® drawing).

 Note

For a Word document to assist you in documenting your decisions, see "NLB Cluster Host Worksheet" (Sdcnlb_1.doc) on the *Windows Server 2003 Deployment Kit* companion CD (or see "NLB Cluster Host Worksheet" on the Web at http://www.microsoft.com/reskit).

Selecting the Number of Network Adapters in Each Cluster Host

At a minimum, you must connect each cluster host in your cluster to a network segment that has connectivity to the client computers. In most solutions, you need to connect each cluster host to other servers and to management and operations consoles in your organization.

With the appropriate cluster network connectivity, your solution will be properly secured, highly available, highly scalable, and easy to manage. Any design deficiencies in the cluster network connectivity portion of the design can compromise the security, availability, scalability, and manageability of the cluster.

Select the number of network adapters in each cluster host by completing the following steps:

1. Identify a network interface, referred to as the *cluster adapter*, which provides connectivity to the client computers.

    Include the appropriate IP configuration (IP address, subnet mask, and so forth) for the cluster adapter, so that the cluster host is on the same physical subnet or virtual subnet.

    All hosts of the same cluster must be on the same physical or virtual LAN (VLAN). In instances where the cluster hosts are not connected to the same physical subnet, ensure that the cluster hosts are connected to a virtual subnet. If all hosts are not connected to the same physical subnet, make sure that your routing and switch infrastructure supports virtual subnets.

2. Specify a network interface, referred to as the *management adapter*, which will provide connectivity to other servers within your organization and to management and operations consoles within your organization.

    Include the appropriate IP configuration (IP address, subnet mask, and so forth) for the management adapter.

 Important

> To prevent unauthorized altering of the Network Load Balancing configuration, enable Network Load Balancing administration only on the management adapter. This is done by restricting traffic through your firewalls or routers.

In instances where only the cluster adapter is included and your applications require peer-to-peer communications between cluster hosts (beyond the cluster heartbeat traffic), see the discussion on unicast mode and multicast mode in "Selecting the Unicast or Multicast Method of Distributing Incoming Requests" later in this chapter.

Figure 8.7 illustrates cluster network connectivity that includes connectivity to clients, other servers in an organization, and management and operations consoles.

Figure 8.7 Cluster Network Connectivity

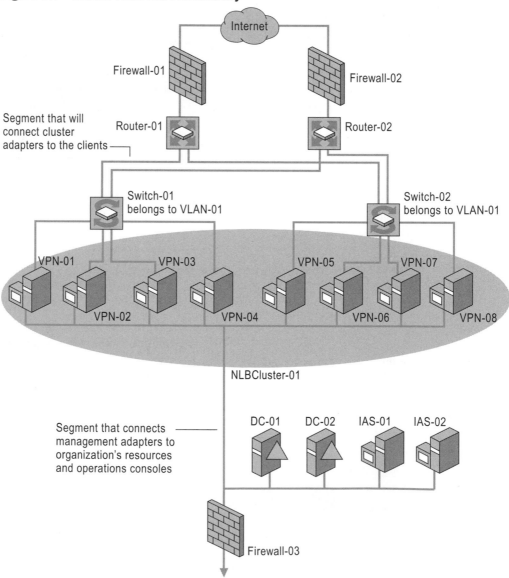

Selecting the Unicast or Multicast Method of Distributing Incoming Requests

All cluster hosts in a cluster receive all incoming client requests that are destined for the virtual IP address that is assigned to the cluster. The Network Load Balancing load-balancing algorithm, which runs on each cluster host, is responsible for determining which cluster host processes and responds to the client request.

You can distribute incoming client requests to cluster hosts by using unicast or multicast methods. Both methods send the incoming client requests to all hosts by sending the request to the cluster's MAC address.

When you use the unicast method, all cluster hosts share an identical unicast MAC address. Network Load Balancing overwrites the original MAC address of the cluster adapter with the unicast MAC address that is assigned to all the cluster hosts.

When you use the multicast method, each cluster host retains the original MAC address of the adapter. In addition to the original MAC address of the adapter, the adapter is assigned a multicast MAC address, which is shared by all cluster hosts. The incoming client requests are sent to all cluster hosts by using the multicast MAC address.

Select the unicast method for distributing client requests, unless only one network adapter is installed in each cluster host and the cluster hosts must communicate with each other. Because Network Load Balancing modifies the MAC address of all cluster hosts to be identical, cluster hosts cannot communicate directly with one another when using unicast. When peer-to-peer communication is required between cluster hosts, include an additional network adapter or select multicast mode. When the unicast method is inappropriate, select the multicast method.

For more information about the interaction between the method of distributing incoming requests and layer 2 switches, see article Q193602, "Configuration Options for WLBS Hosts Connected to a Layer 2 Switches," in the Microsoft Knowledge Base. To find this article, see the Microsoft Knowledge Base link on the Web Resources page at www.microsoft.com/windows/reskits/webresources.

Selecting the Unicast Method

In the unicast method:

- The cluster adapters for all cluster hosts are assigned the same unicast MAC address.

- The outgoing MAC address for each packet is modified, based on the cluster host's priority setting, to prevent upstream switches from discovering that all cluster hosts have the same MAC address.

  The modification of the outgoing MAC address is appropriate for switches. When a hub is used to connect the cluster hosts, disable the modification of the outgoing MAC address. On Windows Server 2003, you can disable modification of outgoing addresses by setting the value of the registry entry **MaskSourceMAC**, of data type REG_DWORD, to 0x0. **MaskSourceMAC** is located in HKLM\SYSTEM\CurrentControlSet\Services\WLBS\Parameters\Interface*Adapter-GUID* (where *Adapter-GUID* is the long GUID assigned to the network adapter in the server).

 Caution

Do not edit the registry unless you have no alternative. The registry editor bypasses standard safeguards, allowing settings that can damage your system, or even require you to reinstall Windows. If you must edit the registry, back it up first and see the Registry Reference on the *Microsoft Windows Server 2003 Deployment Kit* companion CD or at http://www.microsoft.com/reskit.

- The unicast MAC address is derived from the cluster's IP address to ensure uniqueness outside the cluster hosts.

- Communication between cluster hosts, other than Network Load Balancing–related traffic (such as heartbeat), is only available when you install an additional adapter, because the cluster hosts all have the same MAC address.

Although the unicast method works in all routing situations, it has the following disadvantages:

- A second network adapter is required to provide peer-to-peer communication between cluster hosts.

- If the cluster is connected to a switch, incoming packets are sent to all the ports on the switch, which can cause switch flooding.

Selecting the Multicast Method

In the multicast method:

- The cluster adapter for each cluster host retains the original hardware unicast MAC address (as specified by the hardware manufacture of the network adapter).

- The cluster adapters for all cluster hosts are assigned a multicast MAC address.

- The multicast MAC is derived from the cluster's IP address.

- Communication between cluster hosts is not affected, because each cluster host retains a unique MAC address.

By using the multicast method with Internet Group Membership Protocol (IGMP), you can limit switch flooding, if the switch supports IGMP *snooping*. IGMP snooping allows the switch to examine the contents of multicast packets and associate a port with a multicast address. Without IGMP snooping, switches might require additional configuration to tell the switch which ports to use for the multicast traffic. Otherwise, switch flooding occurs, as with the unicast method.

The multicast method has the following disadvantages:

- Upstream routers might require a static Address Resolution Protocol (ARP) entry. This is because routers might not accept an ARP response that resolves unicast IP addresses to multicast MAC addresses.

- Without IGMP, switches might require additional configuration to tell the switch which ports to use for the multicast traffic.

- Upstream routers might not support mapping a unicast IP address (the cluster IP address) with a multicast MAC address. In these situations, you must upgrade or replace the router. Otherwise, the multicast method is unusable.

Including Support for Teaming Network Adapters

Many hardware vendors support *teaming network adapters* to increase network bandwidth capacity and to provide an additional level of network redundancy. Teaming network adapters are multiple network adapters in the same computer that logically act as a single, virtual network adapter. The virtual network adapter can provide load balancing of traffic between the physical network adapters or automatic failover in the event that one of the network adapters fails.

Teaming network adapter drivers and Network Load Balancing both try to manipulate the MAC addresses of the network adapters. As a result, teaming network adapters might work only in limited configurations. As a general rule, avoid including teaming network adapters in your Network Load Balancing solutions.

 Note

Because each implementation of teaming network adapters is vendor-specific, the support for teaming network adapters is provided by the hardware vendor, and it is beyond the scope of Microsoft Product Support Services. For more information about teaming network adapters in your Network Load Balancing solution, consult the teaming network adapter hardware recommendations.

Determining the Network Infrastructure Requirements

The network infrastructure affects your Network Load Balancing solution more than any other component. No matter how much Network Load Balancing enables you to scale out your solution, an inadequate routing and switching infrastructure can create a number of problems.

Even if you optimize the Network Load Balancing cluster, an inadequate routing and switching infrastructure can restrict available network throughput and prevent clients from achieving any improvement in response times. Additionally, an inadequate routing and switching infrastructure can allow a single failure in a router, switch, or network path to disrupt communications with the cluster.

Determine the network infrastructure requirements for your cluster by completing the following steps:

1. Determine the IP subnet requirements for the cluster.

2. Determine how the cluster handles inbound and outbound traffic.

3. Determine when to include switches or hubs to connect cluster hosts to one another.

For more information about how the network infrastructure affects availability, see "Ensuring Availability in NLB Solutions" later in this chapter. For more information about how the network infrastructure affects scalability, see "Scaling NLB Solutions" later in this chapter.

Determining Cluster IP Subnet Requirements

Network Load Balancing requires that all cluster hosts be on the same IP subnet or virtual IP subnet (VLAN). This is because all cluster hosts share the cluster's virtual IP address. The routing infrastructure sends client requests to all cluster hosts by using a virtualized unicast MAC address or a multicast MAC address. For more information about unicast and multicast addressing, see "Selecting the Unicast or Multicast Method of Distributing Incoming Requests" earlier in this chapter.

Determining How the Cluster Handles Inbound and Outbound Traffic

Network Load Balancing cluster traffic is handled differently for inbound and outbound traffic. The differences between inbound client requests and outbound responses affect the network infrastructure and the use of switches and hubs.

Inbound cluster traffic is sent to all cluster hosts by using broadcasts or multicast traffic, which is required so that all cluster hosts can receive the inbound traffic. Switches learn where to send packets by watching the source packets that are sent from the computers directly connected to the switch. After the switch learns a computer's location, the switch sends subsequent packets to the same switch port.

From an inbound-traffic perspective, the behavior of the switch is similar to a hub, because inbound cluster traffic is sent to all switch ports. However, from an outbound-traffic perspective, the switch provides isolation by preventing other cluster hosts from seeing a response to a client from the cluster host that services the client request.

For more information about the behavior of Network Load Balancing traffic, see the Network Load Balancing Technical Overview link on the Web Resources page at http://www.microsoft.com/windows/reskits/webresources.

Determining When to Include Switches or Hubs for Interconnecting Cluster Hosts

For most networks, switches are the preferred technology for connecting network devices to one another. Although many existing network infrastructures have hubs, switches are typically used in new deployments.

Although Network Load Balancing works in most configurations of switches and hubs, some configurations allow for optimal performance, and they provide ease of maintenance and operations. The recommended configuration is to use switches for interconnecting cluster hosts. Configurations that include hubs are also supported, but they require more complex network infrastructure and configuration.

The supported configurations for switches and hubs include:

- Cluster hosts connected to a switch that is dedicated to the cluster.

- Cluster hosts connected to a switch that is shared with other devices.

- Cluster hosts connected to a hub that is connected to a switch.

Cluster hosts connected to a switch that is dedicated to the cluster

In this configuration, the cluster hosts connect to a switch that is dedicated to the cluster. Because the inbound cluster traffic is sent to all ports on the switch, the primary advantage of a switch for inbound traffic — segregating traffic to a limited number of switch ports — is lost.

However, for outbound traffic, only the cluster host responding to the client request is aware of the traffic, because the switch isolates the outbound traffic to the port connected to the responding cluster host. This reduces the congestion of traffic for all the cluster hosts that are connected to the switch.

Cluster hosts connected to a switch that is shared with other devices

In this configuration, the cluster hosts are connected to a switch that is shared with other devices. The switch sends inbound cluster traffic to the other devices as well, creating unnecessary traffic for the other devices.

You can isolate the inbound cluster traffic to only the cluster hosts by establishing a VLAN comprising the ports that connect to the cluster hosts. After you establish the VLAN, inbound cluster traffic is sent only to the cluster hosts and not to the other devices that are attached to the same switch. Using a VLAN to segregate inbound client traffic works for the unicast or multicast method of distributing incoming requests. You can also use the multicast method with IGMP to limit inbound cluster traffic only to the cluster hosts.

Because outbound cluster traffic is sent directly to the client that originated the request, only the cluster host responding to the request sees the outbound cluster traffic. All other cluster hosts, and the other devices connected to the same switch, are unaware of the outbound cluster traffic.

Cluster hosts connected to a hub that is connected to a switch

From the perspective of inbound cluster traffic, a switch provides no additional benefit over a hub, except for being able to define a VLAN that isolates inbound traffic from other devices attached to the switch. Because all cluster hosts receive the inbound cluster traffic, the switch sends all inbound traffic to all ports that are attached to the switch (or ports that are assigned to the same VLAN).

From the perspective of outbound cluster traffic, a switch provides a greater advantage, because it reduces the network contention for outbound cluster traffic. With a switch, only the cluster host originating the outbound cluster traffic is aware of the traffic, because outbound traffic is switched. Using a hub causes network contention for all cluster hosts. With a hub, all cluster hosts receive, and subsequently determine if they need to process, the outbound cluster traffic.

To eliminate the network contention caused by using a hub, install an additional network adapter in each cluster host for the purpose of responding to client traffic. Inbound requests are received through the cluster adapters in each cluster host, while the outbound responses are sent to the clients through the additional network adapter.

Because of the increased complexity of configuration (adding an additional network adapter to each cluster host) and network infrastructure (adding an additional switch to connect all the additional network adapters to the clients), this is not a recommended configuration. Because a switch is required for the additional network adapters, it is easier to eliminate the additional network adapters and connect the cluster adapters to a switch.

If you are considering adding network adapters to improve cluster performance, consider increasing the data rate of the cluster network adapters and corresponding network infrastructure, instead of adding network adapters. For example, to increase available network bandwidth, specify 100 megabits per second (Mbps) network adapters instead of 10 Mbps network adapters (along with the appropriate upgrades to intermediary switches and routers). For more information about increasing the available network bandwidth to the cluster, see "Increasing Available Network Bandwidth to the Cluster" later in this chapter.

Example: Specifying Cluster Network Connectivity

An organization has e-commerce Web applications that are accessed by users on the Internet. The organization's design includes Network Load Balancing to eliminate any application outages and improve performance. The e-commerce Web applications, running on IIS 6.0 and Windows Server 2003, will reside in the organization's perimeter network, which is located between the Internet and the organization's private network.

Figure 8.8 illustrates the existing firewalls, Internet connectivity, and connectivity to the organization's private network.

Figure 8.8   Existing Network Diagram Before the E-Commerce Web Application Solution

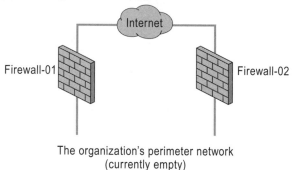

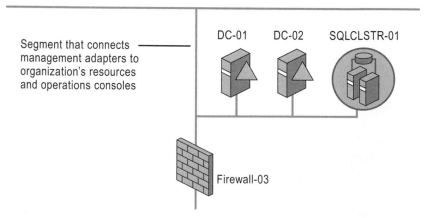

The e-commerce Web application requires support for 1,500 simultaneous users and an acceptable data transfer rate of 10 kilobits per second (Kbps) for each user, for a total aggregate data rate of 15 Mbps.

The organization has conducted lab testing on the devices in the organization's design, including routers, switches, network segments, and servers, and it has determined their capacity as listed in Table 8.16.

Table 8.16 Device Capacity Results from Lab Testing

Device	Results Verified in the Lab
IIS server	▪ Supports 200 simultaneous users. ▪ Provides total aggregate data rates up to 50 Mbps.
Router	▪ Supports virtual IP subnets (VLANs). ▪ Provides total aggregate data rate of 20 Mbps. ▪ Requires manual ARP registration of a unicast IP address with a multicast MAC address.
Switch	▪ Supports virtual IP subnets (VLANs). ▪ Provides total aggregate data rate of 60 Mbps.

Figure 8.9 illustrates the organization's network infrastructure after including the e-commerce Web solution.

Figure 8.9 E-Commerce Web Solution with Network Load Balancing

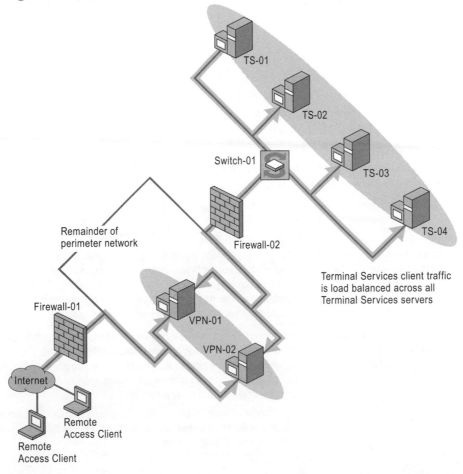

Table 8.17 lists the design decisions in specifying cluster network connectivity and the reasons for making the decisions.

Table 8.17   Cluster Network Connectivity Design Decisions and Their Justification

Decision	Reason for the Decision
Include eight IIS servers (cluster hosts).	Each IIS server supports a maximum of 200 users, and eight servers are required to achieve 1,500 simultaneous users.
Specify unicast mode for distributing incoming client requests.	Network infrastructure supports unicast mode.
Specify VLAN-01 between Switch-01 and Switch-02.	All hosts on the cluster must belong to the same IP subnet.
Place cluster hosts on Switch-01 and Switch-02.	Bandwidth of a single switch is insufficient to handle cluster host traffic.

Ensuring Ease of Cluster Management and Operations

After your Network Load Balancing cluster is deployed, the operations staff in your organization takes primary responsibility for the day-to-day operations of the cluster. In addition to normal administration tasks required to maintain the operating system, such as applying service packs and upgrading the operating system, over the IT life cycle of your cluster, the operations team also maintains and upgrades applications on the cluster.

Follow the guidelines presented in Table 8.18 to help create Network Load Balancing clusters that are easier to manage and operate.

Table 8.18   Guidelines for Designing NLB Clusters for Easy Management

Guideline	Explanation
Include sufficient cluster hosts to support maintenance and failover needs.	Cluster management is easier if enough cluster hosts exist to support client requests when one of the hosts is offline due to maintenance, upgrade, or failure. During lab testing, determine the number of cluster hosts required to support the required client traffic, and then add at least one additional cluster host.
Create a network infrastructure design that can accommodate a change in the number of cluster hosts.	The network infrastructure design must be flexible enough to allow the removal and addition of cluster hosts. When creating the supporting network infrastructure design, include additional ports on the switches or hubs connecting cluster hosts to support the addition of cluster hosts, as required.
	By adding additional network infrastructure support, cluster hosts can be added easily by the operations team without redesigning or recabling the existing network infrastructure.

During the IT life cycle of the cluster, upgrades are performed on the cluster by the operations team. The operations team typically performs these as *rolling upgrades*, by upgrading individual cluster hosts, one at a time, until the entire cluster is upgraded. For more information about performing rolling upgrades, see "Deploying Network Load Balancing" in this book.

Scaling out improves cluster performance by adding cluster hosts to the cluster and distributing client traffic across more cluster hosts. For more information about scaling your cluster, see "Scaling NLB Solutions" later in this chapter.

Example: Ensuring Ease of Cluster Management and Operations

An organization has five mission-critical applications that must be run by remote users. These remote users connect to the organization's private network through a VPN tunnel. The remote users run the applications on servers running Terminal Services.

Because of the number of simultaneous remote users, three servers running Terminal Services are required. The number of servers was determined during the lab-testing phase of the solution. To provide load balancing and fault tolerance, the servers are part of a Network Load Balancing cluster.

The number of remote users that simultaneously access the Terminal Services farm is expected to increase over the lifetime of the farm. Also, the applications running on the farm need to be upgraded periodically, and this requires that the servers be restarted.

Table 8.19 lists the design decisions for ensuring the cluster is easier to maintain and operate and the reasons for making the decisions.

Table 8.19   Cluster Maintenance and Operations Decisions and Their Justification

Decision	Reason for the Decision
Include an additional cluster host.	Ensures that the upgrades to individual servers in the Terminal Services farm can be performed without affecting client response times.
Provide unused ports on Switch-01.	Provides expansion for the addition of cluster hosts (servers running Terminal Services).

Figure 8.10 illustrates the network infrastructure after the optimization of the design to ensure ease of cluster management and operations.

Figure 8.10   Infrastructure Optimized for Ease of Cluster Management and Operations

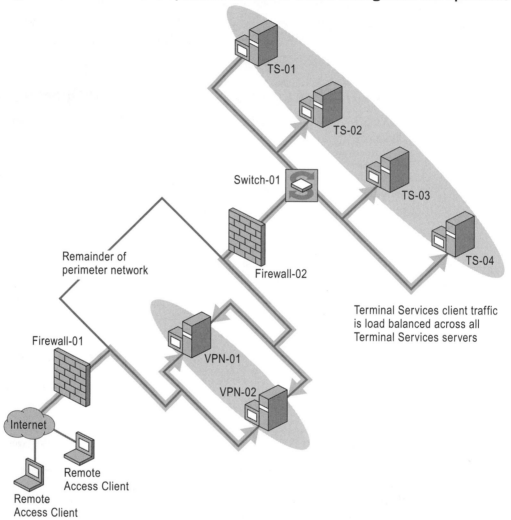

Securing NLB Solutions

The fact that your solution requires Network Load Balancing indicates that the applications and services are critical to the operations of your organization. The stability and integrity of your solution depend on how secure you make the resources that are used by the applications services. Besides protecting confidential data, the security that you include in your design ensures the stability of your applications and services. Use the features of Windows Server 2003 to protect the resources and applications running on cluster hosts. Plan security for your network load balancing solution immediately after determining the core specifications for your Network Load Balancing design, as illustrated in Figure 8.11.

Figure 8.11   Securing Network Load Balancing Solutions

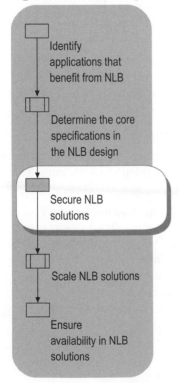

✓ **Note**

For a Word document to assist you in documenting your security settings, see "NLB Cluster Host Worksheet" (Sdcnlb_1.doc) on the *Windows Server 2003 Deployment Kit* companion CD (or see "NLB Cluster Host Worksheet" on the Web at http://www.microsoft.com/reskit).

One of the most important methods of protecting resources and applications on Network Load Balancing clusters is to ensure that only authorized users can remotely manage your clusters. To remotely manage clusters, users must be members of the local Administrators group on every cluster host in the cluster.

 Note
Users who are members of the local Administrators group can administer Network Load Balancing locally, regardless of other restrictions.

Ensure that only authorized users can remotely manage clusters by following these practices:

- Specify that remote management by using Nlb.exe be disabled on all cluster hosts.

  By default, remote management through Nlb.exe is disabled on clusters. Remote administration by using Nlb.exe is not recommended, because this method presents many security risks, including the possibility of data tampering, denial-of-service attacks, and information disclosure.

  If you choose to enable remote control for Nlb.exe, restrict access by specifying a strong remote-control password. Also, include a firewall to protect the Network Load Balancing UDP ports (the ports that receive remote control commands) by allowing access only to authorized client computers.

- Specify that Network Load Balancing Manager be used for all administration.

- Specify that administration be performed only from a secure, trusted computer that is within your organization's private network or that is connected through a VPN remote access connection.

In addition to the security provided by restricting the administration of Network Load Balancing, you can further protect the applications, services, and confidential data on the cluster by using other Windows Server 2003 security features. These security features are specific to the applications and services running on the cluster. For more information about the security features provided by the applications and services running on the cluster, see the security content for the documents listed in "Additional Resources" later in this chapter.

Example: Securing NLB Solutions

An organization has e-commerce Web applications that are accessed by Internet users. The design includes Network Load Balancing to eliminate any application outages and improve performance. The e-commerce Web applications, running on IIS 6.0 and Windows Server 2003, resides in the organization's perimeter network, which is located between the Internet and the organization's private network.

Figure 8.12 illustrates the e-commerce Web farm network design after the placement of the following components:

- Network infrastructure, including firewalls, routers, switches, and network segments
- IIS 6.0 servers into the perimeter network
- Active Directory® directory service domain controllers
- A computer running Windows Server 2003 and SQL Server 2000 on a server cluster
- A computer running Windows Server 2003 and file services on a server cluster

Figure 8.12   IIS 6.0 E-Commerce Web Farm Solution

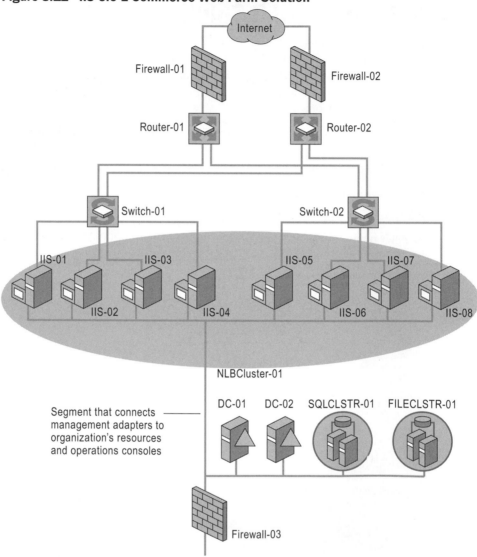

Table 8.20 lists the design decisions that were made to protect the applications and resources on the cluster and the reasons for making those decisions.

Table 8.20   Cluster Security Design Decisions

Decision	Reason for the Decision
IIS 6.0 servers are placed behind Firewall-01 and Firewall-02.	Prevents unwanted client traffic by filtering unnecessary client traffic.
Isolated network for communication is placed between the cluster and other servers in organization.	Prevents users outside the organization from viewing communications between the cluster and other servers in the organization.
Remote management is disabled.	Prevents unauthorized users from managing the cluster.

Scaling NLB Solutions

One of the primary reasons for including Network Load Balancing in your network design solution is to provide the ability to scale out your network by adding additional servers. Any other methods of improving client response times are not directly related to Network Load Balancing, but rather to the network infrastructure and system hardware associated with the cluster. Figure 8.13 illustrates the steps involved in incorporating scaling options in your Network Load Balancing solution.

Figure 8.13   Scaling Network Load Balancing Solutions

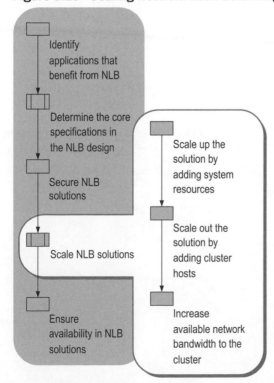

Also, you can ensure the scalability of applications and services by using methods that are specific to the applications and services running on the cluster. For more information about improving the scalability of services running on Network Load Balancing, see "Additional Resources" later in this chapter.

 Note

Document your design on your organization's network diagram. For a Word document to assist you in documenting your Network Load Balancing design decisions, see "NLB Cluster Host Worksheet" (Sdcnlb_1.doc) on the *Windows Server 2003 Deployment Kit* companion CD (or see "NLB Cluster Host Worksheet" on the Web at http://www.microsoft.com/reskit).

Scaling Up the Solution by Adding System Resources

During the lab testing and pilot testing of your Network Load Balancing design, you might discover that the cluster hosts are not responding within the requirements for your solution. Also, as you anticipate the increase in growth that your design must support, the cluster hosts need to continue to respond in accordance with your solution requirements. When a cluster becomes unable to respond the client requests within a specified time, you can improve the performance by *scaling up* your solution.

Take the following actions to scale up your solution:

- Increase system resources (such as processors, memory, disks, and network adapters) for the existing cluster host.

- Replace the existing cluster host with another system that has greater resources.

Scaling up is appropriate in the following situations:

- You want to reduce the total cost of ownership (TCO) by including fewer, more powerful cluster hosts in your design.

- The client response time is insufficient for a cluster host that is supporting the required number of users.

Scale up your solution by adding system resources by completing the following steps:

1. Identify the applications or services running on the Network Load Balancing cluster.

2. Identify the system resources that are consumed by the applications or services running on the cluster.

   Because Network Load Balancing requires only minimal system resources, the applications and services running on the cluster determine the system resources that are consumed first. For more information about the system resource requirements for services running on Network Load Balancing, see "Additional Resources" later in this chapter.

3. Verify the system resource estimates in your deployment lab.

4. Modify the system resource requirements based on the data from your testing in the deployment lab.

5. Document the system requirements in your design.

 Note
You can reduce the system resource requirements for your cluster hosts and avoid scaling up by eliminating any unnecessary applications or services. For more information about the required applications or services in your solution, see "Additional Resources" later in this chapter.

Scaling Out the Solution by Adding Cluster Hosts

Another method that you can use to improve client response time is *scaling out*. You scale out your solution when you add cluster hosts to existing clusters.

Scaling out your solution is appropriate in the following situations:

- You want to reduce TCO by including more, less-expensive cluster hosts in your design.

- You cannot further upgrade the system resources of the existing cluster hosts.

 Tip
To further improve client response time, consider scaling up the cluster host system resources as you scale out.

Scale out your solution by adding cluster hosts to the cluster and completing the following steps:

1. Identify the applications or services that require scaling out.

2. Identify any port rules that are associated with the application or services.

3. Include the additional cluster hosts in the cluster.

4. When appropriate, divide the cluster hosts into separate clusters and use round robin DNS to distribute client traffic across the clusters.

Scaling Out Within a Single Cluster

Determine the number of cluster hosts that are required in your design by estimating the number of clients each host can support and then testing your estimates in your lab. The maximum number of clients that each cluster host can support depends on the applications and services running on the host. For more information about capacity planning for the applications and services running on Network Load Balancing clusters, see "Additional Resources" later in this chapter.

The maximum number of cluster hosts in a cluster depends on a number of factors, such as the network infrastructure or protocols used by the applications and services running on the cluster, in addition to any Network Load Balancing limitations.

The only method of determining the maximum number of hosts in a cluster is by testing your configuration in a lab. When your lab tests indicate that you are unable to support the number of simultaneous clients by scaling out within a single cluster, scale out by using multiple clusters.

Network infrastructure devices, such as routers or switches, can also limit the network throughput to the cluster and ultimately affect how much you can scale out a cluster. To overcome this limitation, you can increase the network infrastructure capacity by changing the number and placement of routers and switches. However, the changes to the network infrastructure capacity might prevent you from keeping the cluster hosts on the same subnet or VLAN. Because all the cluster hosts must be on the same subnet or VLAN, scaling out with a single cluster is inadequate and you must scale out by using multiple clusters on separate subnets or VLANs.

Scaling Out by Using Multiple Clusters

If you are unable to scale out your applications on a single cluster, you can scale out by using multiple clusters. Then distribute the client traffic across the multiple clusters by using round robin DNS.

For example, an organization is getting ready to deploy a new high-volume Web site for its Internet presence. To support the required number of client requests, 72 cluster hosts are necessary. In lab testing, the organization determines that the network infrastructure can support only 9 clusters hosts per VLAN. As a result, eight clusters are required to scale out the organization's Web farm. Table 8.21 lists the clusters and the IP addresses that are assigned to each cluster.

Table 8.21   Clusters and Their IP Addresses in Round-Robin DNS

Network Load Balancing Cluster	Assigned IP Address
IISNLB-01	10.0.1.100
IISNLB-02	10.0.2.100
IISNLB-03	10.0.3.100
IISNLB-04	10.0.4.100
IISNLB-05	10.0.5.100
IISNLB-06	10.0.6.100
IISNLB-07	10.0.7.100
IISNLB-08	10.0.8.100

Figure 8.14 illustrates an IIS 6.0 Web farm in which client traffic is distributed across multiple Network Load Balancing clusters by using round robin DNS.

Figure 8.14   Using Round Robin DNS to Distribute Client Traffic Across Clusters

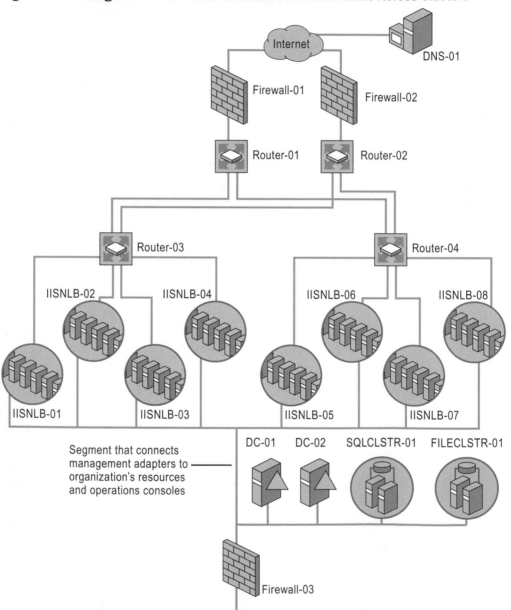

The DNS name of the IIS 6.0 application Web farm is www.contoso.com. The DNS zone for contoso.com contains multiple entries for www.contoso.com, as required by round robin DNS. Each DNS entry corresponds to a Network Load Balancing cluster in the IIS 6.0 application Web farm. Round robin DNS distributes client traffic to the clusters, and then Network Load Balancing distributes client traffic within the cluster.

One of the assumptions in combining Network Load Balancing and round robin DNS is that an entire cluster is never taken offline. When an entire cluster is offline, DNS still directs client requests to the offline cluster and some clients will experience service outages, as they do when round robin DNS entries point to an individual server that is offline. To prevent clients from experiencing service outages, take only individual cluster hosts offline for maintenance or for other reasons.

For more information about round robin DNS, see "Deploying DNS" in *Deploying Network Services* of this kit.

Increasing Available Network Bandwidth to the Cluster

Other steps in improving client response time directly affect the cluster hosts themselves. However, even with a highly optimized cluster, inadequate network bandwidth between the clients and the cluster can increase client response times to unacceptable levels.

Increase the available bandwidth between clients and the cluster by completing the following steps:

1. Identify the intermediary network segments, routers, and switches between the clients and the clusters.

2. Calculate the aggregate bandwidth requirements for the maximum number of simultaneous users.

3. Determine the intermediary network segments, routers, and switches between the clients and the clusters that are unable to support the aggregate bandwidth requirements.

4. Modify your design to increase the available bandwidth, based on the information in Table 8.22.

Table 8.22 Increasing Bandwidth Based on Network Infrastructure Limitations

Available Bandwidth Limited By	Increase Bandwidth by One or More of These Methods
Network segment available capacity	▪ Increase the data rate of the network segment. (Upgrade from Integrated Services Digital Network (ISDN) to digital subscriber line (DSL) or T1.) ▪ Include additional network segments, and distribute the network traffic across the network segments.
Switch capacity	▪ Increase the data rate of the switch and the devices that are connected to the switch. (Upgrade from 10BaseT to 100BaseT or 1000BaseT.) ▪ Include additional switches, and distribute the computers that are connected to the original switch across the switches.
Router capacity	▪ Increase the data rate of the router and the devices that are connected to the router. (Upgrade from 10BaseT to 100BaseT or 1000BaseT.) ▪ Include additional routers, and create redundant routes to load balance the network traffic between the routers.

Example: Scaling NLB Solutions

An organization provides VPN remote access to the organization's users through the Internet. The design includes Network Load Balancing to eliminate any application outages and to improve performance. The VPN remote access servers, which run Routing and Remote Access and Windows Server 2003, reside in the organization's perimeter network, which is located between the Internet and the organization's private network.

Pilot testing of the VPN remote access solution indicates the need for an increase in remote access client performance. Figure 8.15 illustrates the Routing and Remote Access VPN design to be tested.

Figure 8.15 VPN Solution Pilot Test Environment

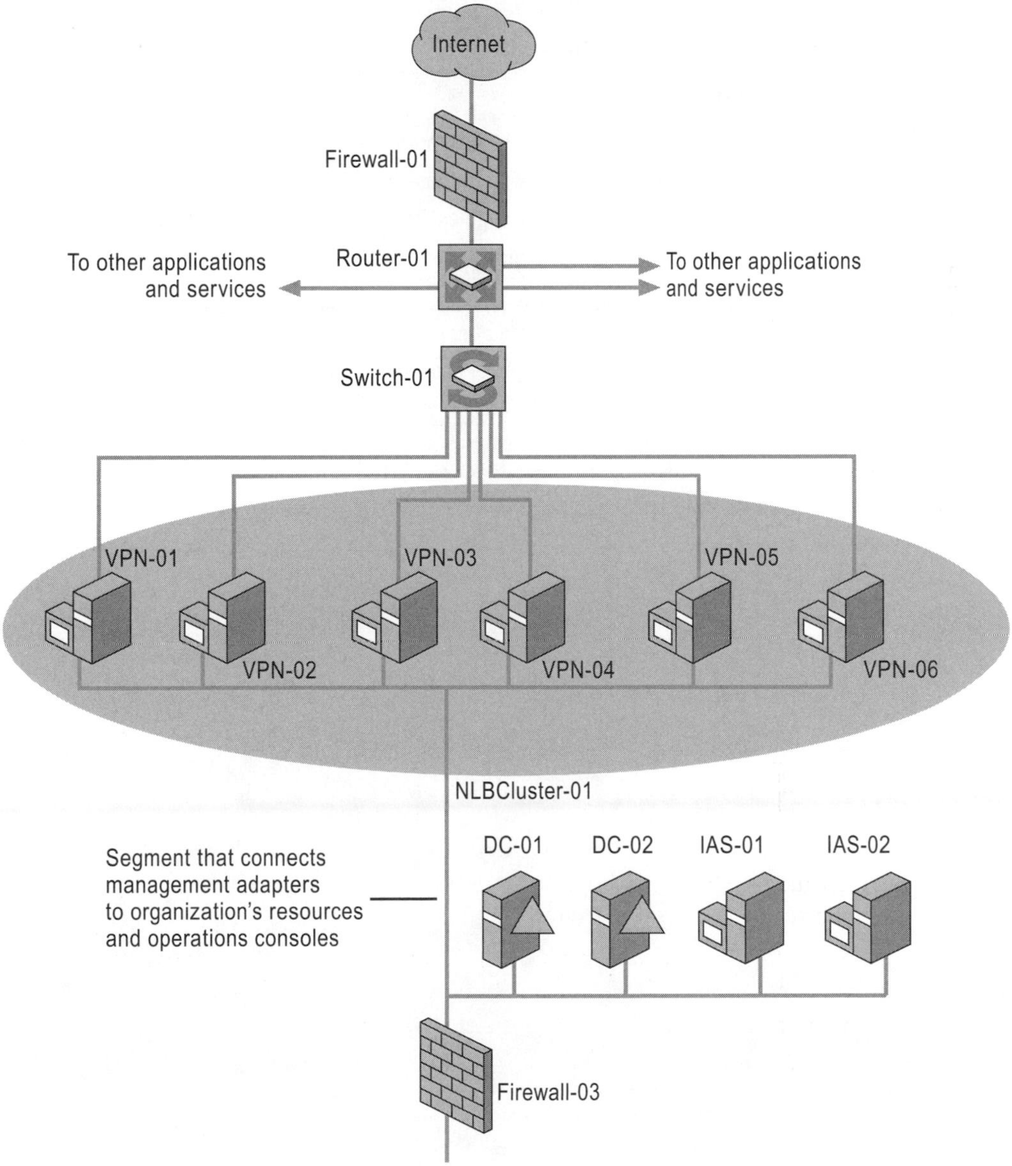

Table 8.23 lists the results of the pilot test for each portion of the design that is illustrated in Figure 8.15.

Table 8.23   Results of VPN Pilot Test

Design Portion Tested	Results
Network infrastructure	▪ Router-01 was saturated with client traffic. ▪ Switch-01 was saturated with client traffic. ▪ The network segment between Switch-01 and Router-01 was saturated. ▪ The connection to the Internet was saturated.
Cluster hosts hardware	▪ Individual cluster hosts lacked sufficient memory to handle the required number of simultaneous users. ▪ The total number of cluster hosts was insufficient to handle total number of simultaneous users.

After the pilot test, the organization modifies the VPN remote access design. Figure 8.16 illustrates the modified version of the VPN design.

Figure 8.16 Revised VPN Remote Access Design

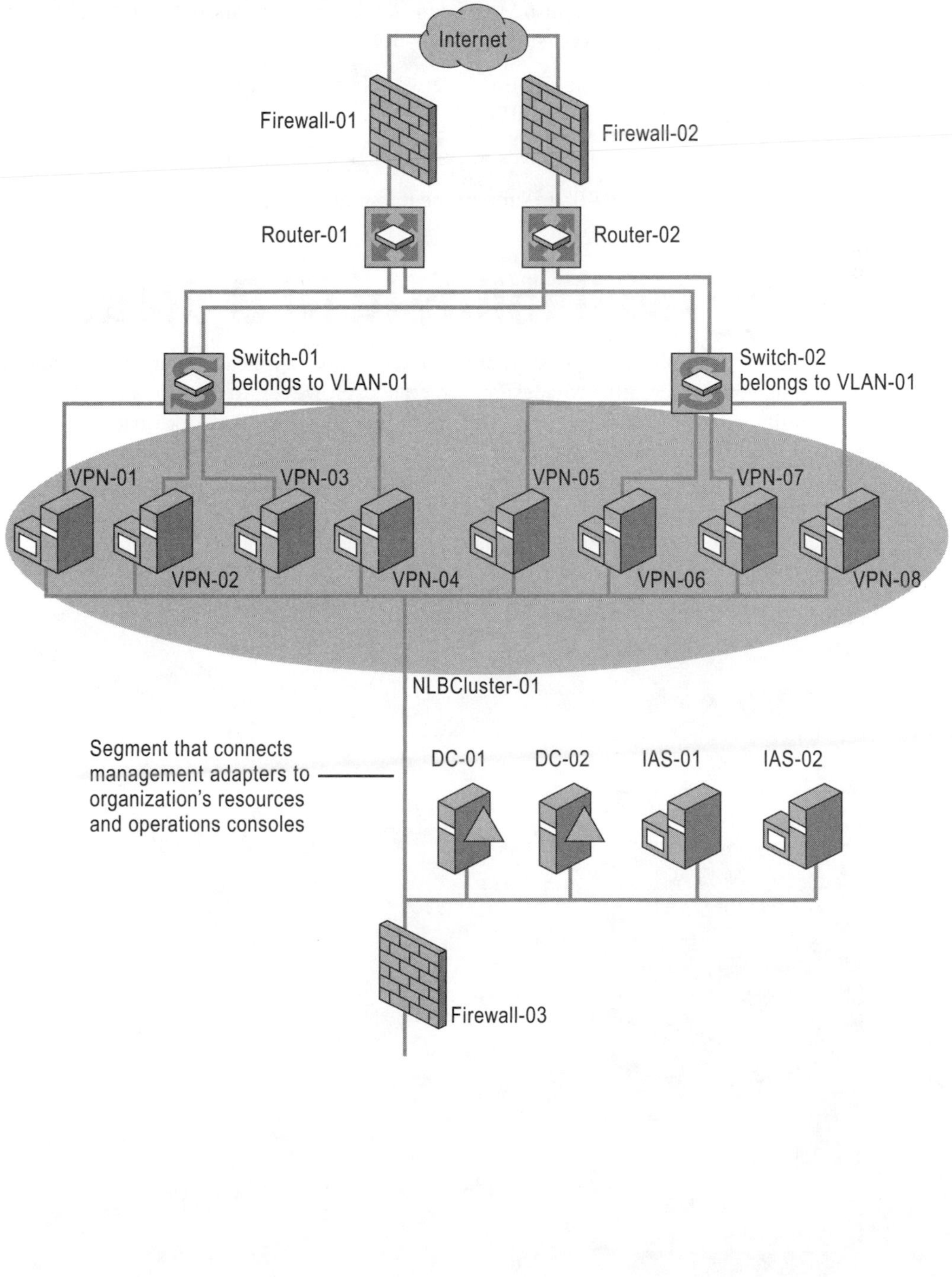

The organization made the following design decisions to improve scalability for the cluster:

- Add Firewall-02 and Router-02 to provide additional network bandwidth to the Internet and to solve the saturation problem on Router-01.

- Add Switch-02 to provide additional network bandwidth to the Internet and to solve the saturation problem on Switch-01.

- Add memory for all cluster hosts to ensure sufficient system resources for the hosts.

- Add VPN-07 and VPN-08 to support the maximum number of simultaneous users.

Ensuring Availability in NLB Solutions

By including multiple cluster hosts that provide the same applications and services, Network Load Balancing inherently provides fault tolerance. However, to provide a complete high-availability solution, your design must include more than just Network Load Balancing. The network infrastructure and system hardware that are associated with the cluster also affect the availability of the applications and services running on the cluster. In addition, include application-level monitoring, such as the monitoring provided by MOM or Application Center 2000, to ensure that applications are operating correctly. Ensuring availability is the final task in designing a network load balancing solution, as shown in Figure 8.17.

Figure 8.17   Ensuring Availability in Network Load Balancing Solutions

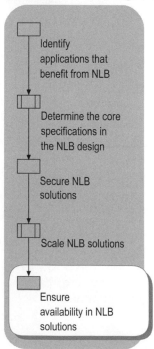

Include the following items to ensure high availability for clients that access applications and services on the cluster:

- Cluster hosts with fault-tolerant hardware

- Signed device drivers and software only

- Fault-tolerant network infrastructure

Also, you can improve the availability of applications and services by using methods that are specific to the applications and services running on the cluster. For more information about improving the availability of services running on Network Load Balancing, see "Additional Resources" later in this chapter.

 Note

After you design the specifications for ensuring availability, document your decisions. For a Word document to assist you in recording your decisions, see "NLB Cluster Host Worksheet" (Sdcnlb_1.doc) on the *Windows Server 2003 Deployment Kit* companion CD (or see "NLB Cluster Host Worksheet" on the Web at http://www.microsoft.com/reskit).

Including Fault-Tolerant Hardware on Cluster Hosts

The cluster host hardware that you specify in your design can affect the uptime of the applications and services in your solution. Including system hardware with a longer mean time between failure (MTBF) can ensure that you experience fewer cluster host failures. In addition, including cluster hosts with fault-tolerant hardware can prevent unnecessary outages in your cluster.

For more information about including fault-tolerant hardware in your design, see "Planning for High Availability and Scalability" in this book.

Including Signed Device Drivers and Software Only

Another method of improving application and services uptime is to include only signed device drivers and software on the cluster hosts. Drivers and software that are signed have been certified by Microsoft, your organization, or third-party companies that your organization trusts. Because unstable drivers and software can affect cluster uptime, including only signed device drivers and software helps ensure the stability of the cluster.

You can specify Group Policy settings in Active Directory to centrally configure the cluster hosts for the appropriate driver signing settings. When you are unable to specify driver signing by using Active Directory, specify the Local Security policies for each cluster host.

For more information about signed device drivers and software, see "Driver signing for Windows" in Help and Support Center for Windows Server 2003. For more information about specifying Group Policy settings, see "Designing a Group Policy Infrastructure" in *Designing a Managed Environment* of this kit.

Including a Fault-Tolerant Network Infrastructure

Even if you perform all the previous steps to ensure fault tolerance for improving application and services uptime, your solution is not complete. Even with a highly optimized cluster, failures in the network infrastructure between the clients and the cluster can reduce uptime for applications and services.

To include a fault-tolerant network infrastructure between the clients and the cluster, complete the following steps:

1. Identify the intermediary network segments, routers, and switches between the clients and the cluster.

2. Determine if any of the intermediary network segments, routers, and switches between the clients and the cluster are potential points of failure that can cause application and services outages.

3. Modify your design to provide a fault-tolerant network infrastructure, based on the information in Table 8.24.

Table 8.24   Providing Network Infrastructure Fault Tolerance Based on Limitations

Potential Failure Points	Include Any of These Fault-Tolerance Solutions
Network connection failure	Redundant network connections to provide fault tolerance in the event that a network connection fails. For example, if you are connected to the Internet by a single T1 connection, a failure of the T1 connection would prevent clients from accessing the cluster. Specify a redundant T1 connection to help prevent this type of failure.
Switch failure	Redundant switches to provide fault tolerance in the event that a switch fails.
Router failure	Redundant routers and redundant routes to provide fault tolerance in the event that a router fails.

Example: Ensuring Availability in NLB Solutions

An organization provides VPN remote access to the organization's users through the Internet. The organization's design includes Network Load Balancing to eliminate any application outages and improve performance. The VPN remote access servers, running Routing and Remote Access and Windows Server 2003, reside in the organization's perimeter network, which is located between the Internet and the organization's private network.

The design includes ISA Server, which protects the VPN remote access servers in the perimeter network. The ISA Server servers are in a cluster (ISANLB-01) that provides load balancing and fault tolerance.

During the pilot testing of the Web content caching solution, with ISA Server, the deployment team experiences a number of outages that affect the entire solution. Figure 8.18 illustrates the Web content caching design, incorporating ISA Server, that is tested.

Figure 8.18   VPN Remote Access Test Environment

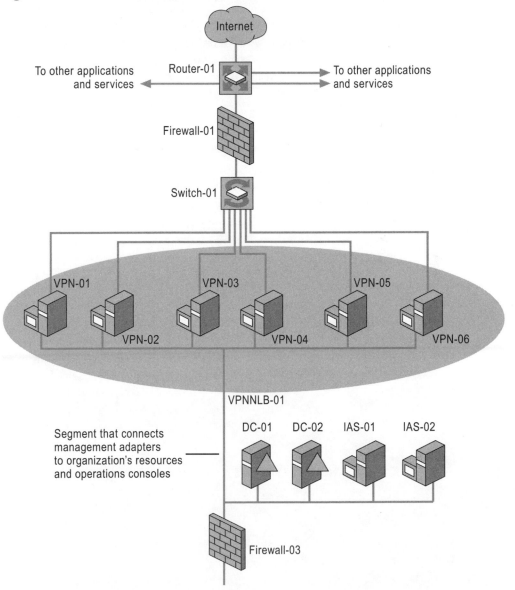

Table 8.25 lists the results of the pilot test for each portion of the design that is illustrated in Figure 8.18.

Table 8.25 Results of VPN Pilot Test

Design Portion Tested	Results
Network infrastructure	▪ A failure of Router-01 resulted in total outage of VPN services. ▪ A failure of Switch-01 resulted in total outage of VPN services. ▪ A total outage of VPN services occurred for failure of the network segment between Router-01 and the Internet, or between Switch-01 and Router-01.
Cluster host hardware	▪ A failure of a disk drive in a cluster host resulted in a total cluster host failure. ▪ Network adapters in the cluster hosts have unsigned device drivers.

After the pilot test, the VPN remote access design is modified. Figure 8.19 illustrates the modified version of the VPN design.

Figure 8.19   Revised VPN Remote Access Design

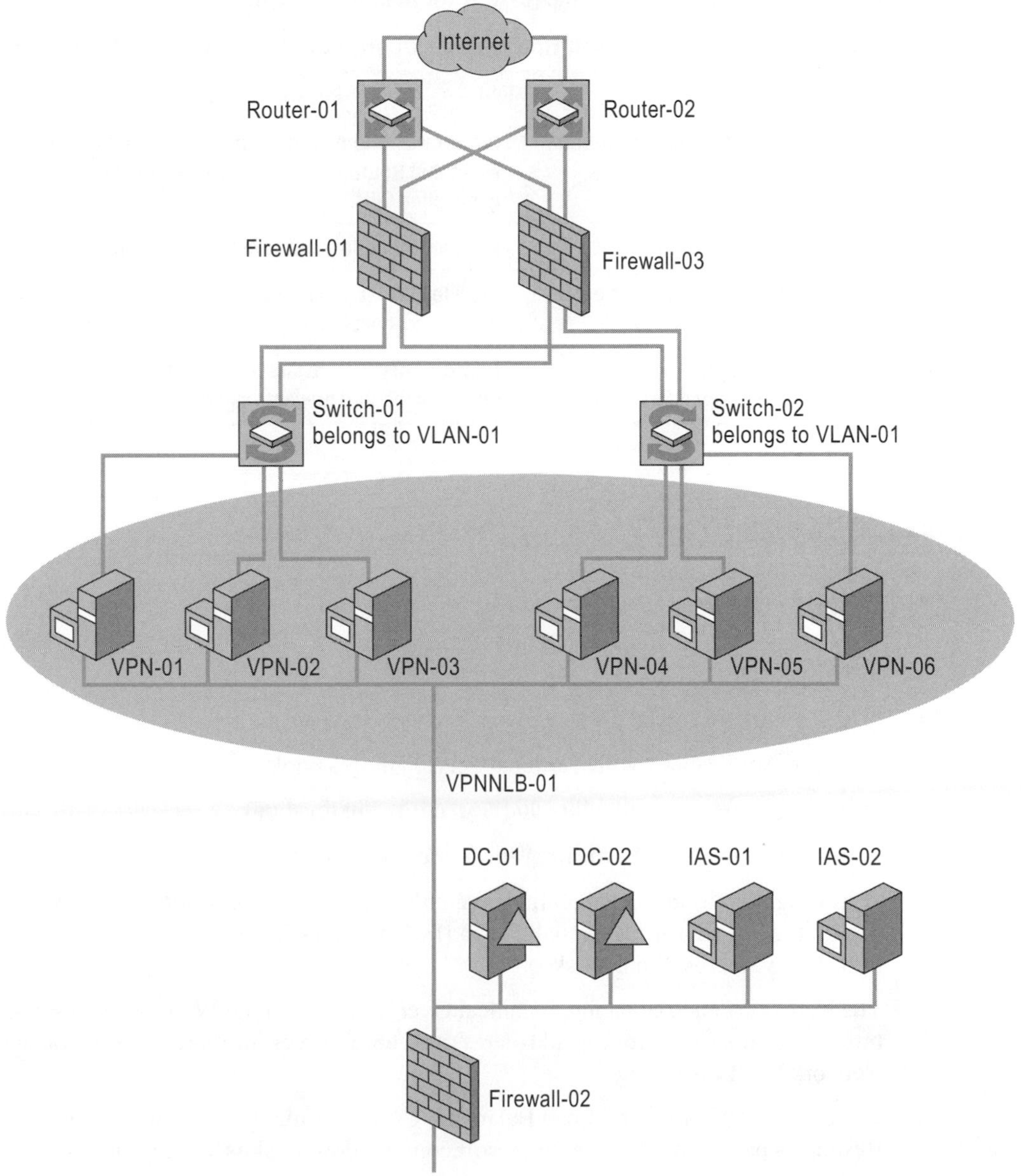

Table 8.26 lists the design decisions that the organization makes to improve the uptime for the VPN remote access solution and the reasons for making those decisions.

Table 8.26   Improving VPN Solution Uptime Design Decisions and Their Justification

Decision	Reason for the Decision
Added Router-02 and additional Internet connection.	Provides a redundant route path to the Internet in the event that Router-01 or the corresponding Internet connection fails.
Added Switch-02.	Provides redundant paths in the event that Switch-01 fails.
RAID disk controllers were used in each cluster host.	Provide disk fault tolerance to help prevent disk failures and cluster host failures.
Group Policy was established to allow cluster hosts to load signed device drivers.	Provides trusted software to help ensure a stable environment, and prevents cluster host failure.

Additional Resources

Related Information

- "Designing Dial-up and VPN Remote Access Servers" in *Deploying Network Services* in this kit.

- "Deploying ISA Server" in *Deploying Network Services* in this kit.

- "Hosting Applications with Terminal Server" in this book.

- "Planning for High Availability and Scalability" in this book.

- "Deploying DNS" in *Deploying Network Services* in this kit.

- "Ensuring Application Availability" in *Deploying Internet Information Services (IIS) 6.0* in this kit (or see "Ensuring Availability in IIS 6.0" on the Web at http://www.microsoft.com/reskit).

- The Network Load Balancing Technical Overview link on the Web Resources page at http://www.microsoft.com/windows/reskits/webresources for more information about Network Load Balancing.

- The Session Directory and Load Balancing Using Terminal Server link on the Web Resources page at http://www.microsoft.com/windows/reskits/webresources.

- Article Q193602, "Configuration Options for WLBS Hosts Connected to a Layer 2 Switches," in the Microsoft Knowledge Base. To find this article, see the Microsoft Knowledge Base link on the Web Resources pageat www.microsoft.com/windows/reskits/webresources.

Related Job Aids

- "NLB Cluster Host Worksheet" (Sdcnlb_1.doc) on the *Windows Server 2003 Deployment Kit* companion CD (or see "NLB Cluster Host Worksheet" on the Web at http://www.microsoft.com/reskit).

Related Help Topics

For best results in identifying Help topics by title, in Help and Support Center, under the **Search** box, click **Set search options**. Under **Help Topics**, select the **Search in title only** check box.

- "Network Load Balancing parameters" in Help and Support Center for Windows Server 2003.

- "Driver signing for Windows" in Help and Support Center for Windows Server 2003.

CHAPTER 9

Deploying Network Load Balancing

9

After completing the design for the applications and services in your Network Load Balancing cluster, you are ready to deploy the cluster running the Microsoft® Windows® Server 2003 operating system in your pilot and production network environments. A successful deployment ensures that your Network Load Balancing cluster meets or exceeds the specifications in the design. In addition, you must ensure that the deployment of your Network Load Balancing cluster does not disrupt the operation of any existing applications or services.

In This Chapter

Related Information

- For more information about the Network Load Balancing design process, see "Designing Network Load Balancing" in *Planning Server Deployments* of this kit.

- For more information about designing server clusters, see "Designing and Deploying Server Clusters" in *Planning Server Deployments*.

Overview of the NLB Deployment Process

A Network Load Balancing cluster comprises multiple servers running any version of the Windows Server 2003 family of operating systems, including Microsoft® Windows® Server 2003, Standard Edition; Windows® Server 2003, Enterprise Edition; Windows® Server 2003, Datacenter Edition; and Windows® Server 2003, Web Edition.

Clustering allows you to combine application servers to provide a level of scaling and availability that is not possible with an individual server. Network Load Balancing distributes incoming client requests among the servers in the cluster to more evenly balance the workload of each server and prevent overload on any one server. To client computers, the Network Load Balancing cluster appears as a single server that is highly scalable and fault tolerant.

The Network Load Balancing deployment process assumes that your design team has completed the design of the Network Load Balancing solution for your organization and has performed limited testing in a lab. After the design team tests the design in the lab, your deployment team implements the Network Load Balancing solution first in a pilot environment and then in your production environment.

Upon completing the deployment process presented here, your Network Load Balancing solution (the Network Load Balancing cluster and the applications and services running on the cluster) will be in place. For more information about the procedures for deploying Network Load Balancing on individual servers, see "New ways to do familiar tasks" in Help and Support Center for Windows Server 2003, and then click "Network Load Balancing Manager".

   Note

As you implement your Network Load Balancing design, use the information for each cluster host recorded by your design team in the "NLB Cluster Host Worksheet" (Sdcnlb_1.doc) on the *Windows Server 2003 Deployment Kit* companion CD (or see "NLB Cluster Host Worksheet" on the Web at http://www.microsoft.com/reskit).

NLB Deployment Process

Deploy your Network Load Balancing solution by implementing the decisions made by the design team. The process for deploying Network Load Balancing clusters is shown in Figure 9.1.

Figure 9.1   Deploying Network Load Balancing

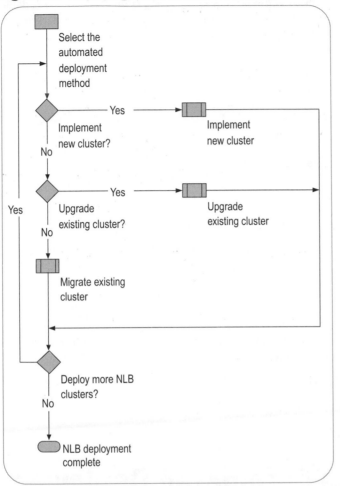

During the Network Load Balancing design process, the design team created and documented the design of the network configuration by using drawing and diagramming software (such as Microsoft® Visio®), and the "NLB Cluster Host Worksheet" job aid that your design team completed for each cluster host. (This worksheet is associated with "Designing Network Load Balancing" in *Planning Server Deployments* of this kit.) The Network Load Balancing design documents describe the number of Network Load Balancing clusters, the placement of the Network Load Balancing clusters in your network environment, the number of Network Load Balancing cluster hosts, and other specifications.

Before deploying Network Load Balancing in your production environment, test your deployment solution in a lab and in a pilot deployment. For more information about testing your design, see "Planning for Deployment" in *Planning, Testing, and Piloting Deployment Projects* of this kit.

After you test your design, you can use different options for deploying each Network Load Balancing cluster, based on the requirements of your organization. Table 9.1 lists deployment requirements and the corresponding options for deploying Network Load Balancing clusters. For each cluster in the Network Load Balancing design, select one of these options for deploying Network Load Balancing clusters.

Table 9.1   Deployment Requirements and Corresponding Options for Deploying NLB Clusters

Deployment Requirements	Implement	Upgrade	Migrate
Fresh installation of Windows Server 2003 is required	●		●
Clusters are to be deployed on new cluster hardware	●		●
Two or more existing clusters to be consolidated into a single cluster			●
A corresponding cluster currently exists in the network environment		●	●
Existing hardware is capable of running Windows Server 2003		●	
Existing Windows registry settings to be retained		●	

When your Network Load Balancing solution includes multiple Network Load Balancing clusters, you might need to use more than one method for deploying Network Load Balancing clusters. For each Network Load Balancing cluster in your solution, read the corresponding section in this chapter for the deployment method you select:

- Implementing New Clusters

- Upgrading Existing Clusters

- Migrating Existing Clusters

Selecting the Automated Deployment Method

Begin the deployment of your Network Load Balancing solution by determining how to automate your Network Load Balancing deployment. Automate the deployment of your Network Load Balancing solution to ensure the consistency of installation, to reduce the time required to deploy your solution, and to assist in restoring failed Network Load Balancing cluster hosts. Manually deploy your Network Load Balancing solution only if creating and testing the automation files and scripts would take more time than manually configuring the cluster. Figure 9.2 shows the process for determining the best method to automate the deployment of your Network Load Balancing solution.

Figure 9.2   Selecting the Automated Deployment Method

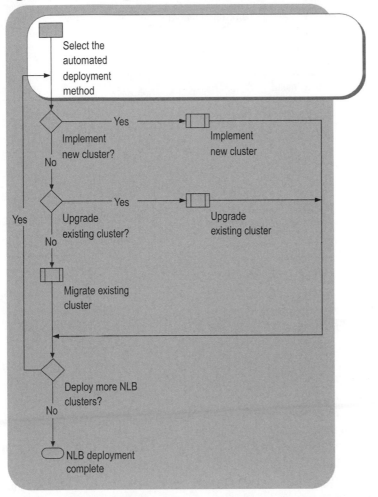

You can automate the deployment of Windows Server 2003 and Network Load Balancing cluster hosts by using one of the following methods:

- Unattended installation

- Sysprep

- Remote Installation Services (RIS)

Table 9.2 compares the characteristics of the various automated deployment methods.

Table 9.2   Comparing Automated Deployment Methods

Deployment Characteristics	Unattended Installation	Sysprep	RIS
Uses images to deploy installation		●	●
Uses scripts to customize installation	●	●	
Supports post installation scripts to install applications	●	●	●
Deployed by using local drives on the target server	●	●	
Initiated by headless servers			●
Deployed from a network share	●	●	

Depending on the requirements of each cluster, more than one method might be required to deploy all your Network Load Balancing clusters. For more information about these methods, see "Designing Unattended Installations," "Designing Image-based Installations with Sysprep," and "Designing RIS Installations" in *Automating and Customizing Installations* of this kit.

The unattended installation and Sysprep methods require that you create script files to automate the deployment. The Network Load Balancing–specific installation and configuration information is required in two sections of the unattended and Sysprep script files: the [MS_WLBS parameters] and [MS_TCPIP parameters] sections.

For more information about the process for configuring the script files, see the *Microsoft® Windows® Server 2003 Corporate Deployment Tools User's Guide* (Deploy.chm). Deploy.chm is included in the Deploy.cab file in the Support folder on the Windows Server 2003 operating system CD. For more information about the parameters used by the script files, see the Windows Preinstallation Environment link on the Web Resources page at http://www.microsoft.com/windows/reskits/webresources. There are no special considerations for automating Network Load Balancing deployment by using the RIS method.

For Network Load Balancing, you need to perform specific tasks when creating the unattended installation and Sysprep script files:

- Review the content in the Microsoft Windows Preinstallation Reference that relates to the [*MS_WLBS parameters*] section.

  WLBS stands for "Windows NT Load Balancing Service," the name of the load balancing service used in Microsoft® Windows NT® Server version 4.0. For reasons of backward compatibility, WLBS continues to be used in certain instances.

- Ensure that the IP addresses for the cluster and all virtual clusters are entered in the IPAddress parameter under the [*MS_TCPIP parameters*] section.

  Typically, Network Load Balancing Manager automatically adds the cluster and virtual cluster IP addresses to the list of IP addresses. Both unattended installation and Sysprep require that you add the addresses to the IPAddress parameter under the [*MS_TCPIP parameters*] section of the script.

Implementing a New Cluster

Many of the mission-critical applications deployed within your organization will be new applications, which require you to deploy new Network Load Balancing clusters. The process for implementing a new cluster involves more than installing Windows Server 2003 and Network Load Balancing on the individual application servers. Implementing a new cluster might require additional network infrastructure, network services, file services, database services, and security services. Figure 9.3 shows the steps that you must complete before and after the implementation of the new cluster.

Figure 9.3   Implementing a New Cluster

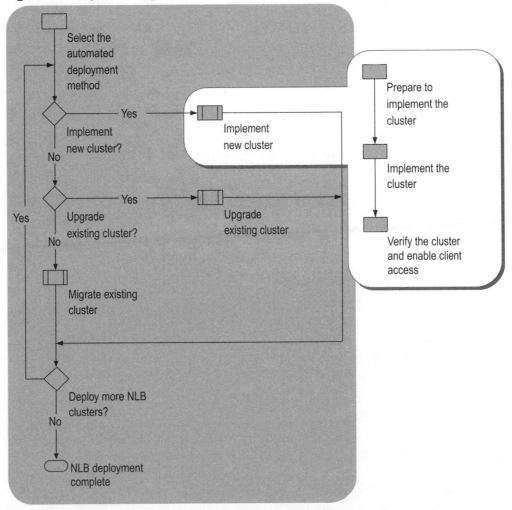

Preparing to Implement the Cluster

Your new cluster is dependent upon the network infrastructure and other network services in your total solution. Ensure that these network infrastructure and other network services are deployed prior to implementing your cluster.

Prepare for the implementation of the new cluster by using the information documented in the "NLB Cluster Host Worksheet" and other documentation (such as Visio drawings of the network environment) that your design team completed for a specific cluster host during the design process. Coordinate with the operations team during this step in the process to review the changes that will occur in your organization's network environment.

To prepare for the implementation of the new cluster, complete the following tasks:

1. Implement the network infrastructure required by the cluster and by the applications and services running on the cluster.

2. Implement any networking services required by the applications and services running on the cluster.

3. Select the method for automating any additional Network Load Balancing configuration.

Implementing the Network Infrastructure

Before you implement the cluster, you must implement the network infrastructure that connects the cluster to client computers, to other servers within your organization, and to management consoles. The network infrastructure components include:

- Network cables
- Hubs
- Switches
- Routers
- Firewalls

 Note
Any references to switches in this chapter refer to Layer 2 switches.

When implementing the network infrastructure, make sure to have specifications about your current network environment available. Specifically, your hardware and software inventory and a map of network topology can be helpful. For more information about creating those documents, see "Planning for Deployment" in *Planning, Testing, and Piloting Deployment Projects* of this kit.

Implementing Any Required Networking Services

Network Load Balancing is independent of the other Windows Server 2003 network services. As a result, you do not need to implement networking services for Network Load Balancing.

However, the applications and services running on the cluster can be dependent on other Windows Server 2003 networking services. For more information about requirements for implementing networking services used by the services and applications running on the cluster, see "Additional Resources" later in this chapter.

Automating Additional Configurations

In many instances, it is possible that Windows Server 2003, Network Load Balancing, or the applications and services running on a particular cluster might require additional configuration after the installation is complete. You can use any combination of the following methods for automating these additional configurations:

- Microsoft Visual Basic Scripting Edition (VBScript)

- Windows Management Instrumentation (WMI)

- Active Directory Service Interfaces (ADSI)

Example: Preparing to Implement the Cluster

An organization is deploying a new Web application that will be accessed by a large volume of Internet users. Because of scaling and availability considerations, the organization will deploy the new, high-volume Web application on a Network Load Balancing cluster. Figure 9.4 illustrates the organization's network environment prior to the implementation of the new cluster.

Figure 9.4   Network Environment Before Implementing New Cluster

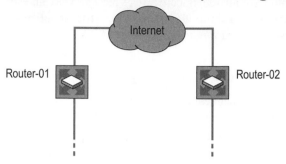

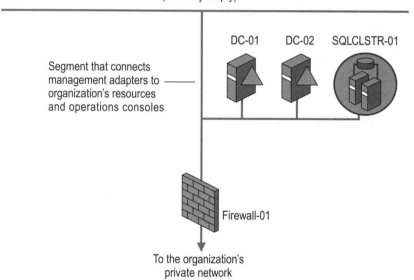

In addition to deciding that the new Web farm will run on a Network Load Balancing cluster, the design team also made the following configuration decisions:

- No single router, switch, or Internet Information Services (IIS) Web farm server failure will prevent users from running the Web application.

- Web application will store data in a clustered SQL server running Microsoft® SQL Server™ 2000 on a server cluster.

- Web application executables Active Server Pages (ASP), Hypertext Markup Language (HTML) pages, and other executable code will be stored on a file server running on a server cluster.

- Accounts used for authenticating Internet users will be stored in Active Directory® directory service.

As the first step in the organization's deployment of the Web application, the IIS 6.0 Web farm, and Network Load Balancing, the organization must restructure the network infrastructure to support the new Web farm and cluster. Figure 9.5 illustrates the organization's network environment after preparing for the implementation.

Figure 9.5   Network Environment After Preparing to Implement a New Cluster

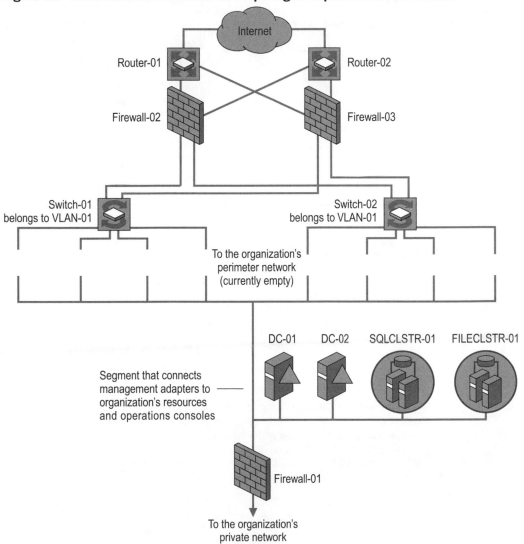

Table 9.3 lists the deployment steps that were performed prior to the implementation of the new cluster and the reasons for performing those steps.

Table 9.3   Deployment Steps Prior to Implementation of the New Cluster

Deployment Step	Reason
Add Firewall-02 and Firewall-03	Provide redundancy and load balancing.
Add Switch-01 and Switch-02	Provide redundancy and load balancing.
Add network segments on Switch-01 and Switch-02	Connect the IIS 6.0 Web farm to the network.
Configure Switch-01 and Switch-02 to belong to the same VLAN	Provide load balancing of client requests by using Network Load Balancing.
Add SQLCLUSTR-01	Provide database support for the Web application on a Microsoft server cluster.
Add FILECLUSTR-01	Provide secured storage for the Web application executables and content on a Microsoft server cluster.
Add DC-01 and DC-01	Provide storage and management of user accounts used in authenticating Internet users.

Implementing the Cluster

To implement the new cluster, complete the following tasks:

1.   Install and configure the hardware and Windows Server 2003 for each cluster host.

2.   Install and configure the first Network Load Balancing cluster host.

3.   Install and configure additional Network Load Balancing cluster hosts.

 Note

When your Network Load Balancing solution includes multiple Network Load Balancing clusters with round robin DNS, complete these tasks for each Network Load Balancing cluster in the solution. For more information about combining multiple Network Load Balancing clusters with round robin DNS, see "Scaling NLB Solutions" in "Designing Network Load Balancing" in this book.

Installing and Configuring the Hardware and Windows Server 2003

The first step in performing the implementation of the new cluster is to install and configure the hardware and Windows Server 2003 for each cluster host. Install and configure all cluster host hardware at the same time to ensure that you eliminate any configuration errors prior to installing and configuring the Network Load Balancing cluster.

To install and configure Windows Server 2003 on the cluster host hardware, you must be logged on as a user account that is a member of the local administrators group on all cluster hosts. Install and configure the cluster host by using the information documented in the "NLB Cluster Host Worksheet" that your design team completed for that host during the design process.

To install and configure the hardware and Windows Server 2003 on each cluster host in the new cluster, complete the following tasks:

1. Install the cluster host hardware in accordance with the manufacturer's recommendations.

2. Connect the cluster host hardware to the network infrastructure.

3. Install Windows Server 2003 with the default options and specifications from the worksheet for the cluster host.

4. Install any additional services (such as IIS 6.0 or Routing and Remote Access) by using the design specifications for the service.

   For detailed instructions on installing additional services, see the resources related to the corresponding service in "Additional Resources" later in this chapter.

5. Configure the TCP/IP property settings and verify connectivity for the cluster adapters.

    Caution
   Configure the dedicated IP address at this time. The cluster IP address and any virtual IP addresses for port rules are added later in the deployment process through Network Load Balancing Manager.

6. If a separate management network is used, configure the TCP/IP property settings and verify connectivity for the management adapter.

   Although not required, it is recommended that you use a separate management network adapter to provide a communication path that is isolated both from the cluster adapter and from the clients. For more information on the benefits of including a management network adapter in your design, see "Selecting the Number of Network Adapters in Each Cluster Host" in "Designing Network Load Balancing" in this book.

7. Configure each server to be a member server in a domain created specifically for managing the cluster and other related servers.

   Although not required, creating a domain for management of the cluster provides a centralized method of controlling security to the cluster. Management of clusters installed in a workgroup is more difficult and time-consuming. When the cluster resides in a perimeter network, create a separate forest for the exclusive purpose of managing servers (including cluster hosts) in the perimeter network.

Installing and Configuring the First Cluster Host

After you have installed and configured the hardware for the cluster, you are ready to install and configure the first cluster host. The first cluster host acts as a master copy when you use an image-based deployment method (such as RIS, Sysprep, or a third-party product) to deploy the remaining cluster hosts.

An image-based deployment is faster and ensures consistency when implementing the remaining cluster hosts, by reducing or eliminating manual configuration. In addition, the same image-based deployment method can be reused after the deployment to restore failed cluster hosts.

Depending on the type of image-based deployment, different methods are used to customize the cluster host after the image has been restored. For example, Sysprep can allow you to interactively customize the image or use a configuration file — sysprep.inf — to customize the image. For more information on customizing the restored image, see "Designing Unattended Installations," "Designing Image-based Installations with Sysprep," and "Designing RIS Installations" in *Automating and Customizing Installations* of this kit.

Perform the following task on the first cluster host by using the "NLB Cluster Host Worksheet" that your design team completed for the first cluster host:

1. If you did not use the automated installation process to create the new cluster, start Network Load Balancing Manager and create a new cluster.

     Tip

    You can start Network Load Balancing Manager by running Nlbmgr.exe.

2. Install the applications and services on the first cluster host.

    Examples of Windows Server 2003 services to be installed at this time include IIS or Terminal Services. For more information about installing Windows Server 2003 services, see the chapters that discuss those services in the *Microsoft® Windows® Server 2003 Deployment Kit*.

    Examples of applications to be installed at this time include, Web applications or Windows applications that run on Terminal Services. For more information about installing the applications running on your cluster, see the documentation that accompanies your application.

3. Enable monitoring and health checking on the first cluster host.

    A Microsoft Operations Manager (MOM) Management Pack exists for Network Load Balancing. When your organization uses MOM to monitor and manage the servers within your organization, include the MOM Management Pack for Network Load Balancing on the cluster hosts.

    For location of additional information about monitoring and health checking the applications and services running on the cluster, review the resources in "Additional Resources" later in this chapter.

4. Verify that the first Network Load Balancing cluster host responds to client queries by directing requests to the cluster IP address.

   Test the first cluster host by specifying the cluster IP address or a virtual cluster IP address in the client software that is used to access the application or service running on the cluster. For example, a client accessing an IIS application would put the cluster IP address or virtual cluster IP address in the Web browser address line.

 Important

Create an entry in DNS for the cluster only after you have completed the deployment of the entire cluster. Prematurely publishing the applications and services in DNS might result in overwhelming the cluster hosts before all cluster hosts are installed

Installing and Configuring Additional Cluster Hosts

After you have installed and configured the first cluster host, you are ready to install and configure the remaining cluster hosts in the cluster. The first cluster host acts as a master copy when you use an image-based deployment method (such as RIS, Sysprep, or a third-party product) to deploy the remaining cluster hosts.

Perform the following tasks on the remaining cluster hosts by using the "NLB Cluster Host Worksheet" that your design team completed for each cluster host:

1. Create an image of the first cluster host that has just been deployed (discussed in the previous section) as required by one of the following image-based automated installation methods:

   - Sysprep

     For more information about creating Sysprep images, see "Designing Image-based Installations with Sysprep" in *Automating and Customizing Installations* of this kit.

   - RIS

     For more information about creating RIS images, see "Designing RIS Installations" in *Automating and Customizing Installations*.

   - Third-party products

     For more information about creating images with third-party products, see the documentation provided with the third-party image deployment software.

2. Restore the image of the first cluster host (created in step 1) to one of the remaining cluster host, following the directions provided in the documentation for the image-base installation method you used.

3. Configure any computer specific information (such as computer name and IP address) on the newly deployed cluster host.

4. Enable monitoring and health checking for the additional cluster host.

    Use the same methods as described for the first cluster host.

5. Verify that the additional cluster host responds to client requests.

    Use the same methods as described for the first cluster host.

6. Complete steps 2 through 5 for each remaining cluster host in the Network Load Balancing cluster.

7. Ensure that the cluster is load balancing requests across all cluster hosts (based on the port rules of the cluster).

The time required to create and test the images used in an image-based deployment can be prohibitive. It might take you less time to install and configure the remaining cluster hosts in the same way that you installed and configured the first Network Load Balancing cluster host. For example, you could deploy a cluster that consists of three cluster hosts. If you decide to deploy the cluster hosts using a method other than image-based deployment, you must ensure that you can restore a failed cluster host.

Example: Implementing the New Cluster

The organization mentioned in "Example: Preparing to Implement the Cluster" earlier in this chapter is now ready to implement the new IIS 6.0 Web farm that uses Network Load Balancing for load balancing and fault tolerance. The network infrastructure and additional networking services have been deployed in preparation for the implementation.

In this step, the organization installed and configured the first cluster host as a model for the remaining cluster hosts. Then the organization deployed the remaining cluster hosts by using an image-based deployment method. Figure 9.6 illustrates the network environment after the implementation of the new IIS 6.0 Web farm and Network Load Balancing.

Figure 9.6   Network Environment After Installing the New Cluster

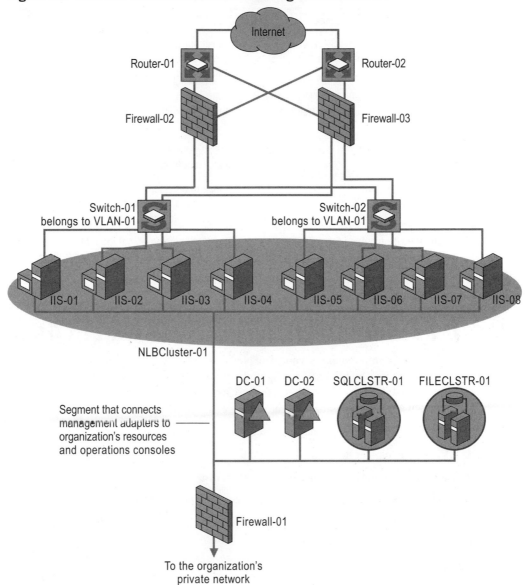

Table 9.4 lists the deployment steps that were performed to implement the new cluster and the reasons for performing those steps.

Table 9.4 Deployment Steps for Implementing the New NLB Cluster

Deployment Step	Reason
Add IIS-01, IIS-02, IIS-03, IIS-04, IIS-05, IIS-06, IIS-07, and IIS-08 server hardware.	Server hardware needs to be connected to network infrastructure in preparation for Network Load Balancing deployment.
Install Windows Server 2003 and Network Load Balancing on IIS-01 by using unattended installation.	Unattended setup is chosen because of the limited number of hosts to be deployed.
Create an image of IIS-01 to use as a model for RIS deployment.	RIS allows the servers to be reimaged in the event of a server failure.
Deploy the image on IIS-02, IIS-03, IIS-04, IIS-05, IIS-06, IIS-07, and IIS-08.	Image deployment ensures a consistent configuration on all servers in the Network Load Balancing cluster.
Verify the Web farm responds to client requests.	Verification ensures that the Web farm is properly configured and that Network Load Balancing is load balancing.

Verifying the Cluster and Enabling Client Access

The final step in implementing your new Network Load Balancing cluster is to ensure that you have properly implemented and configured your cluster. In "Installing and Configuring the First Cluster Host" earlier in this chapter, you verified your implementation of individual servers. Now you must ensure that the entire cluster is secure and is properly monitored and health checked.

To verify the cluster and enable client access, complete the following tasks:

1. Verify the cluster host restoration process.

2. Verify that identified security threats are mitigated.

3. Perform monitoring and health checking on the complete cluster.

4. Verify proper operation of applications and services running on the cluster.

5. Enable client access to the cluster.

Verifying the Cluster Host Restoration Process

Before placing the cluster into a pilot or production environment, you need to verify cluster host restoration to ensure that you can properly restore a cluster host that has failed.

To verify the cluster host restoration process, complete the following tasks:

1. Remove a cluster host from the cluster by performing a drainstop on the cluster host.

   A drainstop prevents a cluster host from handling new client requests. While draining, a cluster host continues to complete any outstanding requests and remains in the cluster until all active requests are completed. Then the cluster host stops all cluster operation.

2. Remove all disk volumes and disk partitions on the cluster host.

3. Restore the cluster host based on the installation method selected earlier in the deployment process.

4. Restart the cluster host.

5. Verify that the System event log of each cluster host contains no errors and that the restored cluster host responds properly to client requests.

Verifying That Identified Security Threats are Mitigated

You need to verify that all the identified security threats are properly handled in your new Network Load Balancing solution.

To verify that the identified security threats are mitigated, complete the following tasks:

1. Connect a client computer to the network such that the clients access the cluster by using the same route path that a typical client computer would use to connect to the cluster.

   For example, when clients connect to the cluster through a series of firewalls and routers to connect to the cluster over the Internet, ensure the client computer used for testing connects to the cluster through the same firewalls and routers.

2. Log on to the client computer with the user rights identified in your security threats.

3. For each identified security threat, reproduce the steps that result in the security compromise of the cluster.

4. Document the results and report the findings to the design team.

5. With the assistance of the design team, resolve any outstanding security issues.

    Important

   Resolve all security threats before proceeding further in the deployment process.

Monitoring and Health Checking the Complete Cluster

Your next step in completing the implementation of your new cluster is to enable monitoring and health checking on the entire cluster. In "Installing and Configuring the First Cluster Host" and "Installing and Configuring Additional Cluster Hosts" earlier in this chapter, you enabled monitoring and health checking on individual cluster hosts. However, in this step you are ensuring that the cluster is monitored as a complete unit. Enable monitoring and health checking on the cluster before allowing users to access the cluster in a pilot or production environment.

As clients begin to access the applications and services in your cluster, continue to provide monitoring and health checking as described in "Installing and Configuring the First Cluster Host" earlier in this chapter. Verify that the cluster performs as expected with live client traffic.

After the deployment process is complete, ensure that your operations staff continues the monitoring and health checking process in their long-term operations processes as part of your ongoing operations.

Verifying Proper Operations of Applications and Services

Before placing the complete cluster into a pilot or production environment, you need to verify that applications and services are running correctly on the cluster.

To verify proper operations of applications and services on the new cluster, complete the following tasks:

1. Temporarily connect a client computer to the same switch used by the cluster.

2. From the client computer, verify that the applications respond to client requests as expected.

3. Disconnect the client computer from the switch.

Enable Client Access to the Cluster

Your last step in the implementation of your new cluster is to allow clients access to the applications and services running on the cluster. Be sure that you successfully complete all previous steps in the process before enabling users to access the cluster in a pilot or production environment.

Enable client access to the applications and the services in the cluster by creating DNS entries. Users will access your applications and services by using user-friendly names or Uniform Resource Locaters (URLs), such as http://www.microsoft.com, which correspond to the individual applications or services on the Network Load Balancing cluster. The DNS entries allow the translation of the user-friendly name to at least one IP address. When round robin DNS is used for load balancing between clusters, you must create a DNS entry for each cluster.

Table 9.5 lists the criteria for determining the number of DNS entries required for your new cluster.

Table 9.5   Criteria for Determining the DNS Entries for Your Cluster

Solution Includes One of the Following	Required DNS Entries
Only one Network Load Balancing cluster.	A DNS entry for the cluster and a DNS entry for each virtual cluster.
More than one Network Load Balancing cluster with client traffic distributed across Network Load Balancing clusters by using round robin DNS.	A round robin DNS entry for each cluster and a round robin DNS entry for each virtual cluster.

Example: Verifying the Cluster and Enabling Client Access

The organization mentioned in the examples earlier in this chapter is now ready to complete the implementation of the new IIS 6.0 Web farm. The Web farm servers are implemented and basic connectivity is provided to the Web farm. The organization has verified that Network Load Balancing is distributing client traffic evenly and that all cluster hosts are servicing client requests.

In this step, the organization verifies that the Web farm and the cluster function as a whole. Although operation of each cluster host was verified during the implementation process, now the organization must ensure that the new Web farm meets or exceeds the design specifications established by your design team before enabling client access to the applications.

Figure 9.7 illustrates the network environment after the implementation of the new IIS 6.0 Web farm and Network Load Balancing.

Figure 9.7   Network Environment After Implementing the New Cluster

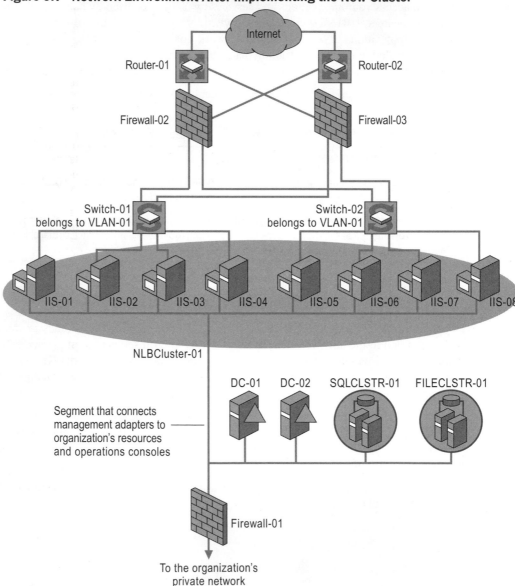

Table 9.6 lists the deployment steps that were performed to verify the new cluster and enable client access.

Table 9.6   Verifying the New Cluster and Enabling Client Access

Deployment Step	Reason
IIS-03 taken off line.	Automatic failover to other Web servers must be proven.
IIS-02 restored.	Restoration process for Web servers must be proven.
Client attached to the Internet and security attacks performed.	Mitigation of security threats must be proven.
Monitoring and health checking enabled on IIS-01, IIS-02, IIS-03, IIS-04, IIS-05, IIS-06, IIS-07 and IIS-08.	Proper operation of the IIS 6.0 Web farm must be verified during and after the implementation process to ensure that load balancing is occurring and that system resources are adequate for client requests.
A DNS entry created for the cluster IP address of NLBCluster-01.	Clients must have a DNS entry to access the Web applications running on the cluster.

Upgrading Existing Clusters

If your organization has applications and services that currently run on the Windows NT 4.0 or Microsoft® Windows® 2000 operating systems, you can upgrade your existing WLBS or Network Load Balancing clusters to take advantage of the improved security and performance of Windows Server 2003 and Network Load Balancing. Figure 9.8 shows the process for upgrading an existing cluster.

Figure 9.8   Upgrading an Existing Cluster

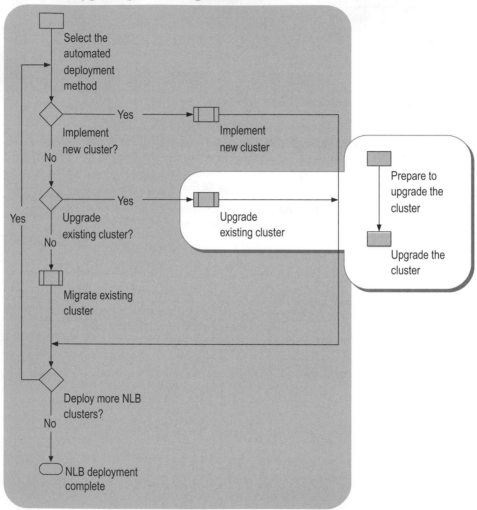

The Network Load Balancing upgrade process assumes the following conditions:

- Your applications are running on an existing IIS 4.0 (on Windows NT 4.0) or IIS 5.0 (on Windows 2000).

- You are upgrading the operating system and services running on your existing application servers.

- The system resources of the computers in your existing application farm are sufficient, or can be upgraded, to support Windows Server 2003 and IIS 6.0.

You can upgrade a cluster by taking the entire cluster offline and upgrading all the hosts, or you can leave the cluster on line and perform a *rolling upgrade*. A rolling upgrade entails taking individual cluster hosts offline one at a time, upgrading each host, and returning the host to the cluster. You continue upgrading individual cluster hosts until the entire cluster is upgraded. A rolling upgrade allows the cluster to continue running during the upgrade.

The decision to use rolling upgrades is based on the applications and services running on your existing cluster. If the applications and services support rolling upgrades, then perform a rolling upgrade on the existing cluster. Otherwise, perform the upgrade process recommended for the applications and services running on the cluster. For more information on the upgrade process for the applications and services running on your cluster, see "Additional Resources" later in this chapter.

Upgrade the cluster by using the information documented in the "NLB Cluster Host Worksheet" that your design team completed for each cluster host during the design process.

Preparing to Upgrade the Cluster

Network Load Balancing runs independently of other networking services provided by Windows Server 2003. On the other hand, the applications and services running on the cluster can be dependent upon the network infrastructure and other network services in your existing environment. Prior to upgrading the existing cluster, deploy any network infrastructure components or networking services that are required by the applications and services running on the cluster.

Prepare to upgrade the cluster by performing the following tasks:

1. Verify that applications and services running on the cluster are compatible with Windows Server 2003.

2. Upgrade the network infrastructure as required by the applications and services running on the cluster.

3. Upgrade any networking services as required by the applications and services running on the cluster.

Verifying Applications and Services Are Compatible with Windows Server 2003

Before you upgrade the existing cluster, ensure that the applications and services running on the cluster are compatible with Windows Server 2003. For help in determining if your application is compatible with Windows Server 2003, use the Windows Application Compatibility Toolkit. To download the toolkit, see the Windows Application Compatibility link on the Web Resources page at http://www.microsoft.com/reskits/webresources.

Upgrading Necessary Network Infrastructure

Before you upgrade the existing cluster, ensure that the final configuration of the cluster can be supported by the network infrastructure that connects the cluster to client computers, to other servers within your organization, and to management consoles. Perform only the network infrastructure upgrades required by the applications and services running on the cluster. Avoid performing upgrades to the network infrastructure for other reasons at the same time that you are upgrading the cluster. This minimizes the number of changes to the environment and reduces the likelihood of problems occurring during the upgrade process.

The network infrastructure to upgrade includes the following components:

- Network cabling
- Hubs
- Switches
- Routers
- Firewalls

 Note

When performing this step, make sure to have specifications about your current network environment available for use. Specifically, your hardware and software inventory, and a map of network topology can be helpful. For more information about creating those documents, see "Planning for Deployment" in *Planning, Testing, and Piloting Deployment Projects* of this kit.

Upgrading Any Required Networking Services

Network Load Balancing is independent of the other Windows Server 2003 network services. As a result, no networking services upgrades are required for Network Load Balancing.

However, the applications and services running on the cluster can be dependent on other Windows Server 2003 networking services. For more information about requirements that the services and applications running on the cluster might have for upgrading networking services, see "Additional Resources" later in this chapter.

Example: Preparing to Upgrade the Cluster

An organization is upgrading their existing virtual private network (VPN) remote access solution. The existing solution has a VPN remote access server farm that supports Point-to-Point Tunneling Protocol (PPTP) and Layer Two Tunneling Protocol (L2TP). Currently the VPN remote access server farm is running WLBS on Windows NT 4.0. Figure 9.9 illustrates the organization's network environment prior to preparing for the upgrade of the existing WLBS cluster that hosts the VPN remote access server farm.

Figure 9.9 Network Environment Before Preparing to Upgrading the Cluster

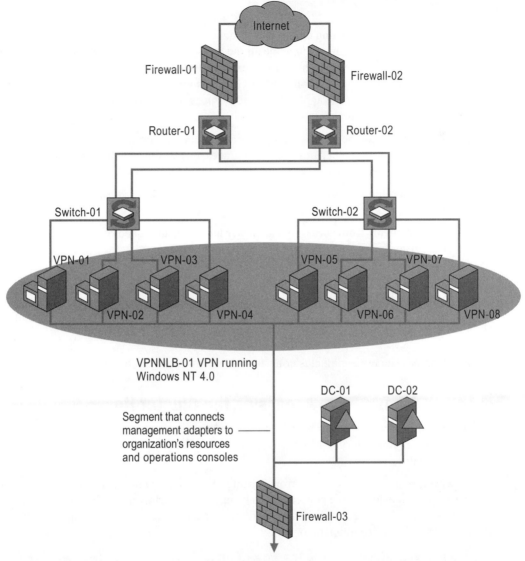

As the first step in upgrading the existing VPN remote access server farm, the organization installs any networking services required by the VPN remote access server farm. No networking infrastructure or networking services upgrades are required for the upgrade.

In the future, the organization plans to deploy Internet Authentication Service (IAS) servers to provide centralized management of remote access policies. However, the deployment of IAS is scheduled to occur after the upgrade to Windows Server 2003 to prevent any unnecessary complications during the upgrade process.

Upgrading the Cluster

The upgrade of your existing cluster can be done one cluster host at a time (a rolling upgrade) or by taking the cluster offline to upgrade all the hosts at the same time (a nonrolling upgrade). It is recommended that you perform a rolling upgrade. Otherwise, perform the upgrade process recommended for the applications and services running on the cluster. For more information on the upgrade process for the applications and services running on your cluster, see "Additional Resources" later in this chapter.

Determine if you can perform a rolling upgrade in your lab prior to your pilot or production deployments. If you can perform rolling upgrades, ensure that you perform the post-upgrade processes described in this section for each individual cluster host.

To perform a rolling upgrade on existing WLBS or Network Load Balancing clusters, complete the following tasks:

1. Prevent clients from accessing the cluster host to be upgraded by performing a drainstop on the cluster host.

2. Monitor client activity on the cluster host until all client activity ceases.

3. Upgrade the cluster host.

4. Verify that the applications and services are running correctly on the upgraded cluster host.

5. Add the cluster host back to the cluster.

6. Upgrade the remaining cluster hosts by performing steps 1 though 5 for each cluster host.

Preventing Clients From Accessing the Cluster Host

Before you upgrade a cluster host, you must ensure that no clients have active sessions running on the cluster host. During the upgrade process, the cluster host is still connected to the network infrastructure.

However, to prevent new clients from starting sessions or applications on the cluster host, perform a drainstop on the cluster host to be upgraded. Performing a drainstop prevents new clients from accessing the cluster while allowing existing clients to continue until they have completed their current operations.

In addition, configure the **Default state** of the **Initial host state** to **Stopped**. Configuring the cluster host in this manner ensures the cluster host cannot rejoin the cluster during the upgrade process. Because the upgrade process requires the cluster host to restart, you need to verify that the upgrade completed successfully before adding the cluster host back to the cluster.

 Tip
You can configure the Initial host state through Network Load Balancing Manager or the property settings of the cluster network adapter.

For more information about performing a drainstop on the source cluster and changing the **Default state** of cluster host, see "Create and Manage Network Load Balancing Clusters" in Help and Support Center for Windows Server 2003.

Monitoring Client Activity on the Cluster Host

After you run the drainstop on the cluster host, monitor client activity on the cluster host to determine when clients are no longer using the cluster host. The method for determining when clients are no longer using the cluster host is specific to the applications and services running on the cluster host.

For example, for a VPN remote access solution, monitor for active VPN connections to the cluster host. When there are no active VPN connections, the cluster host is ready to be upgraded.

For more information about monitoring the applications and services running on the cluster for client activity, see "Additional Resources" later in this chapter.

Upgrading the Cluster Host

After you ensure that no clients are accessing the cluster host, upgrade the cluster host to Windows Server 2003. Ensure that during the upgrade process you apply the latest service packs and hotfixes.

After the upgrade is complete, check the upgrade logs (Setuperr.log in the *windir* folder of the system volume) to identify any problems that occurred during the upgrade process. Many applications and services running on the cluster have log files that identify problems that occur during the upgrade process. For example, IIS 6.0 creates a separate log that documents the upgrade process for IIS components. Make certain that you review any upgrade logs for the applications and services running on the cluster.

For more information about these upgrade logs, see "Additional Resources" later in this chapter.

Verifying the Applications and Services are Running Correctly

After the upgrade of the cluster host is complete, you need to verify that the applications and services are running correctly on the cluster host. You need to do this before starting the cluster service again in order to allow the cluster host to rejoin the cluster. The process presented here is specific to Network Load Balancing. This process might apply to the applications and services running on the cluster, however, the applications and services running on the cluster might have a different verification process. For more information on the verification process for specific applications and services running on the cluster, see "Additional Resources" later in this chapter.

To verify that the applications and services are running correctly after you upgrade the cluster host, complete the following tasks:

1. Temporarily connect a client computer to the same switch used by the cluster.

2. From the client computer, verify that the applications respond to client requests as they did prior to the upgrade.

3. Verify that the identified security threats are mitigated.

    The only action you need to take to mitigate Network Load Balancing–specific security threats is to ensure that unauthorized clients cannot remotely administer the cluster. Unless the network infrastructure, including firewalls or routers, changed significantly since the start of the upgrade, the Network Load Balancing security threats should still be mitigated.

    However, you must mitigate security threats that are unique to the applications and services running on the cluster. For more information about mitigating security threats for specific applications and services running on the cluster, see "Additional Resources" later in this chapter.

4. Enable monitoring and health checking, if they are not already enabled.

    A Microsoft Operations Manager (MOM) Management Pack exists for Network Load Balancing. When your organization uses MOM to monitor and manage the servers within your organization, include the MOM Management Pack for Network Load Balancing on the cluster hosts.

    For more information about monitoring and health checking the applications and services running on the cluster, see "Additional Resources" later in this chapter.

5. Disconnect the client computer from the switch.

Adding the Cluster Host Back to the Cluster

After you complete the upgrade and verify that the applications and services are running correctly, add the cluster host back to the cluster. Because the cluster host is still connected by cable to the existing network infrastructure, adding the cluster host back to the cluster requires you to start Network Load Balancing on the cluster host.

To add the cluster host back to the cluster, use Network Load Balancing Manager to start the Network Load Balancing service on the cluster host. In addition, configure the **Default state** of the **Initial host state** to match the setting that existed prior to the upgrade process. Configuring the cluster host in this manner ensures that the clients accessing the applications and services running on the cluster do not encounter problems when you restart the cluster host and return it to the cluster.

The reason to configure the cluster host with the same settings, instead of selecting **Started**, is that Network Load Balancing loads very early in the operating system boot process. The cluster host can join the cluster before other services are running. This means the cluster host might receive load before other services, such as IIS, are started. Allowing Network Load Balancing to start before other services could result in the denial of service to users until the service starts.

You can use management software, such as MOM, to monitor the services running on the host and to start Network Load Balancing when the appropriate services are running. Using management software to start Network Load Balancing is recommended to prevent users from experiencing outages in service.

For more information on performing a drainstop on the source cluster and changing the **Initial host state** of cluster host, see "Create and Manage Network Load Balancing Clusters" in Help and Support Center for Windows Server 2003.

Example: Upgrading the Existing NLB Cluster

The organization mentioned in the examples earlier in this chapter is now ready to upgrade the existing VPN server farms. In this step, the organization performs a rolling upgrade on each cluster host in the VPN remote access server farm.

Each of the VPN remote access servers were upgraded in turn until the entire VPN remote access server farm was upgraded. Figure 9.10 illustrates the organization's network environment after the upgrade of the cluster.

Figure 9.10   Network Environment After Upgrading the Cluster

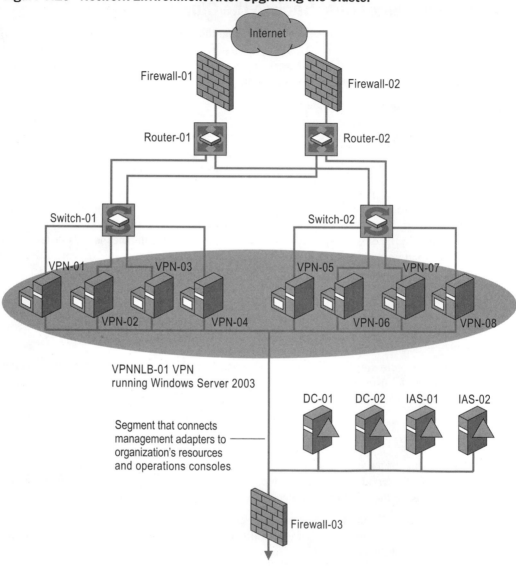

To upgrade the VPN remote access server farm, the following tasks were performed:

1. Prevented client access on the VPN-01 cluster host by performing a drainstop on VPN-01.

2. Monitored client activity on VPN-01 until all client activity ceased.

3. Upgraded VPN-01.

4. Verified that the applications and services are running correctly on VPN-01.

5. Added VPN-01 back to the cluster.

6. Performed steps 1 through 5 on the remaining VPN remote access servers.

Migrating Existing Clusters

Your organization might have applications and services that currently run on Windows NT 4.0 or Windows 2000 clusters. If you want these applications and services to take advantage of the improved security and performance of Windows Server 2003, and if you also want to run these applications on newly installed Windows Server 2003 servers, you can migrate the applications and servers from existing clusters to newly installed Network Load Balancing clusters.

The migration process is appropriate in the following situations:

- You want to migrate one WLBS or Network Load Balancing cluster to a target Network Load Balancing cluster.

- You want to consolidate multiple WLBS or Network Load Balancing clusters onto a target Network Load Balancing cluster.

Migrating WLBS clusters from Windows NT 4.0 or Network Load Balancing clusters from Windows 2000 requires only minimal effort for Network Load Balancing. The majority of the migration effort involves the applications and services running on the cluster. The process for migrating an existing cluster to a target Network Load Balancing cluster running Windows Server 2003 is shown in Figure 9.11.

Figure 9.11   Migrating Existing Clusters

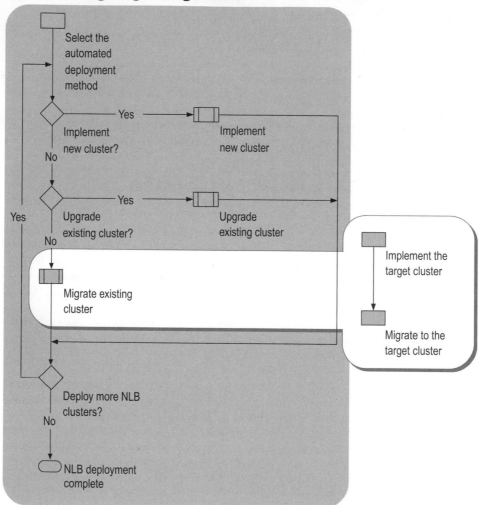

Migrate your WLBS or Network Load Balancing cluster by using the information documented in the "NLB Cluster Host Worksheet" that your design team completed for each cluster host during the design process.

Network Load Balancing Migration Assumptions

The Network Load Balancing migration process to Windows Server 2003 assumes the following conditions:

- Your applications and services are running on an existing cluster running WLBS (on Windows NT 4.0) or Network Load Balancing (on Windows 2000).

- You are installing a new Network Load Balancing cluster as the target cluster.

- Your applications and services are compatible with Windows Server 2003.

In addition to compatibility with Network Load Balancing, the applications and services must be compatible with Windows Server 2003. For help in determining if your application is compatible with Windows Server 2003, use the Windows Application Compatibility Toolkit on the *Windows Server 2003 Deployment Kit* companion CD.

For information about the migration process for the application or service running on your cluster, see "Additional Resources" later in this chapter.

Network Load Balancing Migrations and Consolidations

In addition to migrating an existing cluster to the target cluster, you can use the Network Load Balancing migration process to consolidate multiple existing clusters to the target cluster. The consolidation process is identical to the migration process, except that, for each migration, you are migrating applications and services that formerly ran on multiple clusters onto a single target cluster.

As a part of consolidation, the port rules and cluster virtual IP addresses from all the source clusters must be created on the target cluster. For each cluster that you migrate, you must create port rules on the target cluster that handle the client traffic in the same manner as the traffic was handled on the source cluster. For more information about the migration of port rules, see "Migrating to the Target Cluster" later in this chapter.

Implementing the Target Cluster

The first step in the migration process is to implement the target Network Load Balancing cluster. If the target Network Load Balancing cluster already exists, proceed to the next step in the process, described in "Migrating to the Target Cluster" later in this chapter

The process for implementing the target is identical to the process for installing a new Network Load Balancing cluster. Complete the process described in "Implementing a New Cluster" earlier in this chapter. Ensure that implementing the target cluster does not disrupt applications running on the source cluster. For example, avoid modifying the network infrastructure that actively connects to the source cluster and avoid modifying DNS entries that direct clients to the source cluster.

Example: Implementing the Target Cluster

Contoso Pharmaceuticals is consolidating existing IIS Web farms onto a new IIS 6.0 Web farm. There are four independent IIS Web farms that need to be migrated. Two of the Web farms are running IIS 4.0 and WLBS on Windows NT 4.0. The other two Web farms are running IIS 5.0 and Network Load Balancing on Windows 2000.

During the migration, Contoso plans to consolidate the separate Web farms into one Web farm that supports all of their Web applications. Figure 9.12 illustrates Contoso's network environment prior to the migration of the existing WLBS and Network Load Balancing clusters that host the IIS Web farms.

Figure 9.12   Network Environment Before Migrating the IIS Web Farms

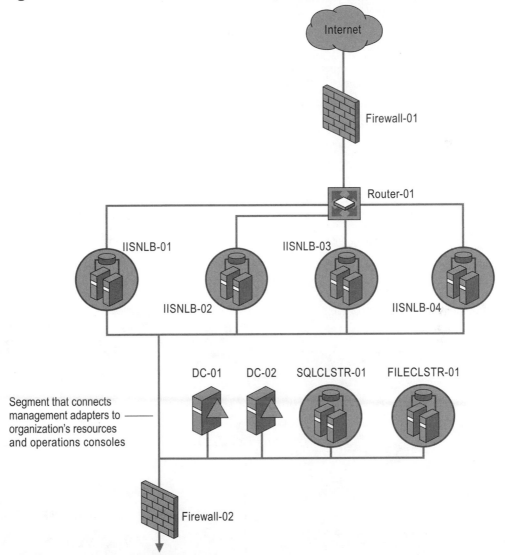

As the first step in Contoso's migration of the Web application server farm, Contoso restructured the network infrastructure to support the new IIS and Network Load Balancing deployment. Additional networking services were deployed in preparation for the implementation.

Then Contoso installed and configured the first server in the Web farm as a model for the remaining servers. Contoso deployed the remaining servers by using an image-based deployment method. Figure 9.13 illustrates Contoso's network environment after the implementation of the target IIS 6.0 Web farm (Network Load Balancing cluster).

Figure 9.13   Network Environment After Installing the Target Cluster

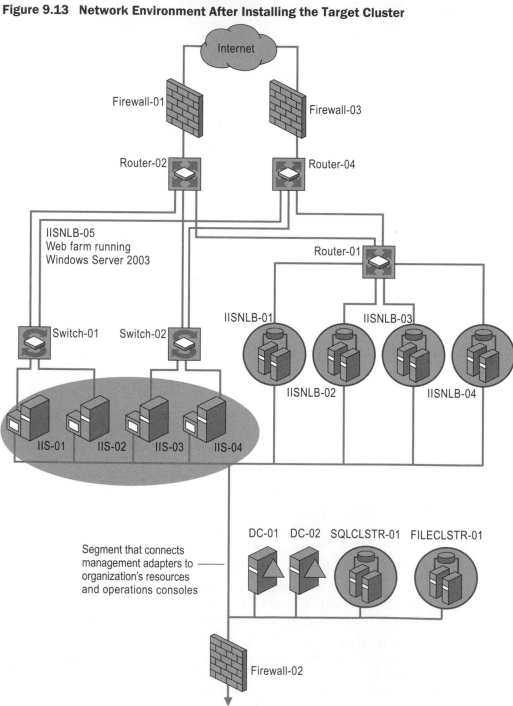

During the implementation of the new target cluster, the existing clusters were not affected. Clients continued to access the applications and services running on the existing cluster during the implementation of the target cluster.

Migrating to the Target Cluster

As discussed in "Implementing the Target Cluster" earlier in this chapter, the only part of Network Load Balancing to be migrated is the port rules. All other aspects of the migration of the cluster are specific to the applications and services running on the cluster. For more information on migrating applications and services running on the cluster, see "Additional Resources" later in this chapter.

Because the number of port rules on a cluster is small, the existing port rules can be easily recreated on the target cluster. If you are consolidating multiple clusters to a target cluster, the creation of port rules is slightly different from the creation of port rules if you are migrating a single cluster to a target cluster. Primarily, when consolidating, you need to ensure that consolidated port rules do not conflict with one another.

Migrate or consolidate the port rules on the source cluster to the target cluster by completing the following steps:

1. Document the port rules on the source cluster.

2. Identify any differences between port rules that exist on the target cluster and the port rules on the source cluster.

3. Create the port rule on the target cluster, as required, with new or different virtual IP addresses.

4. Migrate the applications and services running on the source cluster.

5. Enable client access to the applications on the target cluster.

Documenting Port Rules on the Source Cluster

Document the port rules on the source cluster by completing the following steps:

1. View the port rules in Network Load Balancing Manager or by running Nlb.exe at a command prompt.

   To view port rules in Network Load Balancing Manager:

   a. Start **Network Load Balancing Manager**.

   b. On the **Host** menu, click **Properties**.

   c. On the **Port Rules** tab, view the port rules in the **Defined port rules** box.

   To view port rules by running Nlb.exe, in the command prompt, type **Nlb display** *cluster_IP_address* (where *cluster_IP_address* is the cluster IP address of the source cluster), and then press **Enter**.

   For more information about viewing port rules in Network Load Balancing Manager or by using Nlb.exe, see "Create and Manage Network Load Balancing Clusters" in Help and Support Center for Windows Server 2003.

2. Record the port rules on the job aid "NLB Cluster Host Worksheet" (Sdcnlb_1.doc) on the *Windows Server 2003 Deployment Kit* companion CD (or see "NLB Cluster Host Worksheet" on the Web at http://www.microsoft.com/reskit).

Identifying Differences Between Port Rules

When migrating a source cluster to a target cluster, create port rules that are identical to the source cluster. When consolidating two or more clusters to a target cluster, create port rules that are identical to the source cluster unless port rules exist on the target cluster that specify the same TCP/UDP port number that is specified by a port rule on the source cluster.

During consolidation, two clusters might have port rules that relate to the same TCP/UDP port number, but have different affinity or load weight. In these situations you must differentiate between the different affinity or load weight behaviors by associating each of the source port rules with a different virtual cluster.

For example, you are migrating two clusters, Cluster A and Cluster B, to the same target cluster. Cluster A has a port rule for HTTP (TCP port 80) traffic that specifies no affinity, while Cluster B has a port rule for HTTP traffic that specifies Single affinity. The applications on these servers expect the affinity behavior. To ensure these applications behave as they did on the source servers, specify a port rule, with unique virtual IP address, for each of the affinity behaviors.

Creating Port Rules on the Target Cluster

Create the port rules on the target cluster by using Network Load Balancing Manager. Network Load Balancing Manager is recommended because it ensures that the port rules remain consistent across all the cluster hosts. Other methods require you to manually ensure that the port rules are consistent.

To create the port rules on the target cluster by using Network Load Balancing Manager:

1. Start **Network Load Balancing Manager**.

2. If **Network Load Balancing Manager** does not already list the cluster, connect to the cluster.

3. Right-click the cluster, and then click **Cluster Properties**.

4. Click the **Port Rules** tab.

5. Click **Add**.

6. Using the port rules documented in previous steps, specify values for the following:

   - **Cluster IP address**, which is the virtual IP address that you want this rule to apply to. Enter a specific virtual IP address to create a virtual cluster, or check **All** to apply the rule to all virtual IP addresses.

   - **Port range**

   - **Protocols**

   - **Filtering mode** and as appropriate, values for **Affinity**, and **Load weight**, and then click **OK**.

7. Repeat steps 5 and 6 until all port rules are created.

For more information on creating port rules in Network Load Balancing Manager, see "Create and Manage Network Load Balancing Clusters" in Help and Support Center for Windows Server 2003.

Migrating the Applications and Services Running on the Source Cluster

For information about the specific migration steps for the applications and services running on the source cluster, see "Additional Resources" later in this chapter. After you migrate the applications and services, ensure that the applications and services are running correctly before enabling client access to the applications and services on the target cluster.

Enabling Client Access to the Applications on the Target Cluster

After you have migrated the cluster port rules, applications, and services from the source cluster to the target cluster, you are ready to enable client access to the applications on the target cluster. Enable client access to the target cluster while maintaining the DNS entries to the source cluster. Over a period of time, remove the DNS entries that point to the source cluster.

Enable client access to the applications on the target cluster by completing the following steps:

1. Create the appropriate DNS entries for the applications running on the target cluster.

    For more information on how to create DNS entries for your applications see "Managing resource records" in Help and Support Center for Windows Server 2003.

2. Monitor client traffic to determine if clients are accessing the target cluster.

3. Over a period of time, such as a few hours or a day, confirm clients accessing target cluster are experiencing normal response times and application responses.

4. Remove the DNS entries pointing to the source cluster.

    For more information on how to remove DNS entries for your applications see "Managing resource records" in Help and Support Center for Windows Server 2003.

5. Prevent new clients from accessing the source cluster by performing a drainstop on the source cluster.

    For more information on how to perform a drainstop, see "Create and Manage Network Load Balancing Clusters" in Help and Support Center for Windows Server 2003.

6. Monitor client traffic to the source cluster to determine when clients are no longer accessing the source cluster.

7. When clients no longer access the source cluster, decommission the source cluster hardware.

Example: Migrating to the Target Cluster

The fictitious organization Contoso, mentioned in examples earlier in this chapter, is now ready to migrate their existing applications running on the four IIS Web farms to the target IIS 6.0 Web farm (and subsequently the target Network Load Balancing cluster). Contoso's target Web farm has been installed and their applications have been verified to work with Windows Server 2003 and Network Load Balancing.

Figure 9.14 illustrates Contoso's network environment after the migration of the existing applications to the target Web farm and Network Load Balancing cluster.

Figure 9.14 Network Environment After Migrating Applications and Services

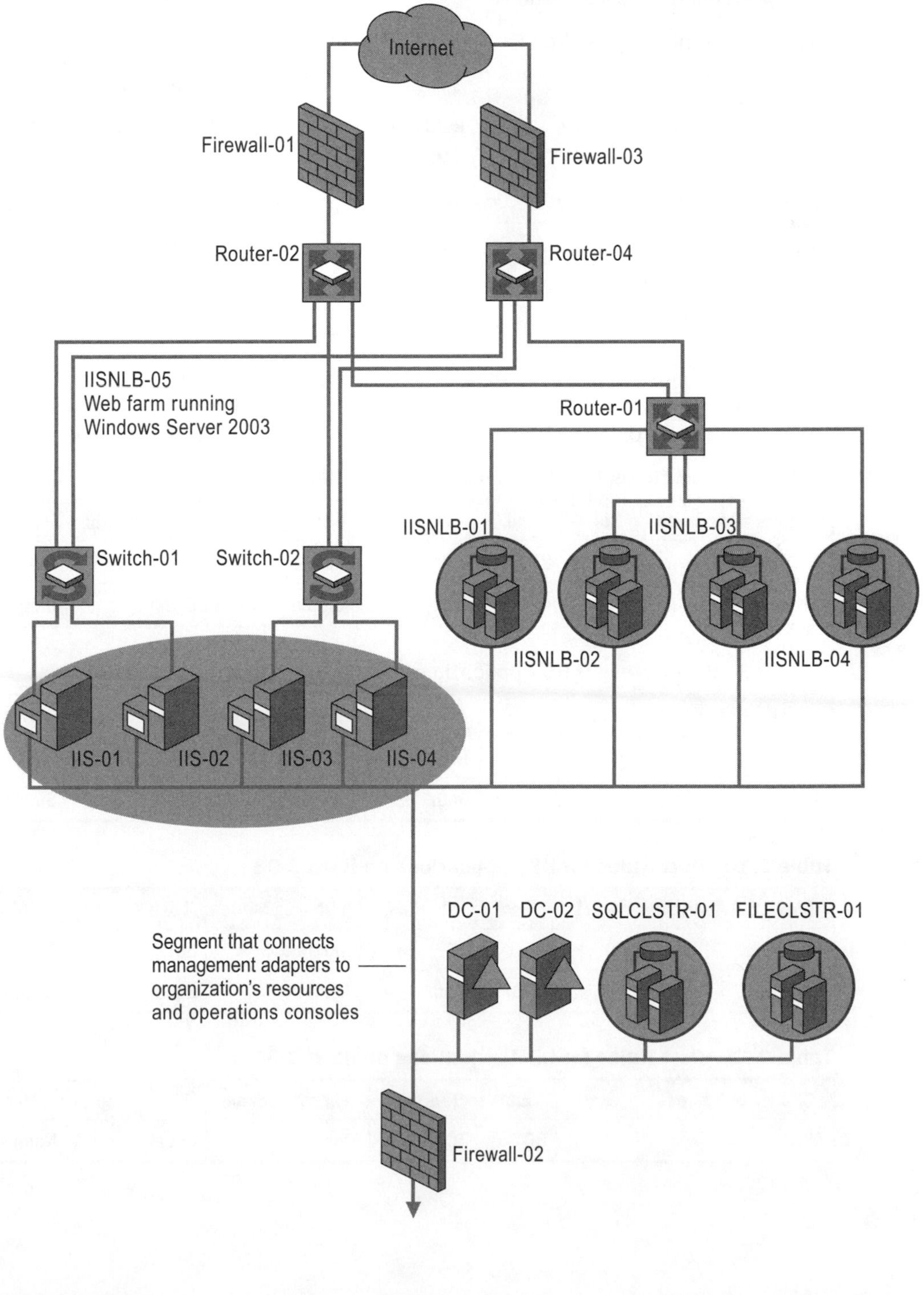

Table 9.7 lists the applications, the Web farms that run the applications, and the DNS entries that correspond to the Web applications.

Table 9.7 Applications, Web Farms, and DNS Entries

Application	Runs on	DNS Entries
Organization's Internet presence	▪ IISNLB-01 ▪ IISNLB-02	▪ www.contoso.com 10.0.0.111 ▪ www.contoso.com 10.0.0.121
Customer support site	▪ IISNLB-03	▪ support.contoso.com 10.0.0.131
E-commerce site	▪ IISNLB-03	▪ sales.contoso.com 10.0.0.132
Nonprofit third-party organization's Internet presence	▪ IISNLB-04	▪ www.treyresearch.net 10.0.0.141

In this step, Contoso creates the port rules on the target cluster based on the port rules from each of the existing clusters (IISNLB-01, IISNLB-02, IISNLB-03, and IISNLB-04). Table 9.8, Table 9.9, Table 9.10, and Table 9.11 lists the port rules for the existing clusters.

Table 9.8 Port Rules for IIS Applications on IISNLB-01

Cluster IP Address	Start	End	Protocol	Filtering Mode	Load Weight	Affinity
All	80	80	TCP	Multiple	Equal	None
All	443	443	Both	Multiple	Equal	Single

Table 9.9 Port Rules for IIS Applications on IISNLB-02

Cluster IP Address	Start	End	Protocol	Filtering Mode	Load Weight	Affinity
All	80	80	TCP	Multiple	Equal	None
All	443	443	Both	Multiple	Equal	Single

Table 9.10 Port Rules for IIS Applications on IISNLB-03

Cluster IP Address	Start	End	Protocol	Filtering Mode	Load Weight	Affinity
All	80	80	TCP	Multiple	Equal	Single
All	443	443	Both	Multiple	Equal	Single

Table 9.11 Port Rules for IIS Applications on IISNLB-04

Cluster IP Address	Start	End	Protocol	Filtering Mode	Load Weight	Affinity
All	80	80	TCP	Multiple	Equal	None

The port rules are recorded for each of the source clusters. Because each of the clusters has different port rules, virtual clusters are created to facilitate the consolidation of the applications onto the target cluster IISNLB-05. Table 9.12 lists the port rules that were created to support the applications on IISNLB-05.

Table 9.12 Port Rules Created for IIS Applications on IISNLB-05

Cluster IP Address	Start	End	Protocol	Filtering Mode	Load Weight	Affinity	Created to Support
All	80	80	TCP	Multiple	Equal	None	All source clusters
All	443	443	Both	Multiple	Equal	Single	All source clusters
10.0.0.153	80	80	TCP	Multiple	Equal	Single	IISNLB-03

The port rules on IISNLB-01 and IISNLB-02 are combined into a pair of port rules on IISNLB-05 because IISNLB-01 and IISNLB-02 support the same application. The two clusters, IISNLB-01 and IISNLB-02, were created to provide scaling in the original design. Because the application — www.contoso.com — is being consolidated onto one Web farm on a single cluster, the port rules can be consolidated as well.

The virtual clusters on IISNLB-03 are created on IISNLB-05 to provide separate virtual IP addresses for support.contoso.com and sales.contoso.com.

A virtual cluster, 10.0.0.154, was created to support the application on IISNLB-04, www.treyresearch.net.

After the applications are migrated to the target cluster, IISNLB-05, and are verified for proper operation, DNS entries are created to direct clients to the applications running on the target cluster. Table 9.13 lists the applications, the Web farms that run the applications, and the DNS entries that correspond to the Web applications that include the target cluster, IISNLB-05.

Table 9.13 Applications, Web Farms, and DNS Entries

Application	Runs on	DNS Entries
Organization's Internet presence	▪ IISNLB-01 ▪ IISNLB-02 ▪ IISNLB-05	▪ www.contoso.com 10.0.0.111 ▪ www.contoso.com 10.0.0.121 ▪ www.contoso.com 10.0.0.151
Customer support site	▪ IISNLB-03 ▪ IISNLB-05	▪ support.contoso.com 10.0.0.131 ▪ support.contoso.com 10.0.0.152
E-commerce site	▪ IISNLB-03 ▪ IISNLB-05	▪ sales.contoso.com 10.0.0.132 ▪ sales.contoso.com 10.0.0.153
Nonprofit third-party organization's Internet presence	▪ IISNLB-04 ▪ IISNLB-05	▪ www.treyresearch.net 10.0.0.141 ▪ www.treyresearch.net 10.0.0.154

After a few days of operation, clients are experiencing no difficulty with IISNLB-05, so Contoso modifies the DNS entries to remove the original Web servers (IISNLB-01, IISNLB-02, IISNLB-03, and IISNLB-04). Table 9.14 reflects the DNS entries after the removal of the original Web servers.

Table 9.14   Applications, Web Farms, and DNS Entries

Application	Runs on	DNS Entries
Organization's Internet presence	▪ IISNLB-05	▪ www.contoso.com 10.0.0.151
Customer support site	▪ IISNLB-05	▪ support.contoso.com 10.0.0.152
E-commerce site	▪ IISNLB-05	▪ sales.contoso.com 10.0.0.153
Nonprofit third-party organization's Internet presence	▪ IISNLB-05	▪ www.treyresearch.net 10.0.0.154

To finalize the completion of the migration, Contoso performs the following tasks:

1. Contoso monitors the source clusters for client traffic.

2. After all client traffic ceases on the source clusters, Contoso decommissions the computers in the source clusters.

Additional Resources

Related Information

- "Deploying Dial-up and VPN Remote Access Servers" in *Deploying Network Services* of this kit.

- "Deploying ISA Server" in *Deploying Network Services.*

- "Deploying DNS" in *Deploying Network Services* for more information on deploying Network Load Balancing with round robin DNS.

- "Upgrading an IIS Server to IIS 6.0" in *Deploying Internet Information Services (IIS) 6.0* (or see "Upgrading an IIS Server to IIS 6.0" on the Web at http://www.microsoft.com/reskit).

- "Migrating IIS Web Sites to IIS 6.0" in *Deploying Internet Information Services (IIS) 6.0* (or see "Migrating IIS Web Sites to IIS 6.0" on the Web at http://www.microsoft.com/reskit).

Related Job Aids

- "NLB Cluster Host Worksheet" (Sdcnlb_1.doc) on the *Windows Server 2003 Deployment Kit* companion CD (or see "NLB Cluster Host Worksheet" on the Web at http://www.microsoft.com/reskit).

Related Help Topics

For best results in identifying Help topics by title, in Help and Support Center, under the **Search** box, click **Set search options**. Under **Help Topics**, select the **Search in title only** check box.

- "Network Load Balancing Manager" under "New ways to do familiar tasks" in Help and Support Center for Windows Server 2003 for more information about the procedures for deploying Network Load Balancing on individual servers.

- "Create and Manage Network Load Balancing Clusters" in Help and Support Center for Windows Server 2003.

- "Managing resource records" in Help and Support Center for Windows Server 2003.

Glossary

A

access control entry (ACE) An entry in an object's discretionary access control list (DACL) that grants permissions to a user or group. An ACE is also an entry in an object's system access control list (SACL) that specifies the security events to be audited for a user or group. See also access control list (ACL).

access control list (ACL) A list of security protections that apply to an entire object, a set of the object's properties, or an individual property of an object. There are two types of access control lists: discretionary and system. See also access control entry (ACE).

ACE See definition for access control entry (ACE).

ACL See definition for access control list (ACL).

ActiveX A set of technologies that allows software components to interact with one another in a networked environment, regardless of the language in which the components were created.

answer file A text file that scripts the answers for a series of graphical user interface (GUI) dialog boxes. The answer file for Setup is commonly called Unattend.txt, but for a network preinstallation, you can name the file anything you like. For a CD-based Setup, the answer file must be named Winnt.sif. The answer files for Sysprep are Sysprep.inf and Winbom.ini. You can create or modify these answer files in a text editor or through Setup Manager.

application programming interface (API) A set of routines that an application uses to request and carry out lower-level services performed by a computer's operating system. These routines usually carry out maintenance tasks such as managing files and displaying information.

auditing The process that tracks the activities of users by recording selected types of events in the security log of a server or a workstation.

authoritative Describes a DNS server that hosts a primary or secondary copy of a DNS zone. See also Domain Name System (DNS).

availability A level of service provided by applications, services, or systems. Highly available systems have minimal downtime, whether planned or unplanned. Availability is often expressed as the percentage of time that a service or system is available, for example, 99.9 percent for a service that is down for 8.75 hours a year.

B

basic disk A physical disk that can be accessed by MS-DOS and all Windows-based operating systems. Basic disks can contain up to four primary partitions, or three primary partitions and an extended partition with multiple logical drives. If you want to create partitions that span multiple disks, you must first convert the basic disk to a dynamic disk by using Disk Management or the Diskpart.exc command-line tool. See also dynamic disk.

basic volume A primary partition or logical drive that resides on a basic disk. See also basic disk.

batch program An ASCII (unformatted text) file that contains one or more operating system commands. A batch program's file name has a .cmd or .bat extension. When you type the file name at the command prompt, or when the batch program is run from another program, its commands are processed sequentially. Also called *batch files*.

boot partition The partition that contains the Windows operating system and its support files. The boot partition can be, but does not have to be, the same as the system partition.

boot volume The volume that contains the Windows operating system and its support files. The boot volume can be, but does not have to be, the same as the system volume. See also system volume.

bottleneck A condition, usually involving a hardware resource, that causes a computer to perform poorly.

C

change journal   A feature that tracks changes to NTFS volumes, including additions, deletions, and modifications. The change journal exists on the volume as a sparse file. See also NTFS file system.

clean installation   The process of installing an operating system on a clean or empty partition of a computer's hard disk.

cluster   In data storage, the smallest amount of disk space that can be allocated to hold a file. All file systems used by Windows organize hard disks based on clusters, which consist of one or more contiguous sectors. The smaller the cluster size, the more efficiently a disk stores information. If no cluster size is specified during formatting, Windows picks defaults based on the size of the volume. These defaults are selected to reduce the amount of space that is lost and the amount of fragmentation on the volume. Also called an *allocation unit*.

In computer networking, a group of independent computers that work together to provide a common set of services and present a single-system image to clients. The use of a cluster enhances the availability of the services and the scalability and manageability of the operating system that provides the services.

See also availability; scalability.

Cluster service   The essential software component that controls all aspects of server cluster operation and manages the cluster database. Each node in a server cluster runs one instance of the Cluster service. See also cluster; node; server cluster.

cluster storage   Storage where one or more attached disks hold data used either by server applications running on the cluster or by applications for managing the cluster. Each disk on the cluster storage is owned by only one node of the cluster. The ownership of disks moves from one node to another when the disk group fails over or moves to the other node. See also cluster; failover; node.

cluster-aware   The classification of an application or service that runs on a server cluster node, is managed as a cluster resource, and is designed to be aware of and interact with the server cluster environment. Cluster-aware applications use the Cluster API to receive status and notification information from the server cluster.

COM+   An extension of the COM (Component Object Model) programming architecture that includes a runtime or execution environment and extensible services, including transaction services, security, load balancing, and automatic memory management. See also Component Object Model (COM).

Component Object Model (COM)   An object-based programming model designed to promote software interoperability; it allows two or more applications or components to easily cooperate with one another, even if they were written by different vendors, at different times, in different programming languages, or if they are running on different computers running different operating systems. OLE technology and ActiveX are both built on top of COM. See also ActiveX.

D

DFS path   The combination of a Distributed File System (DFS) root and a DFS link. An example of a DFS path is *server**dfs**a**b**c**link*, where *server**dfs* is the DFS root, and *a**b**c*\ is the DFS link. See also DFS root; Distributed File System (DFS).

DFS root   The starting point of the Distributed File System (DFS) namespace. The root is often used to refer to the namespace as a whole. A root maps to one or more root targets, each of which corresponds to a shared folder on a server. See also Distributed File System (DFS).

dial-up connection   The connection to your network if you use a device that uses the telephone network. This includes modems with a standard telephone line, ISDN cards with high-speed ISDN lines, or X.25 networks.   If you are a typical user, you might have one or two dial-up connections, for example, to the Internet and to your corporate network. In a more complex server situation, multiple network modem connections might be used to implement advanced routing.

See also Integrated Services Digital Network (ISDN).

digital subscriber line (DSL)   A special communication line that uses modulation technology to maximize the amount of data that can be sent over a local-loop, copper-wire connection to a central phone office. DSL is used for connections from telephone switching stations to a subscriber rather than between switching stations.

Distributed File System (DFS) A service that allows system administrators to organize distributed network shares into a logical namespace, enabling users to access files without specifying their physical location and providing load sharing across network shares. See also service.

domain administrator A person who is a member of the Domain Admins group. Domain administrators can create, delete, and manage all objects that reside within the domain in which they are administrators. They can also assign and reset passwords and delegate administrative authority for network resources to other trusted users. See also resource.

domain controller In an Active Directory forest, a server that contains a writable copy of the Active Directory database, participates in Active Directory replication, and controls access to network resources. Administrators can manage user accounts, network access, shared resources, site topology, and other directory objects from any domain controller in the forest.

domain local group A security or distribution group that can contain universal groups, global groups, other domain local groups from its own domain, and accounts from any domain in the forest. Domain local security groups can be granted rights and permissions on resources that reside only in the same domain where the domain local group is located. See also global group; universal group.

Domain Name System (DNS) A hierarchical, distributed database that contains mappings of DNS domain names to various types of data, such as IP addresses. DNS enables the location of computers and services by user-friendly names, and it also enables the discovery of other information stored in the database. See also IP address; service; Transmission Control Protocol/Internet Protocol (TCP/IP).

dynamic disk A physical disk that provides features that basic disks do not, such as support for volumes that span multiple disks. Dynamic disks use a hidden database to track information about dynamic volumes on the disk and other dynamic disks in the computer. You convert basic disks to dynamic by using the Disk Management snap-in or the DiskPart command-line tool. When you convert a basic disk to dynamic, all existing basic volumes become dynamic volumes. See also basic disk; basic volume; dynamic volume.

Dynamic Host Configuration Protocol (DHCP) A TCP/IP service protocol that offers dynamic leased configuration of host IP addresses and distributes other configuration parameters to eligible network clients. DHCP provides safe, reliable, and simple TCP/IP network configuration, prevents address conflicts, and helps conserve the use of client IP addresses on the network.

DHCP uses a client/server model where the DHCP server maintains centralized management of IP addresses that are used on the network. DHCP-supporting clients can then request and obtain lease of an IP address from a DHCP server as part of their network boot process.

See also IP address; service; Transmission Control Protocol/Internet Protocol (TCP/IP).

dynamic volume A volume that resides on a dynamic disk. Windows supports five types of dynamic volumes: simple, spanned, striped, mirrored, and RAID-5. A dynamic volume is formatted by using a file system, such as file allocation table (FAT) or NTFS, and has a drive letter assigned to it. See also basic disk; basic volume; dynamic disk; mirrored volume; RAID-5 volume; simple volume; spanned volume; striped volume.

dynamic-link library (DLL) An operating system feature that allows executable routines (generally serving a specific function or set of functions) to be stored separately as files with .dll extensions These routines are loaded only when needed by the program that calls them.

E

error detection A technique for detecting when data is lost during transmission. This allows the software to recover lost data by notifying the transmitting computer that it needs to retransmit the data.

Event Viewer A component you can use to view and manage event logs, gather information about hardware and software problems, and monitor security events. Event Viewer maintains logs about program, security, and system events.

extranet A limited subset of computers or users on a public network, typically the Internet, that can access an organization's internal network. For example, the computers or users might belong to a partner organization.

F

failover   In server clusters, the process of taking resource groups offline on one node and bringing them online on another node. When failover occurs, all resources within a resource group fail over in a predefined order; resources that depend on other resources are taken offline before, and are brought back online after, the resources on which they depend. See also failover policy; node; server cluster.

failover policy   Parameters that an administrator can set, using Cluster Administrator, that affect failover operations. See also failover.

fault tolerance   The ability of computer hardware or software to ensure data integrity when hardware failures occur. Fault-tolerant features appear in many server operating systems and include mirrored volumes, RAID-5 volumes, and server clusters. See also cluster; mirrored volume; RAID-5 volume.

file allocation table (FAT)   A file system used by MS-DOS and other Windows operating systems to organize and manage files. The file allocation table is a data structure that Windows creates when you format a volume by using FAT or FAT32 file systems. Windows stores information about each file in the file allocation table so that it can retrieve the file later. See also NTFS file system.

File Replication service (FRS)   A service that provides multimaster file replication for designated directory trees between designated servers running Windows Server 2003. The designated directory trees must be on disk partitions formatted with the version of NTFS used with the Windows Server 2003 family. FRS is used by Distributed File System (DFS) to automatically synchronize content between assigned replicas and by Active Directory to automatically synchronize content of the system volume information across domain controllers. See also NTFS file system; service.

File Share resource   A file share accessible by a network path that is supported as a cluster resource by a Resource DLL.

File Transfer Protocol (FTP)   A member of the TCP/IP suite of protocols, used to copy files between two computers on the Internet. Both computers must support their respective FTP roles: one must be an FTP client and the other an FTP server. See also Transmission Control Protocol/Internet Protocol (TCP/IP).

firewall   A combination of hardware and software that provides a security system for the flow of network traffic, usually to prevent unauthorized access from outside to an internal network or intranet. Also called a *security-edge gateway*.

fully qualified domain name (FQDN)   A DNS name that has been stated to indicate its absolute location in the domain namespace tree. In contrast to relative names, an FQDN has a trailing period (.) to qualify its position to the root of the namespace (*host.example.microsoft.com.*). See also Domain Name System (DNS).

G-H

global group   A security or distribution group that can contain users, groups, and computers from its own domain as members. Global security groups can be granted rights and permissions for resources in any domain in the forest. See also local group.

GUID partition table (GPT)   A disk-partitioning scheme that is used by the Extensible Firmware Interface (EFI) in Itanium-based computers. GPT offers more advantages than master boot record (MBR) partitioning because it allows up to 128 partitions per disk, provides support for volumes up to 18 exabytes in size, allows primary and backup partition tables for redundancy, and supports unique disk and partition IDs (GUIDs). See also master boot record (MBR).

I-K

IEEE 1394   A standard for high-speed serial devices such as digital video and digital audio editing equipment.

image   A collection of files and folders (sometimes compressed into one file) that duplicates the original file and folder structure of an operating system. It often contains other files added by the OEM or corporation.

Integrated Services Digital Network (ISDN)   A digital phone line used to provide higher bandwidth. ISDN in North America is typically available in two forms: Basic Rate Interface (BRI) consists of 2 B-channels at 64 kilobits per second (Kbps) and a D-channel at 16 Kbps; Primary Rate Interface (PRI) consists of 23 B-channels at 64 Kbps and a D-channel at 64 Kbps. An ISDN line must be installed by the phone company at both the calling site and the called site.

Internetwork Packet Exchange (IPX) A network protocol native to NetWare that controls addressing and routing of packets within and between local area networks (LANs). IPX does not guarantee that a message will be complete (no lost packets). See also local area network (LAN).

Intersite Topology Generator An Active Directory process that runs on one domain controller in a site that considers the cost of intersite connections, checks if previously available domain controllers are no longer available, and checks if new domain controllers have been added. The Knowledge Consistency Checker (KCC) process then updates the intersite replication topology accordingly. See also domain controller; replication topology; site.

IP address For Internet Protocol version 4 (IPv4), a 32-bit address used to identify an interface on a node on an IPv4 internetwork. Each interface on the IP internetwork must be assigned a unique IPv4 address, which is made up of the network ID, plus a unique host ID. This address is typically represented with the decimal value of each octet separated by a period (for example, 192.168.7.27). You can configure the IP address statically or dynamically by using Dynamic Host Configuration Protocol (DHCP).

For Internet Protocol version 6 (IPv6), an identifier that is assigned at the IPv6 layer to an interface or set of interfaces and that can be used as the source or destination of IPv6 packets.

See also Dynamic Host Configuration Protocol (DHCP); node.

L

Layer Two Tunneling Protocol (L2TP) An industry-standard Internet tunneling protocol that provides encapsulation for sending Point-to-Point Protocol (PPP) frames across packet-oriented media. For IP networks, L2TP traffic is sent as User Datagram Protocol (UDP) messages. In Microsoft operating systems, L2TP is used in conjunction with Internet Protocol security (IPSec) as a virtual private network (VPN) technology to provide remote access or router-to-router VPN connections. L2TP is described in RFC 2661.

local area network (LAN) A communications network connecting a group of computers, printers, and other devices located within a relatively limited area (for example, a building). A LAN enables any connected device to interact with any other on the network. See also NetBIOS Extended User Interface (NetBEUI); virtual local area network (VLAN); workgroup.

local group A security group that can be granted rights and permissions on only resources on the computer on which the group is created. Local groups can have any user accounts that are local to the computer as members, as well as users, groups, and computers from a domain to which the computer belongs. See also global group.

M

master boot record (MBR) The first sector on a hard disk, which begins the process of starting the computer. The MBR contains the partition table for the disk and a small amount of executable code called the *master boot code*.

Microsoft Management Console (MMC) A framework for hosting administrative tools called *snap-ins*. A console might contain tools, folders or other containers, World Wide Web pages, and other administrative items. These items are displayed in the left pane of the console, called a *console tree*. A console has one or more windows that can provide views of the console tree. The main MMC window provides commands and tools for authoring consoles. The authoring features of MMC and the console tree itself might be hidden when a console is in User Mode.

mirror set A fault-tolerant partition created with Windows NT 4.0 or earlier that duplicates data on two physical disks. Windows XP and the Windows Server 2003 family do not support mirror sets. In the Windows Server 2003 family, you must create mirrored volumes on dynamic disks. See also dynamic disk; mirrored volume.

mirrored volume A fault-tolerant volume that duplicates data on two physical disks. A mirrored volume provides data redundancy by using two identical volumes, which are called *mirrors*, to duplicate the information contained on the volume. A mirror is always located on a different disk. If one of the physical disks fails, the data on the failed disk becomes unavailable, but the system continues to operate in the mirror on the remaining disk. You can create mirrored volumes only on dynamic disks on computers running the Windows 2000 Server or Windows Server 2003 families of operating systems. You cannot extend mirrored volumes. See also dynamic disk; dynamic volume; fault tolerance; RAID-5 volume.

mobile user A user who travels away from a corporate campus such as a salesperson or field technician.

mounted drive A drive attached to an empty folder on an NTFS volume. Mounted drives function the same as any other drive, but are assigned a label or name instead of a drive letter. The mounted drive's name is resolved to a full file system path instead of just a drive letter. Members of the Administrators group can use Disk Management to create mounted drives or reassign drive letters. See also NTFS file system.

N

NetBIOS Extended User Interface (NetBEUI) A network protocol native to Microsoft Networking. It is usually used in small, department-size local area networks (LANs) of 1 to 200 clients. NetBEUI can use Token Ring source routing as its only method of routing. NetBEUI is the Microsoft implementation of the NetBIOS standard. See also local area network (LAN).

Network Load Balancing cluster Up to 32 Web servers from which Network Load Balancing presents a single IP address to Web clients and among which Network Load Balancing distributes incoming Web requests. See also IP address.

node For tree structures, a location on the tree that can have links to one or more items below it.

For local area networks (LANs), a device that is connected to the network and is capable of communicating with other network devices.

For server clusters, a computer system that is an active or inactive member of a cluster.

See also local area network (LAN); server cluster.

NTFS file system An advanced file system that provides performance, security, reliability, and advanced features that are not found in any version of file allocation table (FAT). For example, NTFS guarantees volume consistency by using standard transaction logging and recovery techniques. If a system fails, NTFS uses its log file and checkpoint information to restore the consistency of the file system. NTFS also provides advanced features, such as file and folder permissions, encryption, disk quotas, and compression. See also file allocation table (FAT).

O

organizational unit An Active Directory container object used within domains. An organizational unit is a logical container into which users, groups, computers, and other organizational units are placed. It can contain objects only from its parent domain. An organizational unit is the smallest scope to which a Group Policy object (GPO) can be linked, or over which administrative authority can be delegated.

P-Q

page In virtual memory systems, a unit of data storage that is brought into random access memory (RAM), typically from a hard drive, when a requested item of data is not already in RAM.

Point-to-Point Tunneling Protocol (PPTP) Networking technology that supports multiprotocol virtual private networks (VPNs), enabling remote users to access corporate networks securely across the Internet or other networks by dialing into an Internet service provider (ISP) or by connecting directly to the Internet. PPTP tunnels, or encapsulates, Internet Protocol (IP) or Internetwork Packet Exchange (IPX) traffic inside IP packets. This means that users can remotely run applications that depend on particular network protocols. PPTP is described in RFC 2637. See also Internetwork Packet Exchange (IPX); NetBIOS Extended User Interface (NetBEUI); virtual private network (VPN).

primary domain controller (PDC) In a Windows NT domain, a domain controller running Windows NT Server 4.0 or earlier that authenticates domain logon attempts and updates user, computer, and group accounts in a domain. The PDC contains the master read-write copy of the directory database for the domain. A domain has only one PDC.

In a Windows 2000 or Windows Server 2003 domain, the PDC emulator master supports compatibility with client computers that are not running Windows 2000 or Windows XP Professional.

R

RAID-5 volume A fault-tolerant volume with data and parity striped intermittently across three or more physical disks. Parity is a calculated value that is used to reconstruct data after a failure. If a portion of a physical disk fails, Windows recreates the data that was on the failed portion from the remaining data and parity. You can create RAID-5 volumes only on dynamic disks on computers running the Windows 2000 Server or Windows Server 2003 families of operating systems. You cannot mirror or extend RAID-5 volumes. In Windows NT 4.0, a RAID-5 volume was known as a *striped set with parity*. See also dynamic disk; dynamic volume; fault tolerance.

Redundant Array of Independent Disks (RAID) A method used to standardize and categorize fault-tolerant disk systems. RAID levels provide various mixes of performance, reliability, and cost. Some servers provide three of the RAID levels: Level 0 (striping), Level 1 (mirroring), and Level 5 (RAID-5). See also fault tolerance; RAID-5 volume.

reparse points NTFS file system objects that have a definable attribute containing user-controlled data and that are used to extend functionality in the input/output (I/O) subsystem. See also NTFS file system.

replica set One or more shared folders that participates in replication.

replication topology In Active Directory replication, the set of physical connections that domain controllers use to replicate directory updates among domain controllers within sites and between sites.

In the File Replication service (FRS), the interconnections between replica set members. These interconnections determine the path that data takes as it replicates to all replica set members.

See also Distributed File System (DFS); domain controller; File Replication service (FRS); replica set.

resource Generally, any part of a computer system or network, such as a disk drive, printer, or memory, that can be allotted to a running program or a process.

For Device Manager, any of four system components that control how the devices on a computer work. These four system resources are interrupt request (IRQ) lines, direct memory access (DMA) channels, input/output (I/O) ports, and memory addresses.

For server clusters, a physical or logical entity that is capable of being managed by a cluster, brought online and taken offline, and moved between nodes. A resource can be owned only by a single node at any point in time.

See also node; server cluster.

root target The mapping destination of a DFS root, which corresponds to a shared folder on a server. See also DFS root; target.

round robin A simple mechanism used by DNS servers to share and distribute loads for network resources. Round robin is used to rotate the order of resource records (RRs) returned in a response to a query when multiple RRs of the same type exist for a queried DNS domain name.

S

scalability A measure of how well a computer, service, or application can grow to meet increasing performance demands. For server clusters, the ability to incrementally add one or more systems to an existing cluster when the overall load of the cluster exceeds its capabilities. See also server cluster.

Secure Sockets Layer (SSL) A protocol that supplies secure data communication through data encryption and decryption. This protocol enables communications privacy over networks through a combination of public-key cryptography and bulk data encryption.

Security Accounts Manager (SAM) A Windows service used during the logon process. SAM maintains user account information, including groups to which a user belongs. See also service.

server cluster A group of computers, known as nodes, working together as a single system to ensure that mission-critical applications and resources remain available to clients. A server cluster presents the appearance of a single server to a client. See also cluster; node.

service A program, routine, or process that performs a specific system function to support other programs, particularly at a low (close to the hardware) level. When services are provided over a network, they can be published in Active Directory, facilitating service-centric administration and usage. Some examples of services are the Security Accounts Manager service, File Replication service, and Routing and Remote Access service. See also File Replication service (FRS); Security Accounts Manager (SAM).

simple volume A dynamic volume made up of disk space from a single dynamic disk. A simple volume can consist of a single region on a disk or multiple regions of the same disk that are linked together. If the simple volume is not a system volume or boot volume, you can extend it within the same disk or onto additional disks. If you extend a simple volume across multiple disks, it becomes a spanned volume. You can create simple volumes only on dynamic disks. Simple volumes are not fault tolerant, but you can mirror them to create mirrored volumes on computers running the Windows 2000 Server or Windows Server 2003 families of operating systems. See also dynamic disk; dynamic volume; fault tolerance; mirrored volume; spanned volume.

site One or more well-connected (highly reliable and fast) TCP/IP subnets. A site allows administrators to configure Active Directory access and replication topology to take advantage of the physical network. See also replication topology; Transmission Control Protocol/Internet Protocol (TCP/IP).

smart card A credit card–sized device that is used with an access code to enable certificate-based authentication and single sign-on to the enterprise. Smart cards securely store certificates, public and private keys, passwords, and other types of personal information. A smart card reader attached to the computer reads the smart card.

sniffer An application or device that can read, monitor, and capture network data exchanges and read network packets. If the packets are not encrypted, a sniffer provides a full view of the data inside the packet.

spanned volume A dynamic volume consisting of disk space on more than one physical disk. You can increase the size of a spanned volume by extending it onto additional dynamic disks. You can create spanned volumes only on dynamic disks. Spanned volumes are not fault tolerant and cannot be mirrored. See also dynamic disk; dynamic volume; fault tolerance; mirrored volume; simple volume.

stripe set A volume that stores data in stripes on two or more physical disks. A stripe set is created by using Windows NT 4.0 or earlier. Windows XP and Windows Server 2003 do not support stripe sets. Instead, you must create a striped volume on dynamic disks. See also dynamic disk; striped volume.

striped volume A dynamic volume that stores data in stripes on two or more physical disks. Data in a striped volume is allocated alternately and evenly (in stripes) across the disks. Striped volumes offer the best performance of all the volumes that are available in Windows, but they do not provide fault tolerance. If a disk in a striped volume fails, the data in the entire volume is lost. You can create striped volumes only on dynamic disks. Striped volumes cannot be mirrored or extended. See also dynamic disk; dynamic volume; fault tolerance; mirrored volume.

system volume The volume that contains the hardware-specific files that are needed to load Windows on x86-based computers with a basic input/output system (BIOS). The system volume can be, but does not have to be, the same volume as the boot volume. See also boot volume.

T

target The mapping destination of a DFS root or link, which corresponds to a physical folder that has been shared on the network. See also DFS root; Distributed File System (DFS).

theme A set of visual elements that provide a unified look for your computer desktop. A theme determines the look of the various graphic elements of your desktop, such as the windows, icons, fonts, colors, and the background and screen saver pictures. It can also define sounds associated with events such as opening or closing a program.

thin client A network computer that does not have a hard disk.

Transmission Control Protocol/Internet Protocol (TCP/IP) A set of networking protocols widely used on the Internet that provides communications across interconnected networks of computers with diverse hardware architectures and various operating systems. TCP/IP includes standards for how computers communicate and conventions for connecting networks and routing traffic.

U

universal group A security or distribution group that can contain users, groups, and computers from any domain in its forest as members.

Universal security groups can be granted rights and permissions on resources in any domain in the forest.

Universal Naming Convention (UNC) A convention for naming files and other resources beginning with two backslashes (\), indicating that the resource exists on a network computer. UNC names conform to the *servername**sharename* syntax, where *servername* is the server's name and *sharename* is the name of the shared resource. The UNC name of a directory or file can also include the directory path after the share name, by using the following syntax: *servername**sharename**directory**filename*.

universal serial bus (USB) An external bus that supports Plug and Play installation. Using USB, you can connect and disconnect devices without shutting down or restarting your computer. You can use a single USB port to connect up to 127 peripheral devices, including speakers, telephones, CD-ROM drives, joysticks, tape drives, keyboards, scanners, and cameras. A USB port is usually located on the back of your computer near the serial port or parallel port.

upgrade When referring to software, to update existing program files, folders, and registry entries to a more recent version. Upgrading, unlike performing a new installation, leaves existing settings and files in place.

V

virtual local area network (VLAN) A logical grouping of hosts on one or more local area networks (LANs) that allows communication to occur between hosts as if they were on the same physical LAN. See also local area network (LAN).

virtual private network (VPN) The extension of a private network that encompasses encapsulated, encrypted, and authenticated links across shared or public networks. VPN connections typically provide remote access and router-to-router connections to private networks over the Internet.

virtual server In a server cluster, a collection of services that appear to clients as a physical Windows-based server but are not associated with a specific server. A virtual server is typically a resource group that contains all of the resources needed to run a particular application and that can be failed over like any other resource group. All virtual servers must include a Network Name resource and an IP Address resource. See also failover; resource; server cluster.

volume set A volume that consists of disk space on one or more physical disks. A volume set is created by using basic disks and is supported only in Windows NT 4.0 or earlier. Volume sets were replaced by spanned volumes, which use dynamic disks. See also basic disk; dynamic disk; spanned volume.

W-Z

wide area network (WAN) A communications network connecting geographically separated locations that uses long-distance links of third-party telecommunications vendors. See also local area network (LAN).

Winbom.ini An .ini file that provides a bill-of-materials to incorporate into the Windows installation. Winbom.ini can control different points of the installation and configuration process: for example, it can control Sysprep during Factory mode, Windows preinstallation when starting from the Windows Preinstallation Environment (WinPE), or Windows XP configuration during Windows Welcome.

Windows Internet Name Service (WINS) A Windows name resolution service for network basic input/output system (NetBIOS) names. WINS is used by hosts running NetBIOS over TCP/IP (NetBT) to register NetBIOS names and to resolve NetBIOS names to Internet Protocol (IP) addresses. See also IP address; resource; service.

Windows Management Instrumentation (WMI) A management infrastructure in Windows that supports monitoring and controlling system resources through a common set of interfaces and provides a logically organized, consistent model of Windows operation, configuration, and status. See also resource.

workgroup A simple grouping of computers, intended only to help users find such things as printers and shared folders within that group. Workgroups in Windows do not offer the centralized user accounts and authentication offered by domains.

Index

I-K

O

P-Q

At Microsoft Press, we use tools to illustrate our books for software developers and IT professionals. Tools very simply and powerfully symbolize human inventiveness. They're a metaphor for people extending their capabilities, precision, and reach. From simple calipers and pliers to digital micrometers and lasers, these stylized illustrations give each book a visual identity, and a personality to the series. With tools and knowledge, there's no limit to creativity and innovation. Our tag line says it all: *the tools you need to put technology to work*.

Inside *security information* you can trust

Microsoft® Windows® Security Resource Kit
ISBN 0-7356-1868-2   Suggested Retail Price: $59.99 U.S., $86.99 Canada

Comprehensive security information and tools, straight from the Microsoft product groups. This official RESOURCE KIT delivers comprehensive operations and deployment information that information security professionals can put to work right away. The authors—members of Microsoft's security teams—describe how to plan and implement a comprehensive security strategy, assess security threats and vulnerabilities, configure system security, and more. The kit also provides must-have security tools, checklists, templates, and other on-the-job resources on CD-ROM and on the Web.

Microsoft Encyclopedia of Security
ISBN 0-7356-1877-1   Suggested Retail Price: $49.99 U.S., $72.99 Canada

The essential, one-of-a-kind security reference for computer professionals at all levels. This encyclopedia delivers 2000+ entries detailing the latest security-related issues, technologies, standards, products, and services. It covers the Microsoft Windows platform as well as open-source technologies and the platforms and products of other major vendors. You get clear, concise explanations and case scenarios that deftly take you from concept to real-world application—ideal for everyone from computer science students up to systems engineers, developers, and managers.

Microsoft Windows Server 2003 Security Administrator's Companion
ISBN 0-7356-1574-8   Suggested Retail Price: $49.99 U.S., $72.99 Canada

The in-depth, practical guide to deploying and maintaining Windows Server 2003 in a secure environment. Learn how to use all the powerful security features in the latest network operating system with this in-depth, authoritative technical reference—written by a security expert on the Microsoft Windows Server 2003 security team. Explore physical security issues, internal security policies, and public and shared key cryptography, and then drill down into the specifics of the key security features of Windows Server 2003.

Microsoft Internet Information Services Security Technical Reference
ISBN 0-7356-1572-1   Suggested Retail Price: $49.99 U.S., $72.99 Canada

The definitive guide for developers and administrators who need to understand how to securely manage networked systems based on IIS. This book presents obvious, avoidable mistakes and known security vulnerabilities in Internet Information Services (IIS)—priceless, intimate facts about the underlying causes of past security issues—while showing the best ways to fix them. The expert author, who has used IIS since the first version, also discusses real-world best practices for developing software and managing systems and networks with IIS.

To learn more about Microsoft Press® products for IT professionals, please visit:

microsoft.com/mspress/IT

In-depth, daily administration guides
for Microsoft Windows Server 2003

Microsoft® Windows® Server 2003 Administrator's Companion
ISBN 0-7356-1367-2

The in-depth, daily operations guide to planning, deployment, and maintenance. Here's the ideal one-volume guide for the IT professional who administers Windows Server 2003. This ADMINISTRATOR'S COMPANION offers up-to-date information on core system-administration topics for Windows, including Active Directory® services, security, disaster planning and recovery, interoperability with NetWare and UNIX, plus all-new sections about Microsoft Internet Security and Acceleration (ISA) Server and scripting. Featuring easy-to-use procedures and handy workarounds, this book provides ready answers for on-the-job results.

Microsoft Windows Server 2003 Security Administrator's Companion
ISBN 0-7356-1574-8

The in-depth, daily operations guide to enhancing security with the network operating system. With this authoritative ADMINISTRATOR'S COMPANION—written by an expert on the Windows Server 2003 security team—you'll learn how to use the powerful security features in the latest network server operating system. The guide describes best practices and technical details for enhancing security with Windows Server 2003, using the holistic approach that IT professionals need to grasp to help secure their systems. The authors cover concepts such as physical security issues, internal security policies, and public and shared key cryptography, and then drill down into the specifics of key security features of Windows Server 2003.

To learn more about the full line of Microsoft Press® products for IT professionals, please visit:

microsoft.com/mspress/IT

The practical, portable guides to
Microsoft Windows Server 2003

Microsoft® Windows® Server 2003 Admin Pocket Consultant
ISBN 0-7356-1354-0

The practical, portable guide to Windows Server 2003. Here's the practical, pocket-sized reference for IT professionals who support Windows Server 2003. Designed for quick referencing, it covers all the essentials for performing everyday system-administration tasks. Topics covered include managing workstations and servers, using Active Directory® services, creating and administering user and group accounts, managing files and directories, data security and auditing, data back-up and recovery, administration with TCP/IP, WINS, and DNS, and more.

Microsoft IIS 6.0 Administrator's Pocket Consultant
ISBN 0-7356-1560-8

The practical, portable guide to IIS 6.0. Here's the eminently practical, pocket-sized reference for IT and Web professionals who work with Internet Information Services (IIS) 6.0. Designed for quick referencing and compulsively readable, this portable guide covers all the basics needed for everyday tasks. Topics include Web administration fundamentals, Web server administration, essential services administration, and performance, optimization, and maintenance. It's the fast-answers guide that helps users consistently save time and energy as they administer IIS 6.0.

To learn more about the full line of Microsoft Press® products for IT professionals, please visit:

microsoft.com/mspress/IT